Simon & Schuster's

SUPER

CROSSWORD BOOK

#11

Simon & Schuster's
SUPER
CROSSWORD BOOK
#11

EDITED BY
EUGENE T. MALESKA
and
JOHN M. SAMSON

Gallery Books
New York London Toronto Sydney New Delhi

G

Gallery Books
An Imprint of Simon & Schuster, Inc.
1230 Avenue of the Americas
New York, NY 10020

This Gallery Books trade paperback edition January 2021

GALLERY BOOKS and colophon are registered trademarks of Simon & Schuster, Inc.

For information about special discounts for bulk purchases, please contact Simon & Schuster Special Sales at 1-866-506-1949 or business@simonandschuster.com.

The Simon & Schuster Speakers Bureau can bring authors to your live event. For more information or to book an event, contact the Simon & Schuster Speakers Bureau at 1-866-248-3049 or visit our website at www.simonspeakers.com.

Interior design by Helen Barrow

Manufactured in the United States of America

23   25   27   29   30   28   26   24

ISBN 978-0-6848-7186-8

The puzzles in this treasury have been previously published.

FOREWORD

Welcome to the newest *Super*!

 This eleventh installment brings you 225 excellent crosswords, selected from books in the outstanding Simon & Schuster crossword puzzle series—the first and longest such series in the world.

 Constructors from every corner of the country contributed to this volume, covering many themes. The subjects range from sports, history, literature, and geography to movies, television, music, cooking, and more.

 So sharpen your pencil, put on your thinking cap, and enjoy hours of cruciverbal entertainment!

THE PUBLISHER

P.S. The puzzles designated as winning the "Margaret" award—in honor of Margaret Farrar, who helped launch crosswords as a national pastime—were chosen by the editors as the best in the original books from which this collection is drawn.

COMPLETE ANSWERS ARE AT THE BACK.

For the convenience of solvers who find it awkward to work crosswords in a thick book, the pages are perforated along the spine edge. This makes for easy removal of a single leaf. If you prefer not to remove pages, open the book at several different places and press down gently from top to bottom in the middle. This will help the book lie flat.

1

NOT IN by William P. Baxley

Here's an easy warm-up from Los Angeles. If you find this one is taking more than an hour to complete, good luck with the back-of-the-book beasties!

ACROSS

1 South American rodents
6 Leander's lover
10 Moves swiftly
16 Island off Venezuela
17 Jewish month
18 Educated
19 One with a bag
20 Wheys
21 Main dish
22 Endure longer
24 Greek vowel
26 Lance
27 Wight, for one
28 Scatter hay for drying
30 Telepathy
32 Bone: Comb. form
33 Understand
34 Individualist
36 Oceans
38 Oolong
39 Encountered
41 Russian guilds
45 Stare angrily
48 Withdraw
50 Deserter
51 Avatar of Vishnu
52 Located
53 University of NYC
54 Yellow bugle
55 Rhythm
56 Eucharistic plate
57 Elephant driver
59 Soak flax
60 Swiss river
61 Author of "Exodus"
63 Stupid fellows
65 Vacation spot
68 Insane
71 Negative vote
73 Rubbish
74 Detect
75 Lyric poem
77 Recent: Comb. form
79 Pariah
81 Winter overshoe
83 "Rock of ___"
85 Main trunk
86 Melodious
87 Withered
88 Exterior
89 Accumulated
90 Bird with a forked tail
91 Principals

DOWN

1 Jargon
2 Excite
3 Squid and sepia
4 White poplar
5 Actress Haden
6 Accelerate
7 Netherlands commune
8 Steak order
9 Sermonize
10 Sault___ Marie
11 Fires
12 Frontier settlement
13 Grimm heavies
14 Part of ETO
15 Cordwood measure
23 Greek portico
25 Onager
29 Greek goddess of agriculture
31 Tranquility
34 Protecting shelter
35 Made a grand sound grander
37 Craft
38 Musical syllable
40 Deere's vehicle
42 Part of QED
43 Openwork fabric
44 British gun
45 Stern
46 Volcanic rock
47 Oriental nurse
48 Disencumber
49 Dined
52 Lustrous fabric
53 What Strange breaks
55 Mongrel
56 Dance step
58 Al fresco
60 Alaskan island
62 ___ Salvador
64 Disengage
65 Ancient Greek city
66 Placard
67 Fragrances
68 French artist
69 Isolated
70 Manuscript leaf
72 Leavening agent
74 Kit Carson, e.g.
76 Being
78 S-curve
80 New Mexico resort
82 Coal scuttle
84 Stray

2 NUMBERS GAME by Martha J. DeWitt
A veteran puzzler from South Carolina brings something new to something old.

ACROSS

1 Military greeting
7 Supervisor
11 Inquires
15 Worships
16 Medium for Rembrandt
17 Shuteye
18 Perceptions plus speech and understanding
20 Mother-of-pearl
21 Weaver's reed
22 Over
23 "... ditties of ___": Keats
24 Sandburg's "The People, ___"
25 Merchant ship's officer
27 Lorelei or Circe
28 Winner's spot
31 Outlawed insecticide
34 Burning
36 List of candidates
37 Hebrew lyre
38 Salt solutions
39 Reputation
40 Honeysuckle
41 Uses an abstergent
42 Frequently
44 Wise men
45 Cinnabar and galena
46 "How now! ___?": Hamlet
47 China
48 Money in Bangkok
49 "___ and Whispers": Bergman film
51 He wrote "Night Music"
52 Alphabetic trio
53 Undeveloped nations
55 Nostrils
57 Leisure
58 Utah Beach vessel
61 Confuses
63 Podiatrist's concerns
65 Treasured
66 Fortune-telling card
67 Easter parade site
70 Symbols of hotness
71 Claudia ___ Johnson
72 Urbane
73 King Cyaxeres was one
74 Headland
75 Cords

DOWN

1 Impudent
2 Fred Astaire's sister
3 "___ Labour's Lost"
4 Nobelist in chemistry: 1934
5 Lacrosse team
6 Mountain curve
7 Scenery on 67 Across
8 Its capital is Beauvais
9 A lot
10 Draft bd.
11 Winged
12 ESP
13 "Show Boat" composer
14 Graf ___
17 Bedroom racket
19 Vittles
23 More agreeable
25 Sticks in the mud
26 His dragon was killed by Cadmus
27 Squelched
28 Nonpareil
29 Laid a course
30 Put cargo in a hull
32 Contribution receivers
33 Lock
34 Noah's landfall
35 D
37 Lowered in status
38 Chimpanzee paintings
42 Galloon
43 Just
44 Walk crabwise
46 Rheumatologists' concerns
47 Diana ___, British actress
50 "___ apple cider"
53 Waste allowances
54 ___ of allegiance
56 Book by Admiral Byrd
58 Vladimir Ulyanov
59 Pan fry
60 Kilmer classic
61 Jot
62 Jazzman Brubeck
63 Rank's associate
64 Mud puppies' cousins
65 Best place for wurst
67 Aficionado
68 Quick to learn
69 Pledge

3

BUMPER TO BUMPER by Hank Harrington
Thematic entries refer to irritations of a certain motorist. (If you want to know who that motorist is, he's found at 6 Down.)

ACROSS

1 Iraqui port
6 Hurry up
9 Stated
13 Serum holder
15 Bantam's crest
16 Coil: Comb. form
17 Midshipman
18 A Semite
19 French fathers
20 Motorist's irritation
22 "Bonanza" star
23 Feudal privilege
24 Shanty
25 Disburdened
26 Evil
30 Baseballer Mel
31 Jet-set jet
34 Squabble
35 Peepers
37 Rhapsodize
41 "9 to 5" singer
43 Imelda's addiction
44 Tel ___
45 So long, in Tampico
46 Hard as a rock
47 Extra
48 Threshold
49 Charon's boat
50 Pattern
51 Pell-___
52 Keep back
53 Each
54 Fate
55 Sis kin
57 Drinks in
60 Carpenter's friend
63 Whopper
64 Minor prophet
68 Self-aggrandizing one
69 Motorist's irritation
72 Celtic minstrels
73 Red Wing legend
74 British pantry
75 Dog of song
76 Fires

77 Pop-up item
78 Dirk
79 Son of Odin
80 Inception

DOWN

1 Starr and Simpson
2 Continental pref.
3 Take the podium
4 With frills
5 Hebrew letter
6 Irritated motorist
7 Mosque priest
8 Wane
9 Motorist's irritations
10 Broadcasted
11 "Goodnight ___"
12 Medicated

14 Assam silkworm
15 Creole State Acadian
16 Diagonal spar
21 Vittles
22 Aggregate
27 Cupid
28 Burmese native
29 Political friend
31 Muscle problem
32 A Hawkins
33 Quavering tone
36 Tunis ruler of old
38 Benefit
39 Spica locale
40 Happenstance
42 Motorist's irritation
43 Glacial groove
46 Understand

47 Niš native
49 "Birches" poet
50 Essen article
53 Ted Hughes, e.g.
56 Muscovy pref.
58 Locations
59 Most lucid
60 Jack and Clifton
61 Once more
62 See 22 Across
65 Brainy society
66 Eventuate
67 Trapshooting style
69 Squarish
70 Ship of WW II
71 Prot. sect
73 Panama or stovepipe

4 AT THE ZOO by Bryant White

Most of us are not aware the word *zoo* originated from zoological garden. Not that it matters terribly, it's just that 67 Across would most likely be found in a garden.

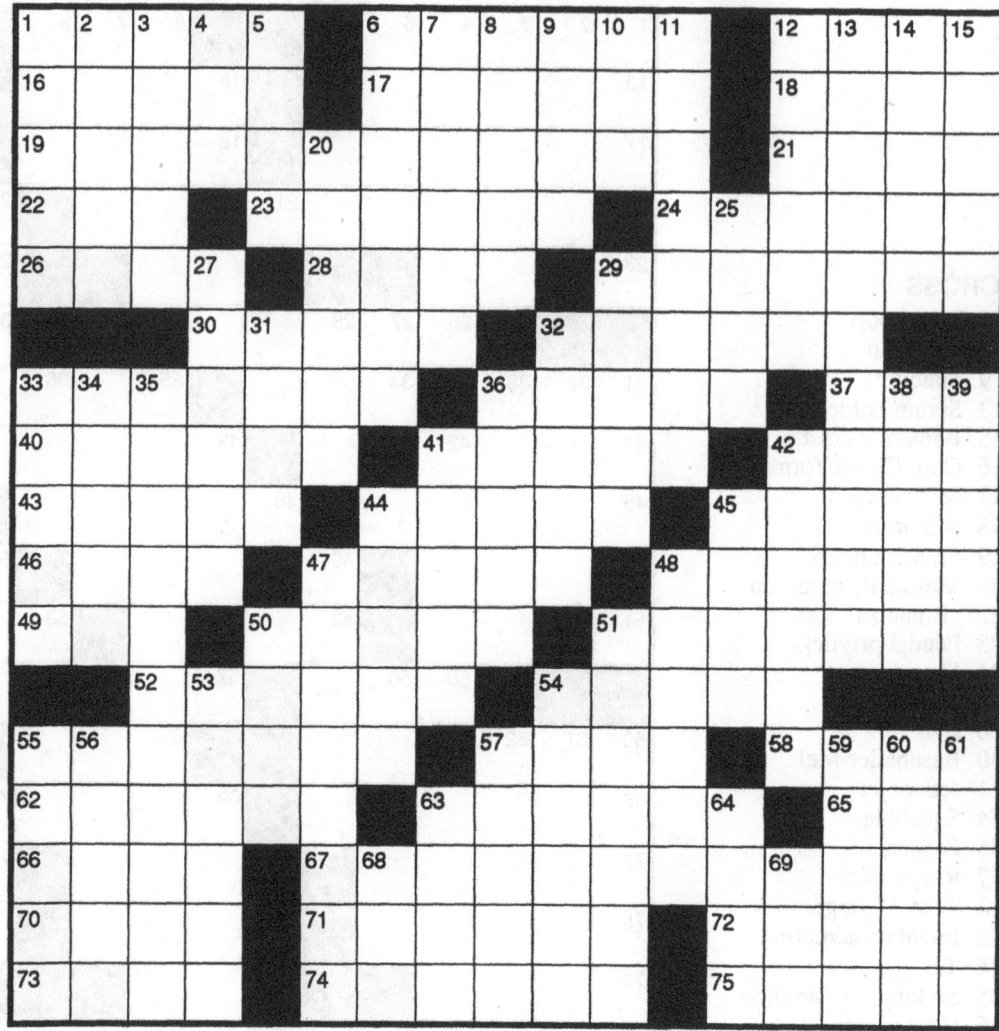

ACROSS

1 Idaho college town
6 Tut's sacred beetle
12 Air pollution
16 Loaded
17 Dravidian language
18 Actress Negri
19 Snoopy's plane
21 "___ Love Her": Beatles
22 Chemical suffix
23 Not ours
24 Lucy of nursery rhyme
26 Musical syllables
28 Merely
29 Tempers
30 He clubbed 61 in '61
32 Lively
33 Deli staple
36 Laments
37 Harden
40 Cooper and Faye
41 Gangster gals
42 Norse god of thunder
43 Cure
44 Prickly pear
45 Oppress, old style
46 Chips off the old block
47 Trident features
48 Hitchcock film
49 Town in Kirghizia
50 Saltpeter
51 Whalebones
52 Writ of execution
54 Turkish monetary unit
55 Made dirty
57 Three-year-old salmon
58 Venomous serpents
62 Paul Newman movie
63 Billiards strokes
65 Whitney
66 Pilaster
67 Taro
70 Gypsy gents
71 Old dog of film
72 Hero Murphy
73 Kind of ranch
74 Large sea ducks
75 Staff notations

DOWN

1 Diamond stops
2 Maine college town
3 Urge forward
4 Baste
5 Amend
6 Vigor
7 De Mille and Fielder
8 Wing-shaped
9 Buccaneer's quaff
10 Iron or Bronze
11 Where LaRussa finds relief
12 Typist's bar
13 Prank
14 Ancient
15 Paces
20 Rambler's protection
25 Fronton cheers
27 Painters' garb
29 "___ We Dance?"
31 "The African Queen" screenwriter
32 Soft drinks
33 Aage Haugland, for one
34 "Miami Vice" star'
35 Brave
36 Spiritless one
38 Red dye
39 Corners
41 "Water Lilies" illustrator
42 Nobel Peace Prize winner: 1979
44 Lustrous
45 Tiny isle N of Flores Island
47 Yellow-brown gem
48 Sable
50 Hawaiian goose
51 College treasurers
53 Pancreatic enzyme
54 According to Hoyle
55 Pottery fragment
56 Japanese painter, Kano ___
57 Syrup source
59 Court rankings
60 Flat fold
61 Begets
63 Pinochle declaration
64 Arcturus, e.g.
68 Waikiki wreath
69 Take to court

5 REMINISCING by James E. Hinish, Jr.
A look back to those nostalgic radio days of the '30s and '40s.

ACROSS
1 Untrue
6 Pianist Templeton
10 Scarum's partner
15 Offhand
19 "___ and Albert"
20 Hester Prynne's mark
21 Heroine of 1939
22 Life of Riley
23 Kay Fairchild (in radio soaps)
25 "Original Amateur Hour" host
27 Mix or Ewell
28 Slammer
29 Vampire
31 Squares, in St. Cyr
32 Soaps director Theodora
34 Radio actor DeKoven
35 Gargantuan
36 "Who is Sylvia? what ___ ..."
38 Letters from Lemnos
40 Wanted one
44 Groups of eight
46 "First Nighter" opener
47 "The ___ Man"
48 Civil rights org.
49 Miseries
50 Show biz sisters of soap opera
54 Literary monogram
55 Ear: Comb. form
56 I winter: Lat.
57 "Learn to Live" author
58 Radio's tavern owner
60 Part of an ocrea
62 Sponge cloth
64 Word on a wall
65 Pickling
67 Tragg et al.
68 Upper crust
71 Wild sheep
72 Arch Oboler's "___ Out"
75 "___ Jazz"
77 Radio-TV attorney
79 Cole Porter song
80 Small crowd
82 Part of TNT
83 Linkletter
84 Radio's water commissioner
87 Dream, to Danielle
88 Vocalist Massey
90 Certain votes
91 Home of 21 Across
92 110 Across, for one
94 Hutch's TV partner et. al.
98 Keeler and Mercer
99 "Tex and Jinx" guests
100 Wall hanging
101 With 117 Across, '40s maestro
103 ___ to the microphone
105 "Indian Love Call" composer
106 Likewise, in Lubeck
107 French TV ntwk.
110 Humorist of the '30s
112 John Reid's alias
115 "African Queen" scriptwriter
116 From head ___
117 See 101 Across

118 Marjorie Forrester, to 84 Across
119 Parks or Lahr
120 Mulligan and mulligatawney
121 Eponymous Hebrew ancestor
122 Violin for Stern

DOWN
1 Burns and Allen theme: "Love ___ "
2 "Lux Video Theatre" host Kruger
3 Radio host who took "the same train every week" to adventure
4 Autumnal mo.
5 Radio story teller Nelson
6 Handicrafter
7 Radio's "Dribblepuss"
8 Gelderland commune
9 Bette's "Juarez" role
10 Men of Menton
11 By ___ (narrowly)
12 Notable in "Kim"
13 Tail: Comb. form
14 On parade
15 "Hit Parade" singer Gibbs
16 Bob and Ray's Interstellar Officer Candidate

17 What "video" means
18 "The Story of ___ Johnson"
24 Capri finish
26 Emerald City's creator
30 Popular soap opera of the '40s
33 Triumphant cries
34 Clergyman
36 Tribe from Sioux City
37 Arthur Godfrey's "Talent ___ "
39 Injure
40 Home for Heidi
41 To laugh, in Lille
42 Beth's predecessor
43 Ms. McGillicuddy
45 ___ Ed McConnell
47 Dennis O'Keefe's radio role
51 Produce a lamb
52 Jefferson, religiously
53 Channel swimmer
56 Famous sportscaster
59 Crew
61 Cigar
63 Tattered Tom's creator
64 Scuffles
66 Swarthout of "The Family Hour"
69 Radio comedy "___ and Esther"
70 "Good . . . day! commentator
73 Provokes

74 Cubic meters
76 Sections of the Met
77 Slickers
78 In ___ (bored)
79 "U.S. Steel Hour" presentation
81 "___ It Now"
85 "To Each His Own" singers
86 "O Canada!" composer
87 Rake
89 One of three
93 "___ of Divorce": radio serial
95 Goad
96 Emergencies
97 "___ False": radio quiz
100 Western series "Straight ___ "
102 Horiz.
103 Popeye, for one
104 Buster Brown's dog
105 Entertain lavishly
106 Meara or Murray
108 Locket, to Lopez
109 Portland's spouse
111 "I've ___ A Secret"
113 Globe
114 King of wit

6 SIGMOID by Lawrence M. Rheingold
If you know how to write a letter from Greece, you'll avoid many a tight squeeze below.

ACROSS

1 Copycat
5 Duo
8 Entry
12 Indispensable
19 Preserve, as ham
20 Savvy
21 Hillside in Hawick
22 Orestes' sibling
23 Cocked hats
25 Decrease
26 More brazen
27 Economic low
28 Suffix with velvet
29 Brief case in grammar
30 Undertow, to Hans
31 Alpine curves
32 Aisne city
34 Fruity dessert
36 Except when
37 Linking
40 Not present: Abbr.
41 Piers
42 Eventuate
45 Felicity or sanctified state
48 I love: Latin
49 Traverses
52 Mason's partner
53 Fourth Estate
54 Male swan
57 Biddy
58 Ayres or Lehr
60 Decibel level: Abbr.
61 It's a long time
62 Triangular cloth insert
63 NYSE watchdog
64 They're on the watch
66 New tax rate settings
69 ___ Pasha (Albanian politico)
71 Sedatives
73 TV alien
74 "Quaint in form and ___": Beers
77 Braided
79 Ancient chariot
82 Plunder
83 Short response
84 ETO general
86 Famed lexicon: Abbr.
87 NHL Hall of Famer
88 Nippon urge?
89 Good earth
90 Conrad the actor
92 Judge's state?
95 Jan. and Feb.
96 Trappings, etc.
98 Lamb work
99 Writer's ___
102 Bell and Kettle
103 Universe theorist
106 Whet
107 Hungarian composer
110 Queen of Carthage
111 Duffer's delight
114 Half the hrs.
115 Goddess of retribution
116 Nucleic acid letters
118 Penitence
120 ___ News, Va.
123 Black Sea port
124 Covetous
125 One who tramples
126 Pudu or muntjac
127 Mountain pass
128 Ret. from a profession
129 Circe
130 Commedia dell ___
131 Raiment
132 Fondle

DOWN

1 Geena Davis, e.g.
2 Soup
3 Blore and Clapton
4 Time-out period
5 Larynx site
6 Remove the chaff
7 Goddess of plenty
8 Competent
9 Salad greens
10 Recent: Comb. form
11 Ruhr city
12 Fragrances
13 Opt
14 Saul's uncle
15 Valve controlling temperature: Abbr.
16 "As ___, it ain't": Carroll
17 Vesicle
18 Bounty
24 Ships of fuels
29 Sister superior
33 Bird's bill
35 ___ of Kutch (salt morass in India)
36 Preceder of dos
37 Omni follower
38 Antiquity, in poesy
39 Loch monster, fondly
41 "___ of potage": Ward
42 Noted publisher: 1858–1935
43 Amerind of Canada
44 Grant
46 "Not ___ fancy": Hamlet
47 "Now have I ___ good day's work": Richard III
48 "Gunsmoke" star
50 Cathedral city
51 Slovenly state
53 Has title to
54 Spiritual guides
55 Scrap; crumb
56 Egyptian god of pleasure
59 Eng. architect's family
61 Inspiration in Ischia
62 Colloid
64 Old English letter
65 Globular: Abbr.
67 Formacid
68 Frantic
70 Realtor, for short
72 More uncouth
74 Nellie the reporter
75 This goes before a buck
76 New Mexico town
78 Old Tokyo
80 Soprano Berger
81 Chic
85 Macedonian city
89 Prune
90 Expansive
91 Viet offensive
93 Twiggy sweepers
94 Hours in D.C.
95 ___ de Stael
96 Lagomorph
97 The Old ___ (Ireland)
99 Gregorians' songs
100 Cesar of old films
101 "Jeopardy" given
102 Slug-a-bed snuggery
104 Kind of image
105 Having lost one's thinking cap?
107 Ecdysiast
108 Law's partner
109 Israeli body
111 ___ facie
112 Ed of TV
113 What atavists do
117 Bern stream
119 Fuel cartel letters
121 Moccasin
122 Keats work
123 Zenana cubicle
124 Math term: Abbr.

7 WORD CROSS by Louis Baron

Our veteran puzzler from New York will always do two things: challenge and amuse. This opus is no exception.

ACROSS

1 Say harshly
5 What a miss is as good as
10 Beat it
13 Is openmouthed
18 Crop-chomping ant
19 Toast start
20 Kooky
21 Man from Qum
22 Realm with a wide throne
25 Untamed
26 Alas, in Arles
27 Sleuth Carter's heyday
29 Wends or Sorbs
30 Windy City sobriquet
31 Name in spydom
32 Rides freely
33 ___ crow
35 Ex-cigar
37 Of an anatomical tissue
39 Nonstop crying jag
45 Peak in W Texas
46 Didn't say ___
49 Spinneret products
50 Literary monogram
51 ___ Dhabi
52 ___ generis
53 Clan
54 Sight from NYC
55 I love, to Cato
56 Set against
58 Most updated
60 London's, when it fell
64 Kin of eau and Wasser
65 Grog
66 Needless activity
67 Pianist Myra
69 Zoo ape's Darwinian query
76 Prolonged account
78 Where David hid from Saul
79 Type of relief
80 Printemps follower
81 The birds
82 What Hudsons guzzled
84 Brooklyn or Japan ender
85 Brian Elias opus
86 Agent of the comics
87 Charisse
88 Paul's "Exodus" role
89 Homestead Act in Canaan
92 Romero film role
94 Kelep
95 Type of wit
96 Each
100 ___ podrida
103 Polynesian banana
105 Dud
109 Arthur
112 Notch-edged
113 Progress slowers
114 Be a Reno court clerk
116 White bird
117 Locale of Camus' "The Plague"
118 "Many ___ is lost for want of meat": Franklin
119 No-see-um
120 European dormice
121 Still
122 "___ Darling Daughter"
123 Penteconter movers

DOWN

1 "And the mome ___ outgrabe": Carroll
2 Ornamental evergreen
3 Inscribed pillar
4 Has a powwow
5 Philip in "China Sky"
6 Ambulance attendant
7 Gossans
8 Somewhat liberal
9 Lett's neighbor
10 French pirate
11 Class of ferns
12 Buddy
13 NFL's 1956 MVP
14 Action area
15 Mozart's Symphony No. 31
16 Stage graphically
17 Attire for Cordero
20 "___ move on!"
23 Its capital is Shillong
24 Alteration site
28 Musical potato
34 The Velvet Fog
36 Pitch
38 Brock of baseball
39 Do the deck
40 Quadri-
41 Bounden
42 Like a baker's apron
43 Father of Peleg
44 Nomad's tent
46 Negev's big city
47 Goddess of plenty
48 Can. capital
52 Plants-to-be
53 Like Sue or Adeline
55 Hit by 34 Down
56 Copywriters
57 Lamb Chop's friend
59 Guiding standards
61 D'Artagnan's creator
62 Atomic arsenal
63 Be unsteady
68 Begin
70 "___ lies all within": Shak.
71 Ohre River's alias
72 Cancún coin
73 Fluid excess in tissues
74 Novarro of films
75 "The Third Man" director
76 Ravi's 100,000
77 Academic growth
83 Kin of unaus
85 Parsons and Taylor
86 Hyde, to Jekyll
88 Confronts
89 Skunk
90 Kindle
91 Clerk type
93 Stick
96 Tenor Schiotz
97 Arctic gravel mound
98 Lake in N Finland
99 Tent caterpillar
101 Royal feline
102 Arm of the Med.
104 Muhammadanism
106 Flaherty film: 1926
107 "Tin Drum" hero
108 Notorious dens
110 Ilium
111 Opp. of tmw.
115 "Silence in the Snowy Fields" poet

WEATHER OR NOT by Barbara Springer

This puzzle, appropriately enough, comes from one of our bright constructors in sunny California.

ACROSS

1 Flatheaded fish
7 Table before a reredos
12 Oodles
17 LIX, eleven times
21 To graft, in a way
22 Africa's Sierra ___
23 Skater's maneuver
24 Pantheon site
25 Environment
26 South American capital
27 Writer Loos
28 ___ City, California
29 Medical suffix
30 Org. in which Michael Jordan played
32 Much ado about little
35 Morning show
37 Player on the dealer's right
38 Holliday of the West
39 Vestiges
40 Function
43 Thing, in court
44 Most iniquitous
46 Callous
48 In any event
51 Tract
54 Wads
58 Type of novel
59 Kind of music
60 In debt
61 City in southern India
62 Accustom
64 Gone from the coop
67 Cancel
69 Too much, in Toulouse
70 Hot ___ (fast driver)
71 Aspect
72 "The lady ___ protest too much:" Hamlet
73 Explosive initials
74 Crummy
76 Sound of triumph
77 Thumb through
79 Karma
80 Eddy's Christian ___
83 Like an ice cream holder
86 Swimsuit style
88 Proceed on
89 Friends and neighbors
91 Hector
92 Light brown
93 Kind of MD
94 Speed
96 Site of the Apennines
98 Ships
102 Needle holder
104 Vice ___
105 Sea near Australia
106 Check; curb
107 With 87 Down, a Borodin opera
109 Future, for one
111 Place for a dance
113 Aware of a hoax
114 People
115 Part of AD
116 Overwhelmed
119 Cornucopia
121 Part of a relay team
123 Chi time
124 Dublin-to-Madrid dir.
125 Desirable quality
128 Bad ___ (German spa)
131 Incensed
132 "Ave ___ vale"
134 Be indecisive
137 Legendary rocker Reed
138 Genie's dwelling
142 Island near Java
143 Occasional
144 Serviceable
146 Part of the Presidential address
148 Henry VI founded it
149 Red head: 1918–24
150 Mister, in Monterrey
151 Headmaster's cousin
152 Excite
153 "Swan Lake" role
154 Rye fungus
155 Measure

DOWN

1 "La Boheme" role
2 Least positive integer
3 Surrealist painter
4 Movie critic Judith ___
5 Surprise in the hole?
6 Confounded
7 Calm
8 Greensward
9 Motion created by a netman
10 Nobelist ___ France
11 Change permitted land use
12 Con game
13 Jackal, for example
14 Kind of acid
15 Uncouple
16 Part of a blind
17 Boring
18 Express
19 Steep
20 Springs
31 Jerome Hines, for one
33 Log-cutting machine
34 Initial
36 Montana's motto: "___ y plata"
40 Fire
41 African capital
42 Fainthearted
44 Country estate
45 True's companion
47 Summit
49 Teased
50 Petulant
52 Place upon a list
53 Type of type
55 Relentless
56 Quickly
57 Rhyme royal stanza, for instance
60 In a risky situation
63 Gaudy
65 Number after siete
66 Alienate, in a way
68 Obloquy
75 Appropriate
78 Just
79 Floral motif
80 Lottery
81 Famous Wimbledon court
82 Apprehend
83 Preferred
84 Marcus Porcius ___ of Rome
85 Gelatin substitute
87 See 107 Across
90 Pie, in Palermo
92 Standing rule
95 Unexpected help
97 Strain
99 Inclines
100 ___ Park, Colorado
101 Reserve
103 Impending
104 Deviate
108 Samite or pekin
110 Kind of boom
112 Right-hand page
116 Retreat
117 Drowsy
118 Sumerian sun god
120 Cleared
122 "Sound of Music" librettist
125 Certain clergymen
126 Ticket
127 Wise lawgiver
129 Ms. Nixon, movie voice
130 "The Medusa and the ___": Thomas
132 Vigilant
133 Choose
135 European capital
136 Unit of force
139 Stake
140 Nuclear particle
141 Saucy
145 Card game of yore
147 Nettle

9 HEARTLESS by Grace C. Pinkston

A talented newcomer from Washington, D.C. presents a challenging theme and lots of refreshing new clues. Pay special attention to her title!

ACROSS

1 Word with walk or step
5 Howdy to Double Doody
9 Used a hawser
14 Rousseau classic
19 Tug's salute
20 Magistrate's command
21 Nicholas Gage bestseller
22 Opthamologist's tool
23 Ray Charles hit
25 Field film: 1984
27 Historical spans
28 Bush and Taft, once
29 Prince hit
30 "___ Stiff": 1953 film
33 "___ grows in size": Ovid
34 Derek Walcott book
35 S Amer. republic
36 Flaubert work
39 Bismarck and Queen Mary
41 U.S. Pacific base
43 Fixed pumps and flats
44 Adult grigs
45 Like Bette Midler
49 Spot
50 "Tell ___ Louella" (Parsons memoir)
51 Current prefix
52 Mitch Miller's instrument
53 Edna St. Vincent Millay gem
58 "Big ___" (of comics)
59 Hitler's architect
60 "Read ___ weep!"
61 ". . . come ___ o'clock"
62 Formal wear
65 Preservative
66 Fortresses' towers
68 Hebrew zodiac's Nisan
69 To some extent, informally
70 DeBakey study subject
71 "If a man ___ talent . . .": Wolfe
72 Duchess of Windsor memoir
78 Name in Norwegian royalty
79 Paroxysm
80 Without warranty
81 Go blithely along
82 Counting word
83 "Giselle" composer Adolphe
84 Looked over the scene of a future heist
86 Whereabouts
87 Progressive series
88 Peter Strauss film
91 A feast ___ famine
92 Exchange rate
95 "Mo' Better Blues" star Lee
96 Emily Litella creator
98 Filmmaker Rene ___
99 Thirty-day mo.
100 Picasso's "La Morte de ___"
101 Keaton/Spacek film
104 Judy Collins memoir
109 Tracking device
110 Calculator key
111 Glut
112 To boot
113 Age units
114 Dilemma parts
115 Carafe's cousin
116 Prepared to drive at Pebble Beach

DOWN

1 Nickname that sounds like an entree
2 A Plato dialogue
3 Stacy Keach film
4 William Clark discovery
5 Score entries
6 "Everybody ___": Nolte film
7 Victorian suffix
8 Napoleonic marshal
9 Acknowledged a letter
10 NFL Hall of Famer Matson
11 Pigeon ___ (tropical shrubs)
12 Ref. work
13 What a gambler casts
14 Slurs over
15 Thornfield in "Jane Eyre"
16 "Life ___ Short": Mickey Rooney memoir
17 Annealing ovens
18 Poetic palindrome
24 Type of rug
26 First black American UN delegate
28 "___ et Lui": book by Sand
30 Comedian Bob of TV
31 Teenager's infatuation
32 Like a dentist's patient
33 ". . . corn, would never see ___": Billy Rose
34 Getty vessel
37 Bagging fibers
38 Kind of court
39 Halcyon
40 ". . . farm ___ some sheep"
42 Words from Goethe
45 Differentiates
46 Moderate
47 Sacred anthem
48 Parts of hammer heads
50 "I seldom go to the place ___ out for": Sterne
54 "The Glamour ___": Kitty Kelley book
55 Caesar's ground
56 Leaves out
57 Hawaiian island
61 "Thou ___ lady": Shak.
62 Sandra Hochman's "Playing ___"
63 Pontiff's vestment
64 "___ Cantos": Pound
65 Puccini opera (with "La")
66 "Ticket ___" (Carpenters hit)
67 Actress Mary's family
69 "King Rat" star
70 Advantage
72 PO forms for lost mail
73 Tackled
74 Café cup
75 Hollywood film company
76 British import from Chile
77 Blade of grass
84 Alice, Gary, and Jackie of films
85 "ain't ___ night out . . .": Fields
87 They perform christies
89 Utensil on a pencil
90 Not necessarily least
92 Carmen of songdom
93 Valli of films
94 TV jungle character
95 Mrs. Sadat
97 "A ___ the Races": Marx Brothers film
99 End of a prank?
100 Adorable, as a child
101 Famous Ailey work
102 Burns's sigh
103 Cathy's mom in comics
104 Literary initials
105 Irritated
106 Outboard motor inventor Evinrude
107 Put to work
108 Distance measure

10 SHINING EXAMPLES by Joan P. Leemhorst
It was natural for Joan to come up with this puzzle. She lives in West Hollywood.

ACROSS
1 Leaders of kings
5 TV spots
9 Riv. ship
12 Tex. time
15 Turning point
19 Beer ingredient
20 What the carpenter shed
21 American poet and critic
22 Airport info.
23 Bury
25 Solo
26 Advents
28 Pile driver weight
29 Nifty
30 Romeo and Juliet
33 Auriculate
34 House or stick preceder
35 Golf appurtenance
36 Yemen money
37 Incipient bks.
38 Remove sodium chloride
41 Small Egyptian cobra
42 Anklebones
43 Ephemerid
46 Tolkien creatures
47 JFK service
49 Possessive pronoun
51 ___ Michel (leading yellow banana)
53 Saint or La Gallienne
54 Yellow pressed cheese
55 Canis Major cynosure
58 Edward Gibson's sobriquet
59 Back talk
60 Rani's garment
61 Red-green blindness
64 Fortification outwork
66 Nursing degree
67 Lake Geneva spa
68 Lentil: Comb. form
70 Well-known initials in movie lore
71 Fowl's shoulder feathers
72 Disparage
73 "___, Macduff"
75 Import
78 Turkish chief
79 Pitcher Maglie
80 Famed ref. book
81 Actor who portrayed Scrooge
83 Eur. country
84 Fabric name derived from Nîmes, France
87 First- and third-quarter moon tides
89 Word feminizers
91 Czech-German river
92 Twelve doz.
93 Waste allowance
94 Gem weight equal to 200 milligrams
95 Vessel for wine
96 Adler and Hagman
100 Special girlfriend
102 Black, to Blake
104 Mellow
106 Straight
107 Galaxy denizen with low surface temperature
108 Western org.
109 Pop
110 Author Chase
111 The Ayatollah's "Great Satan": Abbr.
112 Outside: Prefix
113 Eggplant ___ Baaldi
114 Empire State's capital
116 Kind of parliament
119 Burro
121 Deciding trials
123 HS course
124 Black fly
125 Gold, in Genova
126 High-pitched sound
127 Ayn and Sally
129 Donne's admonition, "Go, and ___"
135 "___ Be Possible?" 1964 song
136 Kind of dye
137 Went back over
138 Insipid
139 Sacramento's Arco, e.g.
140 Wired missive, for short
141 Gold or silver
142 Caesar's 402
143 Semi-erect primates
144 Before, old style
145 Fort ___, Cal.
146 Triumphed
147 Soprano Berger
148 Schism

DOWN
1 Japanese divers
2 Lug
3 Lamb's "Essays of ___"
4 Chinese woody vine
5 Kind of cast
6 Roman emperor and noted pianist
7 Gig implements
8 Glove parts
9 Bogart role
10 Peal
11 Spas
12 Breakfast food
13 "Stella by ___": 1946 song
14 Headgear, in the Highlands
15 Hollywood greats
16 Worried
17 Hit song of 1934
18 Netman Sampras
24 Gangster's gun
27 Alben Barkley
31 Mountain pass
32 ___ Appia
38 Tony ___ (U.S. hurdler in Barcelona)
39 Injure
40 Key contribution to U.S.
41 Certain church member
43 "___ over Miami": 1935 song
44 XXX + XXVI
45 Bark
48 Italian wines
49 Golfer Woosnam
50 Lieutenant general's insignia
52 Caviar
56 Movie ingenue
57 Award named after Antoinette Perry
62 Hudson River fish
63 Month of "darling buds"
65 DDE
69 Tracy and Hepburn
71 Bounder
74 Important Chilean exports
76 Group sums in series
77 Suffix with Annam
80 Frank
82 Cleaver
85 Novelist Wolfert
86 Wouk's "Marjorie ___"
88 Book by Peter Evans
89 Old spelling for egad
90 Defunct British order of knighthood
91 "Love's harbinger": Milton
97 Depend
98 Chitchat
99 Movie fan?
101 ___ culpa
103 French names
104 Actress Rehan
105 "A ___ in Calico": 1946 song
111 Displacement of rock
115 The ___ Press introduced Italic type
117 Incalculable
118 Abbreviated raincoat
119 Tree of Morocco
120 Console
122 Participial ending
125 Full many a time
126 Promotional gimmick
127 Org. headed by Sarnoff
128 Swiss river
129 ___ the Censor
130 Flying prefix
131 USN rank
132 Finish line
133 So be it
134 Part of RIP

11 ALL TOGETHER NOW by Kevin Boyle
Our Long Island constructor has amassed quite a collection of collections
below. Can you uncover all fifteen?

ACROSS

1 Emily or Wiley
5 Turkeys
10 Vault
14 Ziti
19 Islamic God
20 Renew supplies
21 River of Honduras
22 Moral values
23 Collection
25 They occupied Spain until
   1492
26 Use a rudder
27 JFK notice
28 German ice cream
29 French sociologist Gabriel
31 Collection
33 Surface a road anew
35 Deep-fryer contents
36 Assam silkworms
37 Small dog, for short
38 Brazilian resort
40 Sicilian resort
41 Strong water current
42 "The College Widow"
   playwright
43 Fords
45 ___ Arbor
47 Ref. works
49 Bounders
52 Alternative to dn.
53 Collection
57 Small urban plaza
61 Poky
63 Torah section
64 After Diciembre
66 Arab republic, to Rivera
67 "Far better it is ___ mighty
   things": T. Roosevelt
69 Carpet fiber
71 Asian holiday
72 Vaporizes
73 Pottery decorator
75 Amygdala
77 Collection
78 ___ tears (volcanic glass)
80 ___ generis
81 Funny Soupy
83 Collection
87 Uses, as one's influence
90 Binary
95 Betel palms
96 Triumphant interjection
97 Place for un élève
99 Take another spin
100 Daughter of 19 Across
101 "___ 1000 Faces,"
   Lon Chaney film
103 Impervious to light
105 Lost
106 Of the first age
108 Collection
111 Pos. battery cells
112 Python Idle
113 ___ bones (minimum)
114 Blue
115 Cavity: Comb. form
117 Nabokov opus
120 Musical theme
122 Stridulate
125 "___ and Back,"
   Audie Murphy film
127 Guitarist Paul

128 "M*A*S*H" character
129 "___ Goes By"
131 Hawaiian crows
134 Collection
136 Hollow stone
137 Farm female
138 Collection
139 Resembling a wall
140 Opening passage
142 Collection
145 Love
146 Inert gas
147 Skirt feature
148 Sees eye to eye, British dial.
149 Spanish babies
150 Site of Cyclops' smithy
151 Coal beds
152 Mound stats

DOWN

1 Batters guard this
2 Collection
3 Mineo or Bando
4 Stealthy
5 Brothers
6 Coin of Rumania
7 "We're ___ See the Wizard"
8 Rapparee
9 "The Confessions of
   Nat Turner" author
10 Kenyan tongue
11 They marry in haste
12 Dawn goddess
13 Collection
14 Mexican money
15 Alaskan island
16 Tenzing, for one

17 Steering linkage part
18 "Sweet love, was thought
   ___": Blake
19 "Happy Feet" composer
24 Bearing
25 Collection
30 Enjoyed a meal
32 Song of joy
34 Bitter
35 Delay
39 Tzara's movement
43 Fritter away
44 Cromwellian center of
   Puritanism
46 Lacrosse goal
48 Hundred: Comb. form
50 Repugnance
51 Sales pitch
54 Breakfast fare
55 The Great Commoner
56 "It's not whether you
   win ___ . . ."
57 "Rocky III" star
58 "To ___ and a bone . . ."
59 Terza ___ (verse form)
60 Abyssinian weight
62 Battering tool
65 Slippery ones
68 Echo
70 Season
72 Slung mud
74 City on the Ouse
76 "Cheers" or "Amen"
77 Clay, today
79 Penn or Connery
82 Sufficient
83 Bara's nickname

84 Sandarac tree
85 Italian painter Guido
86 Start of a Caesarean
   statement
88 South African people
89 Spanish soup
91 Anatomical openings
92 Collection
93 Ultimate aim
94 Culminate
96 "2001" computer
98 Strings, in pool
101 Collection
102 Collection
104 Destroy
107 Crucial
109 Let
110 Frozen ridge
113 Instrument of Haydn's time
116 Suffix for plug
117 Mexican conservative
   leader Lucas ___
118 Strip
119 F. Hoyle's field
121 Attractive one
123 Plays dirty
124 Waste time
126 "Overboard" star
128 Customary functions
130 Her kettle restored youth
132 Illampu locale
133 Lip
135 Famous also-ran
137 Corrodes
141 Genetic stuff
143 Director Peckinpah
144 Commit a faux pas

CITY SNICKERS by Tap Osborn

Tap invites you to take a whirlwind tour through twelve cities below. You won't see many sights, but you will have a good time.

ACROSS

1 Chimp's cousin
6 Appellations
11 Admiral Zumwalt
15 Give the raspberry to
21 Seascape artist
22 Plain People
23 "Darkness at ___": Koestler
24 "Pretty Maids ___ Row," 1971 film
25 Florida curse?
27 Delaware herb?
29 Portnoy's creator
30 Future fish
31 Ponder
32 Largest of the Ryuku Islands
33 Ryan's co-star in "Love Story"
35 Bus. abbrs.
37 Bluefish tempter
38 Feathers' partner
39 Texas cup?
43 Forum figure
44 Wherewithal
48 Crashes
49 Shoshoneans
50 Trifle in Tours
51 Exchange premium
52 He'll bite your head off
53 These ring true
55 ___ mitzvah: Var.
56 Jujitsu relative
58 Adage
60 Illinois snack?
63 Diamond or Dagover
64 Spectrum maker
66 See 67 Across
67 Liar anagram
68 Fertile, as soil
72 Travails
73 Carton size, for some products
74 Lu Chen's homeland
76 Borden's weapon
77 Josh
78 Germane
80 ___ train
81 Stirring up
83 Wine: Comb. form
84 Ending for journal
85 Midwest capital
86 Nine follower
87 Feudal laborer
88 Garment makers
90 Cuckoopint
91 Skin bruise
92 Libertine
93 Entrepreneurial abbr.
94 Carolina absurdity?
98 Donovan's spy org.
99 Frug's kin
102 Exterminate
103 ___ of (mulct)
104 Of a certain period
106 Herring
107 Scottish swift
109 Luigi's skill
110 Formal and sanctimonious
113 Grayish goose
114 "___ Dreams Ago"
115 Illinois shops?

118 Stick-___-ive
119 Duration
120 ___ moth
121 Bushy evergreen
122 She reads tea leaves
126 Soother
127 ___ Madison: Abbr.
128 Downy surfaces
131 Odor on Puget Sound?
133 Buckeye Belial?
137 Devilfish
138 Baseball's Matty
139 Own up to
140 "The Shepherd's Calendar" poet
141 Acoustic
142 Blue dye
143 Fashion's Geoffrey
144 Sun: Comb. form

DOWN

1 Electrical unit
2 French monarch
3 Texas weeper?
4 Verne's Captain
5 Spunk
6 Yep's opposite
7 Steal ___ on
8 Tropical flowering tree
9 Salinger girl
10 Short
11 Tolerates
12 Rattly
13 Karpov's turn
14 Solidly supportive
15 Mississippi horn warning?
16 Havelock
17 North Carolina college

18 ___ Ridge, 1972 Derby winner
19 Over
20 Avenger King
26 Trace
28 Roadway
31 Stomach or other internal membrane
33 Adenosine diphosphate
34 Medieval poem
36 U. at Raleigh
37 Bachelor of letters deg.
38 Saudi king: 1964–1975
40 Tripod part
41 Gold, to Gaius
42 Straphanger's train
43 Skulls
44 "Cheers" role
45 ___ Khan
46 Canine command
47 Weeding tool
53 Dim
54 Med. course
55 Like Calumet Farm
57 Made full disclosure
58 Pinnacles
59 Francis of TV
61 Pickler's need
62 Ingenuous
65 Pensacola to Miami dir.
69 Connecticut tableware?
70 Wadkins and Ross
71 Inciters
73 New Jersey inlay?
74 Mayhem is one
75 Sounds of disbelief
76 In a stupor
79 Action words

80 "Vanishing Act" star
81 Texas billionaire
82 Goddess, to Nero
85 Smart as a whip
86 Bean curd
89 Evolve
90 Extreme
91 Smithy
92 Maple product
95 "___ of Jeannie"
96 Boarded
97 Soprano Lotte
99 Colorless
100 Bar order
101 Time for a coffee break
105 Nigerian tribesman
108 Polish-born soprano
109 Welcome loudly
110 Recent: Comb. form
111 Move quickly
112 Swerve
116 "Now ___ down to . . ."
117 Southwestern capital
118 Meters
119 Pago Pago locale
122 Terminus
123 Per
124 Outer: Comb. form
125 Darling, in Cork
126 Machete
127 Make tedious
129 "The Nazarene" author
130 Ghostly
132 Untrained
133 Dollop
134 Native suffix
135 Onassis
136 Newcomer

13 A REAL EYE-OPENER by Charles B. Waffell

Charles tells us he was watching "20/20" when the idea for this one came to him.

ACROSS

1 Aral, for one
4 ". . . wish upon ___"
9 Performed an axel
14 Smidgen
17 Foot part
19 French river
20 Make sacred
21 Shade
22 Rat poison
23 Body builders
24 Syrian city
25 LAX acronym
26 "Drink to ___": Ben Jonson
29 "___ the Needle": Follett novel
30 Luanda is its capital
31 Sink
32 Linotype adj.
34 Hwys.
35 Baths
37 Tumultuous
40 Barcelona beaches
43 Grill
44 Hollywood's Ayres
47 Ransack
48 "Close up ___ and draw the curtain close . . .": Shak.
49 Narrow cut
50 Destined
52 South African village
53 Rainbow
54 "The ___": Hartley Coleridge
57 Journey segment
58 Tidy
60 Wheel hubs
61 Wheedle
62 Nuclear wpn.
64 Clear sky
65 Group of geniuses
66 Dolphins or Sharks
67 Jogs
68 Withered
69 Droop
72 Hugo's center, for example
76 "___ Rock": Simon and Garfunkel hit
77 Hide
78 Timbres
79 Kitchen emanation
80 Sign up
81 Fathers
83 Join
84 Pulled
85 Bear Hall-of-Famer
86 A Caucasian
87 Prompts
88 Black: Comb. form
89 Three ___ match
90 Fur trader: 1763–1848
93 Exercises
96 Lod loc.
98 A 1959 hit by The Flamingos
104 Billy ___ Williams
105 Cash register reading
106 Really bad
107 Facial feature
108 Daisy
109 Dudley's rating of Bo in "10"
110 1/24 of un jour
111 Alone
112 Scheldt feeder
113 Risktaker
114 Heraldic wreaths
115 One-A rater

DOWN

1 Where Anna taught
2 Nine: Comb. form
3 City WNW of Boston
4 Certain socks
5 "Well, ___ just . . .": Beatles
6 Singer Tennille
7 What can divide Becker and Edberg
8 Hebrew letter
9 Polynesian drums
10 Book by Nicholas Gage
11 Heidi's home, to her
12 Segar's sailor
13 Kind of general
14 "___ Upon You": Lone Star song
15 Nash, for one
16 Tone follower
18 Eric Carmen song from "Dirty Dancing"
20 Sunken fences
27 Water vessels of India
28 Ski lift
33 Country singer Yearwood et al.
35 Small knife
36 Inventors' friends
38 Controversial apple spray
39 Cheap whiskey
40 Woods of jazz
41 Mantuan money
42 Welcome visage
43 Coagulate
44 Regal reversal
45 Biblical endings
46 Damp
49 Thick piece
50 One hundred
51 Derby
55 "Funny About Love" star
56 0
58 An ancient mariner
59 Archaic ant
63 Separating
64 Made a mistake
65 Sea: Ger.
67 Air
68 Winter deposit
70 Cupid
71 "Buffalo ___"
72 ". . . those ___ blue?": George Macdonald
73 Actor Skinner
74 Reporter's query
75 Coolers
76 "Lost ___: Debbie Gibson song
80 Keep an ___ the ground
82 Protected a deck
84 ___ mater (brain part)
85 Thwarts
87 "Suzanne" composer
88 Guarantee
90 Goose genus
91 Work hard
92 Tenth President
94 Greek seaport
95 Loess and loam
96 Graven image
97 Provocative
99 Oop's gal
100 Steam, in Santiago
101 Jug
102 A lot to see
103 Japanese salad plants

14 GENERALLY SPEAKING by Jack Jumonville

You'll need a good *command* of words to complete this puzzle from a Pelican State neophyte.

ACROSS

1 Backward digs?
4 Veep Barkley
9 Type of sports club
13 Summits
18 Progenitor of Edomites
20 Aptly named novelist
21 Classical concert halls
22 Type of horseplayer
23 U.S.A.'s second 4-star
26 Lana's first husband
27 Child of many an officer
28 Crete's highest point
29 Sailor's gear bag
30 Test anew
31 Burgundy wines
33 Interlocks
34 Egyptian god of turmoil
35 Smashing!
36 ___ de chambre
37 Siegfreid's slayer
40 USMC Commandant
43 Oscar Wilde's forte
46 Anagram of sale
47 Wait-___ (hooked thorn plant)
48 Of the dawn
49 Lift for upright skiers
50 "Gigi" scriptwriter
51 Berlin Airlift 4-star hero
55 Singer Mel from Chicago
56 Vast desert area
57 SW plains Indian
58 "An Officer and a Gentleman" star
59 Indian sirs
60 Chickpeas
62 Debate
63 Pitcher's place
64 Steel girders
66 Film theater, for short
67 Baseball's Boudreau
68 Monogram of the director of "Rocky" and "The Karate Kid"
70 City in Peru
71 A 4-star U.S.A. COS, whose sobriquet was "Lightning"
74 Women kegler's group: Abbr.
76 Three-time House Speaker, ___ Rayburn
77 Peevish
78 Eye layer
79 Deserve
80 Winglike structure
81 Last U.S.A. 5-star
85 Hitler's invalid ethnological term
86 "Nevermore" sayer
88 Tautomeric compounds
89 Pluto
90 Some kind of nut
92 Poet Hart and novelist Stephen
94 Catered clambake cost calculation component
98 Detest
99 Xavier Cugat's fourth wife
100 Inherit
101 Emulates the mouse in Sellers' film
102 First and only USAF 5-star
105 Leguminous plant
106 Opera highlight
107 Greek east-wind god
108 Very willing
109 Key
110 Wee
111 Moved stealthily
112 Balaam's rebuker

DOWN

1 Flask type
2 "A child shall get ___ . . .": Shak.
3 ___ de Mallorca
4 Famous landing place
5 Curtis E. ___, SAC 4-star
6 Fiber sheet for bandage or quilt use
7 Ames and Asner
8 O.T. book
9 Monterey area military reservation
10 Important campus bldg.
11 Is literate
12 Polynesian supernatural power
13 "The ___" (West Point to most of our theme heroes)
14 Sacramental oil
15 A 4-star who relieved both Mac and Ike
16 Adjective for troops of 40 Across
17 Ox yoke bars
19 U.S.A.'s first 4-star
24 "Peer Gynt" creator
25 Alex Trebek, e.g.
31 Civilian clothes, to our theme heroes
32 Spring mo.
33 "The Queen of ___," TV film
35 A spatula is one
36 Brawl
37 Detroit's "Prince ___" (AL MVP 1944–45)
38 ___ vera
39 Ranking WW II U.S.A. 5-star (Nobel Peace Prize 1953)
40 Terminates against
41 Fracas
42 Tibetan antelope
44 Metrical foot
45 Gaul divisor number to Caesar
47 Grads
49 Only U.S.A. General of the Armies
52 Hungarian language group
53 Musical repeat sign
54 Oft-used adjective for "fate"
55 Kind of cross
59 Composer of "Semper Fidelis"
61 "I ___ Camera"
62 Sour in taste
63 Pink Floyd hit
64 Capra's "___ Wonderful Life"
65 Jezebel's deity
67 Kitty's nine
69 "East of Eden" character
71 Actress Collins
72 "___ American Cousin"
73 Allays
75 Arbor antecedent
77 Small merganser
81 Unused type
82 Marshal troops for battle again
83 Vex
84 Late Liberian leader
85 Clothes-drying frame
87 Start of Richard III's cry in battle
89 What Dennis Conner would dread to do
90 Wrist bones
91 Leigh Hunt's Ben Adhem, and others
92 Colette novel
93 Arrested
94 Infield fly
95 Col. Tibbets' mom
96 Mercator title-page figure
97 Dixieland drummer "Baby"
99 Causerie
100 Give a hoot
103 "___ Ramsey,": TV series
104 Half of a Heston role

15

GENERATION GAP by Jan Hurschman

A newcomer from Michigan offers a Stepquote based on a quip by that prolific writer Anon.

ACROSS

1 **Start of a Stepquote**
6 Dished out, in a way
12 Flambeau
17 Spoken or written with ease
18 Circle of color
19 Frittata
21 David's target
22 "___ of the Heart," 1986 film
23 Give the gate to again
24 Suffix with north or south
25 S African township
27 ___ Jack of old comics
29 Howe, to Washington
30 Small anvil
32 **Stepquote: Part III**
34 Guitarist Clapton
35 Go ___ (fight)
36 Analyzes an ore
38 Appointed
40 Pat or Daniel
41 Although: Lat.
42 ___ Adams, "Daisy Mae" of Bwy.
44 You can draw them
45 Jim or John Nance
46 A kind of excuse
48 Foofaraws
49 Datum
50 George Pal's "___ Moon," 1950 movie
54 " . . . haughty, gallant, gay ___": Rowe
58 Boat hoist
59 Market Square in Indianapolis, e.g.
60 Richard Wilbur product
61 Omega
62 Cat-___-tails
63 Placing the tiles again
65 Lend-___ Act, Mar. 11, 1941
67 ___ Peeples, of "Fame"
68 Nights, in Nancy
70 Streisand's "married lady" of songdom
71 "Sit!," to Fido
72 Interpret
74 Indifference
76 Suffixes for human and aster
77 Mafia bigwigs
78 File-folder catch-all, for short
79 SRO shows
82 Submission to a record exec
83 Walter ___ Hospital
85 Refrain syllables
89 Once more
90 Rotated on an axis
92 Glossy, polished
94 Egyptian lizard
95 Pro ___ publico
96 **Stepquote: Part V**
98 Ann ___, Michigan
99 Eng. ___ (frosh course, often)
100 Advertiser's plan or sketch
102 City in NW France
104 Dir. from Warsaw to Lodz
105 Saroyan's "My ___ Aram"
107 Insignificant items
109 Outwitted in a card game
111 Lech's locale
112 More spectral or unearthly
113 Certain Slavs
114 Fasteners
115 Fears greatly
116 **End of Stepquote**

DOWN

1 Excuse for an absence
2 Rapa ___ (Easter Island)
3 Full of froth
4 Aware of
5 **Stepquote: Part II**
6 Milk sugar
7 " . . . to suffer the slings and ___": Shak.
8 Agnus ___
9 Herbert of film, and family
10 AL, HG, PB, etc.
11 Wishes
12 Like a convex lens
13 Augury
14 Rel. of an ump
15 First name of 81 Down
16 Jeanne d'Arc, e.g.
17 Sherwood or Black
20 Sway
21 Ancient people of eastern Europe
26 Actor Morales
28 Operculum
31 "Red ___ the Sunset," 1935 song
33 **Stepquote: Part IV**
35 Main vessel
37 Certain truck
39 Strikebreaker
40 Piazza and Jeter
43 Ancient Roman coin
45 Gangsters' guns
47 Lt.'s order to a PFC
48 Eldest: Fr.
49 ___-not, light-blue flower
50 Fish often seen in tropical aquariums
51 French spa
52 Alpine ridge
53 Dick Tracy's wife
54 Ulyanov
55 Peruses
56 Map within a map
57 River at Frankfurt
58 Therefore, in Tours
60 "Veni, ___, vici": Caesar
64 Russian news agency
66 ___ set ('30s toy)
69 Beans grown in India
73 Capital of Bulgaria
74 Major ___
75 News commentator Leif and family
77 Glutton
79 Ovine noise
80 Groups of eight
81 Editor in whose book the Stepquote quip was found
82 Signified
83 Equips again
84 Whence the Pison flowed
86 "Mister ___," 1948 Heggan and Logan play
87 Does penance
88 Tear up
90 Cowboy Rogers
91 Diverse
93 Mule, to the Army team
95 Lazes in the sun
97 **Stepquote: Part VI**
100 Speech defect
101 Radial
103 Large kangaroo
106 Alfonso's queen
108 By way of
110 "Some ___ meat . . .": Burns

WOULD YOU SPELL THAT PLEASE? by Nancy Nicholson Joline
Cacographers will definitely have trouble with this one! Once again, Nancy has
won the Margaret Award.

ACROSS

1 Dance from Cuba
6 Expand
12 Longed
17 Cordial
18 Bewitch
19 Daniel or Debby
20 Aristophanes'
   Cloudcuckooland
23 French months
24 Flowering shrub
25 Myra and Rudolf
26 "Heidi" author
27 Arkin and Bates
28 Site of ancient Olympics
30 Is in a snit
32 Kept firmly in mind
33 Galbraith's subj.
34 Occurring every eighth day
37 Actor Goodwin
38 '60s student org.
39 Stalin's original surname
42 Bklyn. ___, N.Y.
43 Actress Winningham
44 ___ fours
45 Where to find Isfahan
47 Daisy Duck's niece
50 "___ Loser": Beatles
51 Flavor
53 Takes on
56 Chews the scenery
58 Vic's radio wife
59 Early Scot or Breton
61 Sticky stuff
62 Netherlands sights
63 Trinket, slangily
65 Norman Vincent ___
66 "As it ___, it ain't":
   Tweedledee
67 Islamic sect
68 Indolent
69 "Gigi" lyricist
70 ___ horse
72 Bring up on charges again
74 Cord or Ford
75 O.R. personnel
76 Carson's predecessor
77 Million follower
78 "Le roi est ___, . . ."
79 Tax specialist, sometimes
81 Peace Nobelist: 1961
85 Like McCullers' café
88 Objet d'___
89 These may be growing
90 Hebrides island
91 Kind of line or palm
92 Friar in action
95 "The Thin Man" canine
96 Raptor's weapon
97 Sadat
98 Wise lawgivers
102 Onager
105 Norway or sugar follower
106 Aztec sun god
108 Mores
109 TV producer's concern
110 Sea urchin features
111 Inclines
112 Curly, for one
113 Bob of the PGA

DOWN

1 Nullifies
2 Let go
3 Appearances
4 Unadorned
5 Lotion ingredient
6 ___ gratias
7 Creeping
8 Alençon and Brussels
9 Carter and Irving
10 Clothes
11 Pennsylvania port
12 Humble
13 Preempt
14 Country of Gulliver's
   fourth voyage
15 Beseech
16 Stops
17 Solidified
20 Beery and Webster
21 Christmas display
22 Very, in music
29 Brock of baseball
31 Join (with "in")
33 Poet Pound
34 Christiania now
35 Ecclesiastical

36 Sets
39 Bonneville and Hoover
40 Tastes
41 Treas. Dept. div.
43 ___ van der Rohe
46 Boring tool
47 Corpsman
48 Mennonite group
49 Faulkner's imaginary
   county
51 Arid
52 Fuss
53 Publican's potable
54 Nobelist in medicine: 1970
55 Prognosticators
57 Colorful fish
58 ___-fi
60 Maui crater
63 Quaker pronoun
64 Navy rank below capt.
65 Impudent
67 Sonora shawl
69 Rendered fat
71 ___-di-dah
73 Transgresses
74 Soft drink

77 Maupassant's "Bel-___"
78 Rainier's realm
79 A chewy candy
80 Assume a toe-out stance
82 Fen
83 Kind of cousin
84 Whit
85 Praises
86 Bikini and Kwajalein
87 Tooth: Comb. form
91 Nymph pursued by
   Apollo
93 Copland's "El ___
   México"
94 Curl
95 Allied beachhead of
   WW II
96 Unspoken
99 "Yours, Mine and ___,"
   1968 film
100 "South Pacific" girl
101 Flutist Luening
103 Church part
104 Surpasses
107 Part of XL

17 PUNS AND ANAGRAMS by Nancy Nicholson Joline

Just for a change of pace we present a tricky puzzle by one of our top constructors. For example, "one" might be "I," and "you" might be "U," and "nothing" might be "O."

ACROSS

1 One is among stars in making this flight
7 It's cold, but it may be baked
13 Emitter becomes a nuisance in the home
15 A singer can be effacing
16 Football player takes on section of the barricade
17 Taking you away from troubles for a seafood treat
18 It's gold, or nothing
19 Lesson One translated for jungle queen
21 You and I head east for employment
22 Girl found in grain storage building
24 Eastern epic provides a part
25 Receptacle is a matter for investigation
26 Nero has left to find a film star
28 Any Latvian, I hear, is allowed
29 Stuffed dates, perhaps?
30 Individuals grow old in a domestic establishment
32 100 trees are classified
34 She's a district attorney
35 Card game is a struggle
36 To get a flightless bird, put it in a topless crate
39 Nosier sort of citizen
42 Rosa has small victory to enjoy
43 With the cat out, get a little sleep
45 Rose's about to get ulcers
47 Cupid appears in a European capital
48 Scrimp endlessly to get a curtain
50 Identify a title
51 Man returns to a lake in France
52 Prattle about where to put the turkey
54 Singleton loses one, but a great quantity remains
55 Lee said they're penguins
57 Storied workers in communications
59 Deranged eastern inmate gives theatrical performance
60 Revised, it's different
61 Spinet, repaired, is in harmony
62 Ed Case is terminated

DOWN

1 Tea and rolls can be found in a promenade
2 Romeo at unusal eating place
3 Terrorist group in Rome found in cupboard
4 There's a demon in Wimpole Street
5 Italian money changed for Iranian
6 Remove one's clothing on the main drag
7 A flower emerged
8 Thick slice cut up for some dogs
9 Dunce is at the back of the class
10 Locate where you and I take a test
11 Ken's set brings in the Israeli parliament!
12 Ed, after wild rage, assented

14 Lee and I take to a French star
15 Determines in favor of the Spanish sect, oddly
20 Born on the west side of Needham
23 A D.C. biggie eats with Ron
25 Ira takes corn for a hyena's dinner
27 Bottom of drain put in proper order
29 Examines radar displays
31 Alligator swallows gangster's weapon
33 You, I'm told, are an old lamb
36 Amanda has a right to a month in the East
37 100 joined to save shore birds
38 A scene, dismantled, is put in a container

39 Di's pet treated maliciously
40 They make speeches, of a sort, in Oregon
41 Some err, are transformed, and find contrition
42 Alma is getting something to eat
44 Man works in a museum
46 Sends east for felt
48 Lee is in Spain, briefly, for a rest
49 500 mice ordered for doctor
52 Yearn for a piece of Hawaiian fruit?
53 Privet has split in the middle
56 Landed in a tipsy condition
58 Drink tossed off by Boston partygoers

18 DOWNBEAT by Bert Rosenfield

Bert says he was listening to a Moody Blues album when he constructed this Across-and-Downer.

ACROSS

1 Rubble
7 Bookbinding material
13 Fitted with wings
19 Glide by
20 Acetylene
21 Where Potosi and Sucre are
23 Hugo classic
25 In-port merchandise vessel
26 Rosary bead
27 Mythical man of brass
28 Potato pancakes
30 That, to Tacitus
31 Coarse lacework
33 Cordage fiber
34 "___ nice day"
35 Thine, in Tours
36 Outdo
39 "The ___": 1942 Wayne-Dietrich film
42 Jerk the knee
44 Coronado's quest
45 Papuan port
46 Sarasota, from Clearwater
47 Poly ending
48 Emulates a kestrel
51 Iron: Comb. form
53 London's Hyde Park bridle path
55 To such a degree
59 Cereal grass
62 Geometric abstract
63 Thomas Moore's "___ Rookh"
65 In a sluggish way
66 Cue the cast
68 Live together
70 Bony
72 Grayish-yellow
73 Country house
74 U of UN fame
76 Airline monogram
77 Bach composed over 200
80 Underhanded tactics
83 Draw out
84 Ladder-like
85 Crabwalk
89 Periodot's mo.
92 "The Faerie Queene" heroine
93 Defendants, legally
94 Capt. Hook's expression
95 Unpopular statutes
98 Juan's land
102 Rubberneck
103 Possessing an A-1 physique
104 Chili con ___
106 Former Cambodian ruler ___ Sihanouk
108 Perugia pronoun
109 Flower named for a botanist
111 Basketry fiber
113 "___ tu": Verdi aria
114 Crude clothes presser
116 Quarterback's group
119 Narrow a passage
120 Queen in "King John"
121 Palestinian ascetic of old
122 Builds a skyscraper
123 Gender experts
124 Cervine surnames

DOWN

1 English poet-novelist Walter ___
2 Gives a leg up
3 It underlies the finish
4 Tachometer letters
5 "___ Crime?": song from "Bells are Ringing"
6 TV street
7 Beach in C Florida
8 H-shaped letters
9 QB's neighbor
10 Harry ___ Crosby, A.K.A. Bing
11 Misgiving
12 Partygiver Perle
13 Cleric of Cannes
14 Grant and Piniella
15 German Alpine pasture
16 Resembling a shinbone
17 Grows up
18 Rotary-phone users
22 More relaxed than "parade rest"
24 Part of E.E.
29 Metric units of vol.
32 Culinary utensil
33 Hunter's trail
34 Sacred: Comb. form
37 Minuscule
38 City in S Ohio
40 General assemblies
41 Coxswain's command
43 Boy Scout unit
48 He was RMN's V.P.
49 Diametrically opposed
50 Do a deck job
51 Fog's companion, to the "Macbeth" witches
52 Bypass
54 One of the orch. brasses
56 German ace of WW I
57 Chela
58 Tree toad
59 Org. for Qatar
60 Ancient strongbox
61 Rip in "Summer Rental"
64 U.S. Open golf champ: 1961
67 Button for TV ads
69 Coal scuttles
70 Wahoo
71 German sculptor: 1440–1533
73 Long-tailed parrot
75 Diamond's mo.
78 Final metamorphic stage
79 Albacore or skipjack
81 Peep show
82 Pidgin, for one
86 Muffler
87 Harelike
88 Religious recluses
89 Convent superior
90 Bay at the moon
91 100 Netherlands cents
96 Director May
97 Acad.
98 Yummy British dessert
99 Between a rock and a hard place
100 Prefix for knock
101 Deciphered
105 Pale green
107 Song stylist Della
109 "How ___ thou, man?": Shak.
110 Prop and hex endings
111 "___ out?" (poker query)
112 Turkmen and Uzbek, once
115 Charles Dutton role
117 Houston, from San Antonio
118 Take advantage of

19

ODD COUPLES by Alex K. Justin
When surnames of famous people are combined, strange hybrids emerge.

ACROSS

1 To some extent
7 "___ is a terrible thing to waste"
12 London subway
16 Glyceride
21 La-di-da: Hyph.
22 Crow craft
23 ___ even keel
24 Surgery preceder
25 COLLUSION OF DAVID AND JOYCE
27 HABITAT OF GENE AND ELIOT
29 Sound of Sandy
30 Undivided
31 Candia
33 Damp
34 ___ the way (prepare)
35 Land of Enchantment, old style
36 Greater omentum
37 ___ el Mandeb, strait between Red Sea & Gulf of Aden
40 Lessen the force of
41 Barry Manilow hit
42 FICTION OF BETTY AND TRYGVE
46 Ambassador ___
48 People outside of a profession
49 Fissile rock
50 "___ man answers, . . ."
51 Dry creek bed
52 BOOKS BY EDNA AND PETER
54 Wing: Comb. form
55 Prepare to pray
56 Righteous indignation
57 Unctuous
58 Red cooperative
59 Keep ___ on, observe closely
60 Body of Islamic sacred law: Var.
61 New Kids on the ___
63 Unfriendly
64 Corrida de toros hurrah
65 VENTURE OF BILLY AND TOM
67 Sens scent
68 Olympic category
70 Word before fire
71 Persuaded
72 Money in Cambodia
73 WEARING APPAREL FOR ALEXANDER GRAHAM AND TIMOTHY
77 Dummkopf
80 ELAINE AND LARAINE IN DISTRESS
82 Blasé
83 Long-barreled hunting guns
84 Ornamental network
85 Ghostlike
86 Kind of beer
87 Emulated moles
88 Zygomatic bone
89 Evian evening
90 ONE BROUGHT UP BY PHIL AND JULIA
93 Gulch
94 ___-American
95 French historian: 1846–1919
96 Alda and Arkin
97 Sound, as of music

98 ERIC AND BUDDY UNEMPLOYED, BUT WEALTHY
100 Crystalline compound
101 Nilotic language
102 Receive
103 President of Poland, familiarly
104 Literary style
105 Parisian depot
106 Scream in terror
109 Boadicea was their queen
110 Battle sight on Gilbert Island: 1943
112 Pt. of a crossword puzzle
115 CHARLES KINGSLEY NOVEL FEATURING ADAM, ARTEMUS & DON
117 BLUE RIBBON WINNER BELONGING TO MARGE AND JOHN
120 Coffee ___?
121 Organ stop
122 Roman gold coins
123 Verdi opera
124 Makeshift: Scot.
125 Rail
126 Minimal
127 Casino worker

DOWN

1 "___ Long Way to Tipperary"
2 Famed racehorse
3 Ottoman
4 Opposite of Pac.
5 "The ___," Lloyd C. Douglas novel
6 LEAF OUT OF A BOOK BELONGING TO RIP AND PATTI
7 Up and doing
8 Olympic champion skier
9 Crossword poison
10 Part of Scand.
11 Counterpoints
12 Lofty
13 Harmony
14 Unit of cotton or hay
15 "The ___," Reynolds/DeLuise flick
16 On the way
17 Doddering
18 Calendar abbr.
19 Word before while
20 Blooming
26 Mexican basket-weaving grass
28 Messages between computer experts
32 Do over coloring
35 One of the three virtues
36 Cautious
37 GBS's "___ Methuselah"
38 Lacking a key system
39 SONG FOR BEN, KEN AND ARTHUR
40 Memorable Belgian musician
41 Protective coating
42 Marie mollusk
43 FAVORITE OF RICH AND WENDY
44 "___ a Song Coming On"
45 Sheridan's opponent in 1864
47 Pub potables
48 Discover
49 ___-of-life
52 Pitch and tar: Sp.
53 Gigi's creator
54 TV time
56 By-products of cheese
58 Calls at sea
60 Fishy looking
61 Construct
62 Branch
63 Studies
65 City on the Allegheny

66 Respiratory noise
67 "___ to the wise is sufficient"
69 Northern sea duck
71 Aquiline or Bucephalus
73 Founder of the Salvation Army
74 Serigraph artist
75 Herb used in folk medicine
76 Works hard
78 Rap session?
79 Gardner's character
80 Kenya people
81 ___ as the hills
82 Nobelist in chemistry: 1931
84 Flat bean
86 Pioneer of movie comedies
87 Questionable
88 "Look ___ hands!"
90 "My Friend ___," by Mary O'Hara
91 Novarro of early films
92 Coolly dispassionate
93 TREE BELONGING TO PETE AND PEGGY
95 Part of California landscape
97 Odalisque's quarters
99 Choice groups
100 Small space
101 One of Hancock Park attractions in L.A.
104 Nectar of the gods
105 Chess and checkers
106 Hard work: Brit.
107 Grinder
108 Q–V connection
109 Self produced: Comb. form
110 Novel plantation
111 Pot part
112 Matte
113 French fashion magazine
114 Blossom, in Barcelona
116 Popular vacation wheels: Abbr.
118 Color
119 Arthur or Lillie

20

Don't be misled by Mr. H's title—Hammett's hero is not *our* hero featured at 1 & 5 Across.

ACROSS

1 & 5 Fictional detective
10 Rhyme scheme
14 Related
18 "Arabian Nights" number
19 57.2958°
21 Commercial award
22 Unaspirated
23 Event leading to Junior's romance
25 Our hero's early film portrayer
27 Packs
28 Grissom and Kahn
30 Soft, in Solingen
31 Gus Hall's org.
32 Eye inflammations
33 Coin in Cali
34 Tibia area
35 Stone at 1 Samuel 20:19
36 Bankrolls
40 Helmsley comedy
41 Our hero's portrayer: 1989
45 Yeast acid
46 "___ Otis Regrets"
47 Stereo's forerunner: Hyph.
48 Roentgen's discovery: Hyph.
49 Actress Angeli
50 Coin in Bangkok
51 Hero's sidekick
55 Villains: ___ and the Midget
56 Villain who lived underground
58 Bloom for Amy Lowell
59 Those behind the times
60 More al dente
61 Workplace of 34 Down
62 W. F. Buckley's spy hero
63 Those in our hero's gallery
65 ___ Streona, Ethelred II's son-in-law
67 Level-headed villain
70 Tout d' ___ (at first)
71 Dangerous daughter of another villain
73 Conductor Schmidt
74 ___ print, drapery design
75 Little Face Finney's nemeses
77 Parmesan pronoun
78 Whirl
79 Word with aboard
80 Ex-con wife of 13 Down
84 Snake, for one
85 Places sought by our hero
87 One of Caesar's trio
88 Hopped-up drinks
89 Green moth
90 Cote denizens
91 Elephant king
93 General at Gettysburg
95 Refuge
96 He played Chan
97 Our hero's former partner
99 Villain who tried to starve our hero
104 Villain: B-B ___

105 Our hero's sweetheart
106 Feature of The Blank
107 Lesiure
108 Olfaction
109 Part of R.E.L.
110 Memoranda
111 Pung

DOWN

1 Obscure
2 Excellent number
3 Bill's companion
4 Honchos
5 Mission starter
6 ___ bell (reminded)
7 Says further
8 102, to Tacitus
9 China's Mississippi
10 Sunny Dell ___ (home of 13 Down)
11 Gil or Ruy
12 Afflict
13 Our hero's whiskered friend
14 Shakespeare's England
15 Villain: 88 ___
16 Concerning
17 Weaver or Rorem
20 Vietnam's General Ky
24 Ceramicist's sieve
26 "What did ___?" (reaction to Mumbles)

29 Self, to Schiller
31 Our hero's creator
32 Sequential
33 Kind of sandwich bread
34 Diet ___
36 Grange
37 Member of Junior's law-and-order club
38 Pruneface, to 5 Across
39 Teasdale and Haden
40 Not prof.
41 Gam members
42 To love, in Toulouse
43 Hoover econ. agcy.
44 Kind of V.P.
49 Debra in "Broken Arrow"
51 Planted
52 Difference between canon and cañon
53 The Nutcracker's love
54 Scratching, to 99 Across
55 Kinds of coffee: Var.
57 Povich or Wills
59 Bra padding
62 "Sons ___," Yale refrain
63 Punjabi prince
64 Coins in Corfu
65 Highlands dialect
66 Beloved ones, in Belfort
68 Diversities
69 Hang
71 Short drinks

72 Kind of wt.
75 Former blonde?
76 "Do I dare to ___ peach?": Eliot
78 Emoluments
80 Dutch treat
81 Ukrainian city
82 Surrender
83 N Carolina colonial capital
86 Go by, as time
88 First victim
90 "___ Macabre"
91 18th cen. English composer
92 Agalloch
93 Bread spread
94 Seasons on the Seine
95 Villains: Nilon and Rod
96 "___ Funny Feeling"
97 Good place for 99 Across
98 ___ Aviv
100 Corp. VIP
101 Actor Avery
102 Directional letters
103 Like Junior's hair

21 BIG BLOWS by Elizabeth Arthur
Don't expect to breeze through this one.

ACROSS

1 Whoop it up
6 Humble
10 Tax experts
14 Fishy basket
19 Luigi's love
20 Against
21 SE Kansas city
22 Osprey's home
23 Strong Mediterranean wind
25 Mountainous north wind
27 Pierces
28 Mountain passes
30 N Caucasic language
31 Oklahoma tribe
34 Application
35 Taters
36 Tiny metallic sounds
39 Love affairs
41 Light brown
42 Citizen of Canea
43 Diagram a sentence
44 Tornado origin
47 Knock
49 Lex Luthor's friend
50 Cans
51 Years on end
52 Skier Magoni
53 Carioca's city
54 Traveling urges
58 Dalai Lama's home
59 Landed Scots
61 Theta follower
62 Exhalation
63 Compounds containing NO_2
64 Prefix for pod
65 Socle
66 Kind of hound
67 Hoosegow
68 Operatic airs
69 Deduce
70 Beatitude
73 Monitor
76 Celebes ox
77 Teacher
78 They begin in juin
79 Washbowl pitcher
80 Conan Doyle's title
81 Whole gale's classification
85 Nimble
86 Card game for two
88 Nostrils
89 Sweetsops
90 Cuttlefish ink
91 Exclude
92 Morsel for a pangolin
93 ___ Moines
94 Package: Abbr.
95 Opposed to max.
96 Early heaters
98 Kind of weather balloon
102 Antitrades
107 Utopian
108 Howard and Ely
109 Dog star
110 Tidal bore
111 Famed frontiersman

112 Chooses
113 North Sea feeder
114 Diversion

DOWN

1 Scottish explorer
2 Ratite bird
3 Omnirange: Navig.
4 Son of Aphrodite
5 Chalk talk
6 Perhaps
7 Closures
8 DDE's command
9 Kegler's number 5
10 Stronghold
11 Anchorages
12 Wellaway
13 Composer Stept
14 Like yams, often
15 Stain anew
16 Paleozoic, e.g.
17 German article
18 Yarn measure
24 Colleen
26 Surpass
29 Herculean
31 Flavor
32 Strad relative

33 Determiner of wind direction
35 Lucidity
37 Downward movement of air
38 Catches, biblical style
40 "Enterprise" letters
41 Asian embankments
42 Cote sounds
44 Discovers
45 New Mexican house
46 Rent
48 Way
50 Card for fortune
52 Mortgages
54 Electrician, at times
55 Gam and Moreno
56 Nocturnal lemur
57 Useful
58 Musical groups
60 Confused
62 Rapture
63 Nursemaids
65 Smooth feathers
66 Prejudice
67 Mutt's friend
68 Feeds the kitty
70 Bonny hillside

71 Brock or Costello
72 Discourage
74 CSA general
75 Braid
77 Whorl members
79 Kind of trip
81 Billiards shot
82 Unity
83 Physics Nobelist of 1944
84 Streetcar line
85 Star in Scorpius
87 Way to Rome
89 Avonlea girl
91 "She ___ Say Yes": Kern
92 Perfume
95 L–Q links
96 Punta del ___
97 Buffet
98 Eve's origin
99 Big scene
100 ___ gratias
101 Mouth: Comb. form
103 Sigmoid curve
104 "But ___ on forever": Tennyson
105 Drop the ball
106 Group

22

POUR ME ANOTHER! by Frances Hansen

The editors were ready for a few stiff shots after encountering the pungent puns below.

ACROSS

1 Wash the deck
5 Pahlevi, for one
9 Do Petruchio's job
13 Berate
18 Tennis champ Mandlikova
19 Kind of therapy
20 Take ___ (go swimming)
21 Like some sad socks
22 Leaf angle
23 Scheherazade's milieu
24 Branchlike parts
25 Cow Palace, e.g.
26 The flask seems drained?
30 Extracts flavor by boiling
31 Observes
32 Summon
33 "Mighty ___ Rose"
34 Hard ___ (working busily)
35 Mossback
36 Arafat's org.
39 Cream-sauce base
41 Cartoonist Walker
42 News agcy.
43 Contract a muscle
44 What's worn him out?
50 Merkel of "The Ponder Heart"
51 Cut down on calories
52 Shopping center
53 Uta or Walter
54 Prefix for phone
56 Half of MXXII
57 Bro's sibling
58 Layer
59 They ran into heavy seas?
68 Mongrel
69 Opposite of long.
70 Author Deighton
71 Alley Oop's wife
72 Flu type
75 Senor's affirmatives
77 Sam and J.C.
80 Egg: Prefix
81 But the ship made port?
85 Choler
86 Indian greeting, humorously
87 Cheerleaders do it
88 At a ___ (perplexed)
89 Agreeable altar words
90 Isinglass
91 Chopped down
92 Lt. Kojak
94 Toil
95 Compassionate
96 Made a ducky remark
99 He's glad to be home reading Chaucer?
105 Dr. Jekyll's servant
106 Man not born of woman
107 Silly
108 Help with the dishes
109 Snout-nosed animal
110 Derby winner ___ Ridge
111 Simulated
112 Mighty mite
113 Luster
114 Anna of "Nana"
115 Stadium feature
116 Abominable one

DOWN

1 "Candida" playwright
2 Grew larger
3 Old-womanish
4 Bat?
5 Daisylike mum
6 Start of a toast
7 Revival cry
8 Act of 1862
9 Something to shoot at
10 "All in ___ work"
11 Rodolfo's love
12 Church of England
13 Shilly-___
14 Reef material
15 Designer Cassini
16 Comedian Jay
17 Actress Cannon
19 Clutch member
27 Played a trick on
28 Govern
29 Oliver's wicked tutor
34 "Rule Britannia" composer
35 It keeps the furnace going
36 Give a book a boost
37 ___ majesté
38 They don't laugh at yokes
39 Extend a subscription
40 Orange or Indian
41 "I ___ Bad, and That Ain't Good"
43 Zeffirelli
44 Cronyn of "The Gin Game"
45 Sea duck
46 Barber's call
47 Leave out
48 Carry's partner
49 Huntley
55 Esoteric
57 Cpl.'s superior
58 ___ Kush
60 Thick goo
61 Ingrid in "Casablanca"
62 Unsophisticated one
63 Put into office
64 Partridge's tree
65 Gangland thugs
66 Graceland name
67 Foray
72 Abruzzi bell town
73 Deep-bodied herring
74 Classical villain
75 Daytona Beach racers
76 Hawkeye State
77 Mound of winter wonderland
78 Bright light
79 Pick out
82 Talia of "The Godfather"
83 Vernon's dancing partner
84 Subtracted
90 Part of MOMA
91 Torpedo
92 Tina or Lana
93 Reaped the alfalfa
94 "Jennifer Lorn" novelist
95 Blackguard
96 Tremble
97 La crème de la crème
98 Where town commuters meet
99 Chooses
100 Ancient mariner
101 Run easily
102 Mine entrance
103 ___ B'rith
104 Prefix for sweet

23

CITY CONNECTIONS by Judith C. Dalton

When it comes to cities our Arkansas puzzler knows what she's talking about—her husband is a city manager.

ACROSS

1 Rope fiber
5 Some are white
10 Syringa
15 Gewgaw
18 Moslem ruler
19 Embarrass
20 Ending for dance
21 Domesticate
22 IANM
24 ILOK
26 Songs for Milli Vanilli
27 Wails
29 Small carriage
30 Smudges
32 Suppose
33 Dynasty noted for porcelain
34 Twists
35 City in Belgium
36 Top vaudevillian
40 Blackbeard
41 NJWI
44 He thrilled them in Manila
45 "My treat!"
46 Doublet
47 "Don't be ___ blanket!"
48 Environmental sci.
49 A form of 1501
50 CAMA
54 Incline
55 Semitic love goddess
57 Kingklip catcher
58 Coordinates
59 Millennium members
60 Priam's slain sister
61 Haughty
62 Vilify
64 Ancient Macedonian capital
65 Rich family?
68 Granada goodbye
69 TXNV
72 Diminutive suffix
73 Large grayish deer
74 Cut down
75 Mid-March date
76 Lived
77 Scourge
78 MECO
82 Anabaptist Simons
83 Leaks
85 Appeal
86 Pianist Peterson
87 Son of Zeus and Hera
88 First Egyptian king
89 Catena
91 Colorful beetle
94 Asian antelope
95 Toot
96 CTOH
98 TNKY
103 Ore vein
104 Colorado Indians
105 Raises
106 Beach bird
107 Bar staple
108 Facial communicator
109 Gemma Donati's husband
110 Pulled

DOWN

1 Possessed
2 Long-legged bird
3 Marble
4 Economy
5 Bitter in Bonn
6 Incites
7 Maid
8 Id follower
9 Beatty film
10 13th cen. French morality play
11 One of the Horae
12 Lucerne et Leman
13 Candlenut
14 Siamese set-to?
15 Facial powder
16 Hebrew measure
17 Rock refrain of the '60s
21 Prefix for comedy
23 Put down
25 Utah mountains
28 Sow sound
30 Forks over
31 FLNY
32 Shade, in Salerno
33 Scrooge
34 Leaf orifice
36 Heaviest anchor
37 GAPA
38 Abscond
39 Nettles
41 Cod relatives
42 Gusher product
43 ___ vapore (Italian steamer)
46 French shepherd
48 "Marina" poet
50 Postgraduate exams
51 "Enigma" star
52 Andrea ___ Robbia
53 Spicy stews
54 Animal tracks
56 Vowel sequence
58 Pseudonym
60 Star
61 Ragged Dick's creator
62 "Baby Boom" star
63 Official under Nero
64 UNESCO headquarters
66 Verdugo and Valova
67 Spanish sir
69 Challenges
70 Lives in Las Palmas
71 Netherlands city
74 They're buttons in Britain
76 Overwhelmed
78 Gem weight
79 Industrious
80 Elbow: Comb. form
81 Toward the wind
82 "Sons and Lovers" family
84 Analyze a sentence
88 Gold, silver or Bronze
89 Jest
90 Rub out
91 Thrifty underwriters?: Abbr.
92 Gator
93 Assistant
94 Big truck
95 Peruse
97 Chimney in Paisley
99 Pasture
100 Former South Carolina governor
101 "___ Day At A Time"
102 Natural moisture

DESPAIRING by Jim Page

If you should find yourself despairing over Jim's title, stick a hyphen after the third letter.

ACROSS

1 Of the extremities
6 The Bucs stop here
11 Spanish guy
17 "And found ___ wand'ring mazes lost": Milton
20 Farm machines
21 Idolizes
22 Empress
23 Passes over tyrants
25 Mythical father of Manannan
26 Like Brown's walls
28 Constantly
29 Succumb
30 Writer Blyton
32 United
35 Secondhand
37 "Marnie" actor
38 Plant anew
40 Blocks passion
43 Vague feeling
44 Study
45 Cleveland cager
46 Orsk's 1991 locale
48 Body: Ger.
49 Amatory
54 Wynken's pal
56 Kind of ranch
58 Used a divining rod
60 Kind of palm or line
61 They work with wallflowers?
63 "Old MacDonald" ending
64 Keyboard instrument
66 Bikini events, once
67 Arranged
71 Cummerbunds
72 Two-seater bicycles
74 Unusual
75 Slaw or fries, at times
77 Robt. ___
78 Available, in a way
80 Had on
81 Suffix for insist
82 Sports scribe
84 Glacial ridge: Var.
86 Venomous snakes
88 James MacArthur, to Helen Hayes
89 Baltimore ___
91 Cartoonist Young et al.
94 Ducks kismet
98 Contends in court
100 Flightless bird
101 Persian poet
102 More unctuous
104 Orderly
105 Writer Yutang
106 Diva Stevens
108 Growing outward
110 "TV Guide" abbr.
111 Avoids parachuting
117 More sordid
119 Countenance
120 Coins of Ecuador
121 Houdini, e.g.
122 Lafayette College city
123 Minute
124 Minx

DOWN

1 Branch of the deer family
2 Trig functions
3 Get up anew
4 One more: Abbr.
5 Cato's 452
6 Hindu cymbal
7 Ring great
8 Ancient Persian
9 Advance showings: Var.
10 Future taxpayers
11 "Some ___ meat . . .": Burns
12 ___ bodkins!
13 Swabby's tool
14 Journalist David ___
15 Put out a batter
16 German industrial hub
18 Overruns the Corn Belt
19 Kind of file
20 Dent
24 Scott of history

27 Actor Wallach
31 Strips a German city
33 Thrusting sword
34 Scoffs at Hernando
36 Unravels "The Principles of Philosophy"
37 Cuts up blueprints
39 Six has one
41 Williams's Blanche
42 Perched
47 Robot drama
50 Sport, for short
51 Get rid of some chips
52 Corroborate
53 Check on a boxer
54 Christmas, in Roma
55 Exposed
57 Mil. award
59 Misery
61 Etonian dad
62 Map abbr.
65 New Guinea port
68 Mauna ___
69 Stevenson et al.
70 Mil. award
73 Ital. tobacco union
76 Gershwin

79 Most run-down
80 Small nestlings
83 '60s dress style
85 Polynesian king
87 Sequence of wds.
90 Publish again
92 They're chalked in River City
93 Navy construction arm
94 Meredith's "___ in England"
95 ___-flytrap
96 Chalcedony
97 Yang's opposite
99 Like a Van Gogh night
100 Student: Fr.
103 Naturalness
107 ___ homo
109 "To ___ His Own"
112 "___ ole davil, sea": O'Neill
113 Conceit
114 Coin of Japan
115 Sea eagle
116 Napoleon's marshal
118 Mau ___

SPOTTING CITIES by William Lutwiniak
We counted ten well-known cities hidden below. How many can you find?

ACROSS

1 Samuel Ramey, e.g.
5 Gobble up
10 Citrus coolers
14 Padlock place
18 Stage start
19 Wainscot
20 Ovett or Coe
22 Give ___ (chew out)
23 Red-handed in India?
25 Bugs in Ecuador?
27 Hot spots
28 Word of location
30 Brisk
31 MIT grads
32 Consarn it!
33 Stupefy
34 Analyze
38 One about to say "hello"
40 Special delivery?
44 Eschew
45 Naiveté in Pennsylvania?
48 Actress Merkel
49 NL team
50 ___ me tangere
51 Froth
52 Ski facility
53 Alternative to nothing
54 Warships in New York?
58 Entry in red
59 Sore
62 Ave ___ vale
63 They skirl
64 Man and boy
65 Relished
66 Gibe
67 Fountain treats
69 Big money, in India
70 Got on, timewise
73 Couldn't abide
74 Unusual thing in Alaska?
77 Reliever's stat.
78 Greedy
79 Codger
80 Artist Chagall
81 Sarcastic
82 Political front
83 Prague person in Norway?
87 Timetable, briefly
88 Desert denizen
90 Fly a glider
91 Disrespectful
92 Dinghy duo
93 Peut-___ (perhaps)
94 From Natchez to Mobile
96 Seafood, for some
99 Correo ___ (airmail)
101 Do quickly
106 Avenues in Italy?
108 Similarity in France?
110 Heavy reading?
111 Start of a Dickens title
112 Indulge
113 Program
114 Plane of WW I
115 "___ sow, so . . ."
116 Bleep out
117 Merino mamas

DOWN

1 Bad golf shot
2 Rights org.
3 Name in lights
4 Delphic datum
5 The last frontier
6 Rose prunings
7 Wee colonists
8 Jr. or sis
9 Voracious plant
10 Electrician's tool
11 Name in fashion
12 Choice word?
13 The following: Abbr.
14 ___-miss (sporadic)
15 On high
16 Flight unit
17 Bouquet
21 Countryfolk
24 Titillating
26 Take effect
29 SPGA's Irwin
32 Ipse
33 "The ___ of Dee": Kingsley
34 Org. of Tin Pan Alley
35 Winning coach of Super Bowl VII

36 Ennoblement in Peru?
37 Part of Q-A
38 Conv. voters
39 Rebel
41 Sightseers in Switzerland?
42 Walking ___ (elated)
43 Chapters
45 Provides with
46 Coward and Harrison
47 Seine feeder
52 Algonquin abode
55 Play the fink
56 Alamagordo's county
57 Prized sauterne
58 Sitology subject
60 Unprotected
61 Beat it
63 Nobelist physicist: 1918
65 Singer Franklin
66 Novelist Nwapa
67 Certain rugs
68 ___ ball (revel)
69 Pop. flavor
71 Lake Indians
72 Papa
74 Sonneteers
75 Overact

76 Church area
79 Russian ruler
81 ___ matter of fact
83 Kind of myrtle
84 Boss
85 Scene
86 "Junior look" designer
89 Star-crossed
91 Mopsus, for one
94 NL team
95 Back-up
96 Picks one
97 Field yield
98 Tony Musante role
99 Rehan and Neilson
100 Wriggling
101 Actress Samms
102 Casino pair
103 "Was it a cat ___?"
104 Lit out
105 Phases out
107 ___ glance
109 "___ Mutual Friend": Dickens

26 LADIES-IN-WAITING by Nancy Scandrett Ross

There's an air of mystery surrounding these ladies who are all waiting to be unmasked.

ACROSS

1 Piecrust ingredient
5 Joplin compositions
9 Postal purchase
14 Andrews and Wynter
19 Currency-exchange premium
20 Organic compounds
22 Describing some music
23 Island off Venezuela
24 Othello, e.g.
25 Come to an end
26 Richard Jury's creator
28 Jemima Shore's creator
31 Capable of being sold
32 Organization
33 ___ Aviv
34 Tolkien creations
35 Garden tool
36 Scottish municipal officer
39 Doggie-bag item
40 New Mexico arts center
44 Sojourn
47 Roderick Alleyn's creator
50 Tenzing Norgay, e.g.
52 Train components
53 Big feather
54 Roz Howard's creator
57 "Aeneid" starter
58 Henley essential
59 Cheerleader's quality
60 Floating camels
61 Rogations
63 Alum
66 World event
68 Downy ducks
69 Medium's medium
71 Canasta term
72 French flower
75 A. C. Roebuck's partner
76 Kate Fansler's creator
79 Kind of eclipse
81 Draft org.
82 Inverness native
83 Eastern potentate
84 Clear plastic
85 Somewhat cerulean
87 Catch sight of
88 Performed in class
89 Fixes in folds, à la Dior
93 Linz loc.
95 Lap robe
96 Prevarications
97 Brother Cadfael's creator
99 View from Mt. Desert
102 Highway division
103 Crafts of WW II
104 John Putnam Thatcher's creator
107 Ortrud's victim
108 Haymaker's result
109 Long time
111 Segovia
112 Either half of A.A.
114 Core
116 Bottom line
117 French perfume center
121 Does away with
126 Mrs. Pollifax's creator
130 Alan Grant's creator
132 Clamor
133 Fuzzy bits
134 Vase handles
135 Squeaks
136 Act uppity
137 Novel ending
138 Raises
139 "Riders to the Sea" playwright
140 Lapses
141 Approach

DOWN

1 Fernando of the films
2 "Into the Woods" duet
3 Melees
4 Lord Peter Wimsey's creator
5 Diet, e.g.
6 Dwarf buffalo
7 Boo-boo
8 Calumniate
9 Leading lady
10 Pinnacle
11 Theater org.
12 "Des Knaben Wunderhorn" composer
13 Lament
14 Mends
15 "Tosca" tune
16 Without feeling
17 First victim
18 Ticket orderer's encl.
21 Commuter's stop
22 Verdi heroine
27 Secure
29 Prefix for classic
30 City west of Montgomery
36 Max of the ring
37 Rhône tributary
38 Gaelic
39 Surprised exclamations
40 Some bills
41 Pisa's river
42 Candid
43 Utters
44 Leafless flower stalks
45 Lingers
46 Armed fleets
48 Campus concerns: Abbr.
49 Dines late
50 Enjoyed the slopes
51 Dame Myra
55 Ranch necessities
56 Points for polish
58 Project endings
59 Adam Dalgliesh's creator
62 Hesitant syllables
63 Some kids
64 Hose blemish
65 Adjutant
67 Georgia campus
70 Bridge assets
72 C. B. Greenfield's creator
73 First
74 Lustrous fabrics
76 Sharp
77 Dewy
78 Corded cloth
79 Director Jean-___ Godard
80 Africa-Asia link
82 Smacks
84 Trouser part
85 Most desirable
86 Wound
88 Occult character
89 Strong smell
90 Portoferraio's island
91 Ruse
92 River of NE China
94 REL's alma mater
95 Stadium yells
98 Poet's contraction
99 Less green
100 Containers
101 Printemps follower
105 Pesters
106 Carpers
109 Moral principles
110 "The Four Million" author
113 Dernier ___
114 Pan's music makers
115 Suffix for gray
118 Cuff
119 December visitor
120 Stage direction
121 Open
122 Ulna, e.g.
123 Greek peak
124 Albany's father-in-law
125 Spotted
126 Astronaut Slayton
127 "Advise and Consent" actor
128 Yesterday in Amiens
129 North Sea feeder
131 Label

27

SONS OF EUTERPE by Irene Smullyan
You know the surnames of these composers, but what goes in front?

ACROSS

1 Clerical attire
4 Tiny particle
8 Oakley and Laurie
14 Abraham's concubine
19 Flanders of fiction
21 Reckoning
22 Source of pan y leche
23 Nitrogen compound
24 Butter substitute
25 Von Gluck
28 Japanese theater
30 Greek moralist
31 Squealer
32 Did laundry work
33 Tendon
35 Astronaut's vehicle
36 Australis and Borealis
38 Attempt
39 Chinese: Comb. form
40 Supreme Ct. edict
42 Male bees
44 Speakeasy or bistro
49 Cole mate
51 Victorious utensils?
55 Model Macpherson
56 En ___, René's indeed
58 Nutritive
61 Popular fur
62 Respond
64 One on the run
65 Less attractive
66 Attire for Calpurnia
67 "Call spirits from the
    ___ deep": Shak.
68 Italian wine city
69 Releasing mechanism
70 German river
71 Loser
73 Gluts
75 Breeds
78 Suffix denoting style
79 Cosmetic
81 Remove contents
83 Land of Nod
85 Brit. politicos
88 No longer fresh
90 Biblical city (Gen. 10:10)
92 Cost
96 Treasure chest
98 Australian desert lizard
100 Vital point
102 Articles
103 Top college eleven in
    1991
105 South American rodent
106 Tabula ___
107 Sponsorship
108 Cut of beef
109 Cornice decoration
110 Correct
112 Plexus
113 One kind of war victim
115 Unaccompanied
117 Substances for preserving
    foods
119 Stage shows
122 Moles
124 Wicked
125 Ethiopian prince
128 Scapegraces
130 N.Y.C. subway line
132 Mr. Calhoun et al.
134 Humiliated
136 Rush
137 Finnish lake, to a Swede
139 Controlled
142 Massenet
146 Philippine island
147 Possession
148 Positive electrodes
149 Excellent golf score
150 Listen
151 Leaders
152 English shire
153 Portico
154 Genetic material

DOWN

1 Murderous madness
2 Go-getter of song
3 Blisters
4 German exclamation
5 Hartebeest
6 Bay window
7 Made untidy
8 Perched upon
9 Bite
10 Indian leader
11 Private
12 Newspaper official
13 Garnish for a Margarita
14 Aquatic mammals
15 Ecclesiastical desk
16 Overlarge
17 Austrian psychiatrist
18 Australian pop singer
20 Berlioz
21 Study of natural
    phenomena
26 Volumes
27 Tropical vine
29 Join closely
34 Mozart
36 Pain killer
37 Schumann
41 Debussy
43 Political subdivision
44 Roman emperor: A.D.
    96–98
45 Of the lower intestine
46 Brittle material
47 Controversial sightings
48 Root vegetables
50 Become limp
52 Lyric poem
53 Irks
54 Trap
57 Group of three
59 Feretory
60 Soft consonants
63 Novices
72 Self: Comb. form
74 Cross
76 Tyrannosaurus ___
77 Brown pigment
80 Funeral oration
82 Mother-of-pearl
84 Tchaikovsky
85 Deadly snake
86 Last king of Troy
87 Steep slope
89 North Carolina college
91 Play
93 Israeli desert
94 Hit, Biblical style
95 Curves
97 Affair of the heart
99 Sextet in an inning
101 Not new
104 Preoccupations
111 "Kramer vs. Kramer"
    subject
114 Circumvent
116 Sheeplike
118 Exhaust
120 Prickly: Comb. form
121 Barnacle Bill, e.g.
123 Sultan's decrees
125 Hindu prince
126 Mistreat
127 Garnish for enchiladas
129 Yorkshire city
131 Pay the tab
133 Deride
135 Germ
137 Formerly formerly
138 Therefore
140 Israeli statesman
141 Brain covering
143 Psychotic
144 Recompense
145 Waterfront org.

28 DECEMBER DENIZENS by Jeanne Wilson
We suggest you save this one until the Yuletide holidays.

ACROSS

1 All-inclusive
5 What a bouncer does
11 Pear type
15 Russian info source
19 Blackens
20 Aplenty
21 Spread of a sort
22 Actress Nazimova
23 Goober
24 Up and about
25 Big name in Norway
26 Macintosh, e.g.
27 High (mus.)
28 Wherewithal
30 Yeti's distant cousin?
33 ___ down (lost weight)
35 Sir Flinders ___
    (Br. archaeologist)
36 Kind of bonnet
37 "I hate ___ the evening
    sun . . ."
38 Indicate
41 Constructor
44 Isolde's love
46 Roman goddess of the hearth
47 Residence
52 ___-Croatian
54 Getaway
57 "___ the season to be . . ."
59 ___ O'More, famed Irish
    rebel
60 Sober
62 Lessee
64 Wintry windshield helper
66 "I sent thee late ___
    wreath": Jonson
67 Method
69 Joint: Comb. form
72 "Dundee" for one
73 Wind blast
74 Enthusiast
75 Cashier's abbr.
76 New start of a sort
78 Soul, in St. Lo
79 Johnny Marks' bulbous
    beastie?
82 Ernesto Guevara
85 Barnum's first name
86 "I think, therefore ___"
87 Ice, in Essen
88 Sauté. e.g.
89 Symbol of justice
92 Poorly made
94 "Born in the ___"
95 N France river
96 Intimidations
98 Eat up a storm
100 Studied hard and fast
102 Hebrides isle
103 G. Cooper comment
105 "___, anyone?"
107 "Seven Days ___"
    (Lancaster film)
108 Alex Haley work
110 Nags
113 An asset of S California
115 Aaron or Ruth, e.g.
117 Ravel's well-known
    composition
119 Composer Bruckner
123 Part of ASAP
127 Give the meaning of
129 Milk sugar

131 "Good" Bohemian
    remembered in song
134 Hersey's "___ for Adano"
136 Nesselrode, e.g.
137 Israeli airline
138 Small rodent
139 "___ the money . . ."
141 Drank like a kitten
143 Learning
144 Actor Jack of oaters
145 Gasoline rating
146 Space or limits lead-in
147 "___ Death": Grieg
148 Tiers
149 List; register
150 Nicholas II, e.g.

DOWN

1 "And ___ so rare as . . .":
    Lowell
2 James's creator
3 "Spirit of '76" figure
4 Lauder of cosmetics
5 Richard ___ of 40s films
6 Vessels for preserves
7 Biblical high priest
8 Pamper
9 ___ et quarante (gambling
    game)
10 Madrid mister
11 Thunder claps
12 Earthen jar
13 Connery or Penn
14 Contents of a biggin
15 Mexican fast foods
16 "I have become ___
    name": Rukeyser
17 Blackboard
18 Woodland deity

19 String quartet's bass voice
23 Ago
29 Totals
31 Maggie, to Jiggs
32 ___ avis
34 Poetry specialist
35 ___ de Leon
39 Sorbonne summer
40 Mean
42 Lawyer, in brief
43 "___ oui!"
45 Chit
46 Release
48 Impetuous
49 Slip-up sound
50 Ein, zwei, ___
51 Mrs. Rochester, née ___
52 Whey, for one
53 Like some leaf edges
55 "What's in ___?": Juliet
56 Pear tree dweller?
58 Cliffs
60 It's a long story
61 Suitor
63 Dull sound
65 Compassion
68 Bancroft and Boleyn
70 Primary color
71 Double-reed instruments
74 Like a Cagney character
75 Fabled author
77 Sacro trailer
79 Carla of "Cheers"
80 Morse code sound
81 Stockings material, before
    nylon
82 Punctuation mark
83 Cozy
84 ___ out (barely made it)

85 Trouser fold
88 Remark
89 Fuss
90 Half a little train
91 Florence's river
93 More Morse code sounds
94 Useful
95 Symbol of generosity
97 Religious group
99 Capitulator's cry
101 Spanish stream
104 Caress
106 Guinness or Richardson
109 Come in third
111 Cashes in
112 JEC was one
114 Double-dealing spy
116 "___ saw a moor":
    Dickinson
117 Monte ___ (Italian for
    high Alp)
118 Beginnings
120 Roland Young title role
121 Willow
122 Desire
123 Kipling's wolf pack
    leader
124 Grain storage areas
125 Delusion's partner
126 Eyes amorously
128 Storey
130 Dole
132 ___ contendere
133 Talon
134 Tops
135 Remus' "___ Rabbit"
140 Obese
142 School gp.

WOW! by Judith C. Dalton
Don't be surprised if you find yourself exclaiming Judy's title while confronting those uppercase clues!

ACROSS

1 NFL team
5 "Common Sense" author
10 Rambled
15 Castle barrier
19 Touched down
20 " . . . thumb and pulled out ___"
21 Notwithstanding
22 Spicy stew
23 RENTED PUPPY
25 GRAIN FILE
27 "Old MacDonald" refrain
28 Stitches
30 Nutritional abbr.
31 Crybabies
34 Narrow groove
35 Piano name
39 "Lady ___": 1990 hit song
40 Moslem crusade
41 First-rate
42 Ending for serpent
43 ___ about (approximately)
44 BATTY BARBELLS
48 Housing org.
49 Batty
50 Mature
51 French silk
52 Crisp cookie
53 OED relative
54 Type type
55 Anuran
58 Prefix for vision
59 SICK FEMALES
61 Whatever
62 Bungled
63 Chair name
64 Composer Butler
65 Malay boats
67 Climb
69 " . . . to come ___ o'clock . . ."
70 ADOLESCENT'S ACCESSORIES
73 Coagulated milk
74 They do windows
76 God of war
77 Formerly
78 Tuscany river
79 Buck finisher
80 Black cuckoos
81 Roman 1450
82 Brest beam
83 DULL MANIPULATION
87 Yours, in Tours
88 Valiant's son
89 Five ___ (12:55)
90 Some are double
91 Subdivision of the Sioux tribes
92 Married criminals of Madrid
94 "Over ___"
95 Wee Willie Winkie, for one
97 Train mail sta.
98 Foreign wool particles
99 Twenty: Comb. form
100 WORKER AT KITTYHAWK
104 FOREIGN SPORTS CARS
109 Leander's lover
110 Rose dye

111 Paradigm
112 Branches
113 Receptive
114 British navigational aid
115 Actress Duke
116 NBA team

DOWN

1 Bowl sound
2 Fatima's husband
3 Peace, in Moscow
4 See 1 Across
5 Masher
6 Bedbug
7 Intestine: Comb. form
8 Inner-urban assn.
9 Emotional projection
10 Old TV western
11 Milo in "Ulysses"
12 Competes
13 Author LeShan
14 Belittled
15 Simple organism
16 Like the gray mare
17 Malt liquor
18 Income or sales
24 Passed on
26 Squanders (with away)

29 Bird crop
31 Swimmer Matt
32 Yearly
33 THE CLUE WAS "ERUDITION": THE SOLVER ___
34 Dimension
35 Brazil state
36 VICTOR'S RETREAT
37 Breathe
38 Grounded: Naut.
40 Land of the Rising Sun
44 Violation
45 Presses potatoes
46 Bagging fiber
47 English sluice
52 Tatami material
54 Quince, for one
55 "The Lost Galleon" author
56 Riverine mammal
57 Meticulousness
60 Emerson's middle name
62 Long times
64 A Musketeer
65 Danger
66 Texas AFB
67 Colorful beetle
68 Arrow poison

69 Not worth ___
70 Flavors
71 Mete out again
72 More elusive
74 Like the platypus
75 Gilmore of basketball
80 Stuart queen: 1702–14
81 Pigeons, sometimes
83 Verve
84 Spiny anteater
85 Sharpen
86 Dirigible
91 Ball or brawl
93 Light-bulb gas
94 Gin's friend
95 Paris purchase
96 Base
98 Not fem.
99 "___ a Kick Out of You"
100 First man?
101 Ribbed fabric
102 Anger
103 Garden digger
105 Mount in W. Turkey
106 Vichy water
107 K-O links
108 Family member

30 SUITABLE SUBJECTS by Calista Luminati
Names of fame from the past and present are fair targets for our
Manhasset punster.

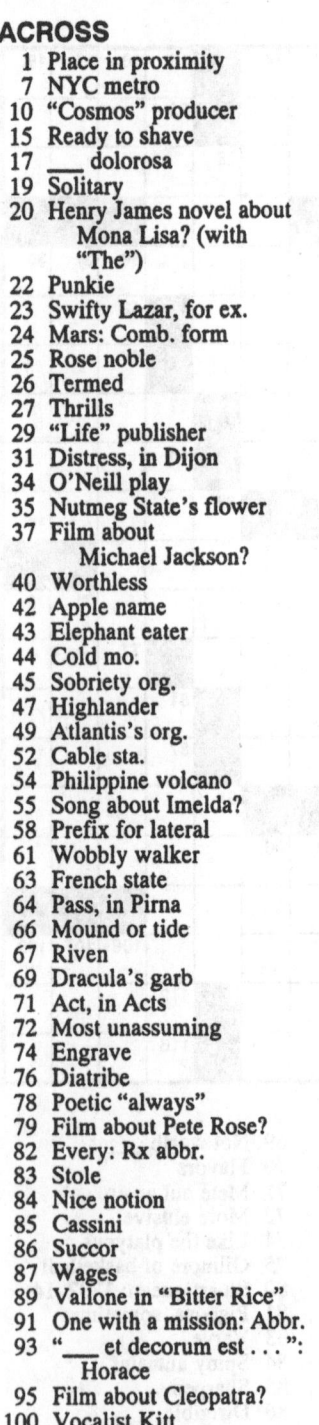

ACROSS

1 Place in proximity
7 NYC metro
10 "Cosmos" producer
15 Ready to shave
17 ___ dolorosa
19 Solitary
20 Henry James novel about
  Mona Lisa? (with
  "The")
22 Punkie
23 Swifty Lazar, for ex.
24 Mars: Comb. form
25 Rose noble
26 Termed
27 Thrills
29 "Life" publisher
31 Distress, in Dijon
34 O'Neill play
35 Nutmeg State's flower
37 Film about
  Michael Jackson?
40 Worthless
42 Apple name
43 Elephant eater
44 Cold mo.
45 Sobriety org.
47 Highlander
49 Atlantis's org.
52 Cable sta.
54 Philippine volcano
55 Song about Imelda?
58 Prefix for lateral
61 Wobbly walker
63 French state
64 Pass, in Pirna
66 Mound or tide
67 Riven
69 Dracula's garb
71 Act, in Acts
72 Most unassuming
74 Engrave
76 Diatribe
78 Poetic "always"
79 Film about Pete Rose?
82 Every: Rx abbr.
83 Stole
84 Nice notion
85 Cassini
86 Succor
87 Wages
89 Vallone in "Bitter Rice"
91 One with a mission: Abbr.
93 "___ et decorum est . . .":
  Horace
95 Film about Cleopatra?
100 Vocalist Kitt
103 Turin-Milan dir.
104 Pollen producer
105 "Middletown" author
107 Quail
108 Badgers of Bari
110 Latvian city
112 ___ la vie
114 Gnaw
115 Tamandua feature
116 Film about Alan?
120 Heights
121 Arabian caliph
122 High crimes
123 Former Attorney General
124 City on the Ouse
125 Wavy, in a sense

DOWN

1 Envelope abbr.
2 Expressions
3 Beurre Bosc, for one
4 Dormer
5 Begin
6 Old Tokyo
7 Print style
8 Harold Grange
9 Stab
10 Simoom
11 Landed
12 Divine
13 Saintly
14 Required
15 Maxims
16 Role for Lasorda in
  "Oliver!"?
17 "Ishtar" director
18 Poplar
20 Weary
21 Emancipated
26 Poetic foot
28 Walked
30 Hot dish
32 Kitchen wrap
33 Nature: Comb. form

36 Sinker
38 "Give all thou ___ . . .":
  Wordsworth
39 Fuss
41 Baby-shower gift
45 "___ Bovary"
46 Peak
48 River of Spain
50 Tribe or helicopter
51 Bristle
53 Type of train
55 Regarding this point
56 Balmy
57 Feared
58 Hartley novel about North?
59 Employment summary
60 Tenor
62 Ten: Comb. form
65 Trick
68 Skim
70 Senator Gramm
73 Gless and Tate
75 Bream
77 Knave
80 Popular Beethoven
  symphony

81 How blue bloods act?
83 Ta-ta
86 Height: Comb. form
87 Atonement
88 Wow!
90 PM
92 La Scala site
94 Milk sugar
95 Beachcomber's find
96 Founder of Taoism
97 Thomas More's crime
98 Nagy in "Hearing
  Voices"
99 Bis!
101 Coin side
102 Pretentious
106 Procrastinate
109 Litigates
111 Game for two
113 Defraud
116 French beverage
117 Linden
118 Ester of guanosine
119 Punkish

31

FROM RUSSIA WITH SKILL by Rosalind Pavane
Since the Cold War has ended, Rosalind feels it's time to honor some famous Americans having a Russian heritage.

ACROSS

1 Backtalk
5 Leather band
10 Removes (a hat)
15 Manufacturer's meas.
18 Waugh or Guinness
19 Grace of "Jane Eyre"
20 Harden
21 Jab
22 Actress from Tula
25 Architect Saarinen
26 Baseball arbiter
27 Pigeons' haven
28 Strode
29 Sausage in Soho
31 Makes a living again
33 Juicy fruit
34 Sums demanded by
   kidnappers
35 Danny of the Phoenix Suns
36 City in North Dakota
37 Carpenter's machine
38 ". . . ___ the garden,
   Maud": Tennyson
39 Conductor from Vyshny
   Volochok
42 Albums for grads
45 Eccentric old man
47 Creatures, in Caen
48 Indonesia's ___ Islands
49 Pt. of speech
52 POW camps
55 These, in Tours
56 With full force
57 Landed property broker
59 Like a gymnast
61 Angry
62 Aviation pioneer from Kiev
64 Period
65 Character actor from Baku
68 Robes for Cicero
69 Cartoonist Dean
71 Kidded
72 "And liddle lamzy ___ . . ."
   ("Mairzy Doats" song)
73 Wintertime menace
74 Machine parts
77 Monk's title
78 More's antithesis
79 Golda's family
81 Clodhopper
83 Belief
84 London-born actor of
   Russo-French heritage
87 French river
91 Rainbows
93 Flower part
94 Unloads
95 Large artery
97 Mason's material
98 Certain Tibetans
100 Rococo
101 Precious ones
102 Catch-all phrase
103 Ex-coach Parseghian
104 Sounds of disapproval
105 Composer from Pskov
   (Vernon Duke)
109 Float for Finn
110 "Age of Anxiety" poet
111 Two under par, on a golf
   hole
112 Man, for one

113 Sandy's bark
114 Fabricators
115 Checks
116 Act

DOWN

1 Warrior of feudal Japan
2 Coastal town in Egypt
3 What Aaron's rod became
4 ___-fi literature
5 Canoodle
6 Race track denizens
7 Mrs. Miniver, for one
8 Matterhorn or Mont Blanc
9 Kitchen gadgets
10 Invalidate
11 Correctly pitched, in music
12 A king of Egypt
13 Sauté
14 Coastal dunes
15 Actor-director from
   St. Petersburg
16 Composer from Indiana
17 Scents
21 "Honi soit qui mal y ___"
23 This equals 160 square rods
24 Oslo's country, to natives
30 Singer Williams

32 Twittering with expectation
33 Port on the Persian Gulf
34 Demolishes
36 Peat, for one
37 Wall or Fleet
39 A sugar
40 Missouri's ___ Mountains
41 Seven-year problem
43 More concise
44 Arizona State's ___ Devils
46 Unclaimed animal, in law
48 Peak in Italy
49 "___ longa, vita brevis"
50 Divine beings
51 Comedian from Odessa
53 "Tam ___": R. Burns song
54 Horse fathers
56 Melodic
58 Theater sections
60 Sour
61 Extemporaneous theater,
   informally
63 Bush and Buckley, once
66 ___ Theater in Sarasota
67 Govt. agcy.
70 A 1974 bestseller by
   Gore Vidal
72 Ovid's 551

73 Honored with
   entertainment
75 Limber
76 Place for fish or oil
79 Like Chaucer's London
80 Prolongs
82 Travel
84 The Great Commoner
85 An 11 on the Beaufort
   Scale
86 Weedy Old World herbs
88 Barrier
89 Scintillate
90 Attempted
92 Cook on a spit
94 Take out, in printing
95 Hooded snake
96 Bellowing
97 Passover feast
98 Passage through a mine
99 Relatives of cods
101 Tzara's art cult
102 Rim
106 Him, to Colette
107 Deserter
108 Cover

OLD-FASHIONED OFFERING by William P. Baxley
Bill's a laid-back Angelino; he prefers a no-nonsense approach to puzzling.

ACROSS

1 Water bottles
8 Popular tropical aquarium fish
15 Russian urn
22 Hillary conquered it
23 Marine food fish
24 Suppose
25 Shine brightly
26 Artist's studio
27 Shed feathers, as an English sparrow
28 Rome's ___ Coeli Church
29 Shipworms
31 Abou Ben Adhem had one
33 Stuffed ___ (kind of sausage)
34 Unseeing nursery trio
36 Macerate
37 Roman bronze
38 Vietnamese New Year
40 Unrestrained revelry
41 Recurring musical beat
43 Chinese skiffs
47 French fathers
49 Unit
50 Early Roman boxing glove
52 Columbia's team
53 Kind of artist
54 Shoulder garments
56 Sir Geraint's wife
58 Baden-Baden, e.g.
59 Stanley Steamer, e.g.
60 Summers in LeMans
61 Opposite of apterous
64 Slogan
66 Wine samplers
68 Cupid
72 Pack down
73 Written order
75 Member of the amaryllis family
76 Pita or dilo
77 Palpebra on the eye
78 Sale of a sort
79 Amphitheaters
80 Spike of corn
81 Dry, as wine
82 Criterion: Abbr.
83 Massachusetts cape
84 Part of a drama
85 Adherent: Suffix
86 Striker
88 In want
90 Bustling excitement
91 Gyrate
92 Malay monetary unit
93 Payment
95 Intrigue
96 Close tightly
97 French coastal region
98 Critter in a Salten story
99 Part of the eye
100 Mild oath
102 Rockies and Andes: Abbr.
103 Cruise stop: Abbr.
104 Small ornamental case
106 Communications satellite
109 Cater-cousin
110 Ancient Celtic priest
112 Accompany for protection
116 Juice or sap: Comb. form
117 Convened anew

119 Caverns
121 At no time
122 Indonesian island
124 June bug
125 Attempt
126 So. Amer. wood sorrel
128 Printer's term for removal
129 Mix
131 CMLI x II
133 Rulers in ancient Persia
137 John ___ Neill (Oz illustrator)
138 Lithe
140 Recluse
142 Persistent tapping
144 "May Lord Christ ___?": Wilde
145 Spanish province
146 Postulate
147 Resume operation
148 Lymphoid tissue
149 Kind of bass

DOWN

1 Earthenware
2 Greed
3 Edits
4 Onassis nickname
5 Exploit
6 Fragrant compound
7 Metric measures
8 Source of roe
9 Roman statesman
10 City in S France
11 Mae West role
12 Tolerates
13 Penitents
14 To be: Fr.
15 Seethe
16 I love: Lat.

17 Tennyson heroine
18 One eying cheesecake
19 Caustic quality
20 Member of the buttercup genus
21 Changes the stamping machine
30 Butcher shop: Fr.
32 Solar disc
35 Muse of music
37 Suburb of Liège
39 Uses a cupel
42 Tanning agent
44 Fine sprays
45 Mexican volcano
46 Collection of anecdotes
47 Share
48 Jeanne D'Arc, e.g.
51 Less complicated
53 Searching; seeking
55 Amerind or orange
57 Greek architectural order
59 Fungicides
60 White-tailed sea eagle
61 Affirms
62 Wyoming city
63 Hymn by S. F. Smith
65 Spread hay for drying
66 Nervous twitch
67 A very long time
69 Narrow strip of silk
70 Popular acclaim
71 Feels annoyed
74 Steering devices on sailboats
75 Guggenheim specialty
79 Common monkshood
81 Opposite of poivre
82 Having a slight luster
84 Building material

87 Tall stories
88 Election month: Abbr.
89 Actress ___ Claire
90 Aspire
91 Joined two pieces of sound tape
93 Spanish hero
94 Implied
97 Assessed
101 Needlefish
103 Golf teacher
105 Branch of mil. service
106 His patron is St. Crispin
107 Having a milky iridescence
108 Harasses
109 One of Hollywood's Westmores
110 Arid
111 Updike's "The Same ___"
113 Give the waiter too large a douceur
114 Discharge
115 Hosted the party
118 Instant
119 Mourn
120 Low steep slopes
123 Small addition to a map
125 Exhausted
127 Separate
130 Copperfield's first wife
132 Tableland
133 Home for a guided missile
134 King of the Huns
135 ___ off (irate)
136 Mob or gang follower
139 Russian village
141 Marie Dressler's great role in 1931
143 Pierre's friend

33 O-ZONE by Cathy Millhauser
A clever idea is combined with fresh, original clues. Nice work, Cathy! You won the Margaret!

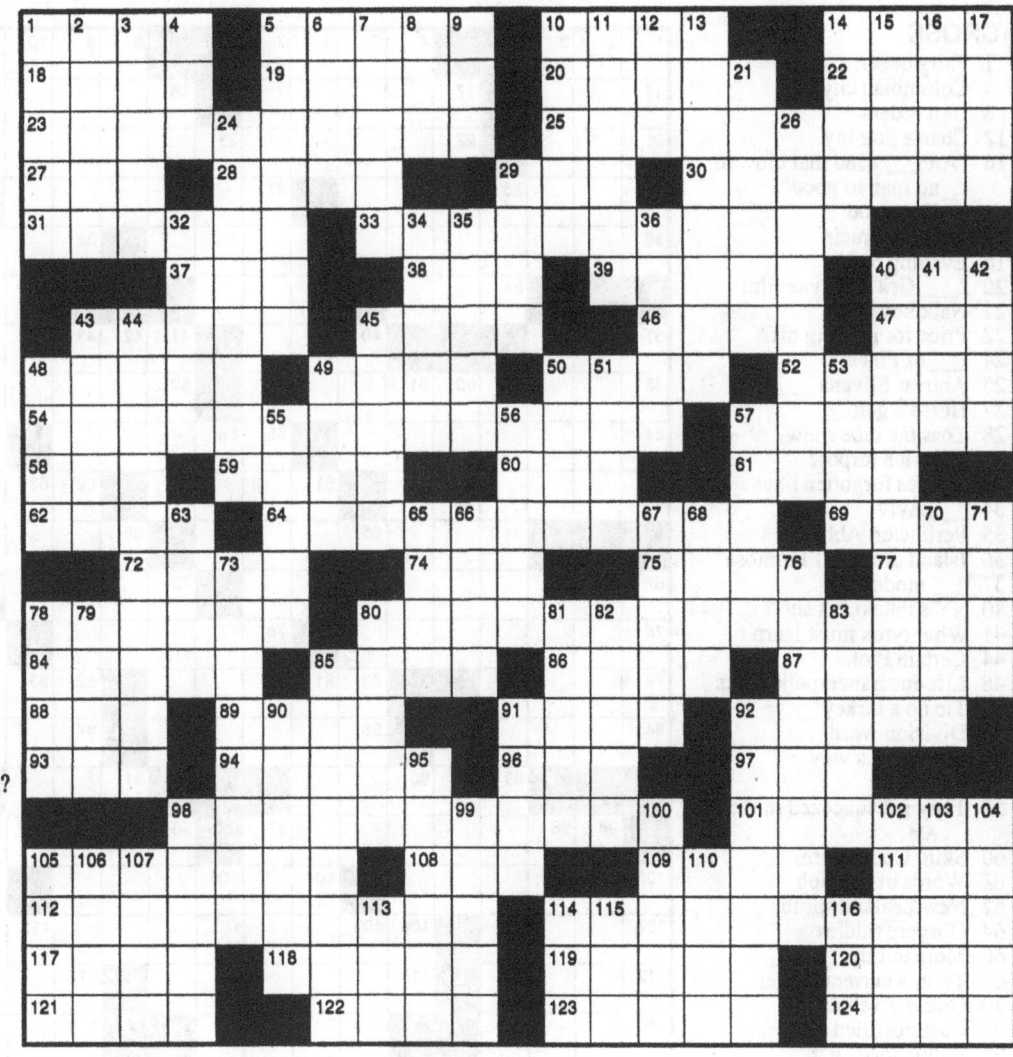

ACROSS
1 "Cave Bears" collective
5 Campfire glower
10 Type of mackeral
14 Metal containers
18 Kedrova of "Zorba the Greek"
19 Actress Gibbs (The Jeffersons' "Florence")
20 Ichabod's Van Tassel, briefly
22 "If I Only ___ Heart"
23 Native American artist's need?
25 Alcott novel about an augury?
27 Einstein's birthplace
28 Lyricist Lerner
29 "___ vobiscum"
30 Glass variety
31 Cheapen
33 Editor, at times?
37 Energy
38 Simmons and Kaline of baseball fame
39 Author Segal
40 Hiatus
43 Fannie Mae offerings
45 Heparin target
46 Perfect report card
47 Genetic designer monogram?
48 She liked Ike
49 Afghanistan title
50 Blocker and McGrew
52 Some map lines
54 TV evaluator on a soapbox?
57 "Cut that out!"
58 Part of NOW
59 Sometime signs at the Martin Beck
60 Mr. McGregor's tool
61 He wrote "Off the Court"
62 Pre-college exam
64 Part of a college?
69 Spanish explorer, De ___
72 What a mendicant does
74 Euclid follower
75 Intense
77 Promise
78 Defoe hero
80 Double form of torture, perhaps?
84 Milk: Comb. form
85 Nothing more than
86 Spotted
87 Chinos, e.g.
88 Torah encloser
89 Apothecary measure
91 Magen David, e.g.
92 Saint ___ Day, May 27
93 "Roundabout" rock group
94 Apollo's birthplace
96 Mapplethorpe's work, controversially
97 Geller, the psychic
98 Oater with a surprise ending?
101 "A Dog's Life" dog
105 Giggles
108 Bee chaser
109 Caspian Sea port
111 Charge
112 See next clue

114 With above, caution re: eggs?
117 Painter Rockwell ___
118 Pops
119 Spill the beans
120 Pacifist
121 Threatening last word
122 Wan
123 Minds
124 Feature of "harassment"?

DOWN
1 Nine, e.g.
2 Heavy thread
3 Gentle as ___
4 Gossip
5 Symbols
6 Naomi's other name
7 Psychologist Bettelheim
8 Chicago loop sights
9 "Ole," in America
10 World's biggest hold-up man
11 Alice Kramden's pal
12 One of the Carsons
13 Kelep
14 "___ night, the stars . . ."
15 Branches
16 London's "Martin ___"
17 Compos mentis

21 Llama's cousin
24 It's no trouble at all
26 Amelia's kin
29 "Ahem!"
32 Advantage
34 "Cheeky" adjective
35 Actress Massey
36 Borneo primate
40 Purple sheep?
41 "___ Love Her": Beatles song
42 Ago
43 Bruins' bases
44 Last dollars?
45 Picked
48 L-Q connectors
49 It opens many a door
50 "Runaround Sue" singer
51 Freshly
53 Ahs partners
55 Appearing gnawed
56 Cogitate
57 Orchid edible
63 Try
65 Raise
66 Alençon product
67 Puff ___ (viper)
68 Muhammad rival of '78
70 Sprees
71 Has

73 Samaritan's act
76 Small plane
78 Dirty Dice
79 Not well
80 Do over the lawn
81 The Jetson's dog
82 Longfellow's "below"
83 It's the pits
85 Dobie Gillis' hang-out
90 Mends seams
91 Your pain was his gain
92 Tragic footwear
95 Of religious rites
98 Kind of wash
99 Sarah ___ (Met soprano)
100 He was deposed by Amin
102 Burns's river
103 Irk
104 Passover repast
105 Bit of bread, in Soho
106 First name in daredevilry
107 Ages upon ages
110 Salt's call
113 Writer LeShan
114 Arafat's gp.
115 Southern Johnny
116 Half of a '66 Broadway musical's title

34

LAZY BONES by Jim Page
You may need a *skeleton* key to unlock the thematic entries in this challenger.

ACROSS
1 Fairy queen
4 Colombian city
8 Deli orders
12 Coarse hominy
16 "An ___ wind that bloweth no man to good": Heywood
17 Burns's Gracie
18 Evening party
20 "___ Grit": Wayne film
21 Nabokov book
22 Price for goofing off?
24 ___ of Pines
25 Actress Silvana ___
27 Horse's gait
28 Toss the dice anew
30 Peruvian torpor?
32 Studies forgotten lines
34 ___ Aviv
35 Perimeter: Abbr.
36 Island group off Formosa
37 ___ mode
40 NY's Pataki, for short
41 What tyros must learn
44 Certain Prot.
48 Life-insurance-policy plus
52 Tie up a turkey
53 Division word
54 Senses, in a way
55 Cloth fold
57 They get squeezed in the AM
60 Skin: Comb. form
61 Words of triumph
62 New Zealand shrub
64 Obscure riddles
66 More untidy
67 Train's current carrier
70 Golfer's vehicle
71 Custard-filled cake
75 Balky horse, e.g.
76 Organic compound
78 Surrounds
79 Yes and yea: Abbr.
80 Civet relative
82 Rodent chasers
84 Writing instruments
86 In a negligent way
87 Vichy, e.g.
88 Syr. neighbor
89 "... how the ___ half lives"
91 Due follower
92 "For that elephant ___ all night": Godwin
95 Noted Broadway family
98 Presley's gyration affliction?
103 One who expiates
104 Like a beehive?
106 Deductive
107 Kind of tree or vase
108 Glass jaws?
111 ___ shelter
112 Lotion ingredient
113 Imprints
114 City near Venice
115 Summer, in Savoie
116 Münster mister
117 Biblical patriarch
118 ___ dog (husky)
119 "___ Ring des Nibelungen"

DOWN
1 "___ Vice"
2 Soviet river
3 France's Mont ___
4 Of an exact duplicate
5 Joseph or Stewart
6 Rent
7 Shiftless Greek ranks?
8 Tug or kayak
9 Long-term jailbird
10 Ancient galleys
11 Japanese coin
12 Horseman's pedal problem
13 Result of a burning desire?
14 Ponders
15 Banana discard
17 "___ of do or die ..."
18 Big name in electronics
19 Plumed wading bird
23 Cowardly Lion portrayer
26 Dieter's target
29 ___ off (slacken)
31 Hearing: Comb. form
33 Catches cattle
37 ___ test
38 Kent's girlfriend
39 Star: Comb. form
40 Fish have them: Abbr.
41 Hwys.
42 English money, once
43 Golfers' range of activity?
45 Actress Swenson
46 Editor's mark
47 Brit's blackjack
49 Comic idler?
50 Provisions; food
51 Clothe
56 ___ Palmas
58 Monarch's terms
59 Writer on Marx and Rimbaud
61 French friend
63 Mend a damaged painting: Abbr.
65 Mouthwash user
66 Loco
67 Refrain syllables
68 Bulk
69 Questionable
70 "___ of Angels"
72 Babylonian god
73 "Rock of ___"
74 Gorby realm, once
77 Actor Gibson
78 Letter after zeta
81 Fellow-resident of our planet
83 Mimic
85 Beatles' "Let ___"
90 Basil and dill
91 ___ off (angry)
92 Subjoin
93 Concise
94 Actor Wallach
95 Set of steps
96 Revere; exalt
97 "O ___ Carlo": Verdi aria
98 Hits the tape first
99 Taft was one
100 Cast a ballot
101 Hot under the collar
102 Brownie scout leader
103 Oriental nurse
105 Siestas
109 All-purpose trk.
110 Package: Abbr.

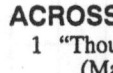

35

QUIZZICAL QUIP by William Lutwiniak
Here's one of the last of over 8,000 crosswords created by a master-puzzler.
Note how deftly he solved a problem at 101 Across. We shall miss our friend
and colleague very much.

ACROSS

1 "Thou ___ it now"
   (Macbeth)
5 Laundered
10 "Once ___ midnight
   . . .": Poe
15 City on the Caspian
19 Nanking nanny
20 John Wayne role: 1954
21 McKinley's birthplace
22 Shroyer spin-off
23 **Start of a quip**
27 Concluding clause
28 Outerwear
29 Experiments
30 Strummers' instruments,
   for short
31 Markka fraction
32 Smeltery deliveries
33 Civic concern
36 Gets coaching
37 Set right
40 **Quip, Part II**
44 Urban structures
46 Formicids
47 Curtaining
48 Holyfield victories
49 To ___ (just so)
50 Coral, for one
51 Mezzo-soprano Marilyn
52 Suit
55 NL-er from Atlanta
56 Orch. offerings
57 "Cosmos" explicator
58 ___ up (chipped in)
59 **Quip, Part III**
65 "My Favorite Year" star
66 Prelims
67 City on the Moselle
68 Cheviot and merino
69 First movie to win an
   Oscar
70 Proscriptions
72 Soc. page person
75 He played Hawkeye
76 Douglas is its capital
77 Stood with
78 Commuting cost
79 Zero
80 **End of quip**
85 Old-hat
87 Disassembles
88 Basso Simon
89 Corrida clamor
90 Hydrophanes
91 Developer's layout
93 Absorb effortlessly
96 ". . . ___ in the affairs of
   men": Shak.
97 Assertive dove
101 This was needed for
   symmetry
104 Escalation
105 Jazzman Condon
106 Izmir people
107 On a par
108 "Diary of ___ Housewife"
109 Ensconces
110 Falstaffian
111 Colorants

DOWN

1 Chuckle
2 "My head is ___ . . . of
   the whole world":
   Fielding
3 "Once in a Blue Moon"
   comedian
4 Down in ___ (depressed)
5 Favored
6 "The Brown Bomber"
7 Danube feeder
8 Kerfuffle
9 "He did ___ but cooed
   and cooed":
   Wordsworth
10 Preternatural
11 Holier-than-thou behavior
12 Motoring pioneer
13 Bottom-line
14 Source of wood for bats
15 Folly
16 Square pillar
17 Eye makeup
18 Manipulates
24 Bumpkin
25 Region of Asia Minor
26 "You ___ Sunshine"
31 Member of the masses

32 Whether ___
33 Masters of ledger-domain
34 TV's Enriquez
35 Speck
36 Like Twiggy
38 Specify
39 Surveying device
41 Turn (into)
42 Inferior
43 Approving
45 Squalid
49 Ball's co-star
51 No-goods
52 Bangkok cash
53 Sponsorship
54 Bleacher creature
55 Struggles
56 Octavia's tunic
57 Men-only affair
58 Phony
59 Sioux City Sue, e.g.
60 Impassive
61 Bean
62 White wine
63 Craving
64 Type of inflorescence
69 Surfers' surfaces

70 Model-actress Cheryl
71 Leverson and Huxtable
72 Pixilated
73 Coloratura Mills
74 Chances
76 ___ at (flirted)
77 Kind of heel
78 Promoted
80 "The Planets" composer
81 'I'll kill you if you ___":
   Burgess
82 Reduces a heap
83 Ukase kin
84 Edify
86 Wool-gathered
91 Free parking, etc.
92 Booboo
93 Other, in Oviedo
94 Dogpaddle
95 ___ Verde Park
96 "A wing ___ prayer"
97 Maison maître
98 Blue hue
99 Words of understanding
100 Grasps: Sc.
102 Keatsian work
103 Keeve

36

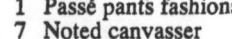

PLAIN GEOMETRY by Rosalind Pavane
According to Roz, the idea for this puzzle came to her while she was occupying a box seat.

ACROSS

1 Passé pants fashions
7 Noted canvasser
13 Small film role
18 Salad green
19 Green-card holders
20 Tweets
22 Endless
23 Colorful flower
24 Horse enclosure
25 Ventilation: Fr.
26 Lariat
27 Rouge et ___, gambling game
29 Mohammad ___, the Greatest
30 Beds for babes
31 Triangular sail
32 Paid news items
33 Storage place
35 Any Costa Rican
36 With 40 DOWN, 92 ACROSS, a precept in "new" geometry?
41 Ancient mystical script
42 Emblem
43 Thread: Abbr.
44 Avowals
45 Rotary tool
47 Solo
49 Soft cheese
50 Tattle
51 Bahamian capital
54 Calliope, e.g.
55 Scented
59 This often follows co.
60 Straitlaced
63 Stiff petticoat
64 Siouans
66 "Up ___," Bill Mauldin cartoon
67 Lorelei's stream
68 Related
69 Aborigine's weapon
71 Direct route
73 Part of a boxer's rec.
74 Most attractive
75 Nurmi or Sibelius
76 Arthurian heroine
78 Dr. Huxtable's 101 Across
79 Defense org. of 1949
80 Closet feature
82 Detroit cager
85 Moisten
86 Pea jacket
87 Cookbook meas.
91 Start of a fairy tale
92 See 36 ACROSS
95 East coast canal
96 Platform
98 Himalayan beast
99 Group
100 Author-critic Judith
101 Offspring
102 So be it
104 British money
107 Not quite
108 Salad ingredient
110 Cattle dealer
112 English sweet
113 Spoil everything
114 Spanish dance
115 One more
116 Luges
117 Kind of journalism
118 Kids

DOWN

1 Clique
2 Vespucci's memorial
3 Certain geometric curves
4 Saturnian features
5 Zoologist's plural suffix
6 Seasoning in potage
7 Summerhouse
8 Inter ___
9 Anathema to serge
10 Russian river
11 Prefix with corn or form
12 "Minding" letters
13 Half of DCII
14 Present time in Tijuana
15 Russian village
16 Mistake in print
17 Having a milky iridescence
18 Does a double take
21 Baker's implement
26 Garand
28 Schl. in Columbus
31 Miter
32 Tennis champion in the '70s
34 Song syllables
37 Hale
38 Snipe's abode
39 ". . . ___ of sympathy with other men": Emerson
40 See 36 ACROSS
46 ___ Lincoln (first movie "Tarzan")
48 Swimmer's length
50 Latin singer, Lopez
51 Mythical weeper
52 Composer Bruckner
53 Hie
54 Fine Chinese porcelain
55 Seed casing
56 Rikki-___-Tavi
57 Point at the base of the skull
58 Use a thurible
61 Heaven: Comb. form
62 Vietnamese money
63 Early Chinese dynasty
65 Infatuated
67 Fame
70 Resound
71 Dracula was one
72 Building addition
75 Portuguese song
77 What follows a disaster-like calculus?
79 Place for a choker
80 Binge
81 Emcee
82 Soothing drink
83 Chants
84 Gossiper's delight
85 Anon
88 Item in a patisserie
89 "Big Band" leader Noble, and family
90 Demonstrative one, in a way
93 Caustic
94 Realtor's concern
97 Saul's successor
100 Girls named for a queen
103 New York nine
104 Kind of tax
105 Daredevil Knievel
106 Agrippina's son
107 River in Italy
109 Temper
111 Caviar
112 Conical cap worn by Muslims

37 JANUS-FACED WORDS by Betty Jorgensen

We would like to add *ravel* and *scan* to Betty's list. This puzzle tied for second place in the Farrar Stakes.

ACROSS

1 Guarantee
7 Rio de la ___, South American estuary
12 Swift
17 An attempt
21 Armored
22 Horse opera
23 Afterward
24 Rich vein
25 TRIM
29 Harold of the old comics
30 "___ my Soul through the Invisible": FitzGerald
31 Cunning
32 Entries in a list
33 Took part in a race
35 Sego lily's state
36 Manicurists
38 Sullies
42 Luck, to the Irish
45 A Roosevelt
46 TRIP
55 Painters' props
56 Actress Moreno
57 Didn't pass
58 Stead
59 Three, in Torino
60 Chemical compound
61 Gross
62 Reeked
63 He wrote "I Like It Here"
65 Leaves out
66 Object of R. E. Lee's allegiance
67 Widow's dower
68 Mae West role
69 Pit
70 Pith helmet
73 Proper
74 SANCTION
82 Helm position
83 Panache
84 Alex Haley's best-seller
85 Help
86 Great fright
89 First-aid procedure, for short
91 Protective embankments
92 City, to a Boer
93 Erroneous
94 Concrete foundations
96 Conduits
97 Roman's 605
98 Beach resort
99 Roma's country
100 Space
101 Plaits
104 CLEAVE
108 Hair style
109 Bog fuel
110 Sports
111 Field and Struthers
114 Rubber trees
117 Kind of head Bottom wears in "A Midsummer Night's Dream"
118 Candy
119 "___ Old Dutch Garden," 1939 song
120 Spray
124 Being, to Brutus

128 WEAR
134 "___ Karenina": Tolstoy
135 Very bitter
136 Gun butt
137 Get there
138 Time frame
139 Saxophone and oboe
140 Drenches
141 Chaff

DOWN

1 Third of a Latin trio
2 Infamous paraphiliac (after "de")
3 Team
4 ___ Bator, Mongolia
5 Primary color
6 Tokyo, formerly
7 Diva Lily
8 Halt
9 Solar disk
10 Camp sight
11 Linkletter
12 Fauna's go-together
13 Coniferous tree
14 Delineate
15 Smoked delicacy
16 Corn or pod preceder
17 List of candidates
18 Sears, for one
19 Name of the 2nd and 6th president
20 Ottoman governors
26 Get rid of the suds
27 Posed
28 Rice dish
33 Moscow money
34 "___ Well That Ends Well"
35 Take advantage of
36 Stands up to
37 Made angry

38 MIT degree
39 Letter between zeta and theta
40 In an old-fashioned way
41 Hebrew dry measures
42 Animal, to a cowboy
43 Colorado's ___ Park
44 Oscar-night sight
45 Hot sauce
47 "Twelfth Night" duke
48 Rank just below cpl.
49 "A Message to ___": Hubbard
50 Narrow inlets
51 Word's final syllable
52 Story-teller
53 ___-Lease, WW II agreement
54 Guffaws
60 Ham it up
62 Switchblades
63 Clerical vestment
64 "O Sole ___"
65 Playful sea mammal
67 Jogs
69 Arias
70 Sesame
71 Eggs, to Ovid
72 Write
73 Hops
75 He-e-ere's Johnny!
76 Sand rat
77 Maxim
78 Door
79 Riga native
80 Pedro's aunt
81 Unmatched
86 Bath powder
87 Author Ludwig
88 Canio's refrain, "___, Pagliaccio"

89 Cigar type
90 Hand part
91 Anatomical sac
92 ___ Flow: British naval base
94 Swizzles
95 Utter
96 Challenge
97 Mild oaths
99 Questionable
101 Heat measures, for short
102 Coll. in Hanover, NH
103 Group honored on Nov. 1
105 One-time family of Edith Wilson
106 Jupiter's mother
107 Adult insect
111 Despicable fellow
112 Sicilian volcano
113 He wrote "The Merry Widow"
114 Opened
115 Praises
116 Printing measures
118 Influence
119 Concerning
120 Explorer Hernando De ___
121 Malay outrigger
122 Take heed, in Ayr
123 Irritates
124 Make wages
125 Actress in "M*A*S*H"
126 Except for
127 Ogler
129 Jack of the sea
130 Sleeve holding
131 Sinuous curve
132 Small amount
133 Eon component

38 MOTTOS by Caroline G. Fitzgerald

Caroline wasn't satisfied with just any mottos. She concentrated on her homeland and squeezed in fourteen of them. Use red, white, and blue pencils to solve this one!

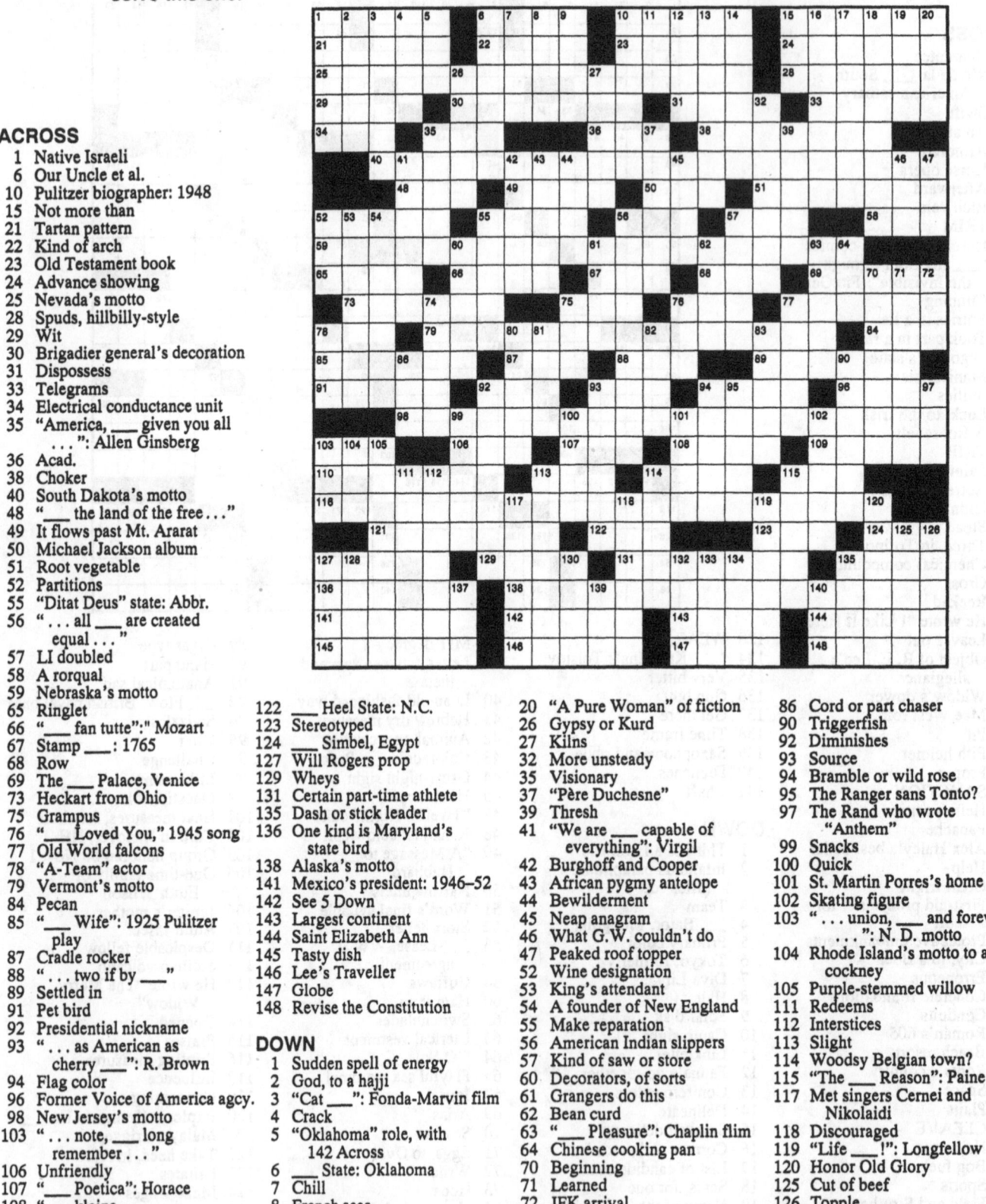

ACROSS

1 Native Israeli
6 Our Uncle et al.
10 Pulitzer biographer: 1948
15 Not more than
21 Tartan pattern
22 Kind of arch
23 Old Testament book
24 Advance showing
25 Nevada's motto
28 Spuds, hillbilly-style
29 Wit
30 Brigadier general's decoration
31 Dispossess
33 Telegrams
34 Electrical conductance unit
35 "America, ___ given you all . . .": Allen Ginsberg
36 Acad.
38 Choker
40 South Dakota's motto
48 "___ the land of the free . . ."
49 It flows past Mt. Ararat
50 Michael Jackson album
51 Root vegetable
52 Partitions
55 "Ditat Deus" state: Abbr.
56 ". . . all ___ are created equal . . ."
57 LI doubled
58 A rorqual
59 Nebraska's motto
65 Ringlet
66 "___ fan tutte:" Mozart
67 Stamp ___: 1765
68 Row
69 The ___ Palace, Venice
73 Heckart from Ohio
75 Grampus
76 "___ Loved You," 1945 song
77 Old World falcons
78 "A-Team" actor
79 Vermont's motto
84 Pecan
85 "___ Wife": 1925 Pulitzer play
87 Cradle rocker
88 ". . . two if by ___"
89 Settled in
91 Pet bird
92 Presidential nickname
93 ". . . as American as cherry ___": R. Brown
94 Flag color
96 Former Voice of America agcy.
98 New Jersey's motto
103 ". . . note, ___ long remember . . ."
106 Unfriendly
107 "___ Poetica": Horace
108 "___ kleine Nachtmusik": Mozart
109 "Ghosts" playwright
110 Work
113 "With God, all things ___ possible": Ohio motto
114 "Live ___ or die": N. H. motto
115 Sixth word of Gettysburg Address
116 Alabama's motto
121 Hell, according to TSE

122 ___ Heel State: N.C.
123 Stereotyped
124 ___ Simbel, Egypt
127 Will Rogers prop
129 Wheys
131 Certain part-time athlete
135 Dash or stick leader
136 One kind is Maryland's state bird
138 Alaska's motto
141 Mexico's president: 1946–52
142 See 5 Down
143 Largest continent
144 Saint Elizabeth Ann
145 Tasty dish
146 Lee's Traveller
147 Globe
148 Revise the Constitution

DOWN

1 Sudden spell of energy
2 God, to a hajji
3 "Cat ___": Fonda-Marvin film
4 Crack
5 "Oklahoma" role, with 142 Across
6 ___ State: Oklahoma
7 Chill
8 French seas
9 Shiism or Sunnism
10 Congregation
11 Chaney from Colorado
12 Concerning
13 Studied
14 "It ___ Advertise": 1931 film
15 Likely
16 Commercial fishing boat
17 Specialties
18 Excesses
19 Trustworthy

20 "A Pure Woman" of fiction
26 Gypsy or Kurd
27 Kilns
32 More unsteady
35 Visionary
37 "Père Duchesne"
39 Thresh
41 "We are ___ capable of everything": Virgil
42 Burghoff and Cooper
43 African pygmy antelope
44 Bewilderment
45 Neap anagram
46 What G.W. couldn't do
47 Peaked roof topper
52 Wine designation
53 King's attendant
54 A founder of New England
55 Make reparation
56 American Indian slippers
57 Kind of saw or store
60 Decorators, of sorts
61 Grangers do this
62 Bean curd
63 "___ Pleasure": Chaplin film
64 Chinese cooking pan
70 Beginning
71 Learned
72 JFK arrival
74 D-J connection
75 S Africa's "___ Paul" Kruger
76 "Esto Perpetua" is its motto: Abbr.
77 Precipitous
78 End of the 19th century
80 Atlanta university
81 "___ tread on me": first U.S. flag motto
82 Want
83 Being utilized

86 Cord or part chaser
90 Triggerfish
92 Diminishes
93 Source
94 Bramble or wild rose
95 The Ranger sans Tonto?
97 The Rand who wrote "Anthem"
99 Snacks
100 Quick
101 St. Martin Porres's home
102 Skating figure
103 ". . . union, ___ and forever . . .": N. D. motto
104 Rhode Island's motto to a cockney
105 Purple-stemmed willow
111 Redeems
112 Interstices
113 Slight
114 Woodsy Belgian town?
115 "The ___ Reason": Paine
117 Met singers Cernei and Nikolaidi
118 Discouraged
119 "Life ___!": Longfellow
120 Honor Old Glory
125 Cut of beef
126 Topple
127 Rich, dark soil
128 Guthrie from New York
130 "Rule, Britannia" composer
132 Utah town on the Colorado
133 "___ Good Day": 1946 song
134 Harris from Indiana
135 Bow or prow
137 Dark rm. product
138 Link
140 "The Good Old ___": 1906 song

39

DISTAFF DILEMMAS by Judith C. Dalton

Some queer queries from noted females lead to wise guys' replies in this fine example of wordplay.

ACROSS

1 Animal feet
5 Sonora Indians
9 British lunchroom
16 Certain Monk's title
19 Railroad operators
21 Thermodynamics scale founder
22 Bull ___ china shop
23 Where do I take my tennis racquet?
25 Rhine feeder
26 Rent
27 Seer
28 Pertaining to certain particles in physics
30 Some are bearded or eared
32 Promote
33 Spanish attacks
35 Roman 2101
36 Where is my show boat?
39 Pain companion
40 Jack or jenny
41 Cauchos
42 ___ Urgel, town in Spain
46 Earthquakes
48 Woody Allen movie: 1971
51 Fall mo.
52 Loki's daughter
53 Where did I leave my rules of etiquette?
57 Scot's since
58 Patriotic women's org.
60 "Water Lilies" artist
61 Bar
63 Louisiana native
65 Seaside plaything
70 Flows
71 Solo instrument compositions
73 Weird
74 Ending with cloth
75 Distribute
76 How will you do this movie shot?
82 Owns
85 A favorite crossword bird
86 Bing Crosby was one
87 First king of all England
89 English novelist Charles: 1814–84
92 Mures River city
93 Hunter or Novak
95 Rajah's wife
96 When is the best time to sing outside?
101 Norse god
102 Certain noblewoman
105 Portrayer of Dr. Kildare
106 Bird sound
107 Bitless headstall
108 Consent
110 Aborigine of India
111 Another favorite crossword bird
112 Where did my Gaelic leading man go?
118 ___ culpa
119 Square cap
120 Gushed anew
121 Serenata
122 Spanish, to Spaniards
123 Portuguese Mmes.
124 Indian mountain pass

DOWN

1 After chi
2 Plant bristle
3 Where did I leave my cookie recipe?
4 Informers
5 Brogan or buskin
6 Yet another favorite crossword bird
7 Covers a house top again
8 Prelim remarks
9 Lapse, in Léon
10 Actor James ___ Jones
11 Aix angel
12 Jamaican pop music
13 "So was ___ joly whistle wely-wet": Chaucer
14 Type of band
15 Singer Clark and namesakes
16 Singer Ross
17 Walking ___ (elated)
18 Chagall and namesakes
20 Ct. adjudicating st. or fed. demands
24 Crush
29 "___ days gone by . . .": Riley
30 Break to pieces
31 Role Jessel often played
32 Marquand's "___ Daughter"
33 Yemen native
34 Agave fiber
36 Kiln
37 Obscure poem
38 Actor Jack of many westerns
43 Where is my latest hat creation?
44 Philanthropist, e.g.
45 Ties
47 Seine feeder
48 Undergrad econ. deg.
49 "Look ___ eyes . . ." (from a Neville Ronstadt hit)
50 Nicknames for Seymour and Silas
54 Diplomat: Abbr.
55 "Ululame" poet
56 "___ Clear Day"
57 Blackthorn fruit
59 S France department
62 Mimicking
63 Chest or closet wood
64 Make amends
66 Ale's cousin
67 Bol. neighbor
68 ___ E. Tee, Derby winner: 1992
69 "Enter the Dragon" star
72 HST, to FDR: Abbr.
77 Malay boats
78 Gladiolus stems, e.g.
79 Rich soil
80 Wave on la mer
81 Roundworm
83 Golfer Palmer
84 Limit the allotment
88 "Little" trophy for Wolverines or Gophers
90 Exertion
91 S Uganda city
93 Pew floor piece
94 Connections that help
97 Caravansaries
98 Of a division of mankind
99 Fabric worker
100 Some are marching
102 Kind of therapy, for short
103 Equipped, as a gig
104 Forearm bones
106 Fuss
108 Envelope or letter letters
109 Boundary in Bilbao
110 Countries' monetary stats per yr.
113 Biochem. globulin
114 Mauna ___, extinct Hawaiian volcano
115 King of Judah: I Kings 15:8–24
116 Pasture
117 Pickup rel.

40 PROPER FITTING by Ernst Theimer

In this Theimer teaser, you should know the meaning of 27 Across. We'll tell you that the capitalized clues call for lopping or stretching.

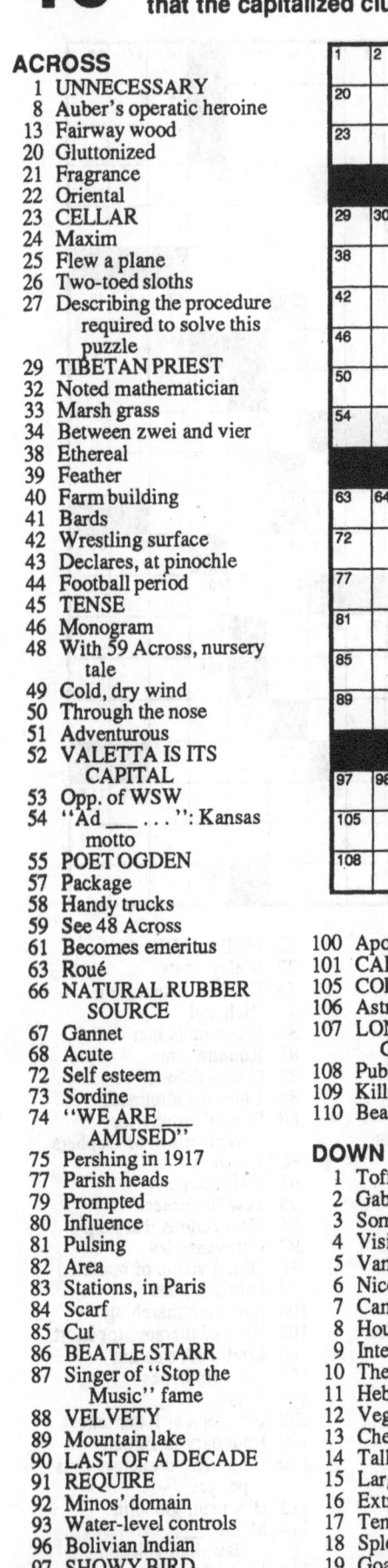

ACROSS
1 UNNECESSARY
8 Auber's operatic heroine
13 Fairway wood
20 Gluttonized
21 Fragrance
22 Oriental
23 CELLAR
24 Maxim
25 Flew a plane
26 Two-toed sloths
27 Describing the procedure required to solve this puzzle
29 TIBETAN PRIEST
32 Noted mathematician
33 Marsh grass
34 Between zwei and vier
38 Ethereal
39 Feather
40 Farm building
41 Bards
42 Wrestling surface
43 Declares, at pinochle
44 Football period
45 TENSE
46 Monogram
48 With 59 Across, nursery tale
49 Cold, dry wind
50 Through the nose
51 Adventurous
52 VALETTA IS ITS CAPITAL
53 Opp. of WSW
54 "Ad ___ ...": Kansas motto
55 POET OGDEN
57 Package
58 Handy trucks
59 See 48 Across
61 Becomes emeritus
63 Roué
66 NATURAL RUBBER SOURCE
67 Gannet
68 Acute
72 Self esteem
73 Sordine
74 "WE ARE ___ AMUSED"
75 Pershing in 1917
77 Parish heads
79 Prompted
80 Influence
81 Pulsing
82 Area
83 Stations, in Paris
84 Scarf
85 Cut
86 BEATLE STARR
87 Singer of "Stop the Music" fame
88 VELVETY
89 Mountain lake
90 LAST OF A DECADE
91 REQUIRE
92 Minos' domain
93 Water-level controls
96 Bolivian Indian
97 SHOWY BIRD

100 Apostle Peter
101 CALIBAN'S MASTER
105 COLONEL'S COMMAND
106 Astrologically auspicious
107 LONGING FOR GREATER THINGS
108 Public speakers
109 Kills
110 Beaver hats

DOWN
1 Toff
2 Gabor
3 Some MIT grads
4 Visionary or restful
5 Vampire
6 Nice summers
7 Cambodian coin
8 Housekeepers
9 Interstice
10 The time being
11 Hebrew measure
12 Vegas sevens
13 Checkmated
14 Talked wildly
15 Largest continent
16 Extraordinary one
17 Tennis unit
18 Spleen
19 Goal

27 Small lakes
28 Vassal
29 Flake
30 Climbing plants
31 Skilled performer
32 Nannies' mates
35 Rue
36 C_2H_6
37 Basketry fibers
39 PAINTER OF WASHINGTON
40 Party
41 POTTERY CLAY
43 Dukedom of 101 Across
44 Quiet
45 Certain roofer
47 Fiery cross in Scotland
48 No bid
49 Feigned illness
51 HONEY BADGER
52 ___ Hari of WW I
56 Observe
57 Strap
58 Aisle attendant
60 Book-jacket review
61 Cross
62 Bondsmen of yore
63 USE STICKUM AGAIN
64 Dame Christie
65 Genuine

67 Koko's weapon
69 Fit for plowing
70 Stew
71 ENTREATIES
73 ROGER, MARY TYLER, OR DINTY
74 ___ fu (karate)
76 Level
78 Convey
79 Agones
80 Weakens
82 Metal used in galvanizing
83 Actors Lorne and Richard
86 HARNESS STRAPS
87 WORD OF OPPOSITE SENSE
88 Heinrich's toast
90 Radio knob
91 Western Indian
92 Harvests
94 VIP conveyance
95 Lass
96 Sky bear
97 Away
98 Celtic Neptune
99 Turkish commander
101 Moccasin
102 Lendl or Trevino
103 Norse goddess of healing
104 Hosp. personnel

41 DEPRECIATION by Bert Kruse

Normally you would write off *depreciation, but in this case we suggest you write* on *it.*

ACROSS

1 Shucks!
5 Island welcome
10 Common contraction
15 René's receipt
19 Medley
20 Theme
21 Earthy color
22 Gabor and Zseller
23 Chaplin classic, with "The"?
25 Top-rated stock shares?
27 Inventor Howe
28 German port
30 With pot or maker
31 Leftovers
33 Rock group and continent: Fr.
34 "___ Three Lives"
35 NE state
36 Sud's opposite
37 Fish spears
41 Did a cobbler's job
42 Early movie theaters?
45 Anger
46 Stamped on
47 Place
48 Phoned
49 Shadow: Comb. form
50 "___ the ramparts . . ."
51 Army supply officers?
55 His dozen has thirteen
56 Proportionately
58 Shower
59 Cuts
60 Dismisses
61 Celerity
62 Oral declaration
63 Shine
65 A hound may lose this
66 Affront
69 Like a tennis lob
70 An unsolicited opinion?
73 Monastic title
74 Links scores
75 Duration
76 Tear
77 Lemur
78 Verse or form start
79 Paul Revere's profession?
83 "Carmen" composer
84 It takes a licking
86 After amas
87 Bacheller's "___ Holden"
88 Uncourtly Nastasie
89 Pizzeria sights
90 Shelters
92 Native habitat
95 Flotilla
96 Tan
97 Mae West role?
99 Jean Harlow
104 Bait
105 Sabbatical
106 Flynn or Leon
107 Orsk's river
108 Buffalo's county
109 Deviated from course
110 Colonial diplomat
111 Torpedoed

DOWN

1 John ___ Passos
2 Clay, today
3 Zilch
4 Ruled
5 Anchor position
6 Dubuque college
7 Work of art
8 ___ nibs
9 Truman's Secretary of State
10 A fine mess
11 Smarts
12 Hebrew letter
13 Take-home
14 Multiplying by three
15 Stash elsewhere
16 Iniquity
17 Cod, for one
18 CIS predecessor
24 Antelope
26 Brown girls
29 Swampy
31 John Williams, at times
32 Paul Newman film, with "The"?
33 Per ___ (yearly)
34 "Reversal of Fortune" star
37 Lachrymose
38 Common?
39 German industrial city
40 Towering tower
41 Lay off
42 Arizona Indians
43 Oxford's width
44 Fear
47 Liquid measure
49 Relish
51 Challenged
52 Arboreal quaker
53 Ready for the sack
54 Waste allowances
55 Amtrak accommodation
57 Observances
59 Cook morels, e.g.
61 Public tiff
62 Veranda
63 Enjoy extravagantly
64 Heavens: Comb. form
65 With goat or grace
67 Bridge expert and family
68 Give out
70 Northern Spy, e.g.
71 Court orders
72 Grain
75 Gregariously
77 Defamatory
79 Eyelashes
80 Disentangled
81 Widgeon
82 Cloaked
83 Slant
85 "No, ___!"
89 Nana Oyl's daughter
90 Wore
91 Mosey
92 Soccer luminary
93 Major Asian border river
94 Actress Austin
95 Weakness
96 Dear, in Milan
98 Roman goddess
100 Before, earlier
101 New Deal agcy.
102 Clown Rice
103 BPOE member

42 POSSESSIVE CASES by James E. Hinish, Jr.

Our Arlington artisan tries to avoid arcane words and crosswordese. Two things he does not avoid are originality and clever clues.

ACROSS

1 Galatea's beloved
5 Emulate Etna
10 Lapham or Marner
15 Skaldic work
19 Rodent of Central America
20 "___ the twain shall meet": Kipling
21 Conductor Leinsdorf
22 Nonsense poet
23 Dunne's dad?
25 Bird's playing field?
27 Donahue's flatware
29 Black suit
30 First estate
32 "___ Skylark": Shelley
33 C&O stops
34 To report, to Rupert
35 Sandal strap
37 Everything
41 Embellish
42 Bush's anger?
44 Mrs. John Lennon
45 Cold: Comb. form
46 Hollow and tubular
47 Gainsboroughs
48 Construction piece
49 Support
50 Von Trapp flower?
54 De Falla's "La Vida ___"
55 Film comedy?
57 Sri Lankan
58 Bright lights
59 Llaneros' weapons
60 Tabloid-style
61 Wild goose
62 Burger's predecessor
64 Penates' companions
65 Richardson heroine: 1748
68 Stulms
69 Wynette's dirt?
71 Brazilian tribe
72 Disney dog
73 Capitol feature
74 Word with star or wolf
75 Mmes. of Madrid
76 Christie sleuth Mortimer
77 Hughes bird?
81 "What's in ___?"
82 Gradual penetrations
84 ___ France
85 City on the Moselle
86 Before aujourd'hui
87 Coin in Callao
88 Whalebone
89 Cat or goat
92 Mrs. Mertz's drink?
96 Sutherland's stream?
98 Rigg's beach?
102 Cooper's tool
103 Patti LuPone role
104 Playful mammal
105 Writer Seton
106 Delaware signer: 1776
107 Amb.'s grp.
108 Courageous
109 Tony Banta drove one

DOWN

1 Nepalese peak
2 Cord or Ford
3 Babilonia's milieu
4 Long Beach's Bay
5 Pulver, for one
6 Answer
7 Grapes, e.g.
8 ___ up (energizes)
9 Quisling
10 Fabric's edge
11 Dies ___
12 NYC commuter line
13 Horiz.
14 Pettifoggers
15 City on the Rio Grande
16 Gogol's "___ Souls"
17 Outer Banks county
18 Refuges
24 Honors, in Hanau
26 Produce roe
28 Hamptons' Island
30 Hardwicke
31 Underwritten span on the Thames?
33 Dolphins coach
34 Parrot

35 Lukewarm
36 Georgetown player
37 Government security
38 Lexington, Va. marker?
39 Jack
40 Ulcers
42 "Les ___": 1957 film
43 Cube or sphere
46 Thanksgiving hymn
48 Man from Meshed
50 "Ryan's Daughter" star
51 ___ und Drang
52 Musical Mariah
53 Faulty
54 Strident sound
56 "___ Carats": 1973 film
58 Cold item in a hothouse
60 Debussy opus
61 On the ___ (disabled)
62 Cambria
63 Saw
64 "Falcon Crest" star
65 "Susan Hopley" novelist
66 Deck hands
67 Jennies
69 Minaret

70 Iris's cousin
73 Worn, like a book
75 Derides
77 Filaments
78 Scullery cloth
79 Blackthorn
80 Cerberus
81 Van Gogh's "Bedroom at ___"
83 Rang up
85 Golden Horde's home
88 Poisons
89 Not closed
90 Difficulty
91 Strip next to Sinai
92 Affliction
93 City in W Mozambique
94 In ___ (in its own place)
95 Reagan's first Interior Secretary
97 Direct ending
99 Actress Alicia
100 Daughter of Chaos
101 Bao ___, former Annamese emperor

43

KING COLE by Jeanette K. Brill

We couldn't agree more with Jeanette's title (and also with her alternate title at 61 Across).

ACROSS

1 Heeds
6 Transfer design
11 Game ragout
16 Tropical fruit
17 Remove a stripe
18 In any case
20 "Find Me a ___" (song for an anthropologist?)
22 Song for merry Andrew?
24 Grampus
25 In the morning
26 Watchful
27 Meadow
28 Alone in Lyons
30 Delightful song
32 Caroled
33 Raison d'___
34 What y's turn into
35 Nosegay
36 Cleverly amusing
37 Let it stand
38 Turner or Koppel
39 U of UN fame
41 CBS founder
42 Fr. holy women
44 Hungry in London
45 Alternative to 5 Down
46 Soothsayer
48 Song for a misandrist?
51 Rail
55 Eremite
56 Calvalry sword
58 Knee
59 Like Hammett's man
60 Fellah, e.g.
61 Alternate title of puzzle
63 Kiln
64 List on a monitor
65 Palindromic name
66 German river
67 Rocky debris
68 Begat
69 Song for a go-getter?
71 L.A. athlete
72 Platform
74 Mistakes
75 Skirt length
76 Turn ending
78 Cripples
80 Tatter
81 Distinction
85 Drinking bout
86 Elapse
87 Swiss river
88 Secluded valley
89 Pierre's peas
90 Song heard all the time?
94 Spanish painter
95 AFL-___
96 "Death, Be Not Proud" poet
97 Threatens
99 Airport abbr.
100 Song for a split personality?
102 Porter musical of 1940
104 Male peregrines
105 Alpine crests
106 Type of theater
107 Piece of plate armor
108 Examples
109 Nintendo button

DOWN

1 Resists
2 Elizabeth ___ Browning
3 Food fancier
4 Tasty tuber
5 Alternative to 45 Across
6 Contrived
7 Edits
8 Pineapple tops, e.g.
9 In the least
10 Author Deighton
11 Adamant
12 Of wings
13 Short speech
14 Wrongful: Comb. form
15 Set apart
17 Simple songs
18 Most skilled
19 Score
21 Sparoid fish
23 Former Hungarian premier
26 Severn feeder
29 Song for every nation
31 Display at MOMA
32 Porter musical of 1955
36 Pale
38 ___ Aviv
39 Titter
40 Canine disease
41 Centerfold
43 Son of Odin
44 Peruvian gold coins
45 Mister, in Mallorca
46 More tender
47 Silly
49 Perspires
50 Dole out
52 Midwest airport
53 Stairway part
54 Prefix for bellum
55 English essayist
56 Units of loudness
57 Ethel, to Caroline
61 Porter the student
62 Devisees
67 NL Rookie of the Year: 1982
70 Believer in Him
71 Trail
73 Porter
75 Musical gourds
76 Damaged
77 "Le Cheval blanc" novelist
78 ___ hitch (knot)
79 North Carolina county
80 Aida's beloved
82 Chemical salts
83 Soup dish
84 Beg
85 Merciful org.
86 Corn flour
87 Siamese twin
90 Oneida Community founder
91 Soprano Lucine
92 Hawaiian geese
93 Slangy assent
96 RAF decorations
98 Mosel tributary
101 "... man ___ mouse?"
102 Waterproof boot
103 Cinque less due

SPORTS SHORTS by Bert Rosenfield
Athletically inclined persons are inclined every which way in this rib-tickler.

ACROSS

1 Compassionate org. founded 1866
6 Beauvais is its capital
10 Out of whack
15 ___ phenomenon, like ESP
18 One way into Rome
19 Defoe's Ms. Flanders
20 Oscar winner: 1939
21 Time past, in poesy
22 What the footballing kennelman did
25 Chess champ: 1960–61
26 Stravinsky's progress-maker
27 Neural contact point
28 Voyager 2's camera subject
30 Versatile plastic
32 What the basketballing barber did
35 Jersey's Midler
36 Draft initials
39 Town in S France
40 Sedaka and Simon
41 "...that face of ___ again": King Lear
43 Seafarer
45 Gyro starter
48 Martha of TV commercials
49 Sizzler from Sampras
51 What the myopic baseballing harpooner did
56 Syndicate biggie
58 Straighten a maze
59 Molasses, in the UK
64 Shank
65 Browning is "Hervé ___"
66 Anatomical ducts
69 Siphon off
70 Humeri companions
72 What the artistic batter did
75 ___ the palm (bribed)
76 Kind of finish
77 Circus trouper
78 Rank's partner
80 "So what ___ is new?"
81 Universally useful liquid
84 Lifesaving specialists in the Coast Guard
86 ___ precedent
87 What the marksman meteorologist did
91 Rimski-Korsakov's "Le Coq ___"
92 Priority item
96 Take a turn for the worse
97 Subject ending
98 Southwest stewpot
100 Ancient potato farmers
102 Bob's road companion
105 Utmost
107 "Stop it!" in Italy
110 What the society stunt driver did
114 Pipe fitter, of a sort
116 Wine made in Sicily
117 Second Amendment word
120 Priestly object of the O.T.
121 Native of Panay
122 What the boxing commuter did

126 Bee chaser
127 ___ pedis (athlete's foot)
128 Sharjah top man
129 ___ Plain (Southwest plateau)
130 He forwards pkgs.
131 Mary or John J.
132 Neighbor of N Dak.
133 Irish river and lough

DOWN

1 "___ in the Sun": Clift-Taylor film
2 What a volleyballing caterer might do
3 Chemistry lab item
4 Calotte or zuchetto
5 "___ of robins..."
6 Bailiwick of Sultan Qabus
7 New Rochelle college
8 Wages mosquito warfare
9 ___ Cook Jr. (Wilmer in "The Maltese Falcon")
10 Cannon ending
11 Outré, not long ago
12 ___ out (erratic)
13 Tapioca base
14 Pedal-operated
15 Deep purple
16 Aslope
17 Otiosity
18 Catch ___ (mishandle an oar)

23 Azine and acridine
24 "Camino ___": T. Williams 1953 drama
29 Wedding-cake feature
31 Paten veils
33 Schnitzel requisite
34 Catch-all case
37 Goggling gentry
38 Frozen-food case name
42 San Antonio cager
44 ___ Billy Graham
46 Leveling letters
47 "___ the ramparts..."
49 Press charges
50 Best-rate freight shipment
52 Where Phillips Univ. is
53 Upset the money market
54 What there ought to be
55 Alter the decor
57 Site of 1970 World Fair
60 Thomas Jefferson's Z-sign
61 What the union umpire did
62 Rests, nautically
63 Make beloved
67 Food colorant and flavorer
68 Tiffin or grub
71 Times immemorial
73 Wear's partner
74 Arp contemporary
79 La Gioconda's tenor lover

82 Light-dawning sounds
83 Old card game
85 Big stat for Levin Mitchell
88 Big brass
89 Popular Chi newspaper
90 Inability island?
92 Canadian Indians
93 Not G. PG, R, or X
94 More alarming
95 Soviet news disseminator
99 Flying island resident
101 ___ fir (Pacific evergreen)
103 Rank and serial number preceder
104 Slithers
106 It had 1750 showings on Broadway
108 ___ de jouy (drapery fabrics)
109 "___ and dangerous"
111 ___ Island Museum (NYC attraction)
112 Cow
113 Guanaco's relative
115 ___ d'ecole: Classical ballet
118 "___ now post time" (Saratoga notice)
119 Young ___ (insurgent)
123 Soil: Comb. form
124 Needlefish
125 The Clermont, e.g.

45

THE VEGGIE CONNECTION by Lawrence M. Rheingold
Five different vegetables provide the impetus for a quintet of interlocking phrases. Kudos to L.M.R.

ACROSS

1 Temptress in "East of Eden"
5 Hake's next of kin
8 LAX data
11 Socko!
14 ___ boy!
18 Bobbin
19 One, to Burns
20 Silent approval
21 Babylonian deity
22 River in NE China
23 Clan
24 Like lovers Romeo and Juliet
27 Reliquary
28 GIBSON ITEM, PAPER AND MISERS
31 Its often stretched
32 Domesday Book money
33 Cordage fiber
34 Aegean isle
35 Linden or Holbrook
37 Kind of judgment
40 Old Nippon city
42 Yawning
44 Birds, to Brutus
46 A return for Seles
48 Grampus
51 Hot item
52 LEGUME, CERTAIN STEMS AND PURSUES QUARRY
59 Word at a pump
60 Fight result, for short
61 Partner of tool
62 Old Irish writing system
64 Pangim is its capital
66 Aurora, to Aristotle
68 Ortler or Todi
70 Soprano Gluck
71 SYMPHONY, PERCHERON AND ROOT
79 Asian nurse
80 Greek tense: Abbr.
81 Ayr avuncular one
82 Eagle plus two
83 ___ del Rio, Veracruz
84 On the ___ (absconding)
86 Plater
88 Awkward gait
93 NAPLES SIGHT, ZODIAC SIGN AND PONE
99 Bill, in brief
100 Harness part
101 Confucian ethic
102 Inst. at Annapolis
103 Cawdor title
105 Half a dance
107 Platter
110 Floppy cap
111 Aunt, in Avila
112 Works of a late modernist
116 Wave in Baja
118 Elman's teacher
120 GREENS, RUNS AWAY AND DIAMOND CIRCUIT
126 ___ time (never)
127 Upper crust

128 Wood sorrels
130 Coward or carol
131 Tippler
132 Polo Grounds hero
133 Pi follower
134 Old portico
135 Lhasa ___
136 Strang gadget
137 Electrical unit
138 ___ Tiki
139 It in Italy

DOWN

1 Ovid's "___ Amatoria"
2 Electronic page
3 Insect spray
4 Kazakh range
5 Old-style type
6 Aware of a scheme
7 BMOC
8 Audience clamor
9 Dangerous windstorms
10 Foofaraws
11 Foundation
12 Concerning
13 Refluxed shores
14 Siberian range
15 Rutabaga
16 Tic followers
17 "Egregiously ___": Othello
25 ___ Branco
26 Schuss, e.g.
29 Apt. components
30 Give a ___ (help)
35 Nimbus
36 With, in Tours
38 Vestment
39 Pound or Sterling
41 Fragment for Fido
43 "Innocents ___": Twain
45 Let it stand, in a score
47 Bush's Secretary of State
49 Scapegrace
50 Pseudonym of a sort
53 Famed playwright
54 Mrs. Arrowsmith
55 Cozy corner
56 Formicid
57 He, to Pasquale
58 Sweet tubers
63 Start of a Chinese game's name
65 "___ in sheep's clothing"
67 Haggard novel
69 Jambalaya item
71 Fairy Queen
72 Mine in Nimes
73 Black Hawk's tribe
74 One of the Graces
75 Potherb
76 Arena in Atlanta

77 Do a double take
78 Saracen
85 Ovine's plaint
87 Prod into action
89 Joanne of films
90 Razes
91 Singer Cantrell
92 Holland product
94 Nine: Comb. form
95 Cloudy
96 Inst. in Chester, Pa.
97 Israeli town near Romla
98 Louis XV, e.g.
103 In fine fettle
104 Army base in Alaska
106 One of the Furies
108 Strong man
109 Kind of card
111 Ethiopian lake
113 Pang
114 Type size
115 One's in Orleans
117 Chopper saves at sea: Abbr.
119 Unevenly edged
121 ___ contendere
122 Mighty mite
123 Listen
124 Galba's successor
125 Temple
129 ___ Paulo, Brazil

SYMBOL-MINDED by Jim Bernhard
Rebus puzzles usually stick to one item, but our man from Texas thinks big.

ACROSS

1 Anatomical duct
4 British dandy
8 Hugh ___ : Fr. king, 987–96
13 Nickname for dad
18 "___ bin ein Berliner": JFK
19 Fissile rock
20 Genus of marine snails
21 Speak on a soapbox
22 Triumphant exclamation
23 Pan or Piper
24 Art collection in Houston
25 Lifts
26 "___, NOW DANCER . . ."
28 Lacking vitality
30 Certain exams
32 Spanish saint's namesakes
34 BIBLICAL PROCURATOR OF JUDAEA
36 Catch-all term
37 Noise
38 Open
39 Show assent
40 October birthstone
43 James's "Portrait of A ___"
45 MORAL ARBITERS
47 Gov't panel of experts
50 Kind of box or bug
51 Wearies
53 Private eyes
55 Prepares potatoes, in a way
59 The 45th state
60 German granny
61 Pt. or qt.
63 Landlady's due
65 Shoulder-bag feature
67 END OF A CHESS GAME
69 Dot-dash "language"
70 Extinct earth-bound bird
72 Mexican salamander
74 Conger
75 Remove
79 Fail
81 Trawler gear
85 Sen. Pete from New Mexico
86 Suit
87 "___ Magic": 1948 hit for Doris Day
89 In the same place in a book
90 Karloff's original name
91 Narcissus's lover
93 Movie skater Sonja ___
95 Shade of green
96 Kind of no.
98 PAR AVION, U.S. STYLE
100 Site of Shah Jehan's monument
101 Romanov, perhaps
102 Adherent
105 Taping devices, for short
107 Flying prefix
109 Emulate Whistler
111 BE RELENTLESS
115 Natives of Nazareth
119 Female legatee
120 Provenance
122 STARTING OVER
123 Actress Shire
124 About a drop
126 Actress Dickinson
128 Join
129 McCowen and Templeton
130 Memorable Massey of films
131 Averages
132 Unit of work
133 Street show
134 Sea or vine lead-in
135 Part of a sign on a family business
136 Hwy. like 66

DOWN

1 Food item
2 This precedes Gesundheit
3 Oboe of yore
4 "What news upon ___?: Shak.
5 Morsel for Mr. Frisky
6 Dogs' bane
7 Feathery greenery
8 TOM PAINE'S OPUS
9 "He always had ___ of childish obstinacy": Mary Wilkins
10 One cause of 80 Down
11 Athlete in blue
12 Mishnah and Gemara
13 KIND OF HAT
14 An Oxford college
15 Baptista Minola, for one
16 "___ the Rear": old song
17 Said aye
19 Exhausted
27 SAM SPADE'S CREATOR
29 Finial
31 ". . . and she bare ___" (Gen. 4:25)
33 STUB EXCHANGED FOR ITEM IN STORAGE
35 Writing on parchment
37 Recolor
40 Opera's singular
41 Panthers' univ.
42 Axillary
44 London's Royal Academy of ___
46 NL 1942 home run champ
48 Napoleon's forces
49 NOTED OFF-BROADWAY THEATRE
52 Japanese prime minister: 1966–72
54 Guitar composer Fernando ___: 1780–1839
56 Corp. head
57 "Howard's ___": E. M. Forster
58 Thérèse of Lisieux, for one
62 "Birdbath" playwright
64 Suffix for a carbohydrate
66 Toe, in ballet
68 Chopper
69 Fabric: Abbr.
71 Cuckoo
73 Ritualistic declaration
75 Computer work: Abbr.
76 Singer Denise of the Garry Moore Show
77 Miss Hogg of Bayou Bend
78 King topper
80 THEY NEED TO BE CHANGED
82 Heron's cousin
83 Mack of "Let's Pretend"
84 German reservoir
86 On behalf of
88 Ocean ships that carry freight cars
92 How to refer to a judge
94 Sound receiver
97 RNs' associates
99 THURBER-NUGENT PLAY, WITH "THE"
102 Babylonian earth mother
103 ". . . ___ few hours from the night": Thomas Moore
104 Hard worker
106 Vast
108 Heckler's weapon
110 Luxurious delicacies
112 Former Met soprano
113 MILITARY ORDER
114 Olga and Masha's sister
115 ___ sanctum
116 Capp's ___ Slobbovia
117 Unable to move
118 Grasslike plant
121 Shakespeare's foot
125 UN org.
127 U.S. watchdog agcy.

47 U.S.A. IMAGUNDI by Joy L. Wouk
The clever title should help you to figure out what tricks Joy has in store for unwary solvers.

ACROSS

1 "___ and the Man": Shaw play
5 Snow, in Aberdeen
8 Nav. officer below Capt.
11 Eating: Comb. form
16 Garner
17 Stone cavity
19 Ballet movement
20 Staff again
21 Atlanta arena
22 De Valera
23 Something delicate
24 Kind of acid
25 Madison corn desserts?
29 Speed
30 Cyclotron item
31 Medicine: Comb. form
32 Tall Asiatic trees
34 Ukase
36 Observatory subj.
40 Elko palm fruit?
44 Biloxi baked dessert?
46 Idolater
47 K-2 is one
48 Hair nets
49 Inhabitant of a holy city of Islam
50 Suffix for a cardinal point
51 Was fresh
55 Asian holiday
56 Maid in Japan
57 New Mexico, to a Mexican
60 Kind of acid or oxide
62 Oregon's capital
64 Sandusky citrus
66 French king, Hugh ___: 987–996
70 Actress in "Phantom Lady": 1946
72 "Wuthering Heights" author
74 ___ Benet, author of "How to Live to Be 100"
75 Fitting
78 Night nuisance
80 Belgian-French river
81 Spreads a secret
83 Responds to a stimulus
85 Ripens
87 Tiffs
88 Laredo spear vegetable
92 Boise sweet stuff
94 Woman's undergarment
95 Lacking a musical key
96 Not alike: Comb. form
97 Farewells, in Florence
98 Of seaweed
100 Chalet feature
104 Olympia deli treat
111 Shun
112 Tanoan Pueblo village in Arizona
113 Famous caravel
114 Gaze at amorously
115 English hymnist
116 Spartan king
117 Wickerwork willow
118 Hawaiian trees
119 Fault
120 Teachers' gp.
121 Abbr. on a map
122 Ascent, in Asti

DOWN

1 In line
2 Decrease
3 Parsonage
4 Virgo star
5 Health-food seasoning
6 Name on a slate
7 Handsome fellow
8 Hospital parts
9 Unequal, in Pisa
10 Distinctions
11 Madrid museum
12 Half: Prefix
13 Uganda's infamous exile
14 Plank preceder
15 Son of Seth
17 DDE rank in WW II
18 Within: Comb. form
19 New Deal agcy.
26 Romanian city
27 Nehru's homeland
28 "The ___ ": 1988 British film
33 Judy of "Laugh-In"
35 Aleuts, e.g.: Abbr.
36 GI address
37 Problem for Lady Macbeth
38 Time's partner

39 Take ten
40 Hottentots
41 Tomato blight
42 Oral
43 Cupid, e.g.
44 "The evil that ___ lives . . .": Shak.
45 Of a Pakistani language
47 Cost, in Bonn
50 The wild blue yonder
52 Irks
53 Indications
54 Printer's instruction
58 Taboo item
59 Sphere
61 Cuban leader
63 Schooner features
65 Van Gogh's last home
67 South Korean seaport
68 Marry on the run
69 Poisonous weed
71 "The rain ___ stays mainly . . ."
73 Lanchester and Maxwell
75 Crafts' partner
76 Strip
77 Place for hack work

79 Hindu melody
82 Repeated
84 Kepi or calotte
86 "The ___ Archipelago": Solzhenitsyn
89 Moslem sword
90 Underground plant parts collectively
91 Connecticut city
92 Angry
93 Stretches
96 Discrimination on the basis of years
97 Fall drink
99 Wolf, to Piero
101 Roused
102 Vim's companion
103 Acclaim
104 Ebb
105 State
106 Glide high
107 Hawaii county seat
108 Our, in Nantes
109 Ford's VP
110 "For ___ jolly . . ."

48

URBS by Roger H. Courtney
Metropolitan monikers and other interesting entries are featured below.

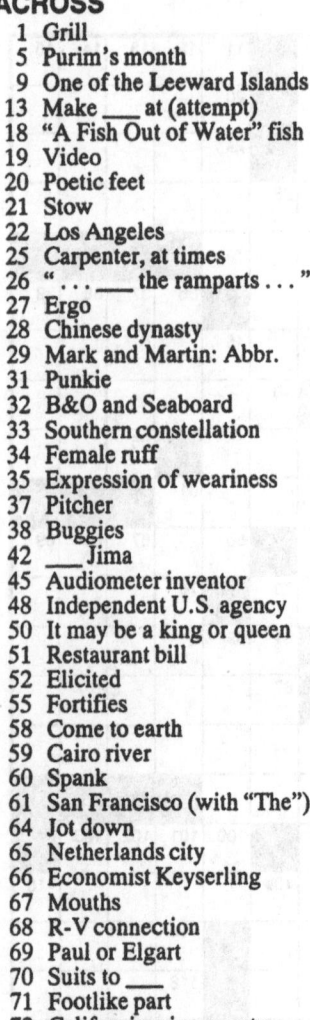

ACROSS

1 Grill
5 Purim's month
9 One of the Leeward Islands
13 Make ___ at (attempt)
18 "A Fish Out of Water" fish
19 Video
20 Poetic feet
21 Stow
22 Los Angeles
25 Carpenter, at times
26 " . . . ___ the ramparts . . . "
27 Ergo
28 Chinese dynasty
29 Mark and Martin: Abbr.
31 Punkie
32 B&O and Seaboard
33 Southern constellation
34 Female ruff
35 Expression of weariness
37 Pitcher
38 Buggies
42 ___ Jima
45 Audiometer inventor
48 Independent U.S. agency
50 It may be a king or queen
51 Restaurant bill
52 Elicited
55 Fortifies
58 Come to earth
59 Cairo river
60 Spank
61 San Francisco (with "The")
64 Jot down
65 Netherlands city
66 Economist Keyserling
67 Mouths
68 R-V connection
69 Paul or Elgart
70 Suits to ___
71 Footlike part
72 California wine country
75 Scottish cap
78 Table scrap
80 Adjective suffix
81 Came to rest
82 Arafat's org.
83 Ditto
85 New York
90 Richard ___
91 Spread for bread
92 Snakeless land
93 Cooking direction
94 More hackneyed
96 Commotion
97 "In ___ Way"
98 Birr
100 Unit of force
101 Senator
102 Omnipotence
106 Rubens of silent films
109 Be overly fond of
111 Oklahoma Indian
112 Orbison
113 French painter Jean
116 South American monkey
118 Morse "E"
121 Devastate
123 Trotyl
124 USIA division
125 Anagram name of "alone"
127 Denver
131 Basted
132 Soft drinks
133 Show of hands
134 Ex-Brave Felipe
135 Watches over
136 Peace Nobelist: 1945
137 Like expensive Scotch
138 Cover at Fenway

DOWN

1 ___ City: Detroit
2 Solvent for fats
3 Fun followers
4 Ad ___ committee
5 Garb
6 Kind of center
7 Mil. address
8 Umps
9 Clay box used in ceramics
10 Brigitte's soul
11 Large kegs: Abbr.
12 Small second
13 Onager
14 Ferber's "___ Door"
15 Gene Pitney hit
16 Confines
17 A Bobbsey twin
20 ___ Mongolia
23 "___ Three Ships"
24 Ambiance
30 Rapid
36 Two before JFK
37 Moose, in Europe
38 Auto-engine part, for short
39 "___ of Capri"
40 Fictional whaler
41 Actress Rowlands
43 Tarry
44 It's heard in "Bolero"
45 Asian palm
46 Dodge
47 Bernie's "It's a ___ When You're Not Around"
49 Golfer Stewart
53 Acclaim
54 Japanese legislature
56 Lack of foresight
57 Lightning flashes
59 Toronto's prov.
62 Nail in a way
63 Hog liver, to a Southerner
68 Lecher
72 Mother-of-pearl
73 Tatyana of TV
74 Penn State's rival
76 Adventitious
77 Design on silk
79 Antique car
83 Castile
84 Singer Nova
85 Wept
86 Take on
87 Author Calderon
88 Eyas' home
89 Pickpockets
95 Boise loc.
97 Alt.
99 Divided into sections
103 Central Illinois city
104 Small travel cases
105 Earth
107 Yearned
108 Fable
110 Drunk
113 Town of central Spain
114 Steam-turbine wheel
115 Satisfy a debt
116 Evaluate
117 Arrow poison
119 Desire
120 Grand
122 St. Petersburg river
126 Magazine needs
128 House addition
129 Chester White
130 Stimpy, for one

49 THE BARD'S BOYS by Vanessa Leigh Patterson
This clever challenger from the Garden State was a strong candidate for the Margaret.

ACROSS

1. Leg. entity
5. Surfing wipeout
8. "Romero" star (with 50 Across)
11. Manassas general
15. Kirgiz mountains
16. Emulate Old Faithful
17. Innumerable
19. Novelist Wister
20. Pisces, for one
21. Italian wine center
22. ___ Domini
23. Prosperity
24. **MODEL MIMER FROM "AS YOU LIKE IT"**
27. **BLOSSOMING BAILIFF IN "MUCH ADO ABOUT NOTHING"**
29. Short airplane trip
30. Interpretation
32. Anchorage inst.
35. Took the point
37. Albacore
38. "The ___ the Worlds"
42. **SHRUBBY SOUL FROM "RICHARD II"**
44. Drain of color
48. Harem room
49. Shavian heroine, in brief
50. See 8 Across
51. Kind of protein
54. **BOORISH BODY IN "TWELFTH NIGHT"**
57. Curving
58. Get up
59. Scottish hymnist
61. Boldly resisted
64. **NARROW NOBLE FROM "KING JOHN"**
71. Defenseless
73. Dumas swordsman
74. Memento ___
75. Inc. relative
76. Draw a picture
78. **FAST FOOL IN "TWO GENTLEMEN OF VERONA"**
79. Also-ran
82. Mackerel shark
83. Pass at Indy
85. Wily
86. Got a fumble
90. "Social Register" word
92. **HOARY HUNCHBACK FROM "THE MERCHANT OF VENICE"**
95. **FAMISHED FELLOW IN "A MIDSUMMER NIGHT'S DREAM"**
100. Turkish pound
101. Pyrenees river
103. Opposer
104. Burn with resentment
105. Ibex, for one
106. **AUTHOR OF "TEN DAYS THAT SHOOK THE WORLD"**
107. Jonathan Steed's friend
108. Fairy-tale beginning
109. Shareholder's stake
110. HST's successor
111. Sibilant
112. Island W of Midway

DOWN

1. Pick the players
2. Hodgepodge
3. Seville stew
4. **TWEAKING TUTOR FROM "THE COMEDY OF ERRORS"**
5. Breath of air
6. Mary in "Red Dust"
7. Buff a brogue
8. Org. with a journal
9. Heavenly bamboo
10. Footnote
11. "Ivanhoe" lady
12. Tall pitcher
13. Attu's chain
14. Exclusively
16. Canadian peninsula
18. Bear or Berra
25. Sacred
26. Snare by nets
28. Obeisance
31. Fond ___
32. Basics
33. Hungarian sheepdog
34. Consumer
36. Fleur-___
39. Rheims roast
40. Frigga's husband
41. **DENTATE DEPUTY IN "II HENRY IV"**
43. Balloonist's necessity
45. Himalayan country
46. Frost a bundt
47. Gemsbuck cousins
50. Stayed put
52. Spirited steed
53. Emulate Scrooge
55. Utah city
56. Never drop this
60. Mirador
61. **BORING BOBBY FROM "LOVE'S LABOR LOST"**
62. Within: Comb. form
63. Crazes
65. Hoe, in Heidelberg
66. Blunders
67. Medieval poem
68. Departs
69. Turgenev's birthplace
70. Antimacassar
72. Left Her Majesty's Navy
77. Relished
78. German admiral: 1861–1941
80. Worker ant
81. Speed Wagon
84. Tool for Vulcan
87. This operator has a handle
88. A day's march
89. Horatio and Claudius
91. **JOSTLING JUSTICE FROM "MEASURE FOR MEASURE"**
92. Russian saint
93. Friend of Androcles
94. Interjection of disgust
96. Shortcuts from AAA
97. Hebrides island
98. Shaving mishap
99. Kind of club
102. Poem for Billy Joe

50

ON LOCATION by Coral Amende
Here are three reasons why we think you'll enjoy solving Coral's crossword: (A.) 121 Across (B.) 47 Down (C.) It's challenging!

ACROSS

1 Census option
6 Yegg's aka
11 Melee
15 That's right!
19 Huntley and Meyers
20 "On Golden Pond" star
21 Mother Bloor
22 Bog down
23 TT
26 Resting
27 Art Deco name
28 Apportion
29 Designer shade
30 Like some expense accounts
32 Legal matter
33 Beadles
35 Lug
37 Actor Wheaton
38 Kind of house or angle
39 Common suffix
41 Docility
45 Artist's hue
48 F
51 Palindromic interjection
52 Like Frost's writing
55 Equitable
56 What the editor did
58 ___ in a poke
59 Band brass
60 Open the castle
62 Fire residues
63 Canal of 1825
65 Howard and Kovics
67 Martin and Risi
69 Biblical verb ending
70 Rave's partner
71 E
74 Coming-out girls
77 Pull
79 Actress Berland
80 Ending for axiom
81 Test type
82 Blouse
84 Big men on campus
86 High: Comb. form
88 Mouths
89 Playground items
91 Rip-off
92 Textbook list
94 Wane
95 E
98 Motor followers
99 Radiation measure
101 Abbr. at JFK
102 Nebr. neighbor
104 Whiz preceder
105 Bus. subject
108 Biblical book
110 Russian jet
113 Shapes in London
116 March 15th
118 Grafting shoot
119 Just okay
120 Sin
121 A
125 Princess in a sari
126 Goatish glance
127 Forty-niner
128 Priest
129 Gen. Robert ___
130 Finishes
131 "Designing Women" star
132 Velocity

DOWN

1 See 45 Across
2 "Over ___"
3 Qualifying races
4 Raison d' ___
5 Alphabet trio
6 Impinge
7 Lehmann or Lenya
8 Come into
9 Humorist George
10 Tantamount
11 Prefix for active
12 All of it: Ital.
13 Toreador's encouragement
14 Canvas cover
15 Chemist's starch substance
16 OA
17 Author Gardner
18 Have to have
24 Arabian gulf
25 Tread the boards
31 Valley girl's superlative
33 Deserve
34 Bollix up
36 Ike Clanton's foe
38 Stroke
40 D
42 French seas
43 "___ Leaving Home": Beatles
44 Turf
45 Berth place
46 Actress Shearer
47 B
48 Skewed
49 Shinbone
50 Fringe, to Franco
53 Constrain
54 Man-town link
57 Better
61 Planter's concern
64 Small cases
66 Pressure
68 Ability
72 Spinach look-alike
73 Outer prefix
75 Ballerina's support
76 Kills with comedy
78 Spliced botanically
82 Fat: Comb. form
83 Trunk adjunct
85 Whack
87 Sesame Street grouch
89 To be, in Bartolomeo
90 Snick's partner
93 Egyptian cotton
96 Cut
97 Being born
100 "South Pacific" heroine
102 Blacksmiths
103 Chinese leader
106 Taste stimuli
107 "___ Blu, Di Pinto Di Blu"
109 Dalai Lama's land
110 Mitterrand's world
111 Rhone feeder
112 Like some skirts
113 Minimal
114 Face shape
115 December 26th event
117 Pump type
119 Piece of cake
122 Painter Shahn
123 Pedro's uncle
124 Tape-speed abbr.

51

ARS GRATIS PULCHRITUDINIS by Gayle Dean
The foremost painter of the Romantic movement in France is the source of this colorful quotation. He can be found at 23 Across.

ACROSS

1 Woody's boy
5 Varied collection
9 Fabled one?
14 Sweep
19 Quick takeover
20 Columnist Rowan
21 Big Bend flora
22 Protective coat
23 Author of quote
26 Electron tube gas
27 Like the OR
28 Intermediaries
29 Capable of movement
30 Square things
32 Feeling poems
33 Nickname on the "Enterprise"
34 Quartet added to 90 Across
37 Stuck
39 Jones of the deep
40 Omnibus conductor
43 One with a crow
44 Turkey ___
45 Seine tributary
46 Dayton product
47 Watermelon remnant
48 **First line of quote**
52 Vanilla ___
53 Limestone region
54 Corroded
55 Wash cycle
56 Little croakers
58 Sea lettuce
59 Stumble
60 Edwin ___ Sparks
61 More vile
62 Spiral
63 Fish hawk
66 Estate
67 Mole at work
71 Soprano Kurz
72 Heathen
73 Whey side-dish
74 Cent-sible guy?
75 **Quote: Part II**
78 Geometric figure
79 German philosopher
80 Brother-at-arms
81 Greek rainbow goddess
82 Manners
83 Toby contents
84 Surfeit
85 Quaker of sorts
87 Fragrant dressing
88 Gypsy's "pack"
90 Musical group
91 Get a grip on
93 King Arthur's retreat
95 Strikes out
97 Skilled sportsman
101 Red River city
102 **End of quote**
104 Xenophobe's nightmare
105 Gemma Donati's spouse
106 Phaeton
107 Corner
108 Raises
109 "I do" place
110 West and Long
111 Out of this world

DOWN

1 Musts for blackjacks
2 Blowout
3 Olympic event
4 Ran
5 Felis pardalis
6 Packed
7 Fury
8 Stewing pot
9 Give consent
10 Made a living
11 Burns's "Wha Hae ___"
12 He has his ups and downs
13 Photos
14 Fine woolen fabric
15 Khania's location
16 All-knowing
17 Fast Eddie's game
18 Piscivorous bird
24 Gunpowder ingredient
25 Tropical rodent
29 Man in a van
31 Departure
33 Lithospheric depression
34 Tar's spar
35 Susan Lucci role
36 Moped forlornly
38 Garret
39 Loon, for one
41 Came up
42 Yield
44 Leash number
45 Broadtail
46 Geraint's thigh protector
48 Reckoning
49 Thinks out
50 Frugal one
51 Learns the ropes
53 Inchon citizen
57 Give the OK
58 Hawaiian veranda
59 "Julia" star
61 Loose and hanging
62 Makes ham tasty
63 Honshu port
64 Part of a calyx
65 Solar system models
66 Macho
67 River sport
68 Petrarch's beloved
69 Waned
70 Actress Witherspoon
72 Cockpit guide
73 Geologist's sample
76 Feature of 63 Across
77 Giveaway
78 Thorough
82 Architect Safdie
84 Sings like Sinatra
85 Bristlelike part
86 Baker's device
87 Compassionate pity
89 "Luck and Pluck" author
90 Hammarskjöld's successor
92 Shabby
93 At a distance
94 Farewell
95 Prosperity
96 Scalp
98 Rochester's beloved
99 Lachrymal secretion
100 Catch sight of
102 Rx regulators
103 Regret

52

IN A SENSE   by Elizabeth C. Gorski
Semanticians should get a kick out of Elizabeth's thematic clues.

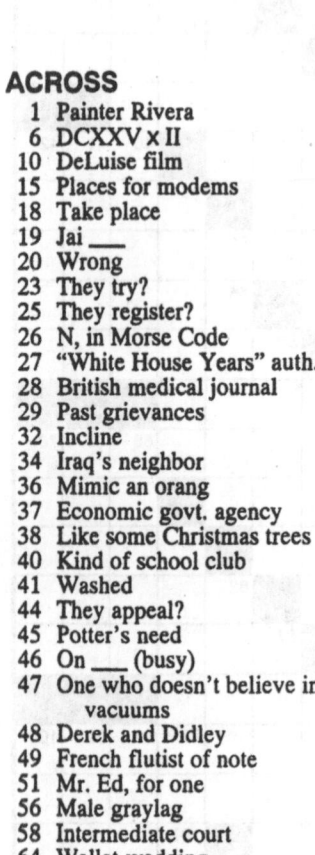

ACROSS

1 Painter Rivera
6 DCXXV x II
10 DeLuise film
15 Places for modems
18 Take place
19 Jai ___
20 Wrong
23 They try?
25 They register?
26 N, in Morse Code
27 "White House Years" auth.
28 British medical journal
29 Past grievances
32 Incline
34 Iraq's neighbor
36 Mimic an orang
37 Economic govt. agency
38 Like some Christmas trees
40 Kind of school club
41 Washed
44 They appeal?
45 Potter's need
46 On ___ (busy)
47 One who doesn't believe in
   vacuums
48 Derek and Didley
49 French flutist of note
51 Mr. Ed, for one
56 Male graylag
58 Intermediate court
64 Wallet wadding
65 Yoko
66 Some verbs have it?
69 Lipid
70 P.O. concerns
72 ___ to China
73 Lower one's rank
75 Vending machines do it
77 Prynne of literature
79 Aged
80 "___ In Dixie": J. Triplet
85 Florida city
88 Solid
90 They cable?
92 Mrs. McEnroe
93 Completed
94 Idyllic times
95 Hereditary letters
96 Postal abbr.
97 Fertilizer
99 Archibald of basketball
100 Crowd chaser
104 Happy
106 Thai language
108 City in France
110 They age?
112 They understudy?
116 Concern of 110 Across
117 Hula Bowl team
118 Drive forward
119 Curve
120 Golfer Bob
121 Explosives
122 Sordid

DOWN

1 It has cts.
2 Here, in Cognac
3 Outside: Comb. form
4 Father Sarducci
5 Biggs played one
6 Hindu monasteries
7 Dolt
8 Monaco princess
9 Eavesdrop
10 Trawls
11 Small wild ox
12 More tasteless
13 ___-fi
14 Florida city
15 H.S. VIP
16 Hoot
17 Make stairs more angled
21 Polish lancer
22 A Lauder
24 Enzyme suffix
29 Fabric measure
30 Casual affirmation
31 They commute?
33 Tea leaf
35 Hwys.
38 Arable
39 Permit

40 Gadget
42 Mild oath
43 Like some stadia
44 City manager's deg.
45 Actress Stark
48 Mingles
50 Argue ___ con
51 Pitt team
52 Philippine denizens
53 They sing?
54 Straight from the bottle
55 Bone: Comb. form
56 Bullion variety
57 Oppositionist
59 Middle East org.
60 Bench
61 Ambassador's bldg.
62 Between Cancer and Virgo
63 Austrian city
67 "Dustin's" letters
68 "___ That": Dizzy Gillespie
   song
71 Seed
74 Penurious
76 Infamous street
78 Comparative endings
80 Ambition

81 Constrictions in the body
82 Rose Bowl winners:
   1986
83 Read matter onto film
84 Mary Martin role
86 Window feature
87 Winglike
88 "Fight ___," Jerry Lewis
   film
89 Charms
90 Twenty grains: Abbr.
91 Most statuesque
93 ___ blank (forgot)
97 "They Call ___ Tibbs"
98 "___ which will live in
   infamy": FDR
100 Throws
101 "How to Hit .300" author
102 County in Ireland
103 "___ Why": Beatles
105 River of NE England
107 Comedian Johnson
109 For fear that
111 Dutch cupboard
113 Protective org.
114 Pop group
115 Stone or Stallone

53

SALAD DAYS by James E. Hinish, Jr.
We hope you're feeling 3 Down after solving this Virginian's vernal challenger.

ACROSS

1 Flanagan's flock
5 Valuable violin
10 Enter
14 Hatter's tea guest
19 ___ about
20 Heights of Palestine
21 Numerical prefix
22 Style of painting
23 Words by Lewis Carroll
  (with 89 & 98 Across)
26 Inner
27 Prince Valiant's son
28 Hardy boy
29 One hundredth of a shekel
30 Call on the set
31 Government by a minor,
  often
33 Ouzo ingredient
34 Sampling
35 Depend or tend ending
36 "Mon ___," Tati film
37 Puerile
40 Beginning
42 Equine juveniles
44 ___ Fail, Irish coronation
  stone
45 Part of B. A.
46 Cable, in Coblenz
47 Grandchildren, in
  Glasgow
48 Racehorse
49 Scorner's word
50 Certain Boy Scout
54 Took care of
55 M. K. Rawlings subject
58 Lots of paper
59 Sea of the Dodecanese
60 Seasonal songs
61 Lamb, to Livy
62 "Inside the Third Reich"
  author
63 Youth ___
65 Curved edge where two
  vaults meet
66 Eire's symbol
69 Junior preppie
70 See 68 Down
72 French faith
73 Sun. talks
74 Ferdinand, for one
75 House, in Hesse
76 Port's opp.
77 William Tell's home
78 Radio soap-opera hero
82 Companion to
  D'Artagnan
83 Snares
85 Marquesses' juniors
86 ___-dieu (kneeling bench)
87 ___ Lucy, Chicken
  Little's friend
88 Western resort
89 See 23 Across
92 Represent by conduct
94 "Waiting for ___":
  Becket
95 Learning of the ages
96 Diamond stat.
97 Name of culinary fame
98 See 23 & 89 Across
101 Bactrian, e.g.
102 Poor boy

103 ___ home (out)
104 "Rock of ___"
105 Little specialty
106 Earl ___ Biggers
107 "Go and Catch a Falling
  Star" author
108 It's often marked

DOWN

1 Czarist aristocrat
2 Honor, Italian style
3 Words by
  Oscar Hammerstein II
4 Mrs., in Madrid
5 AID or CIA
6 Temperamental
7 Confederate
8 Child
9 Early childhood
10 Set sail
11 Palette pigment
12 Willow genus
13 "___ any drop to drink"
14 Enemies of the elderly
15 Measurement
16 Words of I Samuel 2:33
17 Follower of Pluto
18 Elvers' elders
24 Ponderosa, e.g.
25 Spry

30 Praises
32 Tolkien trees
33 "___ woman lived in a
  shoe"
34 Rental sign
36 Due
37 Ma's namesakes
38 Utah range
39 Attack
40 "Dirty Dancing" heroine
41 "Dies ___"
42 Puberty period
43 Nursery et al.
46 Kind of photography
48 Beeper
51 Work, in physics
52 Go back on a promise
53 Satyr's cousins
54 Appear
56 Learning methods
57 Lecher's look
59 Make ___ at (get fresh)
61 As ___ (normally)
62 Expression of indifference
63 German port on the North
  Sea
64 "Hansel and Gretel," e.g.
65 Roundels purpures, in
  heraldry
66 Penn and Astin

67 ___ Hall, Detroit arena
68 Offspring
70 Young professional
71 Greenland settlement
74 Ron Perlman role
76 ___-de-grain yellow
78 "So ___ We Hail"
79 "___ not, here I come"
80 Swift brute
81 Bombastic
82 "Wizard of Oz" composer
84 Stonemason's broad
  chisel
86 Skyjacker
88 "___ is human . . ."
89 "A ___ in White": Collins
90 "___ Irish Rose"
91 Central part
92 Medieval gold and silk
  fabric
93 Fellow
94 Yak butter
95 Avoirdupois wt.
98 Divinity deg.
99 The present, in Dundee
100 Emulated Jack Horner

54

Sid has indulged in fowl play here and there, but his puzzle should make most solvers chirp with delight.

ACROSS

1 Fish sauce
5 Gin pole
9 Mufti for Caesar
13 Wild plum
17 Hip joints
19 Competent
20 Street urchin
21 Pause indicator
23 Circular signature list
25 Petrograd's river
26 "How's that ___?"
27 Infuriate
28 Pass receiver
29 Shrub bearing a globular fruit
31 Censure
33 Ship section
35 ___-Aviv
36 Tears
38 Barrymore
40 Metric wts.
45 Bandeau
48 Box for bucks
50 Entrance for Clementine's dad
52 Imps
54 Earner of twenty-five badges
58 May Day's cousin
60 Anglo-Saxon laborers
61 Serve the purpose
62 Uno, due, ___
63 Gatherings of Rhode Island Reds?
65 Keep
67 Therefore
69 Berlin's its cap.
70 Peale appeal
72 Scand. land
73 Its banks are liquid
78 Broadcast
80 Kind of potato
83 Jelly Roll of jazz
85 Solemn state?
91 ___ Vegas
92 Former president of Italy
93 Turn aside
94 Patronize Delmonico
95 Shower room planks
98 Dreiser's "___ Carrie"
100 Repair
103 Sea thoroughfare
104 Wrestler's pad
105 Reach out and touch someone?
106 Borscht unit
108 Retinal photosensitive receptors
110 Taxing initials
113 So
115 Jungle denizen
118 Old Desk feature
124 "How dry ___"
126 Option
129 Decorate
130 Scent
131 Varicella
133 Sound sense
134 Symbol of peace
135 Peninsula or nut
136 Swiss city (older spelling)
137 Like an eremite
138 Iowa college town
139 Realtor's victory sign
140 Whiskey, bread, and city

DOWN

1 Israeli seaport
2 Web-footed bird
3 Area beyond the suburbs
4 Suez or Erie
5 Author of "The Little Red Book"
6 Secular clergyman of France
7 Act furtively
8 Looked after
9 Enmeshed
10 Certain cookie
11 French dance: Var. sp.
12 Demean
13 Sign of healing
14 Theater area
15 Tent maker
16 Eastern VIP
18 Mystery writer's award
22 Bachrach's "___ Day Now"
24 Pays a bill
30 They have a Grand Exalted Ruler
32 Saga's next of kin
34 Eventful time
37 Indolence
39 Sagacious
41 Freezer
42 Endure
43 Where to see Hawks
44 Graf follower
45 A Wall Streeter?
46 Rants' partner
47 Playing marble
49 Entice
51 Chinese secret club
53 Draft org.
55 Pseudomaniac
56 Palmy Bible spot: Ex. XV: 27
57 Guy Forget's forte
59 Spout forth
63 Messenger
64 Syria once
66 Ancient mariner
68 Fishy cape?
71 Mets, e.g.
74 Hacking knife
75 Length X width, sometimes
76 Take by force
77 Eye at one end of a lariat
79 Peruse
81 Lug
82 "Sesame Street" grouch
84 Raven's haven
85 A CIA predecessor
86 Lash
87 Luxuriant
88 "___ each life . . ."
89 Tommy gun for Tommy Atkins
90 Wild guess
96 Node
97 Festoon
99 Part of a bridle
101 Worships
102 Barbara Bush, ___ Pierce
107 What a trade has
109 Hindu term of respect: Var.
111 TV sitcom
112 City of evil
114 Uncouth lout
116 Sound device
117 Unsteady
118 Pardner
119 He may have feet of clay
120 Kind of dancer
121 Ireland
122 One-third of thrice
123 Golfer Davis ___, III
125 John Stuart ___, English philosopher
127 Nat or Natalie
128 Divorcees
132 Bounder

PLAYING WITH CLICHÉS by Roger H. Courtney
Roger hopes his puzzle will make you happy as a lark.

ACROSS

1 Its capital is Tripoli
6 Kind of duster
10 Actress Deborah ___
14 Cubist Juan ___
18 Folk singer Guthrie and namesakes
19 Vagrant
20 Dies ___
21 Schisms
23 Like a mortal at the portal?
26 Kind of ink
27 Letter addendum: Abbr.
28 Karl Marx's associate
29 Hucksters' cure-alls
31 Greek goddess of victory
32 Pleistocene, for one
33 "The ___ the city was pure gold": St. John the Divine
35 Capp and Pacino
36 Kin of GSA
37 Bright-eyed and bushy-tailed
39 This must be maintained in court
40 Old knife
41 Ft. Worth-to-Wichita Falls dir.
43 Smell and touch
46 Iraqi monetary units
48 Show-offs, of a sort
52 Tatami
53 ___ Zagora: Bulgarian city
55 Peddle
56 Def. positions in football
58 Spoil
61 ___ van der Rohe: U.S. architect
64 County in N. Carolina
65 Altars: Lat.
67 Street carnival
68 Winged
70 Whitelaw ___: U.S. diplomat/journalist
71 Remunerate Tom's dad?
74 Geneviève and Marie: Abbr.
75 Mongrels
77 Doled (with "out")
78 "Take ___ your leader"
79 Coll. entry practice exam
80 Ucayali River location
81 Swiss chemist: Nobelist in 1975
83 Dennis Quaid film: 1988
84 Egyptian dancing girl
85 Impelling actions
87 Tribulation
89 Exact
91 Ham, for one
94 Strong drink: Var.
97 Startled person's vocal sound in comics
98 Author of "Portnoy's Complaint"
99 Heath
102 Millay's "Second ___"
105 D-H connection
108 Dull rote
109 Ranks of equals
112 Stripling
113 West European river
114 Ms. Leghorn is drenched and angry?
116 Stratagem
118 Dugout, in Dijon
119 More recent
120 At the last minute, Nolte!
123 Relieved thirst
124 Abound
125 Antithesis of aweather
126 Challenges
127 Speedy jets
128 Estonia and Latvia, once
129 Kind of pattern
130 Musician Previn

DOWN

1 Bill of ___: receipt for goods
2 Peaceful
3 "What's ___ and read all over?"
4 Sing like a Swiss mountaineer: Var.
5 A king of Judah
6 Nickels and dimes
7 Composer of "South Pacific"
8 Hautboy
9 Reservoirs
10 Relative
11 Items in a school's supply room
12 Showered
13 Tell
14 Misery
15 Gambling city in Nevada
16 Herb Shriner's state
17 Meara's partner, once
22 Answers impudently
24 Close securely
25 Q-U connection
30 British film producer, Sir Alex ___
34 Caviar
37 Plant appendage
38 Pro ___ (for the time being)
40 Gastropod's movement
42 Bare fact?
44 Siesta
45 Win without a blink?
47 "My Friend ___"
48 Drugstore: Abbr.
49 Slacken
50 Type of door
51 Former pro bowler, Bob ___
53 Trickled; oozed
54 "Rockabye baby" spot
57 Creator of Lord Peter Wimsey
59 Cartogram
60 Decorous
62 Emulates a cager at dinner?
63 Vaporizes
66 Kitchen or major ending
69 Cosmetics queen Lauder
72 Goddess who rules Niflheim
73 Crowd sound
76 Certain
82 Gazelle
86 Hail
88 Govt.'s environmental group
90 This may be electrical
91 Mission
92 Some cats
93 Canadian Indians
94 More meager
95 Crone
96 Joins
100 Strikes once again
101 Actresses Dunne and Papas
103 Tumult
104 Thought: Comb. form
106 Old McDonald, for one
107 Former Miami Dolphins quarterback
109 Benefits; added payments
110 Noted British painter of birds
111 French legislative body
113 Old Scratch
115 "He ___ thataway!"
117 Iniquitous
121 "___ Pinafore"
122 Govt. overseers of products

56 BANANA SPLITS AND OTHER GOODIES by Bernard Meren
This clever puzzle comes under the category of What-Will-They-Think-of-Next.
We gave it a second-place award.

ACROSS

1 "Medea" composer: 1946
7 British dandies of the '60s
11 Wet mo.
14 Movie containers
19 Forever, to bards
20 Reeky
21 Spelling contest
22 Heart chambers
23 Opt
24 Art / erial
27 Assam silkworm
28 Four-time Cy Young
   award winner, Carlton
30 Pertaining to Troy
31 ___ alte (an old woman):
   Ger.
32 Build
34 River in old Belorussia,
   USSR
36 More strict
38 Like netting
39 Inocu / lation
42 Shuttle's place
44 Card game for two
45 John Q. or Samuel
50 More hard-of-hearing
53 Old age, of old
55 Kind of shrew
56 NW Afghanistan city
57 En pointe
58 Church calendar
60 Cordon ___
62 Saga
63 Decorative fringe, made
   of coarse lace
65 Smo / king
70 Large bay window
72 Cloth measure of yore
73 Type of boom
74 Nu / clear
79 Art form
83 Name in spydom
84 Posh party nosh
85 Vikki from El Paso
87 Zeno's birthplace
88 Clear a tape
90 Place for old pease
   porridge
91 Sinbad's abductor
92 All mixed up
94 Paradigm
95 One of the Dionne
   quintuplets
98 Diminish
100 Plan / tain
103 Pepper plant
107 Most trite
111 Chesterfield part
112 Measure equaling 1.3080
    cubic yards
113 "The ___ 'e knows . . .":
    Kipling
114 African antelope
117 Parts, in Stuttgart
119 British ___ of Court
120 No / oks
123 Waka and banca
125 She portrayed Scarlett
126 Room in a seraglio
127 French novelist, Claude
    ___
128 Candle-frame at Tenebrae

129 Bobbled fly
130 Ship-shaped clock
131 Byrnes of TV fame and
    hall-of-famer, Roush
132 Central Caucasian

DOWN

1 Is fit for
2 Pied ___
3 Trusts (upon)
4 War / rant
5 Ref. book
6 Exposes to water
7 Emceed a TV panel show
8 Twist
9 Stripped
10 Star wars research prog.
11 Third man
12 Foot: Comb. form
13 Presented old material in
   a new form
14 Preceder of tag or time
15 Wild blue yonder?
16 Rommel
17 Climbing vine
18 Nay or sooth add-on
25 Artemis, to Cato
26 "___ Each Life Some
   . . .": song of 1945
29 Indian pith helmet
33 Ancient Phoenician
   seaport

35 "___ semper tyrannis"
37 Greenland base
40 Hellene
41 Swaggers
43 ___ acid
46 Eye mem / branes
47 Fine steed
48 Its capital is Bamako
49 No dele
50 Nobelist for medicine:
   1943
51 "Ballpark" figure at JFK
52 Chemist's org.
54 Tennis term
59 Peril in the seas
60 Misrepresent
61 Composer of "Symphonie
   Espagnole"
64 Book by Peter Evans
66 Remainder
67 Gardener, at times
68 Snare
69 Here, in old Rome
71 Tumor of fat tissue
74 Attention getter
75 Source of poi
76 Toward the mouth
77 Attended a meeting
78 Sgt., e.g.
80 Not well
81 Society-page word
82 Traipse

86 Vigorous advocate of a
   political cause
89 North Sea feeder
90 U.S. Defense Dept.
   bailiwick
91 Played-again phrase, in
   music
93 He ran for President five
   times
96 Beam
97 Nfld. or Icl.
99 Imperfect: Comb. form
101 Org.
102 Ogled, wickedly
104 Caruso was one
105 Borgnine
106 Tenant
107 Part forming a base for a
    column
108 More faithful
109 Moving
110 Release
115 A-to-F fill-in
116 What fainéants do
118 Kind of pipe organ
121 Her, to Hans
122 No, to Burns
124 He lost to DDE

57

TO A TV NATURE SHOW by Frances Hansen
The alternate title for this puzzle is "Hey, Guys! Enough Is Enough!"

ACROSS

1 Caesar and Niçoise
7 Knocking noise
14 Tipple
19 Brunch offering
20 Issue forth
21 "Oyez!"
22 **Start of a verse**
25 Constrained, as speech
26 King or carte preceder
27 Copy
28 "___ armes, citoyens!"
29 Harvest goddess
31 Letter addenda: Abbr.
32 Periods of comparative ease
36 Entreat
37 See 27 Across
38 Chemist's milieu, for short
41 State firmly
42 Have on
43 Blue dye
44 Pound or Stone
46 **More of verse**
52 Three, Italian style
53 One-tenth of a decade
54 Join the horsy set
55 Exhausted
56 Gusher
58 Iago's wife
60 Unwelcome kind of wicket
61 Miss Havisham's ward
63 Weight equaling 2240 pounds
65 "___ F.B.I.," Mike Connors show
68 West Mongolian border mountains
70 Texas police group
74 Convex molding
75 Come to the surface
76 Garr of "Mr. Mom"
77 ___ number on (humiliate)
78 **More of verse**
84 Lillian of the silent screen
85 "___ Misbehavin'"
86 Word before "sesame"
87 Loses intensity
88 Actress Susan of "L.A. Law"
89 Twice CCCV
90 Take steps
92 King of Naples in "The Tempest"
94 She, in Schweinfurt
95 Yearned
96 Celestial Altar
97 Beethoven's "Moonlight" et al.
101 La-la leader
102 Like Don Juan
106 **End of verse**
111 Turn upside down
112 Soft shades
113 Stick to
114 Winner at Gettysburg
115 Hall of "The Late Show"
116 Stewed to the gills

DOWN

1 Broadcast, in a way
2 Ed of the singing brothers
3 For fear that
4 Jai ___
5 Loose fold under the chin
6 Kind of symbol
7 Wallace or Whitelaw
8 First of a Latin trio
9 Sunbather's reward
10 Capital of Turkey
11 Shadowed
12 Rand's shrugger
13 ___ Aviv
14 Arnaz, Sr. and Arnaz, Jr.
15 Lost in thought
16 Petina of "Song of Norway"
17 Russian refusal
18 Luke of "Kung Fu"
21 Mr. Murphy, to Mrs. Murphy
23 "Tarzan" Barker
24 Flower child
29 Talon
30 A Saarinen
32 Lay down the ___ (read the riot act to)
33 "If ___ I Would Leave You," 1960 song

34 Word after "mene, mene"
35 Coffee-maker
36 Squint
37 Of South America's backbone
38 Lizards' activity, according to Annie
39 Montezuma, notably
40 Verge
42 Moby Dick or Shamu
43 Verdi's farewells, to Met audiences
45 Dist. ___
47 "Grandmother, what big ___ have!"
48 Leather shoe strips
49 William Tell's canton
50 Austrian actress Palmer
51 Tallinn is here
57 Well-to-do
58 Actor Sam ___
59 Island in Taiwan Strait
60 Belle or Ringo
62 Vocal cords' locale
64 Putting area
65 Chinese secret society
66 Egg-shaped
67 Use a divining rod
69 Chalice veil

71 Newman or Booth
72 Wanders
73 Authority
76 Feds
79 Shining
80 Most pleasant
81 Dove shelter
82 "Like two peas in ___"
83 Fuss
90 Transversely
91 Virginal
92 Floating fragrances
93 Texas town of song
94 Ogle
95 Rose distillation
96 Maupassant's "Bel ___"
97 Sink's alternative
98 "Die Frau ___ Schatten," Strauss opera
99 Blazing star
100 Filled with wonder
102 Charlie Chan's phrase
103 Waikiki's island
104 Salt Lake City eleven
105 Beget
107 "Fat farm"
108 Twilight, to Shelley
109 Yalie
110 A Knight to remember

58

LEGALITEASE by Elizabeth C. Gorski
Herewiith a multitalented tyro from the Big Apple makes a pun-filled debut.

ACROSS

1 Cried
5 TV peripherals
9 Male swan
12 Enormous lister
19 "Jacta est ___"
20 Diamonds in Raul's deck
21 Congr. unit
22 Pie stipulation, to a
    splurger
23 Refused to take a nap?
26 Complains; frets
27 Separate piles of paper
28 Japanese port city
30 "___ homo!"
31 Opening night
    performance
32 Envious, in Bonn
33 Vigor, to Solti
34 Killer whales
37 Mexican hors d'oeuvre
39 Entice
41 Mouse: Comb. form
44 ___ Amboy, N.J.
45 Favored with inside
    information?
48 Kind of art or star
49 Author Wiesel
50 Blood fluids
52 "___ Days a Week":
    Beatles song
53 California city
54 Game played with
    counters
55 Medicinal orchid tuber
56 Judicial garb
67 Scrooge, at first
58 Demurs
60 Covered with frost
61 Type of prod or call
62 Racket
63 Provide food for a fee
64 Cave ___! (beware the
    dog)
65 Laconian capital
67 Neighbor of Egypt
68 Muffin ingredient,
    sometimes
71 Pinochle combinations
72 Whey's partner
73 Knights of ___
74 "Right to bear arms" org.
75 Karenina or Christie
76 Danger
77 Bone: Comb. form
78 Kind of ladder or stool
79 Map abbr.
80 Lawyer who pads the
    bill?
83 Some kickers' targets
84 Childhood game
85 Troubles
86 Cow's mamma
88 Waste maker
89 Carson's successor
91 Practical, as a utensil
94 Israeli airline
96 Igneous rock
97 Singer LuPone
98 Kind of verse
101 Some sweaters
104 Horowitz's right-hand
    wrong?

107 Ella Wheeler Wilcox,
    for one
108 Legal tender, in Tokyo
109 Lil ___, 1992 Derby
    winner
110 As neat as ___
111 Woofer's partner
112 Primary color
113 Actor Rip ___
114 Autumnal hue

DOWN

1 Struggle
2 T. A. Edison's specialty
3 Cancun coin
4 Parking-lot party
5 Like some candles:
   Archaic
6 El Greco, by birth
7 Drove
8 Govt. agency that has
   your number
9 "The Seagull" playwright
10 Actor Davis
11 The Divine Miss M
12 Nicotine's cohort
13 Project or merchant
   chaser
14 Narrowed, like some
   fingers
15 Roman friends
16 Not making a heap of
   sense?

17 Nice thought
18 These, in Paris
24 Reduce prices
25 Spine: Comb. form
29 Qualification for
   perpetrator prior to
   conviction
32 Nix something
33 Pitcher Saberhagen
34 Unfolds
35 Ignited again
36 Dressing gown that's too
   revealing?
38 ___-midi (afternoon)
40 Cries of disgust
42 Sing in falsetto
43 Chrysler Building feature
46 Naval officers
47 Book of records
50 Chip dip
51 General Robert ___
53 Infant's guardian, ad ___
55 Mini-plays
56 Coolidge and Hayworth
57 Miracle food
59 Sul una ___ (played on
   one string, in music)
60 Interweave
61 Menu
63 French chemist (nee
   Sklodowska)
64 Young horse
65 Don Adams's TV role

66 Five: Comb. form
67 Lou Fischer song title
68 Untouchable, e.g.
69 "___ We All?"
70 Interruption
72 Con's home
73 Le ___ (Fr. newspaper)
76 ___ Alto, CA
78 ___ Gardens, Pakistan
80 Mosque's tower
81 Underlie, so as to include
82 Improvise
83 "Nutcracker" author, ___
   Alexander
87 Worker who thatches
90 Chew the scenery
92 Mythical sylvan deity
93 "___ Grows in Brooklyn"
95 Thick woolen cloth
96 Kind of plow
98 Latona
99 Chevrotain
100 Sponsorship
101 Likely
102 Suffix denoting an
    enzyme
103 What Ukr. once was
105 Call at Wimbledon
106 Suffix with persist

59 CLASSIFIED ADS by Charles Deber

Despite the title, there are no commercials in this fine contribution from our Canadian doctor.

ACROSS

1 Like Glenn Close's attraction
6 Glasses
11 Lyric poems
15 Study, belatedly
19 Boredom
20 Certain vertebrae
21 Smoke trail
22 Hockey's Gordie
23 L
25 P
27 "Room ___ Top"
28 Summit
30 Turncoat
31 Enclitic contraction
33 Baseball's hot corner
35 W German river
36 Boston "Trail"
39 He wrote "The Hollow Men"
41 Shows disdain
45 "Winterset" hero
46 C
49 Tidy
50 "___ Well That . . ."
52 Singer-songwriter Hendryx
53 Sherbets' next of kin
55 Withered
56 He may get a charge out of fishing
58 T
63 Sm., med., ___
64 Boutiques
66 Mountaintop nest
67 Choice
69 Edicts
71 "Mr. Chips" of the cinema
73 Author Ira ___
74 Of trees
77 Plateaus
79 Sensation
82 "___ Mir Bist du Schön"
83 D
85 Made ___ (succeeded)
86 Qualified
88 Allot
89 Bigfoot's cousin
92 Trudge
93 Archer William
94 B
99 Us, in Bonn
100 Famed cow, and herd mates
103 She plays Claudia in "Knots Landing"
104 Extras onstage
106 Kingston, for one
108 Certain apple trees
110 German tribal districts
111 They ruin it
115 Ripped
116 Basket weave
119 H
121 F
125 Landed
126 Up or down follower
127 Petrol unit
128 After ___ (late)
129 Hurl a hat
130 Karenina or Christie
131 Quick bread
132 These: Sp. Fem.

DOWN

1 Elfin
2 Celebes ox
3 Type of bolt
4 "Mame," to nieces
5 Illuminate
6 San Diego dir. from L.A.
7 Buddy
8 Brilliance
9 Woolwork
10 Log-cutter
11 Acknowledge
12 Famed dress designer
13 Lauder lady
14 Disburses
15 Vexes
16 Clothing, in Callao
17 Amazed, in a way
18 Bare
24 Barbara of "Get Smart"
26 Hammerhead part
29 Mule Sal's canal
32 Trademark
34 Having a rounded roof
36 Sole food
37 W
38 Altar top
40 Blemish: Scot.
42 S
43 N Dakota city
44 Dutch painter
45 Daisy and Ms. West
47 Appointed
48 Illustrator of the Oz books
51 Comic like Chaplin
54 Icy rain
57 Get more weapons
59 Fragrance
60 Inner layer
61 Rental terms
62 MCCXIV ÷ II
65 Early engine power
68 Dyes
70 Hawthorne's birthplace
72 Singer Tucker
74 Subside
75 Rise up
76 Admit
78 Martin or Allen
80 Columbia team
81 Largesse from cheepers, by the dozen
84 Mexican money
87 Bluebloods
90 Nobelist for physics: 1976
91 Charm
95 Kick
96 Registers
97 Of Israel's language
98 Painting with opaque colors
101 ___ S. Gardner of whodunits
102 Midday snooze
105 Spacecraft rockets
107 Mr. Welles
109 Bout
111 Tiff
112 Prince Charles' game
113 Medical suffix
114 Stitched
117 Tight
118 Pound or prophet
120 Genetic material
122 Osprey's cousin
123 Observe
124 Curve

OUT OF AFRICA by Charles R. Woodard
Rest assured Isak Dinesen did not pen that clever rhyme below—the puzzle's creator did.

ACROSS

1 Applaud
5 Opie's aunt
8 Mourning band: Var.
13 Punctuation mark
18 She gets what she wants
19 Rumanian city
20 Disgust
21 Antipathy
22 **Start of the rhyme**
26 Japanese money
27 Greek letters
28 Poet
29 Cognate for Helen
30 Jammed
32 Dens
33 Shula's goal
34 His counterpart
35 Comedian Johnson
36 Iron holders
41 Eclipse type
44 Aves.
45 Noble title
46 Spoken
47 **Rhyme: Part II**
53 "The Bowery" star
54 Signs of victory
55 Blundered
56 Levelled
57 Fore's opposite
58 John Irving hero
59 Court action
60 Beneficiaries
61 Cartoonist Peter
62 Veins
63 San ___ Obispo
64 "It's in the Bag" star
67 Wake
68 Utah senator
69 Peak
72 Habitat
73 Lubricated
74 Mixture
75 Malay tribesman
76 **Rhyme: Part III**
80 "A ___ by any other name . . . "
81 Salt Lake City team
82 Poet's "frequent"
83 Tin Pan ___
84 Performers
86 Actress Winningham
88 Number-issuing org.
89 Pewter component
90 Peeler
91 Honey or sugar, e.g.
95 Newgate or Folsom
99 Kitchen wrap
100 On the sheltered side
101 Female ruff
102 **End of the rhyme**
106 Actress Jergens
107 "Rebel Without a Cause" actor
108 Cafe sign
109 French pantomimist
110 Beef and lamb
111 Severe
112 Printer's measures
113 Feuding Hatfield clan chief

DOWN

1 Hook
2 Reduce
3 Solitary
4 Average
5 Extensive
6 Auricles
7 Summer time in R.I.
8 Recognition
9 Employ again
10 Make ___ at (come on to)
11 Hide
12 Imp
13 Powell and Clive
14 Von Reichenbach's hypothetical force
15 Speck
16 Reflect
17 Final word
19 "___ the Fall": Miller
23 Wilderness
24 Discordant
25 Dress fabric
31 Richard Roundtree film
32 Slats
33 Province
36 Shirley Booth role
37 Crystalline hydrocarbons
38 Remove
39 Street show
40 Sleighs
41 Poet Teasdale
42 Norwegian saint
43 Attic
44 Kind of stool
45 Pound and Benson
48 Bunin and Lendl
49 Infamous fiddler
50 Loss to Cervantes
51 One of the archangels
52 Architectural curve
58 Unseasoned
59 "You've got ___ up . . . ": Berlin
60 Napoleonic general
61 Sakharov or Gromyko
62 Kraus and Zanuck
63 Reclined
64 Iraqi port
65 Detest
66 Hen's home
67 French exclamations
68 Gorge
69 Implement
70 Author Sarah ___ Jewett
71 Promising
73 Frequently
74 Volunteer
75 La Scala's home
77 Excursion
78 Civil War lady of song
79 Sampler
85 Rolling ___
86 Weaver of Raveloe
87 Region of NE Spain
88 Oozes
90 Author of "Common Sense"
91 City maps
92 Indo-European
93 Homonym of 110 Across
94 Spooky
95 Baby buggy
96 Heckle
97 Hunch
98 Alluvium
99 "M*A*S*H" star
100 First gardener
103 Morning abbrs.
104 Formerly
105 Strain ___ gnat

GAMES by Lawrence M. Rheingold
Crossword solving could be considered a game—a pleasant pastime for those fortunate enough to come across amusing clues like Mr. R's. (Below are several examples.)

ACROSS

1 Mating game
6 Letters from Ellás
11 Wellingtons
16 Sired
17 Rockies ridge
18 Machine tool
19 Jalopy
20 Rope
21 Son of Hreidmar
22 Game of endurance
25 Flat spaces: Abbr.
26 Wrenches
27 Cerastes
30 Race: Comb. form
33 Dept. created under
   Carter
34 Lope
37 TV chef
39 Wherry adjuncts
41 Factotum
43 Antler branch
44 Squash necessities
47 Caper
48 Bird's org.
49 Make a gaffe
50 Pourboire
51 ''I think, therefore ___'':
   Descartes
52 Mallard genus
53 In a masterful manner
55 Plate on the mound
57 Wrestling ''trophies''
59 Strain, in Selkirk
60 ''By a winding ___'':
   Bacon
61 V x CCCX
62 Jack of clubs
65 Chutzpah
67 Crete mount
68 Dotty game piece
70 ___ Lingus
72 Marbles game
78 Wart hogs
79 ''So Long, Mary''
   composer
80 Buoy
82 Numbers game
83 Not kindled
84 Soras
85 Arn
86 Dresden donkeys
87 Episcopal meeting

DOWN

1 TV ntwk. of Toronto
2 Grinder
3 Equal, in Epinal
4 Dionysian reveler
5 Turned on skis
6 Adriatic port
7 Rusher Dickerson
8 What Rockne always
   stressed
9 Fragrance
10 Wizened
11 Erased
12 Invectives
13 Sgt. Snorkel's dog
14 Afterward
15 Bombay weight
23 L.A. time
24 Kyushu volcano

27 Play charades
28 Climbed a pole
29 Arcade game
31 Stash away
32 Pearly linings
34 Game that's bet on
35 Card game
36 Nanty ___, Pa.
38 Minimal
40 Pay up
42 Wordsworth, at times
44 Turmeric
45 Masons' doorkeeper
46 Man from U.N.C.L.E.
52 Silo resident
54 Melding game
56 Two-piece piece
58 Underwriter

60 Players in a looking
   game
63 Soul, to Jeanne d'Arc
64 Pool scratch
66 Short holiday
68 Threnody
69 Showy signs
71 Race where 8 Down
   is important
72 Helix
73 Cardholder, in a sense
74 Salute
75 Tolkien trees
76 Actress Pryor
77 Manche capital
78 Fraternal org.
81 O.T. book

62

PRESIDENTIAL PARDONS by Coral Amende
Coral suggests you solve this one on the third Monday in February.

ACROSS

1 Très elegant
5 "___ Girl"
9 Quito loc.
13 Tied
17 Fierce fish
19 Salad tomato
20 Hithers' partners
21 Part of a play?
22 Where, in Madrid
23 Russian lake
24 Radiate
25 Measure, in a way
26 Madison
30 Heel
31 It knows
32 Pub potables
33 Eastern staple
34 German expletive
36 Ripped apart
39 Hank of hair
40 Fill the Lincoln
43 Shake up
45 Said stories
46 Pamphlet
47 Hot air in Spain
48 Skill
50 Entreaty
51 Wake-me-up?
52 Gadget
53 Mount Narodnaya locale
54 "Turn ___ Again"
    (Genesis hit)
56 One-third a wine
57 Actress Verdugo
58 Soul
59 Thinly spread
61 Withered
62 Bad habits
63 Safe place?
64 Forfeit
68 Con men
70 Back biter?
71 Vier
72 Gtr. accessory
75 Other
76 Body: Comb. form
77 Thin, as soup
78 Embryonic
80 Diverted
82 Kind of store
83 Daybreak deity
84 More 59 Across
85 Cap-and-gowner
86 Wallflowerlike
87 Equip anew
88 Musician Mulligan
89 Have ___ (excuse
    oneself?)
91 Corrida cry
92 Unfounded
93 Campus house
94 Bible bk.
97 Mean
99 Arthur
104 Spoken
106 "Lawrence of Arabia"
    director
107 Eye: Comb. form
108 Accepting one
109 Untimely?

110 Zero
111 Amoral
112 Albanian capital
113 Iowa city
114 No ifs, ___ ...
115 Coaster
116 Appear

DOWN

1 Ford
2 Architectural curves
3 ___-European
4 Normandy city
5 Dogged
6 Jack of rhyme
7 Garner
8 Bath powder
9 Microscope part
10 Garfield
11 Joins
12 Canine sleuth
13 Goof
14 Grant
15 Jazz's Fitzgerald
16 Require
17 Unwitting one

18 Before phone or graph
27 In a blue way
28 Spreads
29 Island areas
35 Leg area
37 New York city
38 Jot down
39 Refrain syllables
41 French singles
42 Meter man
43 Makes cynical
44 White poplar
46 People movers
47 Make a point
49 Queues
50 Jimmies
53 Bush
55 Himalayan goat
58 Has the flu
59 First course
60 Best of the best
62 Italian abode
63 Rising star
65 Hoover
66 Mezzo Walker
67 With cunning

69 With lion or half
70 Saunter
71 Actress Oakes
72 Way off yonder
73 Grimace
74 Pierce
76 Light carriage
77 Welt
79 Work hard
81 Dietrich and Hagge
82 Sidewalk sight
85 Twisted
88 Midianites conqueror
89 Wake up
90 Get stuck
93 ___ point
95 Paradise
96 Ballet's Nichols
97 Negri of silents
98 Director Avakian
100 Armbone
101 Unruly crowds
102 Broadway musical
103 Stage award
105 Renowned Brown

63 GRIDIRON GRID by Melvin Kenworthy
A straightforward sporty challenger that belongs in the NFC (No Foolish Clues).

ACROSS

1 Metamorphic rock
6 Glacial deposit
11 Bacon request
16 Comedian DeLuise
19 Domiciles
20 Bête ___
21 Suggestions
22 Arabic robe
23 On the qui vive
24 Paramecium, e.g.
25 Lace tip
26 Abner's father
27 Super Bowl XIX's
   QB-team
30 Part of TGIF
31 Let it stand
32 Expected
33 Lorelei's creator
34 Army off.
37 Joel ___ Spingarn
40 Fall flower
41 Enumerate
42 Soaking
44 Splinter groups
46 Juan's thirst
47 Montreal, e.g.
48 Chalcidice mountain
50 Airborne attacker
52 Redgrave of "Playing For
   Time"
55 Madman
57 Cilia
58 Kind of diet
59 Toward the center
61 French one
62 "King Lear" role
63 "Mary ___ a . . ."
64 Skin
66 A Chief kicker, once
69 "Star ___"
70 Part of e.e. cummings
71 Uses an auger
72 Farrow
73 Sea duck
75 Toled
77 Harpsichordist
   Landowska
79 Dobbin's comments
82 Trip interruption
83 Home of the Sharks
85 Athenian
86 Extorted
87 Warsaw loc.
88 Common contraction
90 Cart
91 Pinkish yellow
93 Took out
95 Watchdog Ralph
97 Fr. holy woman
98 Lyre's cousin
99 Scrutinizes
101 Landing-gear strut
103 Brooch
104 Leading 1976 QB-team
110 Grampus
111 Final deed
112 Stirs up
113 Columbus' birthplace
114 Pedro's uncle

115 ___ fat (emulated Sprat)
116 Veni, to Latin students
117 Loco
118 Lion or poet end
119 Food wrap
120 Title for Wences
121 Pintails

DOWN

1 Herring relative
2 Falana
3 Supplication end
4 Provisions
5 Property
6 Animosities
7 Posthaste
8 Astringent
9 Plowed field
10 Bohemian dance
11 Architectural capital
12 Made amends
13 Rock outcropping of a
   sort
14 An Edinburgh leap
15 Attention getters
16 Leading 1982 QB-team
17 Titania's spouse
18 Poughkeepsie college

28 Units of reluctance
29 Aberdeen girls
33 1961 Oscar winner
34 Term of respect
35 Travel org.
36 Super Bowl XXIV's
   QB-team
38 Pituitary hormone
39 Waltz king
41 Arthur Doyle's middle
   name
43 Particular
45 Charteris character
47 Hero
49 Posed
51 "Driving Miss Daisy" star
52 Hazy
53 Scorch
54 Annexes
56 Wheedled
58 Jujube
60 Challenger
62 Spruce up again
64 Pare
65 Best or Garrett
67 Rorem
68 "Teenage Mutant ___
   Turtles"

69 Outre
71 Slant
74 B.A. or M.A.
76 Grinder
77 Solidarity founder
78 Confused
80 NBA team
81 Ethereal terrier?
83 Answer
84 Signer
87 ___ non grata
89 Honduras seaport
91 "In Cold Blood" author
92 Isis' spouse
93 Mint location
94 Flotsam and jetsam
96 Rules
99 Less than hexa-
100 Golf goof
102 Concert goof
102 Concert hall
104 Parrots of Wellington
105 Spirit
106 San ___: Riviera town
107 Barcelona being
108 Routine
109 Simon ___

64

IN A WORD by Bernard Meren
Thematic entries may be helped by a few split decisions.

ACROSS

1 Madison Ave. awards
6 PGA winner of 1968
11 Crooked
15 Sudden jolts
21 Hair coloring
22 Fragrant
23 Vetch
24 La Scala role
25 Photographer Adams
26 Texas AFB
27 Pelt
28 French White House
29 STEREOTYPE
33 Bobble the ball
34 Parseghian
35 "Three Lives" author
36 Surface for Witt
37 Ooze
39 Pay chaser
41 Old-timer
45 Memorable Gluck
49 Michelle's laugh
51 Duplicate
55 Pour
56 Presently
57 CONSPIRACY
64 Lasso part
65 Insurgent
66 Everybody in Bonn
67 Forever, versified
68 Sleds
69 Forte for 45 Across
70 Do in
71 Tallies
72 Not "fer"
73 Fishy cape
74 Window part
75 Airline inits.
76 PROPOSITIONS
86 Metric measure
87 Wins for Jake the Snake
88 Perfect game spoiler
89 Middle: Comb. form
90 Hordes
93 Snares
94 Lucrezia ___
95 Mr. Cub
96 Uptight
97 Sea eagle
98 Half a spa
99 Pilasters
100 EXCHEQUERS
104 Bone: Comb. form
105 Equal in France
106 Void
107 Giant of Cooperstown
108 Understands
109 Soft shades
111 Cry bitterly
113 A hormone, for short
117 Cereal grain
118 Choose
122 "___ O' My Heart"
124 ___y plata (Montana motto)
125 STAGECOACH
134 Tarry
135 Once more
136 Charged particle
137 Squelched
138 Loath
139 Georgian river
140 Mother-of-pearl
141 Figure of speech
142 Cylindrical
143 Abide
144 Questioned
145 Director Lubitsch

DOWN

1 Irritates
2 Poe maiden
3 Warrant
4 Rarity
5 Latin-American dance
6 Wintry
7 Olive genus
8 Smells
9 Inception
10 Cubic meter
11 Wise goddess
12 Secular
13 Church calendar
14 "___ Gynt"
15 Undergarment for a lady: Hyph.
16 Notifies
17 Chekhov heroine
18 Optimistic
19 Shoe insert
20 Prophet
30 French auto racer
31 Split apart
32 Colonial diplomat
38 Gift
40 Charon's river
42 Refrain syllables
43 Betimes
44 Sushi ingredient
45 Late bloomer
46 Nantes' river
47 Ariel and Titan
48 Daughter of James II
50 Bad time for Caesar
52 The Id is its source
53 "... on thy cold gray stones, ___": Tennyson
54 Zero
57 Product of marriage: Hyph.
58 Hard
59 Agrapha sayings
60 Diviners
61 Corn's cousin
62 Summary
63 Coral reef
70 Omens
71 Type of poem
74 Fish catchers
77 Actor J. Carrol ___
78 Valkyries' leader
79 Bobbin bearer
80 Oxford scholarship
81 Leads
82 A toadstool
83 Busybody
84 Glacial ridge: Var.
85 Prescribed amounts
90 Aromatic herb
91 Remainder, to Rene
92 Symbols of authority
93 Eminent
94 Plain
95 Thai coin
96 Oriental veggies
97 Spurs (on)
98 Marsh
101 Vaquero's rope
102 Edison contemporary
103 Abstemious
109 Almond brown
110 Lots of room
112 Put one's two cents in
114 Increase Mather's son
115 Soldiers
116 Paper wasp
117 Pindar, for example
119 Babylonian hero
120 Suppers in Sevilla
121 Treat alternative
123 "Beau ___"
125 Spoiled child
126 Dream in Dijon
127 Hebrew measure
128 Rhine feeder
129 Gabs
130 Bolt fastener
131 Daughter of Cronus
132 French artist
133 Canadian landscapist

65 YOU MAKE THE WORD by Wilson McBeath

Our man in Akron is tired of giving straight clues; he now tries a two-in-one method to give you a new kind of challenge.

ACROSS

1 Kind of bear or Circle
6 He wrote "The Alteration"
10 Horse doctors, for short
14 Epidermis aperture
19 Hopi's building material
20 In tatters
21 Plant important to cosmeticians
22 Overwhelming fear
23 Swindle a school subject
25 Jailbird eulogy
27 Waste allowance
28 Scurrilous chap
29 Tide
31 Site of "The Masters"
32 Sizzling serves
34 Asseverate
35 Organic compound
36 Kind of security
39 Scenery-chewing histrions
41 Unspoken
45 Tooth: Comb. form
46 Diverges
47 Links area
50 Vocal sound
51 Andy Gump's spouse
52 Type of dress
54 Unsuited
56 Poet Lazarus
57 Places in a mausoleum
59 Note Iranian coin
62 Mas' mates
63 Uneven
64 Asiatic coin consumed
65 108 Across Indian
67 Ratite bird
68 Infuriates
69 Word on Daniel's wall
70 Put a lid on switch positions
72 Melted
73 Savory jelly
75 "___ the Way," 1957 song
76 Thrash polite blokes
78 Case for Wyatt Earp
81 Island near Sumatra
83 Child: Comb. form
84 Princess in Verdi's "Don Carlos"
86 A Gershwin
87 Within: Comb. form
88 Neighbor of Leb.
89 Fasten with a rope
91 Exult
93 Facient
95 Brilliant; preeminent
98 Intones
99 "___ horse!"
102 Of birds
103 Carrie Chapman ___, the suffragist
104 Renew
107 Scandinavian nomad
108 "My Gal ___"
109 Girl in a Salinger story
113 Musical pause precipitated
115 Had dinner put in the earth

118 Bewildered
119 Queue
120 Clinton's canal
121 Twenty
122 Have a craving
123 Hardens
124 Depression
125 Overexcited

DOWN

1 Covenant
2 Redolence
3 Anagram for noel
4 Hold back
5 D.J.'s platter
6 Geometric measures
7 Darn
8 Business abbr.
9 British gun rocky pinnacle
10 Surrender possession
11 Jessica or Lorenzo
12 Freight measure
13 Bristles
14 Tap
15 Arrange an arithmetic table
16 Burden
17 Glove Bench used
18 Zoological suffix
24 Locale of Reykjavik: Abbr.

26 Operate
30 Diner sign
33 Feline quantity
34 Captain Hook's henchman
36 Suffix with hand or tooth
37 Chief Norse god
38 Against pattern
39 Twilight, in poesy
40 Gapes
42 Free of charge ointment
43 Sing-Sing resident
44 Tantalize
46 Holding device
48 Finial
49 Greek vowels
53 Certain wts.
54 Representations
55 Famous
58 Mountain: Comb. form
59 Breed of sheep
60 Pass, as a law
61 Flight predicament
64 Golfer Ed
66 Wahines' wreaths
67 Western London suburb
68 Lawn tools
70 Crete's capital
71 Enervates
73 Nautical call

74 Helios
77 Negative vote
79 Part of QED
80 Cry of disgust
82 Sinatra or Como
84 Dash
85 Tavern
89 Radar signal
90 Passed, as time
92 Potential state
94 Iran's capital
96 Biblical monetary unit
97 Dodges
98 London's "___ of the Wild"
100 Reception
101 West Indian shrubs
103 Early French king
104 Skirmish
105 Neural network
106 She, in Siena
108 Make thread
110 Check
111 Apt rhyme for sheer
112 Hesse river
114 Never, in Nuremburg
116 Depart finish
117 Residue

PENMANSHIP by Jean Hunt
From the Cajun State comes this calligraphic challenger. Get out your
pen-and-pencil set.

ACROSS

1 "The Village" poet
7 Jacks or better
12 Shades of purple
18 Third Reich leader
19 Kind of porch
20 Incense
21 Hams it up
22 Part of Quebec
24 Gusto
25 Dog or turkey
27 Architect Saarinen
28 "He that diggeth ___
    shall fall": Eccles.
29 Black cuckoo
30 Gardens
32 Archaic follower of
    thou
34 Compass dir.
35 Illumination, in Berlin
38 Call forth
40 Allocated
42 Venezuela copper
    center
44 Barcelona bed
46 ___ Rafael
47 Middle-ear bone
50 Destroys documents
52 Cato or Catullus
56 Reimburse
58 Jewish feast
60 Hottentot
61 Nightmarish street
62 Pelts
64 Tear again
66 Sheep ailment
67 Type of tide
69 N Brazil territory
71 Contrition
73 Tennessee ___ Ford
75 Jumps
77 More uncanny
78 Needlefish
80 "___ no more, ladies":
    Shak.
81 Polish river, in Polish
82 Dangled
86 Carols
88 Loki's victim
92 Explosive
93 Weaving defect
95 Type of tea
96 Palm leaf
97 "Is this a dagger which
    ___": Shak.
99 Mars
101 Dumbo's were jumbo
103 Hebrew letter
104 They got Ellsberg in
    trouble

107 Nebraska river
110 Abhor
111 Discourages
112 "My Sister ___"
113 Sorus members
114 Wallop
115 Kay and Ringo

DOWN

1 ___ glass
2 Adriatic seaport
3 Type of energy
4 Sandwich
5 Bumble or killer
6 Once, formerly
7 Newsman Charles
8 Part of the Bible
9 Aurora, to a Greek
10 Lasso
11 Velocity
12 Litotes
13 Mezzo Murray
14 Major or Minor
15 Colombian river

16 Cherbourg church
17 Accommodated
23 Tarkington title
26 Ostrich look-alike
31 Cicatrices
33 Autocrat
36 Occur
37 Lock
39 Moslem prince
41 Flag
43 Honshu seaport
45 Viperides members
47 Play part
48 Charlie Chan actor
49 Capital of Jordan
50 French governing bodies
51 Dehydrated
53 Great: Comb. form
54 Vestment
55 Consumer activist
57 Conway and Tiny
59 Mellowed
63 Hispania
65 Wing: Comb. form

68 Hog haven
70 Jargon
72 "I smell ___!"
74 St. Louis bridge builder
76 Satan
79 Renounces
81 Glacial ridges
82 Allowances
83 Remove a mast from its
    socket
84 Tallow: Comb. form
85 Hamlet
87 File, in French
89 Wobble
90 Click beetle
91 Plunders
94 Droplets
98 Elbe feeder
100 Canned meat
102 Goddess of hope
105 Sugar suffix
106 Record label
108 Drunk as a skunk
109 They go with "carte"

67

FIRST-NAME BASIS by Dorothea E. Shipp
Familiar names are treated with familiarity (and humor) below.

ACROSS

1 Brutus's belly
6 Serving of bacon
12 Climbing palm
18 "Ten thousand saw I at
___": Wordsworth
20 Property
21 Fatigue
22 Anthony after a fight?
24 Hot desert wind
25 Frog genus
26 Amphitrite or Thetis
27 Walked
29 Part of TNT
30 Crimping ___
31 Ricky Ricardo's alter ego
32 Argument
33 Ra's symbol
34 Glyceride
36 Gauze weave
38 Yip or yelp
39 Mountain pool
40 Made a hitch
43 Daytime drama
45 Few and far between
47 Proper floribundas?
52 Cursory
55 Daughter of 31 Across
56 Glaswegian
58 Piscine school
59 In the past
62 Greek resistance of
WW II
63 Witchcraft
65 Historian Crowe
66 French preposition
67 Court star
69 Tomlin in "Nine to Five"?
72 April awards
74 MA or MB
75 Water buffalo
77 What homebodies do
79 Gothic arch
80 Wind dir.
81 Archaic form of
59 Across
83 Fink and Wells
84 Material design
85 MVP of Super Bowl XVII
88 Bumbry's high C?
90 Cowardly
94 Spanish six
96 Magi guide
97 Shankar's music
98 Former tax agcy.
101 Trammel
103 Sound of bagpipes
107 Adjective suffix
108 Barrymore and Peck roles
110 Springlock
113 Mallard relative
115 Tit for ___
116 Town in S Maine
117 Singer Makeba
118 Skin disorder
119 "___ of Honey"
121 Weed that's a royal pain?
124 Temperament
125 Released
126 Double-wide
127 Nutritional no-no
128 Fyn Island port
129 "Rolf Krage" dramatist

DOWN

1 Blazing
2 Gaucho's milieu
3 Empty
4 Anon.
5 Outline
6 Result of West's mistake
7 Ordinances
8 Valuable sire
9 Holds
10 Day's march
11 Soprano Tebaldi
12 Gless's wine?
13 Greedy
14 Pro ___
15 Hambletonian entrant
16 Fans
17 Ticketed one
18 Foxhole
19 Looker
23 North follower
28 Hub: Abbr.
32 Marinate
33 Japanese diver
35 Peut-___ (perhaps)
37 Us, in Madrid
41 It, in Pisa

42 Cryptologist's forte
44 Spanish monetary: Abbr.
46 Ernie and Gomer
47 Importunes
48 Dickensian family of
Maypole
49 Woolly mammoth's time
50 Strindberg's "___ Julie"
51 With baking or cream
53 " . . . down the arches of
___": F. Thompson
54 Coquettish
57 Small dog
59 Slow musical movement
60 Ruler
61 Tall Aryan
63 Dare stagger?
64 Hoary
68 Baltic island
70 Dial number
71 Happening at LAX
73 Belt of the Midwest
76 Eggy drink
78 "___ upon a promontory":
Shak.
82 Rocks, in Berlin

84 Job benefit
86 NBA team
87 Title for Chaplin
89 Downy wool
90 Canea citizens
91 Rapping sound
92 Stir up
93 Hoover
95 Salty solutions
99 Greek letter
100 Shakespearean ghost
102 March 17th event
104 Ponti's homeland
105 Memory
106 Pierced
109 Indebted
111 Metal in terne metal
112 Vernacular
114 Goatish look
116 Other, in Oviedo
117 "Don't Fence ___"
120 Skater Gorsha
122 Cannes season
123 Proverb

68 INTERNATIONAL FARE by Nancy Nicholson Joline

Nancy says if we didn't like this puzzle she was going to send it to *Cosmopolitan*. Don't worry Nancy, we'll always like whatever you send us!

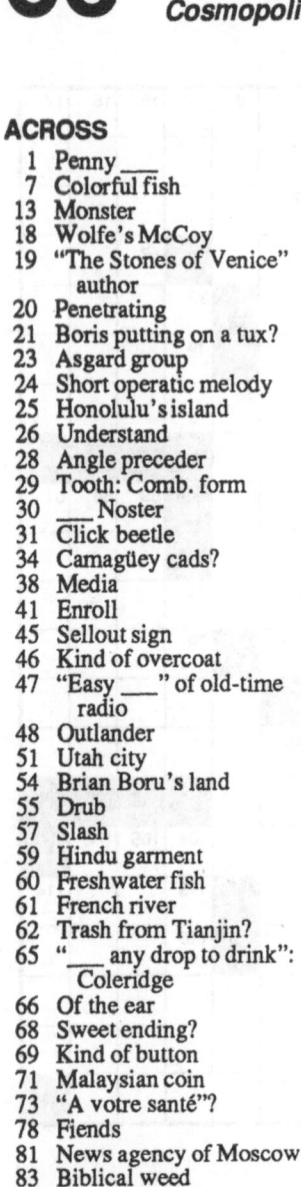

ACROSS

1 Penny ___
7 Colorful fish
13 Monster
18 Wolfe's McCoy
19 "The Stones of Venice" author
20 Penetrating
21 Boris putting on a tux?
23 Asgard group
24 Short operatic melody
25 Honolulu's island
26 Understand
28 Angle preceder
29 Tooth: Comb. form
30 ___ Noster
31 Click beetle
34 Camagüey cads?
38 Media
41 Enroll
45 Sellout sign
46 Kind of overcoat
47 "Easy ___" of old-time radio
48 Outlander
51 Utah city
54 Brian Boru's land
55 Drub
57 Slash
59 Hindu garment
60 Freshwater fish
61 French river
62 Trash from Tianjin?
65 "___ any drop to drink": Coleridge
66 Of the ear
68 Sweet ending?
69 Kind of button
71 Malaysian coin
73 "A votre santé"?
78 Fiends
81 News agency of Moscow
83 Biblical weed
84 Kind of hoop
85 Tom Hanks film
86 Turkish title
87 Where to find Isfahan
88 Petrarch's beloved
90 Ox, to Sandy
91 Commingles
93 Cost-of-living data: Abbr.
96 Comforted
98 Group of seven
99 Dude from Lamphun?
102 Skating star
104 Hindu melodic patterns
105 Murphy of movies
110 Summer cooler
112 Labor gp. founded in 1935
113 "Rock of ___"
114 Baritone Robert
116 Donkey
119 Nerd from Norrköping?
122 Woody Allen's "___ Days"
123 "A gem of ___ ray serene": Gray
124 Displays
125 FDR's columnist cousin
126 Fits
127 Isaac and Otto

DOWN

1 Bret Harte's wily Oriental
2 VCR button
3 Kerr and Woollcott, e.g.
4 Amas follower
5 Actor Andrews
6 It may be dead or deep
7 Christmas decoration
8 Fraternity hopefuls
9 He gives a guarantee
10 Schuss
11 Chars
12 Conductor Lehman
13 Bleat
14 Habitat
15 Slow motion in Sydney?
16 The slammer
17 Actress Garr
18 Unerring
21 Talia Shire film
22 Bay with gray
27 Scenic commune on Sicily
30 "Star Dust" lyricist Mitchell
32 Musical syllable
33 Urged (with "on")
35 Home to Garn and Hatch
36 Maupassant's "___-Ami"
37 Untied
39 Stupor: Comb. form
40 Gibe
41 Informers
42 Kind of chamber
43 Flock watchers in Bavaria?
44 Sculptor/designer Noguchi
49 Samuel's teacher
50 Beethoven's last symphony
52 British rule in India
53 Emulate Vesuvius
56 Vassal
58 "Sans ___, sans eyes, sans taste": Shak.
62 Pellucid
63 Asian Olympic site
64 Small ornamental knob
67 Kind of talent fostered by the Medici
70 Inuit shelter
71 Attempts
72 Golden bird
74 Firearms org.
75 "The ___": Shelley tragedy
76 Wing
77 Béarnaise and Bordelaise
79 Caesar's existence
80 Repel
82 ___ Ana
85 Mens ___ in corpore sano
89 "Arabian Nights" bird
92 FDR or AES, e.g.
94 Flaunts
95 Poetry movement promoted by Ezra Pound
97 Initial participant in a race
99 Delay
100 Discharges
101 Obi, e.g.
103 Speaks imperfectly
106 Name of eight Popes
107 Timely faces
108 Misfortunes
109 Building extension
110 "East of Eden" girl
111 Binary
114 Proper
115 Roof overhang
117 Cariocas' home
118 Alley of Moo
120 Epoch
121 Woolf's "___ Dalloway"

69

If crosswords were game shows, this one would fit somewhere between
Jeopardy and *You Bet Your Life!*

ACROSS

1 Net notable
5 TNT ingredient
11 Lost color
16 Coll. staff
19 Debatable
20 Munchausen, Italian style
21 "___ In the Head": 1959 film
22 Costa Rican peninsula
23 "Has your dog any Chow in him?"
26 Emulate Hammer
27 Poet Siegfried
28 Ha-ha inducers
29 "Auld lang ___"
30 "Like to have my seat?"
37 Vase handles
40 Domesday Book monies
41 Alouettes, par exemple
42 "Buddy, can you spare a dime?"
47 Jumbo weight
48 Diving bell inventor
49 "If I ___ soul shall pity me": Shak.
50 Ward heeler
53 Letter abbr.
54 Wall columns
55 Afrikaners
56 Beaver Cleaver's brother
58 Cooling-off period
60 Jeweler's magnifier
61 Maine's neighbor
62 "Was that spanking necessary?"
66 Like Schönberg's music
68 Ant
69 Second printing
72 Coin of the Mideast
73 Spills the beans
74 Throat clearers
76 Sturm ___ Drang
77 Goddess of plenty
78 Stockholm suburb
79 Egyptian dogheaded ape
80 "I Like ___ Like It": 1951 song
81 "Why do you ride the subways?"
87 Plunderer
89 Seth's boy
90 Caucasus Aryan
91 "Whodunit?"
96 Trawler gear
97 Lends a hand
98 Most breezy
102 After TGIF
103 "What's up, Doc?"
109 Printemps follower
110 Pianist Claudio
111 Loose overcoat
112 Eventful times
113 Common article
114 Lurk about
115 Composer Albinoni
116 Watched loch

DOWN

1 Novelist Kingsley
2 Couch potato's milieu
3 Shed tools
4 Recurring, as winds
5 Detest
6 Ship to remember
7 Brachium
8 Anderson's "High ___"
9 ___ equals 0.035 oz.
10 Inheritor
11 Sham
12 "Gotcha!"
13 "Le Coq ___"
14 'ades
15 "L.A. Law" star
16 Nat King Cole hit
17 As strong ___
18 "R.U.R." playwright
24 Treated to a Mickey
25 Recoiler's word
29 Finish
31 "Stage Struck" star
32 Clear the slate
33 Still on the wagon
34 Claims on property
35 That ___ say . . .

36 Lincoln Center attraction
37 Fed a kitty
38 Not a soul
39 Approves
43 Of the intellect
44 Thackeray's attacker
45 Card game (with "it")
46 Basso Cesare
50 Kiddie outfits
51 Archaic
52 De Putti of silents
54 Sadat
55 Earbenders
56 Occasional N African streams
57 Teal genus
59 Active volcano
60 Near the sacrum
61 Of alchemy
63 Vociferous ones
64 Muscat man
65 E.C. Bentley's sleuth
66 Fuss
67 Cabbie's expectation
70 Loosen
71 ___ of Nantes

73 Black tea
74 Homer king
75 Signe of cinema
78 Caen's neighbor
81 Charged atoms
82 Gump's wife
83 Cull
84 Go ___ flight (fly alone)
85 Afrikaners' rifles
86 "He ___": Easter hymn
87 Mild oath of yesteryear
88 Leg wraparound
91 Map feature
92 Afghanistan's capital
93 Wire measure
94 Biblical weeds
95 Sacred: Comb. form
99 Seine tributary
100 Mex. ladies
101 Hardy heroine
103 Talk a lot
104 Bruin Hall-of-Famer
105 Tail: Comb. form
106 Unprocessed
107 Mil. award
108 School org.

BY THE NUMBERS by William Canine
W.C. from S.C. invites you all to fill in the blanks below. How many can recall the name of that Raye-De Paul hit at 98 Across?

ACROSS

1 Strewed
6 Petty crook
10 Turkish title
14 Withered
18 Fret
19 Whittle
20 Lummox
21 Salver
22 Rallying cry
26 First Egyptian king
27 Seat
28 Arab emirate
29 Director King
30 Rowan
31 In dispute
34 Cpl.
35 Oriental servant
36 Soak
37 Calabrian town
38 Butter maker
40 Amphora
41 Muscle: Comb. form
42 Suns' org.
45 Less complicated
46 Utter
47 Actress Joanne
49 Pressing
52 Neighbor of Syr.
53 Turgenev
55 Houston pro
57 Hasten
58 Hard roll
60 Norse god
63 Capital of Tibet
65 Bargain Day sign
69 Afghan's neighbor
70 Ex-Angel Sandy
71 Brazilian seaport
72 G-Man
73 Miss O'Grady
75 Mary ___ Lincoln
76 Collyer or Wilkinson
79 Wilander and Edberg
81 REL's org.
83 Beiderbecke
84 Edible root
87 ___ Lanka
88 Kind
90 Store
92 Malady
93 German admiral:
    1861–1941
95 Bounder
96 Baronet's wife
97 Prot. denomination
98 1942 song hit
104 Horned viper
105 Patrick or Ryan
106 Singer Lopez
107 Call ___ day

108 Moisten the roast
110 Infers
114 QED center
115 Coy
116 Prefix for drome
117 Queen
118 Blade of yore
119 Connected rms.
120 Danson and Knight
121 Upstairs girls

DOWN

1 Medieval steward
2 Realtor's tactic
3 Helpmate
4 One of Adam's
    grandsons
5 "___ Rosenkavalier"
6 Sensation
7 Crab's sense organs
8 Chemist Remsen
9 Purchasers
10 Addis ___
11 ___ Heights
12 Time for festivity
13 Sandy's remark
14 Trying hard
15 Wear away
16 Babbled

17 Oglers
18 Affair
23 Lord's table
24 Did housework
25 At an end
31 Vespucci
32 Picture of health
33 Search thoroughly
35 Chemical suffix
39 Band
40 Forefront
41 Jessica Lange film
43 "The Hostage"
    playwright
44 Fennel
46 Bovine treat
48 Hindu queen
50 Pocahontas's husband
51 Bergamot or Earl Grey
54 Britten and Ralston
56 Out on a limb
59 Full of enthusiasm
60 Margin
61 WW II org.
62 Misstep
64 Mexicali man
65 Tartan trousers
66 Egret or heron
67 Tills

68 Bygone
69 Doubts
74 Willow
75 Cusp
77 Brazen
78 Calamities
80 Aversion
82 Scale
83 Group
85 Function
86 Hot
89 Omitted
91 Natural home
92 Mindanao seaport
94 Stone
96 Duplicates
98 Broods
99 Entomb
100 Bristles
101 Choleric
102 Ivy and wisteria
103 Oslo ___
108 Bartok
109 Hun king
111 Loos: Abbr.
112 Teensy
113 Someone prized

71

LIFE ON THE FARM by Ernie Furtado
Ernie lives in mid-Manhattan where life can be beastly. This puzzle expresses one of his reveries.

ACROSS

1 Diamond cover
5 "Archie Bunker's Place" regular
10 Dudes
14 Joie de vivre
18 Anatomic canals
19 Noon preceder
20 Funnyman Sahl
21 Hacienda chamber
22 SMALL POTATOES
24 GRADUATE'S PRIZE
26 Trusts
27 Conger fisherman
29 "___ bird to your mountain": Psalms
30 Observed
31 Fast jet
33 Like it or ___
35 King of comedy
36 LIKE SOME BEARDED MEN
40 GI RATION
45 Drs. for expectant mothers
48 Provo sch.
49 Opportune
51 Within: Comb. form
52 Sports transaction
54 PIECE OF CAKE
56 ___ tooth
58 Unit of inductance
59 David's vis-a-vis, once
60 Gumbo: Var.
62 Afore
63 Icelandic literary work
64 More competent
66 To love, in Paris
68 SOME BALLPLAYERS HAVE THEM
70 HORRIPILATION
75 "___ Is Born": Garland film
76 Bombeck and Caldron
77 Motor City gridder
78 Soviet fighter
80 Kafka heroine
82 Rel. title
83 The sixth is one
84 Fire truck
86 JOGGER'S FLOPPER
90 Musical mark
91 Sandhurst weapon
92 Sure winner
93 Block extension
95 Caesar's "but"
96 OATER
100 STUBBORN TUFT OF HAIR
103 Qualifying words
104 Interrogative utterances
106 Implement for a wherry
107 Christiania today
111 Applaud
114 Shankar's instrument
117 Wine cup
119 FRANKIE LAINE HIT
122 ONE-SIDED MILITARY ACTION
124 Black, poetically
125 Precursor to an invention
126 Welcome word
127 Sets of three
128 Hoopster Calvin ___
129 Native of Nish
130 Run-down
131 Code word

DOWN

1 Titter
2 Old-womanish
3 ___ form, used at the Big A
4 Small dog, for short
5 Chess piece
6 Worn out
7 Fit to ___
8 Rod's partner
9 Eve of Hollywood
10 Certain radios
11 "___ Baby Baby": Ronstadt hit
12 Factory-built structure
13 Star: Comb. form
14 Cores
15 "Mighty ___ Rose"
16 Start of Oregon's motto
17 Film starring Anna Sten
18 TV recorders
23 Pope's "___ on Man"
25 Carrots' companions
28 DeMille ballet
32 Poker choice
34 Balsam or resin
37 Mind
38 Whistler was one
39 Ditch diggers
41 Logger cheat
42 Sabotages
43 Ripley's "Believe ___ Not"
44 Unabridged dictionary
45 Tryon's "The ___"
46 Dutch city
47 He lies in wait
50 Col. time zone
53 Dull grays
55 USC rival
56 Twists
57 Poetic foot
61 Julio's house
64 "I could ___ unfold . . .": Shak.
65 Growler
67 Nobelist for medicine: 1970
69 Get ___ (start)
70 Pertaining to bodily motion
71 Re body parts: Comb. form
72 A king of Israel
73 Hustlers after rustlers
74 Hogan rival
78 Interlock
79 Involved with
81 Church section
82 Muscle: Comb. form
83 On ___: built hoping for a sale
85 Disrespectful
87 Elbe feeder
88 Yannick et al.
89 Gershwin's "___, Lucille"
94 Eastwood's ___ Harry
97 It was: Lat
98 Egyptian god
99 Hair dressing
101 ___ out (solved)
102 Legitimate
105 Locations
108 Shop
109 First name in hostelry
110 Left-overs
111 Kind of corner
112 ___ libre
113 Coagulate
115 Cahn/Styne product
116 Johnson of "Laugh-In"
118 A predecessor of Benji
120 Cloth appendage
121 Arrest
123 Arch extender

72

THE OLD WEST by Hank Harrington
The encircled letters, starting at 21 Across and ending at 120 Across, spell out a historic shoot-out.

ACROSS

1 Postulate
6 Gudrun's husband
10 Nicaraguan native
14 Secular clergymen of France
19 Worthless
20 Noted anthropologist: 1858–1942
21 Richard of films
22 Rapid recovery
23 Outlaw target in the Old West
25 Indian target in the Old West
27 Final resting places
28 Kind of signal
29 Italian or Spaniard
30 Numerical prefix
31 Oyl's cry
32 "Money ___ everything"
33 Phoenician city
34 Plastered
36 Sterling or Peerce
38 Works for the accused
40 Bobby of tennis
41 Cotton Mather product
43 Milky Way's shape
44 Home of the Baylor Bears
45 Crowd gone amok
48 Trail bosses of the Old West
51 Suffix for Biblical verbs
52 Cyprinoid fish
53 Arabian bread
54 Butterine
55 Flying Tigers gp.
57 Trinacria, now
59 Ulan ___, Mongolia
60 Gunfighter Hardin
61 Half of a Samoan port's name
62 Cranny's partner
63 Eighth son of Jacob
64 Whistle wetters in the Old West
69 Biblical tower
72 G. Burgess's boorish creature
73 Plasma dose
74 Spaceman Grissom
77 Ooze
78 Kind of tiger
80 Poetic contraction
81 Waldheim of Austria
82 Spasms
84 Serling or Taylor
86 Like some beans
88 Make queries
89 Clown
90 Stumble
92 SE English county
93 Vandyke, e.g.
95 Arachnophobe's bane
98 Sm. land mass
99 Jazz dances
101 Links pegs
102 Arabian gulf
104 "Three men ___ tub"
107 "Dies ___": Ancient hymn
108 "High Noon" and "Hang 'Em High"
111 Hebrew month
112 Growl

113 Sleeve weapons in the Old West
115 Meals-on-wheels vehicle in the Old West
117 Rocky outcrop
118 Custer's last major
119 Pawn
120 Manila resin
121 Road curves
122 The last word
123 Voice votes
124 Out of this world

DOWN

1 Part of "GI"
2 ___ Dame
3 Jesse's brother
4 Work units
5 This crosses the bar often
6 Have an ample amount of
7 Like campfire marshmallows
8 Covered with frills
9 Somewhat like: Suffix
10 Poster word in the Old West
11 Quartz and chalcedony
12 Wise trio
13 Soon
14 Objet d' ___
15 Filipino cutlass
16 Handyman of the Old West
17 Crème de la crème
18 Church assembly
24 D. Rather's network
26 Mild warning
29 Posse get-togethers in the Old West
32 "___ the mouth of hell": Tennyson
33 Schick and Rorschach
35 Past
37 Height: Comb. form
39 For shame!
40 Piquant
41 English sailing barge
42 Breathing sound
44 Union action
46 County in Nebraska
47 Roseanne Arnold's maiden name
49 Darn it!
50 Wise
52 Memorable fashion designer
53 Annie Oakley, sometimes
56 Paperhanger's crime
58 Light sleeper?
59 Thai money
61 Fence picket
64 Gets hitched
65 Cyclotron items
66 Strong ale
67 Les Etats ___
68 Main idea
69 VCR type

70 WW II coalition
71 Old West four-wheeled carriages
74 Showdown figure
75 Yen
76 Scene of Charon's ferry
78 Group of outlaws
79 Eldest sons of dukes
81 Rarity in old western films
83 Kit of the Old West
85 Lose a showdown
87 Strap for Silver
89 Ray gun sound
91 Fruit and veggies
94 Come forth
95 Author of "Tristram Shandy"
96 Individual
97 Fishing boats
99 Move like a crab
100 Kilmer poem
103 Noah's project
105 One of the Judds
106 "L.A. Law" lothario
109 Indian city
110 Rain cats and dogs
111 Popeye's cry
112 Hurricane's little sister
114 Plural conversion
115 Tea type
116 Tiny

73

TO A FUTURE INNOVATOR by Charles R. Woodard
If you're confused by Charlie's toast, substitute "by creating" for the first word at 79 Across.

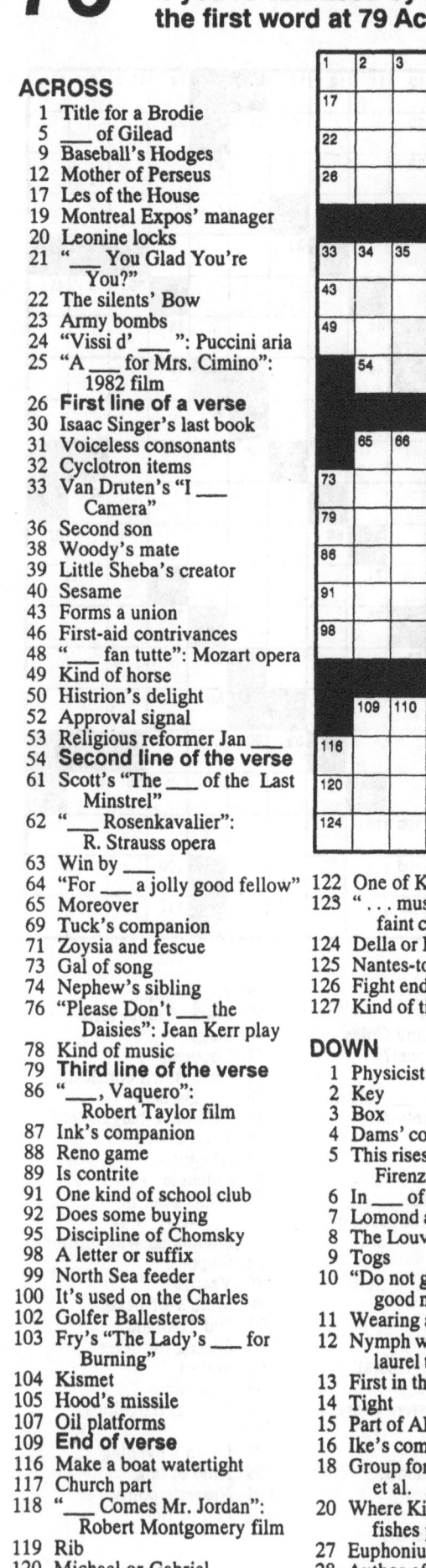

ACROSS
1 Title for a Brodie
5 ___ of Gilead
9 Baseball's Hodges
12 Mother of Perseus
17 Les of the House
19 Montreal Expos' manager
20 Leonine locks
21 "___ You Glad You're You?"
22 The silents' Bow
23 Army bombs
24 "Vissi d' ___ ": Puccini aria
25 "A ___ for Mrs. Cimino": 1982 film
26 **First line of a verse**
30 Isaac Singer's last book
31 Voiceless consonants
32 Cyclotron items
33 Van Druten's "I ___ Camera"
36 Second son
38 Woody's mate
39 Little Sheba's creator
40 Sesame
43 Forms a union
46 First-aid contrivances
48 "___ fan tutte": Mozart opera
49 Kind of horse
50 Histrion's delight
52 Approval signal
53 Religious reformer Jan ___
54 **Second line of the verse**
61 Scott's "The ___ of the Last Minstrel"
62 "___ Rosenkavalier": R. Strauss opera
63 Win by ___
64 "For ___ a jolly good fellow"
65 Moreover
69 Tuck's companion
71 Zoysia and fescue
73 Gal of song
74 Nephew's sibling
76 "Please Don't ___ the Daisies": Jean Kerr play
78 Kind of music
79 **Third line of the verse**
86 "___, Vaquero": Robert Taylor film
87 Ink's companion
88 Reno game
89 Is contrite
91 One kind of school club
92 Does some buying
95 Discipline of Chomsky
98 A letter or suffix
99 North Sea feeder
100 It's used on the Charles
102 Golfer Ballesteros
103 Fry's "The Lady's ___ for Burning"
104 Kismet
105 Hood's missile
107 Oil platforms
109 **End of verse**
116 Make a boat watertight
117 Church part
118 "___ Comes Mr. Jordan": Robert Montgomery film
119 Rib
120 Michael or Gabriel
121 Egg on
122 One of Kipling's twain
123 ". . . music and an ___ faint carouse": MacLeish
124 Della or Peewee
125 Nantes-to-Angers dir.
126 Fight endings called by refs
127 Kind of time

DOWN
1 Physicist Ernst ___
2 Key
3 Box
4 Dams' counterparts
5 This rises and falls in Firenze
6 In ___ of trouble
7 Lomond and Ness
8 The Louvre, e.g.
9 Togs
10 "Do not go gentle ___ that good night": D. Thomas
11 Wearing a sly expression
12 Nymph who became a laurel tree
13 First in the Zodiac
14 Tight
15 Part of AD
16 Ike's command in WW II
18 Group for Petty, Allison et al.
20 Where Kipling's "flyin' fishes play"
27 Euphonium
28 Author of "Exodus"
29 Jan. 1 treats
33 One of the conts.
34 Sound from Garfield
35 Esau's wife
37 First name of 28 Down
39 Activity for Hancock
40 Fencing term
41 Campaign topics
42 Says "th" for "s"
44 Organic compounds
45 Monoski
47 Famed battleship
48 Revolutionary Guevara
51 First home
55 Scottish explorer in 33 Down: 1793–1826
56 Tattooed lady of song
57 Shakespearean sprite
58 Word from a postman's motto
59 Peter and Alexander
60 ". . . ___ deeper into the beauty . . . of things": DuMaurier
65 Mountain mints
66 Slurs
67 Hallow attachment
68 Famous Twenties trial
70 Word with ice or six
72 Lacrosse, e.g.
73 Billow
75 Odd's counterpart
77 Very, in Verdun
80 Barbara Bush, ___ Pierce
81 Approved
82 Dicer's snake eyes
83 County and borough in PA
84 Rack's companion
85 Art ___
90 Fast airliner
92 Thomas of clock-making fame
93 Listing of nobles
94 Poet Teasdale
96 Rara ___
97 Counteract
99 One of eleven
101 Cardinal's garment
104 "The Rockford ___": TV series
105 Vase handles
106 Verb used with havoc
108 ". . . ___ of cold command": Shelley
109 Wax's antithesis
110 Howard of the comics
111 "It came ___ a midnight . . ."
112 Approximately
113 Bell the cat
114 Govt. propaganda group
115 Founder of London police
116 "My Mother the ___": TV sitcom

74

BOTANICAL GARDEN by Elizabeth Arthur
Our Chicago crossworder tells us the idea for this one came to her while drinking some planter's punch.

ACROSS

1 South-of-the-border cheers
5 Piglet
10 "The Ballad of Reading ___": Wilde
14 Physics preceder
18 City on the Adda
19 Composer of "Sunrise Serenade"
20 Helpers
22 Khachaturian
23 Tree for Michael?
25 Vine for David?
27 Kind of silk
28 Appertain
30 Comes up
31 Juan's three
32 Breakers
33 Andy Taylor's son
34 Needle case: Var.
37 Tackles
38 Philippine timber tree
39 Tokyo, formerly
42 Skyrockets
43 Ganymede, Io, and Callisto
44 Remembrance of a good time
46 Beats at bridge
47 Julep garnish
48 Noah, in the Douay Bible
49 Plexus
50 Nice summer
51 Plant for the Alamo?
55 Scruffs
56 Tells a story
58 Turn the clock ahead
59 Material for 65 Across
60 Comes in second at Belmont
61 Fountain treats
62 Michigan city and county
64 Finishes a cake
65 Sun hat from India
66 Example
68 They are often tall
70 Plant for Mr. Ed?
72 Cartoonist Key
73 To-do
74 Goddess of recklessness
75 Singer Seeger
76 Part of n.b.
77 Tensions
80 Jimmies
82 Finished
83 . . — . . . — . . .
84 Snacks for a pangolin
85 Don Adams role
86 Drugbusters
87 Black cuckoos
88 Regulus and Vega
89 Mallard genus
91 Takes care of
94 Shearer of "The Red Shoes"
95 Card games for two
98 Plant for Geronimo?
100 Plant for George?
103 Metal eater
104 Spanish gentleman
105 By and by
106 Kind of sale
107 Allot
108 Part of PIN
109 Irregularly notched
110 Apartment in Soho

DOWN

1 Like the hills
2 "Gentlemen Prefer Blondes" author
3 Word in UNESCO
4 Gun testers
5 Suffix for sea
6 Door fasteners
7 Golden ide
8 Clay, once
9 Topography
10 Boo-boos
11 Buenos ___
12 What your nose knows
13 Guitarist Paul
14 Soprano Wittich
15 Paleozoic and Mesozoic
16 Red or ticker
17 He was Mingo
21 Sugar or flour
24 ___ and penates
26 "Friday Foster" star
29 12/24 and 12/31
32 Penned
33 Double quartet
34 German food
35 Dance like Honi Coles
36 Plants for Monet?
37 Cookout tool
38 "The game is ___": Holmes
39 Plant for Dumbo?
40 Fuss over
41 Is in debt
43 Bogs down
44 Queen ___ lace
45 ___ Dei (by the grace of God)
47 Dust specks
51 Confronts
52 Corners
53 Free-for-all
54 Oleate, e.g.
55 Beethoven's "Choral"
57 Speed skaters
59 Part of a Western chase scene
61 Ethic
62 Monogram mems.
63 Breathtaking
65 Carryalls
66 Dog tag, for short
67 Utopias
68 Recipe amts.
69 Black: Comb. form
70 Stags
71 Copycats
76 Countdown conclusion
78 ___ Barbara
79 Collective bargainers
80 Actor Sharif
81 Allegory
82 Entangle
85 Winchester in "M*A*S*H"
87 Excluding, with "from"
88 Stupor
89 Yearns
90 Mother-of-pearl
91 Old Thailand
92 Ending for defer
93 Redact
94 Golconda
95 This, in Barcelona
96 Ill
97 Loren's evening
99 Kind of talk
101 Nasser's polity
102 Part of IRA

HIGHLY SENSITIVE by Arthur S. Verdesca
**Whether you're thick- or thin-skinned it really doesn't matter; we
found Arthur's opus to have 75 Across. (25 Across would be another descriptive.)**

ACROSS

1 Disconcert
6 Vespid
10 A health food
14 Stimulates
19 Hawk's home
20 Field
21 Musical crowd
22 Tapestry weave
23 Trumpet
25 Fantabulous !
27 Whirl
28 Maxims
30 Native: Suffix
31 Bacon slices
35 Lapham or Marner
36 Farfel's master
40 Heights
41 Arab
42 Nil, to François
44 Linguistics org.
45 Most like a bird?
47 Insipid
49 Eternally, in verse
50 Pen
51 Vive's opposite
53 Individual
54 Soil loosener
55 Small key
56 Standards
60 Valletta's place
61 Star
63 Dismissal
64 Pianist-conductor
   Barenboim
65 Con's theft
66 Links' Palmer
67 Vamp
68 Breakfast fare
70 Platonic dialogue
71 Rubs
74 Two-edged sword
75 Mass appeal
77 Remained inactive
78 Gentle
79 German's honor
80 City on the Humboldt
81 Leaf
82 Colorado mount
83 Aesthetic quality
87 Goethe play
89 Canals on Saint Marys
90 Drier than extra sec
91 Treasure
92 Cooperative group
93 Last
95 Feather
96 Checks
98 Fruitcake
99 Facilitated
100 Mondrian
101 Initial glimpse
105 Is told
111 Farewell
112 Tune in
113 Heraldic border
114 Rumpus
115 Reese sonnet
116 African fox
117 Spanish painter Juan
118 Cobbled

DOWN

1 What to say to the doctor
2 Aunt of Mayberry
3 Scorpio's neighbor
4 Title for Tor
5 1947 De Havilland film
  (with "The")
6 Recompenses
7 The Amu Darya feeds it
8 ___, sette, otto
9 Rice fields
10 Rich oriental fabric
11 Rummages
12 "___ boy!"
13 Modernist
14 Bind
15 Enoch's angel
16 Unit of work
17 ___-di-dah
18 Droop-nosed jet
24 Saul's grandfather
26 Least coarse
29 "___ a Song Go . . ."
31 Basket fiber
32 Kind of clue
33 "I ___ of an Englishman
   . . ."

34 Careful notice
35 Hide
37 Ammonium carbonate
38 Medicated ointment
39 Tusked cetacean
41 Orderly pile
42 Adorée of films
43 Egyptian fertility goddess
46 Follower of Lao-tzu
48 Surge
52 Demote
54 Capital of Crete
56 City on the Moselle
57 Curtain cloth
58 "Harry and ___": 1974 film
59 Vidalia
60 Wetland
62 Sniggled
64 Dances to Summer
66 Fortified
67 River in Minnesota
68 Dialyze
69 Pierre's house
70 French landscapist
71 Burrowed
72 Young bird of prey

73 Filches
75 ___ En-lai
76 Aquarium fish
79 White-plumed birds
81 Dumas ___
84 Cobalt violet
85 Superior
86 Caisson laborer
88 Ships with lateen sails
90 Noblest Roman
94 Indy 500 winner: 1992
95 Glacial hills of Iowa
96 Buenos ___
97 ___ judicata
99 Sponsorship
100 Cliff of Maui
101 Suet
102 Orfe
103 Small bay
104 Mrs. Cantor
106 Be mistaken
107 Word from Slimer
108 Black gold
109 Application
110 Spread alfalfa

76

MODISTE'S MATERIALS by Bernice Gordon
Our puzzle fabricator from Philadelphia has woven several original clues within the checked pattern. One of our favorites is 92 Across.

ACROSS

1 Schlepp
5 Site of Hideyoshi's castle
10 Dravidian language
15 Command to a husky
19 Therefore
20 Hairless
21 Jewish prayer
22 Scope
23 Cotton jersey
25 Contents of a hope chest
27 Beatific
28 Ill-humored
30 Lives
31 On the apex
33 Pinky and Peggy
34 Play by Molnár (with "The")
35 Industrial city in Wisconsin
39 Site of the Jokang Temple
41 Base
45 Took off like ___
46 Summer suiting
48 Different from
49 Bearing
50 Ali of fiction
51 City ENE of Paris
53 Bern's river
54 Author of "The College Widow"
55 Moire
59 Opango's country
61 Poems lacking rhyme
63 I, for one
64 "60 Minutes" regular
65 Eroded
66 Sway
67 Department in NE France
68 Apparel worn by Noel Coward
70 Direction from James Beard
71 Sent an SOS
74 "___ Triste"
75 Sheer fabrics with a crisp finish
77 Wallach or Lilly
78 Bachelor's last words
79 Gave out
81 LSD
82 Norman battle town
83 Like George Apley
85 What men wear with loafers
89 Gave stars to
90 Some amateurs
92 "A billboard lovely as ___": Nash
93 Goddess of the moon
94 Burrow
95 Admission
96 Wrack's partner
98 Draw a likeness
101 Agnew and Malas
103 Carnivore allied to the mongoose
108 Fine fabric from Cork
110 Ovine products
112 Roman known as "The Elder"
113 Habituate: Var.
114 Fully grown
115 Garb for the Forum
116 Enthusiasm
117 Liabilities
118 Where Hercules slew the lion
119 Thrust and counter

DOWN

1 Cupbearer to the gods
2 Large lake
3 Unsightly
4 Some Seles shots
5 Sedative
6 Musical mark
7 Math subj.
8 Sources of Hawaiian timber
9 Ring-shaped
10 Striking scene
11 "Deutschland uber ___"
12 "___ Streets": 1973 film
13 Auberge
14 Indifferent
15 Daytime drama
16 "Trinity" author
17 Thrilled
18 Witches
24 Laughing
26 Final event
29 Ending for end
32 Students at USNA
34 Memorable Valentino role
35 Siamese kings
36 Put apart
37 Unsized material
38 Charged electron
40 Give an audience
41 Person without a home
42 Winter warmer
43 Practice
44 Baby Overacker
46 Darkness Prince
47 Town loudmouth?
50 Ruins
52 Shows contempt
55 After quick or slow
56 Bacchanalian sounds
57 Hugh from Ohio
58 Uppsala resident
60 Mrs. Chaplin
62 Art colony in New Mexico
64 Had a fit
66 Disney pooch
67 Short skirts
68 City in Old Castile
69 A Peace Nobelist
70 Plant capsules
71 More defective
72 Dame Terry
73 Semiconductor
75 Part of M.G.M.
76 Spike a drink
80 Had it coming
82 Mineo
84 "Invisible Man" author
86 Conner and Gordimer
87 See 70 Across
88 Tidbit for an epicure
89 Continue
91 "To ___ His Own"
93 Forty winks
95 Evident
97 Pie served in "David Copperfield"
98 Comic Clay
99 Of time
100 Lebanese bread
101 Give the cold shoulder
102 "The Sweetest Taboo" singer
104 Goes bad
105 Former Surgeon General
106 Chlorination victim
107 Boris of Bulgaria
109 A brilliant finish
111 Queen Mother

77

MOVIE MUTATIONS by Jim Page

Jim has not only mutated well-known titles; he has muted them. Nice work!

ACROSS

1 Child's marble
4 Actress Raines
8 Field hockey pos.
11 Uganda's capital
18 Lifetime
19 Cut of meat
20 ___ code
22 Burrowing rodents
23 Fla. neighbor
24 Sled used in the Olympics
25 De Niro film?
27 Peter Sellers film (after "The")?
30 Indian novelist Raja ___
31 Hernando de ___
32 ___-la-la
33 Cell constituent: Abbr.
34 State of the Commonwealth of Austral.
35 Hero of the Hungarian Revolution of 1848
38 Meat on a skewer
42 Black retriever
45 Bogart film?
50 Made like a racetrack
54 Certain frame
55 Like beer in the fridge
56 Town SE of Rome
57 "The Barefoot ___"
58 Old car
59 "Life isn't all beer and ___": T. Hughes
61 Freshly
62 Gums
64 Mao ___-tung
66 "___ greatest son . . ." (once said of Mussolini)
67 Prizes
71 Catch
73 Major leaguer Max or Hal
75 Poker cynosure
77 Some tableware: Abbr.
78 WW II female corps member: Abbr.
82 Languid
84 Dandy
86 "___ young Lad from Buckingham," (old English country song)
89 Gaelic bard: 3rd cen.
90 Port of ancient Rome
92 Certain lettuce heads
93 Card-table misplay
94 Spencer Tracy film?
96 Sun. talk
97 Unable to act
98 Mr. Van Winkle
99 Costa
102 Center beginning
104 Arab garment
107 Slippery
111 Actress Claire
112 Frank Morgan film?
119 Cary Grant film?
121 Over
122 The 19th Greek letter
123 Of a polyphonic voice part
124 How not to prepare 007's Martini
125 Sonora Indian
126 Boot a grounder
127 Leftover
128 Outside: Comb. form
129 Aspen, e.g.
130 Pumpernickel

DOWN

1 Forms of address for women
2 Frozen asset
3 Winner
4 French magazine
5 Oaf
6 "It gives a lovely ___": Millay
7 Almost, poetically
8 Knocks
9 Physics abbr.
10 "___ Geste"
11 "The Trial" author
12 Chills and fever
13 Mousse shaper
14 Place for pint-sized drinks
15 Done to ___ (cooked perfectly)
16 Actresses Kedrova and Lee
17 ". . . on ___ boat to China"
21 Sour
26 Suffix with nectar: Archaic
28 Cagney film? (with "The")
29 "___ Me Out to the Ball Game"
36 "___ homo!"
37 "Serpico" author
39 Zitherlike instrument
40 Stanford-___ test
41 Indolent
42 James Mason film
43 Model, of a kind
44 Van Heflin film?
45 A framer of Roger Rabbit
46 Sharpen, as a razor
47 Mints, in a way
48 Netman Fraser
49 Vane readings
51 ___ of the valley
52 Suffixes for amyl and ethyl
53 "___ Kapital"
54 U.S. capital airport code: Abbr.
60 "The Keys of the ___"
63 Elec. unit
65 Tannin trio
68 Stored fodder
69 High-school student
70 Fluff up a pillow
72 Set out
73 Renoir painting
74 NBA, e.g.
76 Sheer linen fabric
79 Japanese aborigine
80 Male insect
81 Mil. leaders
82 Songwriter Crane ("White on White": 1964)
83 Tippler
85 "Tonight Show" host, once
87 River to the Sea of Okhotsk
88 Indian garment
91 Certain Muslims
95 Laurel
99 Hardship
100 Toughen
101 Firecracker sounds
102 Official in ancient Rome
103 "___ Joey"
105 Crow
106 "___ Hours" (film with Teri Garr)
108 Journalize
109 "Psychedelic Experience" author
110 "___ Big Boy Now" (Geraldine Page film)
112 Negev material
113 A son of Isaac
114 ___ en point
115 Cato's 1109
116 Drome lead-in
117 Tiresome speaker
118 Ron Howard TV role
120 Merry, in Paris

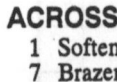

78

CLOAKROOM by William S. McIlrath

A quick glance at the title should steer most solvers in the right direction.
British solvers, however, may be in for a surprise. In England "cloakroom" often
refers to a public rest room.

ACROSS

1 Softened
7 Brazen
13 Honey drinks
18 Jacques ___ François
   Thibault
19 Fuel ferry
20 Repeated
22 When mobsters battle
   over gun moll?
24 Draft receiver
25 Colombian city
26 In ___ (feeling the blahs)
27 Pyretic
28 Actor Gulager
29 Jazz critic Hentoff
30 Sweep
31 What there oughta be?
33 Father of the mystery
   story
34 Rum cake
35 Disburse (with "out")
36 W.V.T. Clark's formal
   affair?
41 Yours, in Tours
42 Station
43 They're on the lam
44 Kayo
45 Slacken
48 Incalculable times
49 Thai bills
50 Fetor
51 Card shark's sartorial
   no-no?
57 Corrida encouragement
58 Pitfall
59 Easing of tension
60 Computerized missiles?
62 Humbugged
65 Popular B.A. major
66 Ortega's others
67 Puzzling buffalo kin
68 Compass pts.
69 Scott's popular quartet
70 Nyet in Nuremberg
71 Tuscan red
73 Photog.'s letters
74 John ___ Lennon
76 Pods at times?
79 Inter ___
80 Burnt pigment
82 Abrupt
83 Admiral William
   Frederick
85 Keystone State founder
86 One way to bake potatoes
90 Breathing sound
91 Other
92 Shop by mail?
94 149, in old Ortia
97 Long Island park
98 But, to Brutus
99 Greenish blue
100 Beep
101 Lat. case
102 Respected ref.
103 Genetic letters
106 "I say!"
108 Ait, to Armando
109 Watering hole
111 Tropical reptile

114 Bard's forever
115 Current unit
116 Ideal
117 Iroquois foe
118 Kind of gasoline
119 Floods

DOWN

1 Anatolian capital
2 Private of comics
3 Entrance courts
4 Wee bairn
5 Novelist Morante
6 Put down
7 Cotton substitute
8 Father of a princesse
9 Foolhardy
10 In addition
11 Lat. gender
12 Quattro minus uno
13 Ariose olios
14 Sandy color
15 "Gotcha!"
16 Lesley-Anne just behind?
17 Tend to
18 Musical org.
21 Immures
23 Ferrigno's incredible role

28 Ovine hut
32 Sapiential, to the core
33 Meadow of France
34 Underlying
36 Negative opening
37 Lover of beauty
38 Lycée kin
39 Sheet
40 East of the choir
42 By
45 Composer Sessions
46 It's ESE of Kirksville
47 Change for thermal wear?
49 Nova precursor
52 "___ to Bountiful"
53 Former Italian President
54 Ibid. and op. cit.
55 Speedster Coleman
56 Hostile craft of the '40s
59 Angel
61 Parade VIP
63 Singer Lennox
64 Postpone
67 "___ not what your
   country . . ."
71 A Thomas
72 Play charades
75 Baby boys of Orense

77 "What though care killed
   ___ . . .": Shak.
78 Ruby's month
79 Canadian export
80 Function
81 Abstemious, in a way
84 Furry alien
86 Early Jewish order
87 Adjured
88 Valencia conqueror,
   El ___
89 Acted the fop
90 Associates
93 Withers
94 Keep
95 Inuit abodes
96 Pick up
100 Lacy loop
102 Camembert's department
103 Sinatra sleuth
104 Wine valley
105 Defrauded, with "out"
107 Dribble
110 Silkworm
111 Ankle-high shoe
112 Jacutinga, for one
113 Oenone's mount

WRITERS' CRAMP by Grace M. Gordon
This crafty constructor from Tappan, N.Y., has come up with a new twist that the literati will especially enjoy.

ACROSS

1 Bible bk.
4 Part of p.t.o.
10 Like some skirts
15 Hellman's attic contents
19 Type of dance or hold
20 Lilli or Arnold
21 A sister of Clio
22 Grocery item
23 Bruins star: 1967–76
24 WOMEN IN LOVE must sometimes eat BITTER LEMONS?
27 Fed. power agency
29 Tenth of a sen
30 War stat.
31 NW Papua-New Guinea port
32 Pronunciation mark
34 UNNATURAL CAUSES induced demise of DUBLINERS?
39 Speaker
40 River into the Elbe
41 Aran Islands language
42 "Cakes and ___": Maugham
45 Mystery novel bane
47 Wiener schnitzels
50 Mauna ___
51 "Fortune" founder
52 Portuguese title
53 Lower deck
55 Springy movement
56 Sound
58 Dig up by the roots
60 Creek
61 Betel palms
63 "___ for St. Cecilia's Day": Dryden
64 Bridal suite at THE HOTEL NEW HAMPSHIRE inspires PASSIONS OF THE MIND?
68 Open freight car
70 ___ et ubique (here and everywhere)
71 Progress
74 ADVENTURES IN THE SKIN TRADE cause DEATH IN VENICE?
79 Mohammedan high rank
80 Isthmus
82 Measure equaling 16.5 feet
83 Hyperventilate, e.g.
84 Sluggish
85 Stentorian
86 A day's march
88 Attack of a sort
89 "His enemies shall ___ the dust": Psalms 72:9
91 Pt. of 1 Down
92 Cut
94 Swamp tree
97 Abstinent, in a way
98 Graf ___
100 Softly, in music
102 Isaac's mother
103 THE LAST LEAF of autumn fell on BLACK SPRING?
106 Vacuous
107 Sofa
110 Of age: Lat. abbr.
111 Free electron
113 Six, to Dante
114 BEN HUR tricked Messala into an ANGLE OF REPOSE?
120 Squeal
122 "Celeste Aida," e.g.
123 Number of drams per ounce
124 Cleave
125 Kind of pkg.
126 Stylish
127 Some legislative bodies
128 City on the Don
129 Still

DOWN

1 DDE terrain
2 Depict
3 ANTHONY ADVERSE works at the PENTAGON?
4 Not c.o.d.
5 "Wizard of Oz" co-star
6 Oval
7 Kitty of "Gunsmoke"
8 Emulate Dorcas
9 Transgress
10 Islamic spirit
11 Killer whales
12 "Norma ___"
13 Flight sched. entry
14 Some Bibles
15 Rich cake
16 Olive genus
17 Shrill cry
18 Single
25 Writer Robert ___ Sherwood
26 Paella ingredient
28 Columbus or Madison, e.g.
32 M.I.T. deg.
33 Ambler or Hoffer
35 "I, Claudius" star
36 Styptic agent
37 Air traveler's distress
38 Approximately
*42 THE COLOR PURPLE is favored by THE MOVIEGOER?
43 "Damn Yankees" girl
44 Greasy spoon sign
46 Lonely
48 Roman cuirass
49 Hibernia
52 Pester constantly for payment
54 In an obvious way
55 Advance
56 Razorback
57 Fuss
59 " . . . it is better to marry ___ to burn": I Corinthians 7:9
62 Horse color
64 Pretty, in Provence
65 Kind of scholar
66 Enthusiasm or pep
67 ___ States: Burmese province
69 Pair
72 Back in time
73 Swerve
75 Kind of bullet
76 Arizona Amerind
77 Helix
78 Gym furnishing
80 Double-runner
81 Sight-see
84 Skedaddles
87 ___ Shen, Chinese poet: 715–770
88 Frustrate
90 ___ dixit
93 Sand bars
94 Headpiece for Diana
95 Pall
96 Diffident
98 Mets' turf
99 Skinned
101 Stable sounds
103 English dramatist: 1652–85 ("Venice Preserved")
104 Courageous or Intrepid, e.g.
105 Runs into
107 Louver
108 Architect Saarinen
109 Eng or Chang
112 Emperor in "Quo Vadis?"
115 Half of CIV
116 Gerontologist's concern
117 Pavement material, sometimes
118 Old Tokyo
119 Increase (with "up")
121 Explosive substance

80

GEOGRAPHY LESSON by Kenneth Haxton
Ken would like to dedicate this one to Mercury, god of thermometers.

ACROSS

1 Reality
5 Broad-topped ridge
9 Broom
14 Fraud
18 Forest buffalo
19 "I will ___ and go now": Yeats
21 Actor in a crowd
22 Five meters
23 Town in Scotland
25 Town in Newfoundland
27 Finis
28 Chew the fat
29 Vast expanse
31 Lounged
32 Nostrils
34 Ermine in summer
35 Cooked in butter
37 English china
39 Ziegfeld's Anna
40 Realms
43 "The Charterhouse of ___": Stendhal
44 Parisian harp inventor
46 Ibert's jackass
47 Woollcott or Benchley
48 Guessed the value
50 Repeating
54 Brouhaha
55 Eisenhower's command
56 Irish fairy folk
57 English river
58 To breathe with difficulty, in Nantes
60 Han or Sung
63 Shade of blue
64 Use a clotheshorse
65 Castle in W Switzerland
68 Cove of S Alaska
70 Zone
73 "Gigi" composer
75 Bohemian ballroom dances
79 Saw-toothed
80 "___ Crooked Ship," Kovacs film
81 Geometric term
83 Turku
84 Schubert-Goethe king
85 "The Backward Son" novelist
87 Roscoe Ates, e.g.
90 Turf
91 Northern Thai
92 Merseyside mom
94 Sea-ear
95 Some caterpillars
98 Opens, in Barcelona
99 Oneness
100 Deep-bodied herrings
101 Aussie cockatoo
102 Grow tardy
104 Painter Durand
106 Scale man
107 Thousand grams
108 Irish sweetheart
111 Arkansas resort
114 Town in Wilts, England
117 Isle
118 Knockwurst go-with
119 Chip off the old block
120 Embassy

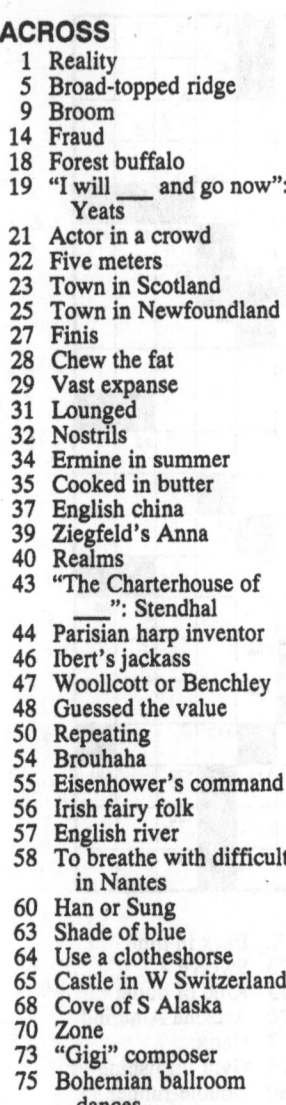

121 Numerous
122 Sawfly saw
123 Being
124 Pantry pests

DOWN

1 Front
2 World's most prolific writer
3 Town in Essex, England
4 Small child
5 Woodworking machine
6 Fragrant root
7 Bearing
8 Hard-rock links
9 Decapitate
10 Letter of excardination
11 Ollie's sidekick
12 Scrap for Sandy
13 ___-jongg
14 Pilchard relatives
15 Mountains of Germany
16 Succulent plant
17 Repair
20 Ham
24 Screech
26 Debussy's "La Damoiselle ___"

30 Town in E Germany
33 African gazelle
34 Spirit
35 Upper house of France
36 Church corner
37 Dispatch
38 Pale
40 Bearded grass
41 Duck down
42 Fib
44 Denatured alcohol
45 Arikara
49 On the move
51 White flag
52 Saarinen
53 Chord
59 Prefix for Dravidian
61 Treads the boards
62 Brogans
63 Perform extreme unction: Archaic
64 Across ship
66 Campo cousins
67 Egg-shaped
69 Gloomy
70 "For all the land that thou ___": Gen.
71 Slip

72 Town in Avon, England
74 Town N of Cape Town
76 Town in Warwickshire
77 As red as ___
78 Contrite
80 Windy City tower
81 Gores as a bull, in Chile
82 Address abbr.
86 Walk laboriously
88 Sheepskin
89 Osprey kin
93 Quiver contents
96 Self-important
97 Cover at Fenway
98 Awn
101 Soothsayer
102 Wheels for wheels
103 Set in a row
104 Psst relative
105 Versatile bean
106 Snarl
107 Golfer Tschetter
109 Balance
110 Some are fine
112 Small stones
113 Choler
115 CATV award
116 Évian, for one

81

ANAGRAMMATIC DOZEN by Lawrence M. Rheingold
From Long Island arrives this challenger featuring logographs (yes, there is such a word) by Larry.

ACROSS

1 Undeclared
6 Bucks
11 Goosefoot
18 Tillable land
19 Baths of Suomi
20 Cuddles
21 It's KEYNES ART MOM
23 Cherub
24 JFK Library designer
25 Removes dowel pins
26 Heavens: Comb. form
27 Tenth of a sen
28 Specter
31 We're URGING ARTIST
   to tune it
34 Eucharist dish
36 Emulate MC Lyte
39 Use a hand shuttle
40 Bursa
41 Vigilant in Vichy
43 Plexuses
46 Depression
49 Former Irani ruler
52 ROB SPACER PAN for
   copiers
54 R&D area
56 Cowboy or Indian
57 Within: Comb. form
58 Partner of pinion
60 Perplexity
62 Four-in-hand fabric
65 Publisher Reid
68 Intention
70 Way to go
71 A DOWEL ROY made
   of it
74 TRAIN MOLE to be a
   circus star
77 Norse goddess of love
78 Four seasons in Valencia
80 Ritchie Valens hit
81 It's sigmoid
82 Myrrh makes it
85 Way off yonder
87 Lough in Fermanagh
90 Classic leader
91 Solution
92 FANCY PELT RIG in
   Arabia
98 Mrs. Al Jolson
100 Two-year-old sheep
102 "The Master Builder"
    playwright
103 Astral
104 Japanese celery
106 In flight, briefly
108 Cartoonist Gardner
110 Be penitent
111 Lizard hides under a
    GOOD DARK MOON
117 Lively dance
119 Not a rural area,
    informally
120 Russian river
121 Praises in Prestwick
124 Crumb
127 Southern Pacific, e.g.
129 NOW DO HEROES in
    Troy
132 Sea goby
133 Caret notation
134 Goddess of the chase
135 Legislatures
136 Travelers
137 Friend of Freud

DOWN

1 Pack down
2 Indonesian isles
3 Container used in TIN
   SCARE
4 Food fish
5 Firth north of Forth
6 Nitpick
7 Perry of TV
8 "White and hairless as
   ___": Herrick
9 Island off Foochow
10 Draft agcy.
11 Philippine island
12 German namesakes of
   Copland
13 Dormice
14 Dir. from Utica to L.I.
15 A feather in SUCH RIPE
   MOLT
16 Admit
17 "A good manner for ___":
   Shak.
19 More rational
20 Ice weights?
22 Quaggy ground
26 Austin col.
29 Savory plant in Savoy
30 Composer Bruckner
32 Source of the Mississippi
33 Promontory
34 Moccasin
35 ___ julienne
37 Altar on high
38 Vitality
42 Subsidize
44 Mackerel gull
45 Chemist Remsen
47 Ortler or Todi
48 Ganoid fish
50 Crested ridges
51 Strawberry clouts
53 Kind of stick
55 Industrial gem
59 Gram or cycle head
61 Scarf
62 Purify
63 Bread maker
64 LUMP INCA BORE long
   before Pizarro
66 EMS report entry
67 Best in "Intermezzo"
69 Mrs. Gump
72 Lixivium
73 Reb's adversary
75 It's a thou
76 Crack agents?
79 In the ___ (likely to
   happen)
80 Volsteaders
83 Clique
84 Uvea site
86 Mass vestment
88 Port of Brazil
89 Sister of Euterpe
93 Ending for bombard
94 Miami-D.C. direction
95 Lawyer RAPS LOOP hole
96 Littoral flier
97 Guy on board
99 Old Tokyo
101 Deep red stone
105 Funny group on Wall
    Street?
107 Bighorn sound
109 Means
111 Iraqi minority
112 "___ Ben Jonson"
113 Pertaining to Dorsets
114 Partakes
115 Maine town
116 Springe
118 Rowan
122 River of Germany
123 E Indian weights
125 Skater Novotny
126 Dynast
128 NYC airport
129 Peruke
130 Zenana cubicle
131 Disencumber

82

An interesting stepquote taken from *The Prick of Noon*, written by 7 Across.

ACROSS

1 **Beginning of a Stepquote**
7 Last name of Stepquote author
14 First name of Stepquote author
19 Straighten
20 Bracelet
22 Remove
23 Actress Rosemary
24 212 or 213
25 Detachments
26 Irish sweetheart
27 Serum in Sicily
29 Taller
31 Little, in Lille
32 Ailments
34 **Stepquote: Part III**
37 Crave
38 Appear
39 White and Blue rivers
41 Close again
43 "Fair ___ had my soul": Wordsworth
45 Motioned
47 Alien transports
49 Snicker follower
50 Disagreement
51 Avoids
53 Predicament
57 Split
60 Emends
62 Playwright William's relatives
63 Reclined
64 Asian sultanate
66 Poet Sara's relatives
68 Scrap
69 One on the move
70 Radiator sound
72 Poker term
73 Miss. neighbor
74 NOW objective
77 "God Knows" novelist
79 Quarry
80 Actress Verdugo
81 Marine passageways
83 Houston athletes
85 Distinction
87 Aircraft guidance system
88 Sculptor Huntington
89 Appear
91 Mary ___ Lincoln
92 Autograph sessions
96 Part of A.M.
100 Dives
102 Grunt
103 Olympian hawk
104 French artist Antoine Jean
106 **Stepquote: Part V**
108 Headliner
109 Prankster
110 Japanese religion
112 "A Passage to India" heroine
114 Soul in Soissons
115 Vassal
117 "Cast ___ on life . . .": W. B. Yeats
120 Black Sea port
122 Pass
123 Joiner of sorts
124 Eskimo of films
125 Greek letter
126 Priestesses of Bacchus
127 **End of Stepquote**

DOWN

1 Jamming
2 Cover
3 Withdraws
4 Scots snow
5 Drones
6 **Stepquote: Part II**
7 Overshadowed
8 Mistakes
9 Contend
10 Pretoria loc.
11 "The Seven Year ___"
12 Remove in law
13 Marsh plants
14 French fear
15 Sea bird
16 Formosa's capital
17 Favor
18 Employment summary
21 Sounds of laughter
28 Heron
30 Delightful places
33 Begins
35 Hors d'___
36 **Stepquote: Part IV**
38 Breastbones
40 Eats
42 Mine find
44 Rule
46 Stallone roles
48 Faction
51 Cosmic cycle
52 Snatches
54 Dazzling
55 Bobby
56 Attempts
57 Pokier
58 Actress Landis
59 Underworld figures
60 Marie and Pierre
61 Lucid
65 Diminutive noun suffixes
67 Bold
69 Chewed
71 Legislator in Spain
75 Greek union
76 Thai money
78 Thriller author Deighton
79 Kind of Indians
82 "A Girl Like I" author
84 Hostels
86 Whinny
88 French river
90 Tallchief and Callas
92 Earth movers
93 Words refusing payment
94 ___ grains? (weighty question)
95 Speeds
96 Posted
97 Stoat
98 Rescind
99 Cpl. or Sgt.
101 Approved
105 Robe for Calpurnia
107 **Stepquote: Part VI**
110 Bristle
111 Ye ___ shoppe
113 Esau's wife
116 Universal time: Abbr.
118 Retreat
119 Epoch
121 Wine combiner

83

COIN COLLECTION by Rosalind Pavane

Hint: When Rosalind bakes, she makes short cakes—and she's very tight with money.

ACROSS

1 Lacking vitality
7 "Enigma Variations" composer
12 Misfit of myth (and of this puzzle)
19 Texas town
20 Sweetie pie
21 Doctor in a clinic
22 Joseph Wambaugh novel
24 Of the heart
25 Coastline city
26 Attention-getting sound
28 Great tennis serve
29 Insult
33 This is 506 to 12 Down
34 Money
38 Leander, to Hero
40 Song from "A Chorus Line"
42 Untrue
43 Hamlet and Borge
44 Devoted beau
46 Congeal
48 "Wild Bill" Donovan's org.
49 Showed apathy
50 ___ Gogh, French artist
52 Muscle spasm
54 City in Florida
56 Fable author
58 El ___, Texas
60 Caviar
61 Edge
64 Suspend
67 Sicilian city
69 Cape ___, Senegal
71 English porcelain
73 Revoke, in law
75 Table decor
77 Hundredfold
78 Jiu ___, a martial art
79 Quick
80 Upward slopes
82 Emit fumes
83 "___ De-lovely"
84 In the, in Italy
86 Bunco is one
88 Coins of France
90 Approximately, in dates
92 Style of English furniture
94 Dye or perfume ingredient
98 Flubs it
100 Ethiopian prince
102 Canine
104 Coarsely textured
105 Nuclear physicist
106 Rough
108 Pixie
110 Asp
111 Mark Twain book
114 Matterhorn
116 These women: Sp.
117 Wedding-announcement word
118 "My Girl ___," Sam Wanamaker film
119 Saved
122 In a more affected manner
125 David McClintick book of 1982

131 Mystery writer Lillian de ___
132 Equipped (with "up")
133 Not singular
134 Chosen
135 Pried
136 Native of San'a

DOWN

1 Ht.
2 Slangy negative
3 Part of familiar palindrome
4 Chess pieces
5 March date
6 Intimidated
7 Architect Saarinen
8 Scottish landowner
9 FDR's alma mater
10 One, to 8 Down
11 Seasons again
12 Master of Latin prose
13 Hindu land grants
14 Nutrition: Abbr.
15 Kennedy or Danson
16 "___ auf Naxos," Richard Strauss opera
17 Not stressed
18 Play time, at school
20 Using trickery
23 Coin of Mexico
27 Swedish actress, Signe ___

29 Bulgar
30 City in Lombardy or California
31 Stratford's river
32 Commission rates
35 Glance: Colloq.
36 Teenager
37 Hub of wine region in California
39 Dream, in Dijon
41 Scream in a comic strip
45 Demolish a Soho flat
47 Facial feature
49 ___ Zedong
51 Off the axis
53 "Feliz ___," amigo's Yuletide greeting
55 Lunar shaped
57 Breath: Comb. form
59 Killer whale
61 Lariat
62 Inactive
63 Submissive
64 Pilgrimage to Mecca
65 Colliery entrance
66 Seines
68 Works of a French sculptor-painter-poet
70 Landing approach
72 Plant with yellow flowers
74 Very generous
76 Painter of "Guernica"
81 Atmospheric problem

85 Speaker's hesitations
87 Unhinged
89 Auricular parts
90 Lake in Italy
91 Semites
93 One of Curly's brothers
95 Andalusian aunts
96 Composer of "My Way"
97 Cereal grasses
98 "Hap" Arnold, for one
99 Jazzman Coleman
101 Bring into court
103 Candied
105 Coda
106 Word with long or light
107 ___ nails
109 Change
112 Cubic meter
113 Inventor of farm equipment
115 Spirited
120 Perfumed
121 Mete
123 Coll. class
124 N.Y. subway system
126 Modernist
127 Total
128 Actress Mary of England
129 Sped
130 Yale student

METAPHORICAL MENU by Warren Reich
If you're counting calories we highly recommend this chef's salad below. It's
low in cholesterol and definitely not fattening.

ACROSS

1 It springs eternal
5 Coagulate
9 Gunner's need
13 Wealth: Comb. form
17 Steppes wind
18 Fortify anew
20 Whiskey drink
21 Like mountain air
22 DESSERT
24 DESSERT
26 Lopes
27 Fresh in France
29 Early Greek
30 Donkeys and mules
31 Airships
32 Worthless
33 Luigi's thirst
34 Former Attorney General
35 Three-time Wimbledon
    winner
37 APPETIZER
40 Archetypically
44 Reuters offering
47 Nigerian city
48 ___ carte
50 Town near Honolulu
51 Bat wood
52 FRUIT
59 Operate
60 Recondite
62 Hoods
63 VCR users
65 Breather
66 Succotash ingredients
67 Crocus
68 Slum
70 End
71 Hermit's sine qua non
75 Pep rally sound
76 ENTRÉE
79 Bamboozle
80 Half the alphabet
82 Paydirt
83 Negative correlative
84 ___ out (got by)
85 Vetoed
88 FRUIT
94 Originates
96 Spy, in Stuttgart
97 Kitty chip
99 Venezuelan Indians
102 Tempest locale?
104 Academic finery
107 State of normlessness
108 Map within a map
109 Spartan governor
110 FRUIT
112 FRUIT
115 Classical theaters
116 American suffragist
117 Indian seaport
118 Tiny circus performers
119 Monstrous lake?
120 Gaelic
121 Posted
122 Semester

DOWN

1 What Alf isn't
2 Chimps' relatives
3 Celebrants
4 ___ cordiale
5 Interbreed
6 Papal name
7 ___ leaf cluster
8 Frivolous one
9 "'There was ___,' quoth
    he": Coleridge
10 Frothy dessert
11 It's the word at times
12 Emulated Gagarin
13 Before birth
14 ___ lazuli
15 Dickens's Heep
16 Bopper preceder
17 MIT degree
19 Artist Caravaggio's real
    name
23 Doctrine
25 "Congo Crossing" star
28 Assenting word
31 Gascon headgear
34 Corpsman
36 Perfume holder

38 Sun: Comb. form
39 Chafes
41 ENTRÉE
42 Mythomane
43 Hankerings
44 Ayr negative
45 Feminine suffix
46 ENTRÉE
49 CD predecessors
52 Hides
53 Lower deck
54 Hockey no-no
55 Kind of relief
56 Overflowing
57 Functional
58 San Raphael's county
61 Relative of fie
64 Remove stones
66 Siegfried and
    Mannerheim
68 Dad's mom
69 Anathema
70 Conifer
71 Disdain
72 Gumbo
73 Female goat

74 He might be tight
77 Cycled
78 Fort Knox holding
81 Percussion instruments
84 Medieval dance
86 Leg bone
87 Extract
89 She-bears, to Conchita
90 Certain teeth
91 Unrestrained
92 Song of praise
93 Implant
95 Sandpipers
98 Escapee
99 "___ a Hot Tin Roof"
100 Battery terminal
101 Ratlines
103 Maternally related
104 Scarlett's love
105 Muezzin's religion
106 Sweetsop
111 Swiss river
113 Uno, due, ___
114 Almond

COWBOY FLICKS* by Bette Sue Cohen
Bette Sue believes that a puzzle with a western theme should have wide open spaces—hence, the asterisks.

ACROSS

1 Obtains
5 Actor in "Ghostbusters"
10 Shul leader
15 Kind of appeal
19 Word with back or head
20 Fill with joy
21 "... what ___ in the papers": Will Rogers
22 Olympic queen
23 *
25 *
27 Like a bird
28 "They Died with ___ Boots On"
30 Arterial trunk
31 Rich soil
32 ___ out (discontinue)
33 Notch
34 Concur
37 Crown
38 "And the stately ___ on": Tennyson
41 Meager
42 *
44 Actress Merkel
46 Bobs gently
47 Become weary
48 Duration
49 Energy
50 Actor Byrnes
51 *
55 Michael Caine role: 1966
56 Richard Burton et al.
58 Fed the kitty
59 ___ de lune
60 Arabian chieftain
61 Stevens of 96 Across
62 Throw
63 Word after home or road
64 Bend in prayer
65 "I am holier ___": Isa. 65:5
68 Jeweler's unit
69 *
71 Egyptian king, briefly
72 ___ Khayyám
73 A wife of Henry VIII
74 "The ___ Breed," 1966 film
75 Penny
76 Cowboy Mix
77 *
81 Molière's forte
82 Attaches
84 "Went to sea in ___": Anon.
85 Fireman, often
86 Crazy: Var.
87 Ruffled border
88 Coagulates
89 Clifton Webb role in "Stars and Stripes Forever"
91 Confronted
92 "One ___ to persuade ...": Plato
96 *
98 *
100 "The King ___"
101 Weird
102 Puts the whammy on
103 Soon
104 "___ Wolf," 1985 film
105 Exhaust
106 "___ Nous," 1983 French film
107 River to the Laptev Sea

DOWN

1 Spar
2 Environmental sci.
3 Done, for short
4 The Mormons in 1847, e.g.
5 State again
6 Fireman's warning
7 Famed owner of a department store
8 Irish ancestor
9 Churns, as if boiling
10 ___ the occasion (meets a challenge)
11 Bandleader Shaw
12 Kind of hug
13 Catch
14 Croce's school of thought
15 Summer wear
16 Straight
17 Film starring Richard Harris: 1977
18 Exclamation from Scrooge
24 Make amends
26 Appropriate: Hyph.
29 Jumble
32 Primp
33 Bake eggs
34 As good ___
35 British potter: 1754–1827
36 *
37 Time: Comb. form
38 Bayard or Grani
39 *
40 Walking ___ (happy)
42 "Save the ___," 1973 film
43 Mink's relative
45 Mimic
47 Like Kate, in the end
49 Incline
51 Spaghetti component
52 Painter of "The Balcony"
53 "___ and the Badman," 1946 film
54 Inscribed pillar
55 Skirt style
57 Sully
59 Stuck; clung; adhered
61 Inward: Prefix
62 What malingerers do
63 Mead's "Coming of Age in ___"
64 Miniature racers
65 Setline
66 Pound part
67 Say
68 Barracks bed
69 Fairway sight
70 Speak slowly
73 George Sand and George Eliot, e.g.
75 Road to Key West
77 Utilize again
78 What the wooden soldiers did
79 Nichols' hero
80 "___ Dream," book by Barbara Taylor Bradford
81 Christie's "Dead Man's ___"
83 Connect to a service outlet
85 Corrupt
87 Character in "Oliver Twist"
88 Dancer/choreographer Champion
89 Rational
90 Wave: Fr.
91 "___ Down Below," 1957 film
92 Teller's call
93 Singer Horne
94 "... the Bird ___ the Wing": Fitzgerald
95 Spirit lamp
96 Stetson
97 With it, in the forties
99 Plymouth Rock, e.g.

86

Harold hopes his jestful jingles will give zestful tingles.

ACROSS

1 Detroit products
5 Sect: Ital.
10 Soiree
14 News summary
19 Woodwind
20 Flub
21 Nichols' hero
22 Rub out
23 Harass Ezra?
25 Causes George to do an about-face?
27 Beat on the market
28 Diamond apparel
30 Clergyman's wear
31 Barren
32 One Day?
33 Football linemen
34 They, to Pierre
35 Canary's cousin
36 Strings' stronger cousins
37 Place for a boutonniere
40 Rescues Peter?
42 Scrooge's favorite word
45 "Woe is me!"
46 Tijuana bull
47 War god
48 Runner on Capitol Hill
49 "L.A. Law" star
50 Coaches Claude?
54 Snake
55 Loses all hope
57 Tardy ___ (Oliver the Late)
58 "Little Miss ___" (Matthau film)
59 Increases the price
60 A god or goddess: Latin
61 Desires
62 Conquered Matterhorn
64 New ___, IL
65 Barrie's "The Little ___"
68 Stratum
69 Discourages Hayley?
71 Actress Gardner
72 Like good wine
73 Billiards sticks
74 At the very least
75 Glaswegian
76 Referendum vote
77 Rush Don?
81 Fountain drinks
82 Prepared apples for baking
83 Vicinities
84 Thread: Comb. form
85 Cooked the potatoes again
88 Full of sauce
89 Straw boss
93 Take into custody
94 Vex
95 Material resting on the waves: Var.
96 Entertain Blanche?
98 Entices Vera?
100 Kind of party
101 Short distance
102 ___ clover (legume)
103 Suffix with establish
104 Church official
105 Gold Coast tongue
106 Boaters' problems
107 Roadhouse sign

DOWN

1 Silver salmon
2 Circa
3 ___ 66
4 Guards
5 Calyx parts
6 Rust
7 Faithful; loyal
8 Scads
9 Town in Oklahoma
10 Quilt stuffing
11 Touches upon
12 Letter opener
13 Rhode Island Red
14 Fastens again
15 Bursts
16 "___ diem!"
17 "Lou Grant" star
18 Gnats, e.g.
24 Cotton fabric
26 Metric units
29 Reddish-blue
32 English county
33 Areas for marinas
35 Hindu dresses
36 Barker, e.g.
37 "Shane" star
38 Nautical word
39 Compensates Helen?
40 Kites
41 Sorties
42 Sponsor Robert?
43 American author (1909–1955)
44 Bonn title
46 Attempted
48 Sections
50 Donee
51 Colleague of 36 Down
52 Loose thread
53 Old World plants
54 Rajahs' mates
56 Heaped
58 Bold; resolute
60 Shasta or gerbera
61 Nilly's partner
62 Homophone for sleigh
63 Canary's confines
64 Piece of pottery: Var.
65 Aping avians
66 Cry at an Athenian orgy
67 "Peanuts" expletive
69 Preserved the beef
70 Vicious eel
73 Surgical tools
75 At an indefinite future day
77 Crane, e.g.
78 Indic language
79 "Battle Cry" author
80 Urban ___
81 Indonesian island
82 Wrinkle
84 Parts of springes
85 "Bring the ___ primrose . . ." (Milton)
86 Little Lord Fauntleroy
87 He wrote about the ego and the id
88 Hardwood
89 Spot
90 Cape ___, Greece
91 Ten percenter
92 Tree houses?
94 Wallet items
95 "Go ___ kite!"
97 Humor
99 ___-de-France

ALL-AMERICAN LINE-UP   by Mary D. Brown
One of our Bay Staters challenges you to a word-play scrimmage.

ACROSS

1 It can be hot
4 Irritated; grated
10 Cause of trysts
16 She was "sweet as apple cider"
19 Mischievous Olympian
20 Imperial sovereignty
21 A food fish
22 Descriptive of some sisters
23 Remick or Grant
24 New York attorney?
26 Tennis term
27 Paints the town red
29 Fixes boat leaks
30 Movie house
32 "Meadows trim with daisies ___": Milton
33 Like some fertilizers
34 Graceful breed of steeds
35 Intense light beams
38 Division word
39 Christens anew
43 Actress much admired by Sherlock Holmes
44 Declare
46 French revolutionary leader
48 Spanish cheer
49 Where the kine form lines
50 Crew
51 River in China
52 Footnote abbr.
53 Kelep
54 Concord 1st grades?
57 Fastener or rule
58 Garfield, for one
59 Sometimes these are sown wild
60 " . . . dark ___ the blaze of noon": Milton
61 Person in a cage
62 Souvenir from Baton Rouge?
67 Rears
69 ___ pieces (get upset)
70 Cuckoopint plant
71 FDR follower
74 Lets up
75 Pensacola piano?
78 An Amerind
79 Invalid
80 Across: Prefix
81 Second in Greece
82 Gov't agent: Hyph.
83 Unclose (to a poet)
84 Shabby
85 World-weary
87 "___ but for the grace of God . . . "
88 Give the lawn another drink
90 Turns right
91 Persian pavilions
92 Legal agreement
93 Furnace
94 End of a loafer
95 Santa's need
98 Parisian potato, pomme de ___
99 Edged

103 Partner of bagels
104 Lansing lush?
107 Unity
108 Black cuckoo
109 Esoteric
110 Golf term
111 Tiresome noise
112 Chanced upon
113 Sandpipers
114 Strip of plaster
115 Famed painter of birds

DOWN

1 Soapstone
2 Willow
3 Nobleman
4 Demand
5 Diverts
6 It has its limits
7 Some desserts
8 Suffix for cardinal points
9 Discourse
10 Spacecraft
11 Obtained by chance
12 Sally Rand's "costume"
13 Three-toed sloths
14 Very popular dessert
15 Dependent
16 Martha's Vineyard is one
17 Judgment Day
18 Biblical title for God (Mark 14:36)

25 Bill of fare
28 Unseals
31 Larry Bird's org.
33 Haven for sun lovers
34 Sharp ridge in moldings
35 Spring-flowering shrub
36 Market Square or Omni
37 A turn in Washington?
40 Alabama abodes?
41 Abridge
42 Passover feast
44 Clans
45 Foot bones
46 California tribe
47 This equals 1076.44 square feet
50 Massenet opera
51 Perch for a camera
52 Evils
54 Some are common; some are proper
55 Estate homes
56 Valued violin
57 Stitches
61 Arborvitae
63 City south of Moscow
64 Emotion at Golgotha
65 Ransacks
66 Home of King Minos
67 Spanish gentleman
68 Popular shade for hosiery
72 Naked preceder

73 Musical qualities
75 Well-known Jacques of song
76 Chap
77 Humble
80 Modern wear
82 Pin providing a fulcrum for an oar
84 Blotches; blots; blemishes
85 Former Yankee player or manager
86 Tables on a map
87 Tinted in the "now" mode
89 French friend
90 Canyons
91 Miss Piggy's name for her beloved Frog
93 Pretense
94 Man about Marseilles
95 Bridge player's thrill
96 One and only
97 This way out
98 "Easier said ___ done"
99 Jefferson's vice president
100 Traveled by horse
101 Camelot lady
102 Sand hill in Great Britain
105 Caesar's two hundred plus one
106 TV series

88 TUBE TEST by Cathy Millhauser
This clever puzzle has won another Margaret Award for our upstate New Yorker.

ACROSS

1 "Untrue!"
6 Fly-by-night?
9 Rolaids' rival
13 He makes a bundle
18 An anesthetic
19 Visually blah
21 Blind part
22 Head of the clast?
23 Omni, e.g.
24 Take-out food?
25 Dame ___ Neagle
26 Crow
27 Graft
29 Hairdressers' program?
32 Perry's creator
33 Munich Mr.
34 Florentine farewell
35 Ave. crossers
36 "___ Be Hard" (song from "Hair")
38 Beat it
40 Caesar, for one
42 Lawyer, for short
43 Yuletide drink
45 Turkish chief
47 Popular game items
51 Mortgage broker's program?
55 Dementia
56 Heavenly way to walk
57 Rhine tributary
58 Sans threads
60 Yarn
61 Saddle part
63 Use a divining rod
66 Hellenic H
68 Gamboling place
69 Cardiac surgeon's program (with "The")
74 Emulate Aladdin
77 Mason or Leyden
78 "Able was ___ . . ."
79 Dream enders, often
83 List shortener
85 Pre-pre-college test
87 Hill dweller
89 Common epithet
90 A Redgrave
93 Editor's program?
97 Close-fitting dress
98 Privy to
99 Chaney or Nol
100 Actor Ayres
101 Savoir ___ (tact)
104 Attempt
106 Narrow bands of leather
109 Chinese chairman of yore
112 Writer Zane
113 ___ out a living (made do)
115 Not well done
116 Cobbler's program?
120 Former Ford
123 Sicily neighbor
124 ". . . unto us ___ is given" (Isa. 9:6)
125 It's a stele
127 Frolic
128 Sect suffix
129 Primer pooch
130 Ms. Lamarr
131 Grover's veep
132 Refine metal
133 ___ Park, FDR birthplace
134 Compass pt.
135 It's on the Aire

DOWN

1 Tide type
2 Ortega's other woman
3 Cheerleaders' program?
4 Men of La Mancha
5 By mouth
6 Uneven, in a way
7 Ire
8 Shaping tools
9 Star anagram
10 Radius' partner
11 Crazed types' program?
12 Sports sites
13 Stock exchange nickname
14 Human rights org.
15 Nutty birds
16 Make into law
17 Family of the author of "Our Gang"
20 Party clean-up find
28 Prudential competitor
30 Fort ___, North Carolina
31 Conference site: 1945
36 Prefix meaning "people"
37 Eugene O'Neill's daughter
39 Smokey ___
41 Force
42 On
44 Teachers, often
46 Ex-coach Parseghian
48 Animal rightsist's eschewal
49 Man or Wight
50 In the Red?
52 Arm
53 Nabisco favorite
54 ". . . pretty maids all in ___"
55 Seaver and Agee in 1969
59 Like rods and cones
62 JFK successor
64 Bleaches
65 "Get it?"
67 "Got it!"
70 California wine region
71 Pile of sheets
72 Russian saint
73 Mr. Cleaver
74 Guns the engine
75 The Beehive State
76 Nemesis
80 Fishermen's program?
81 Stags
82 Pet
84 Sheet
86 Subject of "The Greatest"
88 Some victories of 86 Down
91 Motionless
92 T, e.g.
94 Indian symbol
95 Eely
96 ___ nous
102 Go over
103 Ophthalmologist's program?
105 Beaux mates
107 Imp
108 Word with penny
109 Cass Elliot and Michelle Phillips
110 "Happiness is ___ puppy"
111 Hardy nickname
114 Twosomes
117 Like this: Abbr.
118 Grub
119 Word with penny
121 Do "Time"
122 Speaker of baseball fame
126 "That's all, folks!"

89

NAME MAULING by Tom Allen

Tom tells us that his next opus will feature Donald Tramp, Alan Altar, Goldie Horn, Robert Gulp, and Joe Garage-in-Nola. We can hardly wait!

ACROSS

1 Dovish
8 Summary
13 Model planes' adornments
19 Type of triangle
20 Straighten
21 Self-serve diner
22 Buccaneer broadcaster?
24 Act as a scout
25 River's course, perhaps
26 Fast-lane user
27 Louvre, e.g.
29 Epigram
30 Nomad's home
31 Well-known legal org.
33 Gracie Allen, alternatively
35 Kyushu cutie
39 Spill the beans
42 ___ Lanka
43 Middle of some plays
44 Crayola concern
45 Cobbler's instrument
47 Greek wheeler-dealer?
51 Carmelite Saint
53 Spinning motion, in billiards
55 Raisa's hubby
56 "Keep the ___ burning . . ."
58 Waterfall
59 Laborers on the Volga
61 Discharge
62 Miniseries shot
64 Trouble
65 100 sq. m.
68 Heisting heartthrob?
71 Westheimer topic
72 Hamlet's was bare
74 Society leeches
75 Yemenis
77 Provides evidence
79 In favor of
80 Dyed-in-the-wool
84 ___ Tower, Chicago skyscraper
85 Tending toward
88 Cargo plane
89 Throws a party
90 Memorable Brynner
91 Schwarzenegger part
93 Kuwaiti currency
94 Rooftop fixture
96 Boy from Boise
98 ___ City in "Paint Your Wagon"
99 Canadian issue
103 Soda meas.
104 Pluck
106 Covers a cake
107 Dry beer
109 Tawdry, as a dive
110 2, of 6 and 10: Abbr.
113 Moves toward like a chickadee
115 Literary larcenist?
120 Eggheads' orders?
121 Nantes decree
122 Gemu Gefa native

123 To sit, in 17 Down
124 Link
125 Gray igneous rock

DOWN

1 U.S. Open tennis champ: 1968
2 Pvts.' bosses
3 Child's choice marbles
4 Dockers' org.
5 Who, in Hamburg
6 The ill-fated ___ Doria
7 Satellite's task, for short
8 Recherché
9 Quintet in "La La, Lucille"
10 Dept. using moles
11 A "20 Questions" option
12 Andean nation
13 Coercion
14 Tours summer
15 Panza's parolee?
16 Affair
17 Livy's tongue
18 Stairway
21 Mime
23 One-up one
28 Mergansers
30 Extorting explorer?
31 Where the Bard bathed
32 Plagiarizing playwright?
34 Beautiful bandit?
35 Goliath's home town
36 Canyon call
37 Shopper's purchase
38 Begat
40 ___ du Salut
41 Made a profit
44 Mediterranean fruit
46 Fullback's neighbor: Abbr.
48 La Douce, and namesakes
49 Pinguid
50 Big Apple phone co.
52 De Beauvoir or Signoret
54 Citrus trees
57 Recedes
60 Arrow poison
62 Sing a lullaby
63 The twinkling ___ eye
65 Shame
66 Place to battle cattle
67 Icelandic tales
69 Embrace
70 Harmonium
73 Cattle thief from Springfield, Mass.
76 College protest

78 Informant
80 Hebrides island
81 Darling dog
82 Physical
83 Urgent
86 Penitent
87 Mechanic's need
92 Show backer
95 Speak at length
97 Erode
98 Thrice thrice twice five
99 Antics
100 Part of Caesar's homecoming phrase
101 Withered
102 Mare's fare
105 Work for actors
108 Garden of delight
109 Jersey jumpers
110 Pope (440–61)
111 Lieut.'s superior
112 Hie away
114 Rev.'s talk
116 Veto
117 Certain hosp. area
118 "___ Loves You": Beatles song
119 Sn

90

ACROSS

1 Expectant
5 Preclude
10 Medicate
15 Letters dear to workers
19 Swelling
20 Gentry
21 Saudi vessel
22 Wheedle
23 Dennis Quaid film
26 Colorfully brilliant
27 Term.
28 Stoolies
29 Fallacies
30 ___ Raiders
32 When there's a will
34 Designer Simpson
35 Nobody gives___
36 Duffer's dream
37 Famed New Zealand miler
38 Moues
41 Diving bird
44 Good entrance?
46 Flemish painter's monogram
47 Nay neutralizers
48 Oasis former
49 Muslim prince
50 ___ de soie
51 Capek drama
52 Orgies
56 College figures
57 Upbeat outlook
59 Sustineo ___ (USAF motto)
60 Camp meals
61 Toity's companion
62 Singer Black
63 New kid on the staff
64 Elbow
66 Grecian theatres
67 Place for dressing
70 Handles
71 Castor and Pollux
74 Mil. address
75 DAR doings
76 "Unforgettable" singer
77 Drogheda locale
78 Job opening
79 Diamond call
80 Astronomers' delights
84 Arroyo
85 Bee entrants
87 Aru Islands, formerly
88 Bender
89 Appears
90 Requiem
91 Vincit omnia ___
95 Veracruz capital
97 Southern gen.
98 Persist
99 Start of a marching cadence
100 Arabic letter
101 Cosmic conjecture
105 It's written on checks
106 Hebrides islander
107 "A word spoken ___ season": Proverbs

108 Sigmund's sword
109 German waterway
110 Famous Amos of football
111 Confined
112 "The ___ Girl": V. Herbert

DOWN

1 Feeling of insecurity
2 Rich dessert
3 Think-tank output
4 Yellowish green
5 Thrash out
6 Uplift
7 Keane and Baird
8 Part of ACC
9 Occupant
10 "When lovely woman stoops ___": Goldsmith
11 Ransack
12 New Haven collegians
13 Chalice veil
14 More modish
15 Treeless plain
16 Moon (à la Heywood)
17 Composer Stravinsky
18 Swamps
24 Soupçon
25 "Whatdunit" co-author

31 Dutch liters
33 Keep ___ on
34 "___, and a peculiar grace . . .": Somerville
35 "All ___ quite useless": Wilde
37 Stonecrop
38 Reedlike grass
39 Circumvent
40 Children's Dr.
41 Prefix for scope
42 Enlist again
43 See 16 down
44 Fall guy
45 German specter
48 Hall-of-Famer Hoyt
50 Put forth
52 Grin
53 Nita in "The Marriage Whirl"
54 Outlander
55 Aloha island
56 Mollusk gill
58 Smidgens
60 Kanga's creator
62 One showing promise
63 Don't split these
64 Certain takeoffs
65 In the catbird's seat

67 Loretta and family
68 N.T. book
69 Portnoy's creator
71 Party pursuers
72 Greek underground
73 Chuckle
76 Traveler's-joy
78 Japanese cedar
80 Percheron's footfall
81 Roofing job
82 Like some verbs: Abbr.
83 Iron range of Wisconsin
84 Baseball's Iorg
86 Goldbricker
88 Quipped
90 To trick, in Brit. hazing
91 Ambiguous
92 Spinule
93 Acoustic
94 Bring to a halt
95 Burn out
96 "When I was ___": Gilbert
97 California rockfish
98 Part of STOL: Abbr.
102 "Some like it ___"
103 Literary collection
104 Bighead

91

SHORT PEOPLE by Bernice Gordon
Our Philly puzzler has done some neat tailoring. You'll like her style.

ACROSS

1 Item in a carpentry kit
5 Rock of Gibraltar, in days of yore
10 The lowdown
15 Dry, as champagne
19 Spend time idly
20 Shaq or Ryan
21 Nobel-prize winner in literature: 1948
22 First-rate
23 Decapitated actress
25 Racer without a journey
27 Chicken follower
28 Italian philosopher and critic: 1866–1952
30 Atelier equipment
31 Low-down
32 Transport for baby?
33 Schl. group
34 Rig for drilling a well
37 Arterial trunk
38 Difficult situations
43 Forwards a felony
44 Politician lacking an heir
46 Cheer in the corrida
47 Ancient Asian
48 Root of the taro
49 He lived 905 years
50 Source of roughage
51 Hippie's home
52 Diva without a country
56 Believes; judges
57 Pettifoggers
60 Siouan Indians
61 Do a business letter over
62 Spot
63 The Good-King-Henry
64 Syriac cursive script
65 One prejudiced against the elderly
67 Hollandaise, e.g.
68 Continuous threads
71 Hankers for
72 Director needs a male star
74 Undermine
75 Form of parchisi
76 Hosiery mishap
77 Jeanne Eagels vehicle: 1922
78 Singer James
79 Parabasis
80 Recording artist seeking some ground
84 Well-groomed
85 "___ and West they lie . . .": S. V. Benét
87 Bank transactions
88 Unchangeable, to a poet
89 The law has one
90 Comic-strip pet
91 Losing throw at a dice table
92 Reunion members
95 Kipling's water-boy, ___ Din
96 Antiquated
100 Thespian minus a certain accent
102 "Amadeus" oscar winner wants to get some meat
105 Heinous
106 Leave out
107 Alexander the Great's conquest in 332 B.C.
108 Fiber spun into yarn
109 Guinea pig
110 A 1982 film about growing up
111 Heroine of "Crime and Punishment"
112 Scrivello

DOWN

1 A Nanking nanny
2 His palace was in Venice
3 Pulitzer-winning writer, ___ Gale
4 Lose strength
5 Good-looking
6 Negative terminal of a storage battery
7 Count Tolstoy
8 Score for a golfer
9 Sister of Orestes
10 Soft felt hats
11 Word of regret
12 Fabric with a glazed finish
13 Anderson play, "High ___"
14 What hennins look like
15 Cypress spurge
16 Schoolboy of baseball
17 Single
18 Bell products: Abbr.
24 Provokes
26 Grow toward evening
29 Course in a Cannes meal
32 One of the seven Greek wise men
34 Areas in airports
35 Belief in the West Indies
36 Singer wishing for a pasture
37 Skinks in 107 Across
38 English sand hills
39 Composer Novello
40 Comic needing restraint
41 "Thy word is ___ to my feet . . .": Ps 119:105
42 Meaning
44 Regard with reverence
45 Sound of laughter
48 Drive out
50 Actress-singer Midler
53 A layer of soil
54 Ancient city NW of Carthage
55 Redcap
56 Earl Biggers' middle name
58 Irish port
59 Scottish goblet
61 Hold sway
63 Like Chaplin's trousers
64 Small shoot
65 "___ Me": Steve Martin movie
66 Aged export from the Netherlands
67 Scythe handle
68 Writers O'Casey and O'Faoláin
69 Eroded
70 "Thus ___ Zarathustra" (Nietzsche treatise)
72 M.I.T., e.g.
73 The ocean
76 Conjectured
78 Queen Celeste (Babar's wife)
80 Family of Schumann's teacher
81 Defame
82 Character in "Turandot"
83 Verdi's captain of the guard
84 Keach from Savannah
86 That is to say
88 List of corrigenda
90 Elvis' blue shoes
91 Wrist bones
92 With: Fr.
93 St. Helens' flow
94 Part of UCLA
95 Expression on the Cheshire cat
97 The name that led the angel's list
98 Yellow flag
99 Part of a horse's shoe
101 ___ Pasha, Lion of Janina
103 Two-time Olympic gold medalist Frigerio: 1920–24
104 Rembrandt van ___

92

HAPPINESS IS . . . by Randolph Ross
. . . the fun of solving this puzzle.

ACROSS

1 Drives forward
7 Covered passageway
13 Compile
18 Composer Hamlisch
19 Red wines
21 Oscar winner Matlin: 1986
23 Happy Judy was ___
25 French province known for its wells
26 Caught in a web
27 "___ she blows!"
29 Gazes dreamily
30 Supplicate
31 Half of MCII
32 Happy Ms. Goldberg ___
35 Painter of "Haystacks"
37 Al Yankovich parody
39 Dry conditions
40 The happy angel was ___
42 Duplicates, for short
47 Prepares to drive
48 Malaga moolah
50 Deli order
52 UFO passengers
53 Like some salesmen
56 Movie critic Pauline ___
58 Candid
59 Macbeth and others
61 The happy panther was ___
64 The happy artist ___
66 The happy skydiver ___
68 Gardener's device
69 Wings for Amor
70 Child: Var.
71 Erwin and Udall
72 L.A. player
75 Happenings
78 Official records
82 Ancient ascetic
84 Hacienda housewife
85 Happy Ben Franklin was ___
88 Author Jong
92 Cather's "___ Ours"
93 French legislative body
94 Happy Bob Beamon ___
99 Horace's "___ Poetica"
101 A memorable Arden
102 Suffix with sect
103 "Bus Stop" playwright
106 Gave no stars
108 Happy Mary Lou Retton ___
114 First born
115 Supervise
116 "___ Mountain High Enough," 1967 song
117 Methods: Abbr.
118 Obliterated
119 Prepares to advance on a fly ball

DOWN

1 Limb of the Devil
2 Prefix for content or practice
3 Miens
4 The four Gospels
5 With 30 Down, a Cosby kid
6 Bergen puppet
7 Evangeline was one
8 "Kidnapped" author's monogram
9 Mortarboard
10 Indeed, in Ireland
11 Tooth: Comb. form
12 Emulates Degas
13 The S.G. addresses them
14 Squirellike monkey
15 "Star Wars" droid
16 Knockabout
17 Paris river
20 What an elm provides
22 First word of N Carolina's motto
24 Struck out
28 He defeated JEC
30 See 5 Down
32 Movie theater in Spain
33 Decisions by a P.O. boss
34 Towel word
35 Speck
36 A head scratcher
38 Baksheesh
41 Higher ground
43 Decorous
44 Speedy
45 Presage
46 Swim's anthithesis
49 Steinbeck character
50 Superior black teas
51 Full of baloney
54 Wholly
55 "I've Never ___ Love Before," 1950 song
57 Book of the Bible
59 "___ prisoners"
60 Sen. Daschle's state
61 Via: Abbr.
62 Invests with a gift
63 Masquerade as
64 Without toppings
65 "___ yellow ribbon . . ."
66 Farceurs
67 Useful plant
72 Designs a new kind of wheel?
73 Pilasters
74 Track event
76 Most untried
77 Reddish brown chalcedony
79 Half a train
80 Like Tim
81 Vital statistic
83 Spraying through one's teeth
86 Stored selfishly
87 Some perms
89 "___ Loved You": 1945 song
90 Kind of apartment ownership
91 Citizen of an ancient Greek city
94 Mock
95 Eurasian range
96 Mork's mate
97 Glazier's units
98 Each one: Ger.
100 Mar. honoree
105 Met highlight
107 Wino's affliction
109 Former U.S. Gov't. agency
110 Beast of burden
111 Name at birth
112 Wildebeest
113 Placebo

COST OF LIVING by Cathy Millhauser
Pardon us for saying that we think you'll get a charge out of this puzzle.

ACROSS

1 Hero birthplaces
6 "... cherish ___ and lasting peace": Lincoln
11 Con man's trick
15 Anthony Eden's earldom
19 Heather
20 Actress Siddons
21 As well
22 Big wheel's wheels
23 Shrink's fee?
25 Toymaker's fee?
27 Owing
28 Side order
29 Spotted
30 Chapter in history
31 Proportions
33 Direct opposite
36 Recipe abbr.
39 Brownie or pixie
40 Aforementioned
41 Like a walrus
46 Respiratory therapist's fee?
49 Cosmetician's fee?
51 Mall sights
52 ___ Lanka
54 Buck ender
55 List
56 Airs
57 Pane content
59 Hemmed again
62 Crossword sword
63 "___ nice day!"
64 Donald's cousins?
66 Gp. over 65
67 Obstetrician's fees?
72 Ed.'s reading
75 Clair and Descartes
76 Keep an ___ the ground
77 Throw the blue book at?
81 Chanted
83 Tête toppers
84 Opposite
85 Put on
86 :
89 Female merino
90 Break in a sentence
91 Shepherd's fee?
95 Chiropractor's fee?
96 "Remington ___," of TV
97 It's often smashed
98 Kind of feeling
99 Slalom figure
100 Milk sugar
102 Relish item
105 "Foucault's Pendulum" author
106 Coup d' ___
109 High time
111 Author Mitchison, and Mrs. Judd
115 Diet doctor's fees?
118 Featherweight's fee?
120 Soft cheese
121 Tender
122 Suffix, e.g.
123 Peace pact of '54
124 Pack
125 Handle, to Hadrian
126 "Good ___ You": W. S. Gilbert
127 Ship low deck

DOWN

1 John starter
2 Actress Gray
3 Singing Jenny
4 Less friendly
5 Brazilian dance
6 Gathering in a sch. hall
7 ___ Life (rescue tool)
8 Russian range
9 Story like "Roots"
10 Will-o'-___
11 Took a pew
12 ___ the public (strictly private)
13 Turkish coin
14 Freedom from vanity
15 Apiece, on the court
16 Base
17 Barbra's "Funny Girl" co-star
18 Writer Ephron
24 States
26 Get the better of
32 It's in Seine
34 Nostrils
35 Contender
36 Sample
37 Tummy tightener
38 Lying face down
42 Withered
43 Perceives
44 Computer key
45 Twosomes
47 Let loose
48 Loser to HCH
49 Sight-seer?
50 Bullfighters
52 Barrel part
53 Some reviews
57 Bash
58 Check recipient
60 Brain wave rec.
61 NNW opposite
64 Scold
65 Photo finish
68 White-tailed eagle
69 Light Horse Harry
70 Cuomo's predecessor
71 He brings home a bundle
72 Peeves
73 Nose
74 Lifted
78 Bolt together
79 Casa rooms
80 Deuce beaters
82 Kind of shoppe
83 Former Palm Springs mayor and UZ Singer
84 Ms. ___-Man
87 Speaks superficially
88 Frank L. Baum's canine
90 Green film on old bronze
92 River in Bavaria
93 ___ pin
94 Corrected text
95 Floret or gemule
98 Sea goose
101 "___ a Hot Tin Roof"
102 Bouncer's target
103 Word
104 "Maine Coast" painter
105 Declines
106 Brusque
107 Medley
110 Eugene O'Neill's daughter
112 Ground grain
113 Division word
114 Organ part
116 Royal Botanical Gardens site
117 Plaice's place
119 For

94 SATURDAY MORNING HEROES by Vanessa Leigh Patterson

TV trivia fans have a definite edge on completing this one. On another trivial note, Little Beaver (12 Down) was often portrayed by little Bobby Blake, known now as the actor Robert Blake.

ACROSS

1 Illegal mound move
5 Stephen Dushan was one
9 Catch-all abbr.
12 Hill fort, at Tara
16 Object of an apple test
17 Polyphonic, à la Bach
18 Mars: Comb. form
19 Play a medley
20 THE LONESOME COWBOY
23 Wields the delete key
24 Bed canopy
25 Lead down the garden path
26 Burdensome
28 Soissons state
30 Soybean paste
31 Speck
32 A good way off
34 "THE DAILY SENTINEL'S" CRIME FIGHTER
37 David Copperfield's wife
41 Command to Fido
42 German article
43 Iranian region, once a Soviet republic
44 Canary's cousin
45 Pleasingly ___
48 School org.
50 SAM CATCHEM'S BOSS
53 Repertory members
55 Chinese river
57 Golf iron
58 Congou
59 MASKED RIDER OF THE PLAINS
62 More insipid
64 Napoleon's fate
65 Cabbage lettuce
66 Cervine surname
67 ___ oneself (in a swivet)
69 SHAZAM MAN
74 Span. matron
75 Holy city dweller
77 Prince Valiant's son
78 Hun king
79 EL TORO'S COHORT
81 Dijon donkey
83 Theme
84 Seething with curiosity
85 Pie type
89 Wapiti
91 Possessive pronoun
92 Folding money
93 FOE OF MING THE MERCILESS
96 Brooklyn follower
97 Fish basket
99 Scintilla
100 No, to Nietzsche
102 Out of the weather
105 Narrow waterway
107 ___ Cleves
111 Reserves a table
112 SECRET SQUADRON LEADER
115 European iris
116 Approval word
117 Scans
118 Astronaut Armstrong
119 Hourglass contents
120 Sailor
121 Author Ferber
122 Snatch up

DOWN

1 Tical equivalent
2 Fragrant wood
3 Indy 500 segments
4 Antique drinks mixer?
5 Catch some rays
6 ___ Benedict
7 Inflorescence
8 Scraping snowy streets
9 Jay Gould's railroad
10 Schroeder of tennis
11 Peter in "Timerider"
12 LITTLE BEAVER'S LEADER
13 Exchange premium
14 Ballerina's skirt
15 Concert pianist Myra
17 Scratch for scratch
18 ___ as a cucumber
19 Appear
21 Unplayable tennis serve
22 Chichi fish dish
27 "___ as a Stranger"
29 Journey
31 Polanski's Lady Macbeth
32 Purloin
33 Crucial
35 In one piece
36 "M*A*S*H" character
38 Declaim
39 Spud masher
40 Novelist Seton
41 Young oyster
44 Chemical salt
46 Fairway wreckers
47 Nearest
49 Melvil Dewey's org.
51 French dog
52 British flick
54 More invidious
56 Quechuan
57 Famous Washington hostess
60 Good wirers: Abbr.
61 DDE's gp.
63 Loony
66 Fell on deafened ears
67 Under-the-table sweetener
68 Founder of New Haven
69 Walking sticks
70 Heavenly altar
71 Short stay
72 Fill with delight
73 Ballads
74 Three-handed card game
76 Fossil resin
80 PANCHO'S PAL
82 North Carolina college
86 "___ Chitty Bang Bang"
87 Athenian marketplace
88 Nîmes notary
90 Works the dough
93 Chemin de ___
94 Louvre architect
95 Spoiled a parade
96 Seventh-___ stretch
98 Erstwhile Supreme
101 Serai
102 Nigerian people
103 Asta's lady
104 "Die Nibelungen" composer
105 Rigging support
106 Fed
108 The "Rome of Hungary"
109 Lehua
110 Unit of wk.
113 Alias
114 Miss Lupino

95

A CELEBRATION OF CLOWNS by Nancy Nicholson Joline
Nancy hopes you'll derive some nostalgic joy from this assembly
of the best of yesterday's jesters.

ACROSS

1 Puccini heroine
5 Sour
10 Ad ___ committee
13 Diva Te Kanawa
17 Last word of the Bible
18 Kitchen utensil
19 Popeye's Olive
20 Prognostic
21 Vehicle for clowns at the Met
23 Cole Porter song: 1948
25 Brouhaha
26 NBA team
27 Costumes designer ___-Kelly
28 "Yes!" in Roma
29 Vulpine
30 Maudlin sentimentality
32 Half of sei
34 This may be acute
36 High-muck-a-muck
37 Bills' partners
38 "My Favorite ___": 1942 film
39 Clown who created Weary Willie
44 Sniggler's catch
45 Roulette-wheel color
46 English cathedral town
47 Fort ___, Okla.
50 Fusses
54 Humble
56 Mud, in Madrid
58 Large reception hall
60 Rorschach test ingredient
61 Clowns, often
62 Prototype for modern clowns
64 Soprano role in 21 Across
66 Double this for a Hebrew hymn
67 "As the ___ is bent . . .": Pope
69 Daniels of the silents
70 Attribute
71 Disclose info anonymously
73 Female gallinaceous birds
75 Fleet or Loon preceder
76 Teen trial
77 "___ on parle français"
79 Clown's forerunner
83 "The Gleaners" painter
86 Spelunker's scene
87 "___ Buttermilk Sky," 1946 song
88 Danish seaport
89 Swedish ski resort
90 Like Willie Winkie
91 "Mr. ___": 1983 film
94 Vietnamese celebration
95 Thoreau's "What Sought They Thus ___"
97 A moon of Saturn
100 W Colombia city
102 Film in which Richard Basehart played a clown
104 "King of Clowns"
106 Small ornamental case
107 Rex or Russian Blue, e.g.

108 Uneven, as if gnawed
109 Bruce or Laura of films
110 Informal affirmatives
111 German river
112 No-no's
113 Commedia dell' ___ ("birthplace" of clowns)

DOWN

1 Disables
2 Actuate
3 Farinaceous
4 "Bus Stop" playwright
5 Jackie's ex
6 Mussolini's son-in-law
7 "___ homo"
8 Geom. fig.
9 Cary Grant's birthplace
10 What clowns resemble, often
11 ___ and terminer
12 "Howdy Doody" clown
13 ___ Nidre, Yom Kippur prayer
14 "Cymbeline" heroine
15 Button on a VCR
16 Native

22 On the up-and-up
24 Wagner's Ring ___
31 Elect
33 Rogers and Wilkins
35 ___ di Rienzi (Roman orator)
36 Chapter's partner
37 Walt Frazier's nickname
39 Cloisonné component
40 Kind of home or phone
41 Australian tribal hut
42 Water spirit of Scottish legend
43 Take beyond a law court's jurisdiction
48 Weather-map feature
49 Potential
51 Pedagogue
52 Jean Giraudoux play
53 Hamilton or Witt, e.g.
55 Erhard's therapy
57 Symbol of sovereignty
59 Pismire
63 Type of Broadway show
65 Expunge
68 Traditional clown makeup
72 Oast

74 Cicatrix
78 Composer Franck
80 Like guests at a Lucullan feast
81 Blow or College preceder
82 "Maria ___": 1933 song
83 Garb for 79 Across
84 Think
85 Abates
86 "Forty ___": 1968 play
90 Central part of a ship
91 Coe or Ovett, e.g.
92 Plain
93 French river, site of WW I and WW II battles
96 Chippendale contemporary
98 Grinder or sub
99 North Carolina college
101 Icelandic myth collection
103 "___ nobler in the mind . . ."
105 Love-letter features

PLACES PLEASE by Manny Nosowsky
A San Francisco puzzler makes a delightful debut below. You'll enjoy his refreshing, original clues.

ACROSS

1 Much puzzled patron of the arts
5 Conspirator's "Hey there"?
9 Fox's ally in the Black Hawk War
12 Gad about
16 Set limits
18 Golfers' gp.
19 Goat with large curved horns
20 Good place to start
22 No cad he
23 Picasso's "Dora ___ Seated"
24 Aladdin's discovery
25 Nobelist in chemistry: 1934
26 Jekyll's other self
27 Jerk
28 "¿Que ___?"
29 Eight in a shell
30 Direct the kayak
31 Slow flow
32 Legis. meeting
33 Expressionless
34 Greet the general
37 Havoc of Hollywood
38 Whale's baby
39 Maternally related
40 Ties the flies
41 Was ready to be tied?
45 Get more wrestling points
46 Scandinavian writing of old
47 Grumpy pal
48 Faith of our fathers?
49 Catkin
50 No place for nerds
52 Stock unit
53 Medical fare
54 Ran into
55 Circumstance partner
56 Yielded in the debate
57 Cool down in a way
59 Like Chester on TV, once
60 More than pleasantly plump
61 Ziegfeld et al.
62 Agts.
63 Goes ahead in neutral
64 He's a riot in the court
67 He's a riot on stage
68 Light unit
69 Anglicized first Hebrew letters
70 Stamp sheet
71 Diving bell inventor
72 John in some places
75 Princess of the East
76 Like an untitled flock member
77 Support for a big wheel or even a little one
78 007 foe
79 Literature Nobelist of 1947
80 Bad place to finish
83 Ogden Nash's "The ___ Lama"
84 Wilde or Woolley
85 It's significant
86 Dweeb or dork
87 Help at sea
88 Ase's son
89 It's at the top

DOWN

1 Writer O'Brien's namesakes
2 S Amer. Misses
3 Wild goat of Nepal
4 One with a sheepish look? (Not me, but ___)
5 Word after pretty
6 Magi's letter?
7 Trim the hedges
8 Pair of fives
9 Steeple toppers
10 "Nattering" user
11 Sly
12 Place for a fast foul ball?
13 Went over the top
14 Legal buyer
15 Nonresident doctor
17 On fire
20 "Hallelujah ___ Bum"
21 Takes special care of
28 Powerful, as a drink
29 This word is in its place
30 Final word after the bidding
31 Batty place?
32 Court action
33 "G.I. Jane" of 1942
34 Peruvian put-on
35 It may give birth to the blahs
36 Pin spots
37 Go just for the fun of it
38 Like whitecapped water
40 Legal cases
42 Muslim decrees
43 Lay ___ (nix the rumor)
44 Malmo men
47 In the ___ (sad)
51 Pizzazz
52 Skedaddles
54 "Dial ___ Murder"
58 Clamor in a corrida
59 Christmas thief
63 Youngest sons
64 Country talk
65 Stritch or May
66 One who posts
67 Singers John and Bonnie
68 Matthau or Mondale
70 Good spot for a barbecue
71 Philip Nolan of fiction
72 Peace goddess
73 Subjoin
74 One of Santa's gestures
76 Solons' product
77 Rose holder, once?
78 Fall
81 Napoleon of Fr.
82 SFO abbreviation

FASCINATING FASTENERS by Virginia Yates
This puzzle may be difficult for those who are at loose ends.

ACROSS

1 Give punch punch
6 Pile up
11 Protrude
14 Abstaining from
17 Brown-bag it
18 Voyageur's craft
19 Bio album
20 TV's Peeples
21 Shocker
23 Firmly focused
25 Calumniate
26 "Saw ___ glance": Wordsworth
28 MCE's school
29 For shame!
30 Create a business assn.
32 Ratites of South America
35 Blackbuck
38 Art deco designer
39 "Don't ___ Parade": "Funny Girl" song
41 Top staffer
42 Essentials
44 Bourg's department
45 Had
46 Islamic wraith
47 Up the rates
48 Chinese: Comb. form
49 Tidbit
51 Bums
52 Hot under the collar
53 Humbles
58 "Hedda Gabler" creator
61 CCCLIII x III
62 Jam-filled torte
66 Let
67 Leaf's rib
68 Hematite has it
70 Crete mount
71 Stevedore's org.
72 Homed in on
75 Sandhurst weapon
76 Fools
78 Mt. ___ (Moses' spot for seeing the promised land)
79 Oddity
80 Chinese green tea
81 Tone down
83 Do restaurant clean-up work
84 Ruth's husband
86 Put on a long face
87 Spode pieces
91 Foods that hold well?
94 Vodka quaff
96 Photo
97 Song syllable
98 "From ___ shining . . . "
99 Singer Lopez
100 Bison's kin
101 Cry of pain
102 Van Gogh's "Bedroom at ___"
103 Lemon peel used for flavoring

DOWN

1 Bristle
2 Sounds of disgust
3 Gave ___ (swore off)
4 Animated
5 Gridiron sweep
6 Israeli port
7 Mythical queen of dreams
8 Embrocates
9 Offers some TLC
10 Shindy
11 Shake up
12 Component
13 Suds dispensers
14 Without delay
15 Hamlet's "for shame!"
16 Vogue
22 Superlative suffix
24 Little Sir of Tin-Pan Alley
27 Charge
30 Tabriz locale
31 ___ wallop (has force)
33 Ammonia derivative

34 Diet for bishops?
35 Mine stratum
36 Have an ___ grind
37 Haruspex
38 Cousin of a fish eagle
40 Mamie's mate
42 Chisel
43 Muscle
46 Author Auel
48 Shingle
50 Leave order, to a printer
51 Kind of office or score
52 Restrain
54 Bowdlerizes
55 Drops the ball
56 The Flintstone's pet
57 Footslog
58 Limerick folk
59 Use a piton
60 Rallies
63 Kin of rigatoni
64 River to the Fulda

65 Pecking-order position
67 Dolorosa, for one
68 "Let ___": Beatles song
69 Car named for Mr. Olds
72 Offender's forfeit
73 Gadfly, often
74 Like a fence-sitter
75 Sigh
77 Score for Clyde Drexler
79 Sand stuff
82 ___ nova: jazzy samba
83 Trundle or truckle
85 Goose egg
87 The terrible ___
88 Sheep genus
89 Big top
90 Madras gents
91 What some satellites do
92 Acapulco auntie
93 At times, this is coping
95 Automne preceder

HOLLYWOOD ECHOES by Kenneth Haxton
If you have a sound mind, this puzzle will give you no trouble.

ACROSS

1 Impressario Hurok
4 Met super's prop
9 Agts.' cuts
13 Nanking nursemaid
17 Gator's kin
19 Punch apportioner
20 Gallimaufry
21 Struck, Biblical style
22 Plane or sol prefix
23 "___ unto my feet"
24 Caron film: 1953
25 Ace, king, queen, jack, or ten
26 Berri film: 1969
29 They had a word for it
30 Casual wear
31 Sonnet lines have five of these
32 Tripoli is its capital
33 Dir. from Boston to Portland
34 Actor Davis
36 Susa is its capital
37 Theatre org.
40 Newman-Woodward film: 1968
45 Companion of scepter
48 Ares, to Tiberius
49 Medieval narrative poem
50 The Blue Eagle's initials
51 Koko's weapon
52 Actress Balin
53 Jean Seberg film: 1972
59 So. neighbor of Ky.
60 Phnom Penh is its capital
62 Yuletides
63 Complied
65 Hostess Mesta
66 Dickens's Barnaby ___
67 Get-up-and-go
68 Whirl
70 Cole Porter song: 1929
71 Wreck completely
74 Blunders
75 Tom Conti film: 1983
78 Arith. components
79 QED part
80 Doctors' org.
81 Catherine or Jeanne
82 Star in Lyra
83 Take it on the ___ (beat it)
84 Robards, Balsam film: 1970
90 One who ogles
91 Henry VIII's ultimate
93 Nero, Sellers, or O'Toole
94 Natalie's dad
96 Biplane part
97 Jordan town, N of Amman
99 Rounds the edges
102 Accent
103 Kazan film: 1963
107 Praying figure
108 Kin of etc.
109 Elan
110 Cupid
111 Beans
112 Caron film: 1958
113 Make advances to
114 Element No. 10
115 Dips bait lightly
116 Draft classification
117 Threefold
118 Road map abbr.

DOWN

1 Swindle
2 Mountain nymph
3 Laszlo Loewenstein
4 Hoosegow
5 Becomes livid
6 Red-cased cheese
7 ___ Mater
8 Repeat of a song in a musical
9 High molecular weight compound
10 What Virginia creepers do
11 Mosaic parts
12 ___-disant (so-called)
13 Unicellular protozoa
14 J. Brel French film: 1973
15 Oklahoma Indian
16 Towel marking
18 Eye parts
21 High-pitched
27 Yang opposite
28 Shore bird
29 Type of club
34 Florida city
35 Turkmen tribesman
37 Pert. to an ammonia derivative
38 Sten film: 1934
39 Gleason film: 1942
41 Kate's housemate on TV
42 Talus
43 Collinsworth of NFL fame
44 Computer in "2001: A Space Odyssey"
46 Tennis ace Lacoste
47 Crook
51 Good buy
53 Propeller nozzle
54 Drugstore cowboy
55 Toughen
56 Heavy jacket fabric
57 Painter Fernand ___
58 Singer Lenya
61 Aesop character
64 Fava, for one
66 Ecclesiastical vest
67 Subdued in tone or color
68 Lively dance
69 Odd, in Edinburgh
70 Cougar
71 Instructor
72 Impulse
73 Basil or Feodor
76 Audience
77 De Medici in-law
82 Old hand
84 Accounts in escrow
85 Scraps for Rover
86 Daughter of Polonius
87 "___ Window": Stewart film
88 "And starshine ___ ": RLS
89 Buttercup, e.g.
92 Fields of action
95 "___ Maria"
96 Furrow
97 Shiny cloth
98 Icons, e.g.
99 ___ Rouge, LA
100 Whitewasher
101 Skedaddle
102 Auctioneer's shout
104 Leather, to Mitterrand
105 Italian wine
106 "Rule Britannia" composer
108 Id partner

99 HOMOPHONIES by Jeanette K. Brill
Pardon us if we can't resist the temptation to call this a Brill-iant puzzle.

ACROSS

1 Orwell's "Animal ___"
5 Overcome difficulties
9 Slightly wet
13 Figure of speech
18 Volcano in Guatemala
19 Singletons
21 Wading bird
22 Hoosier poet (1849–1916)
23 Live-in companion?
25 Diet food?
27 Slum dwelling
28 That is, to Brutus
30 American author/ longshoreman
31 Lemon peel
32 Trollope's forte
33 Transport
34 Film star Eastwood
37 Sidetrack
38 Ava Gardner role in 1954
42 Spartan queen, in Greek mythology
43 Music played in Giza pyramid?
46 Possess
47 Compound favored by puzzlers
48 Merit
49 Korean soldiers
50 Walk heavily, as through mud
51 NL team
52 Genoa greeters?
56 Hite, the author
57 Site of Winthrop College
60 Presently
61 Island in SW Florida
63 Selassie
64 Ward off
65 Diligent worker
66 Defame
68 School ___ (old-fashioned pedant)
69 ___ man (anthropologic hoax)
72 Dull surface
73 What a much-married person has?
75 This can precede angle
76 Tolkien creatures
77 Anagram of last
80 "Oh wilderness were Paradise ___"
81 Leg bone
82 Sweater size: Abbr.
83 Lavender, lily-of-the-valley, etc.?
87 Nuisance
88 Turtle
90 "Eadie was ___": 1932 tune
91 Estuary in Scotland
92 Wimbledon champion: 1975
93 Peter I and Ivan IV
94 Young horse
96 Where Gauguin painted in 1892
99 Linear lead-off
100 Easy-flowing manner
104 TBS film library?
106 The cost of uppers and lowers?
108 Heraldic band
109 Companion of mortise
110 Unevenly shaped
111 "Pretty Woman" leading man
112 Senator from Connecticut
113 Limitation
114 Operatic prince
115 Arabian ruler

DOWN

1 Author of "Spartacus"
2 Malaria symptom
3 Undo
4 Motherly
5 Author Octavus Roy ___
6 Upright
7 Fuel
8 Misdo
9 Deprives of authority
10 Demean
11 Coin
12 "___ Love You": Mercer song
13 Rehearsals
14 Shuffle cards
15 King of Norway (995–1000)
16 French papa
17 Observer
20 Roil
24 Give off
26 Expresses appreciation
29 Quixote and Ameche
32 Graph preceder
33 Rhine wine
34 Uncloudy
35 Slow (mus.)
36 Gossip column items?
37 Pertaining to plant development
38 AFL-___
39 Flounder?
40 Took an oath
41 Broadway backer
43 Dionne quint
44 One seeking to grab a cab
45 River in England or N. Carolina
50 Recoiled
53 Vichy leader in WW II
54 Sluggish
55 Opera by Bellini
56 Agitated state
58 Family of a German philosopher
59 Secrete
61 Tap
62 Permits
64 Alphonse D' ___, senator from NY
66 Salmonoid fish
67 Hope or Jessica of films
69 Kind of nail or loafer
70 Carpus
71 Final inning, usually
74 Orchestra instruments
77 Fallacious reasoners
78 Henri's lady friend
79 Alphabet progression
81 Liquid overflow
83 Social class
84 Beginning to develop
85 Louver
86 Piranha
89 Scolded
91 Weather word
93 Wyoming range
94 Film starring Dom DeLuise: 1980
95 Earthy pigment
96 Trampled
97 Baltic island
98 Retained
99 Rajah's lady
100 Ornamental braid fastener
101 Particular
102 Actress Garr
103 French river
105 Asian holiday
107 "___ tu": Verdi aria

CACOPHONY by Joel Davajan
Here's a sound piece of work by a new wordsmith from Las Vegas.

ACROSS

1 Black suits
6 Maple tree genus
10 Hemingway sobriquet
14 Actor Michael from England
19 Eli
20 Roue
21 "Exodus" author
22 ___ a dozen (very cheap)
23 Noisy nitwits?
25 Noisy felons?
27 Most meager
28 Rocker on a stamp
30 Prepares salad
31 Siouan
32 "Pinky" actress, Jeanne ___
33 Memo, in Maidstone
34 Elementary school group
37 David Lean product
38 Saskatchewan city
42 Have ___ for news
43 Feline noises?
45 Alp attachment
46 Mature
47 German philosopher, Immanuel ___
48 Fr. female title
49 Kitchen appliance
51 NYSE group
52 Noisy torpedoes?
56 Pitched pennies or marbles
57 He made a Mona famous
59 Anthony or Barbara
60 In a mortal manner
61 Swedish prizes
62 Culture agcy.
63 Native of an ancient Italian territory
64 Lie back
66 Formal button
67 Fit for waterproofing
70 Mountain crests
71 Noisy comebackers?
73 Long time
74 Impaled
75 Kubrick's computer
76 Ye ___ Sweet Shoppe
77 Aspersion
78 Clock zone
79 Aerial disturbers of the peace
83 Large book
84 Loses hope
87 Fridge assaults
88 Distressed person in melodramas
89 Can. province
90 Droops
91 Irascibility
92 Program
95 Intimidated
96 Slip through slowly
100 Noisy alp?
102 Noisy roadster feature?
104 Fragrant liquid
105 Graf ___
106 Russian river
107 Campaigned again
108 Food fish
109 Watch over
110 Silent actor
111 Roman robe

DOWN

1 Actress Charisse's namesakes
2 Secular
3 This is attached to a ginglymus
4 He "Blew in from Winnetka" in a song
5 Puget Sound city
6 Stand up
7 Tilt
8 Exam ordered by a cardiologist
9 Stockpile
10 Statute proviso
11 Muslim of Punjab
12 Short photos
13 Inquire
14 Jargon
15 "___ Fideles"
16 Golf-ball positions
17 ___ Nagy, Hungarian statesman
18 Headland
24 Zodiac lions
26 Moral attitude
29 Den
32 Terra ___
33 Nat or Natalie
34 Word of mouth
35 Combine
36 Soft drink noise?
37 Tropical fruits
38 "___ the word!"
39 Yule noise?
40 California athlete
41 Like an untended garden
43 Check eggs
44 Verily
47 Actresses Black and Valentine
49 Badgerlike carnivores
50 Guam capital
52 Coddled
53 Musical directive
54 Concert hall
55 "The Cloister and the Hearth" author
56 "___ Aux Folles"
58 Actor in "48 Hours"
60 Demons
63 Liturgical hymns
64 Seethed
65 Irregularly notched
66 One-person performances
68 Armstrong or Prima, affectionately
69 Matriculate
71 Prohibits
72 Crosses
75 Israeli folk dance
77 Maugham's middle monicker
79 Ravi Shankar's instrument
80 Bestowed kingship upon
81 Bundle of hay
82 Noisy container?
83 Stumbles
85 Gasped
86 Member of the birch family
88 Gherkin herb
90 Star in "Judith"
91 A certain belt
92 Character actor Leon ___
93 Deep cut
94 Singer James
95 Overcome difficulty
96 Radio alternatives
97 Aviation prefix
98 Philippine volcano
99 Sicilian volcano
101 FDR VP
103 Scene of the Tell legend

101

FIVE-FINGER EXERCISE by Nancy Scandrett Ross
We think Nancy deserves a hand for this fine opus. Brava!

ACROSS

1 Pub measure
5 "St. Louis Blues" composer
9 Drumstick
12 Plumbum
16 Double curve
17 Inter ___ (among other things)
18 Esau's land
20 Role in Wagner's "Ring"
21 Standard
22 Bombay hemp
23 Stanley Steamer, e.g.
24 Shaw title starter
25 Old-fashioned game
29 Potassium hydroxide solution
30 Siegmund, to Wotan
31 Priestly garment
32 Liquid meas.
35 Gymnastic feats
39 Recent
41 "Un ___ in Maschera": Verdi opera
43 Mississippi novelist-historian
44 Loses momentum or criticizes severely
49 Gladly
50 Eggs on
51 Lennon's lady
52 Graphologist's study
54 Salonga of "Miss Saigon"
55 Western Indian
57 Do some grafting
58 Margaret Atwood novel
64 Too
66 Classical prefix
67 "Water Music" composer
70 Lighted torch
73 "Evita" role
75 Counterpart of patri
77 Thine, in Tours
78 Paraguay's capital
80 Heeded the alarm
81 Diva Mitchell
83 Seat for a cowboy or jockey: Abbr.
84 Adjective for a southpaw
86 Hans of Dada
87 Ga. neighbor
90 Corn holder
92 C minus XLVIII
93 Sometime facial adornments
100 King toppers
103 "___, One Heart": song from "West Side Story"
104 Ratio words
105 "Symphonie Espagnole" composer
106 Berg opera
107 Parched
108 Far from fatty
109 Lohengrin's bride
110 Summer steno, e.g.
111 Reel's partner
112 JFK visitors
113 Stair

DOWN

1 "On Golden ___," 1981 film
2 Borodin prince
3 Agrippina's son
4 Woodworker's pattern
5 Cleaned up
6 Gumshoe's aid
7 Closely associated
8 Pulls abruptly
9 Noted American jurist
10 Sch. purpose
11 City west of Erfurt
12 Page
13 Stray
14 Fleet boss: Abbr.
15 "___ Rheingold"
19 Drudgery
26 Actress Daly et al.
27 Long times
28 "Cabaret" lyricist
32 Bugs Bunny's voice
33 Bounty captain
34 Chaney of the silents
35 Hard-to-manage child
36 Tender
37 Mufti for Caesar
38 B'way sign
40 Excited exclamation
42 Burning
45 Word in U.S. motto
46 "___ creature was stirring . . ."
47 Court order
48 Foch of filmdom
53 World chess champion: 1960–1961
56 "___ Heldenleben": Richard Strauss
58 Pudd'nhead Wilson's creator
59 Haw partner
60 Island off Tuscany
61 Parts for grasping
62 Prefix for liter or meter
63 Manhattan artists' district
64 Fairytale ender
65 Sailing vessel
67 Kind of combat
68 Gaelic
69 Prevaricated
71 N.Z. neighbor
72 Not open and aboveboard
74 Mil. abbr.
75 Racketeering group
76 Magazine features
77 ___ king
79 Quahog
82 Workers' org.
85 Singer John et al.
88 Composer Janacek
89 Dogpatch denizen
91 Exasperates
93 Outlaw's order
94 Plane lead-in
95 Employs
96 Office copy
97 Cop's command
98 Otherwise
99 Daytime TV staple
100 High, musically
101 Billiards necessity
102 Shade tree

102

TOOLING UP by Shirley Soloway
An interesting theme; superb interweaving; many unusual clues—in essence, a solver's delight.

ACROSS

1 Platform
5 Pinball no-no
9 Carl's son
12 Take an oath
16 Arm bone
17 Person who is sui generis
18 Hospital ship
19 Japanned metal
20 SANDER
23 Norse verse
24 Took out
25 TV's Jeannie
26 Shoe for Michael Jordan
28 Toss about
29 Cult film of 1932
31 Mrs. Laughton
32 ___ Thomas, champion U.S. skater in 1987
34 "___ and Glass," 1974 Lennon song
36 Their ism causes a schism
38 Roach or Linden
41 Tear
43 Little bit
45 Gp. formed in Colombia in 1948
47 Phrontistery product
49 Former "first family" of Alaska
52 Gifts for men
55 Negotiates
57 Improve a text
59 Toaster?
60 Bigwig
61 One who has called it a day
63 Seed
64 Chic
67 Actor Keach
68 Varnish
71 Keep up
73 Throat attacker
75 Well-ventilated
76 Solomon, to Bathsheba
77 Inventor of a sign language
79 Functions
81 Rock star Jerry ___ Lewis
82 Mother Roosevelt
85 Relish
88 Some are wild
90 Jubal's invention
92 "___ of the Jedi," 1983 film
94 Florida city near Silver Springs
98 Artificial channels for conducting water
101 Shanghai staple
102 Correct
103 Wherry implements
104 WRENCH
107 Concerning
108 Thrashes
109 Emulate Charles Dudley Warner
110 Penalty
111 Macaulay's "___ of Ancient Rome"
112 Espionage expert
113 Movie-makers' constructions
114 Monoski or komatik

DOWN

1 Desert hills
2 On the qui vive
3 "First ___, first . . ."
4 Bad-mouthed
5 Kermit's cousin
6 Tabard or Admiral Benbow
7 PEAVEY
8 Occupations
9 TV series
10 Berke Breathed's penguin
11 Author of "Games People Play"
12 Sergeant's command
13 SCREWDRIVER
14 "Ye ___ Gift Shoppe"
15 Have on
18 Used the horn
21 Kitten
22 Like Harriet Craig
27 Some Bx. trains
29 NAILS
30 Spanish muralist or city in Turkey
33 Denizen of an alveary
35 SAW
37 Accept
38 Secreted
39 Author of "The College Widow"
40 BOLT
42 Title for Christie or Anderson
44 Mal de ___
46 Soviet unit, once
48 Straighten
50 New Jersey five
51 States of pique
53 Gratuities
54 Loos or Louise
56 Argument
58 NUTS!
62 Neutral shade
64 Bad ___, German spa
65 South Asian landlocked nation
66 Scottish refusal
69 Wrath
70 Comedian Louis
72 In the neighborhood
74 Garbanzo's cousin
78 Turns inside out
80 Bedtime treat
83 Lifts
84 Azimuth
86 Of the ear
87 Pleated strips for trimming dresses
89 Jeers
91 Nudnicks
93 Peg Woffington's creator
95 Tax-return time
96 Former president of Italy
97 Carrying a weapon
98 Type of bank
99 Sister of Natalie Wood
100 Breeze
102 Butter servings
105 "Nor ___ drop to drink": Coleridge
106 Wilde was one

103 WORLDLY-WISE by Cecily Friedlander

We're pleased to publish a first-time creation from a first-rate puzzler. Look for Cecily's byline on future puzzles.

ACROSS

1 Botanical branches
5 Pigeonholes
10 Sings, in a way
15 She pined for Narcissus
19 First place
20 Expel
21 Religious maxims
22 Russian ruler: Var. sp.
23 Tidy
24 Korean quest of conscience?
26 Birdbill protuberance
27 Whole numbers
29 Taxco tender
30 Betel nut palms
32 & 33 Sir Walter, for one?
35 Fidelity
36 Most uncommon
38 Maildrop
39 Aegir or Ran
42 Keats or Pindar
43 Fasting and prayers, e.g.
46 Delete
47 "___ It Romantic?"
48 & 49 Limerick limerick?
51 Mythological German king
52 Israeli airport
53 Hebrew weight
55 Lasso
56 Ages and ages
57 Eye membranes
59 PDQ's cousin
60 See 83 Across
63 Cold-blooded
64 Havens
66 Home of the maple leaf
69 Set
70 Dross
71 Pernicious
72 Sphere
75 Monastery resident
77 Cotyledons
78 Insurance abbr.
80 Bois de Boulogne, e.g.
82 Rasp
83 Sensational Indonesian advertising? (with 60 Across)
84 Foul film
85 Chinese nurses
87 Shakespeare?
89 Yellow pigment
90 Sloth
92 Dots in the Seine
93 Snake bird
94 Notions
95 ___-ski party
97 They lived in Asgard
98 More repulsive
100 Biting fly
101 Welsh rarebit?
104 "Buddenbrooks" author
105 A votre santé?
109 Couple
110 Cork
111 Loose
112 South African bay
113 Sicilian volcano
114 Fixes
115 Searing ray
116 13–19
117 Brit. medals

DOWN

1 Italian painter
2 Arabian gulf
3 Hamburg's developer?
4 Concern
5 Repair a chair
6 Prevent
7 Spanish uncles
8 Old French coin
9 Minister's deg.
10 Unpopular precipitation
11 Seaboard
12 Soil: Comb. form
13 Twitch
14 Bogart film
15 And so forth
16 Brno buddy?
17 ___-kari
18 Hematite and argentite
25 Loci
28 Feat
31 Heckled
33 Watery mire
34 Fr. psychologist, 1857–1926
35 Nickname of Teresa
36 Stir up
37 Assimilate
38 Fathers
39 "77 Sunset ___"
40 Formerly Christiana
41 German negative
43 Punitive
44 Nautical imperative
45 Horned one: Comb. form
50 Refrigerant
53 Minute arachnid
54 Handy watch?
55 Jumbo
58 Tow
61 Units
62 Lummox
64 Student of Socrates
65 Like a scone
66 Stateroom
67 Edam and Gouda?
68 Attraction
70 Bulgars and Croats
71 Trunks
72 Girasol
73 Vishnu avatar
74 South American kook?
76 Cheek
77 Washes
79 Hebrew unit of capacity
81 Scoldings
83 Bundle
84 Skimped
86 Knife of old
88 Glee
89 Tobacco kiln
91 Sharp reprimand
93 Alluvial deposits
95 Little Rooney
96 Niatross, e.g.
97 Jason's father
98 They get booed
99 "Birth" novelist
100 Obtains
101 "Raising Arizona" star
102 Floor covering in Putney
103 Refrain syllables
106 Ribonucleic acid
107 Touch lightly
108 Mano a mano cheer

104 A DAY IN ENGLAND by Joy L. Wouk

The day in Joy's title can be found at 74 Across, and its honoree is at 23 Across.

ACROSS

1 Discordant
6 School dance
10 Power
15 Fine spray
19 Subside
20 Russian convention
21 Buckwheat feature
22 Author Seton
23 Honoree of 74 Across
26 See 49 Across
27 Aleutian island
28 Being
29 Trimmed
30 Humphrey of dance
31 Alluvial plains
33 Eager
34 Port near Liverpool
35 Monarch of 23 Across
39 Mend
40 Norse goddess of destiny
41 Kitchen fixture
42 Hunting-party members
44 IRS employee
47 Ripens
49 Army of Northern
     Virginia of 1861-4
51 Roosevelt and
     Holmes Norton
53 Architectural tooth
55 After pi
56 Bride of 23 Across before
     they married
57 Comedienne Charlotte
58 Words of understanding
61 Tidbit for Dobbin
62 Withdraw by degrees
63 "Delphine" novelist,
     Mme. de ___
66 Novel by 23 Across
69 Basks
70 Epoch of yore
71 Craze
72 "The Edge of Night," e.g.
73 Barrier
74 ___ Day (April 19th)
76 Abner's partner
78 Cruel
82 Most commonplace
83 Feature of leaves and
     marble
86 Ancient portico
87 Still
88 Simon Templar
90 Cribbage term
92 Long time
93 Some are sticky
94 Maiden name of
     56 Across
97 Early-October arrivals
100 Hair, in Pisa
101 Horsemanship
     maneuvering
102 Customary
103 Potvin of hockey
104 Elbe tributary
105 California valley
109 Utah senator
110 Title conferred on
     23 Across by 35 Across
113 Difficult

114 "Accident" director
115 Belfry residents
116 Group of eight
117 Perth native
118 "The Surrender of ___":
     Velazquez
119 Wings
120 Blessed woman

DOWN

1 Bean, in La Habana
2 Help a thief
3 Rave's partner
4 Patron of desperate cases
5 Babylonian god
6 Unspoiled
7 Looter
8 Most peculiar
9 Avril follower
10 Native of Brno
11 Foolhardy
12 Cupidity
13 Kept
14 Skater Babilonia
15 Leave high and dry
16 Idle
17 Novel by 23 Across
18 Armor plate
24 "Omoo" author

25 Ancient Laconian city: Fr.
30 Of the back
32 Printer's measures
34 Most simple
35 Campus feature
36 Goad
37 Paradise
38 Kind of diffusion
39 Beach in SE Florida
43 Discharge
44 Cringe
45 Last king of Troy
46 NAACP and AAAS
48 Rivers
50 Leg part
52 Cities in New Jersey and
     Delaware
54 Suffix for part
59 Rock producer Brian
60 Political parity
63 Juicy
64 ___ Haute
65 Roisterous
66 Timberlane and Canfield
67 He wrote "Waiting for
     Lefty"
68 Whirled
69 Pale
71 Alpine winds

73 Hobgoblins
75 Ceremony
77 North Star state
79 Willow
80 Eight bells
81 Within, in Dijon
83 How the Afrika Korps
     retreated
84 "La vie ___"
85 Edward Lear's forte
89 Corrected
91 But, to Scipio
93 Peace Nobelist: 1971
95 At the summit
96 Doge's domain, once
97 Namesakes of Celtic sun
     god
98 Father of 23 Across
99 Pack animal
100 Intrinsically
103 Portal
106 Mindanao native
107 Braid
108 Po tributary
110 Atty. deg.
111 Arab robe
112 Watch chain

105

If you're halfway through solving this one and still wondering about Coral's title, simply hyphenate it.

ACROSS

1 Itemizes
6 The Final Frontier
11 Ali ___
15 Other
19 Have ___ with (talk to)
20 Pergola
21 Chemical suffix
22 Dramatist Hochhuth
23 Occultist's accessories
25 Fail-safe
27 Musical experimentalist Brian
28 Needlepoint style
29 Arm or leg
30 Nomadic Finns
31 Wee ones
33 Sulfuric or carbolic
35 "What is it all but a trouble ___ . . .": Tennyson
37 Sounds of laughter
39 Roasting fowl
41 Stone Age tool
42 "That's ___ off my mind!"
43 "The Sea Around Us" author
44 Still sleeping
45 SF-Vegas dir.
48 Cupid
49 Screech
50 Like Methuselah
51 Certain wings
52 Prune
53 Scottish landowner
54 La Scala presentation
56 Scoff at
57 Short and stout
58 Bedtime bother
59 Like a lot
60 Descendants
63 Comedian Schreiber
64 Treeless plain
65 Basso from Roma
66 Silliest, slangily
68 Evince contempt
70 Mathematical snake?
71 Payable
72 Like a piano
73 Word from Scrooge
76 City light
77 Ranine home
78 Undid
80 Arm bone
81 B'way sign
82 Freelancer's enc.
83 Weald
84 Sing like Dean
85 Knotted anew
87 Together
88 Conestogas
89 Short race
90 As is, to an ed.
91 Meted
92 "Thou art ___ of honour in my hands" Wordsworth
93 Medical suffix
95 Levy on merchandise
98 Small deer
101 Pulchritude
103 Pupil's purchases, at times
105 Heraldic border
106 Sweetsop
107 On all ___
108 Col. Tibbets' mother
109 Capone's nemesis
110 "___ All Laughed," 1981 film
111 "Stand and Deliver" star
112 Gam and Moreno

DOWN

1 Bathe
2 CRT symbol
3 Play basketball, slangily
4 Little lad
5 Did a store chore
6 Famous singer and infamous marquis
7 Nautical nose
8 Palindrome opener
9 Fall down
10 Vetch
11 Forked
12 Puny particle
13 Yogi's sidekick
14 Wholly
15 Straying
16 Rollercoaster section
17 Eats like a pig
18 Fire and flame starters?
24 Raw deposits
26 Tartan
29 Actor Mark ___-Baker
32 "___ of the Dragon," 1985 film
34 Ensure failure
36 Ran away
37 Dutch-African dialect
38 Elsie's calf
39 Convey
40 Desertlike
41 Bore of a sort
43 Flake, as paint
46 Drink noisily
47 Lauder of cosmetics
49 Snead and Houston
50 Ethereal
51 Senior
53 Containing silver
55 Sweet wine
56 Destined
57 1/12 gross
58 Badminton champ Anderson
60 Bridges
61 Malic beverage
62 Hearst Castle features
63 Betwixt
64 Germ
66 5-year-old's problem
67 Bearded botanically
68 Taste or touch
69 No way, to Nicolai
72 Honed
73 Poppy plant
74 Soon
75 Painter Holbein
77 Trouble
79 Formality
80 Try to convince
82 Before life or waters
83 Lipides
84 Quality
86 Wears
88 Fleece
89 Ensile
90 Actress Spacek
91 Trash
92 Dramatic conflict
94 ___-Ball, midway game
96 Pal
97 Bullfight bull
99 Lawton loc.
100 Those: Sp.
102 Stable scrap
103 Calif. airport
104 Naval CIA

EXPRESS YOURSELF! by Cathy Millhauser
Look for hidden expressions of emotions within the answers to asterisked clues.

ACROSS

1 Field butters
5 P.D.Q. and J.S.
10 Pursuing
15 Soldering ___
19 It has a Minor part
20 Director Morris
21 Practice
22 Bodily bottom
23 A guzzler's is poor*
25 Abbots' habits, in part*
27 Using a scoop
28 Affairs
30 "That made my heart skip ___!"
31 In the main?
32 Used up
33 Spring
34 Grew light
37 " . . . blackbirds baked in ___"
38 Associates
42 Hook's "halt!"
43 Lottery type*
46 Charlotte's construction
48 Holiday in 19 Across
49 Different
50 Kind of blazer
51 Anger
52 Live
53 Highland wear
54 Fishing nets
55 Heal, as the humerus
56 Recount anew
58 Machinate
59 Singer Paul, and family
60 Angel's hair
62 "Jennie" star*
66 "Gee whiz!"
67 Bank take-backs
68 Wedding exchanges
69 It's often ill
71 Elvis's middle name
72 Eucharist plates
75 Lamp resident
76 Literary monogram
79 Cross type
80 Scrub, for NASA
81 Brooklyn institute
82 Olive or Nana
83 Slugger Mel
84 Encoder's output*
86 "Lest we forget our ___": Browning
88 Landed properties
90 Parcels
91 Cheeky, in Cadiz
92 Harvest goddess
93 Toil
95 Confusion
96 En masse
99 Nanki-poo's pop
101 Vigorous
105 Humiliated*
107 Butchers*
109 Soybean product
110 Schlepped
111 ___ one (12:50)
112 Pierre's state
113 ___ dixit
114 Stops in reverse
115 Tourist attraction*
116 Mineo and a mule

DOWN

1 Mechanical mutt in "Sleeper"
2 PDQ
3 Paste used in Japanese cooking
4 Pago-Pago denizens*
5 Misrepresented
6 Kingdome is one
7 Rock projection
8 Non-sharer
9 Closer to Morpheus
10 Madison Ave. workers
11 Façade
12 Turn blue
13 BPOE members
14 See 76 Across
15 Weather-map line
16 "Tamerlane" dramatist
17 Spanish stew
18 Eyases' home
24 Map within a map
26 Guitarist's accessories
29 Gerry or Ford, formerly
32 Accuracy trade-off
33 Namesakes of author Silverstein
34 Intelligence
35 Declare
36 Gargoyles*
37 For a short time
38 "Misery" star
39 Tom Joad, e.g.
40 George Selkirk's nickname*
41 Soap, e.g.
43 Carrel
44 Cooks cherrystones
45 Singer Lopez
47 Palmer or King
49 Iberian cheer
53 Orgs. for parents
54 Scads
55 Matthew Walker is one
57 Berkshire town
58 Quickly
59 Fever with chills
60 Commune near Florence
61 Make bubbly
63 Turn outward
64 Trounces
65 Smallville family
70 Peach part
72 Chapters
73 "Rock-___ Baby"
74 A-one
75 Scrape
77 Harmony
78 Actress Lanchester
81 Academic VIPs
84 Prank
85 Tickled
86 Author Segal
87 Takes out
89 Sneaker part
91 "That was so funny, I ___ to laugh!"
93 Trapshooting
94 Cheryl and Alan
95 The Ohio's is at Cairo
96 Dramatic beginning
97 Hit the mall
98 Klutzes
99 L-Q links
100 Toward
101 Canine tooth
102 Greek cheese
103 CIS river
104 D-Day ships
106 Tag players, at times
108 Souvenir of Honolulu

107

HOMOPHONESE by Robert H. Wolfe

Prepare to be assaulted by some outrageous puns by our vet (in both senses) from Long Island.

ACROSS

1 Lady of Spain
5 Resins
9 Hillbilly's mother
12 Writer Bombeck
16 Bradley and Sharif
18 Baseball name of fame
19 Libation potation
20 Downfall
21 Boxer's aim
22 Midwestern st.
23 Most piquant
25 Goose's dorsum?
27 ___ alba (gypsum)
28 Barrooms
29 Roll-call response
31 Golf course at Miami
34 Comic-book exclamation
35 Nip
37 Waterbird
39 Retain entrance, miners?
44 Maddening
46 A Roman's tongue
47 Insensitive
50 Manorial lands
51 Sight at Newport, R.I.
53 Hamlet's bodkin adjective
55 Moppet
56 Hot times for Bardot
57 Monumental osculation?
60 Nav. officers
64 Brooklyn follower
65 ___ Knievel
66 Tenderest
68 Rejectors
73 Of lyric poems
75 ___-de-Paris, department
    in N France
76 Brick buildings
78 Breeze through a lily?
80 New York city on the
    Thruway
81 Unstressed vowel sound
84 Area east of the Atl.
85 Pelvic bones
87 Charlotte and Norma
88 Attacks
93 Italian river
95 Dashing collars?
97 Dispatch
100 Kind of buggy
101 Inedible orange
102 Posterior
103 Second person
104 Letters before thetas
105 Ringworm
106 Comply
107 École ___ Beaux Arts,
    in Paris
108 Depression
109 Hazard

DOWN

1 Of a dowry
2 Protein acid
3 Taiwan island
4 "Stormy Weather"
   composer
5 Soft leather
6 Inter ___ (among other
   things)
7 Marine mollusks that
   sound like blows on
   the head
8 Submerged
9 Overcame
10 Mont Blanc, e.g.
11 Unearthly
12 Wormy carpets?
13 Repent
14 It's in the lead of lead
15 Exterminator's target
17 York was one
24 Emulated Bing
26 Planter's need
30 Item oft spared
32 "It's ___ to kill a
   mockingbird": H. Lee

33 Gently, to Galba
36 Spock's trips
38 NFL positions
39 Painter of "Locksmith"
40 Starboard side when
   sailing north
41 Wagon follower
42 Zadora and Lindstrom
43 British subway
45 Awry
48 Capital of the Maldives
49 Theatrical shout
52 Perfume ingredient
54 Got by barely
58 Garr, Hatcher, Copley
   and Polo
59 Pelvic bones
60 Cheat
61 Senator from Rhode
   Island
62 City in which to spend
   kroner
63 Fret
64 Insides
67 Kind of weave or pattern

68 Inst. at Dallas
69 Dabs
70 Amer. data org.
71 Bird feed?
72 Hides
74 Most sportsmanlike
77 ___ Na Na
   (entertainment group)
79 Give the boot
82 Gardened, in a way
83 Wise; shrewd
86 Pointed, as a gun
89 Norse gods
90 Man from Qom
91 Winter Olympics
   vehicles
92 Slink
94 Bestow
96 ___ even keel
97 Shortened conjunction
98 Costa
99 Burro, in Brest

108 SOAP OPERA by Sam Lake

Here's a new type of puzzle. Please let us know your reaction.

ACROSS

1. That man's
2. Pistol
3. Existed
4. Drew a bead on; pointed
5. "Casey ___ the Bat"
6. "___ Blue Heaven"
7. Give support to
8. Egotist's favorite word
9. Carpentry tool
10. Playground game
11. Mirrored
12. At home
13. High mark
14. Small, hollow globule
15. "The Man ___ Uncle"
16. Belonging to a third-year high school student
17. Meerschaum, Indian's peace ___
18. Speedy
19. Film director's command
20. See 3
21. Required
22. Following
23. Taking a breath
24. With profundity
25. X – IX
26. Ruptured, as a tire
27. Homophone for hymn
28. Not at home

EXPERTS' ACTIONS by Norman S. Wizer

Our ingenious Keystone Stater takes old phrases literally and makes a new kind of sense out of them.

ACROSS

1 Yemeni or Jordanian
5 "All ___," old song
9 Georgia offering
14 "___, Brute"
18 Espionage communication
19 Shade of blue
20 Literary summary
21 Cry of disgust or defiance: Slang
23 What a meteorologist does?
25 Middle Eastern VIP's
26 Peculiarity
27 Sum total
28 What a bartender does?
30 Elongated fish
31 Lover of beauty
32 Desperado
33 What a demolitionist does?
40 Article in Peru
41 For men only
42 Tale starter
43 Business stat.
46 Acrylic fiber
49 Louise or Turner
50 Abraham's wife
52 Algonquian
53 Stoat's cousin
55 What the underwriter took?
58 Banes
60 "Siddhartha" author
61 Temporary hair coloring
62 Make lace
63 Provide for
65 Church vessel
67 Use
71 Mix film
73 Gives an account
78 What a good waiter does?
83 Equip anew
84 Commiserate
85 Augment
86 Crew members
88 He said, "No man is an island"
89 Cagey
90 Word with spark or fire
91 Coasted
92 Metal mold
93 What sculptors do?
100 Arthurian paradise
103 Public record book
104 Dander
105 What a wainwright does?
108 Redo
113 Come into being
114 Old dance
115 What hairdressers do?
116 Tsar or czar
117 Revere
118 Dyer's device
119 Ensnares

120 Short meeting
121 Fiddler and pianist
122 Cerise and carmine
123 Shoe or family follower

DOWN

1 Israeli port
2 Equine color
3 Entrance to the Comstock
4 Kindly
5 The remainder
6 Stocking stuffers?
7 He played Maude's husband
8 Wapiti
9 Stare toward
10 Catch
11 Emulate "Wrong Way" Corrigan
12 Stopple
13 Greet the villain
14 Become excited about
15 Cylindrical
16 Type of blazer?
17 City on the Mohawk
22 Mulligan
24 Rocky mass
28 Tiger type
29 Reply to a witty point

31 Master
33 Swollen
34 Street show
35 Muslim faith
36 This ends in Oct.
37 Of the ear
38 Israeli dances
39 Go ___ (have a spree)
43 Delighted look
44 Monster's loch
45 Short dog, for short
47 Full of: Suffix
48 What fledglings do
50 Beef fat
51 To boot
52 Dernier ___ (latest vogue)
54 Grassland
56 Colette novel
57 Clothed
59 Left in the lurch
63 Editor's notation
64 First name in architecture
66 Atlantic, to Andre
67 African cobras
68 Face covering
69 Bohemian
70 A college league
72 Touch ___ (iffy)
74 Amerind

75 Musical piece
76 Pick-me-up
77 Stylish
79 Briny
80 Biblical land
81 Czech coin
82 The Graces, e.g.
87 Pt. of a harness
90 Callers
93 Concludes
94 Taste
95 Rossini hero
96 Some steaks: Hyph.
97 Eateries
98 Word with high or low
99 E Mediterranean region
100 At a great distance
101 Disease carrier
102 Relating to a certain straight line
106 Bridge
107 Get one's feet wet
108 Fury
109 ___ out (made a living laboriously)
110 Verify
111 Henri's head
112 Being, to philosophers
115 Bruise

110

FOREIGN LOANS by Peggy Devlin

Peggy has borrowed a lot from the French; but she also owes something to the Dutch, Italians, Spanish, and Irish.

ACROSS

1 Staff symbol
5 Italian bowling game
10 Frosts
15 Happy
19 Nimbus
20 Hunter of the sky
21 Decree
22 Carty of baseball
23 Forefront: Hyph.
25 Commedia dell' arte characters
27 Lozenge
28 Comeback
30 Des ___, Iowa
31 Bellicose, son of Zeus
32 Great bargain
33 Well-informed
34 Relative values
37 Pilose
38 Most insensitive
42 Shackles
43 New beginning
45 Preceder for age or sense
46 Chills and fever
47 Actor Richard from Pa.
48 I. Stone's "___ for Life"
49 Hare's tail
50 Crag
51 Irregular troops
55 Insipid
56 Robots
58 Snow, in Santiago
59 Coarse linen
60 Hall-of-Fame pitcher Wynn
61 Public disturbance
62 Tarts
63 Liquidated, in slanguage
64 With full force
65 Teachers' tools
68 Flora specialists: Abbr.
69 Melee
71 Soak flax
72 Personal pronoun
73 Guinea fowl nestling
75 Tennis calls
76 Palm Springs mayor
77 Author Hyman
78 Outlaws
82 Curly cabbage plants
83 Most diaphanous
85 Remove property from a jurisdiction
86 Street shows
87 Plant of the mustard family
88 Almost an "A"
89 Mt. ___, site of Moses' death
90 Picasso's daughter
93 ___ Archipelago
94 Majors' superiors
98 Vacationer's dwelling: Hyph.
100 Antelope
102 Old-time weapon
103 Clumsy
104 Ship's ___ deck (not a top or bottom one)
105 Mlle., in Madrid
106 Irrational number
107 Armor thigh piece
108 You get a rise out of this
109 Method: Abbr.

DOWN

1 Roughen
2 Scoria
3 Greek underground in WW II
4 Famous French fabulist, La ___
5 Goblins, in Yorkshire
6 Exams for would-be Ph. D's
7 Shiny silk
8 North Atlantic fish
9 Disinclination to move
10 TV sports standbys
11 Everything considered
12 "___ are called but . . ."
13 External: Comb. form
14 British law that colonists opposed
15 Architectural ribs
16 Celebrity
17 Teen woe
18 Soho bunk
24 U.S. satellite
26 Free
29 Gas: Comb. form
32 Less foolish
33 Vases
34 Vaquero's implement
35 Chemical element
36 Extraordinary accomplishment: Hyph.
37 Family of infielder Tommy
38 Effect's partner
39 Baked in a deep dish
40 One of the Americas
41 Explosive
43 Thin; piping
44 Helot
47 Association
49 Bias
51 Skirt inserts
52 Ancient Peruvian
53 ___ wait for (ambush)
54 Actor Bruce
55 Open
57 Scads
59 TV ad awards
61 Struck, old style
62 ___ the bill (treats)
63 African witchcraft
64 Clever; skillful
65 Spend time before a mirror
66 Old-time star Adoree
67 Facing a glacier
70 Town on the Loire
72 "___ Pinafore"
73 Persevere
74 Existence
76 Isak Dinesen's title
78 Plays, collectively
79 Sated
80 ___ breve
81 Valiant
82 Skewered meat
84 Wore away
86 Soften
88 Pats baby's back after a feeding
89 Memos
90 Extra addenda to a missive
91 Japanese aborigine
92 Roué's grimace
93 French stoneware
94 Spanish linen
95 Weird
96 WW II transport
97 RBI, e.g.
99 Spanish queen before Sophia
101 Wonder mixed with fear

111

LEAN YEARS by Barbara Gillis

The distinguished director of "Lawrence of Arabia" and "Dr. Zhivago" is honored in a most original way.

ACROSS

1 Contest
5 Sharif
9 Ancient Italian
14 Turmoil
17 Slacken
18 Not any
19 Lariat
20 Florid
21 Pollster
22 SUNNY SPECIES
25 Baltimore bird
26 ___ la vista
27 Vigor
28 Sweet potatoes
29 Plan
30 Cub Hall-of-Famer
31 Writer Jong
33 Gaze
35 Adj.
37 Showy flower
40 Noted arkwright
44 Poetic pugilist
45 Perfect score
46 Astronomical times
48 Guthrie
49 Pub
52 Rounded off
54 Synagogue official
56 Wallach
57 Black cuckoo
58 Pilaster
59 Rope
60 Blusters
63 Fly catcher
65 Addict
66 Every in pharm.
67 Mischievous
69 Delay
71 Curse
74 Discerned
76 Veranda of Maui
77 Blood of the gods
80 Birds' class
81 Charlotte or Norma
83 Curve
84 Fetter
86 Cutting
89 Beethoven's "Opus 93"
91 One in Munich
92 Turnpike
93 Underworld queen
95 Tribulation
96 Spoils
97 Blum and Errol
98 Ration
99 Dodgers' Little Colonel
101 Question
103 Vines
105 Ornamental tree
110 Soft mineral
113 Cube root of XXVII
114 Throw
115 Pierce
116 SHORT MEETING
119 Carpenter's tool
120 Mature
121 Oxeye relative
122 Journey: Abbr.
123 Furious
124 Steiger
125 Jump
126 Pit
127 Anecdote

DOWN

1 Memento
2 Mete
3 Plant stem
4 Some are great
5 PLACE FOR A BRIDGE
6 California desert
7 Ouzo flavoring
8 Bridle
9 Mouths
10 Crouton
11 Prance
12 Irregular
13 Arrest
14 Region
15 Judge
16 Track term
17 ___ avis
21 Obtained
23 Actress Signe
24 TATUM
32 Worry
34 ___ carte
36 Couch
38 Broadway blinkers
39 Sharp
40 Vex
41 Mr. Roberts
42 Dawn, in Roma
43 NO ALTERNATIVE
46 Ballet position
47 Nova
50 Brio
51 Koch, to Conner
53 TENNIS COURTS AND TRAYS
55 NASA object
61 Gabor
62 Asian peninsula
64 GLEEFUL GHOST
68 Puppeteer Tony
70 Award for Showtime
71 Bolt
72 Benefit
73 Unite
75 Pretentious
78 Buckeye State
79 Hire
82 Repeat
85 Legal thing
87 Bristles
88 Cheekiest
89 At the ___ hour
90 Digit
94 Root
98 Melting device
99 Divulge
100 New York city
102 Utah mountains
104 Healer: Comb. form
106 Dismay
107 Savor
108 Wings
109 Fresh
110 Lift at Vail: Hyph.
111 Jason's ship
112 German song
117 Musical notes
118 Scrap

112 ADD-ONS by Roger H. Courtney

Don't be misled by Roger's title—there's no extra charge for the clever clues below.

ACROSS

1 Cold dish
6 West
9 Hatteras and Horn
14 Duds
19 Aristocracy
20 Unit of resistance
21 Part of Juan's martini
22 Gray gen.
23 Street show
24 Hebrew letter
25 With class or case
26 ___ a high note
27 Civil-rights walk + dismissal notice
31 "Mr." in Bombay
32 Gotcha!
33 Loch monster
34 Happy tune
38 Trim again
41 Tiny arachnid
44 Bit
45 After planet or sol
47 Wine: Comb. form
48 Compose
51 Topper trim + conductor + auto pump
58 AARP member
59 Oklahoma city
60 Woolly
61 Entrance courts
64 Tones down
67 "___ you is born this day . . ."
68 Skeptic + Italian saint
75 Language of Dublin
76 French comedy of yore
77 Mow anew
78 Scoffs
81 Antismoking org.
82 ___ revolt (stirs up)
87 Rug + Dahl's fad + popular music + attendance check
93 Talk a blue ___
94 Prandial time
95 Stand for Klee
96 Needlefish
99 Newts
100 Reveries
103 Like a lawn at dawn
104 Form an opinion
107 John Daly won this in 1991: Abbr.
108 Sharp curve
110 Monetary system + part of CST + something to punch
120 Pablo's fright
121 The Fates
122 Bachelor's last words
123 Nest on high
124 Simple machine
125 Apply: Rx
126 Pro
127 Mezzo Lenya
128 Utopias
129 Pious, formerly
130 ___-by-night
131 City in the Ruhr

DOWN

1 Helot
2 Winglike
3 Pisan coins
4 Suits to ___
5 Acts
6 "___ Dearest," 1981 film
7 Relative of pst
8 Jane Austen novel
9 Sedentary souls + rice alternative
10 Greek letter
11 Australian edible mollusk
12 Tied
13 U.S. marionette maker
14 Monk of Marseilles
15 Advances
16 Most hoary
17 City on the Illinois
18 Perceived
28 "The Wisdom of Eve" author
29 "The Invisible Man" star
30 James T. Farrell hero
34 He roared to fame
35 "Dies ___"
36 ___ D. (Doctor of letters)
37 Duct: Comb. form
39 Prefix for mingle
40 "Half Angel" author
41 SE Florida city
42 Business abbr.
43 GI's limited assignment
46 Friend of Danton
49 Spanish aunt
50 Boredom
52 Thatching grass
53 Laura and Bruce
54 Netherlands cheese
55 Novelist Byrne
56 This, in Tijuana
57 Antique autos
62 Japanese board game
63 Forays
65 Suffix for Stengel
66 Prefix for iliac
68 Offspring: Abbr.
69 Trieste wine measure
70 Consumer
71 Honks
72 Rube
73 Excellence: Abbr.
74 Beneficial
79 Soak flax
80 "Beale ___ Blues"
83 Carangid fish
84 Facility
85 Murdered
86 Confederate
88 Ring official
89 Kind of bread
90 Eyes-in-the-sky org.
91 Female goat
92 Genetic acronym
96 Titter
97 Worshipped
98 Experience again
101 Reminiscence
102 Segovia-Madrid dir.
105 Copywriters
106 Peter and Michael
107 Oral
109 Climb
111 You love: Lat.
112 Swelling
113 Cheap tip
114 Row
115 Pop hero
116 Nucci and Genn
117 Kitchen scraps
118 Mention
119 Honed

113

NOTHING'S ALTERNATIVE by Joan P. Leemhorst
If you were thinking it was *all*, think again.

ACROSS

1 Actor Vallone
4 Lacking luster
9 Gists
13 Scamp
16 Luzon peak
17 Hautboys
18 Algerian port
19 Small Greek theaters
20 Risqué syntax
23 Proximate
24 Maws
25 Ambiguous language
27 Noun feminizer
28 Part of TNT
30 Syllable for Parton
31 180 steps per minute
38 Discredit
42 Kind of answer
45 Flower cluster
46 Hottentot tribe
48 Intelligence
49 Obvious
51 Compass point
52 Toward the mouth
53 Overtake again
54 Steers
55 Grunts
56 Cobbler
57 Certain domino
59 Business alias
60 Secretary of State: 1933–44
62 Sweet bay
63 More devout
66 Observe
67 Classical Nahuatl
68 Fuchsin
69 Drove
70 Prefix for bucks
71 Weizmann of Israel
73 Solidify
74 Welles
76 Tinker-Evers-Chance feat
79 Bashkir city
81 Goal
82 Composer de la Halle
86 Foursome on the town
92 Windward Island
95 His wife's a countess
96 Last half of a popular game show
99 Soprano Mills
100 Tolkien trees
101 Holy, in Rio
102 Info at JFK
103 Lit. submissions
104 Closure
105 Widgeons
106 Trinity member

DOWN

1 Chain of hills
2 Roughly
3 Foible
4 Spy
5 Succor
6 Sloth claws
7 Shotgun gauge
8 Superlative suffix
9 Taboo
10 Indic language
11 Sharp remark
12 Line for a hook
13 Notion
14 Ground seeds
15 Place in Monopoly
19 Rapidly
21 Extorted
22 Redact
26 ___ sewer (dragonfly)
28 Mothering, for short
29 Soak
32 Like Falstaff
33 Vases
34 Masterson

35 "There are no fans ___" (Arab proverb)
36 Pale purple
37 Ant
39 Negotiates
40 Mormon State
41 Boys
42 Through
43 ___ atque vale
44 Pub patrons
47 Latin preposition
50 Hialeah wager
51 Renaissance fiddle
54 Dresser
57 Stunned
58 Expenditure
59 Doctrine
60 Words from St. Nick
61 Over, in Essen
62 Skedaddle
63 Greet
64 Printemps follower
65 "Wind in the Willows" character

68 Lay out
71 CC less IL
72 Enclose
75 AFC + NFC
77 Thorny tree of India: Var.
78 Yakutsk river
80 Mosquito genus
83 Braves
84 Enhance
85 Central American language
86 Believe
87 Sculls
88 "The Haj" author
89 Parental negative
90 Prefix for reverse
91 Three tsps.
92 Hackman or Siskel
93 Routine
94 Lofty poetry
97 Members member
98 Kind of session

114

LOST CHORDS by Bernard Meren

A brand-new idea followed by extensive research and constructive prowess brought about this amazing puzzle. It almost won the Margaret Award.

ACROSS

1 Dangerous gaseous element
6 Zygote is one
10 Disencumber
13 Jamie of "M*A*S*H"
17 Rocket stage
18 "Typee" sequel
19 Japanese apricot
20 Former Congolese Prime Minister
21 Norse god of poetry
22 Type of type
23 Writer Anais
24 Ex-GIs
25 "I Left My Heart in San Francisco"
28 Way out
29 Birthplace of Frederick II
30 "For ___ a jolly good . . ."
31 Switch ending
32 Flaming
33 Helm dir.
35 Oarsmen
36 Not so tight
37 "Bye, Bye, Blues"
42 Dream: Comb. form
44 Donkey, in Dijon
45 "Delphine" author, Mme de ___
46 Vex
49 Hide the loot
51 Turn for the worse
55 "___ o'clock scholar"
56 Defeats, in bridge
57 Mr. Chips portrayer
58 Triumphs
60 Rather's forte
62 Confident
64 Central points
65 Mine-shaft borer
67 Gene Autry's birthplace in Texas
69 Mom's mandate at mealtime
70 Mission
73 "Till the End of Time"
75 N. Y. Island Borough
78 Gross, in a way
80 Buddy
81 Double-jointed
82 To live, to Livy
83 Mayday's cousin
85 Timberwolf
89 "Vissi d'___," Puccini aria
90 "Without a Song"
93 Refrain syllables
94 Elusive one
95 Ancient kingdom near the Dead Sea
96 Beginning or attack
97 Reeky river?
98 Never, in Nuremberg
99 Sommer of Hollywood
100 Of a gland: Comb. form
101 Track event
102 Buzzing insect
103 "The ___ Hunter," De Niro movie
104 Musical symbols

DOWN

1 Jewish spiritual leader
2 See eye to eye
3 Transactions
4 Uninterrupted
5 Dwarf, in Dunkerque
6 Thicket
7 Exudes
8 Bonkers
9 Stevedore, e.g.
10 Fatigued
11 Chemist's ___ group
12 Gainsay
13 "Goodbye, Eyes of Blue"
14 Collins' role in "Dynasty"
15 Call it quits
16 List
26 Belgian port
27 Martian: Comb form
32 Main artery
34 One-time capital of Serbia
35 Instruments Piatigorsky and Casals once played
36 Trygve of the UN
37 Lip
38 Purpose
39 More shipshape
40 Road surfacing
41 Takes advice
43 Ethyl or methyl chaser
47 City near The Hague
48 The Muses, for example
50 "I Aint Got Nobody"
52 Babylonian sky god
53 Dolly from Sevierville, Tenn.
54 Rathskeller mug
59 Some visitors to JFK
61 Toot
62 Actress Alicia
63 Monastic title
64 Okinawa seaport
66 Prince Valiant's son
68 Kind of cab or moth
71 Fledgling
72 Part of 101 Across
74 Chilean president overthrown by Pinochet
75 Winter Olympics event
76 Harangue
77 Churchill's successor in 1945
79 Enlarged an opening
82 "Old MacDonald had a farm, ___"
83 Runner or racer
84 Old card game
86 Place where Bedouins bed down
87 Sportscaster Mussberger
88 Bismarck and Kruger
90 Proceed on
91 Hercules' captive
92 Grayish-white

115 GOING FORMAL by Charles B. Waffell

Don't be put off by the ceremonious title. There are plenty of casual clues and homespun humor below.

ACROSS

1 Japanese wooden clogs
6 Fragrant oil
11 Harvests
16 Extreme
17 Pro ___
18 Politician Stassen
20 Night sticks?
22 Augusta bloom
23 Kind of gram or graph
24 Neighbor of Pa.
25 Made a smart remark
26 Gather
28 Splendid
30 This is made by sitting
31 Hoyden?
36 Late-night flight
38 Meander
39 Revived: Comb. form
41 ___ majesté
42 Author LeShan
45 Kind of corner
46 What Polly put on
49 Noted swearer
51 Via
52 Actress Garr
53 ___ Plaines
55 Hardy and North
56 Handyman?
60 Southern Cal athlete
62 Part of TGIF
63 Leisure, in Lourdes
64 Pay ending
67 Prairie wolves
69 " . . . be seen ___ heard"
71 Port at 104 Across
72 Expressions of doubt
73 New Jersey followers
75 Consume
76 Heckle
77 Building stone
79 Lynx?
83 Mrs. Gump
85 Doctrine
87 Shade of green
88 Peevish
90 Former Portuguese territory
92 Dubai, for one
97 Deficient in hemoglobin
98 Grasshopper?
100 Town out in the sticks
101 Varnish ingredient
102 Change a title
103 See 88 Across
104 Arab republic
105 Love

DOWN

1 Hold
2 Mrs. Al Jolson
3 Scented powder
4 "Peer Gynt" dancer
5 Gawks
6 NFL div.
7 Related
8 More faithful
9 Screenwriter Eric
10 Ethiopian prince
11 Meat cut?
12 Bloodline, in Barcelona
13 Divine answer
14 Lively dance
15 This can be deep
16 Sounds of incredulity
19 Dukakis film
21 Town in Utah
25 Military student
27 Leo XIII, for one
29 Set
31 Snare
32 Word with plate or body
33 Thrills
34 Mortals
35 Still
37 ___ Gift Shoppe
40 Conservative
42 In serial form
43 "Zip-a-___-Doo-Dah"
44 Horace's "___ Poetica"
46 Bluegrass state?
47 Cockney paladin
48 Slippery one
50 Conductor Schmidt
52 Id est
54 Lincoln's Secretary of War
57 Eye, in Español
58 Macaw genus
59 ___ Branco
60 Fort Worth col.
61 Computer memory
65 Clytemnestra's mother
66 Dill, once
68 Tennis star
70 Patriotic org.
71 Humorist Buchwald
74 ___ Juan
77 Hostility
78 Entertain
80 Bavarian brew
81 Southern New York city
82 Controlled a horse
83 North Dakota city
84 ___ France
86 Kind of pole
88 Southern rel.
89 Apply oil: Dial.
91 Alas!
93 Gambling mecca
94 Hebrew month
95 Anagram for item
96 Dutch commune
98 Essential
99 A, in Augsburg

116 UNREAL ESTATE by Stanley Glass
Eight nonexistent locales are hidden below. Can you find them all?

ACROSS

1 Influences
7 Neighbor of Ga. and Ala.
10 Protection
14 Boutique
18 Parisian roughneck
19 Sense
20 Nictitate
21 Glowing circle
22 Scandal-ridden community
24 Slacken
25 Appends
26 Lake Region Indians
27 Bounced
29 Bottom-line element
30 Elation
31 Pismire
32 Malice
33 Connect
36 Finale
37 Discard
38 Destroy
40 Ostentatious
42 Indians of the northern Mississippi
46 Dante's hot spot
48 Go ___ for (support)
51 "The ___ Cometh": O'Neill
52 "Krapp's ___ Tape": Beckett
53 Homo sapiens
54 Drench
55 "Mood Indigo" man
57 Revise
59 Scoffed
60 Pedigreeless pooch
61 Scepter
62 Author Harte
63 Mob disperser
64 Malign
66 Deprived
68 Log maker
72 Remainder
74 Boob; klutz
75 Yawn
79 Beethoven's "Third"
80 Overcome
81 Author of "Myra Breckinridge" & "Burr"
83 Wash out
84 Wrath
85 Elderly
87 Competitors
88 Dice roller's backer
89 King Arthur's realm
91 Insult
92 Subject to ablation
94 Pub offerings
95 Cupid
96 Timetable abbr.
98 Aden native
100 Dice player's "natural"
102 Grumman's moon module
105 Flee suddenly
107 Send a picture electronically
108 Beardless
110 Type of column
112 Netman Camporese
113 Related
115 Oz metropolis
117 Custer's last major
118 Distribute
119 Tenant's obligation
120 Food toppings
121 Mrs. Lincoln's maiden name
122 Gaelic
123 Technique
124 Richard ___ "L.A. Law" senior partner

DOWN

1 Horn or Hatteras
2 "Norma" or "Louise"
3 Stock up on
4 Double quartet
5 Greek R's
6 Indonesian coin
7 Elaborate meal
8 Clergymen's desks
9 Sheltered at sea
10 Ram's mate
11 San Francisco athlete
12 Ripe for harvest
13 Drawing
14 Type of rug or dance
15 Twain's "corrupted" town
16 Bygone
17 Sat
19 Liquid
23 Thirteen were Leos
28 Stupefy
32 Tibetan Utopia
34 House eater
35 Dangerous spot
37 Musial or Hack of baseball
39 Following
41 Would-be spouse
42 Per ___ (method of pay)
43 Org. monitoring rights violations
44 Salmon that has spawned
45 Skip over
46 "At Seventeen" singer
47 ___ Hiken, Sgt. Bilko's creator
49 Cruising
50 Kennedy and Koppel
52 City in New Jersey or Italy
56 Charge at a bridge
58 Obligation
59 Seat of Faulkner's Yoknapatawpha County
62 Free rides to the next round
63 Eye drop
64 Former official in India
65 Writer Douglas Southall ___: 1886–1953
67 Cross
68 Feudal underling
69 Song for Aprile Millo
70 Creation of Charles Dodgson
71 Penny-pincher
73 Overused
75 Yield
76 Jewish month
77 Chums
78 Otherwise
80 Lingerie item
81 "___ lost!"
82 Big shots
84 Freezer compartment
86 Lacy
90 Yale team
91 Sports building
93 See 64 Across
95 Tennis's Chris
96 Cancel abruptly
97 Classical lover
99 Ways out
101 Happening
102 Geometric place
103 Author Jong
104 Kind of box or joint
106 Stepped on
109 Zeus's wife-sister
110 June 6, 1944
111 Type of swelling
114 Wedding-announcement word
116 Hallucinogen, for short

117

WHAT'S A NAME IN? by Louis Sabin

A veteran puzzler has found an ingenious way to give a new twist to Juliet's question.

ACROSS

1 Jaffe role in "Lost Horizon"
5 Whistle wetters
10 Missouri Indian
15 Alphabet series
19 Five-star Bradley
20 "Swan Lake" role
21 Battle site, 394 BC
22 Roof section
23 Three-time NBA MVP
24 Gibson moves in with Pacific islanders?
26 Pace
27 Regard
29 Some are fine
30 Kidd's collection
32 River from Tibet to the Arabian Sea
34 Odeum feature
37 British composer
38 Santa Fe saloons
41 Flower parts
43 Mild gripe
45 Stilt
46 Purposive
48 Mane site
49 Rent again
51 One of Cleopatra's aides
53 Bad-mouth
55 Fabulists
58 Rustic structure
59 Hemingway heroine
61 Commedia dell' ___
62 Elm or Spruce
64 Bashful
65 Apparent
67 Lepidus's 401
69 Auto racers Richard and Mario
71 St.-Lô sky color
72 Every sixty minutes
74 Jessica's stage mate
75 Tip over
79 Cantab's rival
80 Catherine the Great, e.g.
84 Author Santha Rama ___
85 Church figures
87 Danish weights
89 W German port
90 Prepare
92 White fiber
93 Rigel and Mira, e.g.
95 Koran chapter
96 "Oklahoma!" aunt
98 Canter
100 Pigpens
102 Pierce-Arrow or Cord
103 Bristlelike organ
104 Acted furious
106 Retort or recover
108 Temperate, in Tours
110 Finals preceders
112 Express malignant satisfaction
113 States of agitation
116 An Apostle or a Beatle
118 "The Scourge of God"
121 Grumpy
122 Ripken traded to the Angels?
126 Gardened
127 Olympic blade
128 Singer Lopez
129 Witch
130 In the know
131 Funny Foxx: 1922–91
132 Stranger
133 Poker holdings
134 Atl. crossers

DOWN

1 Earring site
2 "Girl, 20" author
3 Balsam gets into betting systems?
4 Impassioned
5 Tribal societies
6 Canticle
7 Actress Kedrova
8 Tocsin
9 Sentenced to Sing Sing
10 Cricket field sides
11 ___ whale
12 He loves: Lat.
13 Categories
14 "La Bohème" prop
15 Divine tidings
16 Darwin, e.g.
17 Above
18 "___ Le Moko": 1937 film
25 Krupp Works site
28 Modify MSS.
31 Antiquing device
33 Maglie plays a medley?
35 Type types
36 Anson's name joins Rockefeller's?
38 Press notices
39 Penthouse
40 Pintado fish
42 Get word of
44 Sikh's snack city?
47 Stevens gets into mail pouch snagging?
50 Pekes and Poms
52 Latin step
54 Alter
56 Buttons gets into deceit?
57 Balto's cargo
60 Landscape for Armstrong
63 Arizona's home of the Sun Devils
66 Actress Patricia and kin
68 Vex extremely
70 Conditions
73 City in S France
75 Exhort
76 A human score
77 Ives gave a mocking representation?
78 Fronton basket
81 Alexander's school problems?
82 Ice peak
83 Lewis Carroll creature
86 Incline
88 Sign that can stop a truck
91 Rerouted
94 Cunard routes
97 Physics Nobelist: 1944
99 Beat
101 Espy
104 Hold back
105 Having two xylem groups
107 Schmaltz
109 Right-hand page
111 Big-band leader
113 Electric company's customer
114 Slangy turndown
115 Glissaded
117 Celebrity
119 Riga native
120 Ruckuses
123 Hero follower
124 Balm of Gilead
125 Song in "A Chorus Line"

118 BE FOREWARNED! by Anne H. Petz
A newcomer from Manhattan comes to the foreground in an unusual way.

ACROSS

1 Stressed consonant
6 Sites
11 Watering device
15 Festive
19 Nativity
20 Bernstein's musical heroine
21 Chorus member
22 Anglo-Saxon money
23 Memorandum notation
26 Charged particles
27 Edmond O'Brien film: 1949
28 Assayed
29 Chinese dog
30 Predict
31 Bucks' mates
32 Jot
34 Verify
35 University in Chicago
38 Heavenly food
40 Sailor's duty period
42 Regarding
43 Cleanse
44 Fury
45 "Ten thousand saw ___ a glance": Wordsworth
48 Raced
49 Creativity helper
50 "___ Song Comin' on."
52 Chief talent
53 Former champ
54 Daggers
55 Ore deposits
56 A little after tea time
57 Without results
59 Has the lead
60 "___ be stronger men!" Phillips Brooks
61 Soothes
63 Sighs
64 Thespian on stage
65 "___ like today . . ."
66 Landlord's sign
68 Sultanate on NW Borneo
69 Dressed to the ___
70 Chocolate substitute
71 Cream-colored cheese
72 D.C. science org.
75 Medics
76 Where the Sforzas reigned
77 "Nothing can need ___": G. Herbert
78 Liquefy
79 Tampa-to-Jacksonville dir.
80 Baum's "Grand ___"
81 "Believe It ___!": Ripley
83 More unfavorable
84 Husband and wife
85 Keels' back section
86 Fall's one
87 Sign on an automobile
90 Playwright Hart
91 Verve
92 Layers
93 One grand
95 Vibration
98 Pea container
101 Butcher shop: Fr.
102 What Galsworthy's Irene became
105 Rocket assisted launch, for short
106 Device for clamping
107 Where Bobby Shaftoe went
108 Dine at home
109 Unhurried
110 Oliver's partner
111 Special individuals
112 Mild expletives

DOWN

1 Footnote abbreviation
2 In ___ (within a living organism)
3 "___ Little Tenderness"
4 Global trade assn.
5 Pitcher's reverie
6 Wrong
7 Carry on
8 New York canal
9 Furnishing
10 Spade
11 "Anne Hathaway, she ___ way . . ."
12 Potpourri
13 Pack
14 Many eras
15 Proceed
16 "___ by any other name . . .": Juliet
17 Bowling alley features
18 Resource
24 Virginia, for one
25 Official records
30 Yen
31 Borge or Hamlet
33 Unique event
34 ___ boy!
35 Type of bank
36 Organic compound
37 Event in a theater
38 Adjective for a perfume
39 Olympic hawk
40 Small birds
41 Indian mulberries
43 Does some knitting
44 Small dam
45 Sutter's Mill denizens
46 Tete-___
47 Pavarotti is one
49 Flavored with marjoram
51 Gourmandize
52 Provender
54 Some La Scala stars
56 Actress Demick
58 Adjutants
59 Literary party
60 ___ chose: Parisian trifle
61 Mr. Nast of a publishing firm
62 Stew ingredient
64 Pome or loquat
66 Stories
67 Spoken
68 Soldiers with bad aim
70 Quote
71 Criminal clique
73 In addition
74 British gun
76 Speck
78 Lament
80 He painted "The Laughing Cavalier"
82 ___ one's laurels (doesn't compete further)
83 What the bride chose to do in a 1937 film
84 Narrator in "Lord Jim"
85 Problem for Santa
86 Blackthorn plum
87 Brain passages
88 Critical
89 Former treaty org.
90 Average, in Arras
91 Madame Bovary's namesakes
93 Go ___ (take a chance)
94 Pelion's supporter
96 Hillock
97 Eternally
98 Pocket bread
99 What ___
100 Studies
102 Fours
103 Ike's arena
104 Start of a Tolstoy title

119

FLOWER GIRLS by Shirley Soloway
Shirley will cast a miss-spell on all you gardeners out there, but it's all in fun.

ACROSS

1 Gaucho's weapon
5 Elec. units
9 Practice for a bout
13 Yugoslav marshal
17 French streets
18 Lugosi of films
19 Port or copter preceder
20 Rafsenjani's domain
21 Pilots
22 Feelings of self-worth
23 " . . . as a bug in ___"
24 Writer Vidal
25 Court star's favorite flower?
28 Domingo, for one
29 Kind of wrestler
30 Alternative to beer
31 Swiss waterway
32 Photo finish
35 Sets down
37 Glue
42 Aka Mars
43 Execs.
44 Throw
45 "Got it!"
46 Item for John Daly
47 Entree item
48 Part of TLC
49 Fix, in a way
50 George of films
52 Golfer Alcott's favorite flower?
54 "___ so it goes"
55 Contentious items?
57 Whitney of the gin
58 "Swing Shift" star's favorite flower?
61 German rulers
65 Spouses
66 Indolent
67 U.S. Open golf champ: 1992
68 Smidgeon
69 On a peak
70 French import
71 Over-emoters
72 Artist Bonheur
73 Molded a second time
75 Old-world instrument
76 More rational
77 Once ___ blue moon
78 "___-de-Lance": 1974 film
79 Babies' perches
81 Chore
84 "Moonlighting" secretary's favorite flower?
90 Mrs. "B. L. Stryker"
91 After a while
92 Nastase of tennis
93 Florence's river
94 One of the Aleutians
95 Lady's man
96 In the vicinity
97 Covers
98 "___ Town": Clark Gable film
99 Grain appendages
100 "A ___ of Robin Hood," by Charles Norris
101 Aberdeen native

DOWN

1 Bric-a-___
2 "That stings!"
3 Sidelong glance
4 Lends a hand
5 Ship position
6 "Agnes of God" star's favorite flowers?
7 Story line
8 Struts
9 Humiliation
10 Land of de Cuellar
11 Tart substance
12 Semi
13 Favorite flowers of actress Palmer and namesakes?
14 Kind of curtain
15 Poi root
16 Super man
26 Litigate
27 Overhead trains, for short
28 Mai ___ (rum drink)
31 Show segment
32 Welcomers at doorsteps
33 Precinct
34 Rock collector
36 Liable
37 "The Bells of St. ___": Crosby film
38 Gas company customer
39 Italian wine region
40 Haws' opposites
41 Always, to Emerson
43 "Ernani" composer
44 Arrived
47 Repairs
48 Sweet stuff
49 Kate's TV friend
51 Mrs. Rogers' favorite flower?
53 Nobelist for literature: 1923
55 Make
56 Seep
58 Stadium receipts
59 Western tribesmen
60 Nobelist Wiesel
61 "The Marrying Man" star's favorite flowers?
62 Black, to Byron
63 Soar
64 Nova, e.g.
65 Spoil
67 Krazy ___ of comics
70 FDR project
71 Causing pain
72 Mischief makers
74 Rocker Adam ___
75 Mr. Iacocca
76 007, e.g.
78 Manages
80 Wide-eyed
81 Chunk
82 "Oz" pet
83 Concerned with
84 Winter whiteness
85 Raggedy
86 Away from the wind
87 Norwegian navigator
88 Loosen
89 Maximum
91 ___ mode

120 PROGRESS by William Lutwiniak
The witticism below applies to everyone—especially toddlers and novice skaters.

ACROSS

1 Country singer Wooley
5 Adolphe Adam ballet
12 Music genre
16 Sometimes it's nuncupative
17 UK German shepherds
19 Preferred helm position
20 **Quip starts**
23 Treated badly
24 Haberdashery items
25 London lunch
26 Run up
27 Unchecked
28 LPGA's Inkster
29 An Allen
31 Ply with port
32 Durable bags
35 Nurtured
36 Inflamed
37 Heavy reading
38 Sis or unc
40 ___ de veau
41 Spencer Tracy movie
42 Farm payoff
43 John's intro
44 Dice
46 Loafer
47 Furnishes
48 **Middle of the quip**
52 Tumbler
53 Shriver and Dawber
54 Learned
55 Time immemorial
56 Uncover
58 Out of
59 Novelist Deighton
60 Le ___ Tho
61 Flyway flock
62 Marian, for one
63 Nav. staff
64 Marquise, for one
66 Clotho, e.g.
67 Lays a lawn
68 Stand OK
69 Records
70 High times
71 Absolve
74 Excellent
75 At bay
79 **Quip ends**
82 Actress Moran
83 Memory
84 AMPAS lead-in
85 Clan subdivision
86 Glengary garb
87 Trust in

DOWN

1. Dog-paddle
2. Supersonic?
3. Ron and Rick
4. Puffed out at the waist
5. Tickled
6. Tas. or Icel.
7. Cracker
8. Auteuil asterisk
9. Crosshatched
10. Minstrel's repertoire
11. Rock artist Brian ___
12. Palm fiber
13. Norwegian king
14. This, in Tours
15. Lament
17. Several
18. Joins together
21. Exploited
22. Mountain runoffs
27. Sinewy
28. Saltation
29. Light-minded
30. Pervasive quality
31. Deteriorated
32. Frenetic fan
33. Succeeded
34. Tulane terms
35. Spanned
36. Pressed a tort
37. Crécy crowd
39. Enjoys the music
41. Conniptions
42. Titlist
43. Conked out
45. "Thanks a Million" man
46. Land of sangria
47. Downcast
49. Stripling
50. Where the living is high
51. Set foot
56. Maneuver a lure
57. Shoe size
58. Diet eschewal
61. Flight unit
62. Purplish-red
63. After V-J Day
65. No-show
66. Miskolc money
67. Box
69. Ashe contemporary
70. Briefed
71. Pro votes
72. Cadre
73. One-liner
74. Papal tribunal
75. Sky sightings
76. Get there fast
77. Of a time
78. Puff of air
80. Lincoln Center attraction
81. Schnapps

121 "LIVE, FROM NEW YORK" by Douglas A. Behrend

A newcomer from Arizona gives you the seven original cast members of "Saturday Night Live," plus the first replacement.

ACROSS

1 Semiprecious blue stone
6 " . . . in like a lion, out like ___ "
11 Diamond surface
16 Avoided detection
18 A Montague
19 In a ___ (excited)
20 Eclipse occurrence
21 TV journalist Sawyer
22 Intestine: Comb. form
23 Pan Am competitor, once
24 "Don't tread ___ "
26 Pro ___ (proportionately)
28 Memb. of "the brass"
29 **Cast member**
34 Slangy affirmative
35 Edna St. Vincent et al.
37 Moonstruck one
38 ___-magnon
39 Inkling
40 Baker, at times
42 Jacob's first wife
44 **Late cast member**
46 Basilica area
49 Married gypsy woman
50 Plant a crop
52 American League's MVP in 1958
54 Wane
57 Kremlin no
58 Composer Khachaturian
60 And so on: Abbr.
61 Imitated a banshee
63 Fez or toque
66 Antelope of SE Africa
67 A Gardner
68 **Late cast member**
74 Some retrievers, for short
77 Campaign for office
78 Equipment
79 Time abbr.
81 Available, as a seat
83 Curved sword
85 Rocker Reed
86 **Cast member**
88 Part of E.T.A.
89 Cézanne's "A Boy in ___ Vest"
90 Opposed to
91 Spotted ___ (endangered bird)
94 Disco light
96 Sky hunter
100 Of an image
102 Percussion-instrument family members
103 Certain orange

104 "___ for the weary"
105 "And ___ all the world, . . .": Shak.
106 Unlike 103 Across
107 Maryland mascots, for short

DOWN

1 Presentation by a prof.
2 Assert
3 Describing a latitude line
4 Wedding words
5 Madame, in Madrid
6 Shakespearean forest
7 Law, in Lyons
8 M.D.'s org.
9 Chess pieces
10 Transvaal conflict
11 Back monetarily
12 Envelope abbr.
13 **Cast member**
14 More spooky
15 Too much, in Milano
17 **Cast member**
19 Minutia item

25 Call a spade a club?
27 Quantity: Abbr.
30 "When I was ___ . . .": W. S. Gilbert
31 Panache
32 Many Renoirs
33 January, to Juan
35 Soviet jet
36 Is he Amin guy?
41 Novelist Wharton
43 Actress Sothern
45 "Judith" composer
47 Fido's doc
48 Ref. book
51 "I met a man who ___ there": Mearns
52 **Cast member**
53 Pianist Gilels
54 Ram's mate
55 Tavern
56 **First replacement**
59 River crossed by Caesar
62 Meadow
64 "And gentle dullness ever loves ___": Pope
65 Landlord's sign

69 Suggestion
70 Unattractive citrus?
71 Sous-chef, frequently
72 Possesses
73 Taxing org.
75 Monster
76 Traps
77 Official absolutions
79 Necklace attachments
80 "Merchant of Venice" heroine
82 Trevi number
84 Knit fabric
87 Macho
92 Mere handful
93 D-Day vessels
95 Province or lake: Abbr.
97 Actress Dawn Chong
98 "___ Got a Secret"
99 Lexicographer's tome: Abbr.
101 Taconite, e.g.

122 FIRST PERSON SINGULAR by Nancy Scandrett Ross
We would like to dedicate this one to Adam.

ACROSS

1 Dies ___
5 Battle souvenirs
10 Dope
14 Signs
15 Editor's mark
16 Method
18 Lover's declaration?
20 Patrol
22 Swarm
23 To be, in Tours
24 Spur
26 Chicago district
27 Farming: Abbr.
28 Julia Child, ___ McWilliams
29 Cantankerous
31 Compass pt.
32 Hideouts
35 Engaging
36 Comprehend
37 Convene
38 Poky
40 Lamb's dam
42 "The world is a bundle ___": Byron
44 Small sum
45 "Betsy's Wedding" star
48 Essence
52 Yarn measure
53 Like a dishrag
55 Spy, in Canaan
56 Gen. Bradley
57 Jekyll's milieu
58 Alamo's boast?
61 Luau staple
62 ___ de Pascua
64 Kind of badge
65 Bearing
66 Stop ___ dime
67 Hot times in Cannes
68 Bright thought
69 Strawberry's weapon
70 ___ down (softened)
72 Squeeze
74 Ado
75 Closure
76 Queen on Mercutio's mind
79 Cavorted
83 Whirls
86 Choler
87 Wage
88 Winter malady
91 Kanga's child
92 Hawk
94 Hulot's portrayer
95 Conspire
96 Formal dance
97 Deli purchase
99 Waist's remark?
102 Magnificent number
103 Wilson's thrush
104 Vexes
105 Trilled
106 Relaxes
107 Pale aqua

DOWN

1 Sour cream's complaint?
2 Twenty quires
3 Short reply
4 Ruhr center
5 Maestro's aid
6 Sugar source
7 Constellation near Scorpius
8 Put back
9 Isaac and Otto
10 Sponge's discovery?
11 Classic prefix
12 Tumble
13 Author of "The Compleat Bachelor"
14 Last letter
17 Treat with tea
18 Printing abbr.
19 Israel follower
21 Rapier
25 Prefix for physical
29 Squeak fixer
30 Bow wood
33 River inlet
34 Phonograph needles
35 Wag
38 Played a gig
39 Current unit
41 Conceit
42 North, to some
43 "Babette's ___"
45 Rhine feeder
46 Vicuna's cousins
47 Ledger entries
49 Enigma's quip?
50 River through Burgundy
51 Three-toned chord
54 Skein's shout?
55 Camper's bed
59 Farrow
60 Stage direction
63 Tree in "Die Walküre"
69 Future flower
71 "A Chorus Line" finale
73 Hikes
74 Supernatural
76 Mile's equal
77 Fields of study
78 Stars of 96 Across
80 Mode preceders
81 Alien's opposite
82 Yalta's peninsula
84 Lounges
85 Boot part
88 Castigates
89 ___ Altos
90 Motorist's maneuver
93 Crater contents
95 Balzac's "Le ___ Goriot"
96 It's posted at 38 Across
98 Porter's "I Hate ___"
100 Parisian possessive
101 Louis IX, e.g.

123 HOLDING PATTERN by Bernard Meren
Our Fayetteville flyer said he was up in the air when he constructed this beauty.

ACROSS

1 Yma from Peru
6 Razorbills, in Granada
11 Burnsian "wee"
14 Choo or plunk preceder
17 Berlin's "All ___"
18 Wary
19 Ductile
21 Hindu queens
22 Sanctum or circle
23 Heartburn soother
24 "We are ___ of singing birds": S. Johnson
25 What Manning tries to avoid
27 Pine
29 Without, in Würzburg
30 Joan Van ___
31 Obligation
33 Stir
35 Kaffiyah cord
37 Fanfare
41 Miami five
42 Baal, for instance
44 Arena of WW II
45 Mire
46 "Ragged Dick" author
48 Inept soldier
51 Informed about
52 Belgian-French river
53 Detective Lupin
56 Slalom
57 Speed
58 Caliph
59 Ethyl or methyl ending
61 Engrave
63 "East of Eden" character
66 Capture
68 Turns inside out
70 Ewe said it?
73 English undershirt
74 Trash throwaway
76 Menotti role
78 Eastern nannies
80 You, in Toulon
81 British informer
84 Elderly
85 "Yes ___!"
86 One-sixth of a drachma
88 ___ volente
89 Pliny's birthplace
90 Perched
92 Neighborhood
94 Rice dish
96 Doubled
101 Rommel
104 Threw out
105 Razorbill
106 Din
107 Festered
108 Out of whack
109 Pierre's year
110 Santa ___
111 Author LeShan
112 Clan units
113 ___ with (supported)

DOWN

1 Teasdale
2 ___ Bator
3 Affluent one
4 Cordial
5 Fronton basket
6 Trued
7 Smooth, phonetically
8 A hundred, in Livorno
9 Franklin from Memphis
10 Hypos
11 Unaccompanied male
12 Altar stone
13 Star in Scorpio
14 Fourth-down choice
15 Author Ducommun
16 Foxx
20 Penitent's wear
26 ___ a pin
28 Troy col.
31 Indian chick-pea
32 Wriggling
34 Margin of victory
36 Foot follower
38 Hawk's leash
39 Charles's family pet
40 Heyerdahl
43 Kirkland of labor
47 Crash
49 Star in Cygnus
50 "Santa Baby" singer
54 Tolled
55 Mosaic piece
58 Abed
60 Author Hunter
62 Gray org.
63 Gardner namesakes
64 Ancient people of Gaul
65 Eskers
67 Monkey bread
69 Minced oath
70 Blowhard
71 Polite interruption
72 Ray or Gucci
75 Museum of Natural History displays
77 Yankee Doodle's feather
79 Mariners' land
82 Quell
83 Japanese carp
87 Soybean for one
91 Tammany bigwig of 1857
93 "Get ___ on yourself!"
95 Horne and Olin
96 Greek Juno
97 Bunin or Boesky
98 Actress Yothers
99 Norwegian canton
100 Whilom
102 Understanding words
103 Poverty

124 NAY SAYINGS by Mark Blakeburn
A negative attitude might prove to be a plus for solvers.

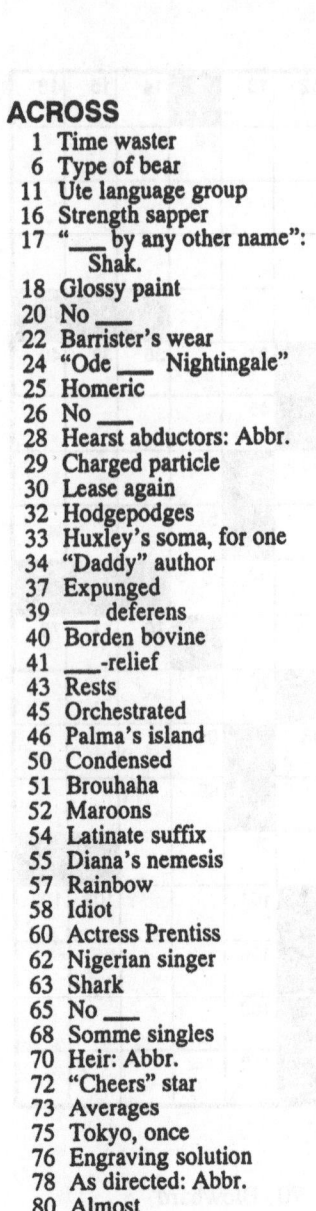

ACROSS

1 Time waster
6 Type of bear
11 Ute language group
16 Strength sapper
17 "___ by any other name": Shak.
18 Glossy paint
20 No ___
22 Barrister's wear
24 "Ode ___ Nightingale"
25 Homeric
26 No ___
28 Hearst abductors: Abbr.
29 Charged particle
30 Lease again
32 Hodgepodges
33 Huxley's soma, for one
34 "Daddy" author
37 Expunged
39 ___ deferens
40 Borden bovine
41 ___-relief
43 Rests
45 Orchestrated
46 Palma's island
50 Condensed
51 Brouhaha
52 Maroons
54 Latinate suffix
55 Diana's nemesis
57 Rainbow
58 Idiot
60 Actress Prentiss
62 Nigerian singer
63 Shark
65 No ___
68 Somme singles
70 Heir: Abbr.
72 "Cheers" star
73 Averages
75 Tokyo, once
76 Engraving solution
78 As directed: Abbr.
80 Almost
82 Totals
83 "The First Time ___ Saw Your Face"
85 Formula-1 cars
86 Odoriferous
88 Foreboding
90 Brother's rel.
91 Woman's hat
92 N.T. book
93 Exclamations of accomplishment
95 Mrs. Mertz
99 " . . . transporting ___ of money": Shak.
100 Church council
102 Chop
104 Uris hero
105 DXXX + DXXI
106 Bank transaction
108 School subj.
109 Aries
110 Apply to
112 No ___
116 Fine wool
117 Hitchcockian
118 She
119 Evans and Carnegie
120 Declivities
121 King novel, with "The"

DOWN

1 Whacky
2 Anti-crack org.
3 K-O connection
4 Sea duck
5 Grated
6 Allotted
7 Ball
8 Cloth mask
9 Houston player
10 Adamant
11 Greek garment
12 Arrow poisons
13 Pedant
14 Pierre's friend
15 No ___
16 In progress
19 "Exit Smiling" star
20 "Yes ___": Beatles song
21 Houston player
23 Stormed: Arch.
27 Slant
31 Wigwam
33 Mesa's cousin
35 Black
36 Fats
38 No ___
40 James and Jones
42 "Ivanhoe" author
44 Silks of Roma
45 Place
46 Address to 13 Down
47 Grate
48 No ___
49 Frogs and toads
51 "Dangerous Liaisons" outcome
53 European wheat
55 Sigourney Weaver film
56 Follet's "Eye of the ___"
59 EFL cousin
61 Hattiesburg sch.
64 Sponge aperture
66 Enrage
67 Copter cousins
69 Sauce and bean
71 Andean country
74 Bandleader Shaw
77 Jong's "___ Woman's Blues"
79 King of Troy
81 Throw out
83 Raised
84 Blue dyes
86 Impress
87 Saracen, for one
88 Wine: Comb. form
89 Swindler
92 Greek god of sleep
94 Jeers
96 "___ and Maude": 1971 film
97 Clear the board
98 Kind of ade
100 French river
101 Embankment worker
103 Ant
106 Irish lower house
107 Novice
111 Refrain syllable
113 Tot
114 Entertainer Sumac
115 Grey in "Three Smart Girls"

UP FRONT ZOO by Jeanette K. Brill
Just for starters, find the eight beasts in this fine offering from a Floridian wordmaster.

ACROSS

1 Printer's ___ (apprentice)
6 Rose perfume
11 Retinue
18 Egg-shaped
19 Laissez-___
20 Fines
21 Absolute
23 Nullifies
24 Tread
25 Indian chief or leader
26 Duo
30 What "video" means
32 Family car
33 Part of TAE
34 Certain legumes
36 Gilbert of tennis
40 ___ out (crush)
42 Yokels
43 Preacher of positive thinking
44 More anxious
46 Greek letters
47 Method of surveying
48 Earphones with attached mouthpiece transmitter
50 Pepys or Nin
51 Pooch in "The Thin Man"
54 Search for and find
57 Clothes-closet culprit
58 Plato, to Aristotle
60 Falls for a married woman
62 Side-show spieler
63 "___ Irish Rose"
65 Take a second look at a book
69 Coral island
70 Like fresh celery
71 Ray
72 Lug
73 Trivial problems
77 Villa d'___
78 Barking dog, at times
79 Word with toe or finger
80 Jazz, for one type
81 Coloring matters
85 What France and Belgium once were
87 Short solo
88 Flighty
95 More courteous
96 "I Want ___," 1911 song
97 Twenty
98 Trappers
99 Slip of memory
100 Cloth used for toweling

DOWN

1 Ward healer
2 LeGallienne
3 Large tub
4 Meteor tail
5 "Daddy Long ___"
6 Again
7 Taiwan's capital
8 Involuntary twitch
9 Heavenly altar
10 Bro. or sis.
11 Actor Lee and namesakes
12 Greek letters
13 One of King Lear's daughters
14 Miner's vehicle
15 Comb. form meaning "outside"
16 Actor in "The Waltons"
17 Being, to a philosopher
22 Of the ear
25 Looks for
26 Ago
27 See 49 Down
28 Lendl of tennis
29 Shaky; dilapidated
31 Warbling Swiss mountaineer
32 Protective agcy.
35 Playful
36 Down time on Wall Street
37 Woody Allen's "___ Days"
38 Heeling, as a ship
39 Start of a Cather title
41 ___ Dee, river in N. Carolina
43 Sch. org.
45 ___ Johnson, 1960 Olympics decathalon winner
46 Neighbor of Leb.
47 Shankar's instrument
49 With 27 Down, epithet for Adenauer
50 Excavated
51 Facing the pitcher
52 Former Asian pact
53 Fortuneteller's card
55 Cravat accessory
56 Amer. kin of 52 Down
59 Norse queen of the underworld
61 Legal thing
63 French city on the Rhone
64 Stein contents in Stuttgart
66 Mitigate
67 "___ boy!"
68 Judge
70 "___ Saturday Night" (after "The"): Burns
73 One who strikes coins
74 Vassar products
75 Likely
76 Disparage
78 Midler or Davis
81 Political patronages
82 Golf club
83 River in S Arizona
84 Golda of Israel
86 Endure
88 Broadway Prince
89 Turkish title of respect
90 Tear
91 Kind of water or cream
92 And not
93 Make a misstep
94 "L.A. Law" actress

126 CONSUMER'S DIGEST by Wilson McBeath

Chef McBeath invites you to partake of his savory creation of fresh clues and peppery puns. (We highly recommend the paradox at 44 Down!)

ACROSS

1 Pod members
5 Hold up
8 A religious faith
13 Nursling
17 Fashion magazine
18 Separate entity
19 Family reunion attendee
20 Nautical term
21 Surrounded by
22 Manipulate
23 Popular Italian restaurants in Soho, New York
25 Gas-grill adjunct
28 Legal document
29 Intersect, geometrically
30 FDR's "Blue Eagle"
32 Twelve: Comb. form
36 Becomes serious
39 Taut
41 Entertain lavishly
43 Deserves
44 Side by side
46 Change the equipment
47 French state
48 Mex. neighbor
49 Negatives
51 Golfer Ballesteros
52 Lit. submissions
53 Of medicine
55 Boards for 57 Across
57 Andrea del ___
59 Swiss river
61 Salon solution
62 Hypotheses
65 Villains
67 Abbr. at the pumps
70 Mr., in Wiesbaden
71 Room in a casa
73 Stole, e.g.
74 Invoice
75 Mine passages
77 Tavern
79 "Golden Hind" captain
80 Think
82 False: Comb. form
83 Up
84 Appraise
86 Continental defense org.
87 Sharp projection
88 Miss Kett
90 Meals on wheels?
95 Glass or grass abode?
100 Alderman, for short
101 Thoroughly cooked
102 Possessive pronoun
103 Singer John
104 Mesabi output
105 Villa d'___
106 Nomadic shelter
107 Choose anew
108 Bottom line
109 Calced

DOWN

1 Anjou, for one
2 Pollster Roper
3 Landed
4 Lees
5 Stirs
6 Beginning
7 Brew
8 Medical trainee
9 Title for Tor
10 Conduct
11 Performed
12 Shooting star
13 See 77 Across
14 ___ Baba
15 TV's Arthur
16 Affirmative
24 More bizarre
26 Short homilies
27 Sluggishness
31 "Pure ___ angel": Talleyrand
33 Discharges
34 Where seniors often eat to meet
35 Animated
36 Appear
37 Percheron's repast
38 Taverns, in Lille
39 Lift at Vail
40 Workers' investment plan: Abbr.
42 Nice summers
44 Takeouts eat-in place
45 Where to find Earl Grey?
48 CIA director
50 Move furtively
53 Without symmetry: Abbr.
54 Churl
56 Annapolis grad.
58 Trunks in trunks
60 Alter a photograph
62 Bangkok native
63 Ibsen's "___ Gabler"
64 Swat
66 Ellington's "___ Indigo"
68 Sommer of films
69 Valley
72 Church area
74 Military units
76 Dutch painter Jan ___
78 Symbol of triviality
79 Attract
81 Biblical book
83 Sock
85 Boa
87 Twenty
89 Hudson or Essex
91 Well-versed in
92 Wow!
93 Aware of
94 Indigence
95 Comprehended
96 Sèvres street
97 Sea eagle
98 Superlative ending
99 Bribe

127

LIVES by Vanessa Leigh Patterson
A no-nonsense work with original clues; autobiographies are hidden within the squares.

ACROSS

1 Boorish one
5 Saint for Ahab
9 Old Possum's theatre cat
12 Tall story
16 General's assistant
17 Poet of the Confederacy
18 Part of R.E.A.
20 Lamb alias
21 Auchincloss memoirs, with "A"
24 Salty septet
25 Health, to Hilaire
26 These can be inflated
27 Shirley Jackson story, after "The"
29 Goddess of discord
32 Haile Selassie's country
34 Tam-o'-shanter
37 Kenneth Clark memoirs, with "The"
39 Ham it up
43 Ice and Iron
45 Always, to Donne
46 Sugar suffix
47 Flapjack cousins
48 Lillian Hellman memoirs
51 New Deal org.
53 Island near Sumatra
54 Dogma
55 Fox hunter's coat
56 Skipjack
58 "___ Irish Rose"
60 Rinds
62 They're lower than violas
65 Auction sign
66 Sidles
71 Kirghiz mountain range
72 Penguins' org.
74 F. Scott Fitzgerald memoirs
76 Rapped out a reply
78 Simian
80 Miss West
81 Roll response
82 Shoe part
83 Anita Loos memoirs, with "A"
86 Hitched
87 Inherently
89 Cheese town
91 Floating debris
94 Whittle
96 Lugubrious noises
100 Famous theater man
101 C. S. Lewis memoirs
105 Song for Aida
106 To ___ (exactly)
107 Woody stem
108 Perthshire loch
109 Sets
110 Nursery product
111 Petitions
112 Span. matrons

DOWN

1 Proverbs
2 Turkish pound
3 Frigga's husband
4 "___ Davis Eyes"
5 Bobble
6 Fleur-de-___
7 Spiked club
8 Kiang
9 Madame Butterfly et al.
10 Happening last mo.
11 ___ approval
12 Frank Lloyd Wright memoirs, with "A"
13 Aweather's opposite
14 Münchausen, for one
15 Kind of chair
19 Sabot sound
22 Saarinen
23 Kettle holder
28 Bleacher unit
30 Gossipy tidbit
31 Embarrassed
33 ___ du Vent
34 Lt.'s goal

35 "Permit Me Voyage" poet
36 Director of "Bonnie and Clyde"
38 Journalist Pyle
40 The Cornish Wonder
41 Salty drop
42 Sibilant
44 Jeanne d'Arc, e.g.
47 Necessity
49 Type of type: Abbr.
50 Heavy wts.
52 Caraway dessert
57 Confused
59 Dr. No's nemesis
60 Word of contempt
61 Ink resin
62 Applaud
63 Tombstone marshal
64 Malcolm Muggeridge memoirs
65 Astral
67 Berliner's exclamation
68 Bias
69 Seine tributary

70 Hurried
71 ___ Dhabi
73 Meaux milk
75 Marsh grass
77 White-tailed birds
79 Attended Choate
83 Complete ranges
84 Words from Hal David
85 Metrical foot
88 Endeavour's org.
90 "Murder à la Mode" author
91 June 14 honoree
92 Mythology
93 ___-de-boeuf
95 Biblical pottage-eater
97 Slightly open
98 Asta's lady
99 Dict. entries
102 Antique auto
103 Compass dir.
104 ___ Moines

128 BIBLICAL BYWORDS by John Greenman

You may be surprised to discover that all six of the common expressions below originated in the Good Book.

ACROSS

1 Gam or Moreno
5 Jacob's sib
9 Valerie Harper role
14 Kind of luck
17 Mystery writer Lesley
18 Roasting rod
19 Roof rims
20 Tune from "A Chorus Line"
21 What charity covers (I Peter 4:18)
24 Pool at Belmont
25 "____ a Camera"
26 Half-score
27 Houston col.
28 Revise
30 Metal fasteners
32 Legal matter
34 Fore's opposite
37 Mispickel and argentite
38 Vic's radio partner
39 Puffs up
42 Burdens
44 Use of threats
46 Wide-awake
48 Explosive
51 Little meaning
54 Be in agreement (Isaiah 52:8)
56 Garden tool
57 Library visitors
59 Budget entry
60 Kind of bean
61 Modifies
62 Elm's offering
64 Orange boxes
66 Grimalkin's cry
67 "Thanks ___!"
68 Fit to drink
69 Sandy's remark
70 Altruistic work (I Thessalonians 1:3)
74 Ar's successor
75 Concorde
76 "Get Happy" tunesmith
77 Most unusual
79 Marilyn or Lena
81 British biscuits
83 Director Avakian
87 Hied
89 ___ of Good Feeling
91 All one's born days
92 Freshman cadet
93 Riot
95 Nothing
97 West of Hollywood
99 Morris or Garfield
100 Pie ___ mode
101 Narrowest margin (Job 19:20)
107 Sportscaster Berman
108 Connection
109 Bog moss
110 Notion: Comb. form
111 Emulated Mehta
112 Altar sites
113 Ruckus
114 Mr. Foxx

DOWN

1 Sends money
2 Tropical lizard
3 Gemara collection
4 Pantry pillager
5 Villa d'____
6 Whirled
7 Succor
8 Colorado tribesman
9 Ring officials
10 ___ la vista
11 Egg: Comb. form
12 Cozy room
13 African fox
14 Controlling forces (Romans 13:1)
15 Cat-___-tails
16 Watches over
22 "___ a Wonderful Life"
23 Eject
29 Rocker's foe in "Quadrophenia"
31 Koppel of TV
32 American Beauty
33 Simple

35 Armada
36 Whig's rival
39 Fox and Bear
40 Dregs
41 Surfeited
43 Gobbled
45 Addict
47 Single
49 Romans-fleuves
50 Taunts
51 Serious stagings
52 Certain fishermen
53 Choicest food and luxuries (Genesis 45:18)
55 Muse of love poetry
58 Natural moisture
60 DOT agency
62 ___ gin fizz
63 Antlers
64 Inlets
65 9W and 66
67 More competent
68 Skin opening
70 Household deity

71 English composer
72 Ranid
73 Kent's coworker
78 Russian chess great
80 Pindar product
82 Young whale
84 Withdraw
85 Ebbed
86 Procedure
87 Wee
88 Martinique volcano
90 Aileen Quinn role
92 Favorite
94 This: Span.
96 Charged particles
97 Arizona-Nevada lake
98 In re
102 1000 pounds
103 Plural ending
104 Elect
105 Combiner for Latin
106 Norse goddess of healing

129

IT'S HARD TO SAY by Dorothy Smitonick

The title refers to the clever query below which begins at 11 Down. (If you're wondering about 44 Across, it's what a parakeet is called in England.)

ACROSS

1 Spaces
6 Cord
11 Overact, with "up"
16 Canine check
17 Chattered
18 Thinks
20 Italian main course, often
21 Chorus section
22 Sage
24 Asparagus stalk
25 Image: Var.
26 Defarge and Bovary: Abbr.
27 Mideast org.
28 Buddies
30 Pert
31 To boot
32 Favors
36 Rap session?
38 Twit's cousin
39 Regulate once more
40 Complete
41 Prohibit
42 English potter
43 Symbol of fitness
44 QUERY: PART III
47 LP features
49 Errs
50 Skip
53 Wild carrot, e.g.
54 Kind of swallow
56 Brontë heroine
57 Styptic sticks
59 Proofread: Brit.
61 Wilde and Underwood
62 Waited
64 Nourishes
68 "___ Sunday Afternoon"
69 Farm
70 Erse
71 SA country
73 Dive
74 American saint
75 Stavanger loc.
76 QUERY: PART VI
77 Hindu title
78 Operative org.
79 Pay to play
80 Asian river
82 Clothe
87 Gobble
89 "___ Runner," 1982 film
90 "Taras Bulba" novelist
91 Squid
92 END OF QUERY
93 Totally
94 Pigs' digs
95 Islamic ruler
96 Curves

DOWN

1 Piz Bernina locale
2 Harvest
3 Spontaneity
4 Travel org.
5 Whetstone
6 Follows
7 Leaves the car at home
8 "___ each life some rain . . ."
9 Tiffin time
10 USNA grad
11 START OF QUERY
12 Each
13 Girl
14 Suffix for serpent
15 In a seductive way
19 Drawing room
23 Alcove
26 Parsonage
29 "We ___ not amused": Victoria
30 Spanker or jib
32 Small braces
33 Agent
34 Arena of WW II
35 QUERY: PART II
36 Did a vinyl job
37 Targets for Elway
38 Inventor, of sorts
40 "___ Easy Pieces"
41 Roll
43 Opponents
44 German political league
45 Comparative ending
46 Suffix for Marshall
48 Temple team
49 Raised
50 USN address
51 Trumpeter Elgart
52 Spurs on
54 QUERY: PART IV
55 Busy as ___
58 Savings acct.
59 Warble
60 QUERY: PART V
62 In general, after "as"
63 Corps
65 Old Testament judge
66 Noise
67 ___-fi
69 Protein substances from flour
70 Yak
71 Ending for confer
72 Change
73 Chinese silk
74 Vocation
76 Wrist bones
77 QUERY: PART VII
80 An astringent
81 Constructed
83 McKarty and Silver
84 Arabian leaders
85 Position at Indy
86 Annexes
88 Bran source
89 Graphics deg.

130 FAIR PLAY by Louis Sabin
Lou suggests that you consider the adage about turning about.

ACROSS

1 Actor Gibson from N.Y.
4 Average ruiner for a batter
9 "Hot corner," e.g.
13 Dividing word
17 Forum salute
18 Kind of code
19 Food quality
20 Ginza glow
21 Hates to bid?
24 Chorister's club
25 Concentrated
26 "___ Cheatin' Heart," 1964 film
27 Black Sea port
29 United
30 Regal settings
33 "Sail ___ Ship of State": Longfellow
34 Atl. crosser
36 Electrolysis products
37 Funnel-shaped flower
41 Limerick product
44 Little Big Horn escapee
46 Time frame
47 This, to Conchita: Fem. form
48 "___ My Love," 1950 song
49 Wary drivers?
53 "Le Coq ___": Rimsky-Korsakov
54 Causes
56 The Venerable ___
57 Couch concern
59 Lay off
60 Argumentative
62 Job security
65 Schubert Alley sign
66 Hawks or Jazz
67 Noted bird watcher
68 Tanner family guest
70 Full houses for young ladies?
74 Medieval lyric poem
75 Gossip
77 Fold
78 Regarding
79 Dispatch
80 Control
82 "Black ___," 1948 film
84 Team lifter
86 Inferior
87 Region
90 "Mule Train" singer
94 Metamorphic rock
97 Flees
98 Went too far
100 Mining site
101 Burly Russians?
104 Word of weltschmerz
105 Cherokee's cousin
106 Wedding, e.g.
107 Aka Horned Frogs
108 Food piercer
109 Destitution
110 Numskulls
111 Needle part

DOWN

1 "Goodfellas" group
2 Buttermilk rider
3 Slow, to Ozawa
4 Bookbinder's units
5 Virginia family
6 Like some gems
7 Puss
8 Child's venue
9 Petty officers
10 C'est ___ (that is to say)
11 Junior
12 "Cogito ___ sum": Descartes
13 Debutante
14 Mandela's doppelgänger?
15 Parts of socks
16 ___ cat (game)
22 Use a thurible
23 Gershwin tune
28 Period
31 The Golden ___, Drake's flagship
32 Tear
35 River to the Ouse
38 Attention
39 Robert of "Quincy, M.E."
40 Bern's river
41 Cookie ingredient, sometimes
42 Word from the bridge
43 Future student-body president?
45 Penny takes two of these
46 Swirl
49 Kind of companion
50 "The Master Builder" dramatist
51 Take-home pay
52 Broadcaster's supply
55 Balin or Balan
58 Kokoon
60 Fastidious
61 Woman, poetically
62 Henry VIII's House
63 Red-brown
64 Geraint's lady
66 Boneless steak
67 Formicarian
68 Pother
69 Sauciness
71 Suited
72 Worn-out
73 Piedmont province
76 Wander
79 Lewis of TV
81 Classified matters, for short
82 Stopped a car
83 Force
85 Watchful periods
88 Ms. Dinsmore
89 Treasured prize
91 Vexed
92 Sluggo's pal
93 Follow
94 Dog chaser
95 City SW of Bogotá
96 Besides
99 Seam opening
102 Suffix with fail or press
103 ___ Levy, aka Yves Montand

131

AVON CALLING by Kenneth Haxton

You don't have to be a Shakespearean scholar to enjoy solving this classical delight. If the Bard had been an answer in this puzzle, we might have been tempted to modify the clue at 20 Across: "Age cannot wither him . . ."

ACROSS

1 Vipers
5 Island in the Seine
8 "___ Days With Me," 1988 film
12 Cubicle
16 Flee
17 Tree knot
18 Not final
19 Nichols hero
20 "Age cannot wither her . . ."
22 Othello's wife
24 Flattened at the poles
25 Lyricist David
26 Baked
27 Hotspur's ally
31 Religious image
34 "Where thou ___, I will . . .": Ruth 1:16
35 Attacks
39 Past or present
41 Memo makers
43 Prefix for lithic
44 Diocese
45 California college town
48 Salieri opera
51 Rod
52 Gain
54 Part of MIT
56 Unfortunates
58 Macbeth's victim
60 Fop in "As You Like It"
62 Time-out
65 Desiccated
67 Map features
70 Gametes
71 Responses to rodents
73 "The Snake Pit" author
75 Berlin grandpa
77 Spanish guitarist
78 Fleet
80 Milk whey
82 More somber
86 Concerning
88 Mad
89 Falstaff's lover
93 Shoe part
96 I.C. and B & O
97 Chafe
100 Katherina's tamer
102 Gentleman of Verona
105 Whooper or whistler
106 Oleo containers
107 State
108 Organic compound
109 Mel and Ed of baseball
110 Widgeon
111 Round Table knight
112 Stitches

DOWN

1 "Nightline" ntwk.
2 Man from U.N.C.L.E.
3 Commoner
4 Runners
5 Mean
6 Household god
7 Koufax had a low one
8 Musically flowing
9 "Soapdish" star
10 Sigma
11 With mite or peak
12 Land invention
13 Black
14 Vocation
15 Clue
17 Actress Capshaw
21 Fido's foot
23 Holiday times
25 Movie Moses
28 Rummy scores
29 Dionyza's servant
30 Kiln
31 Styne's "___ Magic"
32 Prison
33 Singular chap
36 "Picnic" playwright
37 Goneril's father
38 Tosspots
40 Decant
42 Amount to something
46 Salon solution
47 Catchall abbr.
49 Coeur d' ___
50 Friars' fetes
53 "___ to St. Cecelia"
55 Cousin to Justice Swallow
57 "A Boy Named ___"
59 Tatar, formerly: Abbr.
61 Encore!
62 He revolted against Macbeth
63 Bacchanalian cry
64 Eccentric
66 Colombian ponchos
68 Fiesta-taurina charger
69 Urge
72 Malden or Marx
74 Dailey and Coats
76 French soul
79 Anjelica's "Prizzi's Honor" role
81 Possessions
83 Embellishes
84 S Amer. balsam
85 Chooses
87 Old German coin
90 Levi or Gad
91 Eponymous Hebrew ancestor
92 Osprey relative
93 ___ facto
94 Eft
95 Immediately!
98 Emulate Lucullus
99 Enough, once
101 Drone
102 Brewer's back
103 Macanese money
104 Chicago rails

132 MODEST STAR by Shirley Soloway

He played down-to-earth roles, and the quotation reveals that he was the same kind of person in real life.

ACROSS

1 Mare's little one
5 Fraternity letters
9 Enervate
12 St. Louis team
16 Emit light, modern style
17 Fuzz
18 Work the field
20 "His Eye ___ the Sparrow," by Ethel Waters
21 ___ boy!
22 "The Egg ___": MacDonald
23 Impulsive
24 Mayberry youth
25 **Start of the quotation**
29 Wrath
30 Relaxation
31 "Phantom" Chaney
32 With 88 Down, speaker of the quotation
34 Brittany port
37 Gossip: Yiddish
39 Texas inst.
40 Ages upon ages
41 ___ Jacinto River (1836 battle site)
43 **Quotation: Part II**
48 Formulated
52 Actor Ayres
53 Dr. Casey
54 Loc. of Aspen
55 Piece of property
58 Odin's Sleipnir, e.g.
60 **Quotation: Part III**
64 Locale, in law
65 Patio, Hawaiian style
66 This may be a subject
67 D.A.
68 Sounds from 5 Down
69 **Quotation: Part IV**
74 **Quotation: Part V** (Hyph.)
79 St. Tropez summer
80 Winter hazard
81 Hammarskjold
82 Holiday dinner in Israel
84 Start again
86 Singer Cole
90 Taste
91 Pedestal occupant
93 Airport info
94 **End of the quotation**
100 Peruse
102 Title
103 Impression; force
104 Novice
105 Peruvian native
106 Butcher shop, in Brest
107 Peter Gunn's girl
108 D. W. Griffith type of film
109 Utters
110 Mil. title
111 Emulate a skylark
112 Workplace for a pupil or principal

DOWN

1 London apartment
2 Vow
3 Sparkling wine
4 Rental agreements
5 Santa
6 Door holder
7 ___-Chinese
8 Inhibit
9 Short runs
10 King of comedy
11 Models
12 "Flying Down to ___," Astaire-Rogers film
13 Jellied side dish
14 Fancy fabric
15 Show disdain
19 Hook-toothed cutter
26 Tatami
27 Opera by Horatio Parker
28 Rig for a trucker
33 Lady of the cloth
34 Fourposter
35 The Brooklyn Dodgers' Preacher
36 Ltr. holder
37 Chemical suffix
38 Marquand hero
41 Realty agent's sign
42 " . . . rusting in ___ tears": Thompson
44 "___ Talk About Love," Cole Porter song
45 Former labor leader
46 Spore
47 Connecting word
49 Beige
50 Solitary
51 Repair a sock
56 Pt. of the Dark Continent
57 Liner
58 Inner being
59 Tommy of Broadway
60 One of the "Little Women"
61 Con
62 Watering hole
63 Hospital ship
64 Tub
68 Science dealing with health
70 Always, in poesy
71 Brooch
72 Perfect service
73 Evergreen
75 Vitamin info
76 Steatite
77 Caravels, ketches, etc.
78 Emulate Charles Dudley Warner
83 Lyric poems
84 Asian GI
85 Joyful
86 Nostril
87 Field of battle
88 See 32 Across
89 Growing out
91 Area in Ancient Greece
92 TLC giver
95 Fed. agent: Hyph.
96 Adriatic isle
97 Use a keyboard
98 Spring bloom
99 Clock sound
101 "___ Boot," 1981 film

133 QUIZZICAL QUIP by William Lutwiniak
An original witticism and inventive clues highlight this crossword legend's opus.

ACROSS

1 City near Phoenix
5 Rugged cover
9 Kind of trooper
13 "I never ___ purple . . ."
17 Play pieces
18 Wine bucket
19 A Waugh
20 Ivy Leaguers
21 **Start of the quip**
25 Sondheim-Bernstein song
26 Dove house
27 Prisoner
28 Old pro
29 Gainsay
30 Give up
31 Dancer's sleigh-mate
34 Memorable Arnaz
35 Sachet scent
39 Through
40 Wrote Rx's
42 Actor Milland
43 Cushion
44 Potage
45 Claire and Balin
46 Bernhardt's rival
47 Pitcher's choice
49 German spa
51 Activates a beeper
52 **Middle of the quip**
56 Ascent
58 Spreads unchecked
59 Island 2,000 miles west of Chile
62 By itself
63 Literature Nobelist: 1947
64 Common solecism
66 Charge it
67 ID item
68 Doctor's dispensations
71 Noted Scott
73 Coach signal, of yore
74 Pop-ups, usually
75 Jurypersons
76 Makeshifts
77 Overwork
78 Vigor
79 Bluebloods
82 Awful
83 Fine cigars
87 **End of the quip**
90 Avast!
91 Transude
92 " . . . got ___ in Kalamazoo"
93 Respecting
94 Ump's call
95 Quay
96 Father's Day givers, sometimes
97 ___ off (vexed)

DOWN

1 Marshal Dillon
2 Iteration
3 "Nana" star
4 Trembling
5 Too snug
6 Eight, in Erfurt
7 Part of RV
8 Continuing development
9 Peppermint or Duke
10 Lip-salve ingredient
11 Ency., e.g.
12 Accomplishes
13 Tars
14 ___ breve
15 Eminent German skater
16 Tennis great
22 "___ Ideas"
23 Boom type
24 Over
29 Abstruse
30 Bathhouse
31 The law
32 Powerful office
33 Rx items
34 "Red River" actress
35 Wrinkled
36 Rx emporium
37 Comfort
38 Bar members?
40 Study in depth
41 Heckles
44 Belgrade native
46 Speaker's spot
48 Titled lady
49 Engender
50 Peer Gynt's mother
51 Test for a teen
53 They give it a go
54 ___ eye to (intended)
55 Cravings
56 Applaud
57 Trademark
60 Pitcher
61 Beatty film
63 UK liquor store
64 Chamber lead-in
65 "___ Magic"
68 Object
69 Dancer Shearer
70 Triumphant cries
71 Part of FDIC
73 Road show
75 Mantaro locale
77 Oven feature
78 Cartels
79 Award-winning
80 Opposed
81 Leeway
82 Nap
83 Blue hue
84 Ennead
85 Four roods
86 Short timetable
88 Thee, in Tours
89 Swelled head

134 T-MEN by Mark Diehl

When Mark asked the gentleman at 83 Across how he liked the clue, he replied that it suited him to a . . .

ACROSS

1 Spiny-finned fish
5 Stallone role
10 CBS rival
13 Building lot
17 Quarter
18 Tunesmith's org.
19 Minivan asset
21 Glacial stage
22 He loved suckers
24 ___ with (bump off)
26 Woody's son
27 Town SE of Des Moines
28 First name in the Rainbow Coalition
29 Type of sack
30 ___ Jacinto
31 Dit-dit-dit
32 Tuskegee Institute's institutor
37 Feels poorly
38 Some CDs
39 "I cannot tell ___"
40 Food pkg. info
43 "Kidnapped" auth.
44 "Afternoon of a ___": Debussy
45 Companion of aid
46 Bewildered
47 Teen nightmare: Slang
48 Linen
49 Birth-related
50 Enshrined hero of Dogpatch
56 ___ side and down the other
57 Musical brothers
58 French psychotherapist
59 Filmed action sequence
60 Rock-concert equipment
61 Bogus
62 RR stop
65 Ski jumper Nieminen
66 French ecclesiastic
67 Ernest T. Worrell's neighbor
68 Eschew
69 Sulu's commander
73 Econ. yardstick
75 Terhune canine
76 Challenge
77 Spotted carnivore
78 "Legal Eagles" star
80 Sundial number
81 Odors
83 Stepquote inventor
86 Oath responses
88 Number-1 draft picks
89 Morality
90 Lat. gender
91 Forks over
92 "Laus ___"
93 TV's "___ Hope"
94 Art-deco name

DOWN

1 Word with bones or buck
2 Petroleum
3 Spray cans
4 Lustrous fabrics
5 ___ Nui (Easter Island)
6 Pale
7 AT&T competitor
8 Woody Allen film
9 Bellini works
10 Chan's comment
11 Exacta, e.g.
12 Moolah: Slang
13 Sched. listings
14 Goes along with
15 Rakes
16 Oscar relatives
20 Cow
23 Aramaic and Braille
25 Like Winkie
28 Ski-lift type: Hyph.
29 She played Suzie Wong
30 Stew
33 Gaucho rope
34 Cartel
35 Akin to jejunal
36 Prerecorded
41 Put on solid foods
42 Yarn
44 Choice cut
45 Carlson and Jacobsen
46 July-to-July, to Julius
47 Sunflower kin
48 Abridgements
50 Fair-minded
51 "What have you been ___?"
52 In a hearty manner
53 Metrical feet
54 Earthy shade
55 Bays
60 "___ Day at Black Rock"
61 Polka-dotted
62 Guardian angel, perhaps
63 Unfolds
64 "Lonely Boy" singer
66 Culminating
67 Life's spice
68 Manhattan feature
70 Place a mole
71 Turnkey
72 English article
73 Budget-priced
74 Abdul of rock
79 Costner role of 1987
80 "___ Lonesome I Could Cry"
81 Hide
82 Red apples
84 Uno e due
85 ___ Na Na
87 Environmental org.

135
PAX VOBISCUM by Albert J. Klaus
Albert pays tribute to seven recipients of the world's most esteemed prize.

ACROSS

1 South African Peace Nobelist
5 Tucker's partner
8 City SW of Le Havre
12 Auto ID
17 Sale condition
18 Kingston col.
19 "God's Little ___"
20 Work
21 Of a teacher's status
23 German Peace Nobelist
25 Unworldly
26 Intertwines
28 Wk. member
29 Plum part
30 Arab people of Hira
31 Tidbits
35 Exposed
38 Dormouse
39 Water-treatment process
40 Ripsnorter
41 American Peace Nobelist
43 Appeal
44 Prefix for aggression
45 Seal schools
46 Finks on
47 Instance
48 States of low vitality
50 Whelps
52 "Home Run" of baseball
53 Waterbury loc.
54 Up in the air
55 Titicaca locale
56 Isolated
58 Nautical call
59 Anticipate
62 Spar
63 Glaswegian
64 Scoter
65 Fatima's husband
66 Fool
67 Alsatian-German Peace Nobelist
70 Magi guide
71 Sews
73 Grounded birds of yesteryear
74 Copy
75 Costa Brava gentlemen
76 Bring on
77 Payable
78 "Jupiter Symphony" comp.
79 Prefix for lateral
80 Spain and Portugal
84 Polish Peace Nobelist
88 Kegling game
90 Bay window
91 Actor Richard
92 "Butterflies ___ Free"
93 Protective order
94 Walks in water
95 Desire
96 E Indian weight
97 Relax

DOWN

1 Word of departure: Hyph.
2 Employs
3 Color
4 Powermonger
5 Constructed
6 Evangelist Sankey
7 Oodles
8 Chittamwood
9 Emulated Irons
10 Mistakes
11 Maiden-named
12 Thorax linings
13 Least adequate
14 Robe for Omar
15 High fashion
16 Piscivorous bird
22 Invasion
24 Rages
27 Anne Nichols hero
31 Gists
32 Japanese Peace Nobelist
33 Cad
34 Disdain
35 ___ fide
36 Soon
37 French Peace Nobelist
38 Boys
39 Conform
41 Baez or Collins
42 Purport
45 .473 liter
47 Concern
49 Humorist Sahl
50 Line-up
51 Denials
52 A Bobbsey twin
54 Asseverates
55 Pitiful
56 Accumulate
57 Strass
58 Pains
59 Antagonists
60 Vigor
61 Mary Robinson's land
63 Blueprint
64 Empresses
67 Scribbles
68 Fix firmly
69 Tipster
70 Woody Allen film
72 American finch
74 Raise to a third power
76 Dunn or Dey
77 Mel Sharples owned one
79 Prefix for hertz
81 Ruffle
82 Signs
83 Helper: Abbr.
84 Bass
85 Reliever's stat.
86 Spanish hero
87 Actor Ayres
89 Wrath

136

SINLESS by Joy L. Wouk

There's nothing deadly about this puzzle, but we can't say it's easy either.

ACROSS

1 Soho home
5 Mount Pelée product
9 Taiwan island
14 Poke
17 Musical medley
18 Enoch's son: Gen. 4:18
19 Allen or Frome
20 ___ Opey Dildock of comics
21 Pacific atoll for a wine-lovers' convention?
22 ___ mountain, peak in Colorado
23 Emulated Rip Van Winkle
24 Disaster
25 Marx brothers film!
28 Haranguing salesman
30 New Orleans candy
31 Avocet
32 Marsupial "bear"
35 Emden finish
36 Galena, e.g.
37 French magazine
41 Mica!
43 Indonesian channel!
46 Certain votes of assent
48 Claimant to a throne
49 Withered
50 Row
52 Be ready
53 Air Force base in Texas
54 Hansberry play!
57 Above, when referring to part of a text
61 Sgt. and cpl.
62 Dew, to Demetrius
63 Locomotive sound
67 Substance that slows a chemical reaction
69 Giving birth to a colt
71 Aversions!
75 Drool
76 Holly
77 Que. neighbor
78 Commander of David's army
80 Ship that brought Miss Liberty to USA
81 ___ Devi, Himalayan mountain
83 Scorpio's brightest
85 Mosquito larva
88 Locale of St. Catherine's monastery!
92 Fuss
93 Rinds
95 Digital watches' features
96 Wild goat
97 Aviate
98 English poet Stephen ___: 1475–1530
99 Unicorn fish
100 Ardor
101 Afternoon party
102 Flaming crime
103 Concordes, e.g.
104 Mahler's "Das Lied von der ___"

DOWN

1 Silas Marner's need
2 Dieter's spread
3 Lahti native
4 Occurred
5 Tripoli is its capital
6 Suitable for plowing
7 Appraiser's activity
8 Appendices
9 Where sailors eat
10 Expanse east of USA
11 " . . . publish it not in ___ Askelon": 2 Sam. 1:20
12 Having most juice
13 Up to the time of
14 Cheek
15 Lotion ingredient
16 Stadium beverage
26 Wipe out
27 Ooze
29 Everlasting, in poetry
31 More regretful
32 Laos coins
33 Leer's less lascivious cousin
34 Controversial pomologist's spray
38 Bail
39 Fibs
40 To be, to Henri
42 Zeno taught on one
44 Colorful fish
45 Sea swallow
47 Kind of cross
51 Italian cheese
52 Lbs., e.g.
54 Physics Nobelist: 1944
55 Japanese seaweed
56 Havens for GI's
57 Cordage tree (Indian mallow)
58 Les Etats ___
59 Deg. for druggists
60 Nudnik's activity
63 Principal's concern
64 Busy place
65 Singleton
66 Fairy-tale villain
68 ___ and out the other
70 Strange
72 California resort
73 Bewilder
74 Shiny fabrics
79 Enemy plane, to a U.S. ace
82 Omega's partner
84 "The Sun Also ___": Hemingway
85 Float; blow gently
86 Otiose
87 Maja painter
88 Pt. of NAACP
89 Over, in Ulm
90 Guide
91 Truck part
94 Zodiac sign

137

GARDEN VARIETIES by Roger H. Courtney
Believe it or not, the names of the vegetables in this puzzle are indeed genuine!

ACROSS

1 Eton boys' mothers
7 "A" is one
11 Serb or Croat
15 Madison or Fifth
16 First name in mystery writing
17 Basso Cesare ___
18 Ember
19 Olympian who was once imprisoned in a jar
20 Accumulate
21 Liliaceous plant
22 One kind of tide
24 Sequoia's language
26 Political districts
28 W Hemisphere's equivalent of NATO
30 ___ ordinaire (cheap table wine)
31 Singer Nat's cabbage?
35 Kuwaiti royal leader
39 Gone skyward
43 Moros tribe members
44 The Red Baron, e.g.
45 Merrymaking
47 ___ culpa
48 Boccaccio's "The ___ Heart"
50 Gene Autry's horse's radish?
52 Personal angel's corn?
54 Fork prongs
55 ___ gratias
57 Golfer Curtis ___
58 Novelist Levin
59 Distort a report
61 Butt
62 "___ la vie!"
64 Barrie's hero's squash?
66 "Was ___ vision . . . ?": Keats
68 Become flaccid
69 Ventured
74 Ferdinand Magellan's cucumber?
79 Actor McKellen
81 Best seller by Robin Cook: 1977
82 By right
83 "___ Curtain" (Hitchcock film)
85 Keen insight
87 Biblical weeds
88 Kind of root
89 Gas used in rubber manufacturing
90 Took a look
91 Fortune's child
92 Decreases one's bankroll

DOWN

1 Large parrot
2 City in Spain
3 Domingo is one
4 Over
5 Actress McClanahan
6 Wizened
7 Brew containers
8 Transgress
9 Actor Baldwin
10 Screen
11 Former actress Signoret
12 Need a calking
13 Recess at Notre Dame
14 Jawed holding device
17 Hindu wrap
23 ___ vivant
25 Days before holidays
27 Slaps with an open hand: Scot
29 Book by Isaac Singer
32 Letters on the Calvary Cross
33 Actor Vidov
34 Parties in Oahu
36 "The ___ Game": 1959 film
37 Earth's glacial era
38 Preparation used in making cheese
39 Kind of seal or tern
40 Employ once again
41 Ex-Mrs. Trump and namesakes
42 Covered with small figures (Her.)
46 Swiss call: Var.
48 Assignment for junior
49 Jewish month
51 Bandbox ___
53 "___ boy!"
56 "Fin's" units
59 Bowsprit
60 Horse breeder's main man
63 Plowed the earth
65 Peete's org.
67 Hellman's "___ in the Attic"
70 A certain angle
71 A certain candle
72 Correct texts
73 Jutlanders
74 Suffix with usher
75 Roentgen's discovery
76 Unadulterated
77 Do aquatints
78 Libertine
80 Captures
84 Canseco stat
86 Stanley or Walker

138

GO! by Arthur S. Verdesca
The lights are in your favor, so let your pen or pencil fly like 83 Down.

ACROSS

1 Abates
5 Gamma's predecessor
9 Cal or Carnegie
13 Cartoonist Soglow
17 Gladiolus stem
18 Vigorous spirit
19 Vicinage
20 Noah's eldest son
21 Four-star Gilliat film: 1946
24 Name of two Egyptian kings
25 Choice cut
26 Actor Ray
27 Morrow or Eisenhower
29 Shot for a pub crawler
30 Warhol or Pafko
31 Curse
32 Many times
35 Art Deco great
36 Modern medical tools
39 Actor in "Waiting for Godot"
40 Lea
42 Moray
43 Ozark ___ of comics
44 Mythical pome tosser
45 Fatigue
46 First queen of Great Britain
47 Ten-sided figure
49 River to the Rhone
51 Felt compassion
52 Final notice, for short
53 Be very dependent
54 ___ time (never)
55 "___ moi le déluge"
57 Sordid
58 Loose jackets
61 Camera attachment
62 Longfellow's "The Bell of ___"
63 Long, heavy hair
64 Slangy negative
65 Violinist Kavafian
66 Effect in the news
69 Eight reals
70 Catches
72 Put the helm of a ship alee
73 Mixture of sulfides
74 Relating to the throat
75 Diet
76 Label
77 Sterile
79 Letter opener
80 Bullfight cloths
84 Sherbets
85 Milieu for Ethan Allen
88 Suit to ___
89 Second Israeli ambassador to U.S.
90 Opponent
91 Jay's prey
92 Chopin's amie
93 Crust
94 Jersey cagers
95 Very, in Versailles

DOWN

1 Heartbeat rec.
2 Soprano Lucrezia ___
3 Rabbit or Fox
4 Ore refiner
5 Suit
6 College in North Carolina
7 Pitch's source
8 Slow movement
9 Oscar-winning portrayer of Miss Daisy
10 Hence
11 So-so grade
12 Tools, locks, cutlery, etc.
13 James Macpherson or opera by Lesueur
14 Old-time radio serial
15 Yod's predecessor in the Hebrew alphabet
16 Neglect
22 When both hands are up
23 Colonial wooer
28 Slav of SE Germany
30 Brother of 44 Across
31 What bugbears do
32 Foul-smelling
33 Counterfeit
34 Play by Emlyn Williams
35 Innisfail
36 Realm over which Goodman presided
37 Writer Alain ___ LeSage
38 Santa's "wheels"
40 Cave, in poesy
41 Like many a New England pasture
44 Protection
46 Teen bane
48 Burrows and Fortas
49 Done in
50 Intend
51 Asiatic evergreen tree
53 Mother of Proserpina
54 First-rate
55 Insect's wings
56 Middle Atlantic settler
57 Pursue a course of action
58 Groundwork
59 Tobacco kiln
60 Secque or sollaret
62 Orchestrator
63 Terpsichore, e.g.
66 Surname of the girl who went to Oz
67 Lafcadio ___, journalist-novelist: 1850–1904
68 Rower
69 Elaborate public spectacle
71 Reared
73 Brewing grain
75 Demon
76 Modern Carthage
77 Cut diagonally
78 Document, in Durango
79 ___ O'Kelly, ex-president of Ireland
80 Jeff's pal
81 Section of the Met
82 ___ Bundren of "As I Lay Dying"
83 Fast planes
86 Baseball stat
87 United

139

ACROSS

1 Tree juice
4 Italian seaport
8 Film that won an Oscar
   for director Beatty
12 Mellows
16 Kind of wind
17 Another name for
   Jacob's twin
18 "Lord, ___ I?"
   Matthew's query
19 Wept
21 First of a Latin trio
22 Drink greedily
23 Cognomen
24 Took on
25 Three with thirty-one
28 ___ France
29 Otorhinolaryngologist's
   speciality: Abbr.
30 Japanese statesman
31 Smoked delicacy
32 Like the Dust Bowl
35 Early rhyme (1562) on
   this puzzle's theme
42 Part-time paid player
45 Terre ___, Indiana
46 Info at La Guardia
47 Kind of concert
48 A long one has no
   turning
50 Swiss capital: Fr.
51 Suffix with comment
52 One with thirty-one
54 Stand in a queue
55 Three with thirty-one
62 School party
63 One with twenty-eight
   or twenty-nine
64 A long, long time
65 Shade of blue
68 Woman's magazine
69 Gullet
72 Paris street
73 Pepper plant
74 Weird
76 Two with thirty
81 Grocery item
82 Matching pieces
83 Consume
84 Mrs. in Madrid
86 Airport point of
   departure
89 Two with thirty
96 "I ___ if I could, but I
   can't"
97 Entity
98 Hard to find
99 "Hooray" to an
   aficionado
100 Omit
101 Entry flooring
102 Nab
103 Approves

104 Nonesuch
105 Always
106 Notable times
107 Rum portion

DOWN

1 Anna's post
2 Painter ___ - Tadema
3 Stratagem
4 "We've Only Just ___":
   1970 Paul Williams
   song
5 Grown-up
6 Poly's partner
7 Diminish
8 "Bright is the ___
   words": R.L.S.
9 Jacob's twin
10 Grows faint
11 "Let it stand" to a
   printer
12 Accomplish
13 Grating
14 Republic for a Gael
15 Watermelon nuisance
20 HST successor
26 "Return of the ___":
   "Star Wars" sequel
27 Actress Hagen
31 Medieval Italian fortress

32 Nile viper
33 Classic car named for
   the manufacturer
34 Mischievous little one
35 He's had it
36 "Ay, there's ___":
   "Hamlet"
37 Item for a dinghy
38 Sister
39 Repair the roof
40 Zeno was one
41 Blue planet
43 Commoner
44 Hasten
49 Author of "Fear of
   Flying": Init.
50 Pulitzer Prize poet:
   1929
51 Out of town
52 Benedictine titles
53 Confound
55 "Mahogonny" is one
56 Breathing problem
57 Darkroom chemical
58 "Car 54, Where ___
   You?"
59 Straightedge
60 "___ come!" (invitation
   in Dixie)
61 His neighs were words

65 Pock
66 WW II command
67 Potok's "My Name Is
   Asher ___"
69 Wire measure
70 Super serve
71 "___ Will Buy?": song
   from "Oliver!"
73 Veggie chopper
75 Be a nomad
77 Tristan's love
78 Receptionist
79 Kind of relief
80 Forever, poetically
84 Narrow fiber ridge
85 Movie segments
86 Reverent respect
87 Game divided into
   chukkers
88 Wreck
89 Gunny fiber
90 Higher education
   facility: Abbr.
91 River of the Pharaohs
92 Former talk-show host
93 Kick
94 Nevada city
95 Remainder

140

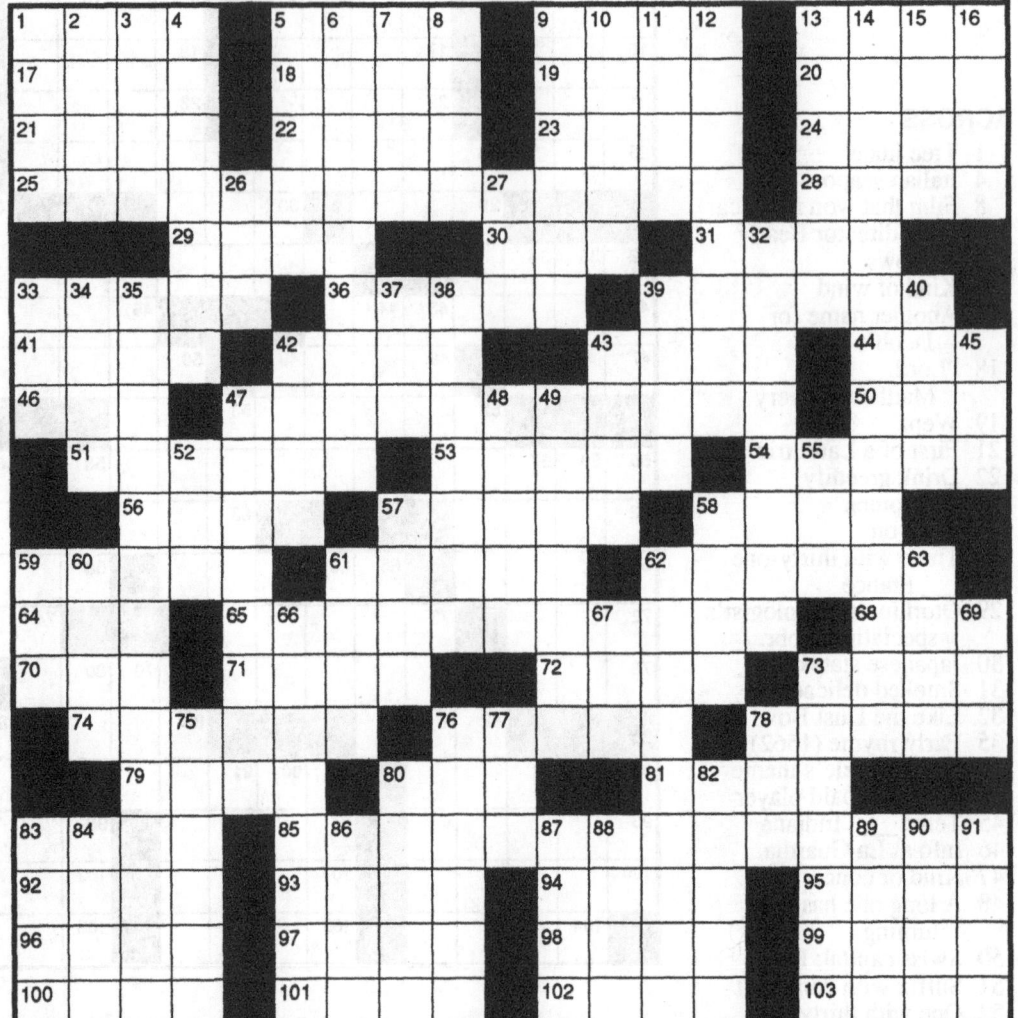

ACROSS

1 Pilaster
5 Mercantile center
9 Junior's ammo
13 Author of "Off the Court"
17 Cats-paw
18 Baseball family name
19 "Thanks ___!"
20 Owner of a magic hammer
21 Athletic field
22 Compact group of people
23 Tandy alone on stage
24 Actor Rip ___
25 Executed with vigor
28 Top-drawer
29 Strong drink
30 High, musically
31 Fail to mention
33 Dublin theatre
36 Mob
39 These make news
41 Forward
42 Galley mark
43 Certain votes
44 Sophisticated, in the Forties
46 Bronx cheer's next of kin
47 Great talkers
50 Double this for a Hebrew hymn
51 Thin
53 An anonym
54 Stroll
56 Execrate
57 Purloin
58 Ice-cream thickener
59 Germ cell
61 Wisdom tooth, e.g.
62 Spectacles
64 Lucrative pool
65 Intermittent drizzles
68 Sup
70 Collection of sayings
71 Give specious aspect to
72 Fine china
73 Pound, the poet
74 Brook
76 Swivets
78 Lend ___ (be attentive)
79 Fender mishap
80 Riv. boat
81 Any D. W. Griffith film
83 South American rodent
85 Abruptly
92 Cherub
93 ___ broom sweeps clean
94 "Uncle Remus" fox
95 Cubitus
96 Quarter pint
97 Eric ___ of the "Monty Python" group
98 Office bigwig
99 Plaintiff
100 Whirlpool
101 "The ___ not Taken," Frost
102 Basilica part
103 ___ off (angry)

DOWN

1 Whit
2 Exploding star
3 Tailless amphibian
4 Stated sans proof
5 He-man
6 Olean's river
7 Crucifix
8 Garb for Susan Jaffe
9 Rook
10 In flight
11 Roper dope?
12 Remain after an evening party
13 Secure
14 Gab
15 Companion of Severinsen
16 Former lightweight champ
26 The old college ___
27 Downcast
32 Communications
33 Low-grade wool
34 Length of fabric
35 Vacillate
37 Antediluvian
38 Incarcerates again
39 Peepers
40 Hawk
42 Causeway
43 Oriental nanny
45 Sky dessert
47 Toy weapon
48 Islamic deity
49 Germ
52 Crossette
55 Garrison
57 "Ae ___ Kiss": Burns poem
58 Ten square chains
59 Spring that may bring some zing
60 Corn bread
61 Unit of distance
62 Inane
63 Mother of FDR
66 Type of missile
67 Smash hit
69 Asphalt ingredient
73 Cover with hard coating
75 ___ beloved
76 Put away
77 Ticket-fare exchange: Abbr.
78 Arch. group
80 Stone pillar
82 Intrinsically
83 Congressional employee
84 Surrounded by
86 Annul
87 Rhyme scheme
88 Yield
89 Turn about
90 ___-jerk reaction
91 Scotland ___

141 BETTER LATE ... by Richard Silvestri

An excellent idea is splendidly executed by a top constructor famed for his refreshing clues.

ACROSS

1 Binge
6 Alley problem
11 Doc and the boys
17 Spinning
18 Lorre in "The Maltese Falcon"
19 Solar-system model
20 Late evangelist?
22 Birds, in the spring
24 Thompson of "Back to the Future"
25 Directly
26 Bondsmen
28 Personal: Comb. form
29 Ninety degrees from norte
31 Does impressions
33 Reduce the fare?
34 Of an age
35 Barge back
37 Idle of comedy
39 Up to snuff
41 Hero ending
42 Future grass
44 Cry out loud
46 Archaeological find
48 Divine drink
51 Setting
53 Jaded
56 Guidonian note
57 Jaipur bigwig
59 Stonewort or fat-choy
60 Quaking tree
61 Use a squeegee
63 Rowdydow
65 Boots one
67 "Caro nome," e.g.
68 The bottom line
70 Green land
72 Glommed
74 Corporate abbr.
75 Blank look
76 Cull
78 Pad
80 "Gunga Din" locale
82 Gal of song
83 ___ buco (veal dish)
84 Hamburger holder
86 Against
88 Dress for Makarova
90 Angelic instruments
94 "___ is as good as a wink": Anon.
96 African antelope
98 Nutty
100 Maryland athlete
101 Mate of 57 Across
102 Unfactual
104 Baker's aide
106 Sales pitch?
107 Imagined
109 Late singer?
112 ___ paper
113 Army groups
114 Stuffed to the gills
115 Fetid
116 Discharge
117 Bleachers features

DOWN

1 Furrier's inventory
2 Leader of the masses?
3 Interact
4 Slippery customer
5 Actor Ron and singer Joe
6 Dug out
7 He goes for the gold
8 Topper
9 Nest-egg accts.
10 Trifled
11 Late golfer?
12 Go against Andre the Giant
13 "___ longa, vita brevis"
14 Tighten the shoelaces
15 Late actor?
16 Homs native
21 Bird that is no more
23 One and only
27 Estuary
30 Prefix for while
32 Spanish ayes?
36 At hand
38 Sarsaparilla alternative
40 Where Napoleon was solo?
43 QED middle
45 Choler
47 Mrs. Victor Laszlo in "Casablanca"
48 Small salamanders
49 Ness
50 Late Secret Squadron leader?
51 Sierra ___
52 Everglades denizen
54 Paris divider
55 Make into law
58 Late police sergeant?
62 Pull down
64 Fixes squeaks
66 Jazz sessions
69 Mother of Castor
71 Straight, as a drink
73 Race for Lewis
77 Night stick
79 Launch or punt
81 Quill-dipping place
83 Pariah
84 Balladeer
85 Deprives of weapons
87 Inauguration words
89 Corrupts
91 Good name
92 Book for a six-year-old
93 Shells out
95 Keaton or Sawyer
97 Excessive
99 Poseidon's domain
103 Tam-tam
105 Neil Young's "___ Never Sleeps"
108 Measure equaling 1/100 inch
110 Never, to Rilke
111 Randy's skating partner

PHRASEOLOGY by Eli Wesoff
This medley from Miami should delight and enlighten even the most blasé solver.

ACROSS

1 Feathered six-footers
5 Lady Chaplin
9 Miami's county
13 Cummerbund
17 Innermost part
18 Puts to work
19 Jay Gould's railroad
20 Comb. form meaning vision
21 On the auction block
24 Commentator Rowan
25 Atelier
26 Major follower
27 Symbolic
29 Riches
32 Frail and slender
33 Hindustani native
37 Weight allowances
38 Earth's path
40 Traditional spanking spot
42 Without a pain killer
46 The North Star
47 Lbs., oz., etc.
48 St. ___, place of exile for Napoleon
49 Menuhin's teacher
51 Nymphs of Moslems' paradise
53 Outcome
54 One behind the times
56 Danny Kaye movie: 1945
58 Vacation seasons in Calais
59 Alter follower
60 "___ o'er silent seas again": T. Moore
61 Escarole
63 Founder of an English news agency
65 Conciliatory gift
66 Actress Del Rio
69 Unlike a taxicab
71 Sobriquets
72 MDCLI + CM
73 "... to keep the strong ___": Shak.
75 What diaskeuasts do
76 Land or sea attachment
79 "He that is not with me ___ me": Matthew
82 Republic between France and Spain
84 The cap'n is his boss
85 Talks big
90 Surf sound
91 Additionally
94 Sweetsop
95 Per ___ wages
96 ___ acid (a contributor to gout)
97 Robert ___ of the C.S.A.
98 Command to Rover
99 Strikebreaker
100 Tropical Asian tree
101 Dried up

DOWN

1 Old French money
2 ___ Blanc
3 Indic language
4 Rank a tennis contestant
5 Super
6 Russian silk city
7 Goaded
8 "There was ___ about my ears": Chesterton
9 ___ rum
10 Prepare for action
11 Calorie counters
12 Unearthly
13 Pertaining to the human condition
14 With speed
15 Cremona creation, for short
16 Yuletide decoration
22 River inlet
23 Singer Ed, or Nancy
28 Leonine groups
30 Sistine Chapel artwork
31 Devour
33 Relative of a vil.
34 A tic-tac-toe winner
35 Distributed sparingly
36 Hersey's town
39 In a sneaky way
41 Russian's Wednesday: Abbr.
42 Cato's "I employ"
43 Moved unsteadily
44 Nine: Comb. form
45 Pops
47 Young wolf or seal
50 Memorable Greek tycoon
52 Pursued until captured
54 Skin: Comb. form
55 Mosque feature
57 "Vaya con ___": 1953 hit
58 Summon forth
60 First ___ (new convict)
62 Long river in central Asia
64 Secular
67 "___ tu," Verdi aria
68 Concorde
70 Like an essay by Lamb
71 Some from down East
73 "___ Rhythm," 1930 Gershwin hit
74 Preakness winner in 1955
76 "The Divine ___" (Bernhardt)
77 Tenth of a grand
78 "... ___ which will live in infamy"
80 Blast in 1945
81 Rocky formation
83 Unloads
86 Ice and Iron
87 Vendition
88 Kind of apron
89 Dagger of yore
92 Bancha or Bohea
93 Sci. course

143 FORMAL EDUCATION by Barbara Weakley
Diplomas are not required here—only a pencil and a sense of humor.

ACROSS

1 Hero's medal: Abbr.
4 Part of etc.
10 "Vera Cruz" star
16 Sound from the stands
17 "Venus" singer
18 Norman Hapgood, e.g.
19 High note
20 Formal advertising media?
22 Loan data: Abbr.
24 Digit
25 Dutch painter
26 Within: Comb. form
27 Sun bear
29 Thickened
31 First lady
32 Pamper
34 One kind of wave
38 Appraise
41 German physicist
42 Card combination
43 Marbles
44 Noddy
46 Mom and Dad
47 Refrain syllable
48 Dignified delirium tremens?
50 Sundial hour
51 Aerie residents
53 Peel
54 Opposite of dextro
55 Animal tracks
56 Remove by force
57 Hot
59 Tawny, in heraldry
60 Porridge type
62 Terminus
63 Significance
65 NHL team
69 Alan Ladd film
72 Chits
73 Part of TEFL
74 Like a fat chance
75 High-class horseplay?
79 Yellow bugle
80 Tithes
81 Sadat's predecessor
82 Masonic org.
83 Danish city
84 Mountain crests
85 Utmost degree

DOWN

1 Imagine
2 Oceanic tunicate
3 Black-tie catering service?
4 Corvine cry
5 Patti LuPone role
6 Claws
7 Model MacPherson
8 French king
9 Home of some Angels
10 Insurgent
11 Dashboard instruments
12 Actress Farrow
13 Being: French
14 These can be spared
15 Approximately
21 Blend, in Bristol
23 Redeems
28 Affirmative
29 Quite properly, his cuisine was lean?
30 Eat
33 Small opening
35 Formal garden bloomer?
36 On the go
37 Sore
38 Certify
39 South American shawl: Var.
40 RBI and ERA
42 Brings under control
45 Printing measures
46 Mean
48 Pessimists
49 Some are blue
52 Actress Ackerman
54 Aches
56 Outward appearance
58 Decimal base
60 Ottoman
61 Composer Bloch
64 Sheriff's group
66 Jibe
67 Fasten firmly
68 Crush
69 Sgt. Snorkel's dog
70 Get rid of
71 Unit of loudness
73 Otherwise
76 Range mem.
77 Regatta need
78 Mos. and mos.

144 MULTIPLE CHOICE by Harry H. Morritt
A new constructor from Vancouver presents six trios and asks you
to select one member of each.

ACROSS
1 Astute
6 "It's ___ unusual day!"
11 Kiddie book elephant
16 Nimbi
17 "Vive ___!"
18 Ancient S. Greek town
19 Loos or Ekberg
20 Within ___ of (very close)
21 Blair or Darnell of movies
22 One of "Three Caballeros" in a 1944 Disney film
24 Put on a play
25 Nap, in Navarra
26 Disinclined
28 Chemical suffix
29 Mother's kin
32 Wild hog
34 One of "Three Holy Children" of O.T.
38 Nordhoff and Hall novel, e.g.
41 Roundish projection
42 Pricey
44 Bing Crosby's birthplace
46 Mountain nymph
48 Sign on a one-way street
50 Jockey
51 Jazz musician Fats ___
53 Greek market place
55 Foster a felon
56 Natural habitat
58 One of three "Old King Cole" requests
60 Clothes, in Cordoba
61 John Jacob or Mary
62 Exclamation of joy or triumph
65 Plotters
67 Mom's word of warning
72 Librarian's devices
74 One of "Three on a Match": 1932 film
77 Main artery
78 Capt. Bligh's landing place after mutiny
79 Tumbler
80 Kind of vein or artery
81 Fictional town in a Hersey book
82 Webber and Rice musical
83 Rejoinder
84 S. V. ___ (U.S. poet)
85 Hold off

DOWN
1 Herring
2 Vietnam capital
3 Garment cut
4 Rosters
5 Book of Biblical songs
6 "When I was ___ I served a term . . .": W. S. Gilbert
7 Dish list
8 A divine revelation
9 Show biz word for "terrific"
10 Connection
11 One of Three Wise Men
12 Moses' adoptive mother, in the Koran
13 Scream of delight?
14 Llama's locale
15 "The Cloister and the Hearth" novelist
23 U.S. mineralogists, James Dwight and Edward Salisbury
24 Ermine
27 Jurist Fortas
30 Official records
31 Chinese year of ___ (1984)
33 Ethnic
34 Mixer setting
35 Goddesses of the seasons
36 Sound as ___ (in excellent health)
37 Wheeler-___
38 Parodies
39 "Let ___ true, but every man a liar": St. Paul
40 Prince, in Kabul
43 Energy unit
45 These are often liberal or fine
47 One of "Three Principles of the People" of Sun Yat Sen
49 ". . . and having ___ Moves on": Khayyám
52 Meal, in Metz
54 Sun-dried brick
57 Capture
59 Scraped the bottom
61 President of Mexico: 1946–52
62 Kentucky pioneer and legislator: 1757–1840
63 Caucasian, to a Polynesian Hawaiian
64 Freed anchor position
66 Put up with
68 Cut in two
69 Efficacy
70 View or prospect
71 Attempt
73 And others: Abbr.
75 ___-deaf
76 Hambletonian, e.g.
78 IOU

145

FOOD FOR THOUGHT by Norma Steinberg
Norma said solving this should be child's play—if you happen to be Julia, that is.

ACROSS

1 Finicky
6 Gross
11 Oriental sleuth
15 Sound before "bless you"
16 Call
17 Stalk
18 Knee to ankle
19 Aftermath of a shelling?
22 Ustinov's title
23 B. J. Thomas hit, with "Most"
25 "Mon ___," Tati film
26 Receivers
28 Tundra denizen
29 Sally ___
31 Kowtow
33 Ad ___ committee
34 He keeps things kosher
38 Check for typos
39 Lifts' locale
41 Stat at Shea
42 Popular one at USC
43 Wrong
44 Perceive
45 Toup
46 Suffix for tele
47 Made yams yummy
49 Threesome
50 Pierre's affirmative
51 "Joy Luck Club" author
52 Tampa or Hudson
53 ___ Mawr
54 Bed and breakfast
55 ___ summer
57 Oz creator
58 Jack Frost targets
60 Cleaning cloth
61 Forty winks
63 Pakistani religion
65 Ho or Corleone
66 Granny, for one
68 Bach composition
70 Goes under
72 Call ___ day
73 See ya, ya nut!
76 Paris' beloved
78 Solecism
79 The end-all
80 "Drums ___ the Mohawk"
81 Talk with God
82 Church council
83 "___ Steal a Million": 1966 film

DOWN

1 Outdated
2 Book of Changes
3 Burnt greens?
4 ___ Tiki
5 Mrs. John Lennon
6 Horrify
7 Sea snail
8 Young mule
9 Us: German
10 Gorcey or Durocher
11 50s dance
12 Pitch
13 Pot penny
14 Degree type
20 "___ gloom of night . . ."
21 Veal piccata, e.g.
24 Ager's "Happy ___"
27 Ill-fated city
29 In favor of
30 "Juno and the Paycock" playwright
32 Actor Tayback
33 Clutch
35 Singer that followed an elder?
36 UCLA player
37 Othello's aide
39 Gimlet ingredient
40 Special diploma
42 Psychologist Bettelheim
43 Dee or Walker
46 Enter
47 Put up
48 Actor McKellen
49 Babar's snoot
51 Hanky's cousin
53 Flying fox
56 "How dry ___ . . ."
57 River edge
59 Fourscore
61 Hotel mogul Hilton
62 Strong
64 Actor Ayres
65 Columbus' son
67 Dance for two
68 So-so
69 Annapolis campus
70 English gun
71 Persian monarch
73 Top off
74 ___ Alamos
75 Actress Irving
77 "Evil Woman" gp.

146 TWINS by David Galef

We hear that David got the inspiration for this one while watching a ball game in Minnesota.

ACROSS

1 Praises
6 "Conductor, when you receive ___": I. H. Bromley
11 Final frontier
16 Start
17 Star in Orion
18 Fife accompaniment
19 Go on ___ (have a wild time)
20 Cram
21 Orange or Indian
22 This creates twins
24 Lobster appendage
26 Hairy
28 Argument
33 Surmounting
37 Twin of its kin?
38 Half a dance
40 Original garden
41 Punitive
43 Condition
45 Worship
46 Forms a twin, perhaps
48 Tiller
50 Golfer Sam's family
51 Loire season
53 Rubbernecks
57 Milk, in Marseilles
59 Acting like many a twin
61 Ph.D. test
64 Scour
66 Transplant
67 Pâté de ___ gras
68 Corporate head: Abbr.
69 Kindle
71 Sutures
72 Padding
74 Stages
77 "I have ___ begun to fight": J. P. Jones
79 Twin
84 "The way of a man with ___": Proverbs
88 Pungent
90 Clobber
91 Pear-shaped instrument
92 Tonga's neighbor
93 White heron
94 Poke
95 Grove
96 Songstress Della ___

DOWN

1 Good earth
2 Prefix with body or dote
3 Addict
4 Steep
5 Hone
6 "___ longa, vita brevis"
7 Suit perfectly
8 Fevers
9 Meditate
10 Fairies' kin: Var.
11 Pelt
12 ___ de deux (ballet dance)
13 Booksellers' org.
14 Gear
15 Before, to Byron
23 Kind of saw
25 Harem room
27 For fear that
29 Twins, sometimes
30 Fuss
31 ___ Borch, Dutch painter

32 Chemical ending
33 Tax times: Abbr.
34 Acne sufferer, frequently
35 Formerly
36 Analagous
39 Egyptian god of eternity
42 Mythical mother of twins et al.
44 On the move
45 Place for a frontal
47 "___ Lay Dying": Faulkner novel
49 Time zone
52 Twin's activity, sometimes
54 Ready
55 Sufficient, to FitzGerald
56 Mil. ranks
58 Monogram of Prufrock's creator
60 Okefenokee denizen
61 Playing badly
62 Parisian monarch

63 Be in the grip of la grippe
65 Twin by design
68 ___-Magnon man
70 Weems or Williams
73 Provide a donation
75 Monument bearing a bust
76 Staid; serious
78 Russian news agcy.
80 Prod
81 Unsheathe
82 Mendacities
83 Being, in Barcelona
84 Perfect serve
85 Movie star Gibson
86 Gown for a priest
87 UN arm supportive of workers
89 A parent

147 FIFTIES FAVORITES by John Greenman

Solvers who were WWII babies will get a special thrill out of the musical memories below.

ACROSS

1 "Old MacDonald had ___ . . ."
6 Declaim
11 Electrical unit, for short
14 Stationed
15 Fables
16 Author of "Danger Is My Business"
18 Therefore, in Tours
19 Cat-___-tails
20 Interweaver
21 Ash or aspen
22 "___ Ballou": 1965 film
23 Fuming
24 Adler and Ross tune: 1954
30 Melancholy, in poesy
31 Suffix with pave or enslave
32 Harbored
35 Relay-race unit
36 Bide
38 Flight on a shuttle
41 Take flight to unite
43 Drapes
44 Netherlands Antilles island
45 Stillman and Allen song: 1955
49 Freshly
50 Month divisions
51 Uprear
52 Composer Rorem
53 He wrote "The Outcasts of Poker Flat"
54 "The Greatest"
56 A Turner
57 "Give a ___ horse he can ride"
58 Piece of cake
60 Artie Glenn tune: 1953
68 Eavesdropped
69 Argentite, e.g.
70 Father
71 Pal of Kukla
72 Stranger
74 Summarize
75 Blossom part
76 Alighieri
77 Actress Glenn ___
78 Aswan, for one
79 " 'Tis good to keep ___ egg": Cervantes
80 Daisylike bloom

DOWN

1 Take ___ (suffer heavy losses)
2 Laissez ___
3 Lou Grant portrayer
4 Mail again
5 Ovid's 1,501
6 Nebraska tribe
7 Deep spite
8 Aka
9 Half a fifth
10 Suffix with Annam or Siam
11 Turkish peak
12 Large parrot
13 Michelangelo masterpiece
16 Customer
17 Earl ___ tea
25 "Get Happy" composer
26 Anne Lindbergh, ___ Morrow
27 Hammarskjöld
28 Icon
29 Belief chosen by Paine and Jefferson
32 Macho one
33 Solo
34 Like an igloo
36 Came out of sleep
37 Punic ___, between Carthage and Rome
38 Nun's garb
39 Rotund
40 Whittled
42 Basilica fixture
43 Opposite of dele
44 Little, to Robert Burns
46 Plucked string's sound
47 Caravansary
48 Author Segal
53 "Messiah" composer
54 Kin of kvass
55 Driver's permit: Abbr.
57 Hopkins of old films
58 White-sale offerings
59 Pointillists' props
60 Karate blow
61 Escorted anew
62 Conference site in 1945
63 Ryan of pitching fame
64 Threefold
65 Lace edging
66 Eradicate
67 Social outcast
72 Susan Hayward film: 1961
73 Take, after taxes
74 NBC's parent co., once

148 POET'S PRECEPT by Martin Ashwood-Smith
A famous versifier gives an essential criterion for assessment of a creative written work.

ACROSS

1 One at ___ (singly)
6 City near St. Petersburg
11 Wise guy?
16 Defamation
17 Ever
18 Poison
19 **Start of a quotation**
22 Ante's cousin
23 RR stop
24 Use a hand glider
25 Blue shade
26 Name of ring fame
27 Spasms
29 Lilliputian
31 **Quotation: Part II**
39 Bert's buddy on TV
40 Brit. award
41 Discombobulate
42 Eleemosynary aid
45 Sunday-supper staple
48 Maynard of westerns
49 Author of the quotation
52 Biblical work?
54 Hierurgies
55 Cloy
56 "___ plaisir!"
58 Dogmatic conclusion?
59 Paralytic arrow topping
63 **Quotation: Part III**
69 "Ca ___ " (French Revolutionary song)
70 The Hague's loc.
71 AWOL chasers
72 Kin of Mr.
75 Sere
78 Author Umberto ___
79 See 2 Down
80 **End of quotation**
85 IRS action
86 Point at, perhaps
87 "He ___ gallant knight . . .": Scott
88 Sows' shelters
89 Ventilated
90 Scatter

DOWN

1 Anatomical wing
2 Barfly
3 ___ Peninsula (Spain and Portugal)
4 Only a pond?
5 North Pole peon
6 Stratagem
7 Cement
8 Mus. scale
9 Calculator button
10 Filmdom's Ray
11 Music lover's purchase
12 Palindromical cry
13 X or y, on a graph
14 Cheese, once
15 Deeply
20 This woman, in Valencia
21 Stare stupidly
26 Backward era?
28 Fencer
30 Fire starter?
32 Push-button precursor
33 Kingklip catcher
34 Cor anglais cousin
35 Nurtures
36 Leave the arms of Morpheus
37 Ending with lion
38 "___ Days That Shook the World": J. Reed
43 DV + DVI
44 "Limp Preludes for a Dog" composer
46 Dieter's last resort?
47 Do some quick addition
49 Aid's partner
50 Untouchable Eliot
51 Persian fairy
52 Mandible
53 Egg, in combinations
57 T'ai ___, Chinese form of meditative movements
60 Mailman?
61 Undertow causer
62 "___ a Wonderful Life": Capra film
64 Qualities
65 Gary or Lorenz
66 Something to do in St. Louis?
67 Engraved
68 "Be off!"
72 Anagram for 55 Across
73 Close
74 Muslim judge
76 Russian log cabin
77 Painter Salvador ___
79 Actress Loretta ___ (of "M*A*S*H")
81 Make a half hitch
82 Former M. East land
83 High and low rtes. to Scotland?
84 Shooting marble

149

STICKHANDLERS by Betty Hinman

Don't be fooled by Betty's punny title; these featured stars never played in the NHL.

ACROSS

1 ___ noire
5 Pro
8 Menu letters
11 Colorado county
15 Dash
16 Diamonds: Sl.
17 Turf
18 "___ the Lonely"
19 Locate
20 Ship-shaped clock
21 Spatula
23 Conductor Klemperer
24 "Paint Your Wagon" heroine
26 Preludes
27 Hungarian-born conductor
29 Pale
30 Seat or boat
31 Pry
32 Toulouse turndown
35 Gingery cookie
37 Calhoun and Sparrow
40 Stretchy
43 Aroma
45 Carina
46 LBJ beagle
47 The past
49 Nip
51 Liberian native
52 Lime coolers
54 Hounds
56 Follower of Aquinas
58 Intoxicate
60 Type of lens
62 Fast times
63 Senator Pressler
65 Of animal life
68 Dark brown
69 London-born conductor
73 Former Union name
74 Conductor Gabrilowitsch
75 Pronghorn
76 Kneeler
78 In the know
79 "Picnic" playwright
80 Large vases
81 "Twin Peaks" bird
82 WW II arena
83 Composer Broman
84 Nikita's negative
85 Capture
86 Ant. of ant.
87 Raced

DOWN

1 Obfuscate
2 Typewriter type
3 Too much, to 27 Across
4 Autographs
5 Least coarse
6 Spotted feline
7 Catalogs anew
8 Very, to 69 Across
9 Trim
10 First name of 69 Down
11 Hitcher
12 Berlin-born conductor
13 Character in "Pericles"
14 Snakestones
22 Belgian painter
25 Gregg specialist
28 "The Golden Girls" star
31 Display
32 Restorative, informally
33 Slur over
34 Met conductor
36 Tack on
38 Beer ingredient
39 Small openings
41 Euripides drama
42 Loony
44 Cheer
48 Self
50 Tooth
53 Most corny
55 Divans
57 Tunesmith
59 ___ and true
61 Fens
64 Quota
66 Location
67 Japan
68 Disappointing
69 English conductor
70 Slow, to 12 Down
71 French artist
72 Peace goddess
73 Created a new company (with "off")
77 Fleecy female

150

David hopes that his puzzle won't cause you any 20 Across or give you a 42 Down
or stir up your 10 Down and make you 6 Down. Otherwise he won't 79 Across.

ACROSS

1 Fret
5 Assessment amount
10 Elation
15 High anxiety
17 Expiate
18 Ill-gotten gain
19 Embarrass
20 Feeling of
    dissatisfaction
22 ___ a button
24 "With ___ by his
    side . . . " Shak.
25 Perfect tennis serve
26 Nationality suffix
27 Attempt
29 Thin and tall
31 Shell-game object
34 Asinine
36 Brother, for one
38 Brimless headgear
41 Throw water around
    gently
43 Sum of 2,563 and 7,437
44 Sad
45 Measurement above the
    hips
46 Actor Alda
47 Comprehend
48 Aristocratic sport
49 Writer Sarah ___ Jewett
51 Newt
54 Erupt
56 Terrify
58 Vegas sight
59 Simon ___, Met
    baritone-basso
61 Accustomed
62 Soldier's or artist's hat
63 Child by marriage
65 Eye layer
67 Proof initials
68 Angers
70 Agitprop, nowadays
71 Roll-call abbr.
74 Doctors' org.
75 "Harper Valley ___"
77 Blank-verse foot
79 Eulogy phrase
84 Kind of toast
85 The Ram
86 Machine for shaping
    wood, etc.
87 Olfactory sense
88 Actress Leigh or Blair
89 Bay window
90 Pitcher Hershiser

DOWN

1 Last frontier
2 Proscriptions
3 Maternally related
4 Sagacious
5 U.K. service branch
6 Gloomy (derived from
    10 Down)
7 Tipster at a track
8 Photographer Adams
9 Tennis call
10 One of the humors
11 Pear-shaped instrument
12 Here in Lyons
13 Capacity-crowd sign
14 E.M.K., e.g.
16 Pure
21 Indian princess
23 Musician Phillips
28 Dismay
30 Word with can or tray

31 Trailblazer
32 Rock star Brian
33 Past
34 Court verb
35 "___ Kapital"
37 Mauna ___
38 Cookbook amt.
39 Bullish cry?
40 Made a search for
42 Effect of 10 Down?
45 Amazing!
46 Dancer Miller
48 His glass is half empty
50 Recuperate
52 Redcoat, to a
    Minuteman
53 Petard material
55 Vim
57 Greek letters
58 A.F.T. rival

59 Brit. honorific
60 Jeanne d'Arc: Abbr.
61 Article in Reims
62 Sushi delicacies
64 Algerian port
66 Prefix with carp or
    center
69 Word with head or mint
71 More competent
72 Kind of belt
73 Dandruff
74 Fits to ___
76 French film comedian
78 Reminder
79 Anglo-Indian ruler
80 Time
81 Pride, e.g.
82 Arafat's gp.
83 Lamprey's cousin

151 '66, ETC. by Melvin Kenworthy

If you re-define *re* as "concerning," then 82 Across will give the theme of Mel's opus.

ACROSS

1 Prowls after prey
7 Oats for Lil' E. Tee
11 Moroccan province
15 Like leaves of the heath
17 Kent of the "Dukes of Hazzard"
18 Pung, e.g.
19 Man with a harmless gun
20 "The ___ American"
21 Berne's river
22 Of age: Lat. abbr.
23 Sprout incisors
25 Fairyland figure
26 Leather workers do this
27 Scat!
28 "___ man answers . . ."
29 Vestige
31 Updike's 1966 opus (with "The")
36 "___ leak will sink . . ." (Eng. proverb)
38 "Because ___ you the truth . . ." (John 8:45)
39 L-P connection
40 Also
42 "Classroom" for Zeno
43 Bauxite and calcite
44 & 48 " . . . Longfellow: Portrait of an ___" (Edward Wagenknecht's 1966 biography)
50 ___ fide
51 Caucasus tribe
53 Urgently threatening
54 Old card game
55 "___ the time . . ."
57 Fads
61 "A Delicate Balance" dramatist: 1966
65 Expiate
66 Actress Grant
67 Fish-eating bird
69 Real ending
70 "The Gumps" maid
73 All
74 Isr. neighbor
75 Pomologist's spray
76 Boorish
77 Of long standing
80 Jacob's third son
81 Malayan boat
82 Makes another schedule
83 Jack London's "Martin ___"
84 Jazzman Thelonius ___
85 Play time

DOWN

1 The Henley is one
2 In ___: behind
3 Mekong Delta site
4 ___ de Queiroz (Portuguese novelist)
5 Grist for a CPA's mill
6 Sevilla seven
7 Orchestra members
8 Last victory for "The Red Baron"
9 Fashion magazine
10 Poet Cecil ___ Lewis
11 Hezekiah's biographer
12 Source of linseed oil
13 Saint Philip ___
14 ___ fixe
16 "I have a ___ . . .": Martin Luther King, Jr.
24 Small case
25 Sgt. Bilko's charge?
27 TV panelist Melvin of "Whodunit?"
28 ___ Republic of Mauritania
30 "Lost Horizon" director (1938)
32 Cirrus or cumulus
33 Father of Ahab
34 Wallet stuffers
35 Misplaced
37 Heroine of Molière's "L'Amour médecin"
41 Where RLS is buried
43 ___ a time (singly)
44 Kind of seaman
45 "___ Indigo," 1931 song
46 Sufficient, to Fitzgerald
47 Coast Guard Academy locale
49 Impressive grouping
52 Menu item
56 It follows Aug. 31
58 Mineral containing silicate
59 Organic catalysts
60 Cassandra was one
62 Gemini 12 commander: 1966
63 John ___ Neale, illustrator of Oz books
64 Goof
68 He shouts "That's a moray!"
70 Hearty's companion
71 "___ Three Lives": Philbrick
72 Wash
73 Large kangaroo
76 Anthony Quinn film: 1970
78 Ike's monogram
79 Tic ___ Dough: TV quiz show

152

MELANGE by Bryant White

Most of the words are familiar, but here and there you may find an addition to your vocabulary.

ACROSS

1 Seraglio
6 Sapphires et al.
12 Mil. medals
16 Plato's market place
17 Eradicate
18 Gudrun's victim
19 Myrrh and gold's companion
21 German sea
22 Your, to Yves
23 Toppings for hamburgers
24 Slowly, to Solti
26 Tennis frames
28 High craggy hills
29 Liquor vessels
30 "Over ___" (Cohan tune)
32 Pumpernickel units
33 Chrysalides
36 Shirt size
37 Copy
40 Turkish hospice
41 Phony jewelry
42 Mason portrayer
43 Stared open-mouthed at
44 Adjutants
45 Court figure
46 Formicary denizens
47 Go in
48 White lead
49 Narrow inlet
50 Hair net
51 Holy
52 City near Lagos
54 Elect a colleague
55 Musical compositions
57 Ronnie ___, former NFL defenseman
58 Vend
62 American League MVP: 1976
63 "___ Walrus" (Beatles song)
65 Small white-spotted rorqual
66 Suffixes for citizens
67 Appraisers of 6 Across: Var. sp.
70 Hoarfrost
71 Pass by
72 Immense
73 Cat's-paw or granny
74 Name of 12 Egyptian kings
75 Canonical hours

DOWN

1 Dagger parts
2 Jibe
3 Criticize severely
4 Gull's kin
5 Speedy shark
6 Certain college students
7 Again!
8 Small singing birds
9 Long, long times
10 ___ Lobos
11 Losses due to theft
12 Mar
13 Ancient armored reptile
14 Liquid part of fat
15 One of the Kikládhes
20 Purpose
25 ___ Clark Five
27 Lays away
29 Dix and Knox
31 Weeded the garden
32 Type of beam
33 Havana, e.g.
34 Muscat native
35 Nautilus skipper
36 Took on freight
38 Verse's opposite
39 Was human
41 Iron peg
42 Explodes
44 Celebes oxen
45 Eugene the ___ ("Popeye" animal)
47 Put in peril
48 Thread-of-life spinner
50 Japanese PM: 1964–72
51 Gin holders
53 Card game or dog
54 Bearing a tuft of soft hairs
55 Affected smile
56 ___ left field (not with it)
57 Lanterns
59 Cambridge's neighbor
60 "___ c'est moi!" (Louis XIV)
61 Tilts to one side
63 Mohammedan priest
64 Omelet ingredients
68 Guido's high note
69 Anger

153

ACROSS

1 Essex or Erskine
4 Rome's Spanish ___
9 Creator of "Li'l Abner"
13 Certain slippers
15 Had the lead in a play
17 Skirts' inserts
18 Priest's vestment
19 John O'Hara's "From the ___"
20 Bullring
21 Permitted
22 Ram's dam
23 AFL-CIO and Teamsters: Abbr.
24 Intended
25 Irk
27 Sassy
28 In a lackadaisical way
29 Jewish month
30 Alien
32 Nostrils
34 Hamlet's "For shame!"
35 Ship's plank curve
36 Civil War general
39 Tease
40 Grim
42 Alpine native
45 Home for more than three billion
47 Well-groomed
50 De Havilland of Hollywood
51 Accent
53 Imbued
56 Six-time tennis champ
57 Closed, as an envelope
59 Fan
61 Silkworm
62 Remedy
65 Terror
67 Anguilla
68 Shamus
69 Pres., Veep or gen., e.g.
70 ___ canto
71 Prepares for action
73 Orbital point nearest sun
75 Diva's delight
76 Needle case
79 Crusaders' headquarters
80 Turning points
83 Mythical weeper
84 Appropriate
85 Edible root
87 TV editor Lou Grant
89 Dostoevsky's "The ___"
90 Builder
92 Name
93 Tarry
94 Calms
95 "___ Mine," 1985 film
96 Formerly, once
97 Clerical council
98 Sr. citizen's nest egg

DOWN

1 Pickling spice
2 "Through the Looking Glass" heroine
3 Narrator
4 Simmer
5 Darnel
6 Blunder
7 Famed park in Vienna
8 Least perilous
9 Prepared baking apples
10 Of a region
11 Cheap offer for thoughts
12 College-entrance exam dry run
13 Evil: Comb. form
14 Colonizes
15 Gary's chief product
16 Lot
17 Urchin
26 Avid desires
27 "The Gold Bug" author
30 Digit
31 Stabilizing device
32 Incipient
33 Stir up
34 Glass-making mixture
36 Martini garnish
37 Worshipped
38 Milk, butter and egg places
39 Mrs. Gorbachev
41 Dawn goddess
43 Jose's hooray
44 Of birth
46 Pertaining to a royal court
48 Modernist
49 "Beowulf" is one
52 But, to Brutus
54 Cousin of etc.
55 Dad's retreat
58 Columba (southern constellation)
60 Hardship
63 Screeds
64 Gourmets
66 Having eyelashes
70 Drone, e.g.
72 "Lone Ranger" theme song composer
73 Sanctity
74 Rapacious
75 Cicatrices
76 Duck down
77 Netting for snaring
78 Untersee craft
81 Penetrate
82 Alabama city where M.L.K., Jr. marched
83 Brood of pheasants
85 Holy Roman Empire founder?
86 Girl studying at MIT
88 Juan Carlos I, e.g.
91 Container for corn or peas

154

ACROSS

1 Research spots
5 Little pest
9 Basie's Buddy
13 Pro ___
17 Nazimova
18 Where Napoleon won in 1796
19 "My Name is ___": Saroyan
20 Jack of oaters
21 Set
23 Set
25 Onuses
26 Shed, as weight
28 Isis' sib
29 Linger
30 First word on the wall
31 Inspires fearful reverence
32 Set
36 Cook badly
40 "Thanks ___!"
41 Some are classified
42 Johnson dog
43 Angels' delight
44 ___ rule
45 Smoked salmon
47 Epigone
49 Hottest red spectral type
51 Continued without break
53 Set
56 Radius' accompanier
57 German engraver
58 Seize suddenly
59 Set
61 NFL team
64 Prince Harry's mom
65 Emit coherent light
66 Pig's digs
67 Follows bull or bear
68 Hgt.
69 ___-de-sac
70 "Exodus" protagonist
72 Mount in Thessaly
73 Whitens
76 Set
79 Inroad
80 Art Deco great
81 British isle
82 Birth
85 Esau's wife
86 Tested
90 Set
92 Set
93 Three, in Toledo
95 Withered
96 One-time
97 Buck heroine
98 Eldritch
99 Chemical compound
100 Regan's dad
101 Aerie

DOWN

1 Innocence symbol
2 Family name in baseball
3 Smudge
4 Type of baseball
5 Projecting wheel rim
6 Ships' records
7 Netherlands piano center
8 Having no purpose
9 French cup
10 Commedia dell' ___
11 Mai ___
12 Authorize
13 Pleasing taste
14 Winglike
15 Hulot portrayer
16 He played Mingo
22 Gang
24 Customer
27 Windsor's prov.
30 Frantic
31 Reroute
32 Bleats
33 More
34 Set
35 Machine with a number
36 William Sydney Porter
37 Set
38 Lake bigger than Huron
39 "High ___": Anderson
45 Weill's wife
46 Harem rooms
47 "... only God can make ___"
48 Gaze
49 Voracious eel
50 Small branch of an antler
52 ___ Bator
53 Noble goals
54 Sisters
55 "___ a Kick Out of You"
59 Nerd
60 Did a crossworder's job
62 To be, to Cicero
63 Coastal food fish
64 Tap
66 Title for Ustinov
69 Mandarin
70 Formicary
71 Hwy.
72 Eight-sided figure
74 Fleet
75 Enos's uncle
76 Epoch
77 Spring holiday
78 Nil ___ bonum
80 Detroit bomb
82 Bone: Comb. form
83 French laughter
84 Road to Rome
85 Field: Comb. form
86 Hammett pooch
87 Eli's home from home
88 Letters from Greece
89 Ding: Informal
91 Pvt.'s big boss
93 Glaswegian denial

155 YOUNG AT HEART by Tap Osborn
Famous octogenarians, nonagenarians, and even a centenarian are featured below.

ACROSS

1 City on Baranof Island
6 Raccoon's cousin
11 December song
16 Wedding worker
17 Birdlike
18 Cooking adjunct
19 He wrote a play at 93
22 Branch
23 Jockey Turcotte
24 Mirth
25 Beach bird
26 Practical one
29 "Cheers" character
31 Indeed
32 Affliction
33 Malarian fever
37 Salary supplement
38 He acted in his 90's
42 Originated
43 Lummox
44 Kicking up one's heels
45 Assam crawler
46 Intuit
47 Early Briton
48 Formerly
49 Horseshoe players
51 Road
52 Hebrew month
53 He coached football at 92
55 Adams, briefly
56 River to the Laptev Sea
57 Herb-of-grace
58 Actress Delany
59 Was radiant
63 Fraction
66 Chit
69 Eye part
70 Sweet one of song
71 Actress Munson
72 He wrote Russian history at 83
77 Insertion mark
78 Shoe stud
79 "The Old Wives' Tale" author
80 Musical Rogers
81 One hundred: Comb. form
82 Conundrum

DOWN

1 "___ Babies"
2 River to the Rhone
3 He invented until age 83
4 Plop's forerunner
5 S Amer. country
6 Henry ___ Lodge
7 Kitchen sight
8 Vent
9 Mediterranean seaport
10 Totally
11 MacArthur at 20
12 ___ poetica
13 Mies van der ___
14 Camporese of tennis
15 It needs cutting
20 Gaelic
21 Portuguese coin
27 Angler's aid

28 Disgruntle
29 Cry of surprise
30 Transport
32 Sound
34 She painted at 100
35 Illusory
36 Glacial ridge
37 Trial release
38 Conjecture
39 Operative
40 Noun suffix
41 Cave dweller
42 Zinc is one
43 Protagonist
46 Moroccan city
47 Summon loudly
50 Catch
51 Pay homage to
52 Dog-faced ape

54 Foot pedal
55 Bursa
58 Forest creature
60 Robust
61 Eggs
62 Date for Tom Jones
63 Owed
64 Talus
65 Kind of cake
66 Approach
67 Wings
68 European capital
70 Card game for three
73 Knowledge
74 ___ room
75 NT letters
76 Newcomer

156

BON APPETIT by Arthur S. Verdesca
Our frugal gourmet from Morristown, N.J., informs us the entire banquet below
only cost him 79¢. (The cost of a number-2 pencil and three erasers.)

ACROSS

1 Twig broom
6 "___ We Dance?"
11 Storm locater
16 Lift
17 " . . . be born, and a
    time ___ ": Eccles.
18 Minneapolis suburb
19 Hawthorne's home
20 European border
21 Quartet member
22 " . . . had a farm, ___
    . . ."
23 Hungarian starch?
26 Suffix for journal
27 Hell
29 Latin abbr.
30 Stop
32 Lake bigger than Huron
34 Drunk
35 Yeast foam
38 No-longer-popular
    vegetable?
42 Cutting remark
46 Only as ___ resort
48 Burn
49 Coe or Coghlan
50 Typewriter type
51 One, to Duncan
52 Skirt type: Hyph.
53 Aid for Stern
54 Incline
56 Existences
57 Let it stand!
58 Encounter at the
    butcher shop?
60 Criterion
61 IOU
63 Common vetch
65 Bind
68 Cries of pain
71 Good sense
75 Misplay
76 Russian bacon?
79 Spanish gold
80 Ruth's mother-in-law
82 As thin as ___
83 "___ is an island"
85 Fragrant compound
86 Luigi's feline
87 Incensed
88 American inventor
89 Fall bloomer
90 "Soap" family

DOWN

1 Harass
2 Oil: Comb. form
3 Dried orchid tubers
4 Follows Capri
5 Card carrier
6 Cluster thickly
7 Goddesses of the
   seasons
8 Acclimatize
9 Pale purple
10 Fewer
11 Keep
12 Summer cooler
13 Feasted
14 Win by ___
15 More remarkable
24 Where the Uinta rises
25 Gaunt

28 Truss the Smithfield?
31 Earl Grey, e.g.?
33 Scale notes
34 Dough roll
35 Max and Buddy
36 Apportion
37 Hike
39 Milan opera house
40 W Rumanian region
41 Nicholas Gage memoir
43 Unextinguished
44 Coty and Descartes
45 Treaty of ___-Litovsk
47 Decimal base
49 ___ de mer
54 Resolute
55 High explosive
58 Spanish painter

59 "Tootsie" star
62 Mohammed's flight to
   Medina
64 Purl anew
65 Doctrine
66 Expunge
67 Runs
68 Gumbos
69 Virgil Earp's brother
70 Malice
72 Body: Comb. form
73 Mount the soapbox
74 Canonical hour
77 Hindu musical work
78 Genus of swans
81 Blanc or Ott
84 Mouths

157 NEPTUNE'S OFFSPRING by Jeanette K. Brill

It was only natural for a Floridian to create this puzzle. By the way, she's a human example of 61 Down.

ACROSS

1 Heavenly bodies having tails
7 Weaken the resistance of
13 Expression of disgust
16 Mountain in the Noah story
17 Greek marketplaces
18 Miller or Barber
19 Desperate
21 Net in reverse
22 Nothing in Nantes
23 German city, canal or bay
24 Titter
26 Memorable Giant
27 What 18 Across aims to surpass
28 Plotters
31 In ___ (in trouble)
35 Amendment to a contract
36 Kyle or Tobin of football fame
37 Jot
39 "___ Kleine Nacht Musik": Mozart
42 British royal family of yore
45 ___ impasse (stymied)
46 ___ S. Cobb
47 Dada's daddy
48 Halfway
51 Yalie
52 Tushingham and Gam
54 Yorkshire river
55 Like some windows
57 German chancellor
58 City in Sicily
59 Herb that's wise?
60 Perspire, e.g.
62 Set sail
66 Extracted the essence by boiling
69 A Burns negative
70 Wharton School deg.
72 Arkansas city near Memphis, Tenn.
73 Musical pause
75 College official
76 Application
77 Persevere
82 Bee chaser
83 Be innate
84 Saws
85 Color that is also called lama
86 Gazed intently
87 Most wan

DOWN

1 Mubarak's capital city
2 Br. of zoology dealing with birds
3 ___ measure (custom created)
4 Ireland, poetically
5 Salt
6 Jeanne D'Arc, e.g.
7 Literary form
8 Windigo
9 Young horses
10 Part of 78 Down
11 Tuck away
12 Fitted together, like some tables
13 In jail: Colloq.
14 Garson of the cinema
15 Sharpens
20 Ray
25 Moslem ruler
27 Actress LuPone
29 Grimalkin
30 He sounds like a song
32 Folk-song symbol
33 What a Diet!
34 Dilapidated building
38 Vetch
40 Subject of a Ludwig book
41 Site of Phillips U.
42 Scottish shirt
43 Tom, Dick and Harry
44 In a predicament
45 P ___ petrol
46 Insect stage
49 Author of "The Divine Comedy"
50 Lessen
53 Star in Perseus
56 In medias ___ (in the middle of things)
58 Superlative ending
59 Aver
61 Successful transplant
63 Not spilled, as tears
64 Become visible
65 Demeans
66 Tennis call
67 Gear for Wyeth
68 Household appliance
71 "___ of robins . . ."
74 Raison d' ___
75 Twofold
78 Explosive initials
79 Eureka!
80 Top
81 Whoopi's role in "Ghost": 1990

158 FAVORITES by Nancy Scandrett Ross

Celebrated people become egotists in this name game conceived in Peekskill, N.Y.

ACROSS

1 Threw a party for
6 Eric the Red's son
10 Greenish-yellow pears
15 Declaim
16 ___ dot
17 Word before linguistics
   or velocity
18 Marilyn's favorite stage
   comedy?
21 Summer coolers
22 Suffix for labor
23 Le Mans-to-Calais dir.
24 Like crudités
25 Showed the way
26 Netman Camporese
27 Old Bailey events
30 Agitated state
31 Nerve cell
34 Bret's favorite
   monologues?
41 Conceptions
42 Dido's lover
43 River isle
44 Stage Edmund
45 Quiche ingredient
47 Superlative suffix
48 Funnyman Johnson
49 Wing of sorts
50 Battery terminals
52 Success stories' Horatio
53 Agnes's favorite novel?
57 Memorizes
58 Actian and Antiochian
59 Nancy ___, late
   comedienne
62 Moselle feeder
63 Capp of Dogpatch et al.
66 Corrida cry
67 Tibetan gazelle
70 Gallery contents
71 Pulitzer novelist: 1958
72 Larry's favorite pop
   singer?
77 Meted
78 Vicuna's habitat
79 Indians conquered by
   the Incas
80 Some partygoers
81 Graphite
82 "___ Ben Johnson ..."

DOWN

1 Kind of point
2 Disintegrate
3 Broken, as a bronco
4 Summers in Aix
5 Society bud
6 Scowl
7 Cathedral near
   Cambridge
8 Sacred image
9 Satyr's cousin
10 Humbug preceder
11 Genovese gold
12 ___ Junipero, famed
   missionary in
   California
13 Panama passage
14 Scads
16 Edible stem
19 Restrict
20 Withdrawal
26 Some bills
28 Spoils
29 ___ nutshell
   (succinctly)

30 Musial of baseball
31 Highlands negative
32 ___ Evans
   (Chubby Checker)
33 Western Indians
34 Used shanks' mare
35 "Die Fledermaus"
   soubrette
36 Domain
37 North Atlantic seabird
38 Slow movement
39 High fliers
40 Gang and mob
   followers
45 Add to
46 Comer's opposite
48 Shakespeare title starter
50 Sailor's direction
51 Future adm.?
52 Churchill's "___
   Country"
54 Kind
55 Flowers' companions
56 One of Thalia's sisters

59 Certain clubs
60 Apportion
61 "The Pearl Fishers"
   heroine
62 Used a toothed tool
63 Meeting place of yore
64 "Gypsy Love"
   composer
65 "___ and Sensibility,"
   by Austen
68 Actinal
69 Lady of the thousand
   days
71 Open a bit
73 Courgette, e.g.: Brit.
74 Freudian concerns
75 Author LeShan
76 PFC's superior

159

ROLE CALL by John Greenman
John tells us he worked full-time on this part-time job. We believe it!

ACROSS

1 Find fault
5 Hooters
9 Native African village
13 On the ___ (fleeing)
16 Is in debt
17 Reagan cabinet member
19 English composer
20 Linguist's ABC's
21 Phileas Fogg
23 Nothing, in Nicaragua
24 Land of ___
25 Bard's "before"
26 Erin
27 Norma Rae
30 Luca ___ Robbia
32 Morning moisture
34 Takes to court
35 Broadway's Barnum
   portrayer
36 Sphere
38 As easy ___
40 Ostrich's cousin
41 Narrow furrow
43 Baptism and
   confirmation
44 Greek consonants
45 Annie Hall
47 Striving
51 Poet Lazarus
52 Bordered
53 Greek cheese
54 Be prone
55 Teachers' org.
56 Mrs. Miniver
58 Neighbor of Syr.
59 Former French coin
60 The Swedish
   Nightingale
61 Virginia willow
62 Growl
63 Adversaries
65 Lawrence of Arabia
68 Commercials
69 Optical maser
70 Prevaricators
71 Mise en ___
74 Parks and Convy
75 Alcove
76 Sarah ___ Jewett
77 "I smell ___!"
78 Cravat
81 Guam and Maui
85 Margo Channing
88 Berliner's "no"
90 Pub quaff
91 Prohibit
92 Winfield or Brubeck
93 Rhett Butler
96 Suffix for journal
97 Ripsnorter

98 Misrepresent
99 Warm
100 Billy ___ Williams
101 Playwright Hart
102 Du Diable and de France
103 As well

DOWN

1 Cyphered
2 Cognizant
3 Make merry
4 Hellenic letter
5 Prefix for present
6 Bizarre
7 Embankment
8 Opposite of NNW
9 "The Bridge at ___
   Rey"
10 Kerry's county seat
11 Rooney and Williams
12 Tone-___ (unmusical)
13 Threadlike
14 Greek god of medicine
15 Drive crazy

18 Half-picas
22 Darling
28 Rockies resort
29 That is
31 Luft or Doone
33 One used to taking
   orders
37 They're rolling in rolls
39 Most stubbornly
   conventional
40 Province of SE China
41 Jacob and Leah's second
   son
42 Spicy Mexican
   concoction
43 Stormed
44 Marquand's sleuth
45 Crowded
46 Idyllic spots
47 Composer Franck
48 Writer Wylie
49 Hemplike fibers
50 ___ Haute
53 More uninhibited

56 Move smoothly
57 Certify
62 Objectives
64 French artist
65 Book section
66 "___ Buttermilk Sky"
67 Mosaic flooring
69 Departers
71 Wept
72 Fold
73 Menu inclusion
74 World Series team of
   1991
77 Hersey's hamlet
79 Totally counted
80 Spooky
82 Tag
83 Cinders and Raines
84 Take care of
86 Esau
87 Science deg.
89 Turner and Snopes
94 Hilo wreath
95 Cry of discovery

160 TAURUS TAUNTER by Sidney L. Robbins
Sid can't recall whether he made this puzzle up after watching Buttons or Skelton.

ACROSS

1 His ___, the Mayor
6 Drummer's gear
11 High-grade harpist?
17 Worshipped
19 Greek column type
20 Grow molars
21 Kindergartners in Moscow?
24 After twelve fifty-nine
25 Devoured
26 Mrs. in Madrid
27 Additions
28 Precise
30 Actress Lee
31 Isomeric
32 Dusting powder
35 Whip handle
37 Choice foods, old style
39 Norse mariner
42 Embarrassed
47 Underseas explorer
48 Show backer
50 Monopoly times two
51 Speck
53 "Sweetheart of Sigma ___"
55 Fold
56 Combing result, at times
60 Football hero, early on
63 Snow vehicle
64 Interstice
66 Yes, to Pierre
67 Immense
69 Cleveland baseball team
71 Tablelands
73 Eagle's nest
78 Auto stopper
80 Misleading clue
82 Nicklaus and Palmer, at first
84 Sign or gas
85 Huey or Shelley
86 Mind
89 Guinea fowl's young
91 Sweet, to Cicero
93 Samoan seaport
94 Half-breed
96 Knightly title
97 "___ my brother's keeper?"
100 Song hit of 1935
104 Fish carriers
105 Straight up
106 Cousin of a hogan
107 Southern meat dish
108 Patriot Warner and clockmaker Thomas
109 Examinations

DOWN

1 Gloriole
2 Host at Valhalla
3 Observe
4 Scrap for Fido
5 Take it easy
6 Cravat
7 Reels' partners
8 Photographer Adams
9 Inge play
10 He once came at 10 o'clock
11 Portico for Pericles
12 Slippery one
13 Wat Tyler was one
14 Coral isle
15 Tribe: Comb. form
16 Spandau inmate
18 Separate
22 Have fun
23 Declaimed
28 Behold, to Ovid
29 Violent squall
31 "___ me, give me liberty . . .": Patrick Henry
32 Kennedy or Weems
33 Onassis' nickname
34 Actress Ullmann
36 Kind of leg?
38 Reasons out
40 Prefix with angle
41 Fault finder
43 Mimics
44 Black gold?
45 Otherwise
46 Colored
49 Admiralty VIP
52 Color at Syracuse
54 Intruded with force
56 Two of a kind
57 "Rule, Britannia" composer
58 A memorable Foxx
59 Emulate an esne
61 Kind of shoe?
62 Kind of gang once seen in a St. Louis ballpark
65 Clergy's need
68 Salt
70 Mideast coin
72 Yen fraction
74 Film director Kenton
75 ___ Grande
76 Tabard or Admiral Benbow
77 Leghorn's largesse
79 Locks?
81 Volunteer
83 "Saturday Night Live" humor
86 Singspiel
87 Dwells
88 Stand for Shahn
90 Doctrine
92 Vinegar bottle
93 ___ of Triumph
94 Fog's fellow traveler
95 Work in acid
97 Cleo's snakes
98 Schoolboy competition
99 Natives of: Suffix
101 Londoner's "bitter"
102 High grounds: Abbr.
103 Barbara Bush, ___ Pierce

161

OOPS! by Mary M. Murdoch
Don't be fooled by MMM's title. There's nothing clumsy about the way this little challenger was put together.

ACROSS

1 Cotton quantity
5 Puerto Rican dance
10 Culture medium
14 Waist-length jackets
16 Total
17 The Fates, e.g.
18 Mere trace, with "A"
20 Torch
21 Sharp-toothed fish: Var.
22 Radames' love
23 Part of AM
24 Barbie's friend
25 "If You Knew Susie" singer
27 Without delay
35 Skater Boitano
36 Spoken
37 Moroccan capital
41 Water vessel of India
42 Eden
45 Prefix for bar
46 Cobbler's tools
47 Literary gp.
48 Literary monogram
49 Bard of Bombay
50 Zuider ___
51 Tom Tryon novel
53 Dalai ___
54 Pliny the ___
56 Bonny hillside
57 Feelings
58 Famous line from "The Ancient Mariner"
62 Slip away
65 ___, amas, amat
66 Parisian playground
67 Columbia letters
71 Swamp
75 Final notice
76 Damon Runyon story
79 Algonquian
80 ___ as pie
81 "El Capitan" composer
82 Crowd
83 Places or shows
84 Flunk

DOWN

1 Sprinkle
2 Eagerly expectant
3 Actress Ackerman
4 ___'acte
5 Canton col.
6 Auk genus
7 Hel's father
8 Prosecuted
9 Connect
10 Peachy city?
11 Subsidy
12 We ___ please
13 U.S. pollster
15 Disturbed
16 ___ Terme (Italian spa)
19 Poetic tear
26 Swiss stream
27 On fire

28 Plastering tool
29 Dubbed
30 Jay of the PGA
31 Blue
32 Refrain syllable
33 Had at a disadvantage, with "on"
34 Beethoven's "Für ___"
38 Language of India
39 Willingham's "End ___"
40 Reprimand, with "take"
42 Word of disgust
43 A protozoan: Var.
44 Sun. talk
49 Becloud
51 Too much, in Tulle
52 Scottish river

55 Constituted
57 Beautifies
59 Lessee's payment
60 Debbie Reynolds role
61 Melville work
62 Period
63 Buffalo skater
64 CNN anchor
68 Words from Chan
69 Spots
70 Wings
72 "... wine with not ___ allaying Tiber in 't": Shak.
73 Jaeger relative
74 Juan's affirmatives
77 Affix for count
78 River in S Sweden

162

T 'n' T by Peter Gordon

Here's the latest example of the fact that new themes with clever titles will never stop coming.

ACROSS

1 Ham it up on stage
8 He plays for pay
11 Famous pooch of filmdom
15 One who edits
16 Former name of Egypt: Abbr.
17 Donahue and Mahre
19 Ta-ta
21 Agent's cut, traditionally
22 After-Christmas store event
23 Stouts
24 Turkish title
25 Hunting expedition
29 Knife maker
31 Affirmative votes
34 Tête
37 Scrapes on children's knees
39 Corbin's "L.A. Law" role
40 Video's counterpart
41 Caesar or Waldorf
43 Embrace
46 Titi
51 Berlin's "___ a Rag Picker"
52 Criminal's false name
53 Established practice
54 ___ petty officer
56 Young chicory plants
58 Toto
63 Superman's insignia
64 Singer Piaf and designer Head
65 ___ around (philandered)
67 Camera part
68 Neck of the woods
70 Sigher's word
74 Former capital of Bangladesh
76 Tutu
80 Burglarize
81 Genesis woman
82 A Gandhi
83 Felix's daughter on "The Odd Couple"
84 Game, ___, and match
85 Most meager

DOWN

1 Spheres
2 "Alice" waitress
3 Wicked
4 ___ of passage (baptism, marriage, etc.)
5 Donkey
6 Corn serving
7 Hear a case in the courtroom
8 ___ Enemy (rap band)
9 Denture wearer Martha
10 Raw metals
11 Likely
12 Enclose in a case, as a sword
13 Have a prickling feeling
14 Tennis player Gibson
18 Fragment
20 Merit
26 "___ and his money . . ."
27 To's counterpart
28 Loser to DDE

29 Kind of apartment, for short
30 Spoon bender Geller
31 Make ill at ease
32 "Believe ___!" ("It's true!")
33 What some jerks serve
35 Actor Alan and spy Nathan
36 Become worn by rubbing
38 "The Family Circus" author Keane
41 Check for a gas leak
42 Abbreviation in a police blotter
43 Get the old ___-ho
44 Cravings
45 This might be educated
47 Butlers' assistants
48 ___ strut (airplane part)
49 Chocolaty candy
50 Letter before omega
54 Type of X-ray image

55 Title for a prince: Abbr.
56 Mag. officials
57 "Domine, dirige ___," London motto
58 Joins pieces of metal
59 Think
60 Galvanized
61 Breakfast dish
62 Intense enthusiasm
66 Capital of Senegal
68 Vigoda and Burrows
69 Great review
71 Lo-cal, in some brand names
72 Gives weapons to
73 Census fig.
75 Pie ___ mode
77 Rheine's river
78 Gregory Hines movie: 1989
79 ___ Na Na (entertainment group)

163 HAWKEYE by Joy L. Wouk
Joy wants to dedicate this one to Alan Alda and everyone in the state of Iowa.

ACROSS

1 Chocolate source
6 He wrote "The Nazarene"
10 Larrigan
13 Czarist Russian Parliament
17 Manila hemp source
18 Irritate
19 A Khan
20 Son of Tereus
21 Sobriquet of 35 Across
23 Actor Cariou
24 Pledge
25 Ferrara family
26 Dale
27 Government of five
29 Loaf
30 Eye cosmetic
31 Underground stem
35 "The Leatherstocking Tales" hero
39 Firth of Clyde island
40 River at Lyon
42 Corday's victim
43 Kind of college
45 Butter, in Oslo
49 Kind
50 Estrange
52 Author Hunter
54 Bishopric
55 Creator of 35 Across
59 Cinnabar or galena
60 Seized
61 Make-believe
62 Coffee vessels
64 Scandinavian rugs
66 Musical genre
69 ___ voce
71 Fay and John of films
73 Aquarium fish
74 Sea tale by 55 Across (with "The")
78 Medieval jerkin
79 Devotees of 55 Across
80 Drop heavily
82 Reversed
85 Bungle
86 Tennis legend
90 Anklebones
91 Guided
92 Sobriquet of 35 Across
94 Man or Wight
95 Assam silkworm
96 Prefix for present
97 Kind of theater
98 Suffix for mob
99 Summer hrs.
100 Boulder Dam lake
101 Bewildered

DOWN

1 Ann or May
2 Down with, in Dijon
3 U.S. suffragist: 1859–1947
4 Pain
5 Clumsy one
6 Desi or Lucie
7 Move sideways
8 Redshank
9 "... robins in ___ hair"
10 Most faint
11 Medium
12 Cambridge grad.
13 Museum displays
14 Luzon brain
15 Legend
16 Pallid
22 Director Reitman
27 Hors d'oeuvres spreads
28 Jack-in-the-pulpit
29 Rather extended
30 Homo sapiens

31 Gal of song
32 Refrain syllable
33 Decoration, in Orvieto
34 Tureen accessory
35 Nights, in Napoli
36 Outlooks
37 Cole Porter song
38 Mink's cousin
40 With rationality
41 Buddha's cousin
44 Touch on
46 Only
47 Culp Hobby's namesakes
48 Contests
51 Part of HRE
53 Continuous
55 Tournament
56 Shaft
57 Killer whales
58 Basket willow
63 Brighter, nocturnally

65 Turf
67 Land measure
68 Lang. for Cato
70 Baltic feeder
72 Literary monogram
75 Handled roughly
76 Slouches
77 Blue-pencil again
78 Male swans
80 Opposites of vacuums
81 Sensational
82 Regretful Miss
83 Great in extent
84 French magazine
85 Wife, in law
86 Actress Theda
87 Hear ye!
88 Bacteriologist Dubos
89 Homecoming attendee
92 Monk's title
93 Boy

164

IN OTHER WORDS by Michael A. Rampino

Our researchers tell us Terence, La Fontaine, and Sophocles share the credit with the good reverend at 23 Across; while Ann Landers and Janet Ace share similar honors at 87 Across.

ACROSS

1 Its capital is Shillong
6 Accumulate
11 Emulates Sol
15 Crystal-lined rocks
17 Matched an arsonist
19 Alpine river to the Rhine
20 Bivouac
21 Christian
22 Breakfast food
23 Rev. Spooner's intended homily
26 Canards
27 Short for psychometry
28 Anguine fish
29 Shoe width
30 Passbook entry: Abbr.
31 Apollo's twin
35 Merits
37 Touchy and quarrelsome
39 Repercussion
41 Blathers
44 Smyrna fig
45 Make beloved
47 Cove
48 Conscription org.
49 Untrammelled
50 Satirize
53 Dec. members
54 Crazes
55 Cummerbund
56 Novelist Matute
59 Declaim
61 Eucharistic wafer
62 Darjeeling or camomile
65 Cerulean or umber
67 Wayward
69 Bamboo eater
71 A kind of bullet
73 Nothing, in Nice
74 Medals
75 Fundamental
77 Tittle
80 Malachite or galena
81 Mineral spring
83 Farming: Comb. form
85 Immerse
86 Entreaty
87 Rev. Spooner's homily
93 Landed
94 Alleviate
95 Authenticate
97 Raise
98 Opener
99 Tirade
100 Anglo-Saxon slave
101 Vow
102 They go to blazes

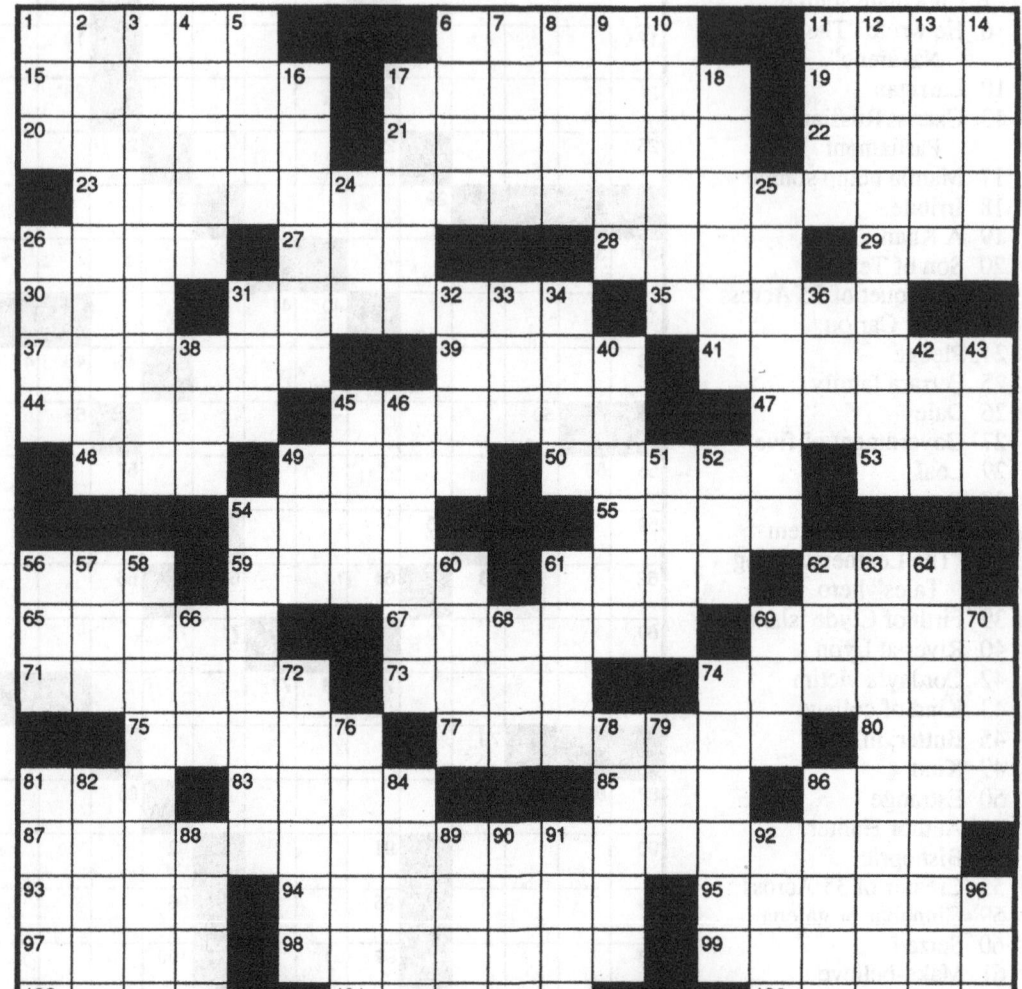

DOWN

1 Turn ten
2 Guards
3 Associations
4 Tarkington's "Alice ___"
5 Self, in Lyons
6 First shepherd
7 ___ sana in corpore sano
8 ___ boy!
9 Fence steps
10 Marketer
11 Star of "Elephant Boy"
12 Staunchly
13 Vocation
14 Meaning
16 Starlike
17 Yawning
18 Gullet skinfold
24 NYC winter time
25 Rhea's cousin
26 Biography

31 Zeus's maddening daughter
32 Ancient Persian
33 H_2O at 31° F
34 Bogus
36 Scottish yearling
38 Short sizes
40 Prayer
42 Racket follower
43 John and Joseph
45 Nibelungs goddess
46 Nide hunter
49 Remote
51 Hog feed
52 Suffix for social
54 Divined
56 Legislation
57 Partner of neither
58 Selma resident
60 Actor Roberts
61 Held cards
62 Pagoda

63 Matriculants
64 Postman's concern
66 Edible tuber
68 Caddoan Indian
69 New Deal org.
70 On the bounding main
72 Hardships
74 Beginnings
76 Vinegar holders
78 Loafer
79 West's Diamond role
81 Glower
82 Dock supports
84 Result of marriage
86 Stone: Comb. form
88 Raison d'___
89 Ominous
90 Stiff hair
91 Affirm
92 Engrave
96 NFL stats

165 VARIATIONS ON A THEME by Jack L. Steinhardt
Four synonyms evoke different combinations in an unusual puzzle from one of our Jerseyites.

ACROSS

1 Swither
6 Asia Minor region of old
11 Beguile
16 Redolence
17 Lariat loop
18 Pen or windshield follower
19 Occasional result of politics
22 Kind of spirit
23 Bickered
24 Daughter of James II
25 ___ Chi, Chinese religion
27 Food, in Frankfurt
29 "___ Kapital"
32 First name of an A-bomb plane
36 Ancient Gallic collar
39 Outré conduct
45 Converses informally
46 Reprimands viciously
47 Bandeau
48 Comic Jay
49 Eyot
50 Endeavor
51 Shelter; dugout
52 Y, e, or et
53 Funicello of films
55 Chopine and Balmoral
56 Peculiar condition
59 Arabian king
60 ___ Fiorentino, suburb of Florence
61 Pennant: Abbr.
62 Formerly Navigators Islands
66 Agricultural beard
68 Escutcheon stigma
71 Type of flight
75 Wrong
79 Halloween attire
82 Poe's "House"
83 Also, to Caesar
84 Mark Twain biographer
85 "___ were the days . . ."
86 Greer or O'Grady
87 Mutate

DOWN

1 Preterit
2 Craft, in Cadiz
3 Bayes or Charles
4 Shiite religious leaders
5 Preserve
6 Poseidon changed her into a mare
7 Snaffles
8 Singletons
9 Bewilder
10 Temptations for Willie Sutton
11 Gimlet
12 Famed Yugoslavian soprano
13 Atop
14 Basted
15 Scotch Gaelic
20 Birthplace of John of Gaunt
21 Asner and Begley

26 Poulards
28 An anagram for seat
29 Vet's advice
30 One-seeded fruits
31 Old Norse peninsula
33 Would-be assassin of Napoleon III
34 Bug and box preceder
35 Height: Comb. form
37 Parts of typewriters
38 Remedy
40 Theater of '44
41 British hunting party
42 Zimbalist Sr. and Jr.
43 "___ There": 1954 song
44 Embossed
49 Old: Abbr.
51 Discovery cry
53 Italian river
54 Insts. for would-be educators

55 Dunnage
57 Heists a heifer
58 Delaying pretext
63 Tue. preceder
64 Succession or sequence
65 Attire, in Amalfi
67 S African province
68 Match
69 Profuse
70 German king: 936–73
72 Egyptian fertility goddess
73 Siamese
74 Pinnacle
76 Particle
77 Actor Auberjonois
78 River into the North Sea
80 "Chances ___,": Mathis hit
81 ___ Locka, city in Fla.

166 MAL DE MER by Kenneth Haxton

This appears to be a 19X19 square puzzle but it's not. It's a 21X21 in disguise. After solving it we think you'll agree with us.

ACROSS

1 Kind of ladder
5 Emulate Duse
8 Peru capital
12 Debussy opus
15 Home of Irish kings
16 Asian mountain range
17 Jannings or Ludwig
18 Secular
19 Golfing great
21 Home of the shamrock
23 ___ but wiser
24 Anti-smoking org.
25 Island or lily
26 Childrens' song
30 City in SW Maine
33 Guido invention
34 States positively
38 Separate
40 Prayer
42 Water for Bardot
43 One who imitates
44 Mohawks and Oneidas
47 "Star Wars" princess
50 Hebrew dry measures
51 Fun place in the home
53 Type type: Abbr.
55 Vitreous
57 Trust, in Dumfries
59 City of Italia
61 A film Dracula
64 Main motif, in music
66 Window decorators
69 Goddess of retribution
70 Masculine
72 Indolent
74 Where Levine conducts
76 Kurosawa's "Lear"
77 Period of heat
79 Candidate list
81 Auto part
85 ___ of hope
87 Vase handle
88 Nicaraguan or Costa Rican
92 Mammoth's epoch
95 Hurry
96 "___ of that which not enriches him": Shak.
99 "The River" author
101 Annoying TV necessities
104 Foster and March
105 Adams or Magnus
106 Stuns
107 ___ uno
108 Fabulist George
109 Hawaii's state bird
110 Flower repository
111 Essence

DOWN

1 Penn, e.g.
2 Sailors
3 Singer Berger
4 No longer owing
5 Tocsin ringers
6 Coolidge
7 Race official
8 Sponges
9 Put under water
10 Ms. Farrow
11 Shady paths
12 Endure
13 Oiseau lifter
14 Songstress Mabel
16 Mimic
18 Hosiery material
20 Writer LeShan
22 E Indian sauces
24 For advertised price
27 Religious image
28 Like matgrass
29 Alborg native
30 Actor Wanamaker
31 Buy ___ in a poke
32 Japanese export
35 Speed Wagons
36 Circus trainers
37 Actress York, to friends
39 Philosophy of Lao-tzu
41 Cooking pot
45 Partial blindness
46 Devilkin
48 Prince and Stravinsky
49 NATO nations
52 Argentine city
54 Argentine city
56 Goal
58 Summers in Dijon
60 Go to next pg.
61 Corde de ___ (Fr. bowstring)
62 Western state
63 Actress Rowlands
65 Emotional status
67 "Call Me Madam" star
68 Tennis units
71 "___ we forget"
73 Chemical compound
75 Camellia sinensis
78 Cadet
80 Wolverine State capital
82 Cigarette butts
83 State flower of 62 Down
84 "Planted a garden eastward ___": Gen.
86 Made solid
89 German river, in Germany
90 Promising people
91 "Nightline" ntwk.
92 "___ La Douce"
93 Fed a line to
94 Come forth
97 Hawaiian island
98 Rice and Fudd
100 Ike
101 Singer Calloway
102 Be indebted
103 Inebriate

167 BLUES CHASER by Jean Hunt

One goal of puzzlers is to make solvers forget their troubles. This delightful creation from Louisiana accentuates the joyous positive.

ACROSS

1 Lobster claw
6 Flower arrangement
11 Peculates
17 Edmonton team member
18 ___ Arena, Washington, D.C.
19 Tycoon
21 "___ of great joy I bring . . .": N. Brady
23 "Too many ___ the fire"
24 Doze
25 Major mountain range
26 Valley
27 Toll rd.
28 Seed covering
30 Part of parrot's bill
31 Quilting and spelling contests
32 Siamese
33 What 72 Across couldn't stop
34 Suburb of Liège
35 Winnows
36 Old Chinese kingdom
37 ___ shrdlu (linotyper's error)
39 Entice
40 ___ Mesta, memorable hostess
43 Aswan, formerly
44 Cornbread
45 Gladdened
47 Process caused by glaciers and oceans
50 Quoth
51 Memorabilia
52 Weir
55 Sitcom that brought fame to Henry Winkler
57 Border
58 Pierre's soul
59 Sup
60 Gus ___, memorable astronaut
63 City SW of Boston
65 Slant
66 "Merry Widow" composer
70 "The Black ___," R. L. Stevenson title
71 Brewer's yeast
72 Early king of Denmark
73 Urge
74 Spiral
75 Within: Prefix
77 "___ corny as Kansas in August"
78 Fades
80 Fight for breath
81 Biblical kingdom
82 "___ me tangere"
83 "Foucault's Pendulum" author
84 Carnelian
85 Craze
87 Printed, as a newspaper story
88 San Francisco 49er of Super Bowl fame
90 Like a really good joke
93 Contestant
94 Swift
95 Dispatch
96 English counties
97 Sylvia Plath poem
98 Square columns

DOWN

1 Words or people of the same descent
2 Mirth
3 Family of cobras and mambas
4 ___ Zeppelin, rock group
5 Gulf of ___ on Greece's coast
6 Abrupt
7 Pincers
8 Launder lightly
9 Sharp-cornered: Abbr.
10 Sandburg's "The People, ___"
11 Beams
12 Biblical weeds
13 ___ Krenz, former E German leader
14 Landers or Rutledge
15 Edwin O'Connor title (with "The")
16 Grass used for cordage
20 Sumerian god of wisdom
22 Quechuan
26 Autry or Kelly
29 Sierra ___, W Africa
31 Reveal
32 Quaker pronoun
35 Streisand movie: 1968
36 Hurried
38 Ending for cash or front
39 Encircle
41 Unaspirated consonant
42 City NE of Amsterdam
44 Meerschaum
45 Isles
46 Steamy sound
48 Buckeye State
49 True grit
50 Ancient Egyptian city
52 Andrews or Wynter
53 Cupid
54 "In the ___ of May": R. Barnfield
56 Small sip
59 Fine feathers
61 Suffix with boff or pay
62 "___ great place are thrice servants": Bacon
64 Sorrows
65 Tease
67 Joker
68 "___ in Calydon," Swinburne poem
69 Sears again
71 Pledge
72 Clown
74 Goldsmith's concerns
75 Gleeful
76 Soundness of mind
78 Township in ancient Attica
79 Sacred images
80 Velvet-like cloth
81 Surround tightly
84 Moselle feeder
86 Burmese tribe
89 Prefix for corn or pod
90 Part of an address
91 Dockers' org.
92 Swedish county

168 FOURSQUARE by William P. Baxley

Here's a nice, straightforward puzzle for those who want a respite from gimmickry. Surprisingly enough, it was created in L.A.

ACROSS

1 Nothing, in Navarra
5 Mine entrance
9 Good conductor of electricity
14 Amino acids, for short
19 An astringent
20 Not a single one, rustic style
21 Expiate
22 Lower in rank
23 Scheming person
25 Loud, sharp noise
27 Disencumber
28 Conspicuous
30 Splendid
31 Naval craft for short
32 Sap
34 Bitter vetch
36 Til
38 Highland flings
39 Oasts
41 Spanish gentlemen
44 Members of the wedding
46 Introducing in steps (with "in")
48 Journalist
49 Sifter
50 Favorable beginning
52 Lab heaters
53 Wings for Amor
54 Four: Comb. form
55 Proceed cautiously
57 Golfers Woosnam and Baker-Finch
58 Deity
59 Wilde's Mr. Gray
60 Solers' next of kin
62 Lamb or Bacon
64 Reserve funds
68 Advantage
71 Coats of arms
73 Gamma-ray dosage
74 African gully
77 Shakespeare's theatre
78 U.S. President after Grant
79 Urn
80 Senile, in a way
82 Body portions of airplanes
84 Spanish rural inn
85 Resources
87 Readjusted musical pitch
88 Fireplace screen
89 Short rest periods
91 Aeries
92 Ancient Japanese
93 Sea between Greece and Turkey
95 U.S. 66, e.g.
96 Checked
99 One of the bipeds
101 New York harbor island
103 Religious recluse
105 Summer drink
106 Between the rows of printed matter
109 Move the furniture around
111 She played Florida in "Maude"
112 Boldness
113 Hawaiian goose
114 Same: Lat.
115 Author Seton and namesakes
116 Ancient chariot
117 Irish gaelic
118 Latvia and Lithuania, once: Abbr.

DOWN

1 Mother-of-pearl
2 Bitter yellow crystalline
3 Birdbrains
4 Danish administrative district
5 Zoologists' interests
6 Ship's cranes
7 "Goodnight" girl in a song
8 Capital of ancient Phoenicia
9 Futon or shiki buton
10 Old English letter
11 What a cicerone heads
12 English princess and queen
13 Rocky outcrops
14 Mode of speech
15 Simple as ___
16 Danseuse
17 King of Judah et al.
18 Clan
24 Midnight rider
26 Alleviates
29 Resident of the Sagebrush State
33 Author of "The Silent Bullet"
35 Tattle: Colloq.
37 Tenon's partner
39 "From the Terrace" author
40 Kind of drum
42 Israel's Abba ___
43 Mtg.
44 Common practice
45 Housings for guided missiles
46 Teacake
47 Jealous
50 Feminine pronoun
51 Attainments of ends via intelligent efforts
54 ___ and froing: Colloq.
56 Nuisances
59 Insoluble coloring matter
61 Some coll. linemen
63 Eisenhower Center's locale
65 Plays up to the crowd
66 Exploit
67 Besmirch
69 "The Master Builder" playwright
70 Vacillate
71 Chorister
72 High dudgeons
74 Brit. servicewoman
75 Amphora adjunct
76 Afar
79 Aphrodite, to Nero
81 Elaborate whatnots
83 Gleamed
84 Protective facing
86 Indeterminate period of time
88 Conifer
90 Brackish
92 Followers of an Alexandrian priest who died A.D. 336
94 Cubs and Mets
96 Asian commander
97 Lawn tool
98 Music critic Taylor
99 Remarkable variable star
100 Prolific auth.
102 Sun. talks
104 Rival of boxer Joe Gans
107 Character in "Charley's Aunt"
108 Salutation for Seneca
110 Three-toed sloths

169 DASH IT ALL! by Norman S. Wizer

If things seem helpless at 26 Across, take another look at Norman's title.

ACROSS

1 Chow
5 Touched clumsily
10 Keogh's kin
14 Season
18 Peak
19 Dispatch boat
20 Long-legged bird
21 Frankenstein's friend
22 Promenade for Plato
23 Calico horse
24 Sèvres school
25 Muses' number
26 Helpless
28 Perpendiculars
31 MGM co-founder
32 Broker's order
33 Happy one
34 Resort
37 Ascend
40 Stone marker
41 Forefront
43 Outbursts
47 Kind of cure?
48 Dressler
49 Mocks
50 Pet
51 Walk
52 Gamin
53 Certain trousers
54 Quickly
55 Trice
57 ABC rival
58 Rubbernecks
59 Cabbage dishes
60 Seis, siete, ___
62 Middling
63 Diverse, shortened
64 British statesman
67 French painter
68 Success
69 Spontaneity
73 Bays
74 War cry
75 Dramatis personae
76 Hightail
77 Silkworm
78 ___ accomplis
79 Meat pie
80 Tally
81 Prime
83 One with gold fever
85 "Ten" star
86 Completely
87 Dramatic genre
88 Lodger
90 Afghan coin
91 A portion
92 Made-to-order
95 Nostrum
99 Amas follower
100 "They seek ___":
    Luke 11:29
101 Twelvetrees
103 Edge treatment
104 Dawdle
105 Trapshooting
106 Get around
107 Press
108 Toward the mouth
109 Hue
110 Nominator
111 Force or master

DOWN

1 Crush
2 Outer: Comb. form
3 Haze
4 Mariner's route
5 Piñata material
6 "A Room with ___"
7 Chinook
8 Winter time in Roanoke
9 Kind of step or stop
10 Uneasy
11 Disorderly profusion of
   color
12 Top performers
13 Stanley's cars
14 Type tersely
15 Lithe
16 Individualist
17 Very in Verdun
20 Musical transition
27 Nothing ___!
29 Ending for flex
30 Blue or White river
34 Files
35 Resort on Lake Geneva
36 Gold coin
37 Teasdale et al.
38 Cheat
39 Citrus drink
40 Luge and pung
42 Greta Gustafson
43 Iron in Milan
44 Sloth
45 Ancient British people
46 Fem. martyrs
49 Tourney
53 Consumer-run store
54 ___ Poetica
56 Spotty
58 Corrida beasts
59 Oblique
61 These in Quebec
62 Truth to Shakespeare
63 Erroll Garner song
64 Aid's cohort
65 Edible root
66 Actuate
67 Baby bunting
68 Waste maker
70 Forsaken
71 Content
72 Corundum
74 Aquaplane
75 Carry off
78 First spar
79 Product of 65 Down
80 Break
82 Prince Dakkar
83 Replete
84 Alaskan cape
86 One of five
88 Homonym of 88 Across
89 Japanese port
90 Washington sound
91 Napped leather
92 Guitar adjunct
93 Well in Orense
94 In the past
95 Happy mollusk
96 City on the Yamuna
97 Grable's were insured
98 An allium
102 Stowe character

170

ACROSS

1 Arms control?
6 Marries sub rosa
12 Self-possessed
18 Bury, in a way
19 Stately dance
20 Decadent
21 "GET I NO KICK FROM CHAMPAGNE"
23 Spalpeen
24 Bird: Comb. form
25 American oil magnates
26 Race round
28 Alley Oop's gal
29 Bank (on)
31 Dos' followers
32 Merchant
35 Noted diarist
36 Looks askance
38 DORIS DENNIS
40 "Let Us Now Praise Famous Men" author
42 Beaut
43 Flying gp.
44 Tart part
47 Secular
49 Visigoths' activity in Rome: A.D. 410
52 Tip-off
53 Misled
55 Gave the low-down to
56 A mean Amin
57 Almost gone
58 "Fixing ___," Beatles song
60 Cell letters
61 Earnings
63 La. parish
65 Warmth
66 Opening
67 Velocity
68 Cries, Irish style
69 Love too fondly
70 Software? (but not Madonna's)
72 Lasting impression
74 ART LETTER
77 Carols collection
81 Tolkien's tree shepherd
82 Immerses
83 Actress Meyers
85 Spore cases
86 Blind item
88 Apt. particulars
89 Easily done
92 M.D.'s
93 Japanese thriller: 1962
95 CIR
98 "How fare you?-___ the best . . .": Shak.
99 Tippi Hedren role: 1964
100 Unguent
101 Continue after halting
102 Actor O'Brien
103 Out on a limb?

DOWN

1 Burns' props
2 Irregular
3 To no purpose
4 That way
5 Cozy
6 Rage onstage
7 Pulls up
8 But
9 Strength
10 Dusk, to Donne
11 Outstanding
12 On and on
13 One-kind connection
14 "___ your heart were touch'd . . .": Shak.
15 "THE CAT AND THE FIDDLE FIDDLE"
16 And other things
17 "Dahlgren" author
22 To the point
27 Landon of Kansas
30 Brewer's ingredient
33 Spud bud
34 Free
37 Mil. unit
38 Actions; events
39 Harrow
41 Plaza denizen of fiction
44 Bird word
45 Enacting clause
46 FLORIDAHO
48 Jellicoe or Jillian
49 Many
50 Curtain fabric
51 Wears away
53 Apply oneself mentally
54 Deep pink
57 Without charge
59 Bowler or boater
62 Saucers on high
64 Alchemize
65 Mighty mites
68 The buck stops here
70 "God ___ from a challenge!": Shak.
71 Torn or tear
73 Some like it hot
74 Hypnotic fellow
75 Smitten
76 Bijou
78 Small knot
79 Show up
80 Chronicled
83 "___ the living Present!": Longfellow
84 Prepared potatoes
87 O'er
90 Cartoonist Peter
91 Formerly, formerly
94 Batter or butter
96 Owned
97 Road runner

171

FOLLOWING THE LEADERS by Dorothy Smitonick
What leaders are Dorothy referring to and who's following them? Find out below.

ACROSS

1 Small residence
4 Ann Landers' twin
8 Squirrel nest
12 Lt.'s superior
16 Celt
18 London trolleys
20 Violin ancestor
22 Ripening agent
23 Corner
24 ___ corporal
25 "He was all white, like ___": E. Bishop
26 Odie's lunch
27 Artist follows the leader
31 Fertilizer
32 Extremely hot: Abbr.
33 Napped leather
34 Chargers
37 Asian range
38 "Golden Boy" playwright
40 Author follows the leader
44 Indiv.
47 Taverns
48 Then: Fr.
49 Cans
50 Persian fairy
51 Movie ratings
52 "Forever ___": Winsor
54 Letters at Dulles
55 "The Age of Anxiety" poet
56 Aba wearer
57 Braid
59 Like a spheroid
60 Actor follows the leader
66 Dog that came home
67 Musical John
68 1/640 square mile
69 Frequently
70 Ruth's sultanate
71 Acclaim
73 Oath response
76 Convertiplane
77 Calvados capital
78 Mosquito genus
80 Seed covering
81 Est., formerly
82 Painter follows the leader
86 Peak
87 Aphids
88 "The Last Leaf" author
89 Northern evergreen forests
91 Author LeShan
92 U.S. furniture designer
94 Author follows the leader
101 Yesteryear
102 Gladden
103 "The Maximus Poems" poet
104 Ultra
106 Nobelist British physicist
107 Friend of Pythias
108 Several: Comb. form
109 Bird of the Outback
110 Jacuzzis
111 Writes
112 Imagines
113 Technique

DOWN

1 S. Meredith, e.g.
2 Prefix for trooper
3 Tenth grader
4 In any case
5 Muscle
6 Bluegrass instrument
7 Inexpensive lodgings
8 Extreme
9 Repeat
10 Deep black
11 Cry from Fido
12 Telegrams
13 Too much of ___ thing
14 Londoner's small change
15 Journey
17 Bookkeeping books
19 Worldly
21 Cupboards
28 Hubert Vallee
29 Former Tatar rulers
30 Guitar relative
34 Suffix for friend
35 Chinese dynasty
36 Piscivorous birds
37 Caesar's love
38 Sedative

39 Johnson and Ameche
41 "___ Ben Ezra": Browning
42 Rubber tree
43 Garret
44 Chair on poles
45 Form of Margaret
46 Irish export
50 Beat
52 "Bad Medicine" star
53 "The ___ Animal," 1942 film
54 Deserve
55 Stop a launch
56 Photographer Adams
57 Penn State rival
58 Papal name
59 Bo Derek film
60 Gift from the dentist
61 Trillions
62 "The Beggar Maid" star
63 Latest
64 Strategies
65 Corkwood
70 Simon ___
71 Rim

72 Wax: Comb. form
73 Something to pump
74 A-line introducer
75 Song of the '50s
77 Erased
78 In spite of
79 Crena
80 Overwhelming
82 Prompt
83 NFL teams
84 "___ an island . . .": Donne
85 1954 sci-fi film
86 Cacomistles
89 Corps
90 Main artery
92 Result
93 Worship
94 Places for pep rallies
95 Applaud
96 Hamstrung
97 Home of the wall game
98 "___ fair in love and . . ."
99 Actress Downey
100 River in Belgium
105 Tsk!

172

ACROSS

1 Canto start
4 Soft cheese
8 Hindu holy man
13 Skiers' mecca
18 He took a ribbing
20 "Five ___ Pieces," 1970 film
21 Re essayist Lamb
22 Sheer fabric
23 TH DA
26 Designer Simpson
27 Red antelopes
28 Kind of closet or chest
29 Like whiskyless punch
31 Hampton or Barrymore
32 USA, Gallic style
33 "Money ___ object"
35 Parched
36 Dancer Michio and skater Midori
37 SU
42 Chaplin's brother
43 Period of 100 yrs.
44 Wife of Zeus
45 Learning method
46 Spanish pelf
48 Crazed
49 Take by force
50 Poker ploys
53 On ___ with (equal to)
55 Farm structure
57 Tartuffe's creator
58 "Lawrence of ___"
60 "___ Misbehavin'"
62 Colonnade
64 South Pacific isle
65 Liner: Abbr.
66 PO
69 Breed of Indian cattle
70 Snips
72 Weed killer?
73 "Trees," for one
74 Trapeze garb
77 Hall of TV
79 One-eyed god
81 Obligation
82 Combined resources
83 Novices
87 Medicinal units
89 Ga. neighbor
90 To dare, in Dieppe
91 Early Peruvian
92 Miler Sebastian
95 Cookbook quartet
97 BU
102 Tuber
103 Engrossed
105 Extensive
106 Napoleonic marshal
107 Scrape away
109 More precipitous
111 Derived from oil
114 Star of "The Pawnbroker": 1965
115 Rhone feeder
116 IC
119 Mother-of-pearl
120 Heeling at sea
121 A Webster
122 Snick's partner
123 Second of two

124 Prepares potatoes, in a way
125 "Gentle ___ Mind," G. Campbell hit
126 Grid scores

DOWN

1 Kingly
2 Descendant of Esau
3 Satirize
4 "What hath then ___ . . . ?": "King Hen. II." IV, i
5 Charlie Brown's expletive
6 ___ Kabibble, memorable musician
7 Ocular gadget
8 Germ
9 "The Four Seasons" star
10 Log keepers
11 Kind of loft
12 Like some heroes
13 Grandparental
14 Fountain treats
15 EI
16 Queen of mystery
17 Was out of
19 Ways' companion
24 Miss or Bull preceder
25 Red and Dead

30 ". . . ___ thousand times no . . ."
32 Make lean
34 Tallow source
38 "Exodus" author
39 Nobelist for Peace: 1949
40 Grant, to Lee
41 Rock's partner
44 Garbo role
47 Undo
48 Fairy queen
49 Habit
50 Crow
51 Like summer quaffs
52 Forecasters
53 Toscanini
54 SP
56 Ananias
57 Full head of hair
58 Tin-Pan Alley org.
59 Garden pest
61 Go one better
62 Lean-to
63 Shyness
67 A tic-tac-toe winner
68 Dove tales?
71 Vend
75 Notion
76 Gloomy one
78 Tide type

80 "___ But the Lonely Heart," 1944 film
83 Fix the salad
84 Having the same chemical properties
85 Ump's cousin
86 Sphere
88 Like ailing throats
92 One working in tandem with another
93 Bade
94 Leaves a grotto
95 Duke in "Twelfth Night"
96 Worries
98 "___ Maria"
99 Evil-tempered one
100 Infantry group
101 Logical start
102 Nursery furniture
104 ___ Haute
108 Hum bug
110 Equal
112 Come in second
113 Newts
114 Where Anna Leonowens taught
117 River of China
118 Long, long time

ACROSS

1 20 quires
5 Botanical opening
10 Puro or maduro
15 Musical Mama
19 Siepi specialty
20 Tennyson's "Enoch ___"
21 "___ Autumn": Keats
22 King of comedy
23 Constructed by Colonna?
25 How Loman canvassed?
27 Actress Valentine
28 "Agnes ___"
30 Naga hills tribesman
31 Cousy's coaster?
34 Hairs, biologically
35 Kaline's calanques?
39 Ill will
40 1982 Levinson film
41 Netman Nastase
42 IMF part
43 "This sceptred ___": "Richard II"
44 Historian Hackman?
46 Actor Gulager
47 Ceramist's furnace
48 Doomsday Book coins
49 Premed. subj.
50 Thatching palm
51 Gen.'s asst.
52 Sinatra's dogs?
56 "Una voce ___ fa": Rossini
57 Tolstoy tigers?
59 Hurons' foe
60 Electrician, at times
61 Cantrell and Turner
62 Armadillos
63 Alberta Indian
65 Reubens' places
67 Khartoum country
68 Weapon for Watson?
71 Designer Cassini
72 Silvers' generosity?
75 Xenophon's X
76 Pleasant resort?
77 Certain votes
78 Zwei's predecessor
79 Ibo's rivals
80 Pretense
81 Allen's pier group activity?
85 Squabbles
86 Cousina's padre
87 Donegal Bay feeder
88 Place to play
89 Ship's garbage, e.g.
91 Land of Veii and Volsinii
93 ___ mecum
94 Master of fauvism
95 ASCAP or ASPCA
96 To ___ phrase
98 Camptown events
99 Little women?
103 Food for Foreman?
108 Agatha's contemporary
109 ___ Semple McPherson
110 Postpone
111 Mrs. Victor Laszlo
112 "The Beverly Hillbillies" star
113 Night lights
114 Hiemal hazard
115 Cassius or Lucius

DOWN

1 Scott's "The ___ Trilogy"
2 Long antecedent
3 SAC center
4 Antony's army?
5 Wales Conference team
6 Aligned
7 Chief god of the Eddas
8 Allen or Ott
9 Lavoisier or Watteau
10 Dale Evans role
11 Kind of syncracy
12 Money in Mannheim
13 One of seven, for short
14 Liechtenstein liberals?
15 Mubarak's capital
16 Word in Herriot titles
17 Maglie or Mineo
18 Curved plank
24 Korea-Manchuria border
26 "___ empta dolore voluptas": Horace
29 Circus performer
31 Soviet lake
32 Kind of NFL kick
33 Blass the numismatist?
34 Byelorussian city
35 "Doubt truth to be ___": "Hamlet"
36 Principal award?
37 Intertwine
38 Lethargy
40 James and Jimmy
41 ___ fatui
44 Alums
45 "Bellefleur" author
48 Occasional, in Orkney
50 Imitative
52 People of good cheer?
53 "___ cold, starve . . ."
54 City pope?
55 Like the "Laughing Cavalier"?
58 Satchel of baseball
60 "King Kong" actress
62 Heartbeat
63 Madame Chiang née ___
64 Current amt.
65 Budge broke bread?
66 Bring out, Wallach style?
67 Use a collander
68 Kate's cousin, in Kiev
69 "___ that lady . . . ?"
70 Request for Kate?
72 Nobleman, to Neal?
73 Aardwolf's cousin
74 19th cen. German poet
79 Like Tatum's talent?
81 Goat antelope
82 Garfield creator and kin
83 Algerian port
84 Skelton performs?
89 Benny's benny?
90 Seasons, in Soissons
92 Poe's Roderick
94 Twinned crystal
96 Crooner from Canonsburg
97 Actor Reginald
98 A Goldberg
99 Loser at Yorktown
100 Writer Levin
101 Corpus ending
102 "___ Meistersinger"
104 "2001" computer
105 107 Down's successor?
106 Botanist Gray
107 Kendall or Kyser

174 ESSCAPADES by Phyllis Fehringer
Our prankish newcomer from Colorado throws you a few curves. We hope you make a hit anyway.

ACROSS

1 Rapid, musically
6 Stair part
10 Pahlavi, wow!?
14 Self-satisfied cup?
18 U.S. Open winner in 1990
19 Close one's trap
21 Faddish hoop
22 Love for Luisa
23 Strike-it-rich hit?
25 Element no. 26
26 Opposite of brevis
27 Diana, the actress
28 Magic finale
29 Fast-paced text?
32 Belief
33 Exec bonuses
35 Unctuous
36 Used a Jacuzzi
37 Morning condensate
38 Inquire
39 Sample
41 Infant's shoe
43 Orient
45 Evangelist McPherson
46 Across: Prefix
47 Greek ars
51 Strips of ground on the Golden Gate?
54 Cents-less
55 Gauntlet
56 Terra ___
57 Baker's baker
58 Retards moos?
59 Part of a rolltop
60 Arthur of the court
61 Holy mmes.
62 Rings a bell
63 Frankfurters: Var.
64 Avail
65 It's in a jamb
66 Horse crazy?
68 Apiece
69 Hostelries
70 Commerce
71 "___ Tú," 1932 pop song
72 Nice NaCl
75 Sputnik?
77 Otherwise
78 Nos. person
79 Fix up old masters
82 Deed holder
83 Tea quantity?
84 Canvas, for short
85 Goals
86 Had expectations
87 Heroic
88 Radium discoverer
89 Ophidian
90 Lesser
91 Barrie brat?
93 Smith, the singer
94 Desire eagerly
95 Sherwood Forest sound
96 Profound
97 More painful
99 "I ___ Song Comin' On"
100 Some sloths
101 Emulate Lithgow
104 Easy walks
106 Sheltered at sea
107 Loamy deposit
109 Bill's partner

110 Fender unbenders?
114 Ago
115 Hide relatives?
116 Jupiter's sister
117 Eye part
118 Where lovers stop the car?
121 Burdened Titan
122 Enlarge a hole
123 Day's beginning
124 Ardent
125 Volume
126 Goes wrong
127 PGA, e.g.
128 Pitchers

DOWN

1 Bungled
2 "To win ___ it all": J. Graham
3 Summer bee-havior?
4 Small drinks
5 Yoko
6 Crept like a dolt?
7 Duty
8 Rhea relatives
9 Objectives
10 Bright
11 Injure
12 Medicinal succulent
13 Metacarpus, e.g.
14 Where patriots suffocate?
15 Game for gamblers
16 Exhorted

17 Equipment
19 Explorer with Lewis
20 Sulfide of 25 Across
22 Winged
24 Cinco de Mayo, e.g.
30 ___ de France
31 Some welcomers
33 Former Turkish title
34 Squares over a fence?
40 Kind of corner
41 Graze
42 Dumbarton ___
44 Pay for a hand
45 Hostile
46 Fishing boat
48 "Battle Hymn" author
49 Finished
50 Parts of a maund
51 Diving duck
52 Bandit chasers
53 Never
54 Botanical sac
55 Bob ___, ex-Dolphin QB
58 Tranquilized
59 Abhor
61 Sub locators
62 Co-owner
63 Sorcerer
65 Bar magnet, e.g.
66 Mulligan holder
67 Like Tom of Coventry
72 Pandora's box?
73 A taxing time

74 Boutonniere site
75 Pin down some rest?
76 Oklahoman
79 Daredevil's delight
80 Ferber or Millay
81 Dining chair?
83 Kind of cord or column
84 Tire liner
86 Busy place
87 Lat. extender
88 Salad green
90 What 37 Across is
91 Fragrant climber
92 He had a bright idea
94 Huntley or Atkins
95 Kin of itsy-bitsy
98 Phylum division
99 Southern st.
100 Norse sea god
102 Phrase maker
103 Some paint company employees
104 Vinegar: Comb. form
105 Danny's daughter
106 John Q.
108 Like the old bucket
110 Strikebreaking taxi?
111 Always
112 Close by
113 Dunce's lip?
115 Cole rule?
119 Wall St. options
120 Turn right

175 MISDIRECTIONS by Arthur S. Verdesca

The highdown is that one of our Jersey jesters is lost on the lowway. Now that you've been given the low sign the going should be easy.

ACROSS

1 Beat the house
4 Softened
9 Shower
13 "I can't believe ___ the whole thing!"
17 Field
19 Small egg
20 Portoferraio's island
21 Schedule
23 Ready to cease hostilities?
25 Becomes less repressive?
27 Emblem
28 Abbot's right-hand man
30 Light units
31 Witnessed
32 Assimilate into a larger group
33 First son
34 Spain's basic monetary unit
37 South America's narrow land
38 ___ and Tobago, West Indies republic
42 Poilu's weapon
43 Reverse maneuver on the slopes?
46 "___ Clear Day"
47 Land measures
49 Suffix with musket or sonnet
50 Type of pressure: Abbr.
51 Former Polish department
52 Equal: Comb. form
53 Richard Adams' sequel?
58 Lorenzo da ___, Mozart's librettist
59 Appoints as supervisor
61 Partial contraction of a muscle
62 Turning points
63 Boss
64 Upbraid
65 Author of "Butterfield 8"
66 Dazzles
68 Bourrée or gigue
69 Admittedly
72 American burbots
73 Refuses to kiss?
75 Vowel sequence
76 Pierre's seraph
77 Tropical American bird
78 Trouble
79 Thin, flat cork
81 Erwin of early TV
82 Being virtuous?
88 Donkey: Ger.
89 Given to ready classification
91 Baird and Mrs. Dithers
92 Sanctioned
94 Caustic substances
95 French painter, Odilon ___: 1840–1916
96 African village
97 "All things were ___ Him": John 1:3
100 Acclaimed person
101 Family of a 16th cen. English poet
105 Makes whole again?
107 Elated look?
109 Belief
110 Kirghiz range
111 Kind of surgeon
112 Dwelling
113 ___, zwei, 99 Down
114 Deflect
115 Noble German ladies
116 ___ judicata

DOWN

1 Ravine
2 Robust
3 Fresh tidings
4 Convertible's cover
5 "Every man walketh in ___ show": Psalms 39:6
6 Japanese village
7 Guernsey or Jersey
8 Plunder
9 Child's creations
10 Ordain
11 Construction beam
12 Industrialists' org.
13 Publisher's activity
14 Groton graduates
15 Measure
16 College in Buckinghamshire
18 Cordial flavoring
22 Minnesota twins
24 "___ a Kick Out of You"
26 Bald
29 Parker house, e.g.
32 Insect sound
33 Pleat
34 A younger brother of Hector
35 Irregular
36 Exciting?
37 Christmas or Bronx follower
38 Andronicus
39 Drops a girl on a two-seater bike?
40 Make ___ of (write down)
41 Vice-President under Coolidge
44 Famous principle
45 Done for
48 At ___ points (antagonistic)
51 France's longest river
54 Rosary beads
55 Was abhorrent
56 Tudor or York
57 Kind of tube
58 Large shrimp
60 Beauty shop treatment
62 Medium-sized dog
64 Implied but unsaid
65 Convex molding
66 Gust of wind
67 Fuzzy
68 Creator of Mr. Dooley
69 Farewell, amigo!
70 Formal reception
71 Surrender
73 Catches
74 Astronomer Carl
80 Two-way communication device
82 Double-purpose couches
83 Submits to
84 Nymph of the deep
85 Makes an error
86 Magniloquent
87 Is foolishly fond of
90 Football group
93 Königsberg philosopher
95 American mountain ash
96 Show clemency
97 LX x XX
98 Bern's stream
99 See 113 Across
100 Japanned metal
101 Book by Isaac Singer
102 Ogler
103 Clair or Coty
104 Droop-nosed flyers
106 Small flounder
108 Pod dweller

176 MUSICAL METEOROLOGY by Jeanette K. Brill
Take a stroll down Memory Lane with hit songs from five past decades.

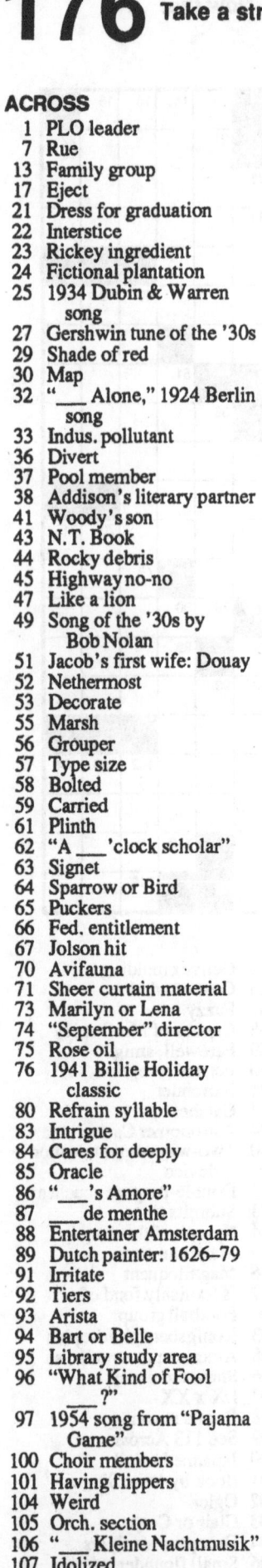

ACROSS

1 PLO leader
7 Rue
13 Family group
17 Eject
21 Dress for graduation
22 Interstice
23 Rickey ingredient
24 Fictional plantation
25 1934 Dubin & Warren song
27 Gershwin tune of the '30s
29 Shade of red
30 Map
32 "___ Alone," 1924 Berlin song
33 Indus. pollutant
36 Divert
37 Pool member
38 Addison's literary partner
41 Woody's son
43 N.T. Book
44 Rocky debris
45 Highway no-no
47 Like a lion
49 Song of the '30s by Bob Nolan
51 Jacob's first wife: Douay
52 Nethermost
53 Decorate
55 Marsh
56 Grouper
57 Type size
58 Bolted
59 Carried
61 Plinth
62 "A ___ 'clock scholar"
63 Signet
64 Sparrow or Bird
65 Puckers
66 Fed. entitlement
67 Jolson hit
70 Avifauna
71 Sheer curtain material
73 Marilyn or Lena
74 "September" director
75 Rose oil
76 1941 Billie Holiday classic
80 Refrain syllable
83 Intrigue
84 Cares for deeply
85 Oracle
86 "___'s Amore"
87 ___ de menthe
88 Entertainer Amsterdam
89 Dutch painter: 1626–79
91 Irritate
92 Tiers
93 Arista
94 Bart or Belle
95 Library study area
96 "What Kind of Fool ___?"
97 1954 song from "Pajama Game"
100 Choir members
101 Having flippers
104 Weird
105 Orch. section
106 "___ Kleine Nachtmusik"
107 Idolized
108 Once more
109 Merits
111 GRF's V.P.
112 Singer Damone
113 Diadem
114 Family of Turkic language
115 Belle Baker sang it in "Betsy"
119 Arlen hit song
125 Anecdote
126 Tied
127 Neater
128 Record cover
129 Hollywood's Best
130 Unit of force
131 Bedaubs
132 Group of four

DOWN

1 WW I troops
2 Cell component
3 Onassis
4 Pro
5 Manila hemp
6 Apartment
7 Undercooked
8 Remove
9 Star of "Pretty Woman"
10 Gypsy man
11 Negatron
12 No. Carolina native
13 Mild cigar
14 London elevator
15 "___, amas, I love a lass . . ."
16 Denier
17 Fashioned
18 Cushion
19 Historic period
20 Manner
26 Plum, for one
28 Mirth
31 Once more
33 Sleeping pads
34 Some New Orleans inhabitants
35 Bob Dylan hit
37 Utter disdain
38 Disburse
39 1939 Parish-DeRose song
40 Isolates
42 ___ a customer (limited amount)
44 Flat-bottomed boat
45 Pilots
46 Helium and nitrogen
48 Expert ending
50 "___ the Fall": Miller
53 Jai ___
54 Kachina
56 Carried
58 Moonwort
59 Brownish-yellow
60 Pointed arches
61 Sullen
63 Germ cell
64 What glads are
65 Diametrically opposite
67 "What's in ___?"
68 Strong push
69 Nonsense
72 Particulars
74 Gulf on the Arabian Sea
75 Parts of shoulders
76 Shone
77 Mrs. John Ridd
78 Customer
79 ___-do-well
81 Commune in Italy
82 Studio
83 Ort
86 ___ Haute
88 Coupled
89 Blot
90 London gallery
91 Baby food
94 One after another
95 Most unsophisticated
97 Marked with spots
98 Prefix for ton
99 San Simeon family
100 Pale yellow
102 Devotion to St. Jude
103 Eye part
105 Minor woodland deities
108 River in N France
109 Gantry or Bernstein
110 Climb
113 Numerical suffix
114 Opera highlight
115 By the ___
116 Stripling
117 Samovar
118 Brown's league
120 Poem
121 Asian holiday
122 LBJ beagle
123 ___ Marie Saint
124 Smith or Barber

JAILS AND GAOLS by Edward Marchese
Featured below are some big houses that are anything but homey!

ACROSS

1 Dance or sauce
6 Nerve: Comb. form
11 Niamey locale
16 Locate
20 "Let's Make ___"
21 Purify
22 "Lulu" is one
23 Confused
24 Capt. Dreyfus was held here
26 "Be a Clown" composer
28 Blue dye
29 Crocus cousin
30 Casualties
32 "Tristan und ___"
33 Increases
35 "Bird thou never ___": Shelley
36 NRC forerunner
37 Apoc. book
38 Sir Walter Raleigh's confinement
43 Al Capone slept here
48 Stat. for Pena
49 City on the Fulda
50 Simon Templar
51 Broil
55 Kazan locale
57 Notify
59 Occupations
61 "Educating ___," 1983 film
62 "___ 17," Holden film
64 Facilitated
66 Berlin prison
68 Lady of Lisbon
69 Phoenician love goddess
73 Perry White, for one
76 East follower
77 Doggie bag contents
78 Howl
79 Perfume ingredient
81 Baking potato
83 Skewered morsels
85 "Little Birds" author
86 Spanish dove
88 Impair
91 Decrease
93 Don Juan's mother
94 Male voice
98 Dos Passos work
99 Aver
101 Small generator
103 Hurler Hershiser
104 "The Prisoner of ___": Byron
106 Lasso
108 Prison near Buffalo
110 Vocalist Basil
111 Kramden's pal
114 Son of Aphrodite
117 Selling point
118 Originates
120 Vexes
121 Cartels
124 Uno + due
125 Voltaire was one of its inmates
127 Dr. Mudd's jail
129 Sara in "Legend"
132 ___ Vegas
133 Greek letters
135 Island off Hong Kong
136 Mysterious
138 Click beetle
141 Concerning
143 Tear down: Brit.
147 Count of Monte Cristo's jail
149 Sea turtles
152 Cheat: Slang
153 Consumer advocate
154 Anodized
155 Aweigh
156 Aphrodite's lover
157 Spanish corn
158 Pancake-house staple
159 Shabby

DOWN

1 Actress Thompson
2 Yemen city
3 PGA Player of the Year: 1990
4 Voyaged
5 Gross
6 Unless: Law
7 Wings
8 Actress Hagen
9 Hand down
10 Society
11 Night: Comb. form
12 City in Malaysia
13 Congeals
14 Sooner than
15 Sword
16 Port in S Portugal
17 Pita plant
18 Wants
19 Challenged
21 Beginnings
25 City near Florence
27 Brenda Fricker's award
31 "___ of Honey"
34 Cocuswood
35 Pickwick's servant
36 Corroborate
38 Song by 26 Across, with "It"
39 Spellbinder
40 Floating
41 East, in Berlin
42 Tiny
44 Greased
45 Gates' org.
46 Also
47 Swiss sculptor: 1860–1920
52 Helpers
53 Gaze
54 Jeer at
56 Ted Stevens' concern
58 Ancient Romans
60 Parasitic protozoans
63 Valiant's quilted garment
65 Cranelike bird
67 ___ lily (calla)
70 "Barney Miller" actor
71 Chart
72 Goose genus
74 Immerse
75 Namby-pamby
80 Inherent
82 Wooden shoes
84 Equal, in Rouen
87 Permit
88 Conduits
89 "___ in the Dark"
90 William Cohen's concern
92 Saunter
95 Awn
96 Distinguish
97 Programmed
100 Sounds at Pimlico
102 Singer Brooks et al.
105 Leg
107 Interpolate
109 "Rinaldo" poet
112 "Le ___ s'Amuse": Hugo
113 Sesame
115 Mouths
116 Town in S Lebanon
119 Henri's hall
122 Emulated Trenary
123 Indonesian island
126 Thai coin
127 Extremely
128 Leaf adjective
129 Arabian coffee
130 Zeus's blood
131 "___ of Libel": Denker drama
134 Succors
137 Western tribe
138 Bishop Sveinsson's discovery
139 Mortgage
140 ___-American studies
141 Aleutian isle
142 Bandleader Fields
144 Israeli seaport
145 Slide
146 Glimpse
148 Political union of 1958–61
150 Lake of Brienz river
151 French stocking

178 ADVENTURES OF A PHYSICIST by Barbara Springer
Warning: You won't find the main entries in an old dictionary. Our California constructor is hip to modern scientific jive.

ACROSS
1 Aquarium problem
4 Pine Tree State
9 Baby buggy, in Brighton
13 Kind of hanger?
18 Long
19 Inflorescence
20 Manufacturer Strauss
21 Uncle Tom's cabin
22 Mideast money
23 Lewis Carroll creation
24 Home of the Iowa State Cyclones
25 Pluperfect
26 Blackbird
27 Pack of camels
28 Castor and Pollux
29 Schulz character
30 Certain interchanges
32 Physicist's racquet enhancer?
35 Hgwy.
36 Spruce
38 Blue-on-white porcelain
39 "___ Take Romance"
42 June bug
44 Like an ice-cream holder
46 Films on copper
49 "Ave ___ vale"
51 Narrate again
54 Dread
55 ___ Kea, extinct Hawaiian volcano
56 Northeast Italy, once
57 Gymnast's move
59 Object of a physicist's trip to Calcutta
61 Menace
63 Austral. state
66 Artificial fly
67 ___ Jima
68 Part of a stereo
69 Slick, with or without pics
70 Litigious person
71 Alas. native
72 Augury
74 Poor surf, to the physicist?
76 At deuce
77 Helps
79 "Fatha" of music
80 Coin for Shylock
83 Lizards
84 Met bass-baritone
85 First state, in a way
88 Out of practice
90 East Lansing inst.
91 California coast's Big ___
92 Watch
96 Roof part
98 A Space Odyssey, in Latin
101 Physicist's very fast scull?
105 Rhinoplasty: Colloq.
107 Windowpane shell of the Philippines
109 ___ lazuli (azure)
110 Like a quercus
112 Chafes; grates
113 Cottonwood
114 Dash
115 Papal court
116 George Sand, to Chopin
117 Survey, for short
118 Prefix for one billionth
119 Rich Little's forte
120 Told a yarn
121 Episode
122 Some times
123 Jam
124 Tee preceder

DOWN
1 Most distant or aloof
2 Physicist's lucky duck call?
3 A greeting
4 Iditarod competitor
5 Forgetful
6 Bridge support
7 Modern squares
8 He has a Grand Exalted Ruler
9 Typewriter part
10 Note
11 Disinclined
12 Blunder
13 Hot stuff
14 "The Thinker" creator
15 Action by Nemesis
16 ___ de soie (silk cloth)
17 Annexes
18 Defense
28 Physicist's strikeout pitches?
31 Run of luck
33 Couple
34 Ribonucleic acid, for short
37 Cuernavaca's state
40 Word with Vegas
41 Suffer
43 Shred
45 Hawaiian goose
47 Comet part
48 Lodge
49 Saunter
50 Rocky slope
52 Floppy
53 Drink like a kitten
56 Swore
57 Rugged rocks
58 Lofty
60 Charter
62 Middle East state
63 Physicist's winning vaults?
64 Embankment
65 Outfit
68 The rain in Spain
70 St. Moritz resident
72 Pocket bread
73 Onager
74 Superman's Miss Lane
75 Subjects
76 Check
78 Fell
80 "___ Kapital"
81 Inuit tool
82 Turtle's protective covering
86 Pop's partner
87 Central Texas town
89 Tug-of-war action
93 Graduated
94 Sevilla is here
95 Large horned mammals, for short
97 Expedition
99 Kind of strip or transformation
100 "A Doll's House" playwright
102 Shakespearean misanthrope
103 Fresh, invigorating air
104 Magnifying glass
106 X out
107 Gondolas, e.g.
108 Actor Clunes
111 Like Death Valley
115 Crow's remark

179

IT AIN'T NECESSARILY SO by Nancy Scandrett Ross

As a footnote to her title Nancy writes: "It all depends on what you consider 95 Across."

ACROSS

1 Schools of seals
5 Prefix for meter
9 Humane org.
13 Appends
17 Actor McCowen
18 Prod
19 Astronaut Shepard
20 Sound the horn
21 Rhythmic pattern?
23 Gov't. agt.
24 King's coif
25 Most deplorable
26 Quarter-moon?
28 "The Elephant of the Célèbes" painter
29 Parisian parent
30 Cowboy's device
31 Walter Mitty actor
32 Old boy
34 He discovered New Zealand
37 Small figures
38 Convention speaker?
43 Compass pt.
44 Cast forth
46 School-support orgs.
47 Something unique
48 Purl's partner
49 Site of Giotto frescoes
51 Bath byproducts
52 Hayworth and Moreno
53 School exercise?
58 West Point parader
61 Opposite of stood
62 Conveyed legally
66 Yemen's capital
67 Wide-mouthed actress
68 Court figure
71 San ___, Riviera resort
72 Word in parentheses
73 Air show highlight?
76 Pose
77 "Vanessa" tenor
79 Periods
80 Ply the blue pencil
82 Forbidden fruit
83 Protracted
85 "... forbear ___ the dust enclosed here": Shak.
87 Farm vehicles?
90 Fragrant flower
93 Pub orders
94 Parched
95 What the dictionary tells us?
96 Spanish surrealist
97 Raced
98 "Manon" melody
99 Start of Bay State's motto
100 Montana specialty
101 First garden
102 Mail
103 NCOs

DOWN

1 Lily leaves
2 The cheaper spread
3 Pressing problems?
4 Creator of Huckle and Lowly Worm
5 Curved moldings
6 Immutable
7 Courtesy's cousin
8 "___ to the West Wind"
9 Less loony
10 Situation
11 Gideon Fell's creator
12 Forebear
13 Early calculator
14 Tumult?
15 Bruce or Laura
16 Dalmation decoration
22 Ate elegantly
26 Moore of the movies
27 Exercise Tyson
29 Maternal flowers?
31 Keystone ___
33 Mauna ___
35 Where Sikkim is
36 Meadowlands denizens
37 Campus org.
39 Edda, e.g.
40 We of Monaco
41 "The Egg ___"
42 Trial
45 Expand
48 Ralph of Cooperstown
50 Ready follower
51 Mother's Day giver
52 Shad delicacy
54 Norway's patron saint
55 Dressing for a BLT
56 Jetty
57 Logical prefix
58 House in Mexico
59 Tennis score
60 Equine gaits?
63 Autograph session?
64 Release
65 Seurat stroke
67 Move
68 Rhine feeder
69 Dep.
70 Cause of itchy eyes: Var.
73 Lady of Spain
74 Gotham City team
75 Canio's wife
78 Maillol sculptures
81 Chemical compounds
83 Chateaux river
84 "As You Like It" forest
86 Mountain nymph
87 Humid
88 Director Kazan
89 Trampled
90 "Bent" actor
91 Part of MIT
92 Ripens
95 "___ Rheingold"

180 ESS-CAPADES by Bert Rosenfield

As usual, Bert has come up with a clever twist. Hint: think about apostrophes!

ACROSS

1 Candlestick (see Rev. 4:5)
7 Piece of Roman armor or port in Colombia
13 Headland
16 Melodic
17 Like an odyssey
18 Down Under ratite
19 Should we extinguish him instantaneously?
21 "___ Affair": U.S.-France 1797 hassle
22 Original baseball czar
23 Old comic strip hero Harold ___
24 Stallone, to pals
25 Part of printemps
27 One more time
29 Mow the lawn again
31 Does it accompany him on "La Mer"?
35 Nix; nothing doing
38 Blackmore's Miss Doone
39 Igneous rock
41 Things frequently common
42 Directory of religious services
45 Hot or long follower
47 Make a doily
48 Is it lost on that Maj. Burns character?
52 WW II air chief ___ Eaker
55 Socks from Steffi
56 Women's club
60 Turku residents
63 Sunk fence
65 Caribbean cruise port
66 Acoustic technology
68 Do they come with pretzels instead of pies?
71 "___ flowing with milk and honey": Exodus
73 "Archduke," e.g.
74 GI shopping centers
75 Mask or meter preceder
77 Trevi throwaway
79 Getting along in years
82 Brazil, for one
83 Well, if hers isn't, then whose is?
87 Burrows
88 Its flower is the sagebrush
89 Part of a fishline
90 Benign bump on the skin
91 Huge African antelopes
92 Evening love song

DOWN

1 John or "L.A."
2 Italian town S of Pescara
3 A billion, to an Englishman
4 Theda's cinema contemporary
5 C ___ Charlie
6 Real estate tenants
7 Real estate tenants
8 ___ Locka, city in Fla.
9 Africa's Great ___ Valley
10 More unfriendly
11 Lurch
12 Handmade lace
13 Does he feed longshots to Archie Goodwin?
14 ___ acetate (banana oil)
15 Movie leading lady ___ Parker
20 Postprandial nosh
25 Ancient 6-time Olympic games victor
26 Old Hebrew zither

28 Short iron stroke in golf
30 GI haven in WW II
32 Dye base
33 "Arma virumque ___ . . .": Virgil
34 Okinawan capital
36 Santa ___, Cal. city near Long Beach
37 Jan. hrs. in 36 Down
40 Kind of leader
43 Blue and yellow macaw
44 Walesa of Poland
46 ___ suiter (wardrobe case)
49 High and pink followers
50 Rainy-day accts.
51 African hartebeest
52 "Talk'st thou to me of ___?": "Richard III"
53 Carioca town
54 If there are no jacks around, is this a winner?

57 Kind of dye: Var.
58 Alpine acrobat
59 "Backjaw"
61 Zero, in soccer
62 Kind of triangle
64 Dawns
67 Weak whining
69 Java almond
70 Sings, Matterhorn-style
72 Danube River feeder
75 Corrode or erode
76 Troyes' department
78 "___, a plan, a canal: Panama"
80 Words of comprehension
81 European region of contention
84 Augment
85 English river to the North Sea
86 Lala preceder

181

VERBA VITAE by Kevin Boyle
Wise words from the Maid of Amherst are quoted by a newcomer from
Manhattan. Beware! Kevin believes puzzles should puzzle.

ACROSS

1 Backward?
5 N California mountain
11 First name of the poet quoted below
16 Religious musical theme
17 Palpitated
18 Riveting gal?
19 **Start of a Dickinson quote**
21 Pervasive quality
22 Enclose
23 Unobtrusive interjection
25 At once, once
26 Coeus or Phoebe
27 Any PGA member
29 Matter of law
31 Gennaio 13, in Genova
32 **Quotation: Part II**
38 ___ la vie
40 Sphere
41 Farrago
42 Husband of MDE
43 Avis modifier
45 Cert. hospital worker
46 Like a bee
48 **Quotation: Part III**
51 Kind of acid
53 ___ de France (Mauritius)
54 Nudnick
55 Playwright Simon, to friends
56 "Giant" novelist's first name
58 Assam native
59 Herring
63 **Quotation: Part IV**
66 Neoplatonism's ultimate reality
67 Scandinavian sea goddess
68 Interrogative utterances
69 Holy grail or Lucifer's tail
71 "Do I dare to ___ peach?": T. S. Eliot
74 Lachrimation product
77 Nightclubs' lowest charges
78 Churchill's communique?
80 **End of the quotation**
83 Cavaedia
84 Slow, to Salieri
85 Chide vehemently
86 Ecclesiastic's daughter
87 Persian and casaba
88 Like potatoes

DOWN

1 Like some measures
2 Old TV western
3 Rabbitlike rodents
4 Oder feeder
5 Play platters
6 Owns
7 Then again
8 Kind of kitchen trashcan
9 Afternoon affairs
10 Sums up
11 Stat for Clemens
12 "Slough of Despond"
13 "The Race ___," 1965 J. Jones hit song
14 Star's vehicle
15 Bear kids
20 Muslim religious practices
24 Speaker of baseball
27 Style of expression
28 Yiddish "mister"

30 Repplier products
32 Had on
33 S African warriors
34 Sawbucks
35 Entry for Clementine's dad
36 Highest mountain of Crete
37 Iniquitous environs
39 Disney movie: 1982
44 Infusarian
45 KOH or NaOH solution
47 Putamina
48 Incites a springer to spring
49 Mountains in the Kirghizia
50 Pertaining to planes
51 A pt. of speech
52 Chinese land unit
57 Make an impression

58 Yggdrasil, e.g.
60 Billie of the blues
61 Work a dummy
62 Spent a half-life?
64 Like "Hamlet"
65 Gerard de ___, French writer: 1808–55
69 River inlet
70 ___ nous (confidentially)
71 John, in Wales
72 Town in the Piedmont
73 Flag
75 Susiana
76 Kato, to the Green Hornet
77 Electrical conductance units
79 Scottish refusal
81 I, to Claudius
82 Coat with solder

UP AND DOING by Rita Yelle
Rita says she spent several sitting hours creating this far-from-sedentary delight.

ACROSS

1 Drift about
6 Aramaic for "father"
10 Peru capital
14 The Scales
19 High nest
20 When shadows are small
21 Son of Seth
22 Archipelago members
23 Dancing Sufi
26 Sounds a horn
27 Negative vote
28 Bric-a-brac stand
29 Remark to the audience
31 Org. with operatives
32 Abbr. on a Spanish letter
33 Gibson and Hall
34 Eggs
36 It's 88 days on Mercury
37 Author Thompson
38 Barriers
39 Sam Malone's former love
41 Lasso
43 Seamstresses
46 Connubiality
48 Gorge
51 Board
52 "Annabel Lee" poet
53 La Scala song
55 Arabian ruler
56 Tribulations
57 Scents
60 Gomer Pyle's org.
62 God of war
63 Tit for ___
64 Expert
65 "Beowulf," e.g.
67 Isolation
69 Oxen of Tibet
71 Subscriber
73 Radioactive gas
74 Old maid
77 Parrot feature
78 German grandpa
79 "___ by Bread Alone":
    Dudintsev
82 Advance
83 Hot times in 100 Across
85 Arctic mammal
87 Chinese: Comb. form
88 Goaded
90 Glide
92 Dawn goddess
93 Weapon of Camelot
94 Stay behind
96 Gas-grill gas
99 Pleaded
100 French city
102 Commence
103 English sandy tract
104 Landing craft
106 Currier's partner
108 Orch. section
109 Boast
110 Calendar abbr.

113 Pierre's friend
114 Anser, for one
116 Requiring the least effort
118 Greek letter
119 Small riot
121 Arachnid activity
124 Poet Nowlan
125 Therefore
126 Math. course
127 Weird
128 List
129 Without
130 Seines
131 Approaches

DOWN

1 Bootlicks
2 Hungarian composer
3 Orissa language
4 Demeanor
5 Turn, to a skier
6 Chronicles
7 Slugger Wade
8 Portend
9 Type of barometer
10 Bulgarian coin
11 Genus of cetacean
12 What a rolling stone isn't
13 More pasty
14 Lettered

15 Prefix for metric
16 Activity of Rhett Butler
17 Networks of nerves
18 Appraise
24 Objects
25 German name for Tallinn
30 Platform
35 Wild ox
38 Lairs
39 Judged
40 Beige
42 Love apple
43 Skewer
44 Eugene O'Neill's mother
45 Australian song
46 Court
47 Chocolate candy
49 Commanded a horse
50 Gaelic
52 Tuning buttons
54 Loving
57 Intense
58 N.T. book
59 Tendon
61 Thunderous sounds
64 Roll-call notation
66 Mrs. Dithers
68 Eddie Cantor's wife
70 Captivate
72 Give in

74 Malicious remark
75 French father
76 Harvest
80 Story starter
81 Two-___ sloth
84 Short salutation
86 Fish eggs
87 Scholar
89 Persevering
91 Building sites
93 Extend
95 Granular snow
97 Communion plate
98 Indict
99 Ron Perlman role
101 Intuits
103 What Freud interpreted
104 Tibetan priests
105 Odor
107 Above
109 Redneck
110 Beethoven wrote only one
111 Seat
112 High and low
115 Gesticulation
117 Dagger of old
120 Poet's even
122 Us, in Jalapa
123 Female ruff

183 ONE-UPMANSHIP by Jean Hunt
From Northern Louisiana comes this careful construction, free from all esoterica and having a most singular theme.

ACROSS

1 Pythias' pal
6 Egyptian actor
12 Copies
18 Serviceable
19 City SW of Fairbanks
20 Affidavit maker
21 Transportation for 85 Across
23 Elbowroom
24 "___ Poetica": Horace
25 Genus of marine worms
26 Rabbit
28 Computer giant
29 Alexis Mikhailovich, e.g.
31 Claret-colored
32 Numb
33 Gudrun's husband
34 Cochlea sites
36 Slender
38 Snicker
39 Financial
42 Inclined
43 Actor Reynolds
44 Russian river
45 Church land
46 Not trigger-happy
48 Caesar's day
49 This precedes 6 Across
50 Certain
51 ___ de cologne
53 Fruity drinks
54 Sable
56 Bristles
57 Gender
58 Gloomy
59 Shooter ammunition
60 Cycle
61 Escape
63 Fine-grained rock
64 Eye makeup
65 Musical ending
66 With all possible speed
67 Architect Norman Bel ___
68 "The Magic ___": Mozart
70 Selected
71 Leaf
72 Nerve network
73 Canter
74 Garland
75 Actress Thompson
79 "___ Lay Dying": Faulkner
80 Average
81 What a klutz does
84 Good, to Pierre
85 They settled the West
87 Paradoxical David Riesman title
90 French doors
91 ". . . now will ___ the waters": Shak.
92 Kind of hit
93 With sword-shaped leaves
94 Most rational
95 Locations

DOWN

1 Ticket: Sl.
2 Penitent ones
3 ___ cantata (sung Mass)
4 Danube tributary
5 Type of sign
6 Gins
7 Lopped
8 Philippines' termite
9 Tatters
10 Cadmus' daughter
11 It's under the hood
12 Loafed
13 Painter Jan van der ___
14 Gibbon
15 Mitchell classic
16 Facilitate
17 Frustrate
22 Vice President: 1813–14
27 Type of race
30 Focuses again
32 Printer's mark
33 Chalice veils
35 Branch
36 With iron or shovel
37 Marimba-like instruments
38 Air
39 Touchy king?
40 Biased
41 "___ Song": Mailer
42 Dispenser of charity
43 Conflagrate
45 Arose
46 Visitor
47 Reb's opponent
50 Jump
52 Consumers
54 Organism's body
55 The Little Colonel
56 Stands fast
58 Floridian county
62 Pigeon house
63 Freshwater bird
64 It may be pulled
66 "How ___ human life": Hannah More
67 With merriment
68 Milkshake
69 Injury
70 Dernier ___
71 Spherule
73 Cup, in Calais
74 Tiglon's mother
76 "Give a man ___ he can sail"?: James Thomson
77 Use a divining rod
78 Amazon's source
80 Worry
81 Penn or Connery
82 Movement for Farrell
83 Teacakes
86 Greek vowel
88 Health org.
89 Stat. for 55 Down

184 SEAGOING ADDRESS by Betty Jorgensen

If you're the type that enjoys a good pun, we highly recommend the four-part groaner below.

ACROSS

1 Creature of the night
4 Type of saxophone
8 Garden plot
11 Room in a casa
15 Escalator clause
16 Alaskan island
17 I love, to Nero
18 "Bananas" star
19 Decrease in numbers
21 Please Mr. Scratch
22 Plagued
23 **Start of a quip**
26 RN concerns
27 Euripides drama
28 Garonne tributary
29 Literary collections
32 Asterisk
34 Almost closed
36 Seven, to Cato
39 **More of the quip**
44 Tarradiddle
45 Bit attachment
46 Involved with
47 Cauda
48 Snakeless land
50 Gauges
52 Chummy
53 Winter time in NYC
54 Sprinkle
55 Indian weight
56 In solitude
59 Hawks' opponents
60 In harmony
64 Delhi dress
65 A Gardner
66 Operatic prince
67 Cause of a bad trip
68 **More of the quip**
73 April acronym
74 Clamp
75 Press
76 Serf
77 Gel
78 Deposed despot
79 Mouths
81 **End of the quip**
91 Pack the groceries again
92 "___ You Lonesome Tonight?"
93 Hopi masked dancers
94 What a miss is as good as
95 Street, in Sorrento
96 Ms. Kett
97 Ms. Hari
98 Observe
99 Pool shape
100 Classic cars
101 Biblical verb ending

DOWN

1 The two
2 Der ___ (Adenauer)
3 Sully
4 Termae of Titus, e.g.
5 The game ended in ___
6 Greek portico
7 It tells only the bright hours
8 Blues street
9 Muslim prince
10 Gentlewoman, in Grenada
11 Emulated Rip
12 As well
13 Vichyssoise ingredient
14 Prefix for room
15 Crow cry
18 Soak up
20 School broadcasts: Abbr.
24 Southern Filipino
25 Grassy plain
29 Hun head
30 Rouge et ___
31 Fit to ___
32 Uttered
33 Pewter constituent
34 "El Dorado" star
35 Iotas
36 South African river
37 Novelist Murdoch
38 In an indolent manner
40 Clean the slate
41 Shipped
42 Ceremonies
43 Japanese city
49 Russian revolutionary
50 "Bolero" composer
51 Devoured
52 Lab dish
54 "The Right Stuff" author
55 Arrest
56 ___ spumante
57 Wry-faced Bert
58 Mine finds
59 Prohibitionists
60 Dramatic conflict
61 Tidings
62 Richard in "Untamed"
63 Prescribed amount
65 Webber-Rice hit
66 Japanese statesman
69 Get even with
70 Man Friday
71 Prankster
72 Earl Grey's hour
77 Marsh
78 Perfect
79 San Juan island
80 Bowl sound
81 Former Iranian coin
82 Start of Scotland's motto
83 Newspaper item
84 Except for
85 Bittersweet covering
86 Actress Nelligan
87 Bismarck
88 ___ the beginning
89 Invective
90 Maritime grp.

185

POTPOURRI by William P. Baxley

From the City of Angels comes this pleasant pastiche full of interesting words. Most puzzlers should solve this one.

ACROSS

1 Desert bloomers
6 Accumulate
11 Union branch
16 Sensational
17 Sinker
18 Japanese seaport
19 Goddess of peace
20 Marsh bird
21 Abstemious
22 Deranged
23 Blackthorn
25 Mrs. Al Jolson
27 Scottish single
28 Political group
30 NYC metro
31 Turmeric
32 Attired
33 Fictional whaler
35 Farm implement in Cornwall
37 Sander
40 Beginning of a refrain
41 Fastidious
45 Severity
46 Hambletonian entrant
48 Metric measure
49 Homophone of I'll
50 Frothier
51 Opera highlight
52 Suds
53 Conspire
54 Choose
55 Kind of shower
57 Weathercock dir.
58 Terminates
59 Entertain sumptuously
61 Muse of history
62 ___ de foie gras
65 Flightless bird
66 Bikini top
67 Replete
71 1960 Gardner biography
72 Actor Roberts
73 Start of a counting out
75 Spanish uncle
76 Singer Mario
78 Gaggle members
80 Sheepish
82 Fragrant compound
83 Above
84 Strong winds
85 "Family Album" author
86 Checks
87 Solar disks

DOWN

1 Scale
2 Pertaining to the ear
3 Religious belief
4 Sn is its symbol
5 Roman calendar date
6 Incorporate
7 French landscapist
8 Black cuckoo
9 Nth degree
10 Sound system
11 What Marciano never did
12 Western Amerind
13 Intrigue
14 Where the action is
15 Enticed
24 Fabricator
26 Famed Scottish comedian
29 Birchbark
32 Greek letter
34 Former White House pet
35 Pledge
36 Needlefish
37 King of Troy
38 Tightly twisted thread
39 Ornamental tag
40 Like the opal
42 Nostrils
43 Instant
44 Irish poet
46 Heavy weight
47 Kind of shirt
50 Counterfeiter
51 Indifferent
53 British track star
54 Teacher in I Samuel
56 Before
58 Tribe
60 "Three ___!" (1986 film)
61 Advances stealthily
62 Fades
63 Nautical command
64 Mother's sister: Fr.
66 Small broom
68 Useful
69 Napery
70 Loamy deposit
72 Peerage member
74 What a guru teaches
77 Zuider ___
79 Summer on the Left Bank
81 Cistern

186 FAUNA IN FLORA by Mary S. Snyder

After uncovering 16 Across, solvers will understand the peculiar phraseology of Mary's title.

ACROSS

1 Spar
5 Go fly ___
10 Suffix for south
13 Varnish resin
14 Venetian coin
15 Prefix for Freudian
16 Cocktail-sauce ingredient
18 Islands, in Palos
21 Furor
22 Japanese aboriginal
23 Most degraded
25 1/1000 of a yen
26 Eagle's org.
27 Condition
28 Glut
29 Seed coats
31 Be under the weather
32 Mint relative
34 Units in cricket
36 USNA grad
37 Rector's residence
40 Deg. in teaching
41 Elfin
42 Chicken crop
45 Christmas ___
46 Italian cheese city
48 Mimic
49 Like a mad hen
50 Boar genus
52 Twice XXVI
53 U.S. organist
   (1853–1937)
55 A very long time
56 Where Jill tumbled from
58 Brown hickory
61 Arena sound
62 Leftovers
66 Came down
67 ___-bitsy
69 Part of ROTC
70 Blow up: Abbr.
71 Elect anew
73 Asian weight
74 Wildebeest
75 Garlic, in Gorizio
76 Green gentian
79 Wapiti
80 Certain singers
81 Conceals
82 Meas. of pressure
83 Belgian violinist
84 Causes of some trips

DOWN

1 Treat
2 Smocks
3 Ol' Blue Eyes'
   monogram
4 Plant dear to Fido?
5 City on the Seyhan
6 African antelope
7 Here, in Toulouse
8 Pendant decorations
9 Heavens
10 Geraint's spouse
11 Fights
12 Mrs. Sprat's request
13 Map
17 Like leavened bread
19 Piedmont city
20 Out of ___
24 Bert Parks, e.g.
27 Orange bloom
30 "___ of thee . . . "
31 Vase handle
33 Some
35 Scamps
37 Cat cry
38 Hail
39 Kind of profit
41 Go under
42 Revolutionary from
   Hunan
43 Prone
44 Miniature
47 Kind of post
50 Former French coin
51 "___ we meet again"
53 Source of digitalis
54 Pick
55 Involves by necessity
56 Inns
57 Doctrine
58 ___-kiri
59 Couturier Cassini
60 Kind of gravy
63 ___ Calabria (Italian
   seaport)
64 Voids
65 Swings around
68 "___ Is Tonight,"
   Harlow novel
69 Cup, in Caen
72 Trickster god
73 City on the Hudson
77 Greek letter
78 Voltaic-cell elem.

187 THE GIRL FROM COUNTY DOWN by Dorothy Elliott
Who is the girl from County Down? Solve 23 Across and find out.

ACROSS
1 Cartographer's output
5 Young or old follower
9 Readily domesticated
16 160 square rods
17 Flintstones' pet
18 Set apart
19 1939 portrayals by Robert Donat & 23 Across
21 Put back
22 ''It ___ Be You''
23 Oscar winner of 1942
25 Inhabitant: Suffix
26 Hwy.
28 Debris
29 Suffix for hobby
30 Top-notch
32 Hic, ___, hoc
33 Words of affirmation
34 Ronald Colman and 23 Across film
38 Food additive
41 Unsettled, as contractual terms
42 Chemistry Nobelist of 1969
44 Blue knights
45 ''___ Cat,'' TV oldie
46 Porter's ''___ Clown''
48 Yorkshire river
49 Rush headlong
51 23 Across in ''Julius Caesar'' (1953)
53 Supplement
54 23 Across's title role of 1944
57 Murray or Peerce
59 Cantinflas film of 1960, with 23 Across cameo
60 ___ Hashanah
61 Cute nose
62 ''American Gigolo'' actor
63 Dandy
64 A Whitney
67 23 Across's title role of 1943
70 Schleswig-Holstein divider
72 Pedestrian to the utmost
73 Clark Gable and 23 Across film
75 ''___ yourself!'' (scram)
76 Ball of yarn
77 ''Time ___ our side'' (Gladstone)
78 23 Across in ''Sunrise at Campobello''
79 Rochester's second wife
80 Eye sore

DOWN
1 Decidedly unwimpy
2 Have ___ (converse)
3 Laurence Olivier & 23 Across film
4 Henri's lucky number
5 ''Star Wars,'' in D.C.
6 Smidgen
7 Tech grad
8 ''___ red, violets . . .''
9 Veranda
10 Lay ___ (flop)
11 Mass, in Monterrey
12 Leopold III's queen
13 23 Across and Walter Pidgeon film (1941)
14 Dormouse
15 Paradise
20 X-rated flicks
24 Hgt.
27 Satan
31 Keats or Horace
32 What misogynists do
33 Call ___ day
34 Nouveau ___
35 Aimée of Paris
36 ''Say what?''
37 Co-screenwriter for ''Pillow Talk''
39 Prefix for comic
40 Gather
43 Marionettes from a Tony
46 Like Mother Hubbard's cupboard
47 BPOE member
50 K–O connection
51 Newfoundland's SE extremity
52 Closed
55 Apparition
56 Paddington Bear's homeland
58 Dame of mystery
61 Word of mouth
62 Canvas primer
63 Excitement
65 One of the Lockhorns
66 23 Across in ''The Forsyte Saga''
67 Part of ARM
68 Signify
69 In casual fashion
71 ''Yes ___'': Beatles song
74 Homophone for you

188 ANIMAL HOUSE by Sidney L. Robbins

Mr. R. was a little double-minded when he came across 31 Down and 80 Across. Sid says if you get stuck at 1 Down, ask a child.

ACROSS

1 Dam site
6 Devoured
11 Building lot
15 Cheat
17 Kind of paper
18 Actor Farrell
19 Deviltry
21 Bridge call
22 Fleecy female
23 Joan Embrey's milieu
24 Offensive of 1968
25 Regret
26 Venerable saint
27 Sniffs
30 Active volcano
33 Off-center
37 Give forth
38 Melodic
40 Org. of the docks
41 Litigate
42 Dirks
44 Wearies
46 Possessed
49 Labor endings
50 Hardy horse
52 Gaucho weapon
53 Rocky peak
54 Tribunal founded in 1899
55 Prudently
57 Actress Arthur
59 Scottish alder
60 Feels
61 Saucy
62 Takes ten
65 Arabian Sea gulf
66 Mocked
68 Kind of concert
70 Buchwald
71 Foolish mo.
74 Paper of today?
75 Koch and Bradley
78 Overstuff
80 Prehensile marsupial
84 Scram
85 Sits
86 Taiwan capital
87 Gal Fri.
88 Weather word
89 Lovers' meeting

DOWN

1 "Who Framed Roger Rabbit" victim
2 Exhibit
3 Zinfandel, for one
4 Inquire
5 Born
6 Repeats
7 Actress Meyers
8 Wigwam
9 Sword
10 Nutcracker suites
11 Daddy Warbucks' henchman
12 Runner's woe
13 Consequence
14 Facilitates
16 Cata follower
20 Soft drink
26 Kind of ball
28 Chow
29 Ratite bird
30 Urania's sister
31 Carnivorous bugs
32 Egg followers
34 Manx mewers
35 Essayist of note
36 Waves the red flag
38 Mine entrance
39 Ms. Bombeck
43 Word of endearment
45 Selves
47 Mel or Marty
48 "___ of Our Lives"
51 Positive
52 Give
54 Despise
56 Neb
58 Muff
61 Dangers
63 Most faithful
64 Mediocre
66 Tel Aviv milieu
67 Wets down lightly
69 Lt.'s boss
72 Tarn
73 Stratagem
75 Discover
76 "I paid my ___"
77 Struck, to Keats
79 Permit
81 Observe
82 Kind of meal
83 Title for Laker

189 HOT STUFF by Sam Lake
In more than one way, this is a nice warm-up puzzle.

ACROSS

1 Scot's tam
4 Famed Canadian physician
9 Eagle or hawk
15 Explorer De ___
16 Stairs over a rural fence
17 Firebird
18 Important New Zealand channel
20 Hardscrabble
21 Of yore
22 "Laborare est ___"
24 Danton's colleague
25 "We might be all ___ of . . .": Shelley
27 Ego
29 Containers in British supermarkets
30 Imminent grads
31 Napoleon slept here
33 Joyous
35 Talks foolishly; slavers
37 Tune
38 Liquidate Darth Vader, e.g.
41 Nosegay
44 Silas Marner's creator
46 Site of Punjab University
48 Adjective for a spinster
50 Muslim faith
52 Jury members
53 Tributary
55 Go ___ for (defend)
57 Piquancy; gusto
58 Angelico or Lippo Lippi
59 Oakland or Marmon
61 "___ for Comedy," 1939 Bway. hit
63 ___ up (united in a project)
66 Cicero's VIII
67 On a holiday
70 Sorrow, in Stuttgart
72 Norms for Greg Norman
74 Rash, impetuous person
76 Modify
78 Kind of bull
80 Famed German lyric poet
81 Tied up a boat at a dock
83 Summer resort off Long Island
85 Region in SE Italy
86 Chignon component
87 Graceful tree
88 Second check-up by a teacher
89 Gügelhopf ingredient
90 Actor Gibson from Peekskill

DOWN

1 Office oasis
2 Disagreeing
3 Fireplace implement
4 East, to a Berliner
5 Spreader of hot lava, north of Sicily
6 Prevaricator
7 Inventor Howe
8 Slightly damaged paper
9 Hijack, as a truck
10 Saroyan hero
11 Henry Morgan was one
12 Earth's hottest area
13 City on the Allegheny
14 Landlord's income
15 Harbor vessels
19 Curl the lip
23 Actress Raines
26 Lotion ingredient
28 Antonym for pass
32 Heeling, as a ship
34 Springe
35 Used eosin
36 Wise legislator
39 Olympic hawk
40 Stone
41 Sound from the Iron Horse
42 Humdinger
43 Persevere in a difficult task
45 Verboten
47 What smog is called in L.A.
49 Ten: Comb. form
51 Unparalleled
54 Freeway feature
56 Memorable Yugoslavian leader
60 Run the harvester
62 Clothes closet culprits
64 Famed English Channel swimmer: 1926
65 Like old barns
67 Narcotic
68 Cone-shaped utensil
69 Author Utley ("The China Story")
70 Truman's birthplace in Missouri
71 Flee to a J.P.
73 Chrysler Building feature
75 Sultan of Turkey: 1512–20
77 Former Brazilian coins
79 Precinct
82 "Tote ___ barge . . .": Hammerstein
84 Adherent

EASY GOING by William P. Baxley
From the City of Angels comes this solvable old-fashioned delight.

ACROSS

1 Maine bay
6 Environmentally modified
10 African antelopes
16 Lucy's friend
17 Unspecified number
18 Rebound
19 Portion
20 Fed
21 Italian seaport
22 Kind of map-maker
25 Doctrine
26 City in Iowa
27 Corroded
28 Wager
30 Fewer
31 Bombay weight
32 Solar discs
34 Tessera
36 Spanish aunt
37 Defeat a bridge contract
39 Peepshows
43 Smart snake?
46 Giraffes
48 Pollute
49 Early
50 Tinge
51 Dashboard sight
53 Flat-topped hills
54 Disposition
55 HST or FDR
56 Encore!
57 Peruse
59 Jewish ceremonial dinner
61 BMOCs
64 Places
67 Sudden flight
69 New Deal org.
70 Gush
71 "Reversal of Fortune" star
73 Tonic
76 Nurture
78 Examine closely
79 Walked
80 Intestine: Comb. form
81 Bitter vetch
82 Metric measure
83 Shouted
84 Carter and Irving
85 Ruhr city

DOWN

1 Fronton baskets
2 Informal reception
3 Molder
4 King mackerels
5 Designer Cassini
6 Manor
7 Offset a defect
8 Oriental nurse
9 Star in Cygnus
10 Failed amendment
11 Mardi Gras follower
12 Expedites
13 Nary a soul
14 Eats in style
15 Louvers
23 Pro ___
24 Soak flax
29 Alpine region

32 Broadcast
33 Hebrews and Canaanites
35 Seat
36 Communications device
38 Like some housing projects
40 Goddess of discord
41 Author O'Brien
42 Commercial luxury jets
43 Little helper
44 Dunce
45 Per ___
46 Neely of the NHL
47 Roman household god
49 Ethical
52 Scottish river
53 Peace in Moscow
56 Tolerate

58 Patriotic org.
60 Pilotless planes
61 Wassail ingredients
62 Early American silversmith
63 Home to Alfred Nobel
64 Yardbird
65 Maine college town
66 ___ Rica
68 "Hostess with the mostest"
70 Baseball-card info
72 Withered
74 Swindle
75 Basilica feature
77 Linear perch

191

SOAP BOX by Albert J. Klaus

After watching TV all afternoon, Al decided to tell the world all about the experience.

ACROSS

1 Accumulate
6 Silent
11 Act with "feeling"
16 Present
17 Related maternally
18 Fast
19 Singer Tucker
20 Ward off
21 River in SE France
22 Extramundane soap?
25 Something unique
26 Submarine
27 Clothe oneself in
29 Soap that needs doctoring up?
37 Ancient Celtic poet
39 Costly
40 How Jack Frost acted?
41 Arabian garment
42 Ottawa Indian
46 Norse goddess of healing
47 XVIII x III
48 Nectar collector
49 Hot time in Paris
50 Defendants
51 Fruit drink
52 Convened
56 Printers' measures
57 Trials
59 Levantine ketch
60 At first, once
61 Revolutionary soap?
66 Space org.
67 Epithet of Athena
68 Cicatrix
71 Soap with a mission?
79 Asphalted
81 Danger
82 Greece
83 Pernod ingredient
84 Disintegrate
85 Sponsorship
86 Portable chair
87 Lavishes affection
88 Droning tone in Glasgow

DOWN

1 Theater gp.
2 Lament
3 ___ mundi
4 Mowed
5 Gull-like bird
6 Fear
7 Once more
8 Guitar adjunct
9 Roman road
10 Relate
11 Son of Gad
12 Tiler's kind of lodge
13 Candid
14 Overtax
15 River in Germany
23 Before
24 Dental deg.
28 Supposed
29 Most serious
30 Trouble
31 Deighton or Dykstra
32 G.R.F.'s secretary of state
33 Bay window
34 Sailors who stow chains
35 Foreigners
36 Erato, for one
37 Golf-ball-cover material
38 Awaits
42 Degrades
43 Paul or Tremayne
44 Plaster of Paris
45 Devoured
53 Auricle
54 Wire measure
55 Alphabetic sequence
58 Saint ___ of Avila
60 Licensor
62 "Till There ___ You"
63 Postpones
64 Gums
65 Peruse again
68 Hot tubs
69 Rattan
70 Eager
72 Imitated
73 Cruel emperor
74 Jog
75 Adjutant
76 Sea lettuce
77 Kind of check
78 Helper: Abbr.
80 Lair

192

"ANYTHING GOES" by Betty Jorgensen
"It's De-Lovely!" is our summation of this <u>hum</u>dinger from Oregon.

ACROSS

1 Vol. measures
4 Entree
10 With said or mentioned
15 Attention-getter
17 Decent
18 Get a runner home
19 Rich soil
20 Eye part
21 Pedro's pal
22 "Anything Goes," e.g.
25 CATV network
26 Angers
27 Conrad in "Slightly
   Used"
28 Stiffened
30 ___ Kong
31 Endings for bombard
35 Kind of frog
36 Capt. Hook's toady
39 Charlotte ___
41 Eria's home
43 Star of 22 Across
46 Big Apple river
48 Russian "AP"
49 Song from 22 Across
54 Rockets
59 Interpolate
60 Standardizing org.
62 Egad!
63 Rind
64 "___ among lords":
   Samuel Johnson
67 Lacedaemon
69 Road to Fairbanks
71 It has a skimmer
73 River island
74 Song from 22 Across
79 City of Light
80 California mountain
81 A Turner
82 Work like a horse
83 Pre-Aztec Indian
84 Object of an apple test

85 Playful sea mammal
86 Curls the lip
87 Wily

DOWN

1 City on the Hooghly
2 What beggars can't be
3 Aquatic routes
4 Agreements
5 Task
6 Handtrucks
7 Anglo-Saxon laborer
8 Camp-stove fuel
9 Able-bodied one
10 Demean
11 Witch's aide
12 Auricular
13 Latvian capital
14 Organic compound

16 Gallic Mrs.
23 Easy comparative
24 Star of the revival of
   22 Across
29 Amphitrite realm
30 Hebrew letter
32 Shady one?
33 Creek
34 Hundredth of a riel
37 Web
38 Usher follower
40 Disarray
42 Painter ___ van Delft
44 Stiff collar
45 Track circuits
47 Set upon
49 Yelp
50 "A Chorus Line"
   number
51 Application

52 Contingent on (with
   "to")
53 Tit for ___
55 Psychic in "Ghost"
56 Orderly displays
57 Analytic
58 Group of acroliths
61 Lines on ice-melt maps
65 Some are waspy
66 Korean seaport
68 Arafat's org.
70 Kind of printer
71 Mail from 79 Across
72 Exterior
74 ___ facto
75 Edith Bolling ___
   Wilson
76 QED center
77 Borecole
78 Venice loc.

193

IN THE FAST LANE by Melvin Kenworthy
Here's one that you can solve in a hurry.

ACROSS

1 Ramada
6 "Le ___ d'Or": Rimsky-Korsakov opera
9 Topeka time
12 Life story, for short
15 Elm or mackerel
16 With a needle: Prefix
17 Blackbird
18 Finale
19 "___ clock scholar"
20 Bossy's milieu
21 Medieval magistrate
23 English proverb
26 Far: Comb. form
27 Saint Philip ___ (1515–95)
28 Scottish landowner
30 Skyline features in Manhattan
33 Bring down a building
35 Decorative vases
36 "___ the Clock": TV game show
37 Acct.
39 Bride of Angel Clare
41 Part of a min.
42 Aleutian island
43 Far from feral
45 "Mayday!" relative
47 Quotation from the Koran
54 Letter carrier: Abbr.
55 ___ Shan: Central Asian mountains
56 Neural network
57 ___ Vegas
60 Between cinco and siete
63 Elev.
64 Lode
65 "Thanks ___!"
67 Treat with disdain
69 Members of a Scottish musical group
71 Whence Columbus sailed in 1492
73 Pile
75 Celestial altar
76 "Festina lente"
81 Appalachian range
82 Make lace
83 Devout
85 JFK predecessor
86 Choose
87 British cathedral city
88 To be, to Tomás
89 Geometer's Latin letters
90 Pawnee's cousin
91 Harrison or Reed
92 Checks

DOWN

1 Govt. agcy. of the '30s
2 Egad, for one
3 Mother of Zeus
4 Establish
5 Owl or angry fan
6 Serene
7 The briny
8 Aspen?
9 Overturn
10 TV interference
11 ___ wave
12 Rouses to action
13 Apprentice doctor: Var.
14 Whoopi's role in "Ghost"
22 Jacob's twin
24 Optional studies
25 Part of 89 Across
29 Mil. decoration
30 "___ thief to catch a thief"

31 Paulsen and Hingle
32 Resorts like Évian and Bath
34 Necessary
36 Tchu!
38 Latin I word
40 Material for a permanent igloo
44 Salamander
46 "Riches ___ man, but command a fool": Eng. proverb
48 Nav. officer
49 Spanish relative
50 Lend a hand
51 Swerve
52 Gleason's "How sweet ___!"
53 Author Deighton
57 What a sitter forms
58 With ice cream, perhaps

59 Comforted
61 "Marry ___ . . ."
62 Brings to court
66 "The Bridges at ___-Ri": 1954 film
68 Man in a box
70 Fit
72 Spanish gentleman's title
74 "Positive Thinking" exponent
77 Motto of Rhode Island
78 Charon's river
79 French naval officer-novelist
80 Tungting feeder
81 Speedy letters
84 Impending H.S. graduates

194

LEADING LADIES by Janet Bender
Three contemporary actresses have unwittingly been cast into
Janet's witty wordplay.

ACROSS

1 Ascend
6 Alpha's counterpart
11 Declined in power
16 Houston athlete
17 Strains
18 Ancient marketplace
19 Native New Zealander
20 Overused
21 Mr. Letterman
22 Actress's scullery items?
25 Bench
26 Site of Iowa State
University
27 Bullfight cheer
28 Tabriz's country
29 Shout from Strange
31 "Fables in Slang" author
34 Peer at Charlemagne's
court
38 Academic period
39 Iraqi missile
40 Gets around
41 Tiny bit
42 Catches flies
43 Actress's rustic retreat?
46 Wind instruments?
47 "Oliver!" director
48 TV antenna
49 Brain passage
50 Poet
51 Citizens of Candia
52 Indian weight unit
53 Escape suddenly
54 Barrel
55 Cakes' companion
56 Choir member
57 Small lizards
61 Actress gets into a
Shavian role?
67 Fragrant wood
68 Paris underground
69 Greeting
70 Fad
71 Get ready for a big date
72 More slick
73 American soprano Emma
74 Classifies
75 Mall business

DOWN

1 Unconscious states
2 Tropical vine
3 Actress Massey
4 Deserve
5 Soft cheese
6 Turkish footstool?
7 Weasel relative
8 Fire escapes
9 Obtains
10 On the QE2
11 Move like a duck
12 Open-mouthed
13 PBS science series
14 Actress Gray
15 Pops
23 Louisiana county
24 Standard of achievement
28 Thoughts

29 Foul-smelling
30 Algerian port
31 Nova Scotia's former
name
32 Andrew in "In Like
Flint"
33 Ford flops
34 Anatomical structure
35 Fly
36 European falcon
37 Calculating serpent?
38 Carried
39 Stop or cake preceder
41 Like argon
42 Well-fed
44 Soviet river
45 Oscar winner for
"Mrs. Miniver"

50 South African
51 Charged particles
53 Proclaims noisily
54 Dry red wine
55 Astound
56 Daisylike flower
57 Expel
58 Large sheet of paper
59 Former German coin
60 Nighttime sound
61 Behold, to Pilate
62 Actress Miles
63 Mr. Ant
64 Little devils
65 Architect Saarinen
66 Not that

195

HARD AS A ROCK by Michael A. Rampino
Don't be fooled by Michael's title. It isn't.

ACROSS

1 Blue pointer shark
5 Supposed
12 Drains
16 Notion
17 Slippery
18 Gingko or tupelo
19 "___ of Our Lives"
20 Forgetful
21 Auricular
22 Boutiques
24 Hag
26 Superlative ending
28 Australian city
30 Aerial navigation aid
33 Drunk
35 Dine
37 She pined for Lancelot
38 Jan Peerce, for one
39 Skater Boitano
41 Rocket stage
42 Function
44 Boxer Firpo
46 Dresden donkey
47 Variety of talc
50 Great: Comb. form
54 H.S. test
55 Authorial concerns
60 Make ___ in (show
      headway)
62 Valuable find
64 All kidding ___
65 Frostier
67 Collection of anecdotes
68 Cadge
69 Tenants
71 Western New York tribe
73 Anguillidae family
      member
74 Pace
75 Play the market
77 Fired
79 Golden
82 General's staffer
85 Flat-bottomed boat
86 Perfect ten
87 Grizzly
88 "Permit Me Voyage"
      poet
89 London playhouse
90 R. E. Lee's alma mater

DOWN

1 Among
2 Critic Huxtable
3 Pennsylvania's symbol
4 Tobacco kiln
5 Put up
6 "___ Gantry"
7 Word wag
8 Exploit
9 "___ the season . . ."
10 Oust
11 Command
12 Fred Flintstone's time
13 Main highways
14 American architect
15 Dry, as in wine
23 "Lucio Silla" and
      "Armide"
25 Wide-mouthed pot

26 Word in Idaho's motto
27 Stair component
29 Hazard from above
31 Avonlea girl
32 Tom in "Detour"
34 Computer gate
36 Tense
39 Ogre
40 She was turned to stone
43 Conical toy
45 Ship's curved plank
48 Prefix for trooper
49 Expire
50 Clayey fertilizer
51 Adams or Magnus
52 Tigereye, for one
53 Pernod's cousin
56 Equal: Comb. form

57 Nonagenarian age group
58 Razor feature
59 Blind a peregrine
61 Abound
63 Version
66 Food and drink
68 Rigorous
70 Dixie
72 Entomb
76 Star of "Elephant Boy"
77 Bath or Baden
78 Embrace
80 Repent
81 Spanish queen
83 Weir
84 Epoch

196

ILL-DISPOSED by Sidney L. Robbins
What does 18 Across have in common with 69 Across? As it turns out, quite a lot!

ACROSS

1 Balm of Gilead source
7 Haitian rum
12 Wet spot
15 Social reformer Bloomer
16 "...birthright for ___ of pottage": Gen.
17 Fiji port
18 "___ Cop": 1984 film
20 Distant
21 Novelist Bagnold
22 Main artery
23 "What's it all about, ___?"
24 Part of a league
26 Clangs
27 Sovereignty
30 LED
34 Landing ship
35 Chest rattles
36 Painting thickly
38 Isle near Scotland
39 Clasped
41 Competent
44 Mint
45 Dark brown furs
46 Stead
47 Sea bird
48 Smith's tools
49 Hair-covered
50 Endless
52 These mortals?
53 Like Father William
55 Delay
56 Strip whale blubber
57 Diamond weight
59 NBA team
60 Hogwash
61 Traitor Pierre ___
64 Tableland
68 Is out of sorts
69 She wrote "Bubbles"
72 Allan-a-___
73 Join
74 Lobe
75 33rd and 42nd
76 Fusses
77 Brushes

DOWN

1 Ruth
2 Last word
3 Jeans man
4 Snow toy
5 Broadcast
6 Prefix for content
7 Nevada lake
8 Eastern VIP
9 Fedora fabric
10 ___ de Pascua
11 Silly one
12 Super Bowl XXV losers
13 Serves
14 Most unusual
17 White ___
19 Shade of blue
23 Mimics
24 Bearing
25 Taxing initials
27 Miscue
28 Camp Henderson practices
29 Horoscope factor
30 Condense
31 Force
32 Undoes
33 Pops
37 Eye-for-an-eye punishment
38 King toppler
39 Mezzo Schwarz
40 Of a body of Roman priests
42 Let
43 A cont.
45 Trading center
49 William Carlos Williams, e.g.
51 Town near Padua
52 South of Ga.
53 They come in eights
54 Rodeo rope
56 Dropped
58 Altar locale
59 Rabbits
61 Gauze weave
62 Eager
63 Turn down
64 Muck
65 She, in Cannes
66 Smack
67 Cleo's snakes
69 On the other hand
70 Certainly
71 Spotted a tool?

197

Gayle shares her title with another _V_—a 1983 TV movie about aliens. Rest assured there aren't any strange or alien entries to be found below.

ACROSS

1 French Nobelist for Literature, 1954
6 Son of Hi and Lois
11 Island greeting
16 Insect stage
17 Faux pas
18 Javier ___ de Cuéllar
19 Cold soup
21 Pinto
22 Suffix for girl
23 Skirt styles
24 ___ de Balzac
25 Hew
27 Deimos' dad
28 ___ nibs
29 Song from "Annie"
30 Fragrant compound
32 Afflictions
34 Started an engine
37 Shakespeare
38 Swiss artist ___ Klee
42 ___ Auxiliary
43 Popular pasta
45 Kiwi-shaped
46 Apollo's birthplace
47 Tarkington's Adams
48 Herbivore
50 Soft
51 First home
52 Numerous
53 Superficial appearances
54 Stumbles
56 Flue sympton
57 "Evita" role
60 Wind dir.
61 Kirkland of labor
62 Polio pioneer
66 Take away
68 Insurgence
70 Buddhist sect
71 Abounding
72 Constant change
74 More despicable
75 First of all
76 Cleanse
77 Wield
78 City on the Meuse
79 "___ Magnolias"

DOWN

1 Public
2 They travel by horse
3 Masculine
4 Yuck!
5 Valuable legume
6 Longed
7 Tuesday worker
8 Stabs
9 Cast
10 Piece of mine?
11 Put side by side
12 Spare
13 Heavenly hunter
14 "Regarding ___," 1991 film
15 Nahuatl language
20 Tickets

24 It's spoken in Mysore
26 Apologetic
28 Damages
31 Shooting sport
32 Magnate
33 Bee participants
34 Pungent spice
35 Carried on
36 Saw
37 Hold fast
39 Comparable
40 Product of stress
41 Mortgages
43 Lodes
44 Queeg's minesweeper
46 Cloak
49 Ammonia derivative

50 Dice throws
53 Deer
55 Go back
56 Bluebeard's last wife
57 Itch for
58 Spiral
59 Francis of hockey
61 Limpid
63 Sky blue
64 Sill
65 Genuflect
67 Part of OTC
68 Bog
69 Canine sounds
72 N.A.R. and D.Q.
73 For shame!

198

WHAT'S THE GOOD WORD? by Bernice Gordon
You'll find the answer to the question above at 19 Across and three other places.

ACROSS

1 Port in western Israel
6 Stiff
11 Athletic competitions
16 Dame ___ Terry
17 Plausible excuse
18 TV showing for night owls
19 Fibber
21 Algonquian beads used as money
22 "___ Through the Tulips"
23 Desire, etc.
25 Division word
27 Like a wintry road
28 Dali or maria
29 Fiber used in basket-making
32 Administered an opiate
36 Toper's problem
37 Producer and writer ___ Schary
38 Slugger Hank
39 Amphibian
41 ___ de vie: brandy
42 "Police Woman" Dickinson
43 Decorated with more openwork
46 Greatly gifted people
48 Swindled
50 Fissile rocks
51 "___ Two-shoes": nursery-rhyme character
52 French pronoun
53 Prefix with corn or cycle
54 Like many an April day
55 Charge to a tenant
56 College in Cedar Rapids
58 Due; profitable
61 Goddess of agriculture
62 Incline
64 Uncle of song
65 Part of Chicago
67 Symbolic representations
71 Girl in an old song
75 Splotch
76 They take care of money
78 Laconic
79 See 71 Across
80 Laborers in olden times
81 Put in a pen
82 Position
83 Author of "Hard Cash": 1863

DOWN

1 Wisecrack
2 High: Comb. form
3 Dud
4 Productive
5 "___ for tennis?"
6 Charlotte of TV
7 Calamities
8 Veneer of gold
9 Portuguese or Spanish native
10 Emulate Mike Nichols
11 "The ___ Happy Fella": 1956 musical
12 Place in office
13 Chemist who won the Fermi prize: 1962
14 Commune in the Atlas mountains of Algeria
15 Grasps
20 New Year in Vietnam
24 Cut of beef

26 Missouri Indians
29 Conception
30 Flies like a condor
31 Honest Abe et al.
33 Sister of Ares
34 Bambi's mother
35 Spoil
38 Feed the kitty
40 Small bit, as tobacco
42 "Many ___ 'twixt the cup and the lip"
43 Recording-star Richie
44 Min Gump's husband (comics)
45 Attend a session with the old grads
47 British writer Wylie
48 Thwart
49 Dots in a radio code
51 Chew the fat
54 Glowing

55 Drive back
56 Pure as the driven snow
57 Paul Getty and his son
59 Up: Comb. form
60 The makings of Paraguay tea
61 Fuel transport
63 Minimum
66 ___ Bull, noted violinist, of long ago
68 Lady Jane Dudley
69 Present name of Castrogiovanni
70 Sheathing; casing
72 Actress Sofer
73 Caused resentment
74 Sum, ___, fui . . .
77 Announcer Husing, of radio fame

199

GLOBAL GIGGLES by Mary S. Snyder
A highly amusing opus from the Keystone State, full of clever right-on-the-money puns. (Although taxpayers may not be amused by 57 Across.)

ACROSS

1 Summarize
6 Tibetan monk
10 Made plumb
15 Verdi output
17 October gem
18 Cochet of tennis
19 Coolidge danced in India?
21 Scents
22 Warned
23 ___ which way
24 Advantage
27 Words of joy
28 Lansbury et al.
32 Sign of success
33 Gumshoe
35 Letter
36 Driver Fabi
37 Cockney's complaint of a Cairo cabbie?
41 ___ populi
42 Sun shelter
44 Not now
45 Wee
47 "___ company . . ."
48 South follower
49 Gloomy
50 Glower
52 Corp. VIP
53 Aubergine
56 ___ de vie
57 Debtor's complaint in Dubuque?
59 Mighty tree
60 Unpredictable
64 Kin to W.C.T.U.
65 U2 hit
66 Downfall
67 Dollop
69 Heady brews
70 Half a dance
71 Not a lot
74 Lots
77 Alabama residences?
81 Muslim decree
82 Verbal
83 Nab runaway Iraqi parent?
84 Duties
85 Actress Theda
86 Crown

DOWN

1 Mythical bird
2 Ecol. org.
3 Cartoon frame
4 Medieval chests
5 Novelist Scarron
6 Hesitant
7 After, in Arras
8 Tennyson's monodrama
9 Math. course
10 Certain sandals
11 Changes the color
12 Card game
13 Mistake
14 Underworld god
16 Sault ___ Marie
20 Gould detective
23 Black cuckoo
24 This, in Toledo
25 Pulled
26 Travel throughout France?
28 Prayerful finish
29 English organ transplant center?
30 River to the Severn
31 Like Marilyn Monroe
33 Companion of mortise
34 Ova
38 Feather: Comb. form
39 Flung
40 High-IQ group
43 Labor union of 1905–1920
45 Builds up
46 Cont.
49 Stain
50 With bag or back
51 Singular
52 Ancient man of Britain
54 Alley
55 Makes do, with "out"
58 Tag
61 Agree
62 Emulates an ecdysiast
63 Hostel
67 Exclude
68 Province of Spain
69 Early Christian sect
71 Rail
72 C.S.A. soldier
73 ". . . head worth ___": Shak.
74 Seed
75 Chemist Remsen
76 Slack
77 Crowd
78 Kin of LSD
79 Hearing
80 Christian denom.

200

ON THE CONTRARY by Walter Covell

When Walter sent this one to us, he asked if we found it too easy to solve. We answered him with his title. We trust you'll agree with us.

ACROSS

1 Waste allowance
5 Peace Nobelist of 1987
10 Headache
16 Dotty
17 Prize
18 Competing at Henley
19 Guerrillas' opponents
22 Menace
23 Offended
24 Changes
27 Felt aggrieved
31 Level
32 Superlative ending
35 Before to poets
36 Guido's high note
37 Gambler's "bones"
38 Office part-timers
40 Granges
42 Neighbor of Leb.
43 Captivate
45 Foam on malt drinks
46 Harmful, not helpful
51 Division word
52 Hebrew tribesman
53 Negative prefix
54 Cosmetician Lauder
56 Potent beam
57 Hasten
58 Make do
59 Consume
60 Lunar mare
62 Old Persia
63 Deliverance usually felt
   to be good
66 Meager
68 Adenauer,
   affectionately, "Der
   ___"
69 Belgian city
72 Responses to attack
79 It comes in sticks
80 Deep-blue paint
81 Chief Justice Warren
82 Pointers
83 William Holden film
84 Come about: Naut.

DOWN

1 Forte of an RN
2 Joey
3 Old Caen coin
4 Type of annuity plan
5 Reluctant
6 Steak order
7 Hip bones
8 Tia in Taunton
9 Parisian possessive
10 Sullenly melancholy
11 Bore
12 Envy's hue
13 ___ Tin Tin
14 Opposed to ext.
15 Booker T.'s group
20 A genuine article
21 Addicts
24 Of Hindu sacred
   scripture
25 Packet boat

26 Regained, as health
27 Scolds
28 Extremities
29 Shade tree
30 "___ Boot"
33 Play the lead
34 Woodworker's pattern
39 Folkways
40 Confront
41 Technique
43 Ending for kitchen or
   major
44 Modern prefix
45 Only
47 Providence-to-Boston
   dir.
48 Calamitous
49 Outspoken
50 Foe
54 Poetic contraction

55 Snow runner
56 One who pulls strings
57 Prepares
59 Appears on stage
61 Catkins
64 Worshipper of Beatrice
65 Lengthen a skirt
67 Printers' measures
69 "All ___," Tomlin film
70 City on the Gulf of
   Gabes
71 Weblike tissue
72 Network letters
73 Not in vogue
74 Western Indian
75 Bone: Comb. form
76 Cistern
77 Historic time
78 Foxy

201 CON OPPOSER by William P. Baxley
This easy puzzle will make you smile.

ACROSS

1 Fortifies
5 Knight of the road
10 Radioactive element
15 Transaction
16 Baseball's alleged creator, ___ Doubleday
17 Central California county
18 Siren in "East of Eden"
19 Calico pony
20 Musical studies
21 Unpolished surface
23 Abel's brother
24 Having branches
25 Young oxen
27 Bakery necessities
29 Followed
31 Hard wood
32 Distress signal
35 Tiny globule
37 Native: Suffix
38 Flatfish
39 Multiply
44 Extremely cold
45 Adjusts the grandfather clock
46 Japanese sash
47 Reach a destination
48 Speak pompously
49 Publisher's assistant
51 Insects
52 Sault Sainte Marie canals
53 National League team
54 Compass reading
55 Spasms of pain
57 Souvenirs from the past
61 Earthly
63 Begin a journey
65 Endorse a nomination
68 Tailless amphibian
70 Crimean city
71 Thirty, in French tennis open
72 Infinitesimal amounts
74 Lower: Var.
75 Enumerated
76 Upper atmosphere
77 Concerning
78 Western movie
79 Spanish baby boys
80 Some votes

DOWN

1 Actress Maude ___
2 Form of discount
3 A carnivorous mammal
4 Lists of candidates
5 Draw upon
6 Baseball stats
7 Baxter and Boleyn
8 Courage
9 What the WCTU fought for
10 International service club
11 Astringents
12 Part of a column pedestal
13 Change for a five spot
14 Nuzzle
17 Tranquil
22 Learned
26 Vassals
28 Pigeon's home
30 Bambi's mother, e.g.
32 Sound
33 Popeye's love
34 Jewish ceremonial feast
36 Postponement
38 Antitoxins
39 Inquiry
40 TV summer fare
41 Missouri amerind
42 Rents
43 Cameroons tribe
44 American journalist: 19th cen.
47 Family of the composer of "Judith"
49 Lake's little sister
50 Sapin
52 Smoothed a rough floor
55 Football player who gets his kicks?
56 Take a nap
58 Where Roma is located
59 Group of pismires
60 Surgical stitch
61 Card game
62 Governor of New Haven colony
64 Weight allowances
65 French commune
66 Silkworm
67 "___ la vie"
69 Large dog
73 Her or his: Fr.

202 TOURIST TIP by Betty Jorgensen

We're not giving you a bum steer when we tell you there's a clever quip just waiting to be discovered below.

ACROSS

1 Himalayan monarchy
6 Malay outrigger
10 Minimal
15 Kashan native
16 Meadowlands
17 Point of view
18 **Start of a quip**
22 Mess duties
23 Score a song
24 Scottish beef cattle
25 Gumbo
27 Man of Oz
28 Meager
30 Portuguese port
33 Anthem starter
37 Dins
40 Neighbors on
42 "Bravo!"
43 Torn apart
44 Giraffe's cousin
45 A Porter
46 **Middle of the quip**
50 Seas of France
51 Perfect
52 City on the Meuse
53 Suffix for differ
54 Distort
55 Libel
57 Guarantor
59 At table
61 Softly, to Segovia
63 Andrea ___ Sarto
64 Fr. holy women
68 Type of stair
71 Helmsley and Mitchell
74 Mel of baseball
75 **End of the quip**
78 Pickling liquid
79 Hibernia
80 Slip away from
81 Beach
82 Algerian titles
83 Islamic commander

DOWN

1 Shaving accidents
2 Blow up
3 Old hat
4 Pismire
5 Big cat
6 Malleable
7 Budget item
8 Caravan stops
9 Horned viper
10 Hiatuses
11 Being
12 Not "fer"
13 Plod heavily
14 Lacrosse teams
19 Kind of pool
20 Moves
21 Flexible
26 ___ Lib
29 Clever actions
31 Ping's pal
32 Suburb of St. Paul
34 Put in the fridge
35 Assert without proof
36 One in want
37 Yalta locale
38 Napery
39 Prevents
41 Spring money
44 Lulu
45 Adheres
47 Ancestry
48 Not give ___
49 Author Paton
54 Mourns
55 British guns
56 Whitman's dooryard flower
58 High country
60 Worships
62 Kukla's friend
65 16th cen. hat
66 Practice piece
67 Take the wheel
68 Pats gently
69 Other, in Oviedo
70 Bear it's partner
72 Weird
73 Flushing stadium
76 Conducted
77 Shade tree

203

A relatively easy puzzle to solve without any stumpers—a remarkable feat in itself when you consider Washington is just full of stumpers.

ACROSS

1 Actor Andrews
5 By and by
10 Spring events
15 Muscovy Johns
17 Worship
18 O. or Patrick
19 Gown material
20 Washington slept here
22 Prevailing weather
24 Raced over
25 Ike's command
26 Used sculls
27 "The Heat ___"
28 Fired
29 Like tuxedos, often
31 Attention getter
32 Gatling ___
34 Wings
35 Marcus Porcius
36 Hayworth and Moreno
40 Kind of eagle
41 Forum wear
42 Lupino
44 Daughter of Loki
45 Show ___
46 Unorthodox
48 Silkworm
49 Cadmus' daughter
50 Tree for ribbons
51 Deuce beater
52 Leisurely drive
53 Korean metropolis
55 Freight boats
56 E Indian tree
57 Ohio college town
59 Ethiopian prince
60 With the cards on the table
62 VIP's jet
65 Var.
67 Kilt feature
68 Out of sorts
69 ROTC member
70 Uncompromising
73 Institution founded in 1846
76 Asperity
77 Embankment
78 Notables
79 Dozer's noise
80 Put up
81 Cher's ex
82 Midge

DOWN

1 Platter
2 Grandparental
3 Ling-Ling's home
4 Vivacious
5 Hebrew letter
6 Fuss
7 Lincoln Memorial, e.g.
8 Che Guevara
9 Rocket type
10 At that time
11 Pronoun
12 Wing
13 Inscribed
14 Church assembly
16 Noose
21 Gaff rope
23 Koppel
28 Blackbird
29 They keep things kosher
30 Sir Galahad's mother
31 Squire-to-be
33 Russian mountains
35 Irish county
37 Building with lots of brass
38 Atmospheric
39 Skulking
41 Oolong
42 Sherbet cousins
43 Doris or Dennis
46 Lading area
47 Irritates
52 Really mad
54 Old Egypt
55 Hall of fame
58 Amo trailer
60 "___ Hickory"
61 Seckels
62 Hosiery thread
63 Inventor Sperry
64 Extant
66 Sacred cows
67 Violet variety
69 Atkins of Nashville
71 Mrs. Charles
72 Weight allowance
74 Gumshoe
75 Jillian

FONETICS by Ernie Furtado
Ernie's clever title is a good example of what lies below.

ACROSS

1 Toon and McGuire
4 Increased
9 Hwy.
12 City near Madrid
14 "As ___ and breathe!"
15 Rubber-legged film
   comedian
17 CERTAIN
   ATTORNEYS
20 Kale cousin
21 Longest river
22 Panama, for one
23 Classic preceder
24 Easy ___ of radio
27 Els
29 TRANSFORMATION
33 Scoff
36 Complete: Comb. form
37 For men only
40 Submit for acceptance
42 Culpability
44 Grain
45 Envelope abbr.
46 MEMBERS OF A
   CLASS
50 Gypsy
51 Sounds of laughter
53 Flintstone pet
54 Purify
56 Ghetto
57 Kind of notes
60 Kitchen utensil
61 URBANE
65 Helix
67 Words with caper or
   figure
68 Investigator: Abbr.
71 Shoe width
72 Rivers of Spain
75 Fisherman of a sort
78 HEALTH EXPERTS
82 ___ nous
   (confidentially)
83 Soprano Mitchell
84 "The history of ___
   ...": Pound
85 Great ending
86 Tin Pan Alley gp.
87 Low's org.

DOWN

1 French aircraft
2 Birthplace of DeGaulle
3 Zigzagged
4 Quick-tempered one
5 Gravel-voiced alien
6 Ovid's dozen
7 Author Hunter
8 Frank's home?
9 College ___
10 Outdated
11 Book with suras
12 Part of NFL
13 Oklahoma city
15 Pitchers
16 WW II craft
18 He was, in Latin
19 Vocal range
25 Highlander uncle

26 Wise
28 Standard steel
30 Goddess of discord
31 Porter's Sweeney
32 Little Joe's number
33 Iranian kings
34 Indigenous
35 Zealots
38 Make amends
39 Pluckier
41 Consent
43 Sun. talk
47 Son, to Simone
48 "You can count ___!":
   2 wds.
49 Withered
52 Cupid
55 Puttering

58 Shield of yore
59 Hovel
62 Burlesque
63 Hip bones
64 "GWTW" plantation
65 Call at home
66 "The Boss" star
69 Lanchester and
   Martinelli
70 Aquarium denizen
73 Earthen pot
74 Fr. holy women
76 Fed. agency: 1941–46
77 Q–U connection
79 NYC subway
80 Ad ___ committee
81 Bambi's aunt

205 ODD COUPLES by Harold B. Counts

Our puzzler from the Bluegrass State has played matchmaker. Can you find the common bond that brought these couples together?

ACROSS

1 Threw out
7 Indiana athlete
12 Largest asteroid
17 Network
21 TV witch
22 Dry as ___
23 Expiate
24 Eight: Comb. form
25 Duane + Helen
27 Martha + Johnnie
29 Suffix for good
30 Canadiens' scores
31 Seines: Brit.
33 Sisters: Fr.
34 Downswing
35 Arias, e.g.
36 Short sheets
37 Stocking: Fr.
40 Georgia tree
41 Attention-getter
42 Loafer insert
46 Curbing
48 Jack + Alex
50 Saharan area
51 Leering
52 Inklings
53 Drift
54 Wizen
55 Pogo's creator
56 "Field of Dreams" actor
57 Steeple
59 Armor plate
60 Disburden
61 Buddy
62 Staff
63 ___ a crowd
64 Nucleic acid
65 Robert + Helen
68 Bully
69 Gets close
71 Zeus' daughter
72 Made of flax
73 Worsted yarn
75 Abbe + Frankie
79 Dentist's deg.
82 Idolize
83 Impressions
84 Frenzied
85 Sèvres sweetheart
86 Turbulent
87 "Photograph" singer
88 Metal disk
90 Salad garnish
91 Director Kenton
92 Benzene: Comb. form
93 Hiss
94 Oratorian
95 Elver's elder
96 Teri + Doug
99 Clothes horse
100 Oversays?
102 Muse of poetry
103 Workers
104 British isle
105 "___ Three Lives": TV oldie
106 Office employee
107 Stage
108 Bubble
111 Chipped in
112 Ho's pal
113 Movie dog
117 Paul + Peggy
119 Ryan + Patricia
122 Banned apple spray
123 Gimlet
124 High-minded
125 Snarl
126 Wallet items
127 Norman and Edward
128 Sugary
129 Defiant gestures

DOWN

1 Existed
2 Wave on the Seine
3 Chance
4 Gewgaws
5 Time
6 "The ___ Conversation": Simon & Garfunkel hit
7 March 17th event
8 White poplar
9 Food fish
10 Goal
11 "Rent-a-Cop" star
12 "Herman" is one
13 Les ___-Unis
14 Rogers and Clark
15 Wind dir.
16 Coast
17 Unassuming
18 Beige
19 Magi guide
20 Heavy barges
26 Act
28 Prominent
32 Joyce in "Roc"
34 Full of thorns
35 Classifies
36 Elbow
37 Agent
38 Lemnos locale
39 Beverly + John
41 Whet
42 Legions
43 Della + Edwin
44 Kills
45 Issue
47 African river
48 Actress Lavin
49 Ritzy street
52 ___ d'oeuvre
54 Moselle feeder
56 Howell and Leno
57 Suburb of St. Louis
58 Tarred a hull
59 Scottish feudal lord
61 Diagram a sentence
62 Butter trees
63 Cogitate
65 Pilar
66 Forty-___
67 Gloomy
70 Roman magistrate
72 Detroit athlete
73 Trade
74 Renée in "Tin Gods"
75 Metric units
76 City in S Turkey
77 By and by
78 Bitter: Fr.
80 Mass book: Fr.
81 "___ Rides Again": 1939 film
85 Onassis and Meyers
87 Tatter
88 Greek philosopher
89 Soil: Comb. form
90 Town SE of Liverpool
92 Fatherly
93 Quits
94 Gifts
96 Corolla lip
97 Hockey players
98 Suffer: Scot.
99 Danube feeder
101 On-off devices
103 Alpine abode
106 Show contempt
107 Positive thinker
108 Old card game
109 He: Latin
110 Cruel
111 Seaweed
112 Cupbearer to the gods
113 Part of A.D.
114 Mormon State flower
115 Chatter
116 Bitters
118 Expected
120 Today
121 Clown Rice

206

SEE 25 ACROSS by Betty Jorgensen
The title of this crossword is the answer found at 25 Across: Other
thematic entries relate to it.

ACROSS

1 Perceptive
7 Powerful person
12 Half a city
17 Blackthorn
21 Shade of brown
22 Soul
23 Perfect
24 Entertainer Turner
25 Bacharach-David hit
29 Corded fabrics
30 Pinza was one
31 Budget item
32 Each
33 Kiwi's cousin
35 Leander's love
36 Devon desserts
38 Dynamo parts
42 Christen
45 ___ Ben Adhem
46 LAND
55 Accent
56 Spydom legend
57 Uppity
58 Helm position
59 Chemical suffix
60 Solti's stick
61 Mountain pools
62 Sting
63 Slaughter
65 Navigation system
66 A West
67 Neil Diamond hit
68 Mutt
69 Misplaces
70 Surfeit
73 Pleasure's antithesis
74 SEA
82 Like embarrassed faces
83 Other
84 Doles out
85 Place for a ring
86 California county
89 Home office
91 After, in Avignon
92 CEO and COO
93 A Darling
94 Flower part
96 Persian fairies
97 Braz. neighbor
98 Like the White Rabbit
99 "Fighting" college team
100 Angered
101 Of offspring
104 AIR
108 Eft
109 Employs
110 Entryway
111 Bamboo eaters
114 Cried
117 Part of Mao's name
118 Moses' mount
119 Engendered
120 Petal perfume
124 Swerve
128 LAND, SEA, AND AIR
134 Native American
135 Persian
136 Shift
137 Reared
138 MD specialists
139 Aplomb
140 Throes
141 Snakes

DOWN

1 Universal sci.?
2 Angry
3 Ensnare
4 "The Haj" author
5 Decimal base
6 High transports
7 Darlings' dog
8 Additional details
9 Shirt savers
10 Melville novel
11 Lamb's lament
12 More knowledgeable
13 Hersey's bell town
14 Fasting period
15 Stripling
16 High peak
17 Rod
18 Mascara's mate
19 Lulus
20 Simple
26 Disconcert
27 Three, in Torino
28 Abate
33 Code name
34 Mythical monsters
35 LBJ pooch
36 Drives the get-away car
37 Sly
38 Draft letters
39 Egyptian king
40 Deductive
41 CD-buying group
42 ___ pin
43 Gentle flower

44 Wail
45 Make up for
47 Turkish inn
48 Real follower
49 Glossy paint
50 Actress Swinburne
51 Sage
52 Panache
53 Very dry
54 Matched pieces
60 Overbearing
62 Moves
63 Old French coin
64 Kind of buoy
65 Fraternal organization
67 Vaults
69 Spindly
70 French seasoning
71 Balaam's beast
72 Neckpiece
73 "For ___ sake!"
75 Gentle
76 Lodger
77 Eugénie was one
78 Mock
79 Boudoir wear
80 Wheels
81 Hesitant sounds
86 Hooters
87 Harvest
88 Pro's foe
89 Shade of blue
90 N.T. letter
91 High nest

92 Chewing tooth
94 Retards
95 Role for 66 Across
96 Papal name
97 Nonsense
99 Virginia willow
101 Source
102 Shoe widths
103 Ghent's river
105 Resort E of Santa Ana
106 Not safe
107 Part of TNT
111 Devoutness
112 Organist Bruckner
113 Nostrils
114 Songbirds
115 Eldritch
116 ASAP!
118 Urban problem
119 ___ B'rith
120 "___ girl!"
121 Double
122 Chinese political party
123 Bible book
124 Empty
125 Gaelic
126 Kassel's river
127 Beatty film
129 Rim
130 DP agcy.
131 Sixth sense
132 FDR's "Blue Eagle"
133 Bounder

207 FOURSOMES by Tap Osborn
A quintet of quartets await uncovering below. (You'll be surprised by the foursome at 73 Across.)

ACROSS
1 Power loss
7 Market move
12 Syndicate
17 Stem the tide
21 Tropical plant
22 Hero Murphy
23 "I feel ___ comin' on . . ."
24 Flag
25 Four writers who failed at the polls
29 Conductor Leibowitz
30 By another way, to Hannibal
31 Sky blue
32 In a pet
33 Ending for fin or pin
34 Was concerned
36 What Popeye raises
38 Smoked salmon
40 Remick
41 City near Osaka
42 Prehistoric prefix
43 Change the decor a bit
45 Four who wrote bestsellers in prison
54 Dream: Comb. form
55 Western NY city
56 Bell, book, or candle
57 Profound
58 Hersey hamlet
59 McCarthy's sidekick
60 Agenda
62 Religious robe
63 Liquor portion
64 ___ Nagpur, India
65 They're court bound
66 Angus, as a youth
69 Assyrian war god
71 Silverheels role
72 Actress Lila
73 Four who never finished grammar school
79 Cow catchers
80 Cremona family of note
81 Handshake
82 Luke and John: Abbr.
83 Stacking platforms
84 Posts
86 Compensation
89 Heroes of WWII
90 "JFK" director
91 White-headed pigeon
92 Starry dragon
94 ___ the start
96 Wooden support
97 Caravansary
98 Spunky
99 Four famous snorers
104 Hat accent
105 As ___ (normally)
106 Be a motormouth
107 Rad. doubled
110 Dada's founder
111 A Brontë
112 Cumbersome
114 Gosh!
117 Estuary
119 Greek god
120 Guitar bar
121 Smell ___
122 Four famed insomniacs
129 Spooky lake?
130 Revolutionary cry
131 Unique artifact
132 Spirit
133 Kicked off
134 Eats with the best
135 Enoch or Eve
136 Smoothing tool

DOWN
1 Earthy color
2 He's all for it
3 Local yokel
4 Suits to ___
5 Mild exclamation
6 Army vol.
7 Chic fur
8 Ghastly
9 Invention basis
10 Prefix for inherit
11 Spitchcock
12 "Mandy" singer
13 Volcanic debris
14 Ball that's a strike
15 Follow follower
16 Yesteryear
17 Fuss and feathers
18 Kind of basin
19 Talk high and mighty
20 Martinique mountain
26 Vocalist Vaughan
27 More gelid
28 Foxy lady
34 Where "Aida" premiered
35 Acastus' ship
36 ___ bar
37 Danish measure
38 St. Louis suburb
39 Candid
41 Frau's proposal turndown
42 Zoologic suffix
43 Subdivision units
44 Biffin's color
45 Horse of a different color
46 "The King ___"
47 Jeté
48 Balzac
49 "___ a song go . . ."
50 Like soldiers at drill
51 In open conflict
52 Experience anew
53 Positive
59 Ignores
60 Moslem sect
61 Riga resident
64 Bar tabs
65 Blackens Mary Poppins
66 River and Horne
67 USN brass
68 Cancel
69 Hear ___ drop
70 Scoria
71 Hebrew letter
72 French ski great
73 Minister, for one
74 Where Castro often is
75 PLO leader
76 Santee
77 "___ the mood . . ."
78 Sour-tasting
83 Condition
84 Dorsey classic
85 Mowbray
86 Prior
87 Corticotropin
88 Toy that sleeps
90 Canseco's nightmare
91 Kind of laugh
92 McLain of baseball
93 Broil
95 Surpass
96 Spatter
97 Temple
98 Carping criticism
100 Rio de la ___
101 Big name in Egyptology
102 Fresh
103 Russian noble family
107 Fortified with a levee
108 Finnish lake
109 Caine film
111 Get the lead out
112 Count of account
113 Writer Sinclair
114 Sound of dismay
115 Golf rarity
116 The heavens
118 ___ out (managed)
119 Lebanon's Gemayel
120 It doth please the cheese
121 City on the Yamuna
123 Lemmon film
124 Kingston sch.
125 Nipper's co.
126 "___ Town"
127 Electrical unit
128 Lon ___

208

ON THE LEE SIDE by Mary Leonard
A noted interior designer was inspired to create this challenger after reading *Iacocca* and 35 Down.

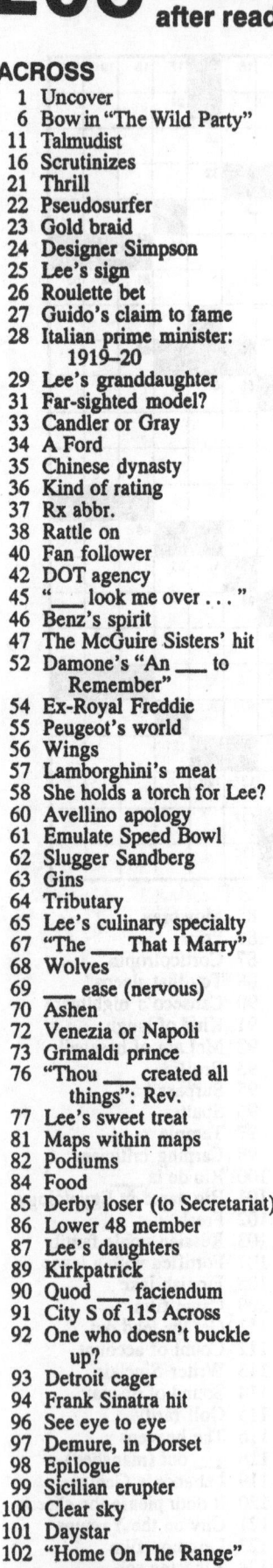

ACROSS

1 Uncover
6 Bow in "The Wild Party"
11 Talmudist
16 Scrutinizes
21 Thrill
22 Pseudosurfer
23 Gold braid
24 Designer Simpson
25 Lee's sign
26 Roulette bet
27 Guido's claim to fame
28 Italian prime minister: 1919–20
29 Lee's granddaughter
31 Far-sighted model?
33 Candler or Gray
34 A Ford
35 Chinese dynasty
36 Kind of rating
37 Rx abbr.
38 Rattle on
40 Fan follower
42 DOT agency
45 "___ look me over . . ."
46 Benz's spirit
47 The McGuire Sisters' hit
52 Damone's "An ___ to Remember"
54 Ex-Royal Freddie
55 Peugeot's world
56 Wings
57 Lamborghini's meat
58 She holds a torch for Lee?
60 Avellino apology
61 Emulate Speed Bowl
62 Slugger Sandberg
63 Gins
64 Tributary
65 Lee's culinary specialty
67 "The ___ That I Marry"
68 Wolves
69 ___ ease (nervous)
70 Ashen
72 Venezia or Napoli
73 Grimaldi prince
76 "Thou ___ created all things": Rev.
77 Lee's sweet treat
81 Maps within maps
82 Podiums
84 Food
85 Derby loser (to Secretariat)
86 Lower 48 member
87 Lee's daughters
89 Kirkpatrick
90 Quod ___ faciendum
91 City S of 115 Across
92 One who doesn't buckle up?
93 Detroit cager
94 Frank Sinatra hit
96 See eye to eye
97 Demure, in Dorset
98 Epilogue
99 Sicilian erupter
100 Clear sky
101 Daystar
102 "Home On The Range" opener
106 Plum or Caniff
107 Plunge
109 Doctrine
112 Lee's vineyard
115 Lee's birthplace
118 Slender as ___
119 "Lady Liberty" star
120 Coupe's couple
121 Farther down the road
122 Big top of Bari
123 Selling point
124 Century plant
125 "The Seven Year Itch" star
126 Coastal fliers
127 Site of 112 Across
128 "Water Lilies" painter
129 Lee's better half

DOWN

1 Lee's sister
2 Writer Canetti
3 Commune SE of Cordoba
4 Lying to, asea
5 Pace, in Pisa
6 The New ___ Minstrels
7 Despoiled
8 Never ___ moment
9 Finger millet
10 Arabian gulf
11 Optimistic
12 Mystical
13 North Carolina fort
14 Breathed's cat
15 Of course!
16 Flower cluster
17 Keats or Pindar
18 Nervy networks
19 John who sang "Friends"
20 Rouen river
30 Viper
32 Pavarotti's plus
35 Lee's no-nonsense book
38 Poodles, to some
39 Rod's pals
40 Makes money
41 Williams
42 Ipso
43 Nomadic Ethiopians
44 Bouffant hairstyles
45 Speed
46 Freelancer's enc.
47 "Plaza Suite" star
48 Iacocca and Arazi
49 Dodge
50 Hologram maker
51 TV's "The Wonder ___"
53 Lee's mother
54 Wine grape
55 Festive
58 "Drive ___": 1975 hit song
59 Worms
60 Scotti's sixth
62 Governs
64 34 Across, for one
66 Good-King-Henry
68 Shearer in "The Red Shoes"
70 Bashaw
71 Sparkling wine
72 Intertwine
73 Star of the 1988 Preakness
74 Caesar's caves
75 Virtuoso Stern
76 How the Heat plays?
78 Porter's "___ Men"
79 Standard
80 Revise
82 Puccini's first Turandot
83 Pianist Watts
84 Ice sheet
87 Aly or Genghis
88 Stretch fader
89 Lee's son-in-law
91 Lake ___-Itza, Guatemala
93 TV hopeful
95 Sierra peaks
96 Home of the Omni
97 Lunar leaving
100 Another Ford
101 Veer
102 Kiwi-shaped
103 He'll use you
104 Yet another Ford
105 ___ la Cité
106 "Tru" star
107 Former GM president
108 Gondoliered
109 Among, to Antonius
110 Fascination
111 Maples
113 Bantu Rhodesians
114 "___ fan tutte"
115 "Giselle" composer
116 Chrysler star, e.g.
117 Guitar sound

209

HOT CROSS PUNS by Robert H. Wolfe
Mother Goose is on the loose. Don't expect to find her below.

ACROSS

1 Tramples (on)
7 Struck
12 Jeanne and Marie
16 Biblical kingdom
21 "Teach us ___ and not
   . . .": Eliot
22 Friend of Danton
23 Expenditure
24 Heathen
25 More innocuous
26 Heart chambers
27 River to The Wash
28 City of Spain
29 Rich Tommy Tucker?
32 Adjust for daylight time
33 Quit
34 Quick-witted
35 Kind of pewter
36 Throe
38 River in Belgium
39 Demean
41 Seasoned rice dish
45 Salon foam
48 Woe!
49 Expressing in posture and
   motion
50 Foot, zoologically
51 Jalopyless Little Bo Peep?
57 Tops
58 Akin to veno-
59 "Then ___ you, and all of
   us": Shak.
60 Pavlova and Magnani
61 Colonist John
65 ___ impasse
66 Look into
68 Snoop
69 Mega or mono follower
70 Partook of
71 City in N France
72 Flue controllers
76 German river
77 Halloween vandal Peter?
81 ___ Bator
82 Malady
84 Trunk in a trunk
85 "Howards ___"
86 Golfer Walters
87 Time for revelry, often
88 Cover for Polonius
89 "It ___ Mean a Thing"
91 Slumber
92 Child's word
95 Town in Zaire
96 Great dame
98 "___ A Dark Stranger,"
   Kerr film
99 Obese Jack Horner?
102 Basso Berberian
105 Film plot
107 Verdi opus
108 Doomed
110 Kane, for one
111 Lassie's friend
113 Netherlands city
116 Nora's dog
117 Ex-Celtic Holman
118 Little fool
119 Cooked to a crisp
122 Conspiracy
125 Cartographic Queen of
   Hearts?
130 Love feast
131 Huamina locale

132 "As leene was his hors as is
   ___": Chaucer
133 More shrewd
134 Empty spaces
135 Last word
136 Compare
137 "Leviathan" star
138 Stately steeds
139 "Promise" is her album
140 Leaven
141 West Pointers

DOWN

1 Rouse
2 Tenor Kramer
3 Bear's-breech
4 Tropical fruits
5 Squeeze
6 Helots
7 Cocky one
8 "Chances Are" singer
9 Senator Hatch
10 Laos neighbors
11 Greek vowels
12 Ranges
13 Wig
14 Ruhr city
15 Suffix for trick
16 Most lean
17 Black sheep with clout?
18 Patronage
19 Bundle
20 Nursing School subj.
30 Kind of slick
31 Czarist decree
35 Speak imperfectly
36 Electrician's unit

37 Dawn of the LPGA
39 Kind of sax
40 Word of disdain
41 Part of ROM
42 Disney film
43 Ethiopian lake
44 Bully cheers?
46 Pahlavi or Jahan
47 Stapes locale
48 B ___ boy
49 Trait carrier
52 Figurine
53 McCartney's "___ In"
54 Mouths
55 Lunar trench
56 "___ Heart," Kern song
60 Branch
61 Coaster
62 Kind of skirt
63 Israel followers
64 Baker and friends tip a few?
66 Powers
67 Exile isle
68 Cowpoke's pal
70 Orbital point
71 Monza money
72 Tooth tissue
73 Nobelist Wiesel
74 Bring the house down in
   London
75 Go bonkers
78 Architectural scheme
79 Book with suras
80 Drift
83 Gardner biography
88 Kind of pilot
89 Before log or pod

90 Coronado's quest
91 Some vaccines
92 Assorted: Abbr.
93 Spore sacs
94 Happening for 37 down
95 "Mission Impossible"
   actress
96 Lamarr in "Algiers"
97 Actor Beatty
99 Worry
100 Super Bowl XXV site
101 LBJ beagle
102 Gooselike
103 Steep
104 Dean Martin film
106 Rhododendrons
109 Carried on
111 Like a wedding cake
112 Resistant
113 Elicits
114 Make mad
115 Before, before
118 Hebrew prayer
119 City in Japan
120 A hundred years before
   the first Xia
   millennium was over,
   to Benedict IV
121 "From the Terrace" author
122 Vena ___
123 Seaweed product
124 Colorado county
125 Dax and Margate
126 PGA winner: 1991
127 Strange lake?
128 Collapsible shelter
129 Mmes.' relatives

210

3PLE PLAY by Ernie Furtado

If you think Ernie's title is about an infield rarity, think again. His theme may be rare, but there isn't one baseball clue below.

ACROSS

1 Pervasive quality
5 "___ to differ!"
9 Desi's daugher
14 Happy letters for 9-to-5ers
18 Guitar ridge
19 Calais calf
20 Vietnam delta
21 Actor Cronyn
22 Balms
24 Exceedingly
25 Historic times
26 Fasten anew
27 Moody of "Allen's Alley"
29 Apparitions
31 THUNDERSQUALLS
34 35.315 cubic feet
35 Tooth extension
36 "Quo Vadis?" figure
38 Sartre novel
42 West of Hollywood
45 ___ Domingo
48 HOME RUNS
51 1925 Berlin hit
53 Equipment for 46 Down
55 Impassive
56 Fail to mention
57 Getz needs
58 Cigar
60 Hot tub
61 Blue Jays or Orioles
62 Pool goof
64 "For ___ jolly . . ."
66 Jack in "Rio Lobo"
69 Ukr., formerly
70 Nothing but
71 STRADDLING
73 October birthstone
75 French soul
78 Posture
80 Scored 100
81 ___ Assembly
85 Falana of song
87 NBA-er Strickland
89 Exclamation of Glasgow
91 In reserve
92 Faded
93 Fathers
95 NFL linemen
96 Bites
97 PARIS LANDMARK
100 ___ la vista
102 Great ending
103 Petty tyrant
104 Kemo ___
106 Annie Oakley
108 To be, in Madrid
111 TERRIFIED
117 Wet
121 Galore
122 Elaine of "Taxi"
123 Ends' companions
124 Not more than
126 Country music
128 Tom or cob
129 Nets
130 Latvian
131 Sign language pioneer
132 Positive replies
133 Poly follower
134 Language of Kerry
135 VIP plates in Manhattan

DOWN

1 Ere
2 An archangel
3 French income
4 New York prison town
5 "___ had it!"
6 Dukakis' running mate
7 "And thus shall ye ___": Exod.
8 Relish
9 Bible bk.
10 They're picked in luaus
11 Marine ___
12 Map on a map
13 SELF-OBSESSED
14 Subsequently
15 Mentor
16 Mosque priest
17 A Parker
20 Famed hypnotist
23 ORDER OF WEIGHTS AND MEASURES
28 It's Grecian in an ode
30 Stratagem
32 Cartoonist Addams
33 Happy signs for angels
37 On the ___ (at odds)
39 Haulers

40 Irish names
41 Sunflower
42 Ares
43 Wilder of song
44 Pitcher with a handle
46 Guitarist Farlow
47 D-Day beach
49 Oater nay
50 Conversations
52 First donor?
54 Cue in group singing
58 Toast
59 AVIAN SUPERHEAVYWEIGHT
63 Dernier ___
65 "Let's Make ___"
67 Parrot
68 1960 BORGNINE FILM
72 A Bunker
74 Horne of song
75 Alan and Robert
76 Shearer of "The Red Shoes"
77 Choice
79 Standard
82 "Street Scene" playwright
83 Cockney cabbies

84 "___ we forget"
86 Deals with
88 Sheriff's assts.
90 Juliette Low's org.
93 ECDYSIAST'S ROUTINE
94 Persian king
96 RR stops
98 "___ of Eden"
99 Hostile craft of WW II
101 Burgeons
105 Sandy stretch
107 Aghast
109 Pot builders
110 Forward
112 White oak
113 Girl watcher
114 Beckett's old man
115 Famed flop
116 They're often counted
117 NYC museum
118 Jazz singer Anita
119 Run in neutral
120 Cooked
125 Sun. talk
127 It starts in juin

211

WALL ST. NEWSPEAK by Edward Marchese
Here's a real challenger! It concerns the jargon of financiers and is based on articles in *The New York Times*.

ACROSS

1 Carp-like Asian aquarium fish
6 Ottoman officials
11 Artist's set of colors
18 Edit
19 Pieces with songs and recitative
20 "___ come to judgment!": Shak.
21 INVESTING IN DISTRESSED SECURITIES
24 Maidens
25 Provider to the poor
26 Haulers
28 Fluid suction tube
29 Adolescent
30 Beef cuts
32 "To ___ and a bone . . . ": Kipling
35 Island near Venice
36 Serf in the distant past
37 Chill
38 TOTALLY DEDICATED CAREER WOMAN
42 "An apple ___ . . ."
43 Ron Howard's early TV role
44 Site of first Olympics
45 Total
49 Broodingly morose
50 Auditorium
51 Kind of scape
54 ANTI-TAKEOVER MEASURES
57 Book by D.S. Freeman
58 Russian river into the Ob
59 Basketry fiber
60 Opera melody
61 ___ canto
62 Mosaic gold
64 Japanese clog
65 More confident
66 King Hussein's capital
68 Seed covering
69 Voided matter
71 Hesitations by speakers
72 Asian weight unit
73 Type size
74 Swiss river
75 Stoneworts
77 FRIENDLY ACQUIRER OPPOSING HOSTILE BID
79 River thru France and Belgium
80 Iranian coin
81 Acute
82 Passageway or entrance
83 Dance
84 Ballpark beverage
85 "Big Board" on Wall St.
87 FIRE-SALE INVESTMENTS IN FAILING FIRMS
91 Informal assent: Var.
92 Sea near Uzbek Republic
96 Specialty field
97 Roman mid-month date
98 Abutment of edges
99 Romeo's kisses
100 Tropical broad-leafed plant
102 Leave
106 He did it his way
108 "Thou shalt not go up ___ as a talebearer . . .": Lev. 19:16
111 GRAMM-RUDMAN TOOL TO BALANCE BUDGET
113 Attack vigorously
114 Type of rapid transit
115 Become aware of
116 Zealous
117 Author of "Jerusalem Delivered"
118 Lock of hair

DOWN

1 Lincoln-Douglas engagement
2 Soap plants
3 Tennis players
4 Recite
5 Animal having teeth: Comb. form
6 Onassis
7 Essences
8 Santa's sounds
9 "Play It ___ Lays": Didion novel
10 Trigonometry function
11 Desk appurtenance
12 Book by Nabokov
13 Light fixture
14 Stores fodder
15 Ornamental clasp for neckwear
16 Skunk-like animal
17 ___ Howard: former Yankee
19 Second largest continent
22 City near Hartford
23 Enologist's concern
27 Bad news for theater latecomer
31 Turkish title of honor
33 Pertaining to open, flat ground
34 Old-time three-masted ship
38 Apprehends
39 Musical work
40 Flange
41 Worker with clay or plastic pieces for coverings
42 ___ Islands in East Indonesia
45 Describing plants growing on the ground
46 Posy
47 Laughs nervously or affectedly
48 The Baleares off Spain, e.g.
49 Composer of "Red Poppy" ballet
50 Protective headgear
51 Safekeeping of goods
52 Earliest flints
53 Neck charms
55 River in Southwest France
56 Artificial or fanciful
57 Stay behind
61 They take a dip
63 Enchantment
65 Composer infamously associated with Mozart
67 Alcoholic malt and hops drink
70 Estonian city
73 Ending for convey or deliver
76 Yawned
77 Rank growth
78 Vale of ___, India's fertile valley
81 Range of perception
83 Substitute
84 Large motor transports
85 A 19th century humorist
86 Unsettled
87 Give up, as an office
88 Muse of astronomy
89 Bank president, at times
90 Gave nourishment
92 Reducer
93 Nubby ply yarn
94 From one side to the other
95 Tropical woody vines
98 Simmers
101 First-rate
103 Gnat or rat
104 Preceder for plane or marine
105 Grates
107 Cartoonist-illustrator: 1840-1902
109 Lbs., for example
110 In no way
112 ___ Paulo, Brazilian state

212

MERE NOTHINGS by Alex K. Justin
The only help we're going to give with this one is: **DON'T BELIEVE THE CLUE AT 1 ACROSS!**

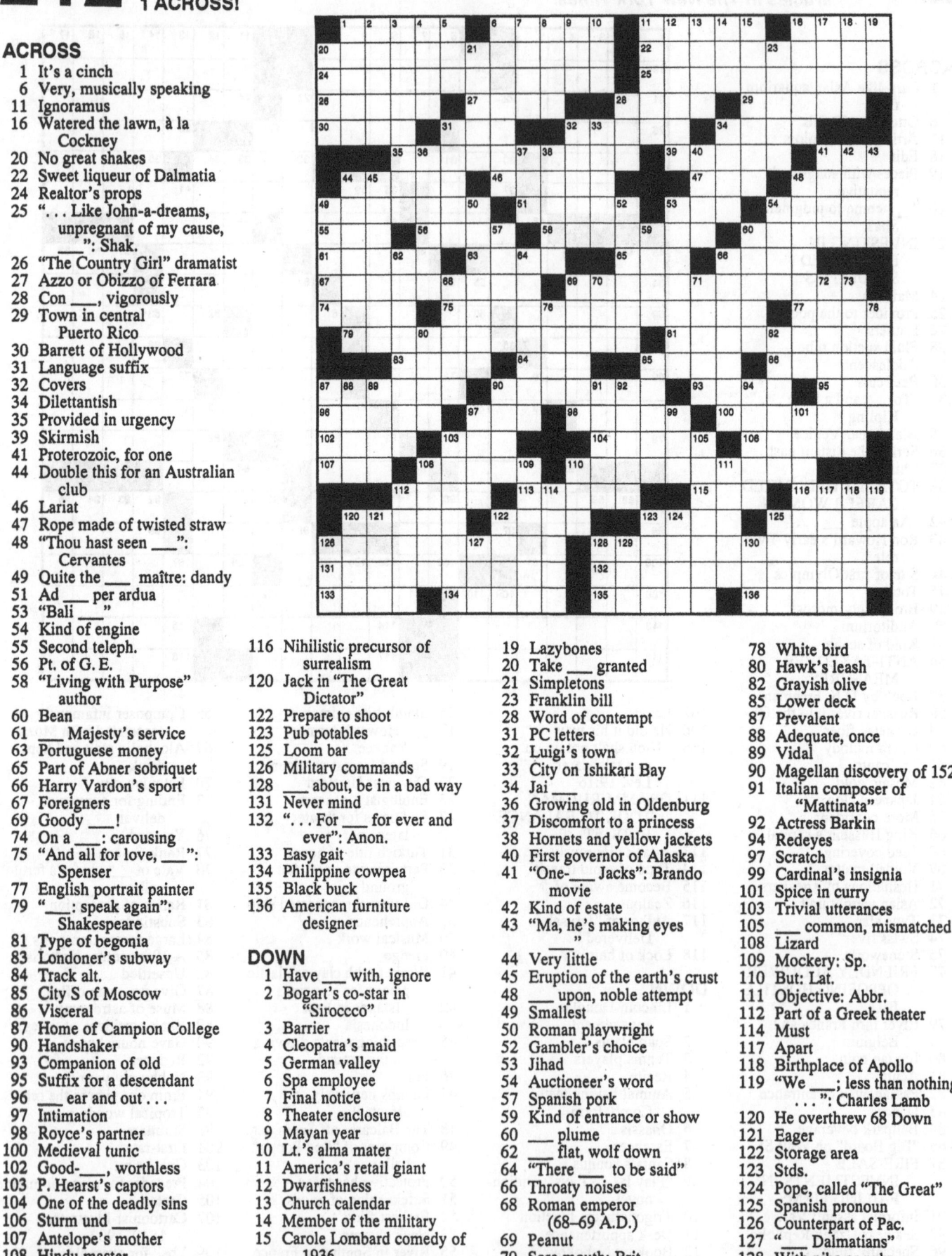

ACROSS

1 It's a cinch
6 Very, musically speaking
11 Ignoramus
16 Watered the lawn, à la Cockney
20 No great shakes
22 Sweet liqueur of Dalmatia
24 Realtor's props
25 ". . . Like John-a-dreams, unpregnant of my cause, ___": Shak.
26 "The Country Girl" dramatist
27 Azzo or Obizzo of Ferrara
28 Con ___, vigorously
29 Town in central Puerto Rico
30 Barrett of Hollywood
31 Language suffix
32 Covers
34 Dilettantish
35 Provided in urgency
39 Skirmish
41 Proterozoic, for one
44 Double this for an Australian club
46 Lariat
47 Rope made of twisted straw
48 "Thou hast seen ___": Cervantes
49 Quite the ___ maître: dandy
51 Ad ___ per ardua
53 "Bali ___"
54 Kind of engine
55 Second teleph.
56 Pt. of G. E.
58 "Living with Purpose" author
60 Bean
61 ___ Majesty's service
63 Portuguese money
65 Part of Abner sobriquet
66 Harry Vardon's sport
67 Foreigners
69 Goody ___!
74 On a ___: carousing
75 "And all for love, ___": Spenser
77 English portrait painter
79 "___: speak again": Shakespeare
81 Type of begonia
83 Londoner's subway
84 Track alt.
85 City S of Moscow
86 Visceral
87 Home of Campion College
90 Handshaker
93 Companion of old
95 Suffix for a descendant
96 ___ ear and out . . .
97 Intimation
98 Royce's partner
100 Medieval tunic
102 Good-___, worthless
103 P. Hearst's captors
104 One of the deadly sins
106 Sturm und ___
107 Antelope's mother
108 Hindu master
110 Paperer's need
112 Twist
113 Köln's river
115 Veteran's org.
116 Nihilistic precursor of surrealism
120 Jack in "The Great Dictator"
122 Prepare to shoot
123 Pub potables
125 Loom bar
126 Military commands
128 ___ about, be in a bad way
131 Never mind
132 ". . . For ___ for ever and ever": Anon.
133 Easy gait
134 Philippine cowpea
135 Black buck
136 American furniture designer

DOWN

1 Have ___ with, ignore
2 Bogart's co-star in "Siroccco"
3 Barrier
4 Cleopatra's maid
5 German valley
6 Spa employee
7 Final notice
8 Theater enclosure
9 Mayan year
10 Lt.'s alma mater
11 America's retail giant
12 Dwarfishness
13 Church calendar
14 Member of the military
15 Carole Lombard comedy of 1936
16 Anthem start
17 Muang Thai, formerly
18 Greek counterpart of Bellona
19 Lazybones
20 Take ___ granted
21 Simpletons
23 Franklin bill
28 Word of contempt
31 PC letters
32 Luigi's town
33 City on Ishikari Bay
34 Jai ___
36 Growing old in Oldenburg
37 Discomfort to a princess
38 Hornets and yellow jackets
40 First governor of Alaska
41 "One-___ Jacks": Brando movie
42 Kind of estate
43 "Ma, he's making eyes ___"
44 Very little
45 Eruption of the earth's crust
48 ___ upon, noble attempt
49 Smallest
50 Roman playwright
52 Gambler's choice
53 Jihad
54 Auctioneer's word
57 Spanish pork
59 Kind of entrance or show
60 ___ plume
62 ___ flat, wolf down
64 "There ___ to be said"
66 Throaty noises
68 Roman emperor (68–69 A.D.)
69 Peanut
70 Sore mouth: Brit.
71 Thief: Slang
72 Sentiment
73 Dried needle of a conifer
76 Honor
78 White bird
80 Hawk's leash
82 Grayish olive
85 Lower deck
87 Prevalent
88 Adequate, once
89 Vidal
90 Magellan discovery of 1521
91 Italian composer of "Mattinata"
92 Actress Barkin
94 Redeyes
97 Scratch
99 Cardinal's insignia
101 Spice in curry
103 Trivial utterances
105 ___ common, mismatched
108 Lizard
109 Mockery: Sp.
110 But: Lat.
111 Objective: Abbr.
112 Part of a Greek theater
114 Must
117 Apart
118 Birthplace of Apollo
119 "We ___; less than nothing . . .": Charles Lamb
120 He overthrew 68 Down
121 Eager
122 Storage area
123 Stds.
124 Pope, called "The Great"
125 Spanish pronoun
126 Counterpart of Pac.
127 "___ Dalmatians"
128 With nibs or nobs
129 Phys. org.
130 Haitian martyr

ECCENTRICITIES by Walter Covell
This is undoubtedly the most unusual (and perhaps most original) crossword
we have ever published. Congratulations to Walter and to all who solve it!

LEFT TO RIGHT

8 Irish luck
18 League
20 Gymnasts
21 An acid salt
22 Entre ___
23 Electra's brother
24 I love: Lat.
25 Imitates St. Helens
27 Cutting tool
29 Irish sea god
30 Gets one's feet wet
32 Bus. subject
34 Pseudonymous initials
36 Hr. part
37 Gully
39 Washington's hat
41 Look for
47 Sings with syllables
50 Gypsy boy
51 River to the Gulf of
    Finland
52 Rubber trees
53 Former European gold
    coin
54 Target for Rypien
55 Brain passage
56 Czech border mountains
58 Suffix for junior
59 Parade time
61 Ampersand's meaning
62 Trains
64 TV awards
65 Tease
67 Noble gas
69 Make over
70 Two-year-old sheep
72 "The Lily Maid of
    Astolat"
74 Empty
76 Pianist Myra
77 Colleague of Nasser
78 Air: Comb. form
82 Tacit teller
83 Ten-percenter
85 Trite saying
86 Pecuniary interests
88 Prescribed amounts
90 Drive of Beverly Hills
92 Hiatus
99 Having many branches
100 Exhort
101 Indian weight
102 Rose or Seeger
105 Early religious cruet
106 Carrot or beet
108 Held an oar horizontally
    again
111 Three-toed sloths
112 Raised
114 Swindled
115 WW II vessel
116 Miss Kett
117 Japanese receptacle set
119 London district
120 One in Pisa
121 Fast-swimming whale
123 Underwater obstacle
125 Narcissism
126 Future grads
127 Spy org. of WW II

RIGHT TO LEFT

7 Anarchy
17 Tumults
19 Surprisingly unusual
46 Throw into confusion
98 Unconventional

DOWN

1 Pro ___
2 Susiana
3 Mus. slow-down
4 Rowed
5 Gin
6 Sudden attack
7 Abysmal
8 Concern
9 "Travels in Hyperreality"
    author
10 Short-barreled
11 Mali people
12 Bird with a bundle
13 Capek play
14 Exist
15 Switch positions
16 Smooth feathers
17 CIS predecessor
26 Kind of life insurance
28 "Atlas Shrugged" author

31 Trouble
33 Obstruct
35 Aides
36 Thawing
37 "The Way We ___"
38 Expiation
39 Lift at Aspen
40 Ascend
42 Dawn goddess
43 Join
44 Animals of Arles
45 Finished
48 Strange
49 Soap-frame bar
53 Cue preceder
57 Caterpillar feature
60 Valais capital
61 Anxious feeling
63 Anger
64 Silkworm
66 Infamous marquis
70 Nearest ones
71 Poetic day's end
73 World col. org.
75 Bridge positions
78 Literary collection
79 Old French coin
80 Legal matter

81 Honshu bay
84 Produce
85 18th Amendment's kind
    of effect?
87 Philippine volcano
89 Guadalajara gold
90 Abbr. at the pumps
91 Nebraskan Indian
93 S African zoos
94 Loose tunic
95 Luigi's skill
96 Press agents
97 Sire
102 Kind of shooter
103 Most groupies
104 Icelandic sagas
107 Bone: Comb. form
109 Architect Saarinen
110 Chops
113 Prevaricate

UP

68 On the bum
112 Johnny in gray
118 Bizarre
122 Classic film comedy
124 Avant-garde
127 Quirky

214

ANATOMIC SURVEY by Edward Marchese
The thematic entries below are easy to find. You carry them around with you every day.

ACROSS

1 Find fault
5 Steadfast
9 Maximally
15 Intriguing group
20 Inter ___ (among other things)
21 Deserve
22 Placate
23 Italian economist-sociologist
24 STUBBORN
26 Worker in photo developing
27 Meat dishes
28 Anne Baxter role: 1950
29 It goes before a fall sometimes
30 FREE SCOPE
32 Vegas lead-in
33 Apollo's birthplace
35 Wound antiseptic
37 French president: 1947–54
39 Droning insect
41 Former republic in Yugoslavia
45 Launce
48 WORN CLOTHING USED BY ANOTHER
54 Cowboy area
56 Pester
57 Cain's victim
58 Cinema ___, documentary film technique
60 "___ and quiet conscience": Shak.
62 Some coll. football linemen
63 ___ Grosso: Brazilia state
64 Son of Seth
65 More inquisitive
67 Beginning
70 Met shortstop
72 Body canal
74 Loin beefsteak
76 Gehrig or Groza
77 Asleep
79 Vietnamese army commander
82 American Indian
86 Signer
88 DEFRAY THE COST
91 Parisian's year
92 Goaded
94 "La ___ Americaine": Truffaut film
95 Hospital supply
97 McCoy or McCarver
98 Backsides
100 Avenue's cousin
102 Author of "Gil Blas"
104 Plays tricks on
107 Seeds used in chocolate
110 Moroccan seaport
112 Ottoman official
113 Anti
114 Pesticide
116 Grown calf
118 Secluded valley
119 "... ___ make dust of all things": T. Browne
122 Ruhr city
123 MAKE OVER-FINE DISTINCTIONS
125 Change abode
127 Stooge
130 Full-house sign
131 Pierces
133 Lacking vitality
137 England's Isle ___
141 Barley beard
143 BROADWAY'S "GOOD LUCK!"
147 Former Lord Epping of movies
149 Witch bird
150 "The ___ Low," 1930 song
152 Site of Black Hawk College, Ill.
153 MISER
155 Kind of information
156 Lacking key
157 Thread a falcon's eyelids
158 County in New York
159 Submachine guns
160 Boxing units
161 MacDonald co-star
162 Antlered ruminant

DOWN

1 Cloaked
2 Active
3 Bright star in Orion
4 Annoyance exclamation
5 Rip
6 Circle parts
7 Hives
8 Finished
9 "... start ___ or two ...": T. S. Eliot
10 Leather ornamenter
11 Ancient Dead Sea kingdom
12 ___ the Great (1st H. R. Emperor)
13 Entertainment: Brit. or Ed Sullivan
14 ___ alba (gypsum)
15 Feline's favorite plant
16 Land measure
17 STAY ACUTELY ATTENTIVE
18 Largest of Andreanof Islands
19 Negative bottom line
23 Scabies
25 England's Derby town
31 Blackbird
34 Less than standard trade quantity
36 "___ It Romantic" (Rodgers & Hart)
38 Pindar specialty
40 Return to former condition
42 One of a golfer's woods
43 Rumanian city
44 Price for playing poker
46 Old ruling Italian family
47 For fear that
48 Pied Piper's town
49 Pearly mollusk
50 Toggle used on a kimono sash
51 Cub Scout group
52 Cry from Juliet
53 "A ___ maketh a glad father" (Biblical proverb)
55 Measured circumference
59 Suffix with persist
61 Impend
66 Should
68 Disquiet
69 Sea gull
71 ___ Dorset (Thos. Sackville)
73 Island off Alaska
75 Relief
78 Postal deliveries in country areas
80 Busy as ___
81 Parasitic plant
83 Stone or metal engravings
84 Equine nay-sayer?
85 Abases
87 Tropical food staple
89 Medicinal herb drinks
90 "___ her ways be unconfined": M. Prior
93 Gaelic
96 Readies
99 Yearning
101 Bib. revision
103 "___ Saints," by Sigrid Undset
104 Healed tissue mark
105 Read studiously
106 Precisely
108 Unreal
109 Ice cream holder
111 Floral wreath
115 Here's opposite
117 Feudal laborer
120 Great weight
121 Beats a rival at an auction
124 First Duke of Normandy
126 Opera by Handel
128 Distraught woman
129 Some are guardians
132 Philippine island
134 ___ di voce: bel canto techniques
135 Annoyed
136 Wept
138 Nice official
139 Oakley or Laurie
140 Chilean expert
141 He wrote "I Like It Here"
142 Inclined
144 Japanese zither
145 Baseball family name
146 Bambi ___: TV dancer of 1950s
148 Sole
151 Diarist Anais ___
154 Guided

215

MOUTHFULS by John Greenman
Lexicologists should appreciate this tour de force. Below are six 23-letter words waiting to be discovered.

ACROSS

1 Mrs. Gorbachev
6 Arson, e.g.
11 Bias
15 Moola
19 Talisman
20 Stormed
21 "___ Mia": 1965 tune
22 Medleys
24 With God depicted as a human form
28 Liner: Abbr.
29 Yellow cheese
30 Relatives of kvass
31 Old French cathedral city
32 Ring
34 Honshu port
35 Invalid
37 Borer
38 Chicago's horal z.
39 "Or I'll ___ hat!"
42 Knackwurst, e.g.
43 Confederates
46 Believer in Eucharistic doctrine
54 Picnic, for one
55 Auspices
56 Long eyeteeth
57 German river
58 "___, I perish, Tranio": Shak.
59 Rx acid
61 ". . . for care and ___ for woe!": Heywood
62 Brazil state
63 Of brain-wave measurement
68 Badger
69 Lodgings
70 Lake near Kyoto
71 Lube
72 Frequently, to bards
73 Fat farms
75 More unadorned
77 Keen
79 Andaman, e.g.
82 One-time Spanish queen
83 Queue after Q
84 Entr' ___
86 Deirdre's land
90 Imperceptibilities
97 "Salut!" is one
98 Smidgen
99 Hardy, to Laurel
100 Tracts between two rivers
101 Max. degrees
102 Realities: Lat.
104 Great Plaines tribe
105 "The Hoodlum Priest" star
106 With bogus civic benevolence
111 Heckart or Brennan
112 Thought
113 "Lola de Valence" painter
114 Hellenic H
117 Classifieds
118 Ripsnorter
119 Join a jury
120 One, in Bonn
124 Rx amount
126 Letter opener
128 Breathing lapses
131 Ewe's plaint
132 Acts promoting ties among sects
137 Papal crown
138 Singular
139 Japanese seaport
140 Rangoon royals
141 Stuff
142 Construction piece
143 Subsides
144 "The Chalk Garden" star

DOWN

1 Totaled
2 Of stars: Comb. form
3 Goethe's I
4 Categorize
5 Your, to Yves
6 Bing and Gary
7 Flaxlike fiber
8 "___ Rhythm"
9 Debussy subject
10 Computer's wk.
11 Revile
12 Headless cabbage
13 Hermes' son
14 Joker
15 Part of the ear
16 Side petals
17 Of the 14th element: Prefix
18 Celeste's family
19 Memorable sitcom
23 Organ grp.
25 Straight down
26 West Indies land
27 Shaw and Corey
33 Deeds of reparation
35 Gulf of ___ (Adriatic arm)
36 Filly feed
37 Sleep like ___
40 Advantage
41 Word of rebuke
42 NBA team
43 "He has ___ on one end . . .": Nash
44 Jargon
45 Land of Nod
46 Moselle city
47 Crease in Pierre's pants
48 Walking, in Paris
49 Sea swallows
50 Romance
51 Gem State
52 Letter line
53 Pamphlet
59 Dwarf tree
60 Wine: Comb. form
61 Sighing phrase
62 Colombian city
64 Laughing
65 Vintner's selection
66 Vandyke
67 Torn apart
74 Gnat or rat
75 Savage
76 Home to over 50% of mankind
78 Godforsaken
79 Slimming exercise
80 Carbon compounds
81 "___ which will live in infamy": FDR
84 More skilled
85 Ovid's 151
87 ". . . it will come: the readiness ___": Shak.
88 Mutiny
89 Lamb product
91 Progeny
92 Hollow
93 Arrived
94 More heated
95 Oahu adieu
96 Elicit
102 Did origami
103 Kong's kin
104 Wavy
105 Uproar
107 Blueprint
108 Therefore: Fr.
109 Foreboding
110 Metal plate
114 Polish prose
115 Quinine water
116 Astral type
118 Abalone
119 Plant spike
121 "Brand" author
122 Titles
123 Impudence
125 Age, old style
126 Uppity one
127 Inner Hebrides isle
128 ___ impasse
129 Swiss river
130 Belgrade native
133 Yalie
134 At the moment
135 Alma-___
136 Actress Balin

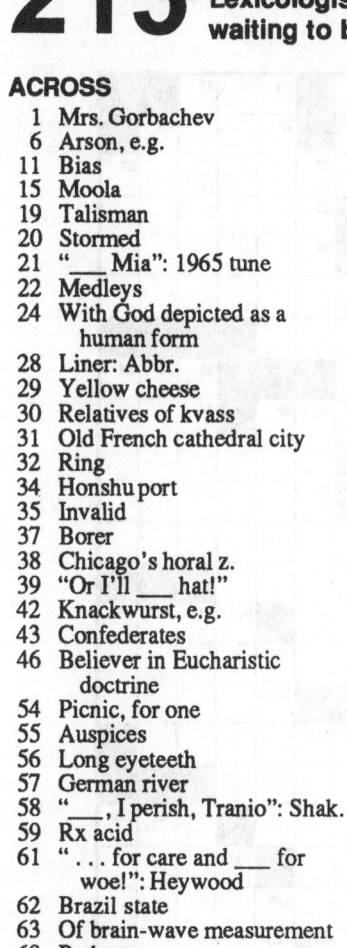

216
ARTFUL ACT by Ernie Furtado
Kudos to our dexterous Gothamite for a fascinating feat in which anagrams and alliterations are combined throughout.

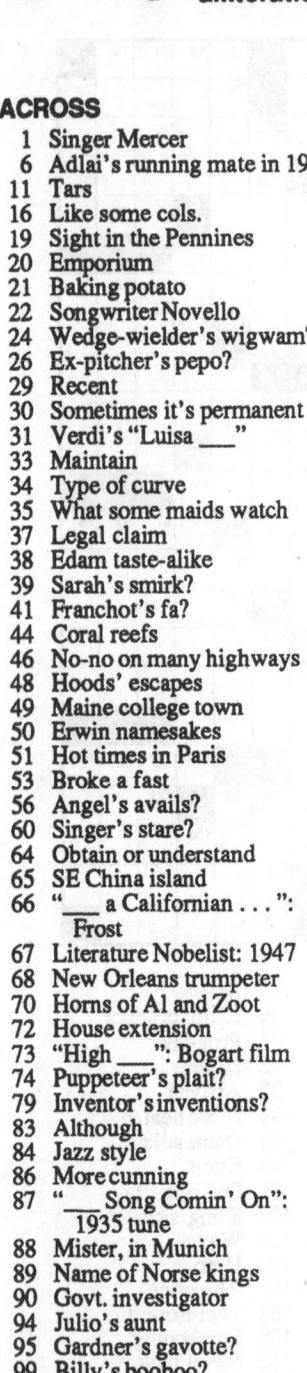

ACROSS

1 Singer Mercer
6 Adlai's running mate in 1956
11 Tars
16 Like some cols.
19 Sight in the Pennines
20 Emporium
21 Baking potato
22 Songwriter Novello
24 Wedge-wielder's wigwam?
26 Ex-pitcher's pepo?
29 Recent
30 Sometimes it's permanent
31 Verdi's "Luisa ___"
33 Maintain
34 Type of curve
35 What some maids watch
37 Legal claim
38 Edam taste-alike
39 Sarah's smirk?
41 Franchot's fa?
44 Coral reefs
46 No-no on many highways
48 Hoods' escapes
49 Maine college town
50 Erwin namesakes
51 Hot times in Paris
53 Broke a fast
56 Angel's avails?
60 Singer's stare?
64 Obtain or understand
65 SE China island
66 "___ a Californian . . .":
   Frost
67 Literature Nobelist: 1947
68 New Orleans trumpeter
70 Horns of Al and Zoot
72 House extension
73 "High ___": Bogart film
74 Puppeteer's plait?
79 Inventor's inventions?
83 Although
84 Jazz style
86 More cunning
87 "___ Song Comin' On":
   1935 tune
88 Mister, in Munich
89 Name of Norse kings
90 Govt. investigator
94 Julio's aunt
95 Gardner's gavotte?
99 Billy's booboo?
101 Part of a sch. yr.
102 ___ spumante
103 Apportion
105 Fatha of jazz
106 Millennia
108 "All kidding ___"
110 Spots
112 Rex's roebuck?
117 Poet's porterhouse?
120 Native
121 Prince of Araby
123 Pilfers
124 Pop
127 Attic
128 Sea or land followers
130 "___ on Down the Road"
131 Handle problems handily
132 Novelist's note-taker?
134 Ollie's annoyance
137 Kind of sch.

138 Che's chum
139 Feral female water buffalo
140 City in Nevada and river
   in Italy
141 Religious gp. (Mormons)
142 Greek island
143 Alums
144 Goodnight girl of
   songdom

DOWN

1 ___ syrup
2 Vicinities
3 Borscht ingredients
4 Major chaser
5 Actress Grant
6 Landed properties
7 Martin and Allen
8 Tipplers
9 Poetic palindrome
10 Appear
11 More inane
12 Partner of young Fred Astaire
13 Plaint
14 God of thunder
15 Solomon, to David
16 Like some spectacle
17 A Waugh
18 Lake Erie port
23 Thesaurus name
25 "Thou ___": Rodgers & Hart
27 Capital of the Beaver State
28 State bird of Hawaii
32 Unjust treatment
35 Director Forman

36 Pornography
39 Gold mine of a sort
40 Live ___ (have a ball)
42 Designer Cassini
43 Space agcy.
44 Composer Khatchaturian
45 In ___ (completely)
47 Goad
49 Alias letters
50 ___ a price on (evaluates)
52 Monogram of "The
   Waste Land" poet
53 "___ Like I": Loos
54 ___ Haute
55 Kett and James
57 A 1957 Fonda film (with
   "The")
58 ". . . government by
   ___": Roosevelt
59 Deborah or Jean
61 Young sow
62 Kind of resistance
63 Choice
69 Disconsolate
71 Circus Maximus official
74 Entices
75 Caine flick: 1966
76 Construction bar
77 European peninsula
78 Mi preceders
80 Make a run
81 Composer Edouard ___
82 Arabian chiefs
85 First showing
88 FDR's successor

91 Thelonious of jazz
92 Brother of Eris
93 Vane readings
96 Cleo or Lois
97 Being, to philosophers
98 A satellite of Jupiter
100 A stadium and former
   pitcher
104 Vietnamese celebrations
106 Respects
107 "Waiting for Lefty"
   playwright
109 Slalom racer's aid
110 Caches
111 Volcano goddess and
   soccer great
112 Manipulates
113 Related maternally
114 Register
115 Mended socks
116 Withdraw
118 Breastbones
119 Occupying an ottoman
122 "Bar at the Folies Bergere"
   painter
124 Lorna of fiction
125 Ring part
126 Thick
128 Ado
129 Obstacle
131 Actress in "Mermaids"
133 Rank of a top noncom
135 Hockey great
136 Prefix with corn

217

OCTOGENARIAN'S DELIGHT by Martin Ashwood-Smith

This quotation from a play by an 18th-century British man of letters is sure to please anyone born in the early part of last century.

ACROSS

1 Seamstress
8 Scacchi and Garbo
14 Sets of six
20 Upset
21 Like some cars
22 Tooth protectors
24 **Start of the quotation**
26 Rodent's knock?
27 Milk curdling enzyme
28 Never, in Navarre
29 Hop house
31 Bond adversary
32 Palindromic Dutch town
33 Cups for thé
36 Gp. that stick to their guns
39 Barkley was one
41 From ___ Z
42 Wood joint
43 Foot feature
45 Shakespearean spirit
47 El ___, Texas
50 **Quotation: Part II**
54 Back talk?
55 Kind of movie
56 Archeological project
57 Laurel-Hardy go-between
58 "We ___ hollow men . . .": T. S. Eliot
60 Part of E.E.C.
61 Wool knot
63 Neither masculine nor feminine
67 Mosaic tile
69 Kiki ___, rock star
71 Flashing device
73 Norse god of strife
74 Eggy concoction
76 Anatomical wings
78 Mer material
79 Another part of E.E.C.
80 Eye, in Oaxaca
82 Author of the quotation
87 Sugary suffix
88 Slip up
90 Songstress Sumac
91 Antlered animals
92 Winner over T.E.D.
93 Possess
95 Like a good experiment
98 Garlic plant: Sp.
100 Mustard pod
104 Early Christian ascetic
105 Chin attachment?
106 Dawn goddess
108 Upshot
109 French coin of yore
110 Ligature
112 Asian capital
114 Contest qualifier
115 **Quotation: Part III**
121 Crossword seabird
122 Beauty's beau
123 Type of harp or mode
124 Calculator button
126 Cal. page
127 She, in Asti
129 "Love ___" (Bel Kaufman novel)
130 Zadoc or Vivaldi
132 Indian sesame
135 Olympian's weapon
137 Siamese coppers

139 ". . . who lived in ___ . . ."
141 Autumn in Avila
143 Tiny room
145 **End of the quotation**
150 Turncoat
151 Nerve cells
152 Roman magistrates
153 Uses a besom
154 Verdant sounding writer?
155 Lists

DOWN

1 Paper quantity
2 Directionless
3 "___ ear and out . . ."
4 Dolly ___ of "Hello Dolly"
5 Vingt et dix
6 Role in Haydn's "Creation"
7 Spooner's title: Abbr.
8 Charles II's Nell et al.
9 Univ. mil. group
10 Booze, basically
11 You, in Quebec
12 Sothern or Jillian
13 Utah's state flower
14 ". . . Julia ___ did give it me . . .": Shak.
15 Maternally related
16 Haida totem pole
17 "___ World my Masters": Middleton
18 Leave the Yankee Clipper
19 Oblique
21 Align
23 "Cheers" props
25 Tangle

30 Athirst
34 Pollen holder
35 London locale
37 Funnyman Foxx: 1922–92
38 Applied unguents
40 Statesman Robert and patriot Thomas
42 Foot, familiarly
43 Dartmoor height
44 Creator of Phil the fiddler
46 Count calories
47 Fuel source
48 City near Haifa
49 With 64 Down, source of quotation
51 Plod
52 Hot under the collar
53 ___ of (exhausted one's supply)
59 Protangonist
62 Pope products
64 See 49 Down
65 Saga
66 Descartes or Coty
68 Soul; life
70 Kind of scout
71 Taco dip
72 Entices
75 Adjective for Humpty Dumpty
77 ___ Sabha, Indian lower house
80 Fairy-tale villain
81 Average guys?
83 Aristotle's institution
84 Bugle call
85 Sure winner: Hyph.
86 Black ___ of Calcutta

89 Armadas
94 One about to blow out birthday candles
96 Provoke
97 "It ___ hard a knot for me to untie": Shak.
99 Artist Arp
101 The eyes have them
102 ___ Bator, city in Mongolia
103 Major ending
107 Part of a Darwin title
111 Emulate Robert Giroux
112 Laze in the rays
113 Perry's penner
115 Demur
116 Frogs, at times
117 A 9th cen. English expanse
118 Post-Lent feasts
119 Cathedra
120 Saint-Saëns' "Danse ___"
125 In disagreement
128 A.K.A. Shropshire
130 Call up
131 Korean soldiers
132 Transparent linen
133 ___-sanctum
134 Rich soil
136 Sculptor Nadelman
138 Palinode
140 Before long
142 Ridicule
144 Salt Lake City athlete
146 Celtic Neptune
147 Owing
148 Shell propeller
149 Sky cat

218 PUNNY MOVIES by Ronald Hirschfeld
Wordplay is what's playing at Ronald's theater-in-the-square.

ACROSS

1 Inside shoe
4 Platform
8 Quartz component: Comb. form
13 "___ Farm" (Orwell satire)
19 History muse
20 Asphyxia
22 Actress Massey
23 Spirit
24 Did farm jobs in a 1972 film?
27 Black Sea port
28 Horses
29 Virginia willows
30 Venture
32 Romaine lettuce
33 ___ the boards (acted)
34 Conflicts in Greek drama
35 Orbital point
38 Frosh, next year
39 Nixon's downfall in a 1968 film?
42 Statutes
43 Vivaldi subjects
46 Image: Comb. form
47 Muse of poetry
49 "Little ___," Poitier film
50 Tine
53 Discord
57 Auberges
58 Pitchman's confederate in a 1983 film?
61 French revolutionary (1759–1794)
62 Penultimate Greek letter
63 Seed covering
64 Suited to ___
65 Health-care provider: Abbr.
66 Dragon slayer
70 Counting-out word
73 "Barry Lyndon" star
78 Vietnamese city
79 Aridity
81 Nut tree
82 Rib steak
85 Sill or earl follower
86 Disparage: Slang (Hyph.)
89 Afternoon social gathering
90 Kind of corner
92 Letters on an F-15
94 Scooby ___
95 Capers
99 Monarch of a patisserie in a 1966 film?
103 Russian ruler
104 Calms one's mind
106 Seeps
107 Neville and Douglas
109 Hopper or Gabler
110 Actor Flynn
112 Cotton fabric
113 Persian fairy
114 Couture comment in a 1959 film?
119 ___ vera
120 Snoops
121 Cries of disgust
122 Type type: Abbr.
125 Chart

126 Arnaz
128 French composer (1866–1925)
129 Weatherman's line
131 Timothy Hutton film
133 Inauspicious portrait time in a 1955 film?
138 Horn: Comb. form
139 Literary device
140 Nine: Sp.
141 Word of division
142 Gets the lead out
143 "___ Marner"
144 Peruse
145 Fuss

DOWN

1 American artist (1861–1933)
2 Broadcaster
3 Common garden flower
4 European crows
5 Gibbon
6 Moody color?
7 ___-the-pants
8 Pulitzer-winning admiral
9 UN org.
10 Moo
11 Serpent follower
12 Expert on woods
13 Omnia vincit ___
14 Knob
15 Wrath
16 Mother's bossy rafting to New York in a 1984 film?
17 Journalist brothers
18 Rover's rein

19 Book pts.
21 In re
25 Stock-trading term
26 Stylish
31 Ninnies
34 Short response
35 From ___ Z
36 Sage of Bombay
37 Plunderers
38 Old Scratch
40 Med. course
41 Heart charts
42 Actress Turner
43 Tonsorial sounds
44 Once: Ger.
45 Coach Bobby attending "Aida" in a 1935 film?
48 Steiger or Carew
50 Dumas the elder
51 Stat for Brett
52 Gretzky, once
54 Weaver's reed
55 Michael Douglas film
56 Organic compound
59 Holy: Comb. form
60 Ohioan President
67 Hearing
68 Toddler's age
69 Mythical bird
71 Observing
72 Madrid-to-London dir.
74 Toward the stern
75 Composer Rorem
76 Component supplier: Abbr.
77 Sgt. or Cpl.
79 ___ quaver (1/32 note)
80 ___ Bearcat
82 Airport listings

83 Hawaiian goose
84 ___ to task
86 Estops
87 ___ fro
88 Like the fox-hunting set
91 82 Across, for one
93 So: Scot.
96 Rhone tributary
97 Muslim magistrate
98 Part of S.O.P.
100 Form of 68 Down
101 Social habit
102 FDR's mother
103 Inexpensive ristorante
105 Files
108 Fevered or chilled
111 Literary monogram
112 Interjections
113 Gravelly gold deposit
115 African antelopes
116 "___ apple a day and keep . . ."
117 Therefore: Lat.
118 "Maya ___" (TV show)
119 Clerical cape
123 "___ of angels coming after me . . ."
124 Milk: Comb. form
126 Palm product
127 Country Slaughter
128 Enunciates
129 On the rocks
130 Between pi and sigma
132 Kettle and Barker
134 Biblical lion
135 OSHA's overseer
136 Genetic helix
137 Gardner or Newton

219

GETTING THE POINT! by Colette McInerney

The editors suggest 14 Down as a good place to start. (Charlie Brown shares that answer with many a frustrated solver!)

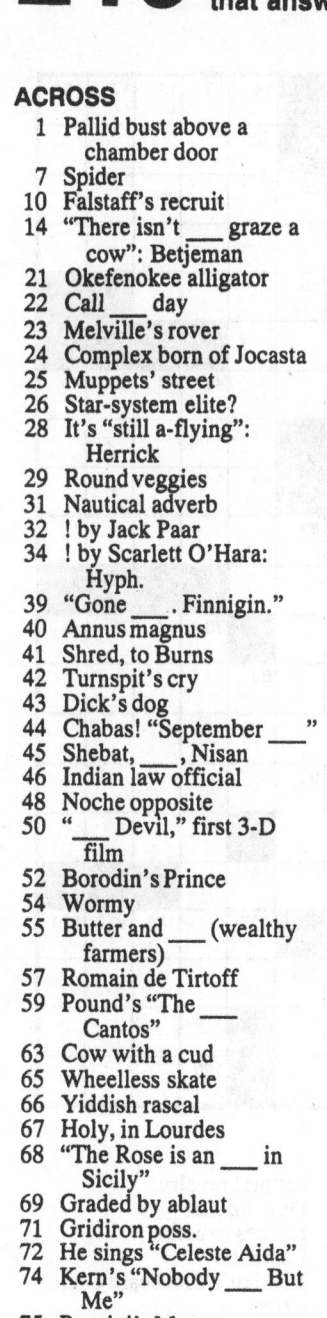

ACROSS

1 Pallid bust above a chamber door
7 Spider
10 Falstaff's recruit
14 "There isn't ___ graze a cow": Betjeman
21 Okefenokee alligator
22 Call ___ day
23 Melville's rover
24 Complex born of Jocasta
25 Muppets' street
26 Star-system elite?
28 It's "still a-flying": Herrick
29 Round veggies
31 Nautical adverb
32 ! by Jack Paar
34 ! by Scarlett O'Hara: Hyph.
39 "Gone ___. Finnigin."
40 Annus magnus
41 Shred, to Burns
42 Turnspit's cry
43 Dick's dog
44 Chabas! "September ___"
45 Shebat, ___, Nisan
46 Indian law official
48 Noche opposite
50 "___ Devil," first 3-D film
52 Borodin's Prince
54 Wormy
55 Butter and ___ (wealthy farmers)
57 Romain de Tirtoff
59 Pound's "The ___ Cantos"
63 Cow with a cud
65 Wheelless skate
66 Yiddish rascal
67 Holy, in Lourdes
68 "The Rose is an ___ in Sicily"
69 Graded by ablaut
71 Gridiron poss.
72 He sings "Celeste Aida"
74 Kern's "Nobody ___ But Me"
75 Puccini's Manon
79 Oxymoronic convertibles?
82 ! by Sandy
83 Canoe-trip treks
84 Comedians
85 Dabbler
87 Cavalier King Charles
89 Take away
90 Pugilistic pariah
92 "___ a cradled child"
96 Oct. 24
99 Loose habits?
100 Other, in Oviedo
101 Give a fillip
102 "___ This Time"
103 Ramp
104 ___ Caves of Maharashtra
106 "Casta Diva" is her song
107 Montreal's '67 show
109 "First Blood" hero
111 ___ vous plaît
112 Xanthippe or Kate
113 Sun. on Mon.
116 Small sizes?
118 Mountain sickness
120 Give a lift
122 Naumann's "___ och Alonzo"
123 Artist Imoko
124 Mexican Amerind
125 ! by the Lone Ranger
128 ! by Ben Bernie
131 Excuse me!
132 Ludwig or Jannings
133 Sardinas in scatola usually are
134 Dostoyevsky's Katerina
137 Emerge as an insect
141 TV attorney
142 Orch. section
143 Selene's sister
144 Approached
145 "It's only ___ in old . . ."
146 "I wol my-selven ___!": Chaucer
147 Tnpk. or hghwy.
148 Rendezvous

DOWN

1 Right of precedence
2 Shebeen quaff
3 Kg.'s 2.2
4 ! by Little Orphan Annie
5 Dangerous partner
6 Exclusive beau
7 Poe's pendulum site
8 "Squat like ___, close at . . .": Milton
9 City in S Florida
10 Pressured
11 Suffix for roller
12 Gless, after Cagney
13 Southern Albanian
14 ! by Charlie Brown
15 Reclining anew?
16 Extra charge: Hyph.
17 In ___ (originally placed)
18 Thorny
19 Her sons are served in a pie
20 Sweeney's "___ River"
27 ! by Road Runner
30 Chassé
33 Wattlebird
34 Carrier Dome mascot
35 "The Gulf Stream" and "The Herring Net"
36 ___ the mouth (rage)
37 Quips
38 Japanese outcast
44 Hitchcock film
45 A cabaletta is a short one
47 Artwork overlay
49 Brotherly love
51 Night lights
53 Roman Rhea
56 Namesakes of "Winterset" hero
58 ___ douloureux
60 Choke
61 Eristics do it
62 Nutcracker suites
64 Welcome mat for a casa
66 Shepard's lunar sport
70 Mariamne's husband
73 Jas., Matt., etc.
75 Chaney or McCallister
76 Harry Haller's wife
77 St. Cloud's county
78 ! by "Jabberwocky's" chortler
79 ___-scarum
80 Bellini's sleepwalker
81 Florid
82 Alder trees
83 Luxurious
85 Stands high
86 Peruvian Indian
87 Caterpillar hair
88 Honey buzzards
90 Pitching Preacher
91 ! by Brunnhilde
93 "See it Now" newsman
94 Capital of Eritrea
95 Saint Lawrence ___
97 Incite
98 Hiccup
99 ! by Annie Rooney
104 Suspension
105 Teeming
108 Make believe
110 DIII doubled
113 Cello virtuoso
114 Mrs. Tibbets and Gay
115 Plants, in poesy
117 Trench or half a trifle
119 Kin of "yours truly"
121 Insane person
124 Bee or jar
125 Well-versed president?
126 "___ Rappaport"
127 Kitchen tool
129 "J'accuse" author
130 Closes a placket
135 "You ___ Too Beautiful"
136 AMEX
138 Alternatives
139 Brother of Osiris
140 Norton and Mr.

220

BEES by Kevin Boyle

'Tis a honey of a puzzle for experts, but neophytes may be stung when they tackle it.

ACROSS

1 Swift steed
5 Longing, long ago
10 Exchange
14 Its capital is Patna
19 Centers
20 Stave off
21 Sacred prohibition
22 Pamplona pineapple
23 Tonsorial symbol
25 Football improvisation
27 Keep ___ on (mind)
28 Ancient script characters
30 Fixes anew
31 East German city
33 Help in a heist
35 Glow with ardor
36 Spanish simpleton
39 Cranium
41 Pickpocket
42 "Behold, ___ went forth . . . ": Matthew 13:3
44 Tides
45 Church dignitaries
50 On one's toes
52 River to the Hudson Bay
54 Redolence
55 Steak accompaniment
58 WW II area
59 Indonesian people
60 Old Irish garment
61 Minutia
62 Cheer
63 Certain buttons on bowling alleys
64 Censorious one
65 First in a series
67 Public brawl
71 TV fare not seen on PBS
72 Marseilles mamas
73 Some MIT grads
77 Ice irregularity
78 Hebrew priest
79 Hot-coal cavity
81 Rubbish
82 Clean up
84 Arsenopyrite variety
85 Examines officially
87 A.K.A.
90 Place for a little picture
91 Blake's "The Book of ___"
92 Second-rate film
94 Pianist Dame Myra ___
95 He foretold Israel's destruction
97 Apply a palliative
98 Becomes gelid
100 Closest to the heart
103 "To ___ a pail of water"
105 Ragout
109 Where many a man keeps his wallet
111 When Picasso was down
113 Botanical sheath
114 Rip
115 Jean de Brunhoff's elephant
116 Crosby, Stills and Nash, e.g.
117 Common archaeological find
118 Araceae family plant
119 Springe
120 Root

DOWN

1 Provençal poem
2 Tanned sheepskin
3 "God's Little ___," Caldwell novel
4 Neonatal preparation
5 Cold comment
6 Set 'em up again
7 Climactic
8 "Candles in the Rain" singer
9 Nat. habitat
10 Religious scholar's deg.
11 First U.S. poet laureate
12 " . . . every fool is not ___": Pope
13 Hawaiian necklace shell
14 Dinah's kitchen companion
15 Contribution of opinions, ideas, etc.
16 Old term for the throat
17 Med. school course
18 Skates
24 One of the Apodes
26 Guitarist Van Halen
29 The Tenth muse
32 In a sudden way
34 Ignoble
36 Salten book
37 Oriental, e.g.
38 Fragrant legume
40 Goes on and on
41 First Bond film
43 Eurofund International on the Stk. Exchange
45 Seasoning
46 First king of Phliasia
47 Big book
48 Let forth
49 Back talk
51 ___ del Rio, town NE of Seville
53 Rash one
56 Mexican dishes
57 Sloth
62 Language group
63 Makes more modest
64 Playboy's place
66 Emergency
67 Piedmont city
68 House plant
69 Brothers
70 Use a scouring pad
73 Littoral revelry
74 Director Lee
75 Rouses to action
76 Lets it be
78 Tolkien's Treebeard et al.
79 Creed
80 Italian one
83 Lights-out signal
86 World: Comb. form
88 Guatemalan crater lake
89 Female demon
92 Floating bridge pontoon
93 Take testimony again
95 Anchor, to a marin or matelot
96 Kind of gas burner
97 Serpentine glacial ridge
99 Adhibit
100 Renowned Nigerian traders
101 To, to Teutons
102 Eight: Comb. form
104 Recedes
106 Milanese money
107 Churn ceaselessly
108 Mumbo jumbo, e.g.
110 Grand Central is one: Abbr.
112 Prefix with determine

221 AMERICAN MOSAIC by Calista Luminati

Here's a fine collection of professionals from all over the world who have made good in the USA.

ACROSS

1 Birthplace of Francis I of France
7 Con game
11 Springsteen's country
14 Textile fiber from casein
19 Rally
20 ___ La Douce
21 ___ Cayes (Haitian seaport)
22 River in state of Para, Brazil
23 Hebetates
24 Corrals
25 "... ___ not hereafter ...": Shak.
26 Shawms
27 Clique
28 Van Gogh's loss
30 Toronto-born broadcaster
33 Collars
35 Arawakan Indian language
36 Siamese measure
37 Blister
39 Nigerian tribesman
41 Squabs
43 Tawdry
44 City on the Brazos
46 Early ascetic
47 Academy Award producer, of Greek parentage
49 Weapon that entangles a steer
51 Call back to work
55 Cardinal suffix
56 Word with Reverend
57 ___ up (became angry)
58 Squatter
59 Use up or pay out
61 Woodsy
63 Milk: Comb. form
64 Subjoin
67 Kind of dye
68 "Kitty Foyle" or "Julia"
69 Former measure of length
71 Berlin's "___ a Ragpicker
72 "... wealth and freedom ___ ...": Goldsmith
74 Faulkland Islands channel
76 Treasure container
78 Dido's love
80 "... unto us ___ is given": Isa. 9:6
81 Rocky mountains
82 Entranced
86 Chatelaine
87 Torn place
88 Actor in "The Cuban Thing"
90 "... What I ___ the papers": Will Rogers
92 A good hand
94 Two-syllable foot
95 Joey
98 "Faerie Queene" heroine
99 Tenzing Norkay et al.
101 Former French coins
102 Andean Empire rulers
104 Exacts compliance
106 He was once a member of Kirov Ballet
109 Owned
110 "Ain't ___ Sweet?": 1927 song
113 It's as good as a miss
114 Debt note
115 Sunflower-oil product
117 Looter's favorite lawbreaker
119 Nimble, in Nantes
120 Music deg.
121 Arm bone
122 Golden Rule group
123 Oppositionists
124 Straddler
125 Caesura
126 Snuggle

DOWN

1 Gharries
2 Wreath for Galahad's headgear
3 Style; taste: Fr.
4 Religieuse
5 Star symbol
6 Mexican-American champion of fruit and vegetable men
7 Taste
8 Inched
9 One with a memory lapse
10 "... like a drunken sailor on a ___ ...": Shak.
11 Smart
12 Tanglewood music man from the Orient
13 Says "I do"
14 "Like ___ of bricks"
15 Orchestra director from India
16 Town near Palisades Park, N.J.
17 Webfoot's home
18 Centaur killed by Hercules
29 Bro., e.g.
31 DDE's territory
32 Court stenographers
33 By birth, 12 Down and 15 Down
34 Politican known for his part in the purchase of Alaska
37 Dell
38 Lake, port or canal
40 Polish-American warbler
42 Tip and Eugene
43 ___ cracking (hurry)
45 "Have you ___ wool?"
46 Scholar, in Savoie
48 ___ paradox (math problem)
50 One of Fran's pals
52 Tingle
53 Network
54 A planetoid
60 Sure cure
61 Wise lawgiver
62 Gandhi follower
64 Yemeni, e.g.
65 Word with grass or fly
66 ___ DeLaurentis
68 Town south of Oslo
70 She starred in "Gigi"
73 Conductor whom Bela Bartok taught
75 Leading political figure, of Italian ancestry
76 Gross
77 Ruffs
79 Bridge-playing actor
81 Number before quattro
83 Provençal love song
84 Papal name
85 Heap, in Havre
89 Descendant of a supposed early American settler
91 Pedantic
93 Balloon's car
95 State in southwest India
96 Shrewdness
97 Adamite
98 Manipulate
100 Letters for a queen
103 "... mercy of ___ stream ...": Shak.
105 Bakers' equipment
107 Sediment
108 Groucho's "You Bet ___ Life"
110 Mauscript mark
111 Barb for flies
112 Gaelic
116 ___ Willie, comics character
118 Expressions of surprise

222

ENTERTAINING NUMBERS by Judith C. Dalton
We hope you can figure out our Little Rocker's ploy.

ACROSS

1 After-shave powder
5 Place for an epi
10 Infield protection, for short
14 Vishnu incarnation
18 Spicy stew
19 Brother of Moses
20 Bear, cap or region preceder
21 What diaskeuasts do
22 101
24 92
26 Folksinger John ___
27 ___-foot oil (leather dressing)
29 New Zealand native
30 Specks
31 Artist Andrea del ___
32 Stable attendant in India
33 Sphagnum, e.g.
34 Smell ___ (be suspicious)
35 Steinbeck's "Sweet ___"
39 Like an old chimney
40 7
43 Honest one
44 Beach birds
45 French head
46 German one
47 Starling's relative
48 Hindu dominion
49 1
53 Model or puzzle
54 Agitate
57 Wing: Comb. form
58 Tracking devices
59 Nostrils
60 Jury members
61 Co-Nobelist with Begin
62 Like McDonald's columns
64 Kind of code or rug
65 Embraced
68 Locations
69 5
73 Flock member
74 Beach toy
75 Rotisserie
76 Actor Andrews
77 Rudder support
78 Statesman Hirobumi
79 13
83 Mixes
84 Bergen et al.
86 Mediterranean gulf
87 Ballpoints
88 Newts
89 ___ Rica
90 Trolley sound
92 All, musically
94 "Iliad" author
95 Office worker in Nice
96 3 (with "The")
98 12
103 Woes
104 Gave thumbs down
105 Increase
106 Bed of roses
107 Flog
108 Rigel is one
109 Simon of the Met
110 Dragon predecessor

DOWN

1 Wool weight
2 A neighbor of Fla.
3 Diamond girl
4 Mixtures
5 French composer of "Socrate"
6 Aches' companions
7 Dies ___
8 Cuban rum
9 Tangle
10 Lone Ranger's partner
11 Hts.
12 Stadium yell
13 High values
14 Tills again
15 Hebrew month
16 Coat or skirt style
17 Supped
20 Plate, in Palermo
23 Craftsy's partner
25 Sacred in Sainte Chapelle
28 Long time periods
30 2
31 Dried orchid tubers
32 Glistened
33 Aesopian ending
35 Shipshape
36 55
37 Capp's Li'l
38 TV's "The Wonder ___"
39 Medieval laborer
40 Listens
41 Ending for abnormal or peculiar
42 Apprehensions
45 Corrupt New York boss
47 Lisa and namesakes
50 Mimicry
51 Precipitous
52 Turkish inn
53 Foot: Comb. form
55 Region in NC Africa
56 ___ bien
58 Mexican sauce
60 Vermicelli or ziti
61 Drama part
62 Jelly-like mould
63 Lasso
66 Water pitchers
67 B.A., M.A., Ph.D. etc.
69 Blunted swords
70 Goals
71 Minneapolis suburb
72 Tin
75 Forces exerted by reduced air pressure
77 Smelly smells
79 Geologic faults
80 Fated
81 Gaelic
82 City ESE of Pittsburgh
83 Activate
85 Loathe
89 What some politicians should run for
90 Actress Glenn
91 Addresses by profs
92 Hawthorne product
93 S Cal. sch.
94 Six: Comb. form
95 Small group of people
96 Lie
97 In shape
99 Trig fig.
100 Author Fleming
101 Post Brownies org., once
102 Like a zoot suiter

223 EGGHEAD SALAD by Gayle Dean

Here's an intellectual salmagundi whipped up by our Tarheel State representative.

ACROSS

1 Tangible tributes
11 Apollo's instrument
15 Drive back
20 Estrangement or derangement
21 Big name in tennis lore
22 Fearful flyer Jong
23 Admirer of the arts
24 **Start of the quotation**
26 Bus terminal: Abbr.
27 Clean with a cloth
28 Quaker of sorts
30 Home movies
31 Early ascetic
33 Sitzmark sitter
34 Eliot's "Adam ___"
35 Taxing gp?: Abbr.
36 Rock resembling flint
37 Early Sikh title
38 Pigeon or catjang
41 Sound from a vireo
44 Bond's Roger
45 Of equal authority
47 Bearish caresses
48 Takes to the sky
49 Ungracefully tall and thin
50 Throw a tantrum
51 In the past
52 Literary composition category
53 Having a sharp flavor
54 Paint-factory employee
55 Makes flawless
57 Item made by the Queen of Hearts
58 Frolic
59 **Quotation: Part II**
63 Darkroom transformation
66 Black
67 Insurance
71 Like a Corman film
72 Loose-fitting
74 Attractive retreat
75 Document transporter
76 Black and Red
77 Rainy-day reserve
78 Come to fruition
79 Bamako's land
80 **End of the quotation**
82 Gambler's choice
83 Editor's mark
84 Reno-to-Vegas dir.
85 Algonquian language
86 Acronym for the Great Lakes
87 Melting ___
88 "Moon-Calf" novelist Floyd
89 Diametrically opposite
90 Certain circus performers
93 Small area around another one
96 Writer's authentic works
97 Camper's umbrella
98 Dinosauria, now?
100 Author of the quotation
102 Ludicrous exaggeration
105 Musical group
106 Cracked
107 Lets off the hook rightly
108 Drivers on golf courses
109 Margaret Mitchell title word
110 Compromise agreement

DOWN

1 Bits
2 Upper-crust
3 Weaver of Raveloe
4 Palmer's peg
5 Schelde River city
6 Morning prayers
7 Parisian storehouse
8 Fonda film, "___ to Five"
9 Little one
10 Stealthy court-wear?
11 Headdress flap
12 Theater guide
13 Attenuated
14 Slippery one
15 Remainder
16 Weatherwear?
17 Pan's instrument
18 Lover of Narcissus
19 Minstrels' song
25 To an excessive degree
29 Father
32 Gawain and Hillary
33 Edward IV's Jane
34 Large and cumbersome
36 Rough
37 It gives a sound at the end of a round
38 Grand one
39 Beaverish?
40 On one's guard
41 Fellow
42 Gargantuan
43 Stravinsky
44 Moon's travel schedule
45 Division of a Pound poem
46 Pullman-strikebreaker Cleveland
48 Cults
49 J.R., for real
52 P.C. Wren's "Beau ___"
53 Cheesy
54 Come to the point
56 Complete
57 Shade
58 Samantha's group?
60 Power
61 ___ Trial, 1925
62 Bow and scrape
63 Pecuniary resources south of the border
64 Anthozoan polyp deposits
65 Beside oneself
68 At a distance
69 American novelist Zona
70 Theater sign
72 Lox adjunct
73 Throb
74 "Easy Rider" rider, e.g.
77 Beautician's tool
78 Wines and dines
79 Spouse
81 Wildcats
82 Khan's emissary
83 Hold a candle to
86 ___ de Balzac
87 Package
88 Fussed over
89 Heathen
90 Corrupt
91 Postman's course
92 Parthenope or Ligea, e.g.
93 Give one's word
94 Puerto ___
95 Outside: Comb. form
96 Stephen King's rabid St. Bernard
97 Foreign text translation
99 For fear that
101 Hobgoblin
103 Tool toted by "Babe"
104 Scottish topper

224 FIRST-NAME BASIS by Nancy Atkinson

Nancy is asking you to play the name game again, but this time she's added a new twist.

ACROSS

1 "My Fair Lady" set designer
7 Nabob
13 The Disciples' language
20 Continental clover
21 "...___, a hand for a hand...": Exodus
22 Eco's bistro
23 DON
26 Cuckoos
27 Home of Syracuse
28 "Barney Miller" actor
29 Moral endings
30 Valley
32 Zero
33 Leaf through
35 Opal's mo.
37 "Twenty-Ninth Street" director
38 Org. founded in 1882
40 Blanche in "The Golden Girls"
41 Namesakes of Jacob's wife
44 Panay people
45 Mil. unit
48 Gravel ridges
50 Bach composition
52 JAY
56 Sondheim subjects
57 Loonlike diver
58 Dabke dancer
59 Jai ___
61 NYC subway
62 D trailers
63 Afternoon socials
65 Inspector Fenwick's daughter
67 Mosaic members
69 LILIES
73 Had a right to
74 Pierre's eye
75 Jot
76 Unknown: Abbr.
77 Olive relative
78 Kind of do-well
80 "The Wanderer" singer
82 John Paul II's cape
84 Zoological mouth
86 PAT
91 ___ hand (reveal)
93 Awards from Eliz. II
94 Demand
95 ___ generis
96 Prefix for pede
97 Honshu shrine center
98 Tack on
100 Liquidate
102 Barcelona bruin
103 Successor to Ramses I
105 Racket chaser
107 Court def.
108 Blue dye
111 Elec. unit
112 Salutational bow
115 Prot. sect
117 LEE
122 Beards
123 Ointment
124 Holed up
125 Kind of liberty
126 Like some sheets
127 "June" painter

DOWN

1 Lower California
2 Stretch
3 BOB
4 Gaudy
5 Go-aheads
6 Modernists
7 Il Duce's followers
8 Corneille tragedy
9 Plug away
10 Former first family of France
11 Part of NATO
12 Roget editions
13 He's "2" or H's "1": Abbr.
14 Aries
15 Palindromic name
16 Turn over
17 Short comings
18 "What's ___ for me?"
19 Rotters
24 "Solar Barque" author
25 Actress Skye
31 From Oslo
34 Tarzan actor, and family
35 Wave on the Ebro
36 Costa Rican coin
37 Lass
39 Pipe of Berlin
42 MARK
43 Begin brunch
46 Vic Damone hit
47 Untried
49 "___ Druids of old...": Longfellow
50 High-ranking eccl.
51 "Toy Soldiers" star
53 Handel's instrument
54 Quebec peninsula
55 Ritard.
60 Chestnut clam
62 Flexible
64 Haifa coin
66 British psychiatrist
68 "A miss is as good as ___"
69 Spread
70 Lessees
71 Help a felon, with "and"
72 Expiate
79 Prophet follower
81 Bones
83 Bridge wood
85 Obelisk
87 ___ Arimathaea
88 Won over
89 Patronage
90 Jeff Davis, for one
92 Vowel sequence
97 Doctrines
99 Remove
101 Shorten the fishline
104 Cay
106 Scottish explorer
108 S constellation
109 Colorfully brilliant
110 "___ giddy as a puppet..."
111 Bat-eared fox
113 Rat chaser
114 Thrice DXVII
116 Pedro's thirsts
118 Corp. VIP
119 Prefix for plunk
120 Wallach or Lilly
121 SOS relative

SOUND SILLINESS by Joel D. Lafargue

Joel's unique humorous style is evident not only in the main entries but also in many of the smaller words.

ACROSS

1 Region: Abbr.
5 Mister from Mandalay
10 "The Sons of Katie ___": Wayne
15 Western temple made from marble?
18 Deuterium discoverer
19 Poet Hart ___
20 "Cabbage"
21 Heart of the matter?
22 Musical that went to the dogs?
25 Part of Welk's count-off
26 Sight ___ (without looking)
27 Had been
28 Sampled
30 Simba's sitting room
32 Hitchcockian
33 Gardener's garment
35 Performer whose name rings a bell?
39 Like O.R. tools
40 Races the motor
41 Actor Bruce ___
42 TV's Jethro Bodine
43 Character in "The Odd Couple"
46 Tramcar contents
47 Because
49 J. R.'s mom, and others
51 Step on it
52 WW II battle site
54 ___ Cristobal
56 ___ majesty
57 Simpleton
58 Cat burglars?
61 Something underfoot?
62 Yellow resin
65 River called Liger by the Romans
66 Underdog's victory
67 She wrote "A Girl Like I"
68 Officer who sings out orders?
74 Country club employee
75 Galway Bay islands
76 "___ Sylphides"
77 Off the books?
81 Item on a Christmas menu
82 Rich from Canada
84 Summons
85 Author Santha Rama ___
86 Preakness winner: 1942
88 Harold of comics
89 Third son of Jacob
90 No ifs, ands or ___
91 Click beetles
93 Feeling sheepish?
96 Herb, Kin and Wil
98 Maternity ward walk
99 Triplets
100 Wear
101 Holyfield's hitter
102 Main course
106 Opposed, in the Ozarks
107 Porky's laryngitis?
113 Big burgers?
114 Ready as a hocky player?
115 Ida Morgenstern's daughter
116 Advocate
117 Before, either way?
118 He wrote "Unsafe at Any Speed"
119 Appoints
120 Hardy heroine

DOWN

1 Famed Chinese poet
2 Innisfail
3 World Series champs: 1990
4 Singer Bobby, and family
5 Lovely to look at, as mountains
6 Abbr. at O'Hare
7 Chinese measure
8 Dick Loudon's establishment on TV
9 Caught in the middle?
10 Manicurist's board
11 Rob the actor
12 TV's Scooby ___
13 "Turn To Stone" rock gp.
14 Attic beam
15 Piccolo pandemonium?
16 Brand of fiber
17 Lawn interlopers
21 Founder of the Barcelona Orchestra
23 Faithful, in Glasgow
24 Schmidt's title?
29 Tuneful to 10 ears?
31 She was Emily Litella
32 Raison d' ___
33 Verdi opus
34 Closer to the truth
35 Former Padres' owner
36 Last of the Caesars
37 At any time
38 Indiana hoopster on the rise?
39 Actor Viscuso
42 City on the Ganges
44 Buy-way
45 Bowler's button
47 Insult
48 Leb. neighbor
50 Capital of Syria?
53 Burroughs' beasts
54 Sweet bread
55 Get high?
59 Loss leader?
60 ___ Borch, Dutch painter
61 Coastal cities: Abbr.
62 Starter for Socrates
63 Fabulous finish, perhaps
64 Hotelier's 21-gun salute?
66 Les Etats ___
68 Cycle go-before
69 Rodent catcher
70 Covers up?
71 Pear-shaped fruit
72 Avoid the draft, in a way
73 Without exception
75 "Captain" Lou of wrestling
78 Cy Young's middle name
79 "I could ___ horse!"
80 Housecleaner's concern
83 Guitarist Paul
84 Give in
87 They're out of this world
89 Speaker's stand
90 Use litmus paper
92 Connecting tissue
93 Grating sound
94 ARCO and Kemper
95 Type of cherry
96 Cliff Robertson's "Batman" role
97 Cartoonist Browne's Viking
98 Actress Laurie
101 Confront
103 Pierre's laugh
104 Trained employees?: Abbr.
105 Supplements (with "out")
108 "Away ___ manger . . ."
109 Imogene's co-star
110 Cry of discovery
111 Gypsy gentleman
112 Cyprinoid swimmer

ANSWERS

1

```
PACAS   HERO    SCOOTS
ARUBA   ADAR    TAUGHT
TOTER   SERA    ENTREE
OUTLAST ETA     SPEAR OSTE
ISLE  TED  ESP  OSTE
SEE   LONER    SEAS
   TEA  MET   ARTELS
GLARE  RETRACT  RAT
RAMA   SITUATE  PACE
IVA  CADENCE   PATEN
MAHOUT  RET   AAR
   URIS  DOLTS   SPA
DAFT  NAY  ROT  SPOT
EPODE  NEO  OUTCAST
GALOSH  AGES  AORTA
ARIOSO  SERE  OUTER
STORED  TERN  STARS
```

2

```
SALUTE  BOSS   ASKS
ADORES  OILS  SLEEP
SEVENSENSES  NACRE
SLEY  ANEW  NOTONE
YES  MATE  SIREN
   FIRSTPLACE  DDT
AFIRE  SLATE  ASOR
BRINES  ODOR  BINE
LAVES  OFTEN  SAGES
ORES  ARAT  DISHES
BAHT  CRIES  ODETS
STU  THIRDWORLD
   NARES  EASE  LST
ADDLES  FEET  DEAR
TAROT  FIFTHAVENUE
OVENS  ALTA  POLITE
MEDE  NESS  TWINES
```

3

```
BASRA   HIE    SAID
AMPULE  COMB  SPIRO
REEFER  ARAB  PERES
TRAFFICJAM  GREENE
SOKE  HUT  RIDDED
   DEMONIC  OTT
SST  ROW  ORBS  RAVE
PARTON  SHOES  AVIV
ADIOS  STONY  SPARE
SILL  FERRY  DESIGN
MELL  REIN  PER  LOT
   BRO  ABSORBS
WALRUS  LIE  AMOS
EGOIST  BOTTLENECK
BARDS  HOWE  SPENCE
BINGO  AXES  TISSUE
SNEE  TYR  START
```

4

```
BOISE  SCARAB  SMOG
ARMED  TELUGU  POLA
SOPWITHCAMEL  ANDI
ENE  THEIRS  LOCKET
SOLS  ONLY  SPLEENS
   MARIS  CHEERY
BOLOGNA  MOANS  SET
ALICES  MOLLS  THOR
SMOKE  NOPAL  PEISE
SONS  TINES  MARNIE
OSH  NITER  BALEENS
   ELEGIT  KURUS
STAINED  MORT  ASPS
HARPER  MASSES  ELI
ANTA  ELEPHANTSEAR
RYES  YELLER  AUDIE
DUDE  EIDERS  RESTS
```

5

```
NOTSO  ALEC  HARUM  GLIB
ETHEL  REDA  OHARA  EASE
STEPMOTHER  MAJORBOWES
TOM  STIR  LAMIA  CARRES
   YATES  ROGER  HUGE
ISSHE  THETAS  CRIMINAL
OCTADS  ACTI  THIN  ACLU
WOES  MYRTANDMARGE  EEC
AUR  HIEMO  SEALE  DUFFY
STIPULA  RATINE  MENE
SOUSING  LTS  THERICH
URIN  LIGHTS  ALLTHAT
MASON  PAREE  THREE  TRI
ART  GILDERSLEEVE  REVE
CURT  NAYS  TARA  SOONER
STARSKYS  COVERT  RUBYS
VIPS  ARRAS  RAPEE
STEPUP  FRIML  AUCH  RTF
WILLROGERS  LONERANGER
AGEE  TOTOE  ERNO  NIECE
BERT  STEWS  EBER  STRAD
```

6

```
APER  TWO  ACCE  ENTIAL
CURE  HIP  BRAE  ELECTRA
TRICORNS  LEEN  NERVIER
RECEION  EEN  ACC  SOG
EES  LAON  SORBET  UNLE
   BETWEEN  ABS  ANTAE
OCCUR  BLEEDNE  AMO
CROSSES  DIXON  PRE  COB
HEN  LEW  EPN  EON  GORE
SEC  EYERS  REASSEMENTS
   EAD  DEPREANTS  ALF
BRIGHTINHUE  TREED  EED
LOOT  ANS  DDE  OED  ORR
YEN  LOE  VEIDT  SOBERNE
   MOS  HARNEES  ESSAY
CRAMP  MAS  ATOMIST
HONE  BARTOK  DIDO  PAR
AMS  ATE  RNA  REMORSE
NEWPORT  ODEA  GRASPING
TREADER  DEER  COL  EMER
SORCERE  ARTE  DRE  CARE
```

7

```
RASP  AMILE  LAM  GAPES
ATTA  HERES  GAGA  IRANI
THELANDOFTHEFAT  FERAL
HELAS  INTHETIMEOFNICK
SLAVS  CHI  MATA  COASTS
   EAT  ASH  TELAR
STORMOFTHEEYE  ORD  BOO
WEBS  RLS  ABU  SUI  SEPT
ATL  AMO  AVERSE  NEWEST
BRIDGEUNDERTHEWATER
   AGUA  RUM  ADO  HESS
AMIMYKEEPERSBROTHER
LITANY  ENGEDI  BAS  ETE
AVES  GAS  ESE  ELM  ABIE
CYD  ARI  PROMISEOFLAND
   CISCO  ANT  NIT
APIECE  OLLA  FEI  LEMON
KINGOFTHEIDYLLS  EROSE
SNAGS  RECORDALLBREAKS
EGRET  ORAN  AMEAL  GNAT
LOIRS  YET  YESMY  OARS
```

8

```
MUDCAT  ALTAR  SCADS  DCIL
INARCH  LEONE  CAMEL  ROME
MILIEU  LAPAZ  ANITA  YUBA
ITIS  NBA  STORMINATEACUP
   TODAY  PONE  DOC  ASHES
ACT  RES  VILEST  HARD
RAINORSHINE  AREA  CLUMPS
DIME  SOUL  OWING  MYSORE
ORIENT  FLOWN  ERASE  TROP
RODDER  FACET  DOTH  TNT
   LOUSY  HAH  LEAF  FATE
SCIENCE  CONICAL  MAILLOT
WEND  KITH  NAG  BEIGE
ENT  ZOOM  ITALY  ROUTES
ETUI  VERSA  CORAL  ARREST
PRINCE  TENSE  BARN  ONTO
SETTLE  ANNO  SNOWEDUNDER
   HORN  ANCHOR  CST  SSE
ASSET  EMS  IRED  ATQUE
BLOWHOTANDCOLD  LOU  LAMP
BALI  STRAY  UTILE  AVENUE
ETON  LENIN  SENOR  RECTOR
SEND  ODILE  ERGOT  EXTENT
```

9

```
SIDE  TWIN  ROPED  EMILE
TOOT  RISE  ELENI  LASER
UNCHAINMY  PLACESINTHE
   ERAS  ELIS  ADOOR
SCARED  ALIE  OMEROS
ARG  ASIMPLE  SHIPS
GUAM  SOLED  EELS  CAMP
ESPY  ITTO  RHEO  OBOE
THEISSLOWTOLEARN  NATE
   SPEER  EMAND  ATTEN
TOPHATS  BRINE  TURRETS
ARIES  SORTA  AORTA
HASA  THEHASITSREASONS
OLAV  RAGE  ASIS  TRIP
EENY  ADAM  CASED  SITE
   SCALE  OFSTEEL  ORA
MARKET  JOIE  RADNER
CLAIR  SEPT  CASA
CRIMESOFTHE  TRUSTYOUR
RADAR  CLEAR  SATE  ALSO
YEARS  HORNS  EWER  TEED
```

10

```
ACES SNOW STR CST CUSP
MALT TEAR POE ETA INTER
ARIA ARRIVALS RAM NEATO
STARCROSSEDLOVERS EARED
JOSS TEE RIAL MSS
DESALT ASP TALI MAYFLY
ENTS USN ITS GROS EVA
EDAM DOGSTAR HOOT LIP
SARI DALTONISM TENAIL
MSN EVIAN PHAC RKO
CAPE DECRY LAYON SENSE
AGA SAL OED SIM AUS
DENIM NEAPS ETTES ELBE
GRO TRET CARAT VAT
LARRYS INAMORATA EBON
AGE NEAT REDSTAR NATO
DAD ILKA USA EXO IMAM
ALBANY RUMP ASS FINALS
ALG GNAT ORO TING
RANDS CATCHAFALLINGSTAR
CANIT AZO RETRACED TAME
ARENA TEL ORE CDII APES
ERER ORD WON ERNA RENT
```

11

```
POST FLOPS LEAP PASTA
ALLAH REFIT ULUA ETHIC
GALLIMAUFRY MOORS STEER
ETA EIS TARDE POTPOURRI
REPAVE HOTOIL ERIAS POM
OLINDA ENNA RACE ADE
WADES ANN ENCS CADS
ACR HODGEPODGE MINIPARK
STIR MAFTIR ENERO SIRIA
TODARE ISTLE TET STEAMS
ENAMELER TONSIL AMALGAM
PELES SUI SALES
VARIETY EXERTS DIATOMIC
ARECAS HAH ECOLE RERIDE
MANAT MANOF OPAQUE ASEA
PRIMEVAL SALMAGUNDI CAS
ERIC BARE SAD COELE
ADA TEMA RASP TOHELL
LES RADAR ASTIME ALALAS
ANTHOLOGY GEODE EWE ANA
MURAL INTRO ODDSANDENDS
ADORE NEON PLEAT GREES
NENES ETNA SEAMS ERAS
```

12

```
ORANG NAMES ELMO JEERAT
HOMER AMISH NOON ALLINA
MIAMIWHAMMY DOVERCLOVER
ROTH ROE MUSE OKINAWA
ALI INCS LURE FUSS
DALLASCHALICE CATO CASH
PILEUPS OTOS RIEN AGIO
OGRE FACTS BAS KARATE
SAW URBANABANANA LIL
PRISM RIAL ARIL ARABLE
ILLS PINT CHINA AXE RAG
RELEVANT GRAVY PRODDING
ENO ESE BOISE TEEN ESNE
SEWERS ARUM SORE SATYR
DBA RALEIGHFOLLY OSS
WATUSI RID DOOUT ERAL
ALEC CRAN ARTE CHURCHY
NENE MANY PEORIAEMPORIA
TOIT SPAN LUNA YEW
SEERESS BALM JAS NAPS
TACOMAAROMA DAYTONSATAN
OCTOPI ALOU ADMIT CLARE
PHONIC WOAD BEENE HELIO
```

13

```
SEA ASTAR LEAPT TAD
INCH RHONE HALLOW HUE
ANTU GENES ALEPPO ETA
MEONLYWITHTHINE S OF
ANGOLA BASIN TTS
RTES SPAS AROAR
PLAYAS CHAR LEW RIFLE
HIS S SLIT FATED STAD
IRIS LOVELIGHTINHER
LEG NEAT NAVES COAX
HBOMB ETHER MENSA
TEAM TROTS SERE SAG
OFTHEHURRICANE IAMA
STOW TONES ODOR ENROL
SIRES WED DREW SAYERS
OSSET CUES ATRO
ONA ASTOR SITUPS
ISR IONLYHAVE S FORYOU
DEE NOSALE AWFUL LID
OX ELEVEN HEURE SOLO
LYS DARER ORLES SSS
```

14

```
DAP ALBEN FARM ACMES
ESAU READE ODEA CHALK
WILLIAMTSHERMAN ARTIE
ARMYBRAT MTIDA DITTY
REASSAY MACONS MESHES
SET SUPER FEMME
HAGEN ALFREDMGRAY WIT
ALES ABIT EOAN JBAR
LOOS LUCIUSCLAY TORME
ERG UTE GERE SAHIBS
GRAMS ARGUE MOUND
IBEAMS CINE LOU JGA
TACNA JOECOLLINS PWBA
SAMT SOUR UVEA EARN
ALA OMARBRADLEY ARYAN
RAVEN ENOLS DIS
CASHEW CRANES PERHEAD
ABHOR CHARO COMEINTO
ROARS HENRYHHAPARNOLD
PULSE ARIA EURUS GLAD
ISLET TINY CREPT ASS
```

15

```
INYOU LADLED TORCH
FLUENT AREOLE OMELET
GOLIATH CRIMES REFIRE
ERN SOWETO SMILIN FOE
TEEST ESOWW ERIC ATIT
ASSAYS ASSIGNED BOONE
ETSI EDIE LOTS GARNER
LAME ADOS FACT
DESTINATION LOTHARIO
DAVIT ARENA VERSE END
ONINE RESETTING LEASE
NIA NUITS SADIE ORDER
CONSTRUE DISINTEREST
OIDS DONS MISC
BOFFOS DEMO REED TRAS
AGAIN REVOLVED SMOOTH
ADDA BONO DAGEA ARBOR
IOI LAYOUT RENNES ENE
NAMEIS TRIVIA EUCHRED
GDANSK EERIER CROATS
SNAPS DREADS DOTES
```

16

```
RUMBA DILATE ACHED
GENIAL ENAMOR BOONE
NEPHELOCOCCYGIA AOUTS
OLEANDER HESSES SPYRI
ALANS ELIS SEETHES
HELD ECON OCTAN NAT
SDS DZHUGASHVILI HTS
MARE PLUS IRAN
MAY IMA SAPOR ASSUMES
EMOTES SADE CELT GLUE
DIKES TCHOTCHKE PEALE
ISNT SHIA IDLE LERNER
CHARLEY RETRY CAR DRS
PAAR AIRE MORT
CPA HAMMARSKJOLD SAD
ART PAINS IONA DATE
ROASTER ASTA TALON
ANWAR SOLONS CATAPULT
MAPLE HUITZILOPOCHTLI
ETHOS RATING SPINES
LEANS STOOGE ESTES
```

17

```
STAIRS ALASKA
TERMITE ERASING
RAMPART LOBSTER
ORO LIONESS USE
LOIS PIECE CASE
LOREN LET SATED
MENAGE SECRET
ADA WAR
RATITE SENIOR
SAVOR NAP SORES
AMOR SCRIM NAME
LAC PLATTER TON
ADELIES EDITORS
MATINEE DIVERSE
INSTEP CEASED
```

18

```
DEBRIS VELLUM ALATED
ELAPSE ETHINE BOLIVIA
LESMISERABLES BUMBOAT
AVE TALOS LATKES ILLE
MACRAME SISAL HAVEA
ATOI ECLIPSE SPOILERS
REACT ORO LAE SSE
ESTER SWOOPS FERRO
ROTTENROW INSOMUCH
OAT OPART LALLA IDLY
PROMPT COHABIT OSTEAL
ECRU MANOR THANT TWA
CANTATAS DIRTYPOOL
EDUCE SCALAR SIDLE
AUG UNA REI SNEER
BLUELAWS TIERRAS GAPE
BUILT CARNE NORODOM
ELLA DAHLIA ISTLE ERI
SADIRON OFFENSIVEUNIT
STENOSE ELINOR ESSENE
ERECTS SEXERS DEERES
```

19

```
INPART AMIND TUBE ESTER
TOOTOO CANOE ONAN NEURO
SOULBROTHERS WILDERNESS
ARF ENTIRE CRETE MOISTY
PAVE FAERY CAUL
BAB BATE MANDY WHITELIE
ATLARGE LAITY SHALE IFA
COULEE BESTSELLERS PTER
KNEEL WRATH OILY ARTEL
TABS SHERI BLOCK CHILLY
OLE OCEANCRUISE AROME
RELAYS AIM SWAYED
RIELS BELLBOTTOMS ASS
MAYDAY BORED ROERS FRET
ASHEN ROOT SPIED MALAR
SOIR FOSTERCHILD RAVINE
ALL FLACH ALANS SONANCE
IDLERICH AMIDE TESO GET
LECH IRONY GARE
SHRIEK ICENI TARAWA DEF
WESTWARDHO CHAMPIONBULL
ORTEA VIOL AUREI OTELLO
TOUSY SORA LEAST DEALER
```

20

```
DICK TRACY ABAB AKIN
IOOI RADIAN CLIO LENE
MOONLANDING RALPHBYRD
GANGS GUSES LEISE
CPUSA STYES PESO
SHIN EZEL FINANCES
AMEN WARRENBEATTY RNA
MISS HIFI XRAY PIER
ATT SAMCATCHEM MAMMA
THEMOLE LILAC FOGEYS
RAWER LAB OAKES
ROGUES EDRIC FLATTOP
ABORD BREATHLESS OLE
JOUY BEES EGLI SPIN
ALL GRAVELGERTIE APOD
HIDEOUTS VIDI ALES
LUNA DOVES BABAR
MEADE HAVEN TOLER
PATPATTON ITCHYOLIVER
EYES TESS NOFACE EASE
NOSE ELEE NOTES SLED
```

21

```
REVEL MEEK CPAS CREEL
AMORE ANTI IOLA AERIE
EUROCLYDON TRAMONTANA
STABS GHATS UDI
SAC USE SPUDS TINKS
AMOURS BEIGE CRETAN
PARSE FUNNELCLOUD TAP
OTIS TINS AEON LARA
RIO WANDERLUSTS TIBET
LAIRDS IOTA BREATH
NITROS TRI PLINTH
BASSET JAIL ARIOSI
INFER BLESSEDNESS CRT
ANOA PROF ETES EWER
SIR BEAUFORTTEN AGILE
ECARTE NARES ANONES
SEPIA DEBAR ANT DES
PCL MINIM ETNAS
RADIOSONDE WESTERLIES
IDEAL RONS ASTA EAGRE
BOONE OPTS YSER SPORT
```

22

```
SWAB  SHAH  TAME  SCOLD
HANA  CHEMO ADIP  HOLEY
AXIL  HAREM RAMI  ARENA
WELLHISENERGYISFLAGON
DECOCTS SEES  CALL
LAKA  ATIT  FOGY  PLO
ROUX  GREG  UPI   FLEX
HESBEENONANOCEANCRUSE
UNA  DIETED MALL  HAGEN
MEGA  DXI   SIS   HEN
EWERGETTINGTHEPITCHER
CUR   LAT   LEN   OOLA
ASIAN SISI  SNEADS OVI
THANKSTOAFINECRUETDID
RAGE  HOW   ROOT  LOSS
IDO   MICA  HEWN  THEO
WORK  KIND  QUACKED
ONLYDECANTERBURYTALES
POOLE ADAM  INANE WIPE
TAPIR RIVA  FAKED ATOM
SHEEN STEN  TIER  YETI
```

23

```
HEMP  SALES LILAC TOY
AMIR  ABASH ARAMA TAME
DUBUQUESTA DECATURLEY
DUETS MOANS FIACRE
SMEARS OPINE MING
SPINS MONS  BIGTIMER
TEACH HOBOKENOSHA ALI
ONME  PAIR  AWET  ECOL
MDI OAKLANDOVER SLOPE
ASTARTE EELER ALINES
YEARS CILLA ALOOF
REVILE PELLA LITTLES
ADIOS DALLASVEGAS ULE
MILU  PARE  IDES  BEEN
ILL CARIBOULDER MENNO
SEEPAGES PLEA OSCAR
ARES  MENES SERIES
SCARAB SEROW SPREE
BRISTOLEDO ALCOALGOOD
LODE  YUMAS REARS ERNE
ICE   SMILE DANTE DREW
```

24

```
ACRAL  TAMPA HOMBRE
NOENDIN BALERS ADORES
TSARINA ELIDESDESPOTS
LIR IVIED EVER DIE
ENID ALLIED USED DERN
RESEED IMPEDESDESIRE
SENSE PERUSE CAV
USSR  LEIB  EROTICAL
NOD DUDE DOWSED DATE
PAPERERS EIO CELESTA
ATESTS CLASSED SASHES
TANDEMS ODD SIDEDISH
ELEE ONSALE WORE ENT
REDSMITH ASAR ASPS
SON ORIOLE CHICS
EVADESDESTINY ARGUES
EMEU SADI OILIER NEAT
LIN RISE ENATE TBA
ELUDESDESCENT SEAMIER
VISAGE SUCRES ESCAPER
EASTON TEENY HUSSY
```

25

```
BASS  SCARF ADES  HASP
ACTI  PANEL MILER ITTO
FLAGRANTLY MOSQUITOES
FURNACES THERE SNAPPY
CES   DRAT  STUN
ASSAY DIALER AIRDROP
SHUN INEXPERIENCE UNA
CUBS  NOLI  SUDS  TBAR
ALL DESTROYERS DEBIT
PAINFUL ATQUE PIPERS
MALES ATEUP FLEER
SHAKES CRORE LATENED
HATED PHENOMENON ERA
AVID  COOT  MARC  ACID
GEO CZECHOSLOVAK SKED
SANDRAT AVIATE SASSY
OARS  ETRE  ESE
OCTOPI AEREO EXPEDITE
PROMENADES COMPARISON
TOME  ATALE HUMOR CARD
SPAD  ASYE  ERASE EWES
```

26

```
LARD  RAGS  STAMP DANAS
AGIO  ENOLS ATONAL ARUBA
MOOR  GOOUT MARTHAGRIMES
ANTONIAFRASER ALIENABLE
SYSTEM TEL  ENTS
HOE BAILIE ORT TAOS
STAY NGAIOMARSH SHERPA
CARS PENNA SUSANKENNEY
ARMA OAR PEP CAISSONS
PRAYERS GRAD SERIES
EIDERS OUIJA MELD LIS
SEARS AMANDACROSS LUNAR
SSS SCOT EMEER LUCITE
BLUISH ESPY RECITED
REPLEATS AUS RUG LIES
ELLISPETERS OCEAN LANE
EBOATS EMMALATHEN ELSA
KAYO EON ANDRES ACK
PITH  NET   GRASSE
ABOLISHES DOROTHYGILMAN
JOSEPHINETEY NOISE LINT
ANSAE CREAKS SNEER ETTE
REARS SYNGE ERRS  NEAR
```

27

```
ALB   ATOM  ANNIES HAGAR
MOLL  SCORE TIENDA AMIDE
OLEO CHRISTOPHWILLIBALD
KABUKI AESOP RAT IRONED
SINEW LEM AURORAS TRY
SINO  DECN  DRONES
NIGHTCLUB SLAW BEATERS
ELLE EFFET ALIBLE LAPIN
REACT GOER UGLIER STOLA
VASTY ASTI DETENT EDER
ALSORAN SATES REARS ESE
ROUGE DRAIN SLEEP
MPS STALE ACCAD EXPENSE
ARCA MOLOCH CRUX ITEMS
MIAMI AGOUTI RASA AEGIS
BARON DENTIL EMEND RETE
AMPUTEE SOLO ADDITIVES
REVUES NEVI EVIL
RAS RASCALS IRT RORYS
ABASED HIE ENARE REINED
JULESEMILEFREDERIC CEBU
ASSET ANODES EAGLE HEAR
HEADS DORSET STOA  RNA
```

28

```
WIDE  EJECTS BOSC TASS
CHARS GALORE OLEO ALLA
PEANUT ARISEN OLAF COAT
ALT MEANS SNOWMANFROSTY
SLIMMED PETRIE EASTER
TOSEE DENOTE FRAMER
TRISTAN VESTA ABODE
SERBO ESCAPE TIS RORY
SERIOUS TENANT SCRAPER
AROSY WAY ARTHRO AUSSIE
GUST  FAN AMT REBIRTH
AME REINDEERRUDOLPH CHE
PHINEAS IAM EIS COOK
SCALES SHODDY USA SOMME
THREATS PIGOUT CRAMMED
IONA YEP TENNIS INMAY
ROOTS CARPS CLIMATE
HITTER BOLERO ANTON
ASSOON DEFINE LACTOSE
KINGWENCESLAS ABELL PIE
ELAL VOLE ONEFOR LAPPED
LORE ELAM OCTANE OUTER
ASES ROWS ROSTER TSAR
```

29

```
RAMS  PAINE ROVED MOAT
ALIT  APLUM ASIDE OLLA
HIREDWHELP WHEATINDEX
EIEIO ACHES RDA
BAWLERS STRIA BALDWIN
INRED JIHAD ACE INE
ONOR CRAZYWEIGHTS NHA
NUTS RIPE SOIE SNAP
DAE PICA HOPTOAD TELE
ILLWOMEN ATALL ERRED
EAMES ARTIE PROAS
SCALE ATTEN TEENWARE
CURD WASHERS ARES NEE
ARNO EROO ANIS MCDL
RAI OBTUSEWANGLE ATOI
ARN OFI CHINS BRULE
BIGAMOS THERE ALARMER
RPO MOITS ICOSI
WRIGHTHAND HIGHWHEELS
HERO EOSIN IDEAL RAMI
OPEN DECCA PATTY SUNS
```

30

```
APPOSE  IRT   SAGAN
LATHERED MATER ALONE
PORTRAITOFALADY MIDGE
AGT AREO RYAL TITLED
LIFTS LUCE MISERE ILE
LAUREL THECOCACOLAKID
LOSEL IDA ROC DEC
MADD GAEL NASA HBO
APO HEYBIGSPENDER TRI
DODDERER ETAT REICHEN
AGGER TORN CAPE DOEST
MEEKEST ETCH HARANGUE
EER THEFALLENIDOL OMN
BOA IDEE OLEG ABET
PAY RAF AMB DULCE
JEWELOFTHENILE EARTHA
ENE ANTHER LYND COWER
TASSOS RIGA CEST EAT
SNOUT THEKINGOFCOMEDY
ACMES HASAN TREASONS
MEESE ELY PERMED
```

31

```
SASS  STRAP DOFFS GRO
ALEC  POOLE INURE PROD
MARIAOUSPENSKAYA EERO
UMP COTE LOPED BANGER
REEARNS BERRY RANSOMS
AINGE FARGO SANDER
INTO KOUSSEVITZKY YBS
GEEZER ETRES ARRU
ADJ STALAGS CES AMAIN
REALTOR LITHE IRATE
SIKORSKY ERA TAMIROFF
TOGAE ABNER SPOOFED
DIVEY FLU STATORS FRA
LESS MEIRS GALOOT
ISM PETERUSTINOV OISE
IRIDES STALK DUMPS
CAROTID STONE SHERPAS
ORNATE DEARS ETAL ARA
BOOS VLADIMIRDUKELSKY
RAFT AUDEN EAGLE ISLE
ARF LIARS STEMS DEED
```

32

```
CARAFES SCALARE SAMOVAR
EVEREST HALIBUT IMAGINE
RADIATE ATELIER MOULTED
ARA TEREDOS DREAM DERMA
MICE RET AES TET RIOT
ICTUS SAMPANS PERES ONE
CESTUS LIONS CON STOLES
ENID SPA CAR ETES
ALAR MOTTO TASTERS AMOR
TAMP PRESCRIPTION AGAVE
TREE LID AUCTION ARENAS
EAR SEC STD ANN ACT ITE
SMITER NEEDING ADO SPIN
TICAL COMPENSATION PLOT
SEAL RIVIERA BAMBI LENS
EGAD MTS POC ETUI
COMSAT PAL DRUID ESCORT
OPO REMET GROTTOS NEVER
BALI DOR TRY OCA DELE
BLEND MCMIII SATRAPS REA
LISSOME EREMITE RATATAT
ENTERIN SEVILLE PREMISE
RESTART ADENOID STRIPED
```

33

```
CLAN  EMBER ATKA  ORES
LILA  MARLA TRINA HADA
OSAGEBRUSH LITTLEOMEN
ULM ALAN PAX OPALINE
DEBASE OMISSIONARY
VIM ALS ERICH GAP
LOANS CLOT AAAA RNA
MAMIE KHAN DANS ROADS
NIELSENORATING STOPIT
ORG SROS HOE ASHE
PSAT OBERLINWALL SOTO
BEGS EAN DEEP VOW
CRUSOE RACKANDOPINION
LACTO MERE SEEN PANTS
ARK DRAM STAR BEDES
YES DELOS ART URI
WESTWARDOHO SCRAPS
TEEHEES CEE BAKU FEE
OVOIDWHERE PROHIBITED
KENT SODAS LETON DOVE
ELSE PALE OBEYS ONER
```

34

```
MAB   CALI    BLTS    SAMP
ILL  ALLEN  SOIREE   TRUE
ADA  COSTALOAFING   ISLE
MANGANO  CANTER  REROLL
INCUSAPATHY   RELEARNS
     TEL  CIR    MATSU
ALA     GOV  ROPES  EPISC
CASHVALUE  TRUSS    INTO
INTUITS  PLEAT  ORANGES
DERMAT  AHAS  TREEHEATH
ENIGMAS     MESSIER
THIRDRAIL  CART  GATEAU
REFUSER  AMIDE  ENRINGS
AFFS   GENET  RATSNAKES
STYLI  LAXLY  SPA    ISR
     OTHER   TRE  ATE
SHUBERTS  WEARYPELVIS
ATONER  HONIED  APRIORI
MING  BUMMANDIBLES  TAX
ALOE  STAMPS  UDINE  ETE
HERR   ENOS    SLED   DER
```

35

```
HAST  CLEAN  UPONA   BAKU
AMAH  HONDO  NILES   ENOS
HAVEYOUNOTICEDTHATTHE
APODOSIS  COATS  TRIALS
UKES   PENNI    ORES
CRIME  TRAINS  REMEDY
PEOPLEWHOSAYMONEY  ELS
ANTS  VOILE  KOS   ATEE
SEA  HORNE  BEFIT  BRAVE
    SELS  SAGAN  PONIED
ISNTEVERYTHINGUSUALLY
OTOOLE  HEATS    METZ
WOOLS  WINGS  TABUS  DEB
ALDA  MAN  SIDED   FARE
NIL  HAVEQUITEALOTOFIT
DEMODE  UNRIGS    ESTES
    OLES  OPALS  PLAT
OSMOSE  ATIDE  PEACENIK
TWENTYONELETTERPHRASE
RISE  EDDIE  TURKS  EVEN
AMAD  SEATS  OBESE  DYES
```

36

```
CAPRIS  GALLUP    CAMEO
ROMAINE  ALIENS  CHIRPS
ETERNAL  ZINNIA  CORRAL
AERAGE  REATA  NOIR  ALI
CRIBS  JIB    ADS  ATTIC
TICO  TOFORMASQUA  RUNE
SEAL  FIL  OATHS  REAMER
    ALONE  BRIE  TELL
NASSAU  MUSE  AROMATIC
INC  PRUDISH  CRINOLINE
OTOS  FRONT  RHINE  AKIN
BOOMERANG  BEELINE  KOS
ENTICING  FINN   ELAINE
    THEO  NATO  SHELF
PISTON  BEDEW  POD  TBSP
ONCE  DLYCORNERSS  ERIE
STAND  YAK    SET  CRIST
SON  AMEN  PENCE  ALMOST
ENDIVE  DROVER  TREACLE
TEARIT  BOLERO  ANOTHER
   SLEDS  YELLOW  JOSHES
```

37

```
ASSURE  PLATA  FLEET  STAB
MAILED  OATER  LATER  LODE
ADDADORNMENTSORCLIPAWAY
TEEN  ISENT  ARCH   ITEMS
    RAN    UTAH  FILERS
BEFOULS  CESS    SARA
STUMBLEORSTEPGRACEFULLY
EASELS  RITA  FAILED  LIEU
TRE  ESTER  CRASS  STANK
AMIS  OMITS  CSA  THIRDS
LIL  STONE  TOPI    PRIM
BOYCOTTORGIVEAPPROVALTO
ALEE  ELAN  ROOTS    AID
TERROR  CPR  BERMS  STAD
AMISS  SLABS  DUCTS  DCV
LIDO  ITALIA  AREA  BRAIDS
CLINGFIRMLYORSPLITAPART
AFRO   PEAT   MUTANTS
SALLYS   ULES    ASS
SWEET  INAN  SPRIG  ESSE
WITHSTANDUSEORERODEAWAY
ANNA  ACRID  STOCK  ARRIVE
YEAR  REEDS  SOAKS  BANTER
```

38

```
SABRA  SAMS  CLAPP  ATMOST
PLAID  OGEE  HOSEA  PREVUE
ALLFOUROURCOUNTRY  TATERS
SALT  ONESTAR  OUST  WIRES
MHO  IVE  SCH    STIFLER
UNDERGODTHEPEOPLERULE
OER  ARAS  BAD    PARSNIP
SEPTA  ARIZ  MEN  CII  SEI
EQUALITYBEFORETHELAW
CURL  COSI  ACT  OAR  DOGES
EILEEN  ORC  IFI  SAKERS
MRT  FREEDOMANDUNITY  NUT
CRAIGS  MOM  SEA  NESTED
MYNAH  RON  PIE  BLUE  USIA
LIBERTYANDPROSPERITY
NOR  ICY  ARS  EINE  IBSEN
OPERATE  ARE  FREE   AGO
WEDAREDEFENDOURRIGHTS
ONESELF  TAR    SET   ABU
LASSO  SERA  SEMIPRO  SLAP
ORIOLE  NORTHTOTHEFUTURE
ALEMAN  ANNIE  ASIA  SETON
MORSEL  STEED  BALL  AMEND
```

39

```
PAWS  SERI  TEASHOP   DOM
SWITCHMEN  RANKINE   INA
INTOCOURTMARGARET   AAR
    HOLE  ORACLE  MUONIC
SEALS  BOOST  ASALTARS
MMCI  OFFSHOREDINAH
ACHE  ASS   ULES   SEODE
SEISMS  BANANAS   NOV
HEL  ATAPOSTEMILY  SYNE
DAR  MONET    SALOON
CAJUN  BEACHBALL  POURS
ETUDES   EERIE    IER
DOLE  UPCLOSEGLENN  HAS
ANI  CROONER   EGBERT
READE  ARAD  KIM   RANI
INSUMMERDONNA   ODIN
COUNTESS  AYRES  TWEET
HALTER  ACCEDE   GOND
ERN  BACKTOIRELANDJILL
MEA  BIRETTA  RESPOUTED
ODE  ESPANOL  SRAS  GHAT
```

40

```
NEEDLES  MANON  BRASSIE
OVERATE  AROMA  EASTERN
BASEMEN  TENET  AVIATED
    AIS  PROCRUSTEAN
LLAMA  BOOLE  REED  DREI
AIRY  PINNA  BARN  POETS
MAT  MELDS  HALF  TAUGHT
INITIALS  PUSS  MISTRAL
NASALLY  RASH  MALT  ENE
ASTRA  GNASH  BALE  UTES
    INBOOTS  RETIRES
RAKE  LATE  SOLAN  SHARP
EGO  MUTE  KNOT  GENERAL
PASTORS  CUED  LEVERAGE
ATHROB  ZONE  GARES  BOA
SHEAR  RING  ARMEN  PLUS
TARN  TENT  KNEED  CRETE
    SLUICEGATES  URO
FLAMING  SIMON  PROSPER
REGIMEN  TRINE  ASPIRIN
ORATORS  SLAYS  CASTORS
```

41

```
DANG  ALOHA  HASNT  RECU
OLIO  TOPIC  OCHER  EVAS
SILVERRUSH  WHITECHIPS
    ELIAS  EMDEN  BOILER
SCRAPS  ASIES   ILED
CONN   NORD   TRIDENTS
SOLED  PENNYODEONS  IRE
TROD  LIEU  RANG   SCIA
OER  DIMEMASTERS  BAKER
PRORATA  SPRAY  SEVERS
    FIRES  SPEED  PAROL
LUSTER  SCENT  OUTRAGE
ARCED  ACENTSWORTH  DOM
PARS  SPAN  RACE   LORI
UNI  COPPERSMITH  BIZET
POPSICLE  AMAT   EBEN
    ILIE  OVENS  HAVENS
PATRIA  FLEET   CAMEL
EMERALDLIL  LEADBLONDE
LURE  LEAVE  ERROL  URAL
ERIE  YAWED  DEANE  SANK
```

42

```
ACIS  ERUPT  SILAS  EDDA
PACA  NEVER  ERICH  LEAR
IRENESPAPA  LARRYSPARK
    PHILSSILVER  SPADES
CLERGY   TOA    STAS
MELDEN  THONG  THEWORKS
ADORN  GEORGESBURN  ONO
CRYO  PIPY  OILS   IBAR
AID  MARIASCALLA  BREVE
WCSFIELD  TAMIL  FLARES
    BOLAS  LURID  BRANT
WARREN  LARES  CLARISSA
ADITS  TAMMYSGRIME  GES
LADY  DOME  LONE   SRAS
EGG  HOWARDSHAWK  ANAME
SEEPAGES  ILEDE  TREVES
    HIER  SOL   BALEEN
ANGORA  ETHELSWATER
JOANSRIVER  DIANASSAND
ADZE  EVITA  OTTER  ANYA
READ  DELEG  GUTSY  TAXI
```

43

```
OBEYS  DECAL    SALMI
PAPAW  DEMOTE  ATLEAST
PRIMITIVEMAN  BEACLOWN
ORC  MATINAL  ALERT  LEA
SEUL  ITSDELOVELY  SANG
ETRE  IES  POSY   WITTY
STET  TED  THANT  PALEY
    STES  LEER   SINK
SIBYL  IHATEMEN   SORA
LONER  SABER  GENU  THIN
ARAB  YOURETHETOP  OAST
MENU  ANNA  WESER  SCREE
BRED  LETSDOIT   LAKER
    DAIS  ERRS  MAXI
STILE  MAIMS  RAG  NOTE
SPREE  PASS   AAR  GLEN
POIS  NIGHTANDDAY  SERT
CIO  DONNE  MENACES  ARR
ALLOFYOU  PANAMAHATTIE
TERCELS  ARETES  ARENA
TASSE  CASES   RESET
```

44

```
ASPCA  OISE  AMISS   PSI
APPIAN  MOLL  DONAT  ELD
CLIPPEDANAI  REDALE  TAL
RAKE  SYNAPSE  NEPTUNE
ACETATE  SHAVEDPOINTS
BETTE  SSS  ALET  NEILS
HERS  TAR  AUTO   RAYE
ACE  SPEAREDALINER
CAPO  UNRAVEL  TREACLE
CRUS  RIEL  VASA  DRAIN
ULNAE  DREWAWALK  OILED
SOCKO  SEAL  FILE   ELSE
ETHANOL  SURFMEN  SETA
SHOTTHEBREEZE   DOR
MUST  SOUR  ION    OLLA
INCAS  BING  NTH  BASTA
CRASHEDABALL  ADAPTOR
MARSALA  MILITIA  URIM
ATI  SLUGGEDATURNSTILE
CEE  TINEA  EMIR  STAKED
SDR  ASTOR  SASK  ERNES
```

45

```
ABRA  COD  ETA  BAM  ATTA
REEL  ANE  NOD  ANU  LUAN
SEPT  STARCROSSED  ARCA
PEARLONIONSKINFLINTS
LIMO   ORA  ISTLE   IOS
HAL  SNAP  EDO    AGAPE
AVES  LOB  ORCA    TUB
LENTILBEANSTALKSPREY
OCTANE  TKO  DIE   OGAM
GOA  EOS  ALP    ALMA
MASTERWORKHORSERADISH
AMAH  AOR   EME    PAR
BOCA  LAM  NAG   WADDLE
ISLEOFCAPRICORNBREAD
INV  HAME  TAO    USNA
THANE  CHA  DISC   TAM
TIA  ERTES  OLA   AUER
SPINACHLEAVESHOMERUN
ATNO  ARISTOCRATS  OCAS
NOEL  SOT  OTT  RHO  STOA
APSO  TEE  MHO  KON  ESSO
```

46

```
VAS  TOFF  CAPET  POPSY
ICH  SHALE  OVULA  ORATE
AHA  PETER  MENIL  RIDES
NOW-ER  ANEMIC  MAKEUPS
DOMINICS  PONTIUS  LATE
ETAL  DIN  UNDO  NOD
OPAL  LADY  CORS  NAC
PILL  TIRES  TECS  RICES
UTAH  OMA  AMT  ROOMRENT
STRAP  ✓MATE  MORSECODE
MOA  AXOLOTL  EEL
ELIMINATE  FALLb  SEINE
DOMENICI  FIT  ITS  IBID
PRATT  ECHO  HENIE  NILE
TEL  AIRd  AGRA  TSAR
IST  VCRS  AER  ETCH
STOP@NOTHING  ISRAELIIS
HEIRESS  ORIGIN  AT☐ONE
TALIA  MINIM  ANGIE  WED
ALECS  ILONA  MEANS  ERG
RAREE  CORAL  BROS  RTE
```

47

```
ARMS  SNA  CDR  PHAGE
REAP  GEODE  PLIE  REMAN
OMNI  EAMON  WISP  AMINO
WISCONSINDIANPUDDINGS
TEAR  ANION  IATRO
ACLES  DECREE  ASTR
NEVADATE  MISSISSIPPIE
ADORER  PEAK  SNOODS
MECCAN  ERN  SASSED  TET
AMAH  ESTADO  NITRIC
SALEM  OHIORANGE  CAPET
RAINES  BRONTE  SULA
APT  SNORER  LYS  LETSON
REACTS  AGES  SCRAPS
TEXASPARAGUS  IDAHONEY
SLIP  ATONAL  ANISO
CIAOS  ALGAL  EAVE
WASHINGTONGUESANDWICH
AVOID  HANO  PINTA  OGLE
NEALE  AGIS  OSIER  KOAS
ERROR  NEA  MTS  ERTA
```

48

```
MESH  ADAR  SABA  ASTAB
OTTO  TAPE  IAMBS  STORE
THECITYOFANGELS  SAWER
OER  SIC  SUNG  STS  GNAT
RRS  ARA  REE  PHEW
EWER  CARRIAGES  IWO
BELL  EPA  SHEET  TAB
EVOKED  ARMS  LAND  OHIO
TAN  CITYBYTHEBAY  NOTE
EDE  LEON  ORA  STU
LES  ATEE  PES  NAPA  TAM
ORT  IAL  ALIT  PLO
SAME  THENAKEDCITY  III
OLEO  EIRE  STIR  TRITER
ADO  HARMS  PEP  DYNE
POL  GREATNESS  ALMA
DOTE  OTO  ROY  ARP
TITI  DIT  RUIN  TNT  VOA
ENOLA  THEMILEHIGHCITY
SEWED  COLAS  VOTE  ALOU
TENDS  HULL  AGED  TARP
```

49

```
CORP  GAS  ANA  RENO
ALAI  GUSH  MANY  OWEN
SIGN  ASTI  ANNO  WEAL
TOUCHSTONE  DOGBERRY
HOP  RENDITION
APU  LED  TUNA  WAROF
BUSHY  ETIOLATE  ODA
CLEO  ALICIA  ELASTIN
SIRTOBYBELCH  ARCING
ARISE  BONAR
DEFIED  THELORDBIGOT
UNARMED  ARAMIS  MORI
LTD  DESCRIBE  SPEED
LOSER  MAKO  LAP  SLY
RECOVERED  NEE
OLDGOBBO  STARVELING
LIRA  EBRO  ANTI  BOIL
GOAT  REED  PEEL  ONCE
ANTE  DDE  ESS  WAKE
```

50

```
OTHER  ALIAS  RIOT  AMEN
CHETS  FONDA  ELLA  MIRE
HEARTOFTHEMATTER  IDLE
ERTE  METE  ECRU  PADDED
RES  MACERS  TOTE  WIL
PENT  ING  TAMENESS
UMBER  STARTFIRES  OHO
POETICAL  FAIR  PROOFED
PIG  TUBA  UNBAR  SMUTS
ERIE  RONS  DINOS  ETH
RANT  BUTTOFAJOKE  DEBS
TUG  TERRI  ATIC  ORAL
SHIRT  DEANS  ALTO  ORA
SEESAWS  SCAM  GLOSSARY
EBB  FINISHLINE  CADES
ROENTGEN  ETA  SDAK
GEE  ECON  ESTHER  MIG
MOULDS  IDES  CION  SOSO
EVIL  ABSOLUTEBEGINNER
RANI  LEER  MINER  PADRE
ELEE  ENDS  POTTS  SPEED
```

51

```
ARLO  OLIO  AESOP  SCOPE
COUP  CARL  CACTI  ARMOR
EUGENEDELACROIX  XENON
STERILE  AGENTS  MOTILE
ATONE  ODES  BONES
SEPTET  GLUED  DAVY  CAD
PRIER  TROT  OISE  TIRE
RIND  THEFIRSTVIRTUEOF
ICE  KARST  EATEN  RINSE
TADPOLES  LAVER  FALTER
ERLE  BASER  COIL
OSPREY  MANOR  TUNNELER
SELMA  PAGAN  CURDS  ABE
APAINTINGISTOBEA  CUBE
KANT  ALLY  IRIS  MORES
ALE  CLOY  ASPEN  POMADE
TAROT  TRIO  GRASP
AVALON  WHIFFS  ATHLETE
FARGO  FEASTFORTHEEYES
ALIEN  DANTE  AUTO  TRAP
REARS  ALTAR  KEYS  EERY
```

52

```
DIEGO  MCCL  FATSO  PCS
OCCUR  ALAI  INACCURATE
LITIGATORS  SOCIALITES
DASHDOT  HAK  LANCET
BYGONES  LEAN  IRAN  APE
OEO  TINSELED  GLEE
LAVED  MINISTERS  KILN
THEGO  PLENIST  BOS
RAMPAL  PALOMINO
GANDER  APPELLATE  ONES
ONO  DOUBLEMEANING  FAT
LTRS  ASLOWBOAT  DEMOTE
DISPENSE  HESTER
OLD  ASUPPER  TAMPA
FIRM  STITCHERS  ONEAL
DONE  CAMELOTS  RNA
RRC  MARL  NATE  PLEASER
ELATED  LAO  ORLEANS
WINEMAKERS  SPELUNKERS
AFTERTASTE  EAST  IMPEL
ESS  ESTES  TNTS  SEAMY
```

53

```
BOYS  AMATI  GOIN  ALICE
ONOR  GOLAN  OCTO  GENRE
YOUAREOLDFATHER  ENTAL
ARN  ANDY  AGORA  LIGHTS
REGENCY  ANISE  TASTE
ENCY  ONCLE  YOUTHFUL
BIRTH  TWOYEAROLDS  LIA
ARTS  SEIL  OYES  PONY
BAH  TENDERFOOT  SAWTO
YEARLING  REAMS  AEGEAN
NOELS  AGNUS  SPEER
HOSTEL  GROIN  SHAMROCK
UPPER  YOUNGSTERS  FOI
SERS  BULL  HAUS  STBD
URI  PEPPERYOUNG  ATHOS
MANTRAPS  EARLS  PRIE
GOOSY  TAHOE  WILLIAM
ACTOUT  GODOT  LORE  RBI
CHILD  THEYOUNGMANSAID
CAMEL  HERO  NOTAT  AGES
APERY  DERR  DONNE  TEST
```

54

```
ALEC  MAST  TOGA  SLOE
COXAE  ABLE  ARAB  COMMA
ROUNDROBIN  NEVA  AGAIN
ENRAGE  END  GOOSEBERRY
BLAME  KEEL  TEL
RIPS  DREW  KILOS
BRA  TILL  ADIT  SCAMPS
EAGLESCOUT  SOS  ESNES
AVAIL  TRE  HENPARTIES
RETAIN  HENCE  GER
SERMON  NOR  WABASH
AIR  IDAHO  MORTON
OWLISHNESS  LAS  LEONE
SHUNT  EAT  DUCKBOARDS
SISTER  DARN  LANE  MAT
PHONE  BEET  RODS
IRS  VERY  BEAST
PIGEONHOLE  IAM  CHOICE
ADORN  ODOR  CHICKENPOX
LOGIC  DOVE  KOLA  BASLE
LONE  AMES  SOLD  RYES
```

55

```
LIBYA  CROP  KERR  GRIS
ARLOS  HOBO  IRAE  RENTS
DEADASADOORNAIL  INDIA
INCL  ENGELS  SNAKEOILS
NIKE  AGE  STREETOF  ALS
GCA  ALERT  ORDER  SNEE
NNW  SENSES  DINARS
PEDANTS  MAT  STARA
HAWK  RTS  PAMPER  MIES
ASHE  ARAE  RAREE  ALATE
REID  PAYTHEPIPER  STES
MUTTS  METED  METO  PSAT
PERU  PRELOG  DOA  ALME
URGES  WOE  PRECISE
EMOTER  SHNAPS  EEK
ROTH  ERICA  APRIL  EFG
RUT  PEERAGES  LAD  SAAR
ASAWETHEN  DEVICE  ABRI
NEWER  INTHENICKOFTIME
DRANK  TEEM  ALEE  DARES
SSTS  SSRS  TEST  ANDRE
```

56

```
BARBER  MODS  APR  REELS
ETERNE  OLID  BEE  ATRIA
SELECT  DIVIDEDHIGHWAY
ERIA  STEVE  ILIAN  EINE
ERECT  ORESSA  STERNER
MESHY  PARTINGSHOT
ORBIT  ECARTE  ADAMS
DEAFER  ELD  ERD  HERAT
ATIP  ORDO  BLEU  TALE
MACRAME  BREAKTHEHABIT
ORIEL  ELL  SONIC
ATOMICFISSION  ETCHING
HARI  PATE  CARR  ELEA
ERASE  POT  ROC  ADDLED
MODEL  EMILIE  TAPER
BANANASPLIT  BETEL
STALEST  SLEEVE  STERE
ORSE  SABLE  TEILE  INNS
CUTTINGCORNERS  CANOES
LEIGH  ODA  ANET  HEARSE
ERROR  NEF  EDDS  OSSETE
```

57

```
SALADS  RATATAT  DRINK
OMELET  EMANATE  HEARYE
WESAWALIONKILLHISPREY
STILTED  ALA  IMITATE
AUX  CERES  PSS
LETUPS  PLEAD  APE  LAB
AVER  WEAR  ANIL  EZRA
WEKNEWHEWOULDDEFEATIT
TRE  YEAR  RIDE  SPENT
OILWELL  EMILIA  STICKY
ESTELLA  LONGTON
TODAYS  ALTAIS  RANGERS
OVOLO  RISE  TERI  DOA
NOWTURNYOURCAMERAAWAY
GISH  AINT  OPEN  DIMS
DEY  DCX  ACTON  ALONSO
SIE  ACHED  ARA
SONATAS  TRA  AMOROUS
WHOWANTSTOSEEHIMEATIT
INVERT  PASTELS  ADHERE
MEADE  ARSENIO  SOUSED
```

58

```
WEPT VCRS COB TITANIC
ALEA OROS HSE ALAMODE
RESISTEDAREST REPINES
COLLATE AKITA ECCE
GALA SCHEEL BRIO
ORCAS NACHO LURE MYS
PERTH PRIVYLEGED POP
ELIE SERA EIGHT LODI
NIM SALEP ROBES MISER
STICKLES RIMED CATTLE
NOISE CATER CANEM
SPARTA SUDAN CORNMEAL
MELDS CURDS MALTA NRA
ANNA PERIL OSTE STEP
RTE MALFEESANT SHINS
TAG ILLS UDDER HASTE
LENO USABLE ELAL
SIMA PATTI LEONINE
ANGORAS TREBLEDDAMAGE
POETESS YEN ETEE APIN
TWEETER RED TORN RUST
```

59

```
FATAL SPECS ODES CRAM
ENNUI SACRA WISP HOWE
YOUNGFELLOW NOTEPAPER
ATTHE ACME RENEGADE
ITLL THIRD EDER
FREEDOM ELIOT SNIFFS
MIO NOGENTLEMAN NEAT
ALLS NONA ICES SERE
EELER SMALLCHILD LGE
STORES AERIE ELECTION
FIATS DONAT LEVIN
ARBOREAL MESAS TINGLE
BEI MALEPARENT ITBIG
ABLE METE YETI SLOG
TELL MISBEHAVING UNS
ELSIES NOONE ENCORES
TRIO SORBS GAUE
SPOILERS TORE NATTE
POSSESSED LATESTCRAZE
ALIT TOWN LITRE HOURS
TOSS ANNA SCONE ESTAS
```

60

```
CLAP BEE CRAPE COMMA
LOLA ARAD REPEL ODIUM
AWORDFORTHEHALFFLYTSE
SEN ETAS ODIST AILEEN
PRESSED LAIRS WIN
HER ARTE HOLSTERS
SOLAR STS EARL ORAL
ALOFTINTHEPUZZLEGLARE
RAFT VEES ERRED RASED
AFT GARP TRIAL DONEES
ARNO LODES LUIS
BARNES VIGIL GARN TOR
ABODE OILED OLIO MORO
SHORNOFVITALFUNCTIONS
ROSE UTES OFT ALLEY
ARTISTES MARE SSA
TIN PARER PETNAME
PRISON SARAN ALEE REE
RIDINGAWINGANDAPRAYER
ADELE MINEO EATS TATI
MEATS STERN EME ANSE
```

61

```
CHESS BETAS BOOTS
BEGAT ARETE LATHE
CRATE RIATA OTTER
OLYMPICMARATHON
RMS WRESTS
ASP ETHNO DOE JOG
CHILD OARS DOALL
TINE RACKETS DIDO
NBA ERR TIP IAM
ANAS ADEPTLY SLAB
BELTS SILE STAIR
MDL PAM NERVE IDA
DOMINO AER
CHINESECHECKERS
BOARS COHAN ELATE
BINGO UNLIT RAILS
ALDER ESELS SYNOD
```

62

```
CHIC THAT ECUA EVEN
PIRANA ROMA YONS ROLE
ADONDE ARAL EMIT RULE
WISCONSINSCAPITAL CAD
NOSE ALES RICE ACH
ASUNDER TRESS GASUP
JAR TOLD TRACT SOLANO
ABILITY PRAYER COFFEE
DEVICE URALS ITON EST
ELENA ANIMA SPARSE
SERE VICES CACHE LOSS
SHILLS MOLAR RIVAL
AMP ELSE SOMAT WATERY
FOETAL AMUSED GENERAL
AURORA RARER GRAD SHY
REFIT GERRY ANALIBI
OLE IDLE FRAT EZEK
PAR DUDLEYMOORECOMEDY
ORAL LEAN OCUL ABIDER
LATE NONE BASE TIRANA
AMES ANDS SLED SEEM
```

63

```
SLATE ESKAR CRISP DOM
HOMES NOIRE HINTS ABA
ALERT MONAD AGLET NER
DANMARINODOLPHINS FRI
STET AWAITED LOOS
MAJ ELIAS ASTER COUNT
ASOP SECTS SED PORT
ATHOS STRAFER VANESSA
MANIAC HAIRS BALANCED
ENTAD UNE REGAN HAD
PELT JANSTENERUD WARS
EDW BORES MIA EIDER
ENAMELED WANDA NEIGHS
LAYOVER SANJOSE GREEK
BLED POL ARENT DRAY
CORAL DELED NADER STE
ASOR PERUSES OLEO
PIN KENSTABLERRAIDERS
ORC ENVOI RILES GENOA
TIO ATENO ICAME NUTTY
ESS SARAN SENOR SMEES
```

64

```
CLIOS BOROS ALOP STARTS
HENNA OLENT TARE TENORE
ANSEL REESE HIDE ELYSEE
FOURSPEAKERRECORDPLAYER
ERR ARA STEIN EIS
SEEP OLA VETERAN ALMA
RIS CLONE RAIN SOON
ITLEDTOHISINCARCERATION
NOOSE REBEL ALLE ETERNE
LUGES ARIA SLAY SCORES
AGIN COD SILL EAL
WHATNFLNOSEGUARDSPLAYED
ARE PINS HIT MESO
ARMIES GINS BORI BANKS
UNEASY ERNE BADEN ANTAE
DISCHARGEDSTORECASHIERS
OSTE EGAL EGEST OTT
SEES PASTELS SOB ACTH
OAT ELECT PEG ORO
BROADWAYTHEATERDIRECTOR
REMAIN ANEW ANION SATON
AVERSE KURA NACRE TROPE
TERETE STAY ASKED ERNST
```

65

```
POLAR AMIS VETS STOMA
ADOBE RENT ALOE PANIC
CONSCIENCE CONTRIBUTE
TRET CAD NEAP AUGUSTA
ACES STATE ENOL
SOCIAL EMOTERS TACIT
ODONT VEERS TEE TONE
MIN ALINE INAPT EMMA
ENTOMBS MEMORIAL PAS
EROSE SENATE SALUTE
EMEU ENRAGES MENE
CAPONS DEICED ASPIC
ALL TANGENTS HOLSTER
NIAS PAEDO EBOLI IRA
ENTO SYR BELAY GLOAT
AGENT STELLAR CHANTS
GETA AVIAN CATT
FRESHEN LAPP SAL ESME
RESTRAINED SUPPLANTED
ATSEA LINE ERIE SCORE
YEARN SETS DENT HYPER
```

66

```
CRABBE OVERS MAUVES
HITLER STOOP ENRAGE
EMOTES GASPE INSULA
VIM TROT EERO APIT
ANI HOES DOST ESE
LICHT EDUCE DISSED
AROA CAMA SAN
STAPES SHREDS ROMAN
COM SATE SEDER NAMA
ELM SKINS RERIP GID
NEAP AMAPA RENTANCE
ERNIE STARTS EERIER
GAR SIGH ODRA
SUSDED NOELS OTTER
TNT SCOB TSIA OLA
ISEE ARES EARS TAV
TAGONPAPERS PLATTE
DETEST DAMNS EILEEN
SPORES SMITE STARRS
```

67

```
ALVUS RASHER RATTAN
AGLANCE ESTATE OVERDO
BLACKEYEDSUSAN SIMOOM
RANA NEREID PACED TRI
IRON ARNAZ SETTO ATEN
ESTER LENO ARF MERE
TIED SOAP SPARSE
PRIMROSES SKETCHY
LUCIE SCOT SHOAL AGO
EDES VOODOO EYRE DES
AGASSI DAYLILY OSCARS
DEG ARNI DINEIN OGEE
SSE AGONE IDAS PRINT
RIGGINS GRACENOTE
CRAVEN SEIS STAR
RAGA IRB TRAP SKIRL
ETIC AHABS LATCH TEAL
TAT ORONO MIRIAM ACNE
ATASTE QUEENANNESLACE
NATURE UNTIED TRAILER
STEROL ODENSE EWALD
```

68

```
ARCADE WRASSE BEAST
SHERMAN RUSKIN ACUTE
RUSSIANDRESSING AESIR
ARIETTA OAHU GET TRI
DENTI PATER ELATER
CUBANHEELS ORGANS
REGISTER SRO RAGLAN
ACES ALIEN OREM EIRE
THRASH SLIT SARI DACE
SOMME CHINESEJUNK NOR
AURAL TEE PANIC
SEN FRENCHTOAST OGRES
TASS TARE HULA SPLASH
AGHA IRAN LAURA OWSE
BLENDS CPI CONSOLED
SEPTET SIAMESECAT
HAMILL RAGAS AUDIE
ADE CIO AGES MERRILL
BURRO SWEDISHMEATBALL
RADIO PUREST REVEALS
ALSOP SPASMS STERNS
```

69

```
ASHE AMATOL FADED FAC
MOOT BARONE AHOLE OSA
IFEEDHIMREGULARLY RAP
SASSOON GAGS SYNE
IPREFERTHESLIMLOOK
ANSAE ORAE OISEAUX
NOANDMYNAMEISBETTY
TON EADS DIENO POL
ENC ANTAE BOERS WALLY
DETENTE LOUPE CANADA
ITWASYOURBIRTHDAY
ATONAL EMMET REISSUE
DINAR BLABS AHEMS UND
OPS SOLNA AANI IT
IMTHEIRWORSTCRITIC
SPOILER ENOS OSSET
IDUNNOASKMEANOTHER
NETS AIDS AIRIEST
SAT YOURBLOODPRESSURE
ETE ARRAU ULSTER ERAS
THE PROWL TOMASO NESS
```

70

```
SOWED SPIV AGHA SERE
REPINE PARE BOOR TRAY
ONEFORALLANDALLFORONE
MENES LAP DUBAI VIDOR
ASH ATSIXESANDSEVENS
NCO AMAH RET ACRI
CHURNER VASE MYO NBA
EASIER SAY DRU URGENT
LEB IVAN ASTRO HIE
BAGEL HOENIR LHASA
TWOFORTHEPRICEOFONE
IRANI ALOMAR BELEM
FED ROSIE TODD BUD
SWEDES CSA BIX TURNIP
SRI ILK SHOP DISEASE
SPEE CAD DAME BAP
MISTERFIVEBYFIVE ASP
ONEAL TRINI ITA BASTE
PUTSTWOANDTWOTOGETHER
ERAT CUTE AERO ELLERY
SNEE STES TEDS MAIDS
```

71

```
TARP MEARA FOPS ELAN
VENAE AFTER MORT SALA
CHICKENFEED SHEEPSKIN
RELIES EELER FLEEASA
SEEN SST NOT ALAN
GOATEED DOGBISCUIT
OBS BYU TIMELY ENTO
TRADE DUCKSOUP WISDOM
HENRY CHET OCRA ERE
EDDA ABLER AIMER
RABBITEARS GOOSEBUMPS
ASTAR ERMAS LION
MIG OLGA MSGR SENSE
ENGINE PONYTAIL PRESA
STEN SHOOIN ADE SED
HORSEOPERA COWLICK
ORSO EHS OAR OSLO
ACCLAIM SITAR TASTER
MULETRAIN TURKEYSHOOT
EBON IDEA ENTER TERNS
NATT SERB SEEDY AREA
```

72

```
INFER ATLI RAMA ABBES
SORRY BOAS EGAN RALLY
STAGECOACH WAGONTRAIN
URNS BUSY LATINO OCTO
EEK ISNT TYRE TANKED
JAN DEFENDS RIGGS
TRACT DISC WACO MOB
RAMRODS ETH DACE CITE
OLEO RAF SICILY BATOR
WES PAGO NOOK ASHEN
WATERINGTROUGHS
BABEL GOOP UNIT GUS
EXUDE BENGAL TIS KURT
TICS CARS ROD STRINGY
ASK ZANY TRIP ESSEX
BEARD SPIDERS ISL
STOMPS TEES OMAN INA
IRAE OATERS ADAR GNAR
DERRINGERS CHUCKWAGON
LEDGE RENO HOCK ELEMI
ESSES AMEN AYES EERIE
```

73

```
MISS BALM GIL DANAE
ASPIN ALOU MANE ARENT
CLARA ROCS ARTE PIANO
HERESTOTHEUNBORNHERO
SCUM SURDS IONS
AMA ABEL MIA INGE TIL
FEDERATES SLINGS COSI
ROAN ROLE AOK HUSS
WHOLLONEDAYWINTHECUP
LAY DER ANOSE HES
BESIDES NIP GRASSES
SAL NIECE EAT RAP
USINGANOVELCROSSWORD
RIDE PEN KENO RUES
GLEE SPENDS SEMANTICS
ESS TEES OAR SEVE NOT
FATE ARROW RIGS
WHICHRUNSACROSSANDUP
CAULK APSE HERE TEASE
ANGEL GOAD EAST EERIE
REESE ENE TKOS REAL
```

74

```
OLES SHOAT GAOL META
LODI CARLE AIDES ARAM
DOUGLASFIR FROSTGRAPE
SCHAPPE REFER ARISES
TRES WAVES OPIE
ETWEE TRIES ACLE EDO
SOARS MOONS AFTERGLOW
SETS MINT NOE RETE
ETE FORGETMENOT NAPES
NARRATES RESET PITH
PLACES MALTS IONIAS
ICES TOPEE INSTANCE
TALES HORSERADISH TED
STIR ATE PETE BENE
PRESSURES OPENS SLAIN
SOS ANTS SMART NARCS
ANIS STARS ANAS
SEESTO MOIRA ECARTES
INDIANPIPE BUSHCLOVER
ACID SENOR LATER FIRE
METE PERS EROSE FLAT
```

75

```
ABASH WASP BRAN FUELS
AERIE AREA ROTE ARRAS
HEARINGAID OUTOFSIGHT
REEL DICTA ITE
RASHERS SILAS NELSON
ACMES STEED RIEN MLA
FREEST TASTELESS EER
FOLD ABAS UNIT CLAW
ISL TOUCHSTONES MALTA
ASTERISK CONGE DANIEL
HEIST ARNIE SIREN
OMELET CRITO MASSAGES
SABER COMMONTOUCH SAT
MILD EHRE ELKO PAGE
OSO GOODTASTE STELLA
SOO BRUT HOARD ARTEL
ENDURE PINNA ARRESTS
NUT EASED PIET
FIRSTSIGHT HEARSABOUT
ADIEU DIAL ORLE NOISE
TEARS ASSE GRIS SOLED
```

76

```
HAUL OSAKA TAMIL MUSH
ERGO PELON ALENU AREA
BALBRIGGAN BLANKETING
ELYSIAN SULLEN EXISTS
ATOP LEES SWAN
RACINE LHASA SHAMEFUL
ASHOT SEERSUCKER ELSE
MIEN BABA REIMS AAR
ADE WATEREDSILK CONGO
SESTINAS VOWEL ROONEY
EATEN POWER MARNE
ASCOTS BLEND SIGNALED
VALSE MOUSSELINES ELI
IDO DEALT ACID STLO
LATE NYLONSOCKS RATED
ATHLETES ATREE SELENE
LAIR ADIT RUIN
DEPICT SPIROS MEERKAT
IRISHLINEN LAMBSWOOLS
CATO ENURE ADULT TOGA
ELAN DEBTS NEMEA SPAR
```

77

```
MIB ELLA RFB KAMPALA
AGE LOIN AREA AGOUTIS
ALA LUGE PEACEFULBULL
MOUSETHATSQUEAKED RAO
SOTO TRA RNA NSW
BEM KABOB LAB
THECAINESITIN OVALED
DOORCASE ONICE LATINA
CONTESSA REO SKITTLES
ANEW ULA TSE ITALYS
ESTEEMS ENSNARE
LANIER POT STG WAAC
LISTLESS FOP ADASHING
OSSIAN OSTIA ROMAINES
RENEGE THELASTMURMUR
SER INERT RIP
RIB EPI ABA EELY
INA SEDATEMANOFBORNEO
GUNGASILENCE ATOP TAU
ORGANAL STIR SERI ERR
RESIDUE EXO TREE RYE
```

78

```
ABATED ARRANT MEADS
ANATOLE COALER ECHOED
SKIRTSTHEISSUE DRAWEE
CALI ARUT HOT CLU NAT
AREA ALAW POE BABA
PAY NECKTIEPARTY ATOI
POST ESCAPEES STUN
RELENT EONS BAHTS
ODOR HALFSLEEVE OLE
GIN DETENTE IBMS HAD
ENG OTROS ANOAS ENE
RAJ NEIN MASCARA ENL
ONO PEAJACKETS ALIA
OCHER CURT HALSEY
PENN ESCALLOP RALE
ELSE SUITYOURSELF CIL
RIIS SED TEAL PAGE
ABL OED RNA EGAD ISLA
TAVERN BOACONSTRICTOR
ETERNE AMPERE EIDOLON
ERIES LEADED SPATES
```

79

```
EPH PLEASE GORED TOYS
TOE PALMER ERATO OLEO
ORR DHLAWRENCEDURRELL
TVA RIN MIA AITAPE
BREVE PDJAMESJOYCE
SAYER SAALE ERSE ALE
CYANIDE CUTLETS LOA
LUCE DOM ORLOP LILT
HALE STUB RIA ARECAS
ODE JOHNIRVINGSTONE
GONDOLA HIC HEADWAY
DYLANTHOMASMANN AGA
STRAIT ROD PANT SLOW
LOUD ETAPE FIT LICK
EUR SCISSOR CYPRESS
DRY SPEE PIANO SARAH
OHENRYMILLER EMPTY
SETTEE AET ION SEI
LEWWALLACESTEGNER RAT
ARIA EIGHT ADHERE CTN
TONY DIETS ROSTOV YET
```

80

```
FACT LOMA BESOM SHAM
ANOA ARISE EXTRA POLE
COLDSTREAM HEATHERTON
END CHIN OCEAN LAZED
NARES STOAT SAUTE
SPODE HELD DEMESNES
PARMA ERARD ANE WIT
ESTIMATED ITERANT ADO
ETO SHEE TRENT RALER
DYNASTY AZURE AIRDRY
CHILLON COLDBAY
SECTOR LOEWE REDOWAS
EROSE SAILA AREA ABO
ERL SPENDER STAMMERER
SOD LAO MATER ORMER
TRACTORS ABRE UNITY
SHADS ARARA LATEN
ASHER GUIDO KILO GRA
HOTSPRINGS WARMINSTER
EYOT KRAUT SCION POST
MANY SERRA ESSE ANTS
```

81

```
TACIT CLAMS SALSOLA
ARADA SAUNAS CARESSES
MONEYMARKETS AMORETTO
PEI UNPEGS URANO RIN
SHADE GUITARSTRING
PATEN RAP TAT SAC
ALERTE RETIA SAG SHAH
CARBONPAPERS LAB PRO
ENDO RACK PROBLEM
REP OGDEN AIM ROUTE
EARLYWOOD LIONTAMER
FREYA ANO DONNA ESS
INCENSE AFAR ERNE
NEO KEY FLYINGCARPET
ERLE TEG IBSEN STARRY
UDO ABN REA ATONE
KOMODODRAGON GALOP
URB DVINA ROOSES ORT
RAILLINE WOODENHORSES
DRAGONET INSERT DIANA
SENATES GOERS ADLER
```

82

```
WORSHI DEVRIES    PETER
EVENUP WRISTLET  ERASE
DECAMP AREACODE  UNITS
GRA SIERO  HIGHER  PEU
ILLS NGFROM  NEED  SEEM
NILES RESEAL  SEEDTIME
GESTURED  UFOS   SNEE
   SPAT  EVADES  SCRAPE
SCHISM CORRECTS  INGES
LAIN  BRUNEI  TEASDALES
ORT GOER SSS  ANTE  ALA
WOMENSLIB  HELLER  PREY
ELENA SEALANES  OILERS
RENOWN  SHORAN   ANNA
   SEEM  TODD  SIGNINGS
MERIDIAN SWOOPS  SNORT
ARES GROS  ORKAND  STAR
IMP SHINTO  ADELA   AME
LIEGE  ACOLDEYE  ODESSA
ENACT SOLDERER  NANOOK
DELTA  MAENADS  GHOURS
```

83

```
ANEMIC  ELGAR  CENTAUR
LAREDO DEARIE  INTERNE
THENEW¢URIONS  CARDIAC
   SEAPORT  AHEM    ACE
SLAP DVI DOLLARSAND¢S
LOVER ONE  NOTSO  DANES
ADORER GEL   OSS  MOPED
VIN¢VAN  KINK   OCALA
AESOP  PASO  ROE    RIM
HANG ENNA VERDE  SPODE
ADEEM ¢ERPIECES  ¢UPLE
JITSU RAPID  AS¢S  REEK
ITS NEI  SCAM   ¢IMES
   CIRCA ADAM  COALTAR
GOOFS RAS  DOG  GRAINY
FERMI HARSH  ELF  SNAKE
INNO¢SABROAD  ALP  ESAS
NEE TISA   RESCUED
ARTSIER INDE¢EXPOSURE
LATORRE GEARED  PLURAL
ELECTED NOSED   YEMENI
```

84

```
HOPE CLOT  AMMO    PLUT
BURAN REARM SOUR  RARE
SMARTCOOKIE HUMBLEPIE
CANTERS FRAIS   IONIAN
ENGINES BLIMPS  TRASHY
   SETE MEESE  EVERT
  REDHERRING IDEALLY
NEWS EDE  ALA   LAIE
ASH POLITICALPLUM  MAN
ESOTERIC COWLS  TAPERS
LULL LIMAS  IRID
GHETTO FINIS  SOLITUDE
RAH SPRINGCHICKEN  CON
ATOM  ORE   NOR   EKED
NEGATED  SOURGRAPES
  RISES  SPION  ANTE
CARIBS TEAPOT  REGALIA
ANOMIE INSET  HARMOST
TOPBANANA ROTTENAPPLE
ODEA CATT  SURAT FLEAS
NESS ERSE   SENT  TERM
```

85

```
GETS RAMIS  RABBI  SNOB
ACHE ELATE  IREAD  HERA
FORTAPACHE STAGECOACH
FLUTTERY THEIR  AORTA
   LOAM PHASE  SLOT
ASSENT CREST  SHIPSGO
SPARE THESHOOTIST  UNA
NODS TIRE   TERM  SNAP
EDD WAGONMASTER ALFIE
WELSHMEN ANTED  CLAIR
EMEER INGER   SLING
STEAD KNEEL  THANTHOU
CARAT CATTLEDRIVE  TUT
OMAR PARR   RARE  CENT
TOM REDTOMAHAWK FARCE
APPENDS ABOWL  DOUSER
LUNY FRILL   GELS
SOUSA FACED  NOBLELIE
HANGEMHIGH THEWAYWEST
ANDI EERIE  HEXES  ANON
TEEN SPEND  ENTRE  YANA
```

86

```
CARS SETTA  BASH  RECAP
OBOE ERROR  ABIE  ERASE
HOUNDPOUND TURNSBURNS
OUTTRADE MITTS  TIPPET
STERILE DORIS  CENTERS
ILS SERIN  CORDS
LAPEL SAVESGRAVES  BAH
ALAS TORO  ARES   PAGE
DEY TRAINSRAINS  RACER
DESPAIRS HARDY  MARKER
HIKES DIVUS   WANTS
SCALED SALEM  MINISTER
LAYER CHILLSMILLS  AVA
AGED CUES   ONLY  SCOT
YES HURRYMURRAY COKES
CORED AREAS   NEM
REFRIED BRINY  FOREMAN
ARREST TEASE  FLOATAGE
TREATSWEET WILESMILES
HOUSE INCH  ALYCE  MENT
ELDER TSHI  LEAKS  EATS
```

87

```
TIP RASPED  AFFAIR  IDA
ATE EMPIRE  PLAICE  SOB
LEE QUEENSCOUNSEL  LOB
CAROUSES CALKS  CINEMA
PIED MARLY   ARAB
LASERS INTO  RENAMES
IRENE STATE  MARAT  OLE
LEAS TEAM   TARIM  IBID
ANT NHPRIMARIES SLIDE
CAT OATS  AMID   TELLER
LOUISIANAPURCHASE
STERNS GOTO  ARUM  HST
EASES FLORIDAKEYS  OTO
NULL TRANS  BETA  TMAN
OPE SEEDY  BLASE  THERE
REWATER GEES   KIOSKS
MISE FORGE   HEEL
SLEIGH TERRE  BORDERED
LOX MICHIGANRUMMY  ONE
ANI ARCANE  DORMIE  DIN
MET STINTS  SCREED  EDE
```

88

```
NOTSO OWL   TUMS  BALER
ETHER DRAB  SLAT  ICONO
ARENA DATE  ANNA  GLOAT
PAYOLA THEBRAIDYBUNCH
ERLE HERR   CIAO   STS
EASYTO SCAT   SALAD
ATT NOG AGHA   TRIVIA
THELOANRANGER MADNESS
ONAIR AAR   BARE   TALE
POMMEL DOWSE ETA  LEA
BOBNEWHEARTSHOW
RUB JAR IEREI  ALARMS
ETAL PSAT  ANT   GREAT
VANESSA LETSMAKEADELE
SHEATH INON  LON   LEW
FAIRE STAB   STRAPS
MAO GREY  EKED   RARE
AWLINTHEFAMILY ESCORT
MALTA ASON  SLAB  CAPER
ARIAN SPOT  HEDY  ADLAI
SMELT HYDE   SSE  LEEDS
```

89

```
ANTIWAR RECAP  DECALS
SCALENE ALINE  AUTOMAT
HOWARDCORSAIR PRENOTE
ESS ROUE  MUSEE   QUIP
TENT ABA  MRSBURNS
GEISHA DIVULGE   SRI
ACTII COLOR AWL  IXION
THERESA ENGLISH GORBY
HOMEFIRES LIN  BOATMEN
DEMOB CAMEO  UNEASE
ARE ROBBERREDFORD  SEX
BODKIN SNOBS  ARABS
ADDUCES FOR  INGRAINED
SEARS PRONETO  AIRTAXI
HOSTS YUL  CONAN  DINAR
ROD IDAHOAN  NONAME
DISUNION BTL   GRIT
ICES LAGER  NEON   LCF
DARTSAT DANIELLESTEAL
OMELETS EDICT  ETHIOPE
SEDERE NEXUS  SYENITE
```

90

```
ATIP DEBAR  TREAT  TGIF
NODE ELITE  OILER  URGE
GREATBALLSOFFIRE NEON
STA RATS  IDOLS  NADERS
TESTATE ADELE  ADARN
ACE SNELL  GRIMACES
GREBE PEARLYGATES  HVE
YEAS WADI   EMIR  PEAU
RUR SATURNALIAS COEDS
OPTIMISM ALAS  MESSES
HOITY CLINT   HIREE
JOSTLE ODEA  SALADBAR
ANSAE GEMINITWINS APO
TEAS COLE   EIRE  SLOT
OUT CLEARNIGHTS GULCH
SPELLERS AROES   JAG
LOOMS DIRGE  VERITAS
JALAPA RELEE  LAST  HUT
ALIF THEBIGBANGTHEORY
DATE IONAN  INDUE  GRAM
EDER STAGG  CAGED  ONLY
```

91

```
ADZE CALPE  FACTS  BRUT
MOON ONEAL  ELIOT  AONE
AGNESMOORE DARRELLWAL
HEARTED CROCE  EASELS
VILE STORK   PTA
ROTARY AORTA  DILEMMAS
ABETS ADLAISTEVEN  OLE
MEDE EDDO   ENOS  BRAN
PAD JOANSUTHER  DEEMS
SHYSTERS OTOES  RETYPE
PLACE BLITE   SERTA
AGEIST SAUCE  SPIREMES
LONGS INGMARBERG  SAP
LUDO SNAG   RAIN  ETTA
ODE DUSTYSPRING SLEEK
FARNORTH LOANS  ETERNE
ARM SANDY   CRAP
ALUMNI GUNGA  ARCHAIC
VANESSARED MURRAYABRA
EVIL ELIDE  EGYPT  NOIL
CAVY DINER  SONIA  TUSK
```

92

```
IMPELS ARCADE   AMASS
MARVIN CLARETS  MARLEE
PLEASEDASPUNCH ARTOIS
SNARED THAR   MOONS
BEG DLI CRIEDWHOOPEE
MONET EATIT   SERES
ONCLOUDNINE  REPROS
TEESUP PESO  PASTRAMI
ETS GLIB  KAEL   OPEN
THANES TICKLEDPINK
PAINTEDTHETOWNRED
WALKEDONAIR  SEEDER
ALAE TIKE  STUS   RAM
GOINGSON ACTA  ESSENE
SENORA HIGHASAKITE
ERICA ONEOF   SENAT
JUMPEDFORJOY ARS  EVE
ARIAN INGE   ROTATE
PANNED DIDHANDSPRINGS
ELDEST OVERSEE  AINTNO
SYSTS ERASED  TAGSUP
```

93

```
DELIS AJUST  SCAM  AVON
ERICA SARAH  ALSO  LIMO
MINIMUMWAGE TOPDOLLAR
INDEBT SLAW  SEEN   ERA
RATIOS INVERSE
TSP ELF SAID   TUSKED
AIRFARE APRETTYPENNY
STORES SRI  EROO  ROTA
TUNES STAMPS  RESEWED
EPEE HAVEA  SMEES  SRS
DELIVERYCHARGES
MSS RENES  EARTO  TEST
INTONED BERETS  POLAR
FOOL ISTO   EWE  PAROLE
FOLDINGMONEY  BACKPAY
STEELE ATOM  GUT   ESS
LACTOSE RADISH
ECO ETAT  NOON  NAOMIS
BULKRATES DOWNPAYMENT
BRIE SORE  ENDER  SEATO
STOW ANSA  DAYTO  ORLOP
```

94

```
BALK   SERB   ETC   RATH
ALAR  FUGAL  AREO  SEGUE
HOPALONGCASSIDY  EDITS
TESTER  SEDUCE  ONEROUS
   ETAT  MISO  ATOMY
 FAR  GREENHORNET  DORA
SIC  EIN  GILAN  SERIN
PLUMP  PTA  DICKTRACY
ACTORS  ILI  MASHIE  TEA
THELONERANGER  INANER
  EXILE  COS  DEERE
 BESIDE  CAPTAINMARVEL
SRA  MECCAN  ARN  ATTILA
KITCARSON  ANE  ESSAY
ABOIL  PECAN  ELK  ITS
TENS  FLASHGORDON  ITE
  CREEL  IOTA  NEIN
INDOORS  STRAIT  ANNEOF
BOOKS  CAPTAINMIDNIGHT
ORRIS  OKAY  READS  NEIL
SAND  TAR  EDNA  GRAB
```

95

```
MIMI  ACERB  HOC  KIRI
AMEN  RICER  OYL  OMEN
IPAGLIACCI  BEACLOWN
MELEE  NETS  ORRY  GIA
SLY  GOO  TRE  ACCENT
   VIP  COOS  BLONDE
EMMETTKELLY  EEL
NOIR  ELY  SILL  ADOS
ABASE  LODO  SALA  INK
MIMES  PIERROT  NEDDA
ELI  TWIG  BEBE  TRAIT
LEAK  HENS  VAN  ACNE
  ICI  COURTJESTER
MILLET  CAVE  OLE
ODENSE  ARE  WEE  MOM
TET  AFAR  RHEA  NEIVA
LASTRADA  FELIXADLER
ETUI  CAT  EROSE  DERN
YEPS  EMS  DONTS  ARTE
```

96

```
ESTE  PSST  SAC  ROVE
DRAWALINE  PGA  IBEX
INTHEBEGINNING  GENT
MAAR  LAMP  UREY  HYDE
ASS  PASA  CREW  STEER
  OOZE  SESS  WOODEN
SALUTE  JUNE  CALF
ENATE  BAITS  HADFITS
REPIN  RUNE  DOC  TROW
AMENT  INGROUP  SHARE
PILL  MET  POMP  CEDED
EASEOFF  GIMPY  OBESE
  FLOS  REPS  COASTS
JESTER  RICH  WATT
ALEFS  PANE  EADS  IAN
RANI  LAIC  AXLE  DRNO
GIDE  ATTHEBITTEREND
ONEL  WIT  MILESTONE
NERD  SOS  PEER  APEX
```

97

```
SPIKE  AMASS  JUT  OFF
EATIN  CANOE  ANA  NIA
THUNDERBOLT  RIVETED
ASPERSE  IATA  TECH
  TUT  INCORP  RHEAS
SASIN  ERTE  RAINONMY
EXEC  BRASSTACKS  AIN
ATE  JINN  HIKE  SINO
MORSEL  BEGS  RILED
  TAKESDOWNAPEG
IBSEN  MLIX  LINZER
RENT  VEIN  IRON  IDA
ILA  PINPOINTED  STEN
SAPHEADS  NEBO  QUIRK
HYSON  SUBDUE  BUS
 BOAZ  POUT  TEAPOTS
STAPLES  SCREWDRIVER
PIC  TRA  SEATO  TRINI
YAK  YOW  ARLES  ZESTS
```

98

```
SOL  SPEAR  PCTS  AMAH
CROC  LADLE  OLIO  SMOTE
AERO  ALAMP  LILI  HONOR
MARRYMEMARRYME  GREEKS
DENIMS  IAMBS  LIBYA
 ENE  OSSIE  ELAM
ANTA  RACHELRACHEL  ORB
MARS  LAI  NRA  SNEE
INA  KILLKILLKILL  TENN
CAMBODIA  NOELS  OBEYED
 PERLE  RUDGE  STEAM
ROTATE  PAREE  TOTALOUT
ERRS  REUBENREUBEN  NRS
ERAT  AMA  STE  VEGA
LAM  TORATORATORA  EYER
 PARR  PETER  NAT
STRUT  SIHAN  BEVELS
STRESS  AMERICAAMERICA
ORANT  ETAL  GUSTO  AMOR
LIMAS  GIGI  HITON  NEON
DAPS  ONEA  TRINE  RTE
```

99

```
FARM  COPE  DAMP  TROPE
AGUA  ONERS  IBIS  RILEY
SUITEHEART  VANITYFARE
TENEMENT  IDEST  HOFFER
  RIND  PROSE  HAUL
CLINT  SHUNT  CONTESSA
LEDA  CHEOPSSTICKS  OWN
ENOL  EARN  ROKS  SLOG
ATL  CIAOLINE  SHERE
ROCKHILL  ANON  SANIBEL
 HAILE  AVERT  PLIER
SLANDER  MARM  PILTDOWN
MATTE  ALTAREGO  TRI
ENTS  SALT  ENOW  SHIN
LGE  COMMONSCENTS  PEST
TERRAPIN  ALADY  FIRTH
  ASHE  TSARS  FOAL
TAHITI  RECTI  FACILITY
REELESTATE  BERTHRATES
ORLE  TENON  EROSE  GERE
DODD  STINT  IGOR  EMIR
```

100

```
CLUBS  ACER  PAPA  PALIN
YALIE  RAKE  URIS  ADIME
DINGALINGS  RACKETEERS
SCANTEST  ELVIS  TOSSES
  OTOE  CRAIN  CHIT
PUPILS  MOVIE  MOOSEJAW
ANOSE  CATERWAULS  INE
RIPE  KANT  MME  RANGE
OTC  BANGALORES  LAGGED
LEONARDO  EDEN  FATALLY
 NOBELS  NEA  PICENE
RECLINE  STUD  SEALABLE
ARETES  BOOMERANGS  EON
GORED  HAL  OLDE  SLUR
EST  SONICBOOMS  FOLIO
DESPAIRS  RAIDS  DAMSEL
 ALTA  LOLLS  BILE
AGENDA  COWED  FILTRATE
MATTERHORN  RUMBLESEAT
ESTER  SPEE  URAL  RERAN
SHADS  TEND  MIME  STOLA
```

101

```
PINT  WCOY  LEG  LEAD
OGEE  ALIA  EDOM  ERDA
NORM  SUNN  AUTO  ARMS
DROPTHEKERCHIEF
 LYE  SON  ALB  BBL
STANDS  NEW  BALLO
FOOTE  RUNSDOWN  FAIN
URGES  ONO  WRITING
LEA  UTE  INARCH
 THEMAIDSTALE
ASWELL  NEO  EL
FLAMBEAU  CHE  MATRI
ATOI  ASUNCION  AROSE
LEONA  SDL  LEFTUED
ARP  FLA  EAR  LII
LEBARMOUSTACHES
ACES  ONE  ISTO  LALO
LULU  SERE  LEAN  ELSA
TEMP  ROD  SSTS  STEP
```

102

```
DAIS  TILT  ROB  AVOW
ULNA  ONER  HOPE  TOLE
NEWSMANVANOCUR  EDDA
ERASED  EDEN  SNEAKER
STREW  FREAKS  ELSA
 DEBI  STEEL  SECT
HAL  REND  DRAM  OAS
IDEA  EGANS  TIETACKS
DEALS  EMEND  DRINKER
 VIP  RETIREE  PIT
ELEGANT  STACY  STAIN
MAINTAIN  STREP  AIRY
SON  EPEE  USES  LEE
 SARA  SAVOR  OATS
HARP  RETURN  OCALA
SLUICES  RICE  PROPER
OARS  SNATCHAWAYFROM
INRE  TANS  EDIT  FINE
LAYS  SPY  SETS  SLED
```

103

```
RAMI  RATES  SCATS  ECHO
EDEN  EVICT  LOGIA  TZAR
NEAT  SEOULSEARCH  CERE
INTEGERS  PESO  ARECAS
 GREAT  SCOTT  TROTH
RAREST  SLOT  SEADEMON
ODIST  PIOUSACTS  ERASE
ISNT  ERSE  VERSE  ATLI
LOD  MANEH  LARIAT  EON
RETINAS  ASAP  HOO
 BRUTAL  PORTS  CANADA
 GEL  SLAG  BANEFUL
ORB  OBLATE  LOBES  TLO
PARC  GRATE  BALI  SCUM
AMAHS  AVONMAVEN  OCHRE
LAZINESS  ILES  DARTER
 IDEAS  APRES  AESIR
UGLIER  GNAT  CELTMELT
MANN  FRENCHTOAST  PAIR
PLUG  UNTIE  ALGOA  ETNA
SETS  LASER  TEENS  DSOS
```

104

```
HARSH  PROM  MIGHT  MIST
ABATE  RADA  OCREA  ANYA
BENJAMINDISRAELI  REBS
ATTU  ESSE  PARED  DORIS
 DELTAS  AVID  BOOTLE
QUEENVICTORIA  DARN
URD  SINK  STANDERS  CPA
AGES  LEESMEN  ELEANORS
DENTIL  RHO  MRSLEWIS
 RAE  ISEE  OAT  WEAN
STAEL  CONINGSBY  WARMS
AERA  FAD  SOAP  BAR
PRIMROSE  LUM  UNKIND
PROSIEST  VEINING  STOA
YET  THESAINT  NOBS  EON
 BUNS  MARYANNEEVANS
LIBRAS  PELO  PESADE
USUAL  DENIS  ISER  NAPA
GARN  LORDBEACONSFIELD
HARD  LOSEY  BATS  OCTAD
SCOT  BREDA  ALAE  BEATA
```

105

```
LISTS  SPACE  BABA  ELSE
ACHAT  ARBOR  ITOL  ROLF
VOODOODOLLS  FOOLPROOF
ENO  CREWEL  LIMB  LAPPS
 TYKES  ACID  OFANTS
TEHEES  CAPON  EOLITH
ALOAD  CARSON  ABED  ESE
AMOR  SHRIEK  AGED  ELLS
LOP  LAIRD  OPERA  FLOUT
 DUMPY  SNORER  ADORE
SCIONS  AVERY  STEPPE
PINZA  LAMEST  SNEER
ADDER  OWING  KEYED  BAH
NEON  POND  OPENED  ULNA
SRO  SASE  FOREST  CROON
 RETIED  ASONE  WAGONS
SPRINT  STET  DOLED
ATOOL  OSIS  OCTROI  ROE
GOODLOOKS  SCHOOLBOOKS
ORLE  ATES  FOURS  ENOLA
NESS  THEY  OLMOS  RITAS
```

106

```
RAMS  BACHS  AFTER  IRON
ASIA  ERROL  DRILL  SOLE
GASMILEAGE  MONKSCOWLS
SPOONING  EVENTS  ABEAT
     ASEA  SPENT  SPA
DAWNED  APIE   COHORTS
AVAST  SWEEPSTAKES  WEB
TET   OTHER  TRAIL  IRE
ARE  PLAID  SEINES  KNIT
    RETELL  PLAN  ANKAS
PASTA  LEEREMICK  GOLLY
REPOS   VOWS   REPUTE
ARON  PATENS  GENIE  TSE
TAU   ABORT  PRATT  OYL
OTT  CRYPTOGRAMS  EDENS
ESTATES  LOTS  FRESCA
    OPS  SLAVE  MOIL
ASONE  MIKADO  FORCEFUL
CHAGRINNED  SLAUGHTERS
TOFU  TOTED  TENTO  ETAT
IPSE  SPOTS  SIGHT  SALS
```

107

```
DAMA  LACS   MAW   ERMA
OMARS  ALOU  ALE  RUIN
TITLE  MINN  SPICIEST
ANSERSBACK  TERRA
LOUNGES  HERE  DORAL
   EEK  SNORT  OUSEL
KEEPADIT  DERANGING
LATIN  NUMB  DEMESNES
ESTATE  BARE  KID
ETES  STELAKISS  CPOS
    ITE  EVEL  SOREST
SPURNERS  ODIL  VILLE
MASONRIES  ALOEBLOW
UTICA  SCHWA  EUR
SACRA  RAES  ASSAILS
   ADIGE  ETONTHERUN
TRANSMIT  DUME  OSAGE
HIND  EVE  ETAS  TINEA
OBEY  DES  DENT  RISK
```

108

```
HIS GUN WAS AIMED
AT MY BACK. I SAW
IT REFLECTED IN A
BUBBLE FROM JUNIORS
PIPE. FAST ACTION
WAS NEEDED! AFTER
INHALING DEEPLY, I
BLEW HIM AWAY.
```

109

```
ARAB  OFME  PEACH  ETTU
CODE  TEAL  ENVOI  NERTS
RAINCHECK  EMIRS  TRAIT
ENTIRETY  BREAKSTHEICE
   GAR  BEAST  OUTLAW
BRINGSDOWNTHEHOUSE
LAS  STAG  ONCE  GNP
ORLON  TINA  SARAH  CREE
WEASEL  CALCULATEDRISK
NEMESES  HESSE  RINSE
    TAT  SEETO  AMA
AVAIL  OATER  REPORTS
SERVESONERIGHT  RETOOL
PITY  ADDTO  OARS  DONNE
SLY  PLUG  SLID  DIE
CHIPOFFTHEOLDBLOCK
AVALON  LIBER  IRE
FIXONESWAGON  RENOVATE
ARISE  PAVAN  MAKEWAVES
RULER  ADORE  AGER  NETS
SESS  NEROS  REDS  TREE
```

110

```
CLEF  BOCCI  RIMES  GLAD
HALO  ORION  ENACT  RICO
AVANTGARDE  PANTALOONS
PASTILLE  RALLY  MOINES
   ARES  STEAL  UPON
RATIOS  HAIRY  CRASSEST
IRONS  RENAISSANCE  NON
AGUE  GERE  LUST  SCUT
TOR  GUERRILLAS  FLAT
ANDROIDS  NIEVE  CRASH
   EARLY  SCENE  FLANS
OFFED  AMAIN  POINTERS
BOTS  DONNYBROOK  RET
HERS  KEET  LETS  BONO
MAC  DESPERADOES  KALES
SHEEREST  ELOIN  RAREES
   RAPE  BPLUS  NEBO
PALOMA  GULAG  COLONELS
PIEDATERRE  HARTEBEEST
SNEE  INEPT  TWEEN  SRTA
SURD  TASSE  YEAST  SYST
```

111

```
RACE  OMAR  OSCAN  ADO
RELAX  NONE  RIATA  RED
GALLUP  THISHAPPYBREED
ORIOLE  HASTA  PEP  YAMS
TACTIC  EVERS  ERICA
   STARE  ASST  CANNA
NOAH  ALI  IOO  PARSECS
ARLO  TAVERN  FILLEDOUT
GABBAI  ELI  ANI  ANTA
LASSO  RAVES  WEB  USER
    OMN  KNAVISH  LAG
DAMN  SAW  LANAI  ICHOR
AVES  RAE  ARC  TETHER
SARCASTIC  EIGHTH  EINE
HIGHWAY  HEL  WOE  ROTS
LEONS  DOLE  REESE
    ISSUE  IVIES  PLATAN
TALC  III  HEAVE  IMPALE
BRIEFENCOUNTER  RIPSAW
AGE  ASTER  TRAV  IRATE
ROD  START  HOLE  TALE
```

112

```
SALAD  MAE  CAPES  FLOPS
ELITE  OHM  OLIVA  RELEE
RAREE  MEM  UPPER  ENDON
FREEDOMMARCHINGORDERS
   SRI  AHA  NESSIE
LILT  RECLIP  MITE  TAD
ARIUM  OENO  INDITE
HATBANDMASTERCYLINDER
RETIREE  ADA  LANOSE
   ATRIA  TAMES  UNTO
DOUBTINGTHOMASAQUINAS
ERSE  SOTIE  RECUT
SNEERS  ACS  RAISESA
CARPETROCKANDROLLCALL
   STREAK  NOON  EASEL
GAR  EFTS  DREAMS  DEWY
IDEATE  PGA  ESS
GOLDSTANDARDTIMECLOCK
GRIMA  MOIRA  IDO  AERIE
LEVER  ADMOV  FOR  LOTTE
EDENS  SEELY  FLY  ESSEN
```

113

```
RAF  MATTE  NUBS  IMP
IBA  OBOES  ORAN  ODEA
DOUBLEENTENDRE  NEAR
GULLETS  DOUBLETALK
ETTE  TRI  LAH
   DOUBLETIME  REBUT
PAT  BRACT  NAMA  DATA
EVIDENT  RHUMB  ORAD
REPASS  BEEVES  UGHS
   PIE  DOUBLET  DBA
HULL  LAUREL  HOLIER
OBEY  AZTEC  MAGENTA
HERD  MEGA  CHAIM  SET
ORSON  DOUBLEPLAY
UFA  AIM  ADAM
DOUBLEDATE  GRENADA
EARL  DOUBLEJEOPARDY
ERIE  ENTS  SANTO  ETA
MSS  STOP  SMEES  SON
```

114

```
RADON  CELL  RID  FARR
AGENA  OMOO  UME  ILEO
BRAGI  PICA  NIN  VETS
BELONGSTODADDY  EXIT
IESI  HES  EROO  AFIRE
   NINE  CREW  LOOSER
SINGINTHE  ONEIRO
ANE  STAEL  NETTLE
STASH  RELAPSE  ATEN
SETS  DONAT  WINS
NEWS  ASSURED  NODES
TREPAN  TIOGA  EAT
ERRAND  ONMYHANDS
STATEN  EARN  PAL
LITHE  ESSE  SOS  LOBO
ARTE  WITHAINMYHEART
LALIA  EEL  MOAB  ONSET
ODER  NIE  ELKE  ADENO
MEET  DIOR  DEER  RESTS
```

115

```
GETAS  ATTAR  CROPS
ARRANT  FORMA  HAROLD
WILLIAMCLUBS  AZALEA
SPECTRO  DEL  CRACKED
   REAP  REGAL  LAP
THOMASBOY  REDEYE
ROVE  NEO  LESE  EDA
AMEN  KETTLE  TROOPER
PER  TERI  DES  OLLIES
   JOHNOFALLTRADES
TROJAN  FRI  AISE  OLA
COYOTES  ANDNOT  ADEN
UMS  ITES  EAT  RIDE
ASHLAR  ROBERTCAT
   MIN  TENET  NILE
BILIOUS  GOA  EMIRATE
ANEMIC  KATHERINEDID
PODUNK  ELEMI  RENAME
TESTY  YEMEN  ADORE
```

116

```
COLORS  FLA  EGIS  SHOP
APACHE  FEEL  WINK  HALO
PEYTONPLACE  EASE  ADDS
ERIES  OUSTED  NET  GLEE
ANT  SPITE  ATTACH  END
   SHED  RAZE  SHOWY
DAKOTAS  INFERNO  TOBAT
ICEMAN  LAST MAN  SOUSE
ELLINGTON  EDIT  JEERED
MUTT  ROD  BRET  TEARGAS
   VILIFY  BEREFT
SAWMILL  REST  OAF  GAPE
EROICA  BEST  GOREVIDAL
RINSE  IRE  AGED  RIVALS
FADER  CAMELOT  ASPERSE
   ERODE  ALES  EROS
ARR  YEMENI  SEVEN  LEM
BOLT  FAX  SHAVEN  DORIC
OMAR  AKIN  EMERALDCITY
RENO  METE  RENT  SAUCES
TODD  ERSE  ART  DYSART
```

117

```
LAMA  COLAS  OSAGE  MNOP
OMAR  ODILE  NEMEA  EAVE
BIRD  MELANESIANS  STEP
ESTEEM  ARTS  TREASURE
INDUS  MUSIC  ELGAR
CANTINAS  PETALS  EGAD
LEG  TELIC  NAPE  RELET
IRAS  SMEAR  LIARS  SILO
PILAR  ARTE  STREET  SHY
SEEMING  CDI  ANDRETTIS
   BLEU  HORAL  HUME
UNBALANCE  ELI  EMPRESS
RAU  ELDERS  ESER  EMDEN
GIRD  SISAL  STARS  SURA
ELLER  TROT  STIES  CAR
SETA  RAMPED  SNAPBACK
   SOBRE  SEMIS  GLOAT
UNQUIETS  PAUL  ATTILA
SOUR  CALIFORNIAN  HOED
EPEE  TRINI  CRONE  ONTO
REDD  ODDER  HANDS  SSTS
```

118

```
IVTIS AREAS HOSE GALA
BIRTH MARIA ALTO ORAS
IVYOURINIVMATION IONS
DOA TESTED CHOW IVSEE
DOES IOTA ATTEST
DEPAUL MANNA WATCH
ANENT PURGE WRATH IAT
TORE MUSE IFEELA IVTE
ALI DIRKS VEINS IVTEN
VAINLY STARS PRAYTO
COMIVTS AHS FEIGNER
ONADAY TOLET BRUNEI
NINES CAROB GOUDA NAS
DOCS MILANO ALIE MELT
ENE HOTEL ORNOT WORSE
MATES SKEGS SEASON
IVSALE MOSS ELAN
TIERS IOOO TREMOR POD
ETAL IVSYTESIVMERWIFE
RATO VISE TOSEA EATIN
SLOW STAN ONERS DRATS
```

119

```
BOLA AMPS SPAR TITO
RUES BELA HELI IRAN
ACES EGOS ARUG GORE
CHRISANTHEMUM TENOR
SUMO ALE AAR
MATTE LAYS MUCILAGE
ARES VIPS CAST ISEE
TEE MEAT CARE ALTER
SANDERS AMYRYLLIS
AND BONES ELI
GOLDIEROD KAISERS
MATES LAZY KITE BIT
ATOP WINE HAMS ROSA
RESHAPED LUTE SANER
INA FER LAPS
STINT SWEETALLYCEUM
LONI ANON ILIE ARNO
ATTU LORD NEAR LIDS
BOOM AWNS GEST SCOT
```

120

```
SHEB GISELLE ROCK
WILL ALSATIANS ALEE
IFYOUFALLONYOURFACE
MISUSED TIES TIFFIN
SEW WILD JULI
FRED WINE BURLAPS
BRED SORE TOMES REL
RIS FURY CROPS DEMI
IVORIES SHOE GIVES
DONOTDESPAIRATLEAST
GLASS PAMS ERUDITE
EONS STRIP FROM LEN
DUC SKEIN MAID PERS
SETTING FATE SODS
RATE LOGS UPS
ACQUIT RARE UPATREE
YOUAREMOVINGFORWARD
ERIN RETENTION ACAD
SEPT TARTANS RELY
```

121

```
LAPIS ALAMB FACET
EVADED ROMEO DITHER
CORONA DIANE ENTERO
TWA ONME RATA VIP
LARAINENEWMAN YEP
MILLAYS LUNATIC CRO
IDEA KNEADER LEAH
GILDARADNER NAVE
ROMI SOW JENSEN
EBB NYET ARAM ETC
WAILED HAT SUNI
ERLE JOHNBELUSHI
LABS POLITIC GEAR
CPM UNTAKEN CUTLASS
LOU GARRETTMORRIS
ARR ARED ANTI OWL
STROBE ORION ICONIC
PIANOS NAVEL NOREST
SAYTO SEEDY TERPS
```

122

```
IRAE SCARS INFO
OMENS CARET MEANS
IMPASSIONATE POLICE
TEEM ETRE URGE LOOP
AGR NEE ORNERY NNE
LAIRS WINSOME SEE
SIT JAIL EWE
OFHAY AMT ALDA GIST
LEA LIMP CALEB OMAR
LAB IMMEMORABLE POI
ISLA MERIT MIEN ONA
ETES IDEA BAT TONED
HUG FUSS END
MAB PRANCED REELS
IRE SALARY FLU ROO
SELL TATI PLOT BALL
SALAMI IMMEASURABLE
SEVEN VEERY ROILS
SANG EASES NILE
```

123

```
SUMAC ALCAS SMA KER
ALONE LEERY TENSILE
RANIS INNER ANTACID
ANEST GETTINGSACKED
YEARN OHNE ARK
DEBT PEN AGAL ECLAT
HEAT IDOL ETO SLUSH
ALGER SADSACK ONTO
LYS ARSENE SKI TEAR
IMAM ENE ETCH
ARON NAB EVERTS BAA
VEST GLADBAG AMAHL
AMAHS TOI NARK AGED
SIREE OBOL DEO COMO
SAT AREA PILAF
HITATWOBAGGER ERWIN
EVICTED MURRE NOISE
RANKLED AMISS ANNEE
ANA EDA SEPTS SIDED
```

124

```
IDLER POLAR PIMAN
ANEMIA AROSE ENAMEL
IFSANDSORBUTS PERIWIG
TOA EPIC PROBLEM SLA
ION RELET OLIOS PILL
STEEL DELED VAS ELSIE
BAS REPOSES STAGED
MAJORCA DEWED SETTO
ABANDONS ENT ACTAEON
ARC STUPE PAULA SADE
MAKO TRESPASSING UNES
DESC ALLEY MEDIA EDO
ETCHANT EMP NARROWLY
RUINS EVERI LOTUSES
SMELLY OMENING SIS
TOQUE HEB TADAS ETHEL
ASUM SYNOD MINCE ARI
MLI DEPOSIT GEOM RAM
PERTAIN SKINOFFMYNOSE
MERINO EERIE FEMALE
DALES DROPS STAND
```

125

```
DEVIL ATTAR CORTEGE
OVATE FAIRE AMERCES
CATEGORICAL NEGATES
STEP SAGAMORE
PAIR ISEE SEDAN
ALVA CHICKPEAS BRAD
STAMP HICKS PEALE
TENSER IOTAS STADIA
HEADSET DIARIST
ASTA FERRETOUT MOTH
TEACHER NIAGARA
BARKER ABIES REREAD
ATOLL CRISP SKATE
TOTE MOLEHILLS ESTE
BITER NAIL TEAM
PIGMENTS GAUL
ARIETTE HAREBRAINED
POLITER AGIRL SCORE
SNARERS LAPSE TERRY
```

126

```
PEAS ROB ISLAM BABY
ELLE ONE NIECE ALEE
AMID USE TRATTORIAS
ROTISSERIE DEED
MEET NRA DODECA
SOBERS TENSE REGALE
EARNS ABREAST REFIT
ETAT GUAT NOES SEVE
MSS IATRIC PALETTES
SARTO AAR RINSE
THEOREMS DEMONS REG
HERR SALA TOOK BILL
ADITS TAPROOM DRAKE
IDEATE PSEUD ARISEN
ASSESS EDC SNAG
ETTA CHUCKWAGON
GREENHOUSE POL DONE
OURS ELTON ORE ESTE
TENT REOPT NET SHOD
```

127

```
SLOB ELMO GUS TALE
AIDE RYAN ELEC ELIA
WRITERSCAPITAL SEAS
SANTE EGOS LOTTERY
ERIS ETHIOPIA
CAP OTHERHALF EMOTE
AGES EER OSE CREPES
PENTIMENTO SSA NIAS
TENET PINK ELATER
ABIES PEELS
CELLOS SOLD EASES
ALAI NHL THECRACKUP
BARKED APE MAE HERE
UPPER GIRLLIKEI WED
INNATELY EDAM
FLOTSAM PARE MOANS
LOEW SURPRISEDBYJOY
ARIA ATEE CANE EARN
GELS SOD SUES SRAS
```

128

```
RITA ESAU RHODA POT
EGAN SPIT EAVES ONE
MULTITUDEOFSINS WIN
IAM TEN UST EMEND
TNUTS RES AFT ORES
SADE BLOATS LOADS
DURESS ALERT TNT
DEF SEEEYETOEYE HOE
READERS RENT FAVA
ALTERS SHADE CRATES
MEOW ALOT POTABLE
ARF LABOROFLOVE ESS
SST ARLEN RAREST
HORNE SCONES ARAM
SPED ERA AGE PLEBE
MELEE NIL MAE CAT
ALA SKINOFONESTEETH
LEN TIEIN PEAT IDEO
LED APSES TODO REDD
```

129

```
AREAS TWINE HAMIT
LEASH RANON OPINES
PASTA ALTOS WISEMAN
SPEAR IKON MMES PLO
PALS SAUCY TOO
PREFERS SEANCE GINK
RETUNE FINISH BAN
SPODE FIDDLE BUDGIE
GROOVES BUNGLES
FLEE WEED BARN EYRE
PENCILS SUBEDIT
OSCARS ABIDED FEEDS
ONA GRANGE GAELIC
ECUA PLUNGE CABRINI
NOR COULD BABU
CIA ANTE AMUR DRAPE
ENGORGE BLADE GOGOL
SEAPEN FUDGE INALL
STIES AMEER ESSES
```

130

```
MEL  SLUMP  BASE  INTO
AVE  PENAL  ODOR  NEON
FANCIESPASSING  GLEE
INTENSE  YOUR  ODESSA
ASONE  THRONES  ONO
   SST  IONS  PETUNIA
LACE  RENO  ERA  ESTA
ALL  BENDMINDERS  DOR
REASONS  BEDE  EGO
DESIST  TESTY  TENURE
SRO  FIVE  AUDUBON
ALF  MAIDENHANDS  LAI
DIRT  PLY  ASTO  SEND
OPERATE  BART  RAH
SAD  TERRAIN  LAINE
SCHIST  LAMS  OVERRAN
CAMP  HUSKYSIBERIANS
ALAS  ERIE  EVENT  TCU
TINE  NEED  DOLTS  EYE
```

131

```
ASPS  ILE  AFEW  CELL
BOLT  KNAR  NISI  ABIE
CLEOPATRA  DESDEMONA
OBLATE  HAL  OVENED
OWENGLENDOWER
IKON  DIEST  ASSAILS
TENSE  NOTERS  NEO
SEE  FRESNO  ATAR  GAT
PROFIT  INST  LOSERS
DUNCAN  LEBEAU
RECESS  SERE  INSETS
OVA  EEKS  UNDSET  OPA
SOR  ARMADA  SERUM
SEDATER  ANENT  SORE
DOLLTEARSHEET
INSOLE  RRS  ABRADE
PETRUCHIO  VALENTINE
SWAN  TUBS  AVER  ENOL
OTTS  SMEE  TOR  SEWS
```

132

```
FOAL  CHIS  SAP  RAMS
LASE  LINT  PLOW  ISON
ATTA  ANDI  RASH  OPIE
THISMUGOFMINEIS  IRE
EASE  LON  SPENCER
BREST  YENTA  SMU
EON  SAN  ASPLAINASA
DEVELOPED  LEW  BEN
COLO  ASSET  STEED
BARNDOORWHYSHOULD
VENUE  LANAI  NOUN
ATT  HOS  PEOPLEPAY
THIRTYFIVE  ETE  ICE
DAG  SEDER  RENEW
NATALIE  SIP  IDOL
ARR  CENTSTOLOOKATIT
READ  NAME  DINT  TYRO
INCA  ETAL  EDIE  EPIC
SAYS  ENS  SOAR  DESK
```

133

```
MESA  TARP  PARA  SAWA
ACTS  ICER  ALEC  ELIS
THEHIGHCOSTOFHEALTH
TONIGHT  COTE  INMATE
VET  DENY  CEDE
COMET  DESI  LAVENDER
OVER  PRESCRIBED  RAY
PAD  SOUP  INAS  DUSE
SLIDER  BADEN  PAGES
CARETHESEDAYSIS
CLIMB  RAGES  CASTER
LONE  GIDE  AINT  OWE
AGE  TREATMENTS  DRED
POSTHORN  OUTS  PEERS
RIGS  TIRE  PEP
BARONS  DIRE  CORONAS
ENOUGHTOMAKEYOUSICK
STOP  OOZE  AGAL  INRE
TIME  PIER  SONS  TEED
```

134

```
SCAD  RAMBO  ABC  ACRE
AREA  ASCAP  HEADROOM
WURM  PHINEASTBARNUM
DOAWAY  ARLO  BUSSEY
JESSE  KNAP  SAN  ESS
BOOKERTWASHINGTON
AILS  IRAS  ALIE  NTWT
RLS  FAUN  ABET  ATSEA
ZITS  CREA  NATAL
JUBILATIONTCORNPONE
UPONE  AMES  COUE
STUNT  AMPS  SHAM  STA
TONI  ABBE  VERN  SHUN
CAPTAINJAMESTKIRK
CPI  LAD  DARE  HYENA
HANNAH  IIII  SMELLS
EUGENETMALESKA  IDOS
ALLSTARS  ETHIC  NEUT
PAYS  DEO  RYANS  ERTE
```

135

```
TUTU  BIB  CAEN  PLATE
ASIS  URI  ACRE  LABOR
TENURIAL  STRESEMANN
ASTRAL  LACES  TUE
PIT  IBAD  MORSELS
BARED  LOIR  AERATION
ONER  JANEADDAMS  SUE
NON  PODS  RATS  CASE
ANEMIAS  SNIPS  BAKER
CONN  ALOFT  PERU
APART  AVAST  FORESEE
MAST  SCOT  COOT  ALI
ASS  SCHWEITZER  STAR
STITCHES  MOAS  CLONE
SENORES  SPUR  DUE
WAM  MULTI  IBERIA
LECHWALESA  NINEPINS
ORIEL  EGAN  ARE  ELKS
WADES  WANT  SER  REST
```

136

```
LOFT  LAVA  MATSU  JAB
OLIO  IRAD  ETHAN  OLE
OENO  BALD  SLEPT  WOE
MONKEYBUESS  SPIELER
PRALINE  STILT
KOALA  ENDE  ORE  ELLE
IGLASS  GAPORESTRAIT
PLACETS  PRETENDER
SERE  OAR  WAIT  REESE
RAIINTHESUN
SUPRA  NCOS  ROS  CHOO
INHIBITOR  FOALING
DICLINATIONS  SLAVER
ASSI  ONT  JOAB  ISERE
NANDA  ANTARES
WIGGLER  AIPENINSULA
ADO  PEELS  LEDS  IBEX
FLY  HAWES  UNIE  ZEAL
TEA  ARSON  SSTS  ERDE
```

137

```
MATERS  TEAM  SLAV
AVENUE  ERLE  SIEPI
CINDER  ARES  AMASS
ALOE  EBB  CHEROKEE
WARDS  OAS  VIN
KINGCOLE  EMIR
ARISEN  SULUS  ACE
REVELRY  MEA  EATEN
CHAMPION  GUARDIAN
TINES  DEO  STRANGE
IRA  SLANT  TARGET
CEST  PETERPAN
ITA  SAG  DARED
EXPLORER  IAN  COMA
TRULY  TORN  ACUMEN
TARES  CUBE  BUTANE
EYED  HEIR  SPENDS
```

138

```
EBBS  BETA  TECH  OTTO
CORM  ELAN  AREA  SHEM
GREENFORDANGER  SETI
SIRLOIN  ALDO  DWIGHT
TOT  ANDY  SWEAR
OFTEN  ERTE  SCANNERS
LAHR  GREENSWARD  EEL
IKE  ERIS  TIRE  ANNE
DECAGON  SAONE  ACHED
OBIT  CLING  ATNO
APRES  SEAMY  BOLEROS
LENS  ATRI  MANE  NAH
ANI  GREENHOUSE  PESO
ENSNARES  EASE  MATTE
GULAR  FARE  TAG
BARREN  SIRS  MULETAS
ICES  GREENMOUNTAINS
ATEE  EBAN  ANTI  NEST
SAND  RIND  NETS  TRES
```

139

```
SAP  BARI  REDS  AGES
ILL  EDOM  ISIT  CRIED
AMO  GULP  NAME  HIRED
MAYJULYAUGUST  ILEDE
ENT  ITO  EEL
ARID  GRAFTONSVERSE
SEMIPRO  HAUTE  ETA
POP  LANE  BERNE  ATOR
DECEMBER  WAIT
OCTOBERJANUARYMARCH
PROM  FEBRUARY
EONS  DELFT  ELLE  MAW
RUE  BETEL  ELDRICH
APRILNOVEMBER  OLEO
SET  EAT  SRA
APRON  JUNESEPTEMBER
WOULD  UNIT  RARE  OLE
ELIDE  TILE  NAIL  OKS
ONER  EVER  ERAS  TOT
```

140

```
ANTA  MART  CAPS  ASHE
TOOL  ALOU  ALOT  THOR
OVAL  CLOT  SOLA  TORN
MADETHEDUSTFLY  AONE
GROG  ALT  OMIT
ABBEY  HORDE  EVENTS
BOLD  DELE  AYES  HEP
BOO  WINDJAMMERS  ELI
TWEAKY  ALIAS  AMBLE
HATE  FILCH  AGAR
SPORE  MOLAR  SCENES
POT  RAINSHOWERS  EAT
ANA  GILD  BONE  EZRA
ENDURE  STEWS  ANEAR
DENT  STR  EPIC
PACA  OUTOFACLEARSKY
AMOR  ANEW  BRER  ULNA
GILL  IDLE  BOSS  SUER
EDDY  ROAD  APSE  TEED
```

141

```
SPREE  SPLIT  DWARFS
AREEL  CAIRO  ORRERY
BILLYMONDAY  NESTERS
LEA  SOON  SERFS  IDIO
ESTE  APES  DIET  ERAL
STERN  ERIC  ABLE  INE
SEED  SOB  RELIC
NECTAR  MILIEU  BLASE
ELA  RAJA  ALGA  ASPEN
WIPE  TODO  ERRS  ARIA
TOTAL  ERIN  EYED  INC
STARE  SELECT  TABLET
INDIA  SAL  OSSO
BUN  ANTI  TUTU  HARPS
ANOD  KUDU  BATS  TERP
RANI  WRONG  ICER  PIE
DREAMED  DONNAAUTUMN
MANILA  UNITS  SATED
SMELLY  EGEST  TIERS
```

142

```
EMUS  OONA  DADE  SASH
CORE  USES  ERIE  OPTO
UNDERTHEHAMMER  CARL
STUDIO  DOMO  TYPICAL
   AFFLUENCE  REEDY
TODA  TRETS  ORBIT
WOODSHED  UNSEDATED
POLARIS  WTS  HELENA
  ENESCO  HOURIS  END
DODO  WONDERMAN  ETES
EGO  TOSAIL  ENDIVE
REUTER  SOP  DOLORES
METERLESS  MONIKERS
  MMDLI  INAWE  EDIT
SCAPE  ISAGAINST
ANDORRA  BOSN  BOASTS
ROAR  INTOTHEBARGAIN
ATTA  DIEM  URIC  ELEE
HEEL  SCAB  ASOK  SERE
```

143

```
DSC  CETERA  ROMERO
RAH  AVALON  EDITOR
ELA  WILLIAMBOARDS
APRS  TOE  HEEM  ESO
MALAYAN  JELLED
  EVE  SPOIL  TIDAL
ASSESS  OHM  TENACE
TAWS  TERN  PARENTS
TRA  JAMESJAMS  III
EAGLETS  PARE  LEVO
SPOORS  PRY  STOLEN
TENNE  PEASE  END
  IMPORT  RANGERS
OSS  IOUS  ENG  SLIM
THOMASFOOLERY  IVA
TENTHS  NASSER  OES
ODENSE  ARETES  NTH
```

144

```
SHARP  AMOST  BABAR
HALOS  LEROI  ASINE
ANITA  ANACE  LINDA
DONALDDUCK  STAGED
SIESTA  LOATH  OSE
   ENATE  BOAR
SHADRACH  SEASAGA
LOBE  STEEP  TACOMA
OREAD  ARROW  RIDER
WALLER  AGORA  ABET
ELEMENT  FIDDLERS
  ROPA  ASTOR
AHA  CABAL  BEHAVE
DATERS  BETTEDAVIS
AORTA  TIMOR  GLASS
ILIAC  ADANO  EVITA
REPLY  BENET  DELAY
```

145

```
PICKY  AWFUL  CHAN
ACHOO  PHONE  HUNT
SHANK  PEASONEARTH
SIR  OFALL  ONCLE
ENDS  ELK  FORTH
GROVEL  HOC  RABBI
EDIT  GARAGE  ERA
BMOC  SIN  SEE  RUG
GRAM  CANDIED  TRIO
OUI  TAN  BAY  BRYN
INN  INDIAN  BAUM
NOSES  RAG  CATNAP
ISLAM  DON  KNOT
FUGUE  SINKS  ITA
CASHEWLATER  HELEN
AINT  OMEGA  ALONG
PRAY  SYNOD  HOWTO
```

146

```
LAUDS  AFARE  SPACE
ONSET  RIGEL  TABOR
ATEAR  STUFF  OSAGE
MIRROR  TELSON
  PILOSE  DEBATE
ATOP  PEA  CHA  EDEN
PENAL  STATE  ADORE
RECREATES  HELM
SNEADS  ETE  STARES
  LAIT  IMITATING
ORALS  SCRUB  REPOT
FOIE  CEO  LIT  SEWS
FILLER  PHASES
  NOTYET  DOUBLE
AMAID  ACRID  BRAIN
CELLO  SAMOA  EGRET
ELBOW  STAND  REESE
```

147

```
AFARM  ORATE  AMP
BASED  TALES  CRAIG
AINSI  ONINE  LACER
TREE  CAT  IRATE
HERNANDOSHIDEAWAY
  DREAR  MENT
HAD  LEG  AWAIT  HOP
ELOPE  SWAGS  SABA
MOMENTSTOREMEMBER
ANEW  WEEKS  RAISE
NED  HARTE  ALI  TED
  MANA  SLICE
CRYINGINTHECHAPEL
HEARD  ORE  SIRE
OLLIE  ALIEN  RECAP
PETAL  DANTE  CLOSE
DAM  ANEST  ASTER
```

148

```
ATIME  TAMPA  SWAMI
LIBEL  ATALL  TOXIN
APERFECTJUDGEWILL
PRE  STA  SOAR  SKY
ALI  TICS  WEE
READEACHWORKOFWIT
ERNIE  OBE  FAZE
ALMS  ROAST  KEN
ALEXANDERPOPE
JOB  RITES  SATE
AVEC  ISM  URARI
WITHTHESAMESPIRIT
IRA  NETH  MPS
ESQ  ARID  ECO  SOT
THATITSAUTHORWRIT
AUDIT  BLAME  DIEDA
STIES  AIRED  STREW
```

149

```
BETE  FOR  ALA  BACA
ELAN  ICE  SOD  ONLY
FIND  NEF  SPREADER
OTTO  ELISA  INTROS
GEORGSOLTI  ASHEN
  SETTEE  SNOOP
REJET  SNAP  RORYS
ELASTIC  ODOR  KEEL
HIM  YORE  DRAM  VAI
ADES  NAGS  THOMIST
BESOT  ZOOM  LENTS
  LARRY  FAUNAL
SEPIA  BARBIROLLI
SOVIET  OSSIP  DEER
PRIEDIEU  HEP  INGE
URNS  OWL  ETO  STEN
NYET  NET  SYN  TORE
```

150

```
STEW  RATAL  BLISS
PANIC  ATONE  LUCRE
ABASH  FRUSTRATION
CUTEAS  ATE  ACE
ESE  STAB  LANK  PEA
  STUPID  SIBLING
TOQUE  PLASH  IOOOO
BLUE  WAIST  ALAN
SEE  POLO  ORNE  EFT
  SPEW  UNMAN  NEON
ESTES  USUAL  BERET
STEPSON  SCLERA
QED  IRES  HYPE  ABS
  AMA  PTA  IAMBIC
RESTINPEACE  MELBA
ARIES  LATHE  SMELL
JANET  ORIEL  OREL
```

151

```
RAVENS  FEED  IFNI
ERICOID  LILA  SLED
GREASER  UGLY  AARE
AET  TEETHE  PIXIE
TAN  BEATIT  IFA
TRACE  MUSICSCHOOL
ASMALL  ITELL  MNO
  PLUS  STOA  ORES
AMERICAN  HUMANIST
BONA  IMER  DIRE
LOO  NOWIS  CRAZES
EDWARDALBEE  ATONE
LEE  OSPREY  IZE
HILDA  ENTIRE  SYR
ALAR  RUDE  OLDTIME
LEVI  PROA  REDATES
EDEN  MONK  RECESS
```

152

```
HAREM  JEWELS  DSOS
AGORA  UNROOT  ATLI
FRANKINCENSE  MEER
TES  ONIONS  ADAGIO
SETS  TORS  FLAGONS
  THERE  LOAVES
COCOONS  LARGE  APE
IMARET  PASTE  BURR
GAPED  AIDES  JUROR
ANTS  ENTER  CERUSE
RIA  SNOOD  BLESSED
  IBADAN  COOPT
SONATAS  LOTT  SELL
MUNSON  IAMTHE  SEI
ITES  GEMMOLOGISTS
RIME  ELAPSE  GREAT
KNOT  RAMSES  SEXTS
```

153

```
CAR  STEPS  CAPP
MULES  STARRED  GORES
AMICE  TERRACE  ARENA
LICIT  EWE  TUS  MEANT
NETTLE  PERT  IDLY
  ELUL  FOREIGN
NARES  FIE  SNY  ORD
RAG  STERN  TYROLEAN
ASIA  SOIGNE  OLIVIA
ICTUS  STEEPED  EVERT
SEALED  ROOTER  ERIA
ANTIDOTE  PANIC  EEL
TEC  VIP  BEL  GIRDS
  PERIGEE  SOLO
ETUI  ACRE  CRISES
NIOBE  DUE  OCA  ASNER
IDIOT  ERECTOR  TITLE
DELAY  SEDATES  ENEMY
ERST  SYNOD  IRA
```

154

```
LABS  FLEA  TATE  RATA
ALLA  LODI  ARAM  ELAM
MOUNTAGEM  STIPULATE
BURDENS  LOSE  OSIRIS
    LAG  MENE  AWES
BECOMEFAST  OVERHEAT
ALOT  ADS  HER   SRO
ASA  LOX  APER  MSTAR
SEGUED  INTENTIONAL
  ULNA  DURER  GRAB
PLAYSCENERY  EAGLES
DIANA  LASE  STY  ISH
ALT  CUL  ARI  OSSA
BLEACHES  ENTRENCHED
  RAID  ERTE  AIT
ORIGIN  ADAH  ASSAYED
SITONEGGS  INSTIGATE
TRES  SERE  LATE  OLAN
EERY  ENOL  LEAR  NEST
```

155

```
SITKA  COATI  CAROL
USHER  AVIAN  AROMA
GEORGEBERNARDSHAW
ARM  RON  GLEE  FRN
REALIST  LILITH
  SURE  WOE  AGUE
PERK  GEORGEBURNS
MADE  HULK  ONALARK
ERI  FEEL  PICT  NEE
TOSSERS  LANE  ADAR
ALONZOSTAGG  SAML
LENA  RUE  DANA
GLOWED  DECIMAL
TAB  UVEA  SUE  ONA
ALEKSANDRKERENSKY
CARET  CLEAT  PEELE
KENNY  HECTO  POSER
```

156

```
BESOM  SHALL  RADAR
ELATE  TODIE  EDINA
SALEM  URALS  TENOR
EIE  BUDAPASTA  ESE
TOPHET  ETC  HINDER
       ARAL  WINO
BARM  HASBEAN  BARB
ALAST  SCALD  MILER
ELITE  ANE  ALINE
ROSIN  SLANT  LIVES
STET  MEATING  TEST
     CHIT  TARE
TETHER  OWS  REASON
ERR  GORKYPORK  ORO
NAOMI  ARAIL  NOMAN
ESTER  GATTO  IRATE
TESLA  ASTER  TATES
```

157

```
COMETS  SOFTEN  UGH
ARARAT  AGORAE  PRO
INDIRESTRAITS  TEN
RIEN  KIEL  TEHEE
OTT  PAR  SCHEMERS
HOTWATER  RIDER
ROTE  ATOM  EINE
STUART  ATAN  IRVIN
ARP  MIDSTREAM  ELI
RITAS  AIRE  BARRED
KOHL  ENNA  SAGE
EGEST  PUTTOSEA
DECOCTED  NAE  MBA
EARLE  REST  DEAN
USE  STAYTHECOURSE
CEE  INHERE  ADAGES
ELK  STARED  PALEST
```

158

```
FETED  LEIF  BOSCS
ORATE  POLKA  AREAL
COMEBLOWYOURHORNE
ADES  ITE  NNE  RAW
LED  OMAR  TRIALS
   SNIT  NEURON
HARTETOHARTETALKS
IDEAS  AENEAS  AIT
KEAN  EGG  EST  ARTE
ELL  ANODES  ALGER
DEMILLEONTHEFLOSS
   LEARNS  ERAS
WALKER  SAAR  ALS
OLE  GOA  ART  AGEE
OLIVIERNEWTONJOHN
DOLED  ANDES  CARAS
STAGS  LEAD  ORARE
```

159

```
CARP  OWLS  STAD  LAM
OWES  MEESE  ARNE  IPA
DAVIDNIVEN  NADA  NOD
ERE  EIRE  SALLYFIELD
DELLA  DEW  SUES  DALE
   ORB  ASPIE  HERON
STRIA  RITES  MUS
DIANEKEATON  CONTEST
EMMA  EDGED  FETA  LIE
NEA  GREERGARSON  ISR
SOL  LIND  ITEA  GNAR
ENEMIES  PETEROTOOLE
   ADS  LASER  LIARS
SCENE  BERTS  ELL
ORNE  ARAT  TIE  ISLES
BETTEDAVIS  NEIN  ALE
BAR  DAVE  CLARKGABLE
ESE  ONER  BELIE  HEAT
DEE  MOSS  ILES  ALSO
```

160

```
HONOR  TRAPS  SERAPH
ADORED  IONIC  TEETHE
LITTLEREDSCHOOLBOYS
ONE  ATE  SENORA  ELLS
EXACT  LILA  ALLO
TALC  CROP  CATES
ERICTHERED  REDFACED
DIVER  ANGEL  DUOPOLY
IOTA  CHI  CREASE
PART  REDGRANGE  SLED
AREOLA  OUI  VAST
INDIANS  MESAS  AERIE
REDLIGHT  REDHERRING
TEERS  NEON  LONG
OBEY  KEAT  DULCE
APIA  MESTEE  SIR  AMI
REDSAILSINTHESUNSET
CREELS  ERECT  TEEPEE
HASLET  SETHS  TESTS
```

161

```
BALE  SALSA  AGAR
ETONS  ALLOUT  TRIO
●INTHEBUCKET  LAMP
PIRAYA  AIDA  ANTE
   KEN  CANTOR
ATTHE●OFTHEHAT
BRIAN  ORAL  RABAT
LOTA  PARADISE  ISO
AWLS  AML  TSE  BHAT
ZEE  THEOTHER  LAMA
ELDER  BRAE  AURAS
NORANY●TODRINK
ESCAPE  AMO
PARC  NASA  MORASS
OBIT  THELEMON●KID
CREE  ASEASY  SOUSA
HERD  LOSES  FAIL
```

162

```
OVERACT  PRO  ASTA
REVISOR  UAR  PHILS
BRITSBYEBYE  TENTH
SALE  ALES  AGHA
SAFARI  CUTLER
AYS  FRENCHFORHEAD
BOOBOOS  ARNIE
AUDIO  SALAD  HUG
SMALLMONKEYOFPERU
HES  ALIAS  USAGE
CHIEF  ENDIVES
WIZARDOFOZDOG  ESS
EDITHS  MESSED
LENS  AREA  ALIAS
DACCA  BALLETSKIRT
STEAL  EVE  MAHATMA
EDNA  SET  SPAREST
```

163

```
CACAO  ASCH  PAC  DUMA
ABACA  RILE  AGA  ITYS
PATHFINDER  LEN  OATH
ESTE  VALE  PENTARCHY
   LAZE  MASCARA
STOLON  NATTYBUMPPO
ARRAN  SAONE  MARAT
LANDGRANT  SMOR  SORT
ALIENATE  EVAN  SEE
JAMESFENIMORECOOPER
ORE  HELD  PRETENSE
URNS  RYAS  CLASSICAL
SOTTO  WRAYS  TETRA
TWOADMIRALS  CORSET
READERS  PLOP
OVERRULED  FLUB  BORG
TALI  LED  DEERSLAYER
ISLE  ERI  OMNI  ARENA
STER  DST  MEAD  DAZED
```

164

```
ASSAM  AMASS  SETS
GEODES  ABETTED  AARE
ENCAMP  GENTILE  BRAN
TIMEHEALSALLWOUNDS
LIES  ESP  EELS  EEE
INT  ARTEMIS  RATES
FEISTY  ECHO  PRATES
ELEME  ENDEAR  INLET
SSS  FREE  MIMIC  YRS
   FADS  SASH
ANA  ORATE  HOST  TEA
COLOR  ERRANT  PANDA
TRACER  RIEN  AWARDS
BASIC  CEDILLA  ORE
SPA  AGRI  DIP  PLEA
TIMEWOUNDSALLHEELS
ALIT  RELIEVE  ATTEST
REAR  STARTER  SCREED
ESNE  SWEAR  HOSES
```

165

```
PANIC  TROAS  AMUSE
AROMA  HONDA  WIPER
STRANGEBEDFELLOWS
TEAM  HASSLED  ANNE
     SHE  ESSEN
DAS  ENOLA  TORC
ECCENTRICBEHAVIOR
CHATS  STRAFES  BRA
LENO  AIT  TRY  ABRI
AND  ANNETTE  SHOES
WEIRDCIRCUMSTANCE
SAUD  SESTO  STD
   SAMOA  AWN
BLOT  ORBITAL  AWRY
OUTLANDISHCLOTHES
USHER  ETIAM  PAINE
THOSE  ROSIE  ALTER
```

166

```
STEP   ACT  LIMA  LA(MER)
TARA  ALAI  EMIL  LAIC
ARNIEPAL(MER)  EMER  ALDISLE
SADDER  ACS  EASTER
FAR(MER)INTHEDELL
SACO  SCALE  ASSERTS
APART  ORISON  EAU
MI(MER)  A(MER)INDS  LEIA  O(MER)S
GA(MER)OOM  ITAL  GLASSY
LIPPEN  NAPOLI
LUGOSI  TEMA  TRIM(MER)S
ATE  MALE  OTIOSE  MET
RAN  ESTRUS  SLATE
CHASSIS  RAYOF  ANSA
CENTRALA(MER)ICAN
ICEAGE  HIE  ROBSME
RU(MER)GODDEN  COM(MER)CIALS
MEGS  EDIE  AWES  NU(MER)O
ADE  NENE  BED  GIST
```

167

```
CHELA  SPRAY  STEALS
OILER  ULINE  MAGNATE
GLADTIDINGS  IRONSIN
NAP  ANDES  GLEN  TPK
ARIL  CERE  BEES  THAI
TIDE  ANS  FANS  SHU
ETAOIN  LURE  PERLE
SYENE  PONE  CHEERED
EROSION  SAID  ANA
DAM  HAPPYDAYS  HEM
AME  DINE  GRISSOM
NORWOOD  BIAS  LEHAR
ARROW  BARM  CANUTE
YEN  COIL  ESO  IMAS
DIMS  PANT  ELAM  NOLI
ECO  SARD  MANIA  RAN
MONTANA  RIBTICKLING
ENTRANT  FLEET  HASTE
SHIRES  DADDY  ANTAS
```

168

```
NADA  ADIT  METAL  PABAS
ALUM  NARY  ATONE  ABASE
CONTRIVER  THUNDERCLAP
RID  EMINENT  REGAL  LST
ENERVATE  ERS  SESAME
REELS  OVENS  SENORES
USHERS  PHASING  SCRIBE
SIEVE  HEADSTART  ETNAS
ALAE  TETRA  CREEP  IANS
GOD  DORIAN  HEELERS
ESSAYIST  NESTEGGS
BENEFIT  CRESTS  REM
WADI  GLOBE  HAYES  VASE
ANILE  FUSELAGES  VENTA
ASSETS  RETUNED  FENDER
CATNAPS  NESTS  AINUS
AEGEAN  RTE  ARRESTED
MAN  ELLIS  EREMITE  ADE
INTERLINEAR  REARRANGE
ROLLE  NERVE  NENE  IDEM
ANYAS  ESSED  ERSE  SSRS
```

169

```
MESS  PAWED  IRAS  SALT
ACME  AVISO  STILT  IGOR
STOA  PINTO  ECOLE  NINE
HOG-TIED  RIGHT-ANGLES
LOEW  BUY  SMILER
REPAIR  SCALE  STELE
AVANT-GARDE  FLARE-UPS
SINE  MARIE  JEERS  SNIT
PAD  ARAB  CORDS  APACE
SNAP  CBS  TOURS  KRAUTS
OCHO  SO-SO  MISC
ATTLEE  COROT  HIT  EASE
BARKS  WHOOP  CAST  LAM
ERIA  FAITS  PASTY  TOTE
TOP-NOTCH  FORTY-NINER
DEREK  QUITE  COMEDY
ROOMER  PUL  SOME
CUSTOM-BUILT  CURE-ALL
AMAT  ASIGN  HELEN  OGEE
POKE  SKEET  EVADE  URGE
ORAD  TINT  NAMER  TASK
```

170

```
CUFFS  ELOPES  POISED
INURN  MINUET  EFFETE
GETOUTOFLINE  RASCAL
AVI  GETTYS  LAP  OOLA
RELY  RES  SELLER  NIN
SNEERS  DAYAFTERDAY
AGEE  ONER  USAF
CRUST  LAIC  SACKING
HINT  CONNED  CLUEDIN
IDI  GOING  AHOLE  DNA
RETURNS  STMARY  GLOW
PREFACE  RATE  KEENS
DOTE  BRAS  SCAR
MISSINGLINK  HYMNAL
ENT  STEEPS  ARI  SORI
SLAT  RMS  FACILE  DRS
MOTHRA  SHORTCIRCUIT
EVERAT  MARNIE  SALVE
RESUME  EDMOND  TREED
```

171

```
APT  ABBY  DREY  CAPT
GAEL  TRAMS  REBEC  AGER
TREE  LANCE  ADOLL  BONE
ANDREWJACKSONPOLLOCK
GUANO  UHT  SUEDE
STEEDS  ALAI  ODETS
HARRYTRUMANCAPOTE  SGL
INNS  ALORS  TINS  PERI
PGS  AMBER  ETAS  AUDEN
ARAB  PLAIT  OBLATE
FRANKLINPIERCEBROSNAN
LASSIE  ELTON  ACRE
OFTEN  SWAT  ECLAT  IDO
STOL  CAEN  AEDES  ARIL
SSR  ULYSSESSGRANTWOOD
CREST  LICE  OHENRY
TAIGA  EDA  EAMES
GROVERCLEVELANDAMORY
YORE  ELATE  OLSON  MOST
MOTT  DAMON  PLURI  EMEU
SPAS  PENS  SEES  ART
```

172

```
BEL  BRIE  SADHU  ASPEN
ADAM  EASY  ELIAN  VOILE
SOMEOFTHESEDAYS  ADELE
IMPALAS  CEDAR  UNLACED
LIONEL  EUA  ISNO  SERE
ITOS  LUMPSOFSUGAR  SYD
CEN  HERA  ROTE  ORO
MANIC  WREST  BLUFFS
APAR  SILO  MOLIERE
ARABIA  AINT  STOA  NIUE
STR  POTATOCHIPS  GIR
CUTS  HOER  POEM  TIGHTS
ARSENIO  ODIN  DUTY
POOLED  TIROS  DOSES
FLA  OSER  INCA  COE
OES  PATSOFBUTTER  CORM
RAPT  VAST  NEY  ABRADE
STEEPER  OLEIC  STEIGER
ISERE  TIPOFTHEICEBERG
NACRE  ALIST  NOAH  SNEE
OTHER  RICES  ONMY  TDS
```

173

```
REAM  STOMA  CIGAR  CASS
ARIA  ARDEN  ODETO  ALAN
JERRYBUILT  WILLYNILLY
KAREN  OFGOD  AOR
BOBSLED  PILI  ALCOVES
ANIMUS  DINER  ILIE  INT
ISLE  GENEALOGIST  CLU
KILN  ORAS  ANAT  ATAP
ADC  FRANKFURTERS  POCO
LEOPARDS  ERIES  WIRER
LANAS  PEBAS  SARSI
DELIS  SUDAN  TOMAHAWK
OLEG  PHILANTHROPY  CHI
NICE  AYES  EINS  AROS
ACT  STEVEDORING  ROWS
TIO  ERNE  ARENA  JETSAM
ETRURIA  VADE  MATISSE
SOC  COINA  RACES
RICHWIDOWS  CHUCKSTEAK
ERLE  AIMEE  TABLE  ILSA
BAER  NEONS  SLEET  CLAY
```

174

```
MOSSO  STEP  SHAH  SMUG
IRWIN  CLAMUP  HULA  AMORE
SLAPOFLUXURY  IRON  LONGA
DORS  IAN  SPRINTEDMATTER
ISM  PERKS  OILY  BATHED
DEW  ASK  TASTE  BOOTEE
EAST  AIMEE  TRANS  RHOS
SPANHANDLES  BROKE  GLOVE
COTTA  OVEN  SLOWS  DRAWER
ASHE  STES  PEALS  WEINERS
USE  DOOR  SADDLEPATED
PER  INNS  TRADE  ERES  SAL
SPACESETTER  ELSE  CPA
RESTORE  OWNER  SPOT  TARP
IDEALS  HOPED  EPIC  CURIE
SNAKE  MINOR  STINKERBELL
KATE  COVET  TWANG  DEEP
ACHIER  FEELA  AIS  ACT
AMBLES  ALEE  LOESS  COO
SCARATTENDANTS  AGO  SKIN
CERES  UVEA  SPARKINGLANE
ATLAS  REAM  YESTER  EAGER
BOOK  ERRS  ASSN  EWERS
```

175

```
WIN  TAMED  RAIN  IATE
AREA  OVULE  ELBA  SLATE
DOWNINARMS  CLAMPSUPON
INSIGNIA  PRIOR  LUMENS
SEEN  COOPT  CAIN
PESETA  CHILE  TRINIDAD
ARME  UPHILLSKIING  ONA
ROODS  EER  ATM  LWOW
ISO  WATERSHIPUP  PONTE
SETSOVER  TONUS  CRISES
HIRER  TAUNT  OHARA
BLINDS  DANSE  AVOWEDLY
LINGS  PUCKERSDOWN  AEI
ANGE  ANI  AIL  SHIVE
STU  DOWNTONOGOOD  ESEL
TYPEABLE  CORAS  OKAYED
LYES  REDON  STAD
MADEBY  TOAST  SPENSERS
CARVESDOWN  UPCASTEYES
CREED  ALAI  NEURO  TENT
EINS  BEND  DAMEN  RES
```

176

```
ARAFAT  REGRET  CLAN  SPEW
ENROBE  AREOLA  LIME  TARA
FAIRANDWARMER  AFOGGYDAY
CERISE  CHART  ALL
PCB  AMUSE  STENO  STEELE
ARLO  EPH  SCREE  SPEEDING
LEONINE  COOLWATER  LIA
LOWEST  ADORN  FEN  BASS
ELITE  FLOWN  TOTED  SOCLE
TENO  SEAL  CAGER  PURSES
SSI  APRILSHOWERS  ORNIS
NINON  HORNE  ALLEN
ATTAR  GLOOMYSUNDAY  TRA
SCHEME  LOVES  SEER  THAT
CREME  MOREY  STEEN  PEEVE
ROWS  AWN  STARR  CARREL
AMI  STEAMHEAT  SOPRANI
PINNIPED  EERIE  STR  EINE
ADORED  AGAIN  EARNS  NAR
VIC  TIARA  ALTAIC
BLUESKIES  STORMYWEATHER
YARN  EVEN  TIDIER  SLEEVE
EDNA  DYNE  SMEARS  TETRAD
```

177

```
SALSA  NEURO  NIGER  FIND
ADEAL  FILTER  OPERA  ASEA
DEVILSISLAND  COLEPORTER
ANIL  IRIS  DEATHS  ISOLDE
EKES  WERT  AEC  ESD
LONDONTOWER  ALCATRAZ
ERA  KASSEL  SAINT  ROAST
TATAR  TELL  TRADES  RITA
STALAG  EASED  SPANDAU
DONA  ASTARTE  EDITOR  ERN
ORTS  MOAN  IRIDIN  RUSSET
KEBOBS  NIN  PALOMA
DAMAGE  LESSEN  INEZ  BASS
USA  ASSERT  MAGNETO  OREL
CHILLON  RIATA  ATTICA
TONI  NORTON  EROS  ASSET
STEMS  ROILS  TRUSTS  TRE
BASTILLE  SHARKISLAND
MIA  LAS  RHOS  AMOY
OCCULT  ELATER  ASTO  RASE
CHATEAUDIF  LEATHERBACKS
HOSE  NADER  PLATED  ATRIP
ARES  GRANO  SYRUP  SEEDY
```

178

```
ICH   MAINE  PRAM   CRAPE
ACHE  UMBEL  LEVI   HOVEL
RIAL  SNARK  AMES   IDEAL
MERL  HERD   STARS  LINUS
OSMOSES      SUPERSTRING
RTE  TRIM  NANKEEN    ILL
  DOR  CONIC    PATINAE
ATQUE   RETELL    ANGST
MAUNA  VENETIA   CHIN
BLACKHOLE  IMPERIL   QLD
LURE IWO AMP MAG    SUER
ESK  PRESAGE  LIGHTWAVE
  TIED  SUCCORS  HINES
DUCAT   SAURIA    ESTES
ALABAMA   RUSTY     MSU
SUR  OBSERVE  EAVE   MMI
  ATOMICSHELL  NOSEJOB
CAPIZ  LAPIS  OAKY  RUBS
ALAMO  ELAN  CURIA  AMIE
RECON  NANO  APING  SPUN
SCENE  ERAS  WEDGE   ESS
```

179

```
PODS  OCTO  SPCA    ADDS
ALEC  GOAD  ALAN    BEEP
DECADENCE  NARC     AFRO
SORRIEST  DECRESCENT
  ERNST  MERE   SPUR
KAYE  ALUM     TASMAN
NOS  DENOMINATOR  ESE
SPEW  PTAS  ONER   KNIT
ASSISI    SUDS   RITAS
  DECOMPOSITION
CADET  LAIN    DEEDED
ADEN  RAYE  ASHE  REMO
SIC  DEFORMATION   SIT
ANATOL   ERAS    EDIT
  NONO  LATE  TODIG
DETRACTORS   GARDENIA
ALES  ARID   DEMEANING
MIRO  TORE  ARIA  ENSE
PASS  EDEN  SEND  SGTS
```

180

```
LAMPAD   LORICA      RAS
ARIOSE   EPICAL      EMU
WILLIAMSAFIRE       XYZ
  LANDIS   TEEN      SLY
MAI    ANEW       RECUT
ISAACSTERN      NOSOAP
LORNA    SIAL     NOUNS
ORDINAL  SHOT       TAT
  LORETTASWIT
IRA   ACES      SOROSIS
FINNS   HAHA      ARUBA
SONICS   SOUPYSALES
  ALAND   TRIO      PXS
GAS   LIRA       OLDISH
NUT  EVAMARIESAINT
ABE   NEVADA    LEADER
WEN   ELANDS    SERENA
```

181

```
DRAW  SHASTA     EMILY
RAGA  PANTED     ROSIE
AWORDISDEAD      AROMA
SHUTIN   PSST     ANON
TITAN   PRO        RES
IDI   WHENITISSAID
CEST  ORB  MESS    DDE
RARA   LPN      APIAN
  SOMESAYISAYIT
AMINO   ILE      PEST
DOC  EDNA  AOR    SHAD
JUSTBEGINSTO       ONE
  RAN   EHS     RELIC
EATA   TEAR    MINIMA
VSIGN   LIVETHATDAY
ATRIA   ADAGIO    RATE
NIECE   MELONS    EYED
```

182

```
FLOAT  ABBA  LIMA  LIBRA
AERIE  NOON  ENOS  ISLES
WHIRLINGDERVISH   TOOTS
NAY  ETAGERE  ASIDE  CIA
SRA MELS OVA YEAR    KAY
  DAMS   DIANE    RIATA
SEWERS  WEDLOCK  STODGE
PLANK  POE  ARIA  EMEER
ILLS  AROMAS  USMC  ARES
TAT ACE EPIC  SOLITUDE
  ZEBUS  DONOR   RADON
SPINSTER  CERE  OPA NOT
LEND  ETES  WALRUS SINO
URGED  SAIL  EOS  LANCE
REMAIN  PROPANE  BEGGED
  ARLES   START   DENE
LST IVES STR BRAG   OCT
AMI  GENUS  EASIEST PHI
MELEE  SPINNINGATHREAD
ALDEN  ERGO  GEOM EERIE
SLANT  SANS  NETS NEARS
```

183

```
DAMON   SHARIF    IMAGES
UTILE   NENANA    DEP1NT
CISTOGAWAGON      LEEWAY
ARS  NEREIS  BRER    IBM
TSAR  RED  DEAD     ATLI
  EARS  SVELT     TEHEE
M1TARY  ATILT      BURT
ISHIM  GLEBE     GUNSHY
DIEM  OMAR  SURE    EAU
ADES  ST1MARTEN   AWNS
SEX  DOUR  PEAS    BIKE
  DECAMP  CHERT   LINER
  CODA  SO1ST    GEDDES
FLUTE  CHOSE     PAGE
RETE  TROT  LEI    SADA
ASI  FAIR  SPILLS   BON
PI1ERS  THELILLYCROWD
PORTES  IRAISE   1BASE
ENSATE  SANEST   SITES
```

184

```
BAT  BASS  BED      SALA
COLA ATTU AMO      ALLEN
ATTRITION  SIN     BESET
WHENTHEADMIRALSPOKE
  IVS    ION        LOT
ANAS  STAR  AJAR    VII
TOTHESAILORSONBOARD
LIE  REIN  INTO    TAIL
IRELAND  RATES    PALSY
  EST   WATER      SER
ALONE  DOVES    ATTUNED
SARI  ERLE  IGOR    EGO
THENAVYFLATTOPITWAS
IRS  VISE  IRON    ESNE
  SET    IDI       ORA
KNOWNASADECKORATION
REBAG  ARE    KATCHINAS
AMILE  VIA  ETTA   MATA
NOTE   ELL  REOS    ETH
```

185

```
CACTI   AMASS     LOCAL
LURID   DONUT     OTARU
IRENE   SNIPE     SOBER
MAD  SLOE  ERLE    ANE
BLOC  IRT  REA    CLAD
  AHAB   PLOUGH
PLANER   TRA     DAINTY
RIGOR  TROTTER    ARE
ISLE  FOAMIER    ARIA
ALE  CONNIVE    ELECT
METEOR  SSE     CLOSES
  REGALE   CLIO
PATE EMU BRA     FULL
AVA  ERIC  EENY    TIO
LANZA  GEESE     OVINE
ESTER  ONTOP     GALES
STEEL  STEMS     ATENS
```

186

```
  GAFF  AKITE      ERN
COPAL   DUCAT      NEO
HORSERADISH       ISLAS
ADO  AINU     SEEDIEST
RIN  BSA  TERM     SATE
TESTAE  AIL      CATNIP
  INNINGS     ENS
MANSE  MSE  FEY    MAW
EVE   PARMA        APE
WET  SUS  LII     FOOTE
  EON   HILLTOP
HOGNUT   OLE     EXTRAS
ALIT  ITSY  TNG    ENL
REBALLOT  TAEL     GNU
AGLIO  DEERSTONGUE
  ELK  ALTOS     VEILS
  TSI   YSAYE     EGOS
```

187

```
MAPS   STER     TAMABLE
ACRE   DINO     ENISLED
CHIPPINGS       RESTORE
HADTO  GREERGARSON
OTE  RTE  SLAG     IST
  AONE   HAEC      IDO
RANDOMHARVEST      MSG
INDISPUTE        HASSEL
COPS  THE  BEA    AIRE
HURTLE   CALPURNIA
EKE  MRSPARKINGTON
  JAN   PEPE     ROSH
PUG  GERE  FOP     ELI
MADAMECURIE      EIDER
TRITEST       ADVENTURE
GOCHASE  CLEW    ISON
ELEANOR  EYRE    STYE
```

188

```
ASWAN   EATEN      ACRE
CHISEL  CREPE      SHEA
MONKEYSHINES      PASS
EWE   ZOO  TET     RUE
  BEDE       SMELLS
ETNA  ASKEW       EMIT
ARIOSE   ILA       SUE
DAGGERS  TIRES     HAD
ITES  MUSTANG     BOLA
TOR  HAGUE      SOBERLY
  BEA   ARN     SENSES
PERT  RESTS       ADEN
JEERED        ROCK
ART   APR  USA     EDS
FILL  MOUSEOPOSSUM
FLEE  POSES      TAIPEI
ASST  SLEET      TRYST
```

189

```
CAP   OSLER      RAPTOR
SOTO   STILE     ORIOLE
COOKSTRAIT       BARREN
OLDEN   ORARE     MARAT
WEDREAM   SELF     TINS
SRS  ELBA       ELATED
  DROOLS  AIR      ZAP
POSY  ELIOT      LAHORE
UNWED  ISLAM      PANEL
FEEDER  TOBAT      ZEST
FRA   CAR        NOTIME
  TEAMED  OCTO     OFF
LEID  PARS      HOTSPUR
ALTER  PAPAL      HEINE
MOORED  FIREISLAND
APULIA  TRESS      ITEA
RETEST  YEAST      MEL
```

190

```
CASCO   ECAD  ELANDS
ETHEL   SOME  RECOIL
SHARE   TMAN  ANCONA
TOPOGRAPHER   TENET
AMES  ATE  BET  LESS
SER   ATENS   TILE
   TIA  SET  RAREES
ADDER  CAMELOPARDS
SOIL  MATINAL   TINT
SPEEDOMETER  MESAS
TEMPER  DEM  BIS
   READ  SEDER  SRS
LOCI  LAM  NRA  SPEW
IRONS  RESTORATIVE
FOSTER  SCAN  PACED
ENTERO  TARE  STERE
ROARED  AMYS  ESSEN
```

191

```
AMASS  TACIT  EMOTE
NONCE  ENATE  RAPID
TANYA  REPEL  ISERE
ANOTHERWORLD  ONER
      HERO   DON
   GENERALHOSPITAL
BARD   DEAR  ICILY
ABA  ALGONKIAN  EIR
LIV  BEE   ETE  REI
ADE  ASSEMBLED  ENS
TESTS  SAIC  ERST
   ASTHEWORLDTURNS
      ESA   ALEA
SCAR  SANTABARBARA
PAVED  PERIL  ELLAS
ANISE  ERODE  AEGIS
SEDAN  DOTES  DRANT
```

192

```
CCS   ACCESS  AFORE
AHEM  CHASTE  BATIN
LOAM  CORNEA  AMIGO
COLEPORTERMUSICAL
USA  IRES   NAGEL
TENSED  HONG  IERS
TREE  SMEE   AMALIE
ASSAM  ETHELMERMAN
       EAST  TASS
YOURETHETOP  SOARS
INSERT  ANSI  DRAT
PEEL  AWIT  SPARTA
   ALCAN  POOL  AIT
IGETAKICKOUTOFYOU
PARIS  SHASTA  LANA
SLAVE  TOLTEC  ALAR
OTTER  SNEERS   SLY
```

193

```
PORCH  COQ  CST  BIO
WAHOO  ACU  ANI  END
ATENO  LEA  PODESTA
HASTEMAKESWASTE
   TEL  NERI  LAIRD
SPIRES  RAZE   URNS
BEAT  CPA  TESS  SEC
ATTU  TAME   SOS
HASTEISOFTHEDEVIL
   ENV  TIEN  RETE
LAS  SEIS  ALT  VEIN
ALOT  SNUB  PIPERS
PALOS  HEAP  ARA
MAKEHASTESLOWLY
POCONOS  TAT  PIOUS
DDE  OPT  ELY  ESTAR
QED  REE  REX  REINS
```

194

```
CLIMB  OMEGA  WANED
OILER  TAXES  AGORA
MAORI  TRITE  DAVID
ANNIEPOTTSANDPANS
SEAT  AMES   OLE
   IRAN  FORE  ADE
PALADIN  TERM  SCUD
EVADES  IOTA  SHAGS
LINDAHUNTINGLODGE
VANES  REED  AERIAL
ITER  BARD  CRETANS
SER  BOLT  CASK
   ALE  ALTO  EFTS
EVAMARIESAINTJOAN
CEDAR  METRO  HELLO
CRAZE  PREEN  ICIER
EAMES  SORTS  STORE
```

195

```
MAKO  REPUTED  SAPS
IDEA  ELUSIVE  TREE
DAYS  AMNESIC  OTIC
   STORES   CRONE
EST  PERTH  TELERAN
STONED  EAT  ELAINE
TENOR  BRIAN  AGENA
OPERATE  LUIS  ESEL
     SOAPSTONE
MEGA  PSAT  BYLINES
ADENT  TROVE  ASIDE
RIMIER  ANA  SPONGE
LESSEES  ERIES  EEL
   TEMPO  INVEST
SHOT  AUREATE  AIDE
PUNT  STUNNER  BEAR
AGEE  THEATRE  USMA
```

196

```
BALSAM  TAFIA   BAR
AMELIA  AMESS  SUVA
BEVERLYHILLS  AFAR
ENID  AORTA  ALFIE
   MILE   PEALS
EMPIRE  DIODE  LST
RALES  IMPASTO
ARRAN  HASPED  ABLE
COIN  MARTENS  LIEU
ERNE  ANVILS  PILAR
   ETERNAL  FOOLS
OLD  STALL  FLENSE
CARAT   HEAT
TRIPE  LAVAL   MESA
AILS  BEVERLYSILLS
DALE  UNITE  EARLAP
STS  TODOS  SWEEPS
```

197

```
CAMUS  DITTO  ALOHA
IMAGO  ERROR  PEREZ
VICHYSSOISE  PAINT
ISH  ALINES  HONORE
CHOP  ARES  HIS  NYC
   ESTER  BANES
CRANKED  BARD  PAUL
LADIES  VERMICELLI
OVATE  DELOS  ALICE
VEGETARIAN  SILKEN
EDEN  MANY  VENEERS
   TRIPS  FEVER
CHE  ENE  LANE  SALK
REMOVE  MUTINY  ZEN
ALIVE  VICISSITUDE
VILER  PRIMO  PURGE
EXERT  SEDAN  STEEL
```

198

```
JAFFA  RIGID  MEETS
ELLEN  ALIBI  OLDIE
STORYTELLER  SEWAN
TIPTOE  STREETCARS
   INTO  ICY  TREE
ISTLE  SEDATED  DTS
DORE  AARON   EFT
EAU  ANGIE  LACIER
ARTISTES  FINAGLED
SHALES  GOODY   LUI
   TRI  RAINY  RENT
COE  PAYABLE  CERES
HILL  NED   LOOP
ALLEGORIES  LAURIE
SMEAR  BANKTELLERS
TERSE  ANNIE  ESNES
ENSTY  STAND  READE
```

199

```
RECAP   LAMA  TRUED
OPERAS  OPAL  HENRI
CALCUTTARUG  ODORS
   ALERTED  ANY
EDGE  AHS  ANGELAS
SRO  TEC  MISSIVE
TEO  EGYPTME   VOX
AWNING  THEN  TEENY
   TWOS  ERN  SOUR
FROWN  PRES  PURPLE
EAU  IOWALOT   OAK
ERRATIC  ATS  ONE
DESCENT  DAB  ALES
   CAN  SEVERAL
PILES  MOBILEHOMES
IRADE  ORAL  BAGDAD
TAXES  BARA  TIARA
```

200

```
TRET  ARIAS  MEGRIM
LOCO  VALUE  OARING
COUNTERINSURGENTS
   THREAT   SORE
VARIES   RESENTED
EVEN  EST  ERE  ELA
DICE  TEMPS  FARMS
ISR  ENAMOR  BARM
COUNTERPRODUCTIVE
   INTO  LEVITE  NON
ESTEE  LASER  RACE
EKE  EAT  SEA  ELAM
RIDDANCE  MEASLY
   ALTE  OSTEND
COUNTEROFFENSIVES
BUTTER  SMALT  EARL
STEERS  TEXAS  STAY
```

201

```
ARMS  TRAMP  RADON
DEAL  ABNER  SOLANO
ABRA  PINTO  ETUDES
MATTE  SETH  RAMOSE
STEERS  SLICERS
ENSUED  EBONY   SOS
   DROP  ITE  SOLE
PROLIFERATE  GELID
RESETS  OBI  ARRIVE
ORATE  PROOFREADER
BUGS  SOO  NINE
ENE  PANGS  RELICS
   MUNDANE  SETOUT
SECOND  TOAD  YALTA
TRENTE  IOTAS  LOUR
LISTED  OZONE  INRE
OATER  NENES  AYES
```

202

```
NEPAL   PROA  LEAST
IRANI   LEAS  ANGLE
CUSTOMSINSPECTION
KPS  NOTATE  LUINGS
STEW  TIN  SCANT
   OPORTO  OSAYCAN
CLAMORS  ABUTS  OLE
RIVEN  OKAPI  COLE
INENGLANDISCALLED
MERS  IDEAL  LIEGE
ENT  GNARL  SLANDER
ASSURER  EATING
  PIANO  DEL  STES
DOGLEG  LEONAS  OTT
ATRAVELLERSCHEQUE
BRINE  EIRE  ELUDE
SANDS  DEYS  AMEER
```

203

```
DANA  LATER  THAWS
IVANS  ADORE  HENRY
SATIN  MOUNTVERNON
CLIMATE  RERAN  ETO
 OARED  ISON  AXED
RENTED  PST  GUN
ALAE  CATO  RITAS
BALD TOGA IDA HEL
BIZ HERETICAL ERI
INO OAK TREY SPIN
SEOUL  ARKS  TEAK
 ADA  RAS  OPENLY
LEAR  MISC  PLEAT
ILL CADET ADAMANT
SMITHSONIAN RIGOR
LEVEE LIONS SNORE
ERECT SONNY GNAT
```

204

```
 ALS  WAXED  TPK
AVILA  ILIVE  ERROL
FILADELFIALAWYERS
COLLARD  NILE  HAT
NEO ACES  TRAINS
  METAMORFOSIS
SNEER  TELEO  STAG
HANDIN  ONUS  IOTA
ATT SOFOMORES ROM
HAHA DINO REFINE
SLUM LINER RICER
  SOFISTICATED
SPIRAL  CUTA  DET
AAA RIOS  TROLLER
FYSICALTHERAPISTS
ENTRE  LEONA  ANART
EST  ASCAP  GSA
```

205

```
BOOTED PACER CERES MESH
ENDORA ABONE ATONE OCTO
EDDYANDREDDY RAYEANDRAY
NESS GOALS NETTS SOEURS
 SLIDE SOLOS SHTS
BAS PINE HOLLO SHOETREE
REINING LORDANDCORD ERG
OGLING HINTS ROVE SEAR
KELLY JONES SPIRE TASSE
EASE PARD STAVE THREES
RNA HAYSANDHAYES HARASS
 NEARS IRENE LINEN
CADDIS LANEANDLAINE DMD
ADMIRE IDEAS AMOK AMIE
ROILY STARR PATEN CRESS
ERLE PHEN ALGER PRIEST
EEL GARRANDBARR DRESSER
RESTATES ERATO CREW ELY
 ILED STENO PHASE
SIMMER ANTED HEAVE ASTA
KLEEANDLEE ONEALANDNEAL
ALAR AUGER NOBLE TANGLE
TENS LEARS SWEET SNOOKS
```

206

```
ASTUTE NABOB WALLA SLOE
SORREL ANIMA IDEAL TINA
TRAINSANDBOATSANDPLANES
REPS BASSO RENT EVERY
 MOA NERO AFTERS
STATORS NAME ABOU
SUPERCHIEFORIENTEXPRESS
STRESS MATA SNOOTY ALEE
INE BATON TARNS SMART
ENOS LORAN MAE STONES
CUR LOSES SATE PAIN
UNITEDSTATESILEDEFRANCE
 EGGY ELSE METES EAR
ORANGE DEN APRES MGRS
WENDY SEPAL PERIS BOL
LATE ILLINI IRED FILIAL
SPIRITOFSTLOUISENOLAGAY
 NEWT USES INGRESS
PANDAS WEPT TSE
SINAI BRED ATTAR VEER
METROLINERQETWOCONCORDE
OTOE IRANI STINT RAISED
GYNS POISE PANGS ADDERS
```

207

```
OUTAGE SLIDE MAFIA STOP
CROTON AUDIE ASONG TIRE
HGWELLSBRESLINHUGOVIDAL
RENE ALIA CIEL IRATE
ERY CARED SAILS LOX LEE
 NARA PALEO PAPER
RALEIGHHITLERWILDENEHRU
ONEIRO OLEAN NOUN DEEP
ADANO SNERD SLATE ALB
NIP CHOTA SUERS LADDIE
 ASHUR TONTO KEDROVA
CHAPLINEDISONTWAINMONET
LARIATS AMATI CLASP
EVANGS SKIDS MAILS PAY
RAF STONE BALDY DRACO
INAT SLAT SERAI FEISTY
CATOPLUTARCHLINCOLNOTHO
 PLUME ARULE RANT
DIA ARP EMILY BULKY GEE
INLET ARES CAPO ARAT
KAFKADUMASPROUSTVANGOGH
ERIE ARISE CURIO MORALE
DIED DINES ARDEN PLANER
```

208

```
DECAP CLARA RABBI PORES
ELATE HODAD ORRIS ADELE
LIBRA ROUGE SCALE NITTI
MARYCAITLIN EAGLEVISION
ASA EDSEL TANG OCTANE
 DTD PRATE MAIL
FAA HEY SEELE SINCERELY
AFFAIR PATEK MONDE ALAE
CARNE MISSLIBERTY SCUSA
TROT RYNE SNARES FEEDER
OSSOBUCO GIRL MASHERS
 ILLAT PASTY PORTO
RAINIER HAST LICORICE
INSETS ROSTRA FARE SHAM
STATE KATHIANDLIA JEANE
ERAT PHILA IDIOT PISTON
NICEANDEASY AGREE MIM END
 ETNA ETHER SOL
OHGIVE MILT SWOOP ISM
VILLANICOLA ALLENTOWNPA
AREED LOREN DOORS LATER
TENDA ASSET AGAVE EWELL
ERNES SIENA MONET DARLA
```

209

```
STAMPS SMOTE STES SHEBA
TOCARE MARAT COST PAGAN
INANER ATRIA OUSE AVILA
RINGSFORHISSUPPER RESET
 TOSSITIN KEEN LEY
ACHE LYS ABASE RISOTTO
MOUSSE ALAS GESTURAL
PES HASLOSTHERHEAP AONE
 ARTERIO IAND ANNAS
SMITH ATAN DELVE PRY
LITH ATE LILLE DAMPERS
EDER PUMPKINBEATER ULAN
DISEASE AORTA END LISA
 EVE ARRAS DONT SLEEP
MAMMA BUTA HEROINE
ISEE FATINTHECORNER ARA
SCENARIO AIDA DAMNED
CITIZEN TIMMY EDE ASTA
NAT SIMP OVERDONE
CABAL SHEMADESOMECHARTS
AGAPE PERU ARAKE CAGIER
VACUA AMEN LIKEN CRENNA
ARABS SADE YEAST CADETS
```

210

```
AURA IBEG LUCIE TGIF
FRET VEAU MEKONG HUME
OINTMENTS EVERSO ERAS
RETIE TITUS SPECTRUMS
ELEC3CSTORMS STERE
 ACHE NERO NAUSEA
MAE SANTO ROUND3PPERS
ALWAYS AMP STOIC OMIT
REEDS CLARO SPA NINE
SCRATCH HESA ELAM SSR
 MERE AS3DE OPAL
AME MIEN ACED GENERAL
LOLA ROD HAIGS ONICE
DIED SIRES LTS SNACKS
ARCDE3OMPHE HASTA EST
SATRAP SABE PASS
 ESTAR HORRORS3CKEN
MOISTENED AGOGO NARDO
ODDS ATMOST BLUEGRASS
MALE SEINES LETT EPEE
AYES ESTER ERSE DPLS
```

211

```
DANIO AGHAS PALETTE
EMEND ARIOSI ADANIEL
BOTTOMFISHING DAMSELS
ALMONER TOTERS PIPET
TEEN RIBS ARAG LIDO
ESNE ICE CORPORATENUN
 ADAY OPIE ELIS
ENTIRE GLUM HALL SEA
POISONPILLS RELEE TOM
ISTLE ARIA BEL ORMOLU
GETA SURER AMMAN ARIL
EGESTA ERS TAEL AGATE
AAR ALGAE WHITEKNIGHT
LYS RIAL KEEN ACCESS
 STEP BEER NYSE
VULTUREFUNDS YEH ARAL
AREA IDES SEAM BACI
CANNA DEPART SINATRA
ANDDOWN SEQUESTRATION
TIEINTO SUBWAY SENSE
EARNEST TASSO TRESS
```

212

```
 TOIT MOLTO KNOW OSED
TOBRAGABOUT MARASCHINO
FORSALESIGNS ANDCANSAY
ODETS ESTE BRIO COAMO
RONA ESE COATS ARTY
 CAMEUPWITH MELEE ERA
NULLA REATA GAD YET
LEPETIT ASTRA HAI STEAM
EXT ELEC PAULSON NOODLE
ATHER REIS LIL GOLF
STRANGERS GOODYGUMDROP
TOOT AND FORREWARD OPIE
 WILLCOMEOF ANGELWING
TUBE OTB OREL INNER
REGINA GREETER FERE ITE
INONE CUE ROLLS SURCOAT
FOR SLA SLOTH DRANG
EWE SWAMI STEPLADDER
 SKEW RHEIN VES DADA
OAKIE LOAD ALES EASER
ATTENTIONS HAVETOSMILE
THINK OFIT IMGOINGTODO
LOPE SITAO SASIN EAMES
```

213

```
REDROSID CESS SRAORPU
ALLIANCE OCNU TURNERS
TARTRATE NOUS ORESTES
AMO ERUPTS BURR LER
 WADES ECON AKA MIN
WADI TRICORN SEEK
ETALUBOBMOCSID SOLFAS
ROM NEVA ULES PISTOLE
END ITER SUDETES ITIS
 EASTER AND RETINUES
EMMIES NEEDLE ARGON
REDO TEGS ELAINE
INANE HESS SADAT AERI
ATM AGENT SAW USANCES
 DOSES RODEO PAUSE
KCARTNETAEBEHTFFO
RAMOSE URGE TOLA PETE
AMA ROOT REFEATHERED
AIS BASRELIEF CHEATED
LST ETTA INRO KEW UNA
SEI REEF EGO SRS OSS
```

214

```
CARP TRUE ATMOST CABAL
ALIA EARN SOOTHE PARETO
PIGHEADED COATER STEAKS
EVE PRIDE ELBOWROOM LAS
DELOS IODINE AURIOL
DOR SERBIA SANDEEL
HANDMEDOWN RANGE TEASE
ABEL VERITE ASTILL RTS
MATO ENOS NOSIER OUTSET
ELSTER MEATUS TBONE
LOU ATREST GIAP AMERIND
INKER FOOTHEBILL ANNEE
NEEDLED NUIT ENEMAS TIM
DORSA STREET LESAGE
SPOOFS CACAOS SALE AGHA
CON ETHION VEALER GLEN
ARTTO HERNE SPLITHAIRS
REHOUSE YESMAN SRO
ENTERS ANEMIC OFMAN
AWN BREAKALEG ERROL ANI
MOONIS MOLINE SKINFLINT
INSIDE ATONAL SEEL ERIE
STENS ROUNDS EDDY DEER
```

215

```
RAISA CRIME SKEW CASH
MASCOT RAGED CARA OLIOS
ANTHROPOMORPHOLOGICALLY
STR TILSIT ALES RHEIMS
HOOP UBE VOID AWL CST
EATMY MEAT ALLIES
TRANSUBSTANTIATIONALIST
REPAST EGIS FANGS EDER
IPINE BORIC AFIG CEARA
ELECTROENCEPHALOGRAPHIC
RIDE INNS OMI OIL OFT
SPAS BARER AVID
SEA ENA RST ACTE EIRE
INDISTINGUISHABLENESSES
TOAST IOTA OLLIE DOABS
ULTS FACTA OTOE DULLEA
PSEUDOPHILANTHROPICALLY
EILEEN IDEA MANET
ETA ADS ONER SIT EINS
DOSAGE SIRS APNEAS BAA
INTERDENOMINATIONALISMS
TIARA LONE OTARU RANEES
CRAM IBAR WANES EVANS
```

216

```
MABEL ESTES SALTS RET
ARETE STORE IDAHO TVOR
PEETESTEPEE LEMONSMELON
LATE WAVE MILLER ALLEGE
ESS METERS LIEN LEYDEN
MILESSMILE TONESNOTE
ATOLLS UTURN LAMS
ORONO STUS ETES ATE
KATESTAKE PAGESGAPE GET
AMOY IMET GIDE ALHIRT
TENORS ELL SIERRA
BAIRDSBRAID TESLASTALES
ALBEIT BOP CAGIER
IFEELA HERR OLAV TMAN
TIA ERLESREEL ROSESSORE
SEM ASTI METE HINES
EONS ASIDE SPECKS
REEDSDEER KEATSSTEAK
INNATE EMIR STEALS DAD
GARRET SCAPES EASE COPE
STONESSTENO NORTHSTHORN
ELEM FIDEL ARNEE RENOS
LDS CRETE GRADS IRENE
```

217

```
QUILTER GRETAS HEXADS
UNNERVE TWOTONE ENAMELS
ILOVEEVERYTHING RATATAT
RENIN NUNCA OAST DRNO
EDE TASSES NRA VEEP ATO
TENON TOENAIL ARIEL
PASO THATSOLDOLDFRIENDS
ECHO HORROR DIG AND
ARETHE EUR NEP NEUTER
TESSERA DEE STROBOSCOPE
TYR NOG ALAE EAU ECON
OJO OLIVERGOLDSMITH OSE
GOOF YMA ELKS HST OWN
REPLICATIVE AJO SILIQUE
ESSENE ESE EOS RESULT
ECU TIE TAIPEI HEAT
OLDTIMESOLDMANNERS ERNE
BEAST AEOLIAN CLEAR
JAN ESSA ETC PRIEST TIL
EPEE ATTS ASHOE OTONO
CELLULE OLDBOOKSOLDWINE
TRAITOR NEURONS AEDILES
SWEEPS GREENE ROSTERS
```

218

```
PAC DAIS SILIC ANIMAL
CLIO APNEA ILONA MORALE
HARROWEDANDMOWED ODESSA
STEEDS ITEAS DARE COS
TROD AGONS APSIS SOPH
PLANOFTHETAPES LAWS
SEASONS ICONO ERATO
NIKITA PRONG DISSONANCE
INNS THEBIGSHILL DANTON
PSI ARIL ATEE HMO
STGEORGE EENY RYANONEAL
HANOI DRYNESS BEECH
ENTRECOTE IEST BADMOUTH
TEA AMEN USAF DOO
ANTICS KINGOFTARTS TSAR
SETSATREST OOZES AARONS
HEDDA ERROL ORGANDY
PERI SOMELIKEITHAUT
ALOE PRIES WAGHS ITAL
MAP DESI SATIE ISOBAR
ICEMAN BADDAYATBACHRACH
CERATO IRONY NUEVE INTO
ERASES SILAS READ ADQ
```

219

```
PALLAS PAN WART GRASSTO
ALBERT ITA OMOO OEDIPAL
SESAME TOPBRASS OLDTIME
PEAS ALEE IKIDYOUNOT
OHFIDDLEDEEDEE AGIN ERA
ROON YIP SPOT MORN ADAR
AMALA DIA BWANA IGOR
NEMIC EGGMEN ERTE PISAN
GRAZER RAIE GONIF SACRE
ESTATE APOPHONIC RGS
RADAMES ELSE LESCAUT
HARDTOPS ARF PORTAGES
AMUSERS TYRO SPANIEL
RID ROUNDHEEL CALMAS
UNDAY GOWNS OTRA AROUSE
MAYBE LEEK AJANTA NORMA
EXPO RAMBO SIL SHREW
YEST LRGS VETA AID CORA
ONO MAYA HIYOSILVERAWAY
YOWZAYOWZA AHEM EMIL
OLEOSAS IVANOVNA ECLOSE
MATLOCK PERC EOS NEARED
ASHANTY SLEE RTE TRYSTS
```

220

```
ARAB BRAME SWAP BIHAR
LOCA REPEL TAPU ANANA
BARBERPOLE BROKENPLAY
ANEYE OGAMS READJUSTS
PLAUEN ABET DOTE
BATO BRAINPAN DIP
ASOWER NEAPS PRELATES
MINDFUL THELON AROMA
BAKEDPOTATO ETO YAMIS
INAR TRACE RAH RESETS
BLAMER OPENER
AFFRAY ADS MERES BSCS
SERAC ELI BARBECUEPIT
TRASH NEATEN DANAITE
INSPECTS ALIAS LOCKET
LOS BPICTURE HESS
AMOS EASE ICESUP
INNERMOST FETCH SALMI
BACKPOCKET BLUEPERIOD
OCREA TEAR BABAR TRIO
SHERD ARUM SNARE YELL
```

221

```
COGNAC SCAM USA AZLON
AROUSE IRMA LES TUERE
BLUNTS PENS TIS OBOES
SET EAR PETERJENNINGS
ARRESTS TAINO NIOU
VESICLE IBO OTTOMANS
GARISH WACO ESSENE
ELIAKAZAN BOLA REHIRE
TEEN VERY BLEW SITTER
SPEND SYLVAN LACTO
ADD AZO MOVIE ELL HES
REIGN SMYLIE CHEST
AENEAS ASON TORS RAPT
BROOCH RENT RAULJULIA
READIN ONER IAMBUS
KANGAROO UNA SHERPAS
ECUS INCAS COERCES
RUDOLFNUREYEV HAD SHE
AMILE IOU OLEO RIOTER
LESTE SMD ULNA OTHERS
ANTIS HOE REST NESTLE
```

222

```
TALC SPIRE TARP RAMA
OLIO AARON POLAR EDIT
DALMATIANS INTHESHADE
PRINE NEATS MAORI
MOTES SARTO SICE
MOSS ARAT THURSDAY
SOOTY HILLSOFROME ABE
ERNS TETE EINS MYNA
RAJ WAYPASSAGE POSER
FLUSTER PTER SONARS
NARES PEERS SADAT
ARCHED AREA CLASPED
SITES EASYPIECES EWE
PAIL SPIT DANA SKEG
ITO RUEMADELINE STIRS
CANDICES ORAN PENS
EFTS COSTA CLANG
TUTTI HOMER CLERC
FACESOFEVE OCLOCKHIGH
ILLS NIXED BOOST EASE
BEAT STAR ESTES SNAP
```

223

```
TESTAMENTS LUTE REPEL
ALIENATION ASHE ERICA
DILETTANTE PHILOSOPHY
STA WIPE ASPEN VIDEOS
ESSENE SKIER BEDE
IRS CHERT GURU PEA
CHIRP MOORE COLLEGIAL
HUGS SOARS LANKY RAGE
AGO GENRE TANGY TONER
PERFECTS TART CAVORT
ISTHEMICROSCOPE
PRINTS INKY COVERAGE
EERIE BAGGY BOWER FAX
SEAS CACHE RIPEN MALI
OFTHOUGHT POKER CARET
SSE CREE HOMES POT
DELL POLAR TAMERS
AREOLE CANON TARP OIL
VICTORHUGO CARICATURE
OCTET AJAR EXONERATES
WOODS GONE SETTLEMENT
```

224

```
BEATON FATCAT ARAMAIC
ALSIKE ATOOTH TAVERNA
JOHNSONSTITLEINMADRID
ANIS SICILY SOO ISTS
GLEN NIL SCAN OCT
GALLO SAR RUE LEAHS
ATI REGT OSAR CANTATA
LENOSBRIGHTBIRD TEMAS
GREBE ARAB ALAI IRT
EFG TEAS NELL SMALTI
FLOATINGPADSALATOMLIN
EARNED OEIL IOTA IGN
ASH NEER DION ORALE
STOMA SAJAKSGENTLETAP
TIPONES OBES NEED SUI
CENTI ISE ADD ERASE
OSO SETI EER RESP
ANIL AMP SALAAM EPIS
REMICKSSHELTEREDPLACE
GOATEES OLEATE LAIRED
ONSHORE FITTED INNESS
```

225

```
TERR SAHIB ELDER TAW
UREY CRANE MOOLA CORE
FIDDLERONTHEWOOF AONE
UNSEEN WERE TASTED
LAIR EERY OVERALLS
KNELLCARTER STERILE
REVS DERN BAER OSCAR
ORE SINCE ELLIES HIE
CORALSEA SAN LESE ASS
PURRPETRATORS SOLE
AMBER LOIRE UPSET
LOOS TRILLSERGEANT
PRO ARAN LES UNLISTED
HAM LITTLE CALLS RAU
ALSAB TEEN LEVI BUTS
ELATERS REDASABLEAT
SHRINERS PACE TRIO
HAVEON FIST ENTREE
AGIN DISAPPEARINGOINK
MACS ONICE RHODA URGE
ERE NADER NAMES TESS
```

THE MEGA SERIES

continues the grand crossword tradition begun by Simon & Schuster in 1924.

Simon & Schuster Mega Crossword Puzzle Books

AND COMPLETE YOUR COLLECTION WITH THESE CLASSIC TITLES

Simon & Schuster Super Crossword Books

The <u>Original</u> Crossword Puzzle Series

71209

Available wherever books are sold or at SimonandSchuster.com